The Norton Scores

NINTH EDITION | VOLUME II

NINTH EDITION | IN TWO VOLUMES

The Norton Scores

A Study Anthology

Edited by Kristine Forney

Professor of Music
California State University, Long Beach

with textual notes
by Roger Hickman

Professor of Music
California State University, Long Beach

VOLUME II: SCHUBERT TO THE PRESENT

W. W. NORTON & COMPANY
NEW YORK • LONDON

Printed in the United States of America

Manufacturing by Maple-Vail
Copy Editor: Jan Hoeper
Project Editor: Claire McCabe
Production Manager: Roy Tedoff

ISBN 0-393-97946-6 (pbk.)

W. W. Norton & Company, Inc., 500 Fifth Avenue, New York, N.Y. 10110 www.wwnorton.com

W. W. Norton & Company Ltd., Castle House, 75/76 Wells Street, London W1T 3QT

1 2 3 4 5 6 7 8 9 0

Contents

Preface ix

How to Follow the Highlighted Scores xii

A Note on the Recordings xiv

1. Franz Schubert (1797–1828), *Erlkönig (Erlking)*, D. 328 1
2. Schubert, *Die Forelle (The Trout)*, D. 550 9
3. Schubert, Quintet in A major for Piano and Strings (*Trout*), D. 667, fourth movement 15
4. Hector Berlioz (1803–1869), *Symphonie fantastique*
   - Fourth movement, *Marche au supplice (March to the Scaffold)* 32
   - Fifth movement, *Songe d'une nuit du sabbat (Dream of a Witches' Sabbath)* 53
5. Fanny Mendelssohn Hensel (1805–1847), *Bergeslust (Mountain Yearning)*, Op. 10, No. 5 109
6. Felix Mendelssohn (1809–1847), Violin Concerto in E minor, Op. 64, first movement 115
7. Frédéric François Chopin (1810–1849), Prelude in E minor, Op. 28, No. 4 165
8. Chopin, Nocturne in C minor, Op. 48, No. 1 167
9. Robert Schumann (1810–1856), "Und wüssten's die Blumen" ("And if the flowers knew"), from *Dichterliebe (A Poet's Love)*, No. 8 174
10. Franz Liszt (1811–1886), *La campanella (The Little Bell)*, from *Transcendental Etudes after Paganini*, No. 3 179
11. Richard Wagner (1813–1883), *Die Walküre*, Act III, Finale 189

12. GIUSEPPE VERDI (1813–1901), *Rigoletto*, Act III
    Aria, "La donna è mobile" ("Woman is fickle") 200
    Quartet, "Un dí, se ben rammentomi" ("One day, if I remember right") 205

13. CLARA SCHUMANN (1819–1896), Scherzo, Op. 10 225

14. BEDŘICH SMETANA (1824–1884), *Vltava (The Moldau)*, from *Má vlast (My Country)* 236

15. JOHANNES BRAHMS (1833–1897), *Ein deutsches Requiem (A German Requiem)*, fourth movement 301

16. BRAHMS, Symphony No. 3 in F major, third movement 313

17. GEORGES BIZET (1838–1875), *Carmen*, Act I
    No. 3. Chorus, "Avec la garde montante" ("Along with the relief guard") 331
    Recitative, "C'est bien là" ("It's right there") 340
    No. 4. Chorus, "La cloche a sonné" ("The bell has rung") 343
    No. 5. *Habanera*, "L'amour est un oiseau rebelle" ("Love is a rebellious bird") 354

18. PETER ILYICH TCHAIKOVSKY (1840–1893), *The Nutcracker*, Three Dances
    March 366
    Dance of the Sugar Plum Fairy 390
    Trepak (Russian Dance) 399

19. ANTONÍN DVOŘÁK (1841–1904), Symphony No. 9 in E minor *(From the New World)*, first movement 414

20. GIACOMO PUCCINI (1858–1924), *Madama Butterfly*, Act II, "Un bel dí" ("One beautiful day") 467

21. GUSTAV MAHLER (1860–1911), *Das Lied von der Erde (The Song of the Earth)*, third movement, *Von der Jugend (Of Youth)* 473

22. CLAUDE DEBUSSY (1862–1918), *Prélude à "L'après-midi d'un faune" (Prelude to "The Afternoon of a Faun")* 485

23. AMY CHENEY BEACH (1867–1944), Violin Sonata in A minor, second movement 518

24. SCOTT JOPLIN (1868–1917), *Maple Leaf Rag* 526

25. ARNOLD SCHOENBERG (1874–1951), *Pierrot lunaire*, Op. 21
    No. 18. *Der Mondfleck (The Moonfleck)* 530
    No. 21. *O alter Duft aus Märchenzeit (O Scent of Fabled Yesteryear)* 536

26. CHARLES IVES (1874–1954), *The Things Our Fathers Loved* 541

27. MAURICE RAVEL (1875–1937), *Rapsodie espagnole (Spanish Rhapsody)*, fourth movement, *Feria* 544

28. BÉLA BARTÓK (1881–1945), *Concerto for Orchestra*, fourth movement, *Interrupted Intermezzo* 596

29. IGOR STRAVINSKY (1882–1971), *Le sacre du printemps (The Rite of Spring)*, Part II:
Glorification de l'élue (Glorification of the Chosen One) 608
Evocation des ancêtres (Evocation of the Ancestors) 622
Action rituelle des ancêtres (Ritual Action of the Ancestors) 626

30. STRAVINSKY, *L'histoire du soldat (The Soldier's Tale)*, *Marche royale (Royal March)* 637

31. ANTON WEBERN (1883–1945), Symphony, Op. 21, second movement 647

32. ALBAN BERG (1885–1935), *Wozzeck*, Act III
Scene 4 656
Interlude 670
Scene 5 675

33. SERGEI PROKOFIEV (1891–1953), *Alexander Nevsky*, seventh movement 682

34. GEORGE GERSHWIN (1898–1937), Piano Prelude No. 1 696

35. SILVESTRE REVUELTAS (1899–1940), *Homenaje a Federico García Lorca (Homage to Federico García Lorca)*, third movement, *Son* 701

36. AARON COPLAND (1900–1990), *Billy the Kid*, Scene 1, *Street in a Frontier Town* 718

37. OLIVIER MESSIAEN (1908–1992), *Quatuor pour la fin du temps (Quartet for the End of Time)*, second movement, *Vocalise, pour l' Ange qui annonce la fin du Temps (Vocalise, for the Angel who announces the end of Time)* 760

38. JOHN CAGE (1912–1992), *Sonatas and Interludes*, Sonata V 769

39. BILLIE HOLIDAY (1915–1959), *Billie's Blues* 772

40. BILLY STRAYHORN (1915–1967)/DUKE ELLINGTON (1899–1974), *Take the A Train* 777

41. DIZZY GILLESPIE (1917–1993)/CHARLIE PARKER (1920–1955), *A Night in Tunisia* 808

42. LEONARD BERNSTEIN (1918–1990), *West Side Story*
Mambo 810
Tonight Ensemble 833

43. GYÖRGY LIGETI (b. 1923), *Désordre (Disorder)*, from *Etudes for Piano*, Book I 850

44. PIERRE BOULEZ (b. 1925), *Le marteau sans maître (The Hammer Without a Master)*
No. 1. *Avant "L'artisanat furieux" (Before "Furious Artisans")* 856
No. 3. *L'artisanat furieux (Furious Artisans)* 862
No. 7. *Après "L'artisanat furieux" (After "Furious Artisans")* 865

45. George Crumb (b. 1929), *Ancient Voices of Children*, first movement, *El niño busca su voz (The Little Boy Is Looking for His Voice)* 870

46. David Baker (b. 1931), *Through This Vale of Tears*, sixth movement, *Sometimes I Feel Like a Motherless Child* 874

47. Arvo Pärt (b. 1935), *Cantate Domino canticum novum (O sing to the Lord a new song)* 881

48. Joan Tower (b. 1935), *For the Uncommon Woman* 894

49. Paul Lansky (b. 1944), *Notjustmoreidlechatter*, excerpt 928

50. John Adams (b. 1947), Chamber Symphony, third movement, *Roadrunner* 931

51. Abing (Hua Yanjun, 1883–1950), *Er quan ying yue (The Moon Reflected on the Second Springs)* 969

52. Traditional Cajun Music, *Jongle à moi (Think of Me)* 971

Appendix A. Reading a Musical Score 977

Appendix B. Instrumental Names and Abbreviations 979

Appendix C. Glossary of Musical Terms Used in the Scores 984

Appendix D. Concordance Table for Recordings and Listening Guides 993

Acknowledgments 997

Index of Forms and Genres 1000

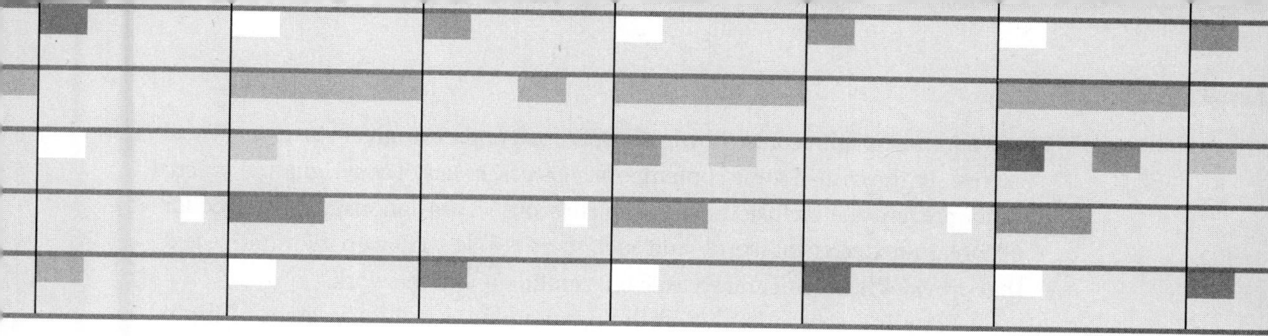

Preface

The Ninth Edition of *The Norton Scores* provides a comprehensive approach to the study of the masterworks of Western music literature, from the earliest times to the present. Presented in two volumes, the anthology meets a number of teaching and study needs in the field of music, including the following:

- as a core anthology, or an ancillary, for a masterworks-oriented music class, to aid in the development of listening and music-reading skills;
- as a study anthology for a music history class focused on major repertory, genres, or styles of Western music;
- as a core repertory for analysis classes, providing a wide variety of styles, forms, and genres;
- as a central text for a capstone course in musical styles focused on standard repertory, listening, or score study;
- as an ancillary to a beginning conducting course and a help in reading full orchestral scores;
- as an independent study resource for those wishing to expand their knowledge of repertory and styles;
- as a resource for music teachers in a wide array of courses.

The Norton Scores can be used independently, as described above, or in conjunction with an introductory music text. The repertory coordinates with *The Enjoyment of Music*, Ninth Edition, by Joseph Machlis and Kristine Forney. Recording packages are available for use with this edition: 8 CDs (in two volumes matching the contents and division of the score volumes) and 4 CDs (selected works).

The anthology presents many works in their entirety; others are represented by one or more movements or an excerpt. Most selections are reproduced in full scores; however, opera excerpts are given in piano/vocal scores. (In the case of some contemporary pieces, issues of copyright and practicality prevent the inclusion of a complete score.) Translations are provided for all foreign-texted vocal works, and each score is followed by an informative text that provides historical and stylistic information about the work.

The full scores in this anthology employ a unique system of highlighting that directs those who are just developing music-reading skills to preselected elements in the score, thus enhancing the music-listening experience. Students with good music-reading skills will, of course, perceive many additional details. Each system (or group of staves) is covered with a light gray screen, within which the most prominent musical lines are highlighted with white bands. Where two or more simultaneous musical lines are equally prominent, they are both highlighted. Multiple musical systems on a page are separated by a thin white band. For more information, see "How to Follow the Highlighted Scores" on p. xii. This highlighting system has been applied to most instrumental works in full scores; in vocal works, the text generally serves as a guide throughout the work.

The highlighting is not intended as an analysis of the melodic structure, contrapuntal texture, or any other musical aspect of the work. Since it emphasizes the most prominent line (or lines), however, it often represents the principal thematic material in a work. In some cases, the highlighting may shift mid-phrase to another instrument that becomes more audible.

Here are some considerations regarding the repertory included in this anthology:

- Music is divided into two volumes:
  - Volume I: Gregorian Chant to Beethoven
  - Volume II: Schubert to the Present
  - 8-CD set matches this division
- All major Classical genres are represented:
  - New genres in this edition include Baroque trio sonata, Italian cantata, nocturne, Mexican art music, prepared piano, spiritual minimalism
  - Complete multi-movement works for study (Baroque concerto, Classical symphony, concerto, chamber music, sonata)
- Seven works by women composers:
  - Middle Ages to contemporary (Hildegard von Bingen, Barbara Strozzi, Clara Schumann, Fanny Mendelssohn Hensel, Amy Cheney Beach, Billie Holiday, Joan Tower)
  - Wide-ranging genres (chant, Italian cantata, piano music, song, chamber music, jazz, orchestral music, among others)

- Numerous works influenced by traditional and world musics:
  - Traditional music of the Americas (Ives song, Copland ballet, Revueltas symphonic work, Bernstein musical theater work, Cajun dance tune)
  - European traditional music (Haydn quartet, Gay ballad opera, Bizet opera, Ravel orchestral work)
  - Eastern influence (Mozart sonata, Puccini opera, Mahler song cycle, Cage prepared piano work)
  - African influence (Ligeti piano etude, jazz selections)

The appendices to *The Norton Scores* provide some useful pedagogical resources for students and faculty. These include the following:

- table of clefs and instrument transpositions;
- table of instrument names and abbreviations in four languages (English, Italian, German, and French);
- table of voice designations in English, Italian, and Latin;
- table of scale degree names (in four languages);
- glossary of all musical terms in the scores;
- table of concordances between scores, recordings, and listening guides in *The Enjoyment of Music;*
- index by genre and form of all selections in the anthology.

Volume I also has a helpful explanation of some performance practice issues in early music, and, where needed, editor's notes explain particular markings in a score that might not be widely understood.

There are many people to be thanked for help in the preparation of this Ninth Edition of *The Norton Scores*: my California State University, Long Beach colleagues Roger Hickman, for his informative texts on each musical selection, and Gregory Maldonado, for his expert work on the highlighting of new scores; research assistants Carla Reisch, Denise Odello, Patricia Dobiesz, and Jeanne Scheppach, for their invaluable help on this project; John Muller of The Juilliard School of Music, for his assistance in the coordination of the scores with the recordings; Claire McCabe and Allison Benter, both of W. W. Norton, who ably collected the scores and handled the permissions; Jan Hoeper, for her capable copyediting of the scores and texts; Kathy Talalay of W. W. Norton, for her skillful and painstaking work on the entire *Enjoyment of Music* package; and Maribeth Payne, music editor at W. W. Norton, for her support and guidance of this new edition. I am deeply indebted to them all.

How to Follow the Highlighted Scores

By following the highlighted bands throughout a work, the listener will be able to read the score and recognize the most important or most audible musical lines. The following principles are illustrated on the facing page in an excerpt from Beethoven's Symphony No. 5 in C minor (first movement).

1. The musical line that is most prominent at any time is highlighted by a white band shown against light gray screening.
2. When a highlighted line continues from one system (group of staves) or page to the next, the white band ends with an arrow head (>) that indicates the continuation of the highlighted line, which begins on the next system with an indented arrow shape.
3. Multiple systems (more than one on a page) are separated by narrow white bands across the full width of the page. Watch carefully for these bands so that you do not overlook a portion of the score.
4. At times, two musical lines are highlighted simultaneously, indicating that they are equally audible. On first listening, it may be best to follow only one of these.
5. When more than one instrument plays the same musical line, in unison or octaves (called doubling), the instrument whose line is most audible is highlighted.
6. CD track numbers are given throughout the scores at the beginning of each movement and at important structural points within movements. They appear in a □ for the 8-CD set and in a ◇ for the 4-CD set, where appropriate.

36
63
310
320
330
1.
p
Fl.
Ob.
Cl.
Fg.
Cor. (Es)
Timp
Vl.
Vla.
Vc.
Cb.
cresc.
1
2
3
4
5
6

A Note on the Recordings

Sets of recordings of the works in *The Norton Scores* are available from the publisher. There is an 8-CD set that includes all the works in the two volumes of the anthology and a 4-CD set that includes selected works from both volumes. The location of the work in the recording sets is noted at the top of each score, to the right of the title.

Example (for Schubert's *Erlkönig*)
8CD:5/ [1]–[8]
4CD:1/ [80] – [87]

The number after the colon designates the individual CD within the set; the boxed numbers after the diagonal slash gives the inclusive tracks on that CD. For an overview of which works appear on the various recording sets, see Appendix D *Concordance Table for Recordings.*

For the 8-CD set, the first set accompanies *The Norton Scores*, Volume I, and the second set accompanies *The Norton Scores*, Volume II.

Note: Occasionally, there are differences between the notated scores and the recordings; an editor's note is generally included in the score to explain these performance choices.

Electronic Listening Guides

There are interactive Listening Guides available from the publisher for each work on the 8-CD and 4-CD sets. These provide study tools to help students understand the form and style of each work.

The Norton Scores

NINTH EDITION | VOLUME II

-each character has its own voice register + projects its own mood
-narrative ballad

Lieder

1. Franz Schubert

Erlkönig (Erlking), D. 328 (1815)

8CD: 5/1–8
4CD: 1/80–87

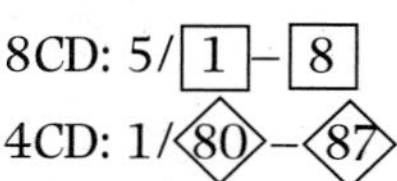

1 80

Schnell. ♩ = 152.
Singstimme.
Pianoforte.
→ triplets = horse racing
Wer rei - tet so spät durch Nacht und Wind?
Es ist der Va - ter mit sei - nem

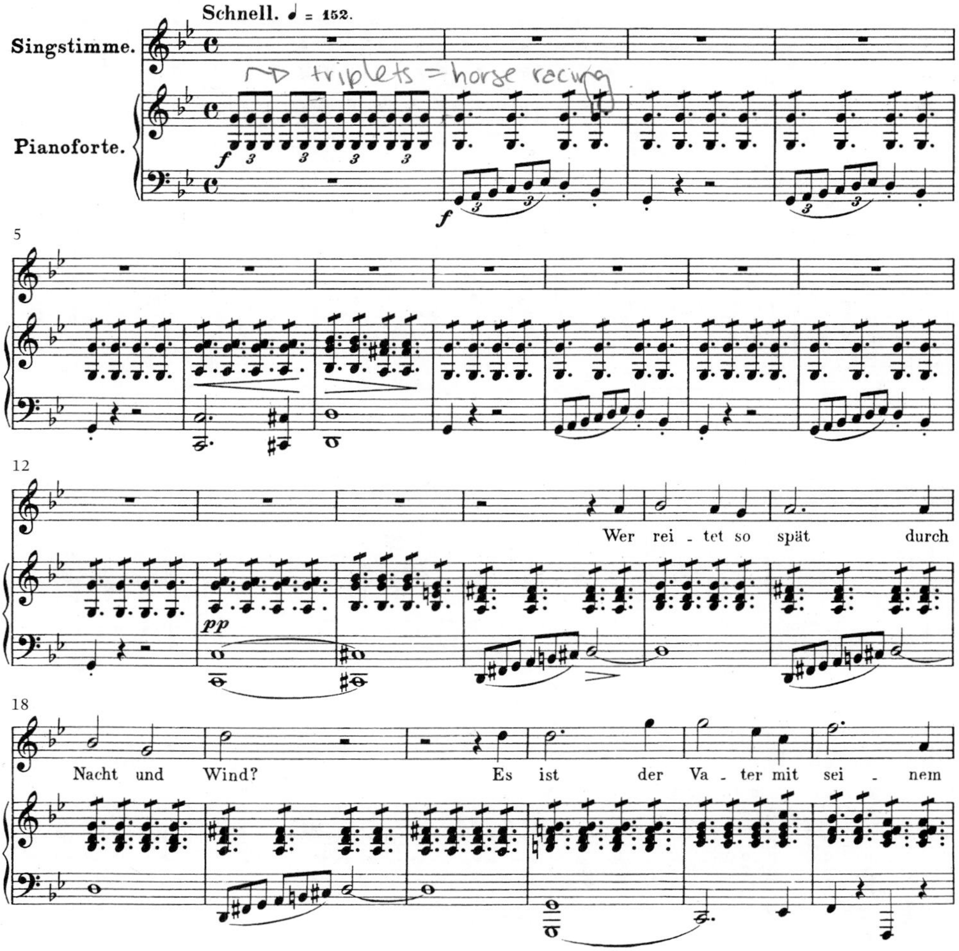

Editor's note: In performance, this Lied is often transposed to F minor, and occasionally to E minor.

24
Kind; er hat den Kna - ben wohl in dem Arm, er fasst ihn
30
sicher, er hält ihn warm. Mein
f
pp
37
Sohn, was birgst du so bang dein Ge - sicht? Siehst, Va - - ter,
f
(pp)
43
du den Erl - kö - nig nicht? den Er - - len -
mf
p
48
kö - nig mit Kron' und Schweif? Mein Sohn, es ist ein
mf

2
81
54
Ne - belstreif. „Du lie - - bes Kind, komm,
(ppp)
60
geh mit mir! gar schö - - - ne Spie - le
64
spiel' ich mit dir; manch bun - - - te Blu - men sind
68
an dem Strand; mei-ne Mut - ter hat manch'
3
82
71
gül - - den Ge - wand“. Mein Va - ter, mein Va - ter, und hö - rest du
f

76
nicht, was Er-len-könig mir lei - se verspricht? Sei ru-hig, bleibe
p
decresc.
82
4
83
ru-hig, mein Kind; in dür-ren Blättern säu-selt der Wind. „Willst,
87
fei - ner Kna - be, du mit mir gehn? mei-ne Töch - ter sol - len dich
ppp
90
war - ten schön; mei-ne Töch - ter führ - ren den nächt - li-chen Reihn, und
93
wie - gen und tan - zen und sin - gen dich ein, sie wie - gen und tan - zen und sin - gen dich ein".
f

5
84
97
Mein Va - ter, mein Va - ter, und siehst du nicht dort Erl -
102
kö-nigs Töchter am dü - stern Ort? Mein Sohn, mein Sohn, ich
decresc.
108
seh' es ge - nau; es scheinen die al - ten Wei - den so grau.
cresc.
ff
6
85
113
„Ich lie - be dich, mich
p
pp
118
reizt dei-ne schö-ne Ge - stalt; und bist du nicht wil - lig, so brauch' ich Ge-

7
86
123
walt". Mein Va - ter, mein Va - ter, jetzt fasst er mich an! Erl - kö - nig
fff
129
hat mir ein Leids ge - than!
8
87
Dem Va - ter
fz
f
134
accelerando
grau - set's, er rei - tet geschwind, er hält in Ar - men das
cresc.
139
äch - zen - de Kind, er - reicht den
ff
fz
144
Recit.
Hof mit Müh' und Noth; in seinen Armen das Kind war todt.
Andante.
fz
fp
pp
p
f

Text and Translation

Wer reitet so spät durch Nacht und Wind?
Es ist der Vater mit seinem Kind;
er hat den Knaben wohl in dem Arm,
er fasst ihn sicher, er hält ihn warm.

"Mein Sohn, was birgst du so bang dein Gesicht?"
"Siehst, Vater, du den Erlkönig nicht?
den Erlenkönig mit Kron' und Schweif?"
"Mein Sohn, es ist ein Nebelstreif."

"Du liebes Kind, komm, geh mit mir!
gar schöne Spiele spiel' ich mit dir;
manch' bunte Blumen sind an dem Strand;
meine Mutter hat manch' gülden Gewand."

"Mein Vater, mein Vater, und hörest du nicht,
was Erlenkönig mir leise verspricht?"
"Sei ruhig, bleibe ruhig, mein Kind;
in dürren Blättern säuselt der Wind."

"Willst, feiner Knabe, du mit mir geh'n?
meine Töchter sollen dich warten schön;
meine Töchter führen den nächtlichen Reih'n
und wiegen und tanzen und singen dich ein."

"Mein Vater, mein Vater, und siehst du nicht dort,
Erlkönigs Töchter am düstern Ort?"
"Mein Sohn, mein Sohn, ich seh' es genau,
es scheinen die alten Weiden so grau."

"Ich liebe dich, mich reizt deine schöne Gestalt,
und bist du nicht willig, so brauch' ich Gewalt."
"Mein Vater, mein Vater, jetzt fasst er mich an!
Erlkönig hat mir ein Leids gethan!"

Who rides so late through night and wind?
It is a father with his child:
he has the boy close in his arm,
he holds him tight, he keeps him warm.

"My son, why do you hide your face in fear?"
"Father, don't you see the Erlking?
The Erlking with his crown and train?"
"My son, it is a streak of mist."

"You dear child, come with me!
I'll play very lovely games with you.
There are lots of colorful flowers by the shore;
my mother has some golden robes."

"My father, my father, and don't you hear
the Erlking whispering promises to me?"
"Be still, stay calm, my child;
it's the wind rustling in the dry leaves."

"My fine lad, do you want to come with me?
My daughters will take care of you;
my daughters lead off the nightly dance,
and they'll rock and dance and sing you to sleep."

"My father, my father, and don't you see
the Erlking's daughters over there in the shadows?"
"My son, my son, I see it clearly,
it's the gray sheen of the old willows."

"I love you, your beautiful form delights me!
And if you are not willing, then I'll use force."
"My father, my father, now he's grasping me!
The Erlking has hurt me!"

Dem Vater grauset's, er reitet geschwind,	The father shudders, he rides swiftly,
er hält in Armen das ächzende Kind,	he holds the moaning child in his arms;
erreicht den Hof mit Müh and Noth:	with effort and urgency he reaches the courtyard:
in seinem Armen das Kind war todt.	in his arms the child was dead.

JOHANN WOLFGANG VON GOETHE

The Romantic spirit is largely indebted to a generation of poets whose works deal with images of love, heroes, nature, and the supernatural. In the late eighteenth century, musical settings of such poems were homophonic and strophic; thus the music remained subordinate to the text. But Franz Schubert (1797–1828), who composed over six hundred Lieder, elevated the genre to a new artistic level with beautiful melodies and imaginative piano accompaniments. Written in 1815, *Erlkönig (Erlking)* is one of Schubert's earliest masterworks in the genre. The song is a narrative ballad, a subgenre of the Lied that tells a story, usually tragic. Passages of dialogue are not uncommon. This poem, by the great German literary figure Johann Wolfgang von Goethe, relates a story based on the legend of the king of elves, whose touch is deadly to humans.

Schubert avoids the more typical strophic setting for telling such a story and creates a dramatic through-composed structure. Following an opening statement by a narrator, a dialogue among the father, the boy, and the seductive elf king ensues. Each character in the story has its own voice register and projects its own mood. The climax is created by the rising sequential repetition of the son's terrified, dissonant cries. Unifying the diverse vocal styles is an unrelenting triplet accompaniment in the piano that creates a visual image of the racing horse. The energetic motion only ceases when the narrator returns and tells of the tragic ending.

2. Franz Schubert

8CD: 5/[9]–[11]

Die Forelle (The Trout), D. 550 (1817)

17
sah in sü - ßer Ruh des mun - tern Fischleins Ba - - de im
21
kla - ren Bächlein zu, des mun - tern Fischleins Ba - - de im
25
kla - - ren Bächlein zu.
p
10
29
pp
Ein Fi - scher mit der Ru - - te wohl
p

33
an dem U - fer stand, und sah's mit kal-tem Blu - - te, wie
37
sich das Fischlein wand. So lang' dem Was-ser Hel - - le, so
41
dacht ich, nicht ge - bricht, so fängt er die Fo - rel - - le mit
45
sei - ner An-gel nicht, so fängt er die Fo - rel - - le mit

49
sei - ner An-gel nicht.
p
11
53
Doch end-lich ward dem Die - be
pp
57
die Zeit zu lang. Er macht das Bäch-lein tük-kisch
cresc.
p
cresc.
61
trü - be, und eh ich es ge-dacht, so zuck-te sei-ne
p

65
Ru - te, das Fisch - lein, das Fisch-lein zap-pelt dran, und
p
69
ich mit re-gem Blu - - te sah die Be-trog-ne an, und
73
ich — mit re - gem Blu - - te sah die Be-trogne an.
77
dim.
pp

Text and Translation

In einem Bächlein helle, Da schoss in froher Eil' Die launische Forelle Vorüber wie ein Pfeil. Ich stand an dem Gestade Und sah in süsser Ruh' Des muntern Fischleins Bade Im klaren Bächlein zu.	In a bright little stream the good-natured trout darted about in joyous haste like an arrow. I stood on the bank and watched in sweet repose the bath of the lively little fish in the clear water.
Ein Fischer mit der Rute Wohl an dem Ufer stand, Und sah's mit kaltem Blute, Wie sich das Fischlein wand. So lang' dem Wasser Helle, So dacht, ich, nicht gebricht, So fängt er die Forelle Mit seiner Angel nicht.	A fisherman with his rod also stood on the bank and cold-bloodedly watched the little fish swimming to and fro. As long as the water stays clear, I thought, he won't catch the trout with his rod.
Doch endlich ward dem Diebe Die Zeit zu lang. Er macht Das Bächlein tückisch trübe, Und eh' ich es gedacht, So zuckte seine Rute, Das Fischlein zappelt dran, Und ich mit regem Blute Sah die Betrog'ne an.	But finally the wait grew too long for the thief. He made the brook all muddy, and before I knew it, his rod quivered, the little fish wriggled at its end, and I, my blood boiling, gazed at the betrayed one.

C. F. Schubart

3. Franz Schubert

8CD: 5/12–18

Piano Quintet in A major (*Trout*),
Fourth Movement (1819)

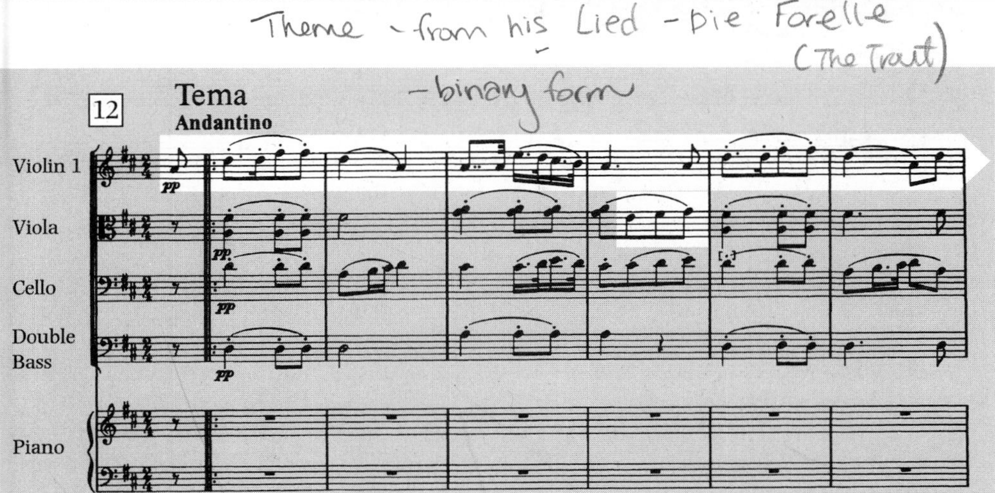

13

14

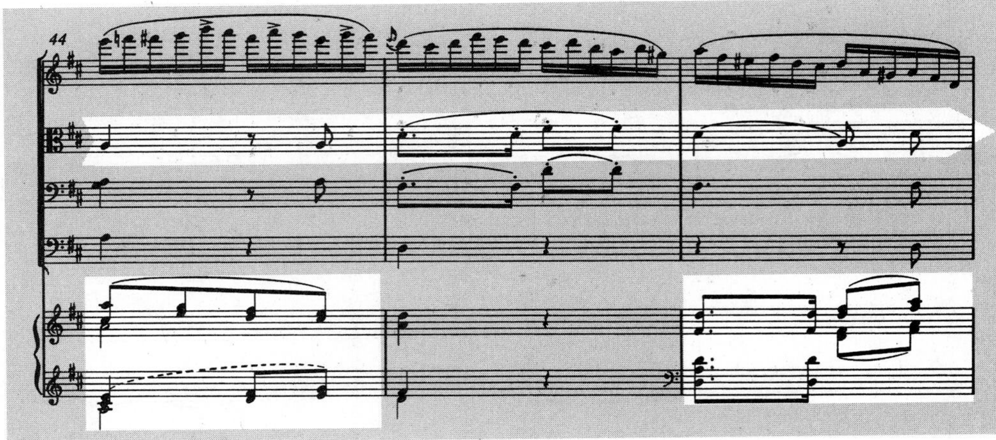
44

47
1
2

50
p

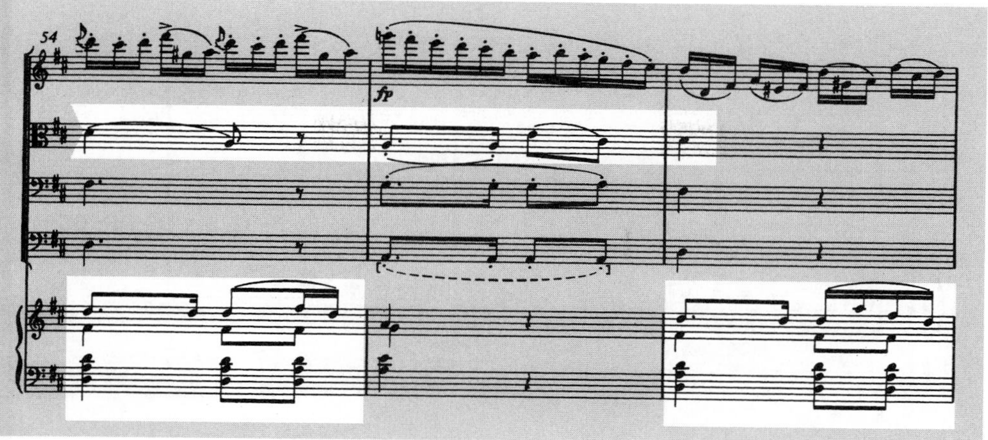

15

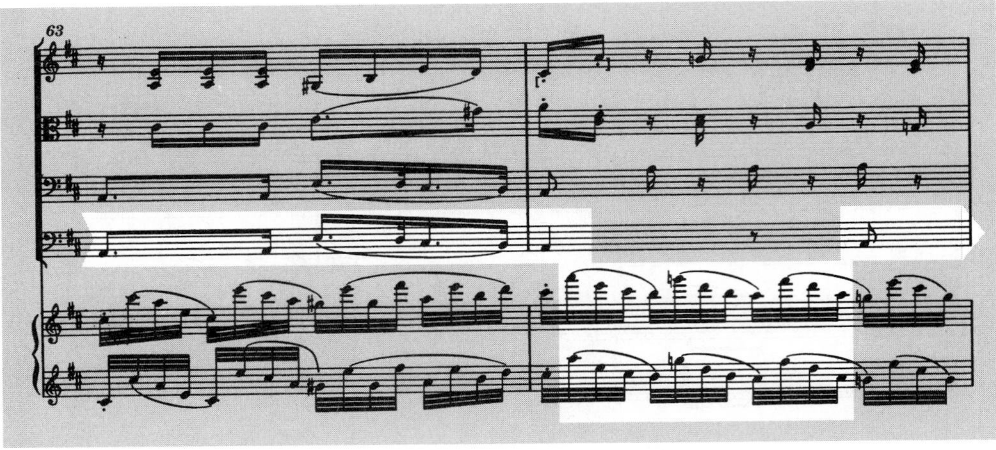
63

65

67
1

68
2

70

72
[>]
8

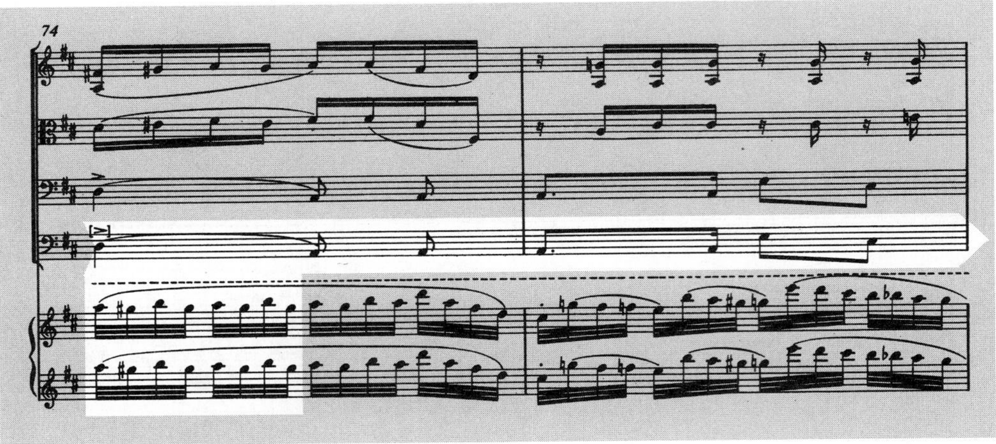
74

76
8

78

16

89
pp
pp
[pp]
pp
pp

91

94
[p]
decresc.
pp
cresc.
p
decresc.
pp
cresc.

97
tr
pp
[pp]
p
decresc.

17

Var. V
101
pp
p
p[p]

105
cresc.
[cresc.]
[p]
[pp cresc.]
p
1

108
pp
pp
[pp]
pp
cresc.

113
pp
pp

117
[>]

121
pp
decresc.

125
[dim.]
[dim.]
dim.
[dim.]
dim.

18
like a 6th variation - brings back main theme
+ piano accomp. from song
128 Allegretto
p
6
p

132
p

138
[p]
p
p

140

144
p

149

154
p
[p]
[p]
[p]

159

164
decresc.
decresc.
[p]
6
6

168
pp
dim.
pp
[dim.]
pp
6
[dim.]
pp
dim.
decresc.
pp
dim.

Franz Schubert's brief life span coincides with a fascinating period in Viennese history. On the one hand, Vienna was the home of one of the greats of the Classical era, Ludwig van Beethoven. He died just one year before Schubert. On the other hand, Schubert's Vienna embraced fully the Romantic operatic sensations of Rossini. This Classical-Romantic dichotomy is evident in Schubert's instrumental music, in which he fashioned a distinctive combination of Romantic style and Classical structure in his symphonies, piano sonatas, and chamber music. This fusion is critical to nineteenth-century chamber music in general. Of all of the Romantic instrumental genres, chamber music retains the strongest and most consistent ties to Classical structures. But within this Classical framework, composers like Schubert placed an emphasis on melody, color, and theatricality, prominent features of the pervading Romantic spirit.

The expanding color palette of nineteenth-century chamber music is evident in Schubert's *Trout* Quintet, which is scored for the unusual combination of piano, violin, viola, cello, and string bass, rather than the standard ensemble of a piano and string quartet. Typical of Romantic chamber music, the virtuosic weight of the composition lies in the piano part. Composed in 1817, the *Trout* Quintet is set in five movements, reflecting the early freedom of Schubert's chamber works, which range from one to six movements in length. The fourth movement, inserted between a scherzo and the finale, functions as a second slow movement in the cycle. Schubert casts this movement in a standard Classical form of a theme and variations and borrows its theme from his own Lied, *Die Forelle* (*The Trout*).

The song itself is typical of Schubert's Lieder. The poem, by the critic and composer Christian Schubart, has three stanzas and relates a delightful tale of the demise of a trout at the hands of a clever fisherman. The subject matter reflects Schubert's interest in nature, although some symbolism might be read into the tale. The vocal line mirrors the innocence and simplicity of the story with its repeated diatonic phrases, and the piano accompaniment suggests the image of splashing water. The modified strophic form also reflects the simplicity of the narrative; the only variation in the form occurs during the climactic action of the third stanza.

In the Quintet, the theme is reshaped into a binary structure. Each variation features different combinations of instruments, and the theme is increasingly treated more freely. The final section, which can be viewed as a sixth variation, brings back a clear statement of the original theme and incorporates the piano accompaniment material from the song as well.

-programed symphony
-reoccuring theme "idée fixe" appears in all 5 mvts

4. Hector Berlioz

Symphonie fantastique,
Fourth and Fifth Movements (1830)

8CD: 5/19 – 31
4CD: 3/9 – 14

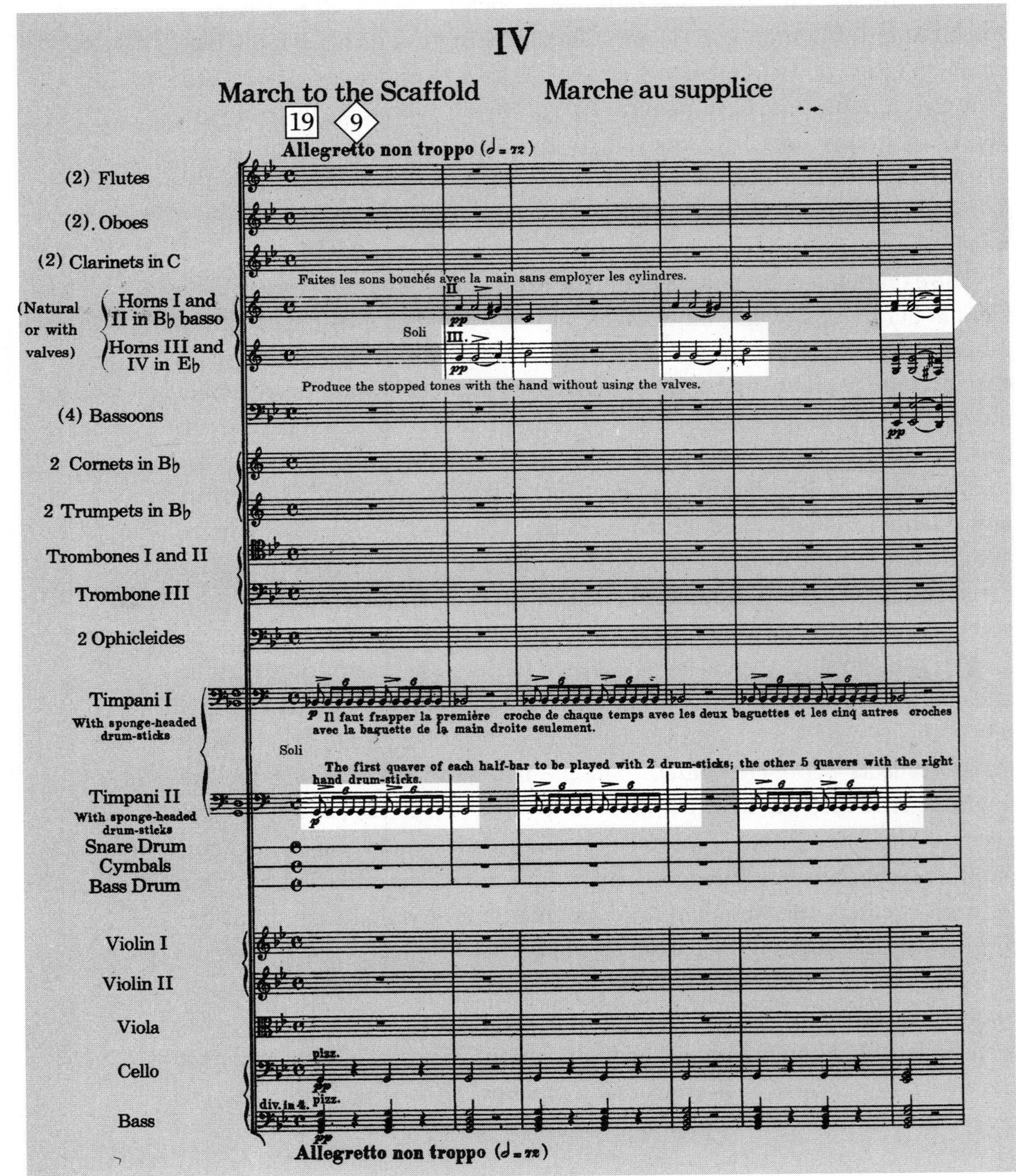

7
II.
I.
p
cresc. poco a poco

15
20
10
Clar.
Corni
Fag.
unis.
Soli
C^tti
Tr.
Tromb.
Oph. I.
cresc.
Timp.
cresc. molto
cresc.
pizz.
arco
Viol.
unis.
dim.
26
Cor. III. IV.
Fag.
cresc
Timp.
Soli
Viol.
Vello. e C.B.
unis.
dim.

34
Timp.
Viol.
dim.
p
39
Fl.
Ob.
Clar.
Corni.
Fag.
C^tti
Tr.
Tromb.
Oph. I.
Timp.
ff
mf
p
Viol.
f
dim.
(dim.

44
Fl.
Ob.
Clar.
Corni.
Fag.
Soli unis.
Timp.
Viol.
pizz.
pizz.
pizz.
pizz.

50
Fag.
Viol.

55
Fag.
unis.
Viol.
dim.

21
11
60
Fl.
Ob.
Clar
Corni.
avec les cylindres tous les sons ouverts.
with the valves, all tones open
Fag.
Ctti
a 2.
Tr.
Tromb.
Oph. I.
cresc.
Timp.
cresc.
Cinelli.
Gr. Tamb.
arco
Viol.
Vcllo.
C.B.
53

68
pizz.

22 12

75

poco f p

cresc. f

p cresc.

arco

pizz.

83
I.
Soli
Soli
II.
Oph. I.
Soli
poco f
f cresc.
poco f
cresc.
Cinelli
Solo
Gr. Tamb.
Solo
arco
pizz.
arco
pizz.
arco
pizz.
arco
pizz.
arco
pizz.
arco
pizz.
arco
arco
arco
pizz.
arco
cresc.
cresc.
cresc.

91
a 2.
a 2.

96
(>)
(> >)
mf
cresc.
ff
f

101
diminuendo
poco f
Soli
Soli
cresc.
cresc.
cresc.
cresc.

106

a2.

I.

Soli

Soli

unis.

Soli

Soli

pizz. arco pizz. arco

pizz. arco pizz. arco pizz.

pizz. arco pizz. arco pizz.

pizz. arco pizz. arco pizz.

pizz.

114
a 2.
a 2.
mf
cresc.
arco
ff
sempre più forte

23
13
119
a 2.
Baguettes de bois
Wooden drum-sticks
cresc.

125
dim.
p
pp
ff
a 2.
I.
mf

136

a 2.

a 2.

a 2.

a 2.

a 2.

unis.

a 2.

sul G

sul G

144

a 2.

a 2.

a 2.

unis.

a 2.

151

2 Oph.

muta in B♮

158

a2.

24 14

I. Solo

pp dolce assai ed appassionato

Trois Timbaliers
Three drummers

167

rall. poco a tempo

I. II.

a 2.

Fag.

III. IV.

a 2.

a 2.

a 2.

1. Timpanista.

2. Timpanista.

Soli

3. Timpanista.

Tamburo.

Cinelli.

étouffez le son
damp the tone

Gr. Tamb.

étouffez le son avec la main
damp the tone with the hand

pizz.

pizz.

pizz.

pizz.

pizz.

arco

arco

arco

arco

arco

rall. poco a tempo

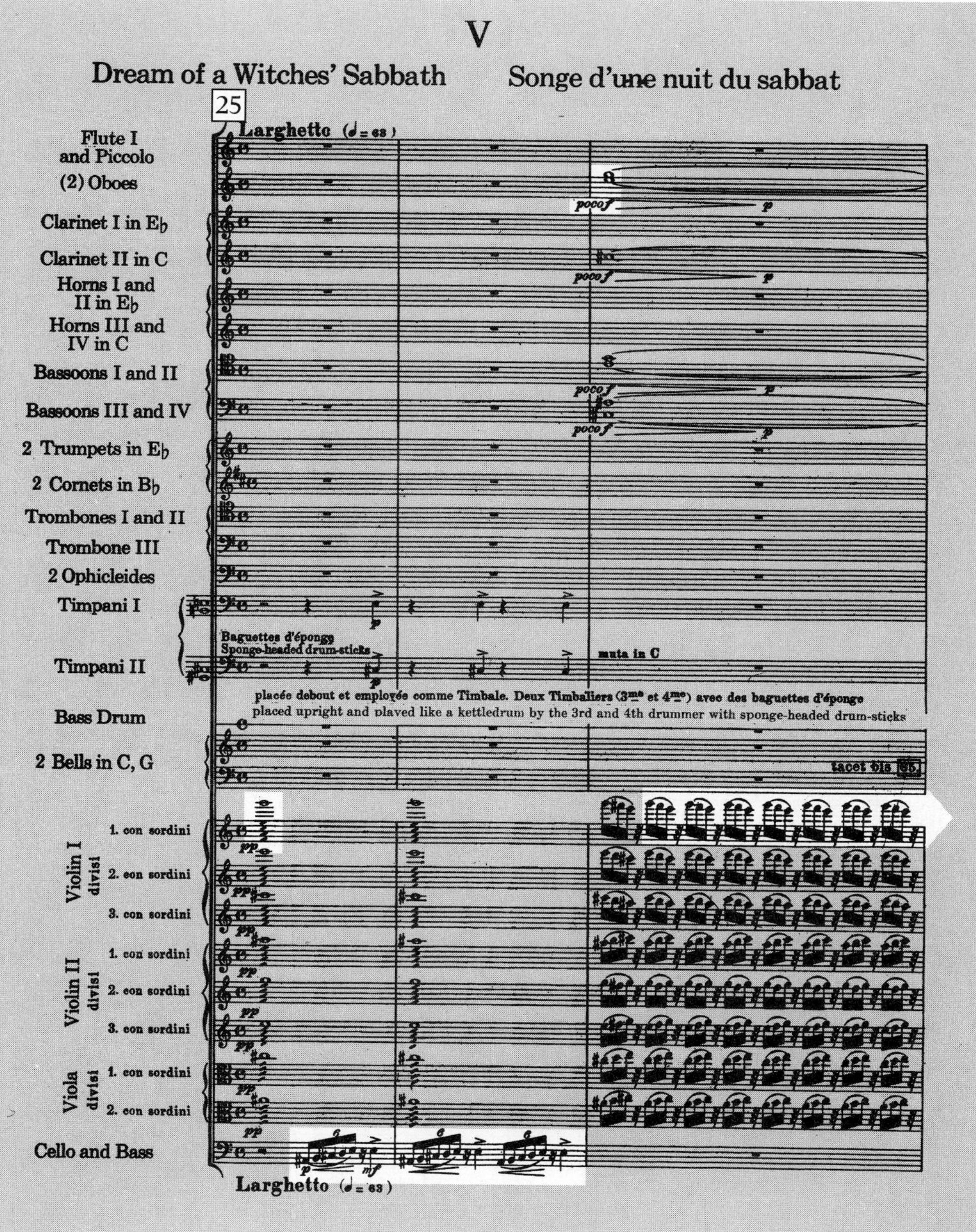
V
Dream of a Witches' Sabbath
Songe d'une nuit du sabbat
25
Larghetto
Flute I and Piccolo
(2) Oboes
Clarinet I in E♭
Clarinet II in C
Horns I and II in E♭
Horns III and IV in C
Bassoons I and II
Bassoons III and IV
2 Trumpets in E♭
2 Cornets in B♭
Trombones I and II
Trombone III
2 Ophicleides
Timpani I
Baguettes d'éponge
Sponge-headed drum-sticks
Timpani II
muta in C
placée debout et employée comme Timbale. Deux Timbaliers (3me et 4me) avec des baguettes d'éponge
placed upright and played like a kettledrum by the 3rd and 4th drummer with sponge-headed drum-sticks
Bass Drum
2 Bells in C, G
tacet bis
Violin I divisi
1. con sordini
2. con sordini
3. con sordini
Violin II divisi
1. con sordini
2. con sordini
3. con sordini
Viola divisi
1. con sordini
2. con sordini
Cello and Bass
Larghetto

4

f dim. p

pizz.

div.

Vcllo.

C.B.

ppp

mf

7
Fl. Solo
Fl. picc. Solo
a 2.
Soli
dim.
I. Solo
Solo III. bouché avec les cylindres
ppp stopped, with valves
II.
Deux timbaliers, roulement avec des baguettes à tête d'éponge sur la Grande Caisse placée debout
Two timpanists, rolling with sponge-headed sticks on the upright Bass Drum.
arco
unis.

13

muta in G

16
Solo I.
mf
dim.
sf > pp
Solo. III. bouché avec les cylindres
pppp
f
éponges
pp
ôtez les sourdines
ôtez les sourdines
ôtez les sourdines
ôtez les sourdines
ôtez les sourdines
ôtez les sourdines
div.
div.

26

21

Allegro (♩. = 112)

Allegro assai (𝅝 = 76)

Solo lointain distant

ppp

cresc.

ouvert avec les cylindres

open, with valves

a 2.

ff

I.

p *cresc.* *poco a poco*

Sur les deux timbales

p

cresc. *poco a poco*

cresc. *poco a poco*

p

sans sourdine

sans sourdine

Allegro (♩. = 112)

Allegro assai (𝅝 = 76)

32

a 2.

a 2.

a 2.

40
Allegro (♩. = 104)
Fl. picc.
Ob.
poco f
Clar. I in E♭
Solo
poco f
cresc.
Clar. II in C
poco f
Fag.
unis.
mf
Viol. I unis.
Viol. II unis.
Viola unis.
Vcllo.
C.B.
Allegro (♩. = 104)
49
Fl. picc.
Ob.
Clar.
Fag.
Viol.
pp
pp

55
Fl.
Fl. picc.
Ob.
Clar.
Cor.
Fag.
Viol.
61
Fl.
Fl. pic.
Ob.
Clar.
Cor.
Fag.
Viol.
cresc.
(cresc.)
a 2.

67

Fl.

Fl. picc.

Ob.

Clar.

Cor.

a 2.

Fag.

unis.

Tr.

C^tti

Tromb.

Oph.

Timp.

Viol.

ff

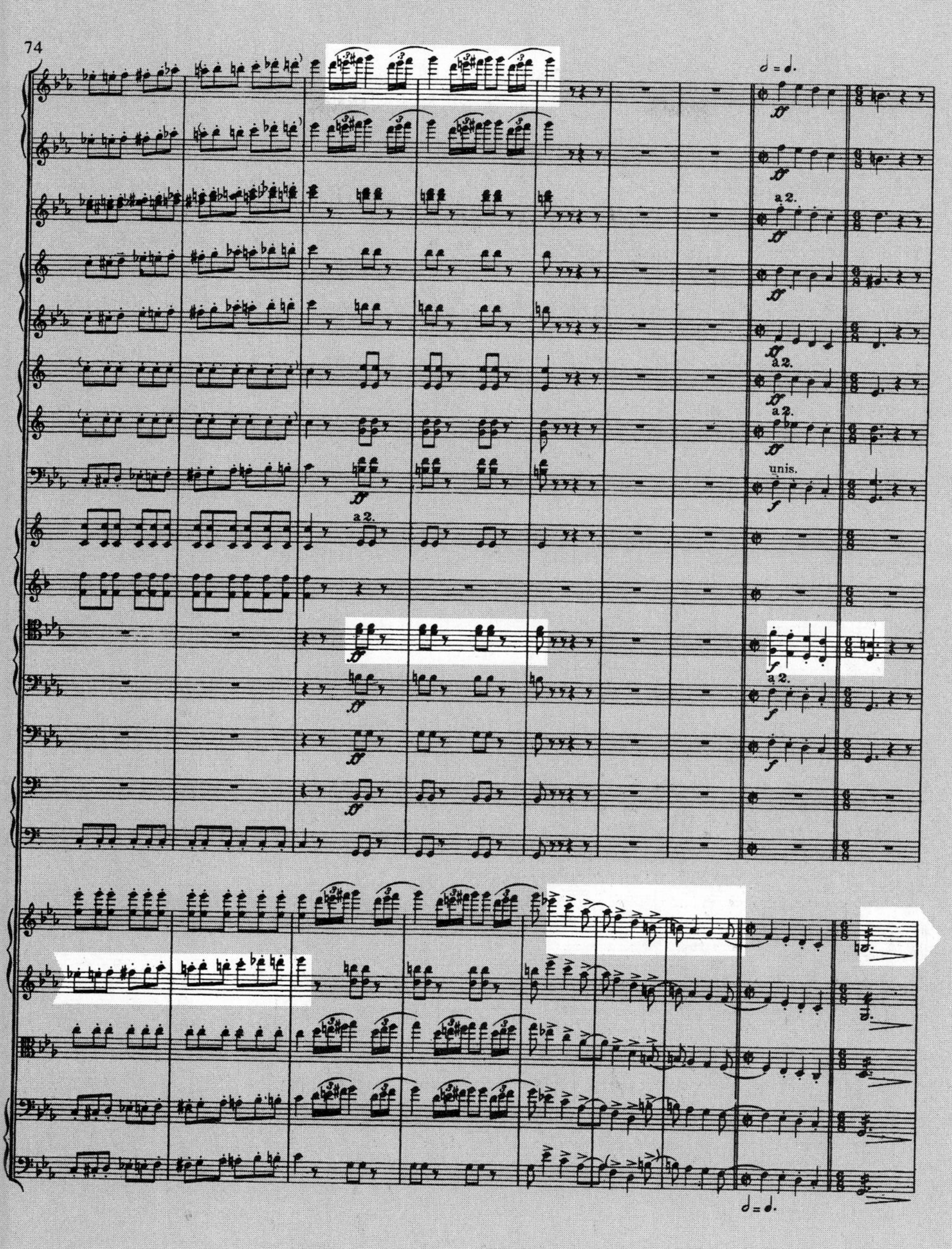
74
a 2.
unis.

83
Fag.
unis.
sf>p
(dim.)
ppp
Viol.
p
f
sf
102
27
Tromb.
Timp.
derrière la Scène
behind the Scene
Due campane (2 Glocken) in C (Ut) G (Sol)
con Ped.
A défaut de Cloches derrière le Théâtre, plusieurs Pianos sur l'avant-scène.
In the absence of Bells behind the scene, several pianos on the apron.
Soli
poco f
ff

115
Ob. I. Solo
mf
a 2.
Cor.
Tr.
Tromb.
Timp.
Camp.
p
pp
Viol.
mf
28
127 Dies iræ sans presser
Fag. unis.
Oph. a 2.
Soli
f
Camp.
Viol.
sans presser

146
29
Fl.
Fl. picc.
Ob.
Clar.
Cor.
Fag.
Tr.
Ctti
Tromb
Oph.
Gr. Tamb.
Camp.
pizz.
Viol.
pizz.
pizz.

159
arco
pizz.
H.B.1.

171
pizz.
pizz.
pizz.

184
arco
arco
arco
arco
arco
tenu
tenu

196
f

209
pizz.
pizz.
pizz.

221

G-Caisse roulante, deux Timbaliers

Bass-Drum roll, two timpanists

a 2.

a 2.

arco

arco

arco

231
Fl.
Fl. picc.
Ob.
Clar.
Cor.
Fag.
Tr.
Cttⁱ
Tromb.
Oph.
Baguettes d'éponge
Sponge-headed sticks
Timp.
Viol.
cresc.
a 2
a 4.

30

Ronde du Sabbat
Witches' round dance

241 **Un peu retenu**

Un peu retenu

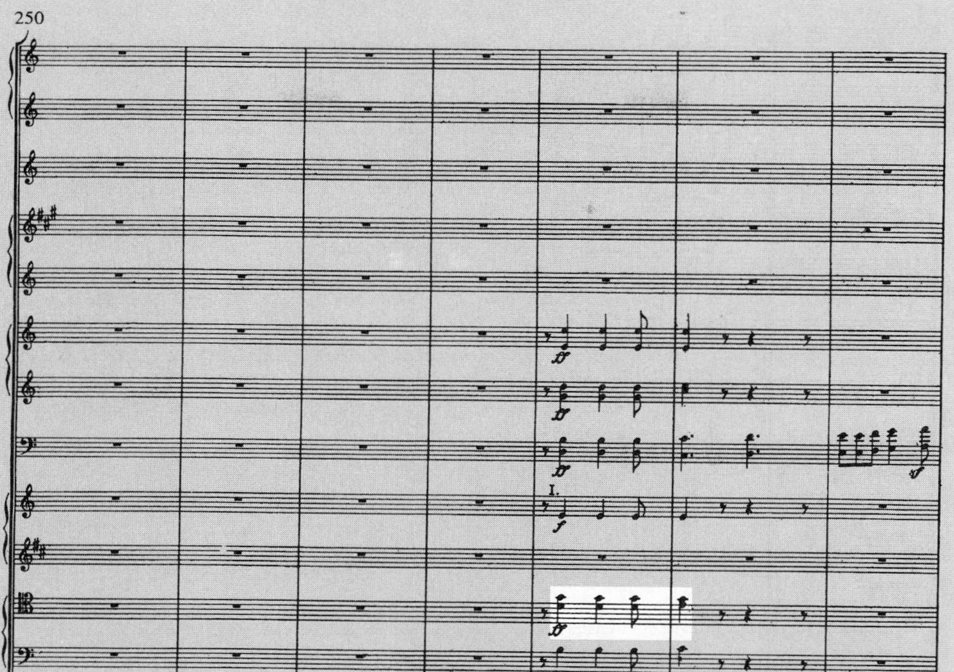

250

257
I.
a 2.
a 2.
unis.

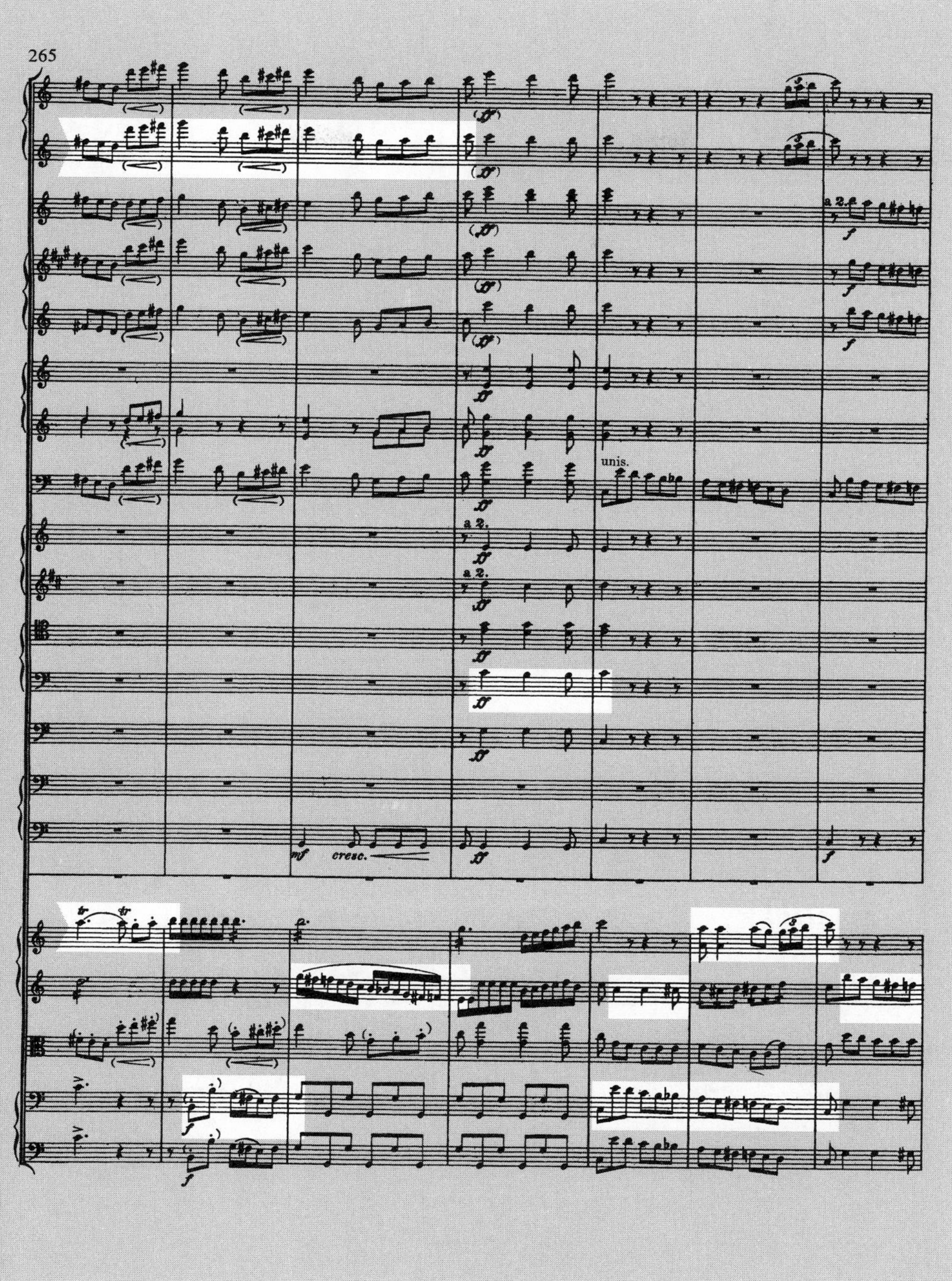
265
unis.
a 2.
a 2.
a 2.
mf
cresc.

272
a 2.
f
cresc.
ff

280

289
I.
(cresc.)
(cresc.)

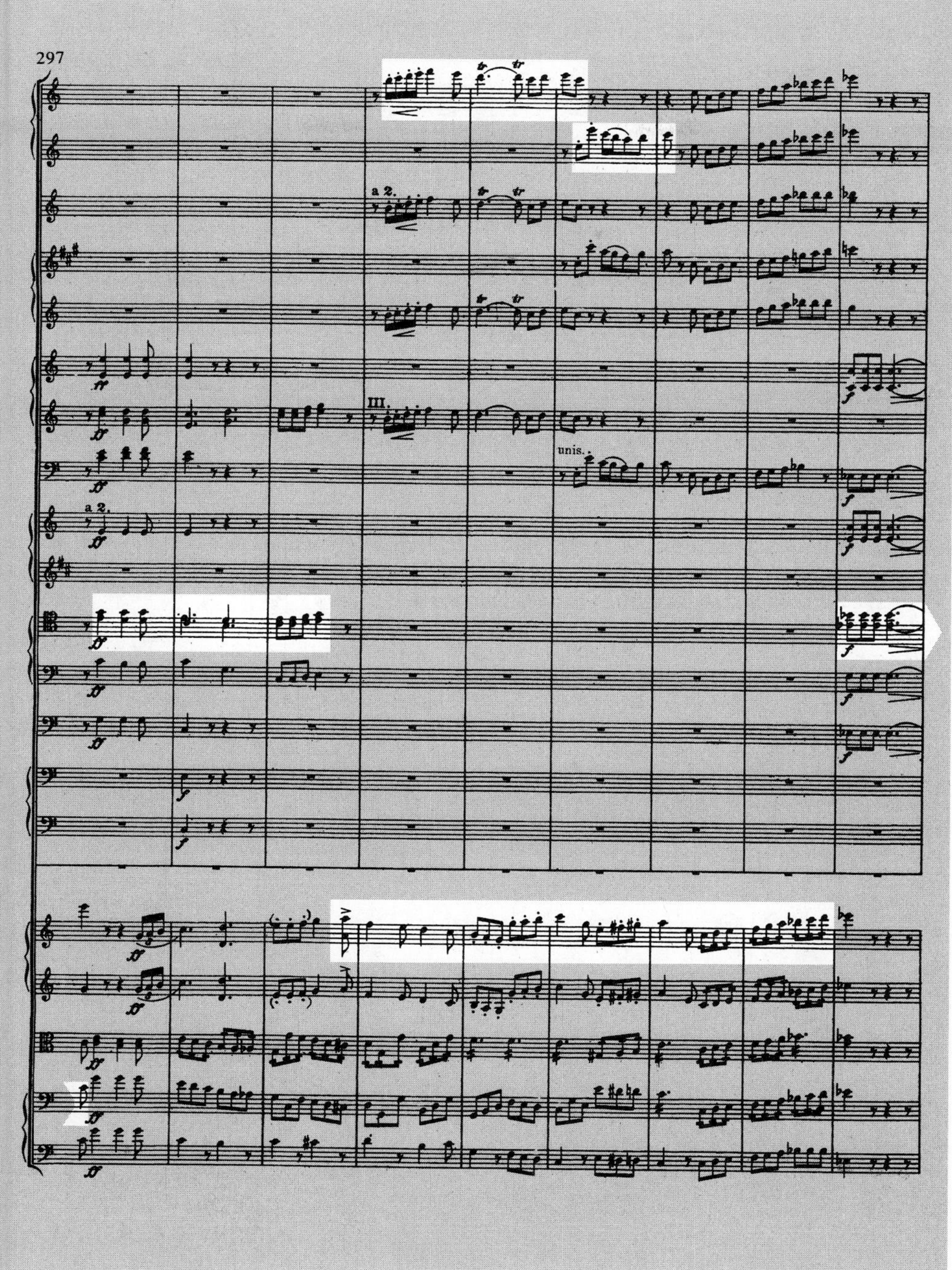
297
a 2.
III.
unis.
a 2.

306
Soli
éponges
pizz.
arco

313
f dimin.
f dimin.
f (dimin.
f dimin.
f dimin.
a 2.
ff
p
a 2.
ff
p
ff
pp
ff
pp
pizz.
f
arco
ff
pizz.
f
arco
ff
ff
f
ff
ff
f
ff
ff
f

320
a 2.
unis.
a 2.
a 2.
a 2.
pizz.
pizz.

327
I.
III.
Soli
dim.
pp
unis. Soli
sf
arco
en dim. toujours
(en dim. toujours)
pizz.
poco f

335
sf > pp
sf > pp
sf > pp
sf > pp
p
dim.
ppp
dimin. sempre
ppp
ppp
p
pp
pp
p
pp

345
II.
Solo
poco f
IV. Solo
poco f
II.
pp
IV.
pp
ppp
II. Solo
presque rien
mf
ppp
presque rien
mf
ppp
pizz.
pp
div. arco
mf
div.
Soli
ppp
arco
mf
dim.
Soli
presque rien
arco
pppp
mf
dim.

361

cresc. poco a poco - - - - - - - - -

II.

bouché avec les cylindres

IV.

poco sf > *p*

crescendo

Un Timbalier
One drummer

Solo

pp

cresc. poco a poco -

pp

cresc.

Soli

pp

crescendo - - - - - - -

371

bouché avec les cylindres

II.

poco sf > p

Les deux Timbaliers réunis

Both drummers together

p cresc. poco a poco

p

p

cresc. poco a poco

poco a poco

poco a poco

380
mf
cresc.
I.
mf
cresc. sempre
cresc. poco a poco
f cresc. sempre
cresc. sempre
mf

389
ff
mf
mf
f
unis.
a 2.
cresc. molto
div.
unis.

398
ff

107

31

414

Dies irae et Ronde du Sabbat ensemble

Dies irae and witches' round dance together

a 2.

unis.

a 2.

a 2.

a 2.

mf

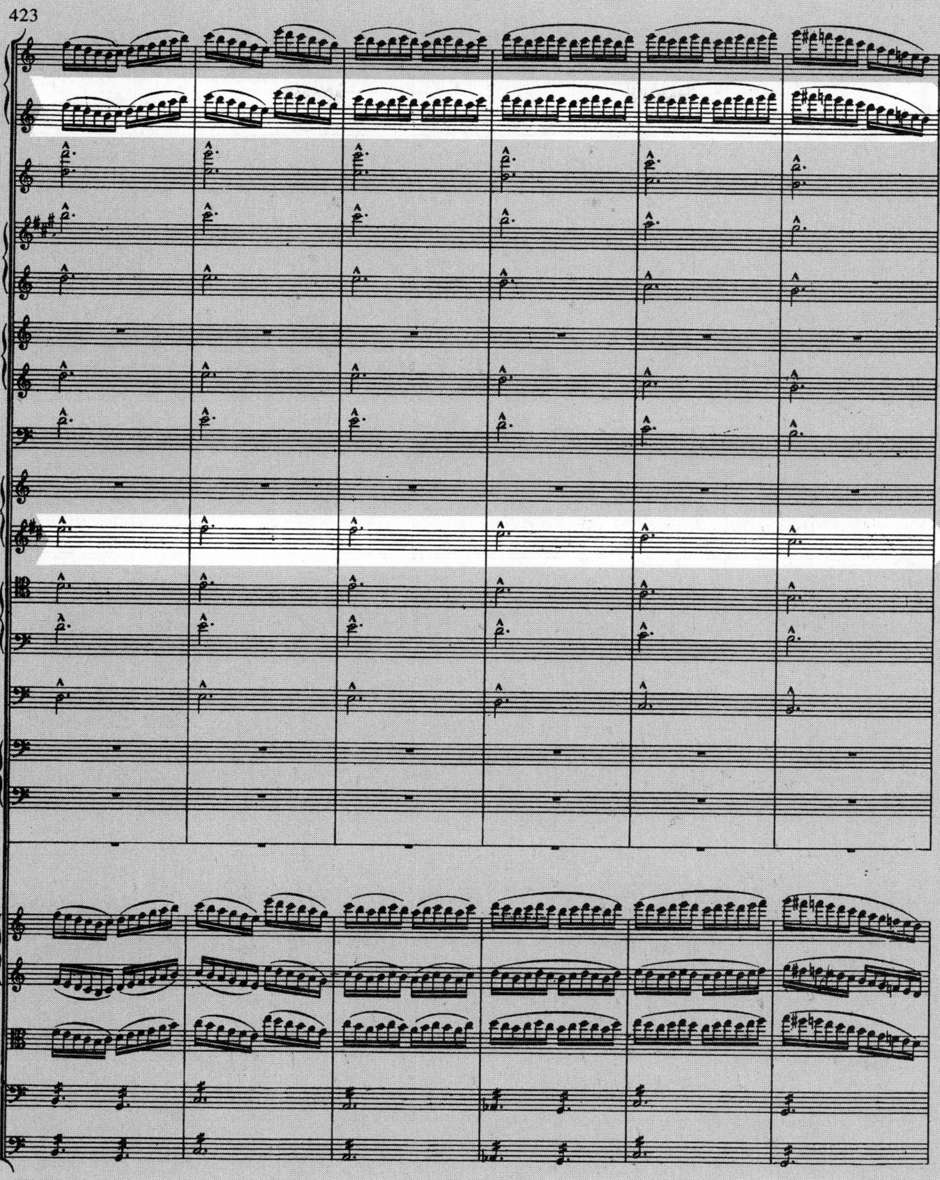

423

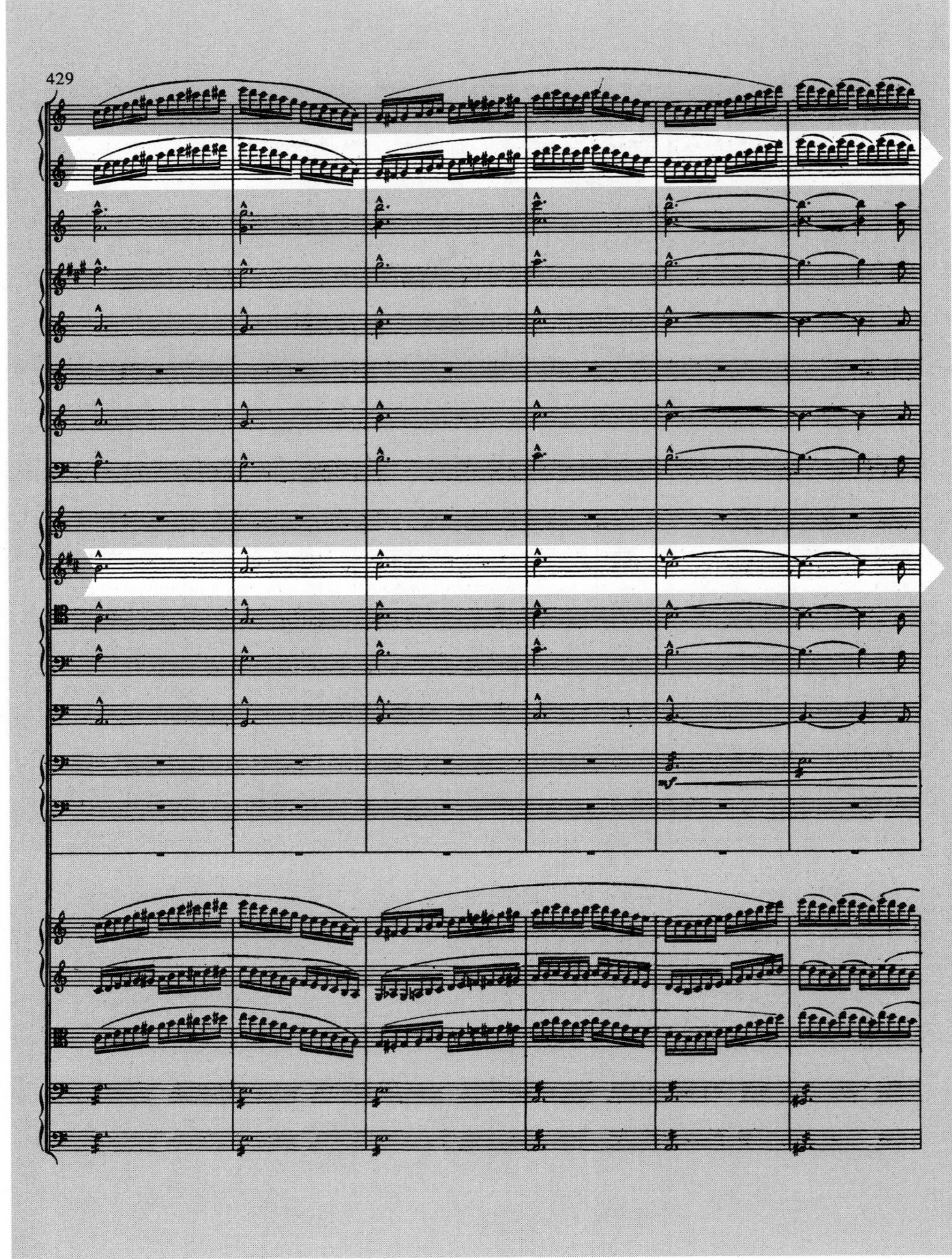
429
mf

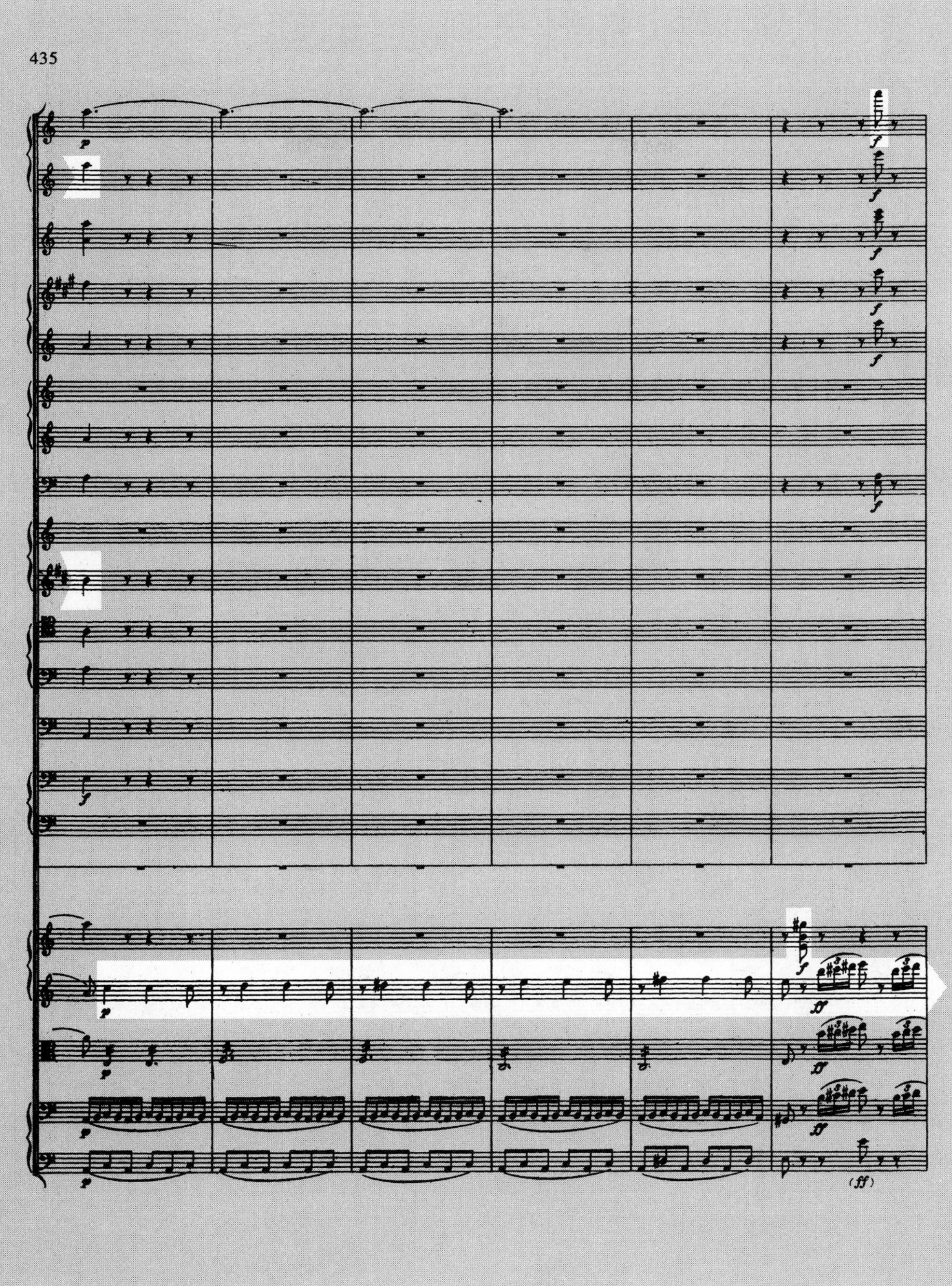
435

441

a 2.

mf

unis.

frappez avec les bois de l'archet

frappez avec les bois de l'archet

frappez avec les bois de l'archet

(col legno battuta)

div.

448

pizz.

pp

pizz.

pp

456

Soli

p légèrement

I.

p légèrement

p légèrement

I.

p légèrement

arco

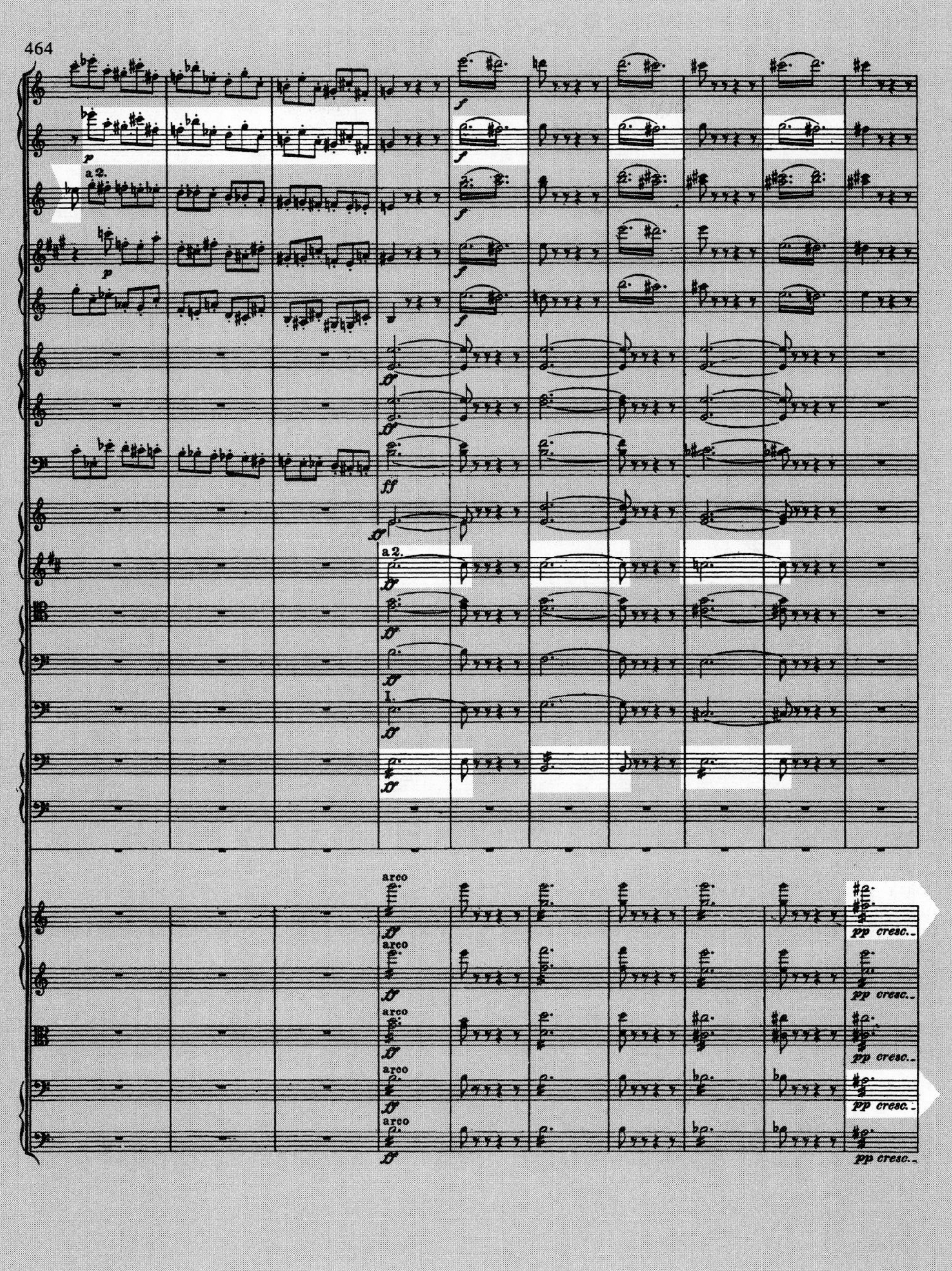
464
a 2.
p
f
ff
a 2.
I.
arco
pp cresc.

474
Soli
I.
a 2.
unis.
mf
cresc.

483
Solo II.
a 2.
unis.
a 2.
a 2.
cresc. molto
a 2.

animez un peu

493

a 2.

a 2.

I.

animez un peu

504
unis.
a 2.
a 2.
I.
div.
unis.

515

tenu

unis.

Coup frappé sur une Cymbale avec une baguette couverte d'éponge ou un tampon
Struck on a cymbal with a sponge-headed drum-stick or a padded stick

Cinelli.

The early Romantic tendency toward the colossal is best seen in the imaginative works of Hector Berlioz (1803–1869). Expanding both the size and the range of colors of his operas, choral works, and symphonies, Berlioz created innovative works that dazzled the Parisian public. *Symphonie fantastique* (1830), a program symphony with five movements, stands as one of the masterpieces of the early Romantic era because of its fanciful story, effective use of thematic transformation, and brilliant orchestration.

For the most part, Berlioz pays only passing homage to Classical structures. While the first three movements primarily present musical tableaus of the poet and his love, the fourth and fifth abound in specific imagery. In his opium state, the poet dreams that he has killed his lover, and, in the marchlike fourth movement, he is led to a scaffold and beheaded. In a later revision of the symphony, Berlioz added a repeat of the opening section of this movement, which is heard in our period-instrument recording. The intent of the repetition was likely to lengthen the movement, not to suggest any underlying structure. In the last movement, the poet is transported to a Faustian scene, where witches, including his beloved, revel in his demise.

A recurring theme, labeled the *idée fixe* (fixed idea) by Berlioz, appears in all five movements of the symphony. Representing the poet's lover, the melody is continuously transformed to meet the moods of the story. In the fourth movement, it appears briefly at the end, as the poet's last thought is about love. In the finale, the theme, played by the E-flat clarinet, is a rollicking, grotesque jig, reflecting the true image of his love.

Masterful orchestration is evident throughout both movements. The string instruments explore contrasting colors with passages of pizzicato and *col legno* (hitting the strings with the wood side of the bow). The woodwind families are expanded with instruments such as the E-flat clarinet, the English horn, and the contrabassoon, and the flutes are asked to make an unusual sound effect by rolling the mouthpiece away from their lips at the beginning of the fifth movement. The low brass section is also expanded with the addition of two *ophicleides* (obsolete brass instruments, replaced today by tubas). As is evident at the beginning of the fourth movement, the role and size of the percussion section are also increased. One of the most striking passages of orchestration occurs in the fourth movement: following measures 82 and 109, the principal theme is presented with continuously changing colors, often on a note-by-note basis, including a "note" by the unpitched cymbals. But the most stunning moment in the entire symphony occurs at measure 127 of the finale, when the sacrilegious intoning of the *Dies irae* (*Day of Wrath*) chant by the low brass is heard against church bells ringing in the background.

stanza 1+3 = A+
" 2 = A−, free motion

5. Fanny Mendelssohn Hensel

8CD: 5/32–34

Bergeslust (Mountain Yearning), Op. 10, No. 5 (1847)

– strophic
– last completed work

13
ü - ber sich den blau - - - - - - - - - - - - - - - - - - - en, tief -
17
kla - ren Him - mels - dom.
21
33
Vom Ber - ge Vö - gel flie - - gen und Wol - ken so ge -
25
schwind, Ge - dan - ken ü - ber - flie - - gen die Vö - gel und_ den

29
Wind; ___
Ge - dan - ken ü - ber -
33
flie - - gen
die Vö - gel und den
37
Wind,
die Vö - - gel
und
den
Wind. ___
41
34
Die

46
Wol - ken ziehn her - nie - - der, das Vög - lein senkt sich gleich, Ge -
50
dan - ken gehn und Lie - - der bis in das Him - mel - reich, Ge -
54
dan - ken gehn, Ge - dan - - - - - - - - - - - - - - - ken bis in das Him - mel -
f
p
59
p
poco rit.
reich. Ge - dan - ken gehn und Lie - - der
poco rit.

dramatic ending.

Text and Translation

O Lust, vom Berg zu schauen Weit über Wald und Strom, Hoch über sich den blauen, den klaren Himmelsdom.	What longing to gaze from the mountaintop far across forest and stream, with, high above, the blue, clear dome of heaven.
Vom Berge Vögel fliegen, Und Wolken so geschwind, Gedanken überfliegen Die Vögel und den Wind.	From the mountain, birds fly and clouds speed away, thoughts soar over the birds and the wind.
Die Wolken zieh'n hernieder, Das Vöglein senkt sich gleich, Gedanken geh'n und Lieder Bis in das Himmelreich.	The clouds drift downward, the little bird will soon alight, but thoughts and songs reach to the realm of heaven.

Joseph Freiherr von Eichendorff

Like her younger brother Felix Mendelssohn, Fanny Hensel (1805–1847) was extremely talented both as a composer and as a pianist. She accepted her role as a woman in nineteenth-century European society, and devoted herself to her husband, her family, and her child. But she also found time for some concertizing and composition, most notably of piano music and Lieder.

The Lied *Bergeslust (Mountain Yearning)* is Hensel's last completed work. Her highly literate upbringing likely influenced her choice of text; the poem by Joseph von Eichendorff is a high-quality expression of the Romantic vision of nature. The three stanzas are set in a modified strophic form. The first and third stanzas, in A major, are essentially identical, while the second stanza, beginning in A minor, moves more freely, reflecting the images of motion expressed in the poem. The compound meter suggests the simplicity of nature, and the harmonic underpinning and vocal line capture the inspired spirit of the poet. This quality is reinforced in the song's dramatic ending.

6. Felix Mendelssohn

8CD: 5/35–43

Violin Concerto in E minor, Op. 64, First Movement (1844)

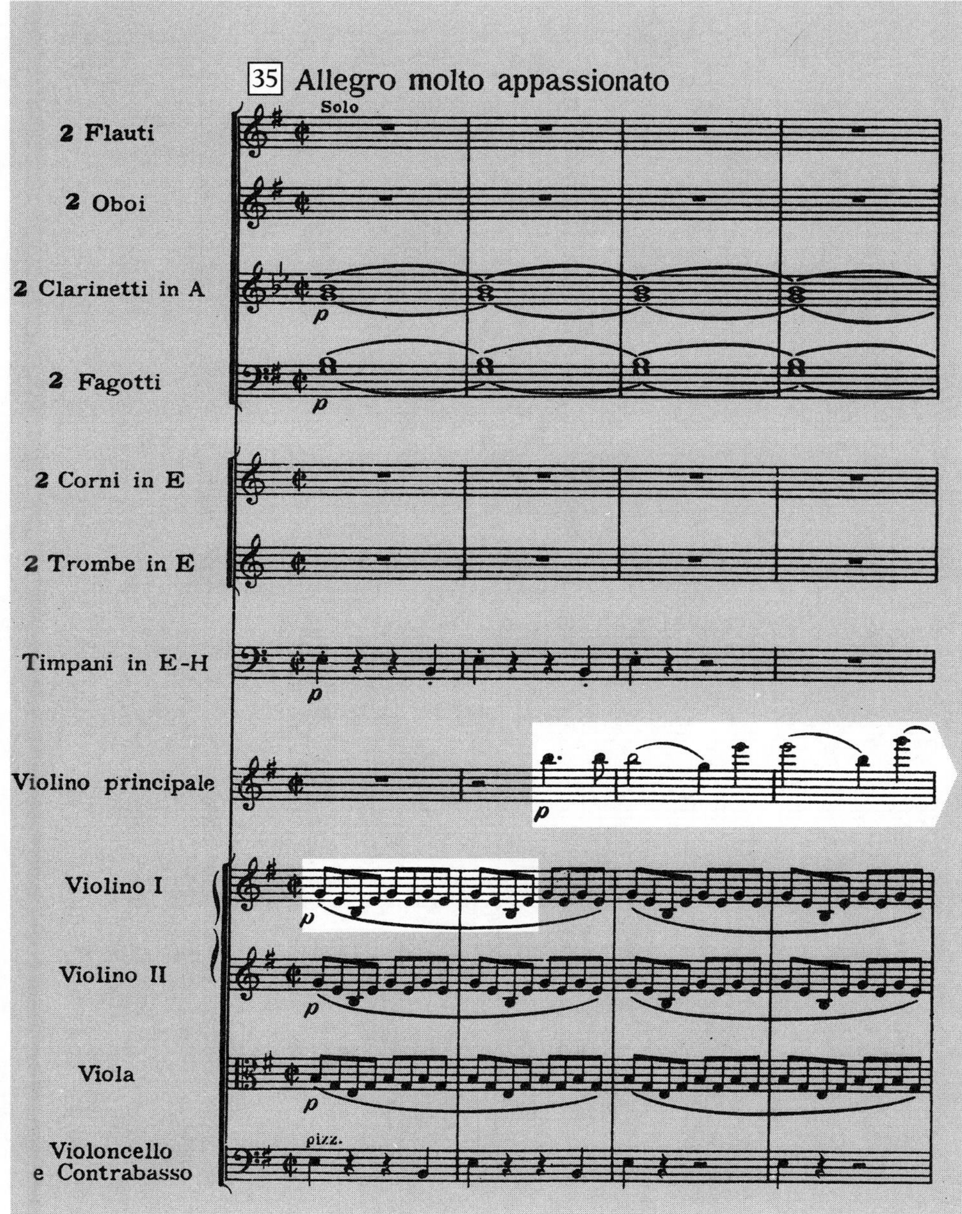

Cl.
Fg.
Vl.pr.
Vl.
Vla.
Vc.
e Cb.

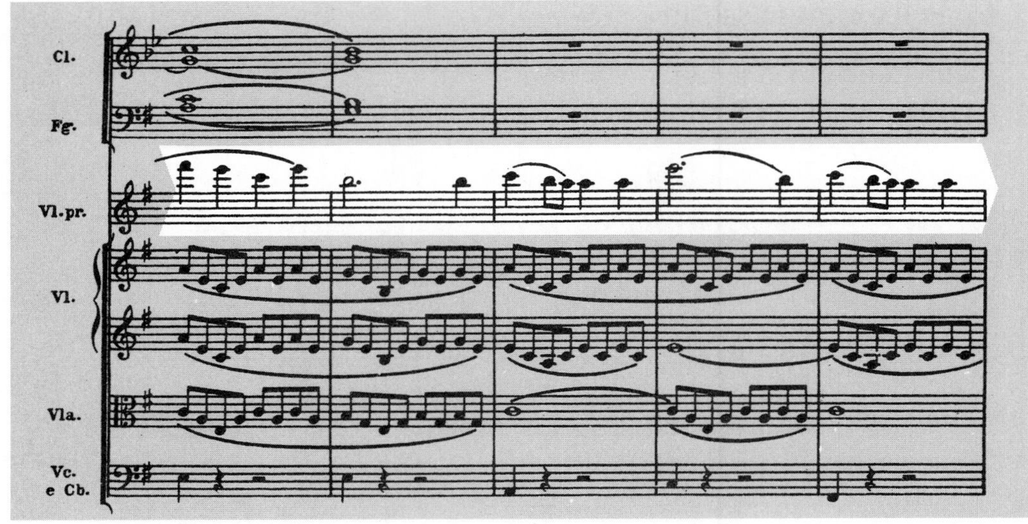

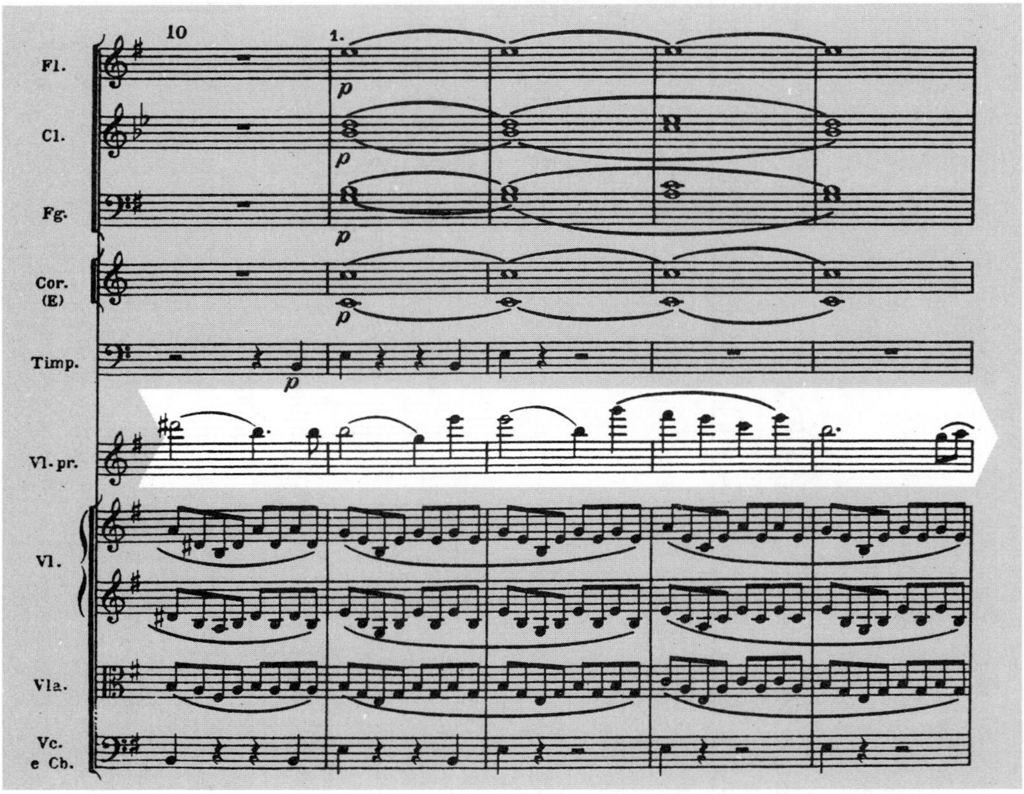
10
1.
Fl.
Cl.
Fg.
Cor.
(E)
Timp.
Vl.pr.
Vl.
Vla.
Vc.
e Cb.
p

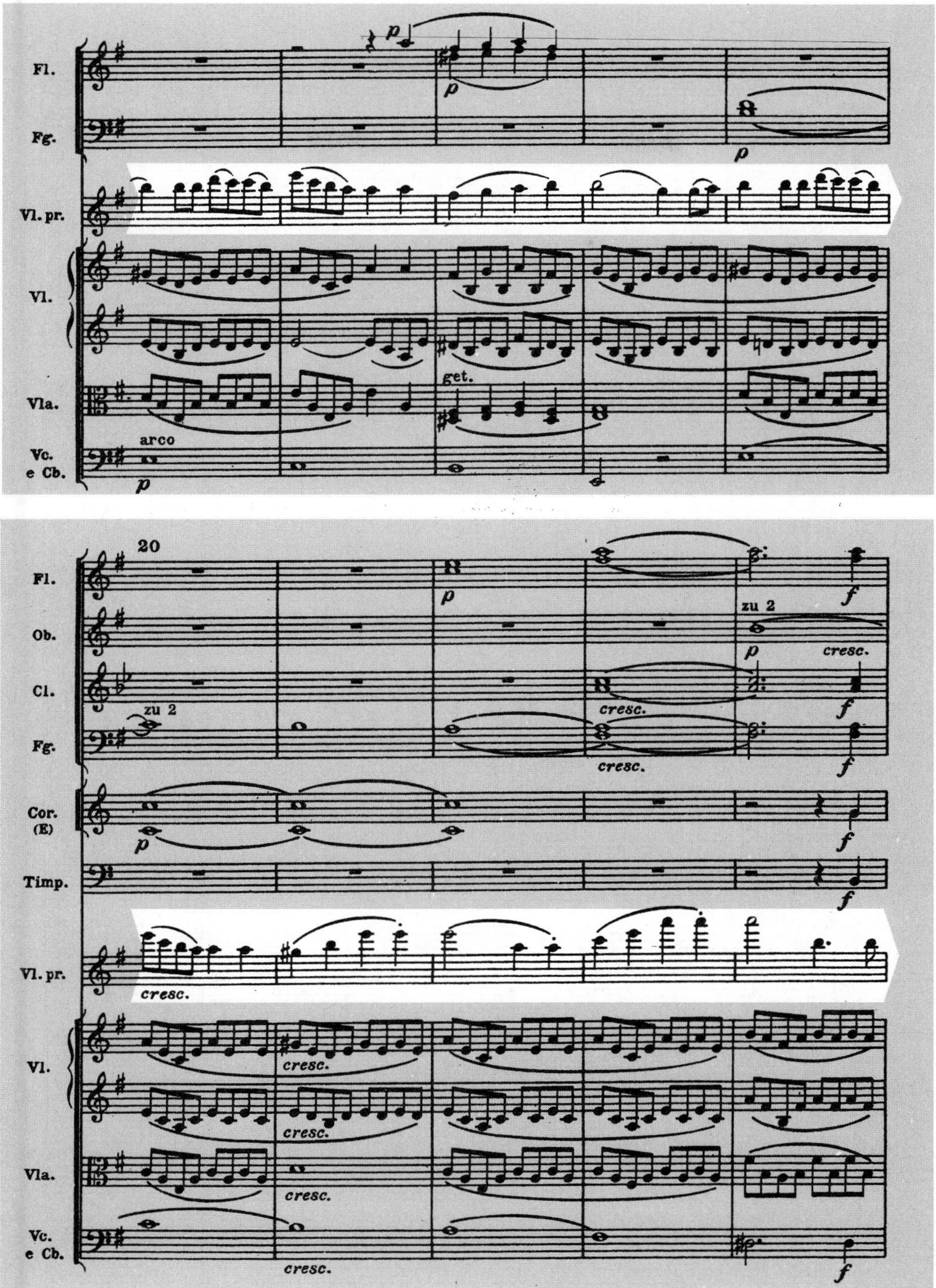

Fl.
Fg.
Vl. pr.
Vl.
Vla.
Vc. e Cb.
get.
arco
20
Ob.
Cl.
Cor. (E)
Timp.
zu 2
cresc.
p
f

Fl.
Ob.
Cl.
Fg.
Cor. (E)
Timp.
Vl. pr.
Vl.
Vla.
Vc. e Cb.
30
zu 2

Fl.
Ob.
Cl.
Fg.
Cor. (E)
Timp.
Vl. pr.
Vl.
Vla.
Vc. e Cb.
mf
4ta
cresc.
p
fp
1.
40
sf
f
tr
cresc.

zu 2
Fl.
Ob.
Cl.
Fg.
Cor. (E)
Tbe. (E)
Timp.
tr
Vl. pr.
3
Vl.
Vla.
Vc. e Cb.
f

50
Tutti
zu 2
Fl.
Ob.
Cl.
Fg.
Cor. (E)
zu 2
Tbe. (E)
tr
Timp.
Vl. pr.
Vl.
Vla.
Vc. e Cb.
ff
sf

Fl.
Ob.
Cl.
Fg.
zu 2
f
Cor. (E)
Tbe. (E)
tr
Timp.
Vl.
Vla.
Vc. e Cb.
60
ff
sf
zu 2

zu 2
Fl.
zu 2
Ob.
zu 2
Cl.
Fg.
Cor. (E)
Tbe. (E)
Timp.
Vl.
Vla.
Vc. e Cb.
zu 2

36
70
Fl.
Ob.
zu 2 p
Cl.
Fg.
Cor. (E)
Tbe. (E)
Timp.
Vl.
Vla.
Vc. e Cb.
Solo
80
Vl. pr.

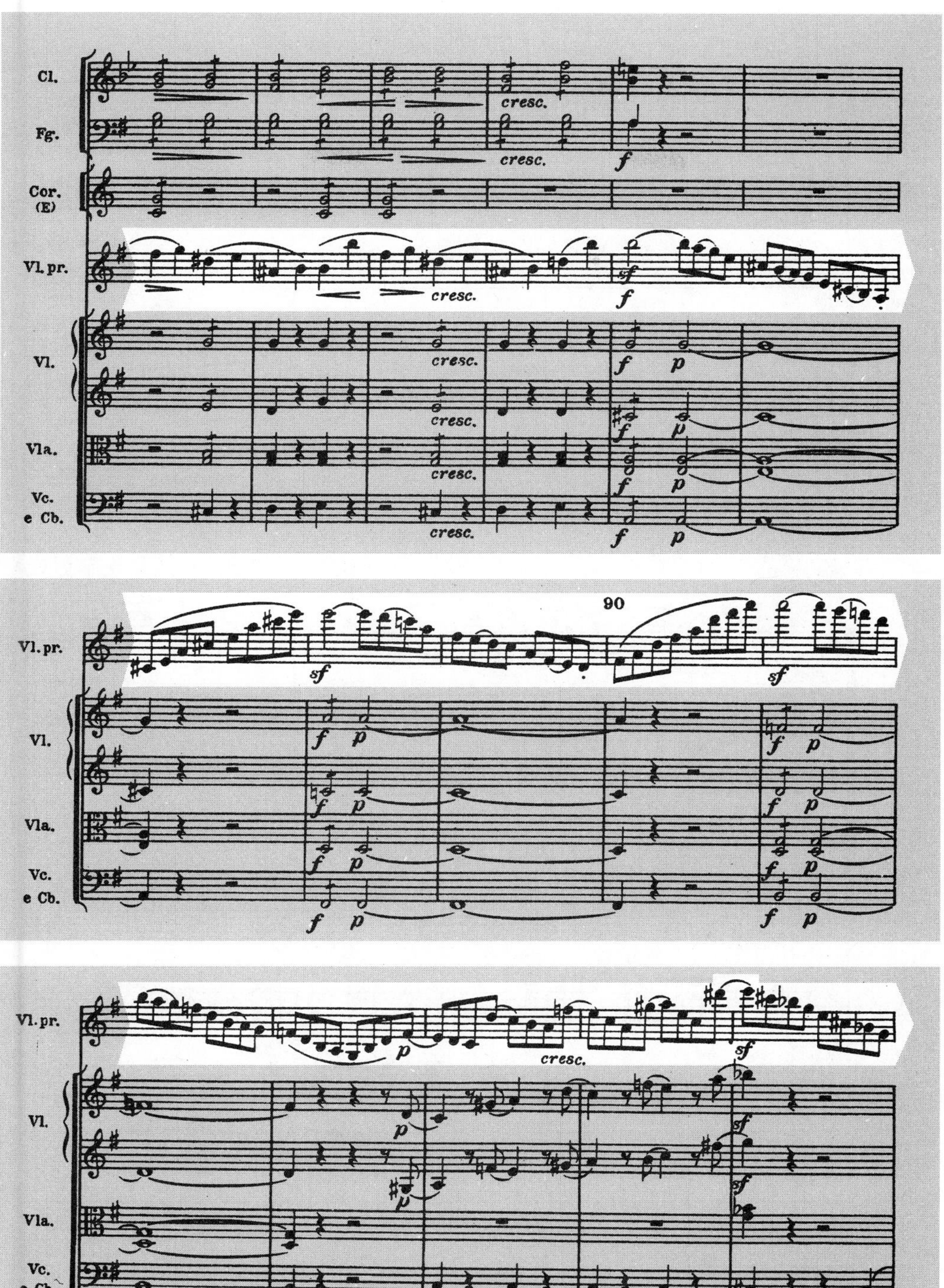
Cl.
Fg.
Cor. (E)
Vl. pr.
Vl.
Vla.
Vc. e Cb.
cresc.
f
p
sf
90
Vl. pr.
Vl.
Vla.
Vc. e Cb.
Vl. pr.
Vl.
Vla.
Vc. e Cb.

1.
Fl.
p
3
Vl. pr.
cresc.
Vl.
p
p
Vla.
p
Vc.
e Cb.

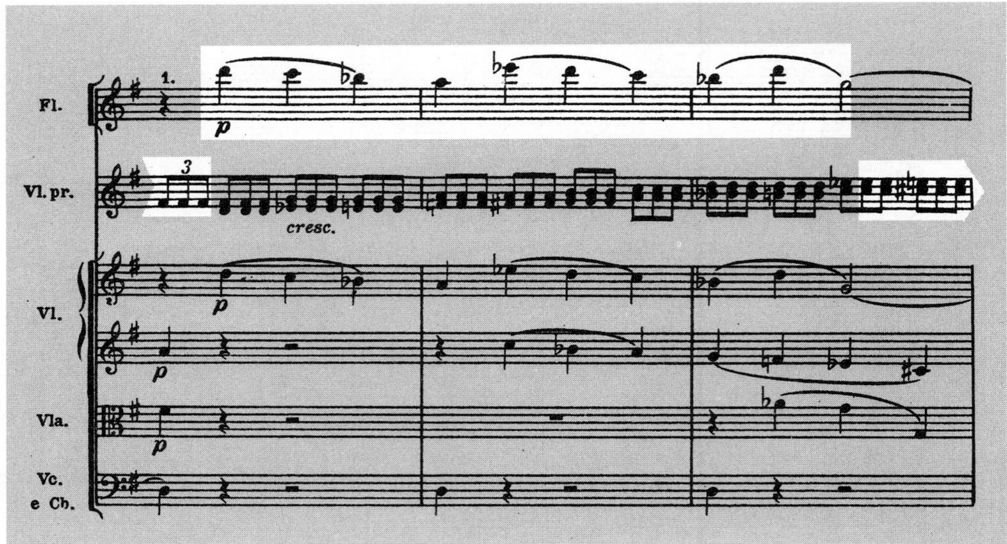

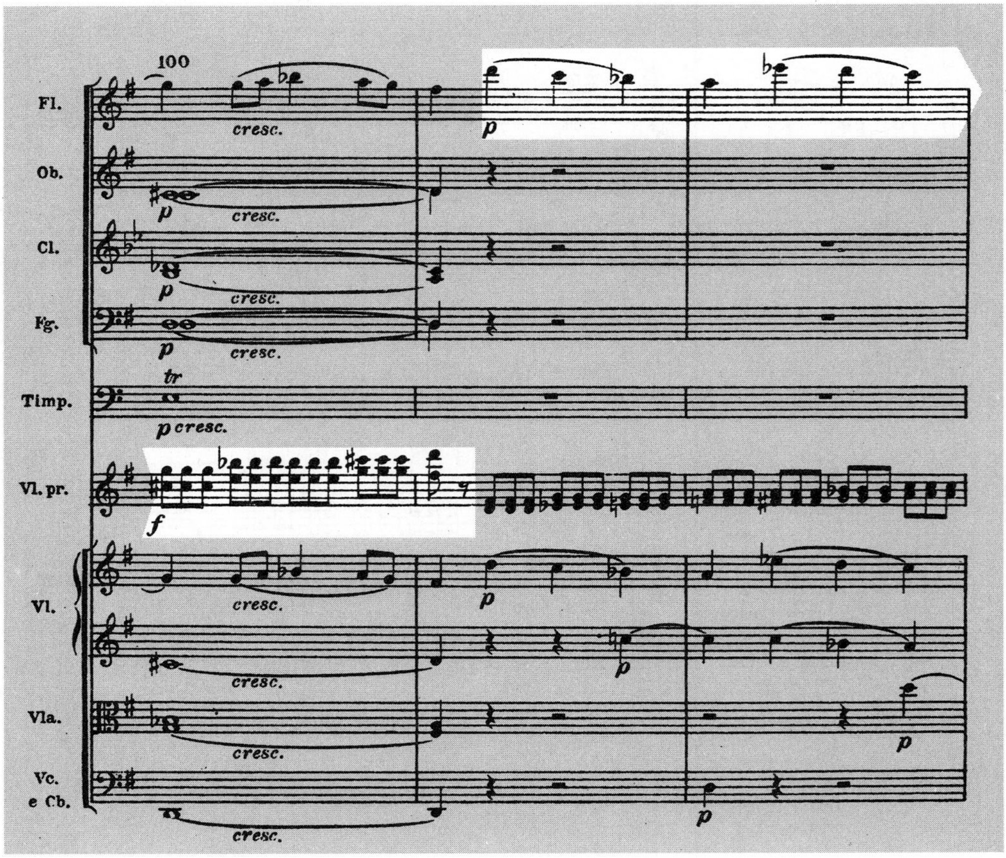
100
Fl.
cresc.
p
Ob.
p
cresc.
Cl.
p
cresc.
Fg.
p
cresc.
tr
Timp.
p cresc.
Vl. pr.
f
Vl.
cresc.
p
cresc.
p
Vla.
cresc.
p
Vc.
e Cb.
cresc.
p

Fl.
cresc.
p
Ob.
cresc.
Cl.
cresc.
Fg.
cresc.
Timp.
tr
cresc.
Vl. pr.
p
Vl.
cresc.
dim.
cresc.
dim.
Vla.
cresc.
dim.
Vc.
e Cb.
cresc.
dim.

110
Fl.
Vl. pr.
cresc.
Vl.
cresc.
cresc.
Vla.
cresc.
Vc.
e Cb.
cresc.

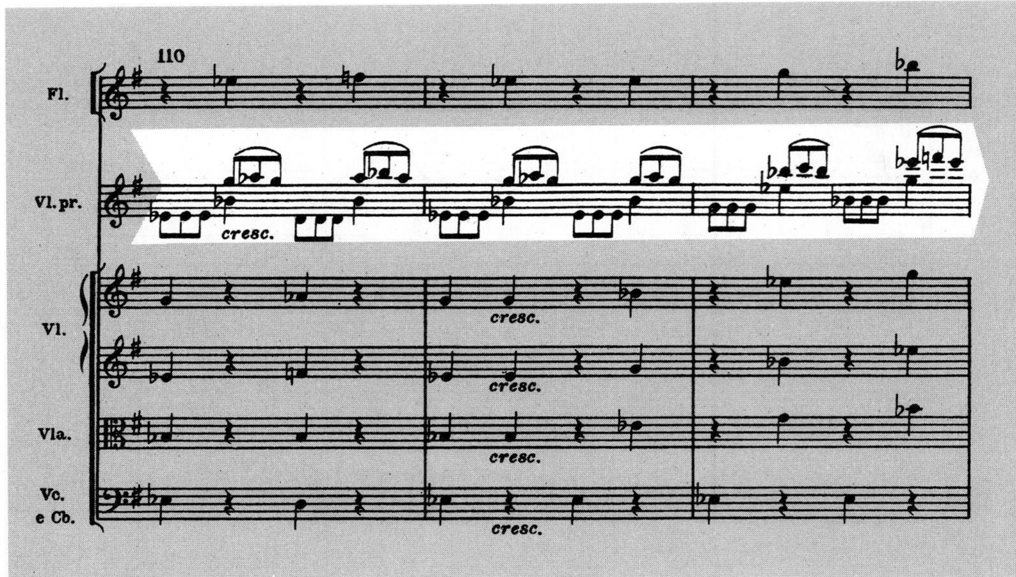

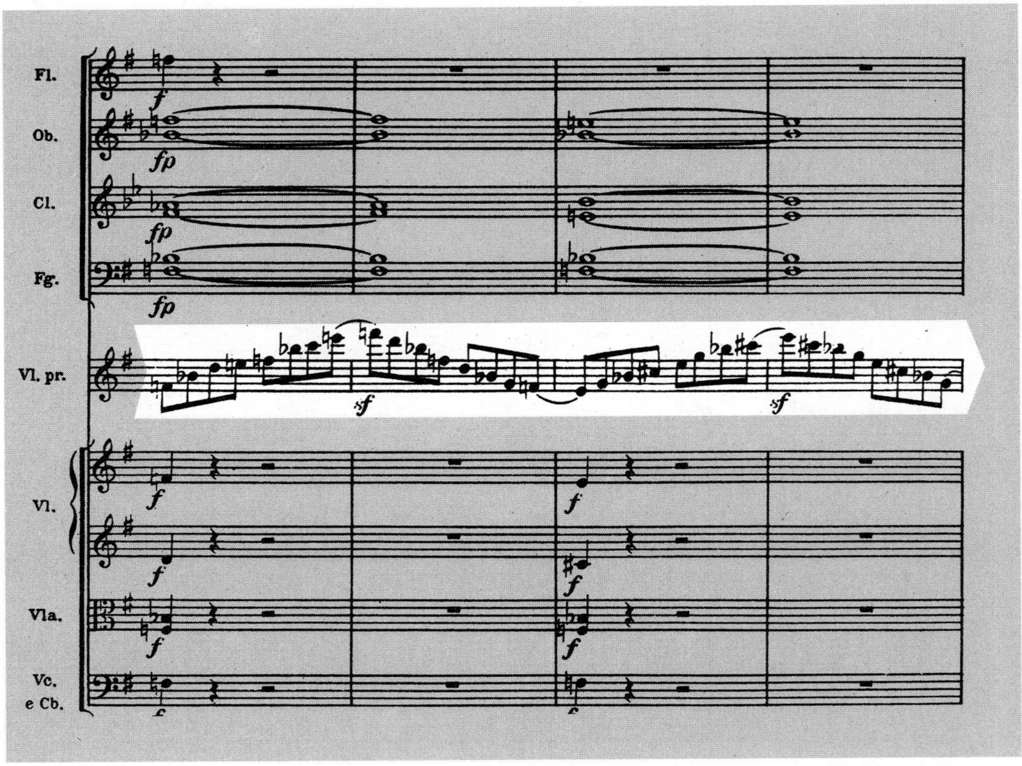

Fl.
f
Ob.
fp
Cl.
fp
Fg.
fp
Vl. pr.
sf
sf
Vl.
f
f
f
f
Vla.
f
f
Vc.
e Cb.

120
Ob.
Cl.
Fg.
Vl. pr.
Vl.
Vla.
Vc. e Cb.
dim.
f
sempre dim.
p
37
130
Fl.
tranquillo
pp
pp tranquillo
p tranquillo

Fl.
Cl.
Vl.pr.
140
pp
pp
pp tranquillo
p cresc.
150
Vl. pr.
Vl.
Vla.
Vc.
sf
160
p
cresc.

38
Cl.
Fg.
Vl.pr.
Vl.
Vla.
Vc. e Cb.
pp
cresc.
pizz.
pp Bassi
170
Ob.
p
sf
arco
leggiero
f
cresc.

180
Vl. pr.
cresc.
sf
p
pizz.
Vl.
pizz.
pizz.
Vla.
pizz.
Vc.
e Cb.
Fl.
1.
p
Ob.
1.
p
Cl.
p
Fg.
p
Vl. pr.
pp
Vl.
pp
pp
Vla.
pp
Vc.
e Cb.
pp
Fl.
Ob.
Cl.
1.
Fg.
Vl. pr.
cresc.
arco
Vl.
arco
arco
Vla.
arco
Vc.
e Cb.

Cl.
cresc.
cresc.
Fg.
cresc.
cresc.
Vl. pr.
cresc.
p leggiero
Vl.
cresc.
cresc.
pp
Vla.
cresc.
pp
Vc.
e Cb.
cresc.
pp

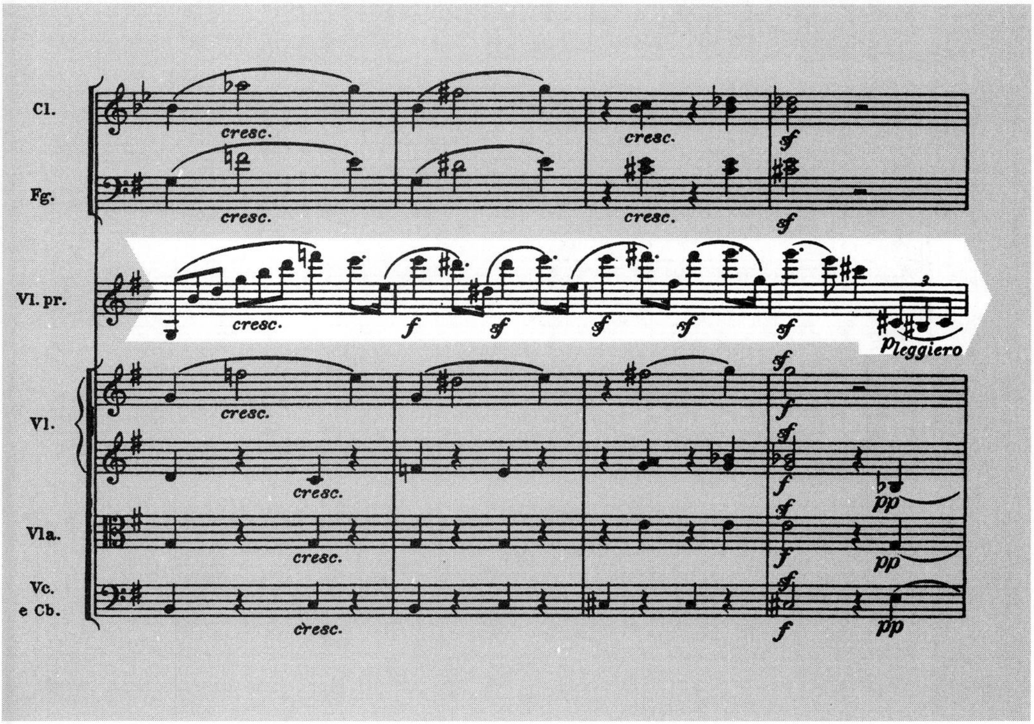

200
Fl.
Ob.
Cl.
Fg.
Vl. pr.
Vl.
Vla.
Vc.
e Cb.

Fl.
Ob.
Cl.
Fg.
l. pr.
cresc.
Vl.
Vla.
Vc.
Cb.

Fl.
Ob.
Cl.
Fg.
Cor. (E)
Vl. pr.
Vl.
Vla.
Vc. e Cb.
zu 2
210
Tbe. (E)
Timp.
con forza

220
zu 2
Fl.
Ob.
Cl.
Fg.
Cor. (E)
Tbe. (E)
Timp.
Vl. pr.
Vl.
Vla.
Vc. e Cb.
dim.
39
230
zu 2
agitato
pizz.
cresc.

Tutti
zu 2
Solo
Fl.
Ob.
Cl.
Fg.
zu 2
Cor. (E)
Tbe. (E)
Timp.
Vl.pr.
p tranq.
Vl.
Vla.
arco
Vc. e Cb.

Fl.
Ob.
Cl.
Vl.pr.
Vl.
Vla.
Vc.
e Cb.
p
p
Vc.

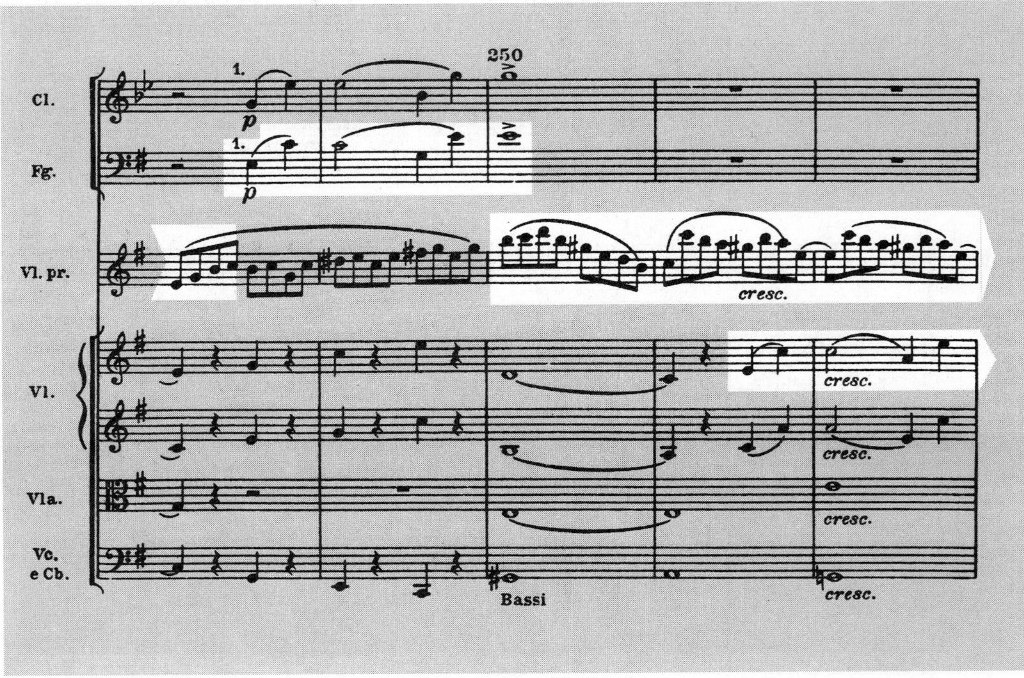
Cl.
Fg.
Vl. pr.
Vl.
Vla.
Vc.
e Cb.
250
1.
1.
p
p
cresc.
cresc.
cresc.
cresc.
cresc.
Bassi

Fl.
Ob.
Cl.
Fg.
Cor. (E)
Tbe. (E)
Timp.
Vl. pr.
Vl.
Vla.
Vc. e Cb.
zu 2
f
p

260
Fl.
Ob.
Cl.
Fg.
Cor. (E)
Tbe. (E)
Timp.
Vl. pr.
Vl.
Vla.
Vc. e Cb.
f
p
dim.

Cl.
Fg.
Timp.
Vl. pr.
Vl.
Vla.
Vc. e Cb.
pp
pp
pp
p dim.
p
p
p
p

270
Cl.
Fg.
Timp.
Vl.pr.
Vl.
Vla.
Vc. e Cb.
pp
sempre più p
dim.
sempre dim.
dim.
sempre dim.
dim.
sempre dim.
dim.
sempre dim.

Vl. pr.
Vl.
Vla.
Vc. e Cb.
pp
280
Cor. (E)
sempre pp
Vc.
Bassi
290
Ob.
Cl.
Fg.
Tbe. (E)
Timp.
poco a poco cresc.
cresc.

Fl.
cresc.
sf ff
Ob.
Cl.
Fg.
Cor. (E)
Tbe. (E)
Timp.
tr
ff
Vl. pr.
Vl.
Vla.
Vc. e Cb.
40
Cadenza ad lib.
300
8
f

6. Mendelssohn, Violin Concerto in E minor, Op. 64: I

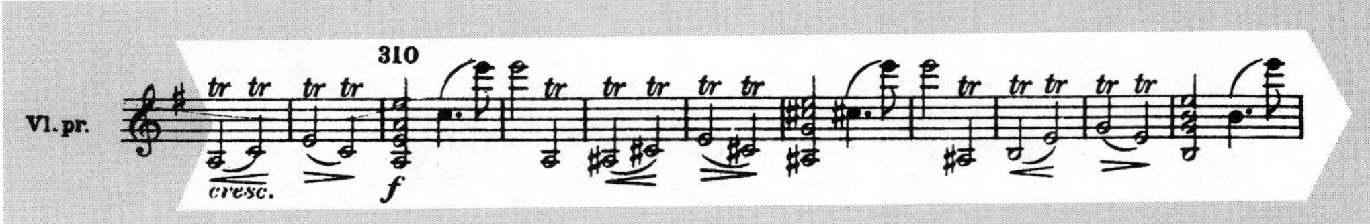

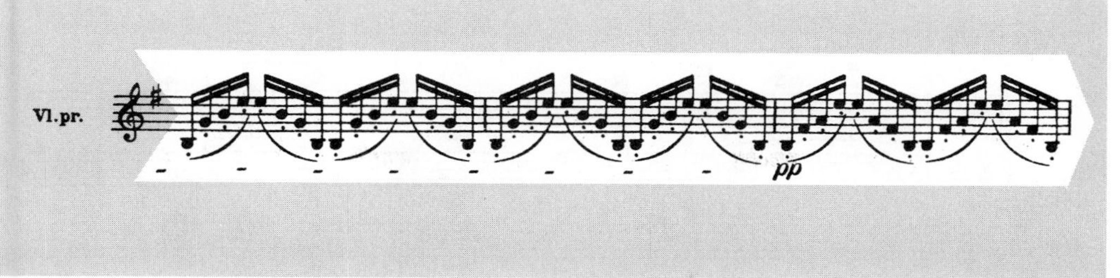

41

Fl.
1.

Ob.
1.
pp

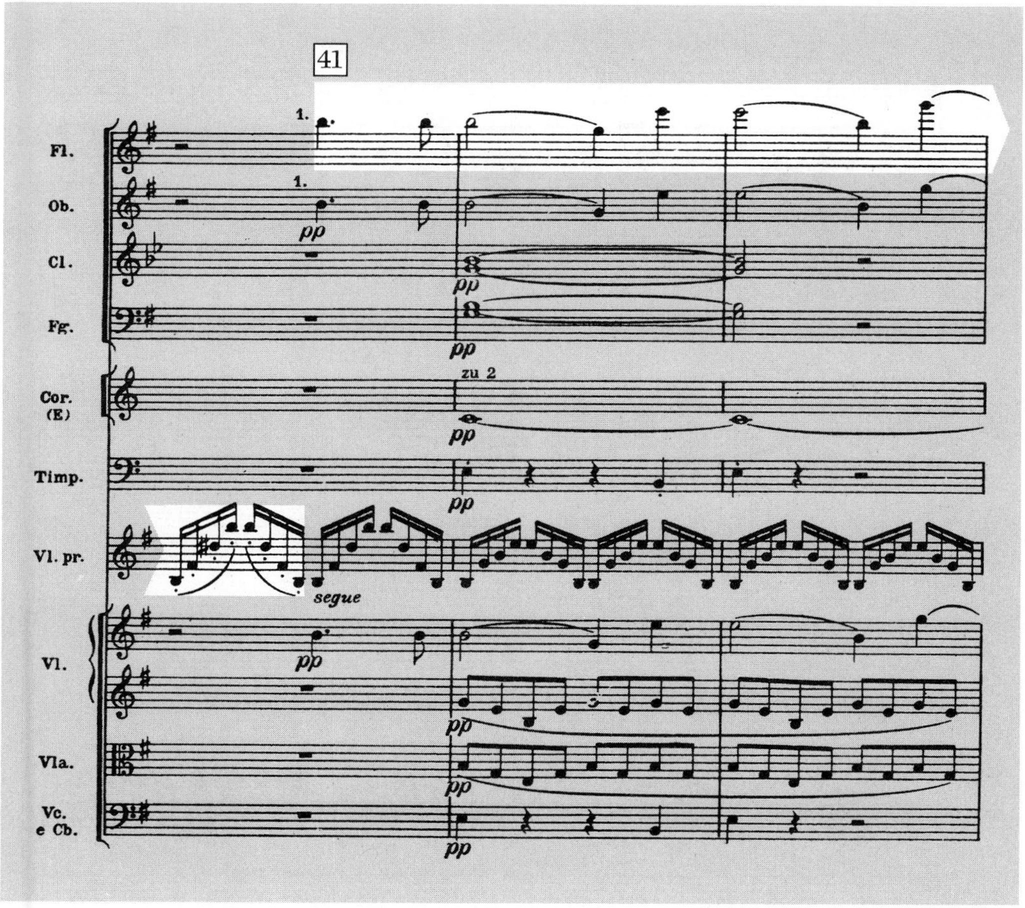

Cl.
pp

Fg.
pp

Cor. (E)
zu 2
pp

Timp.
pp

Vl. pr.
segue

Vl.
pp
pp

Vla.
pp

Vc. e Cb.
pp

340
Fl.
Ob.
Cor.
(E)
Vl. pr.
Vl.
Vla.
Vc.
e Cb.

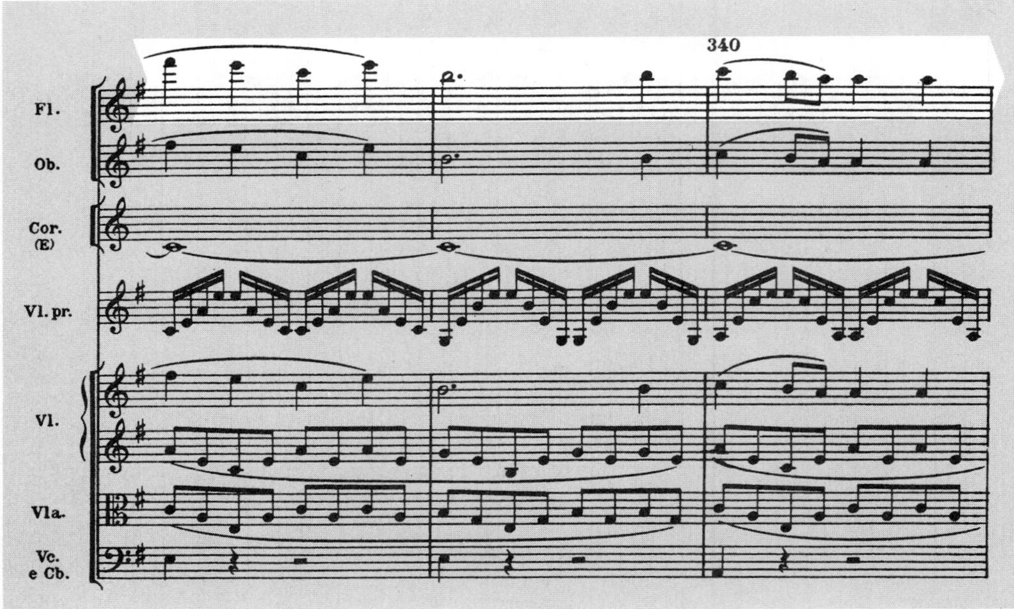

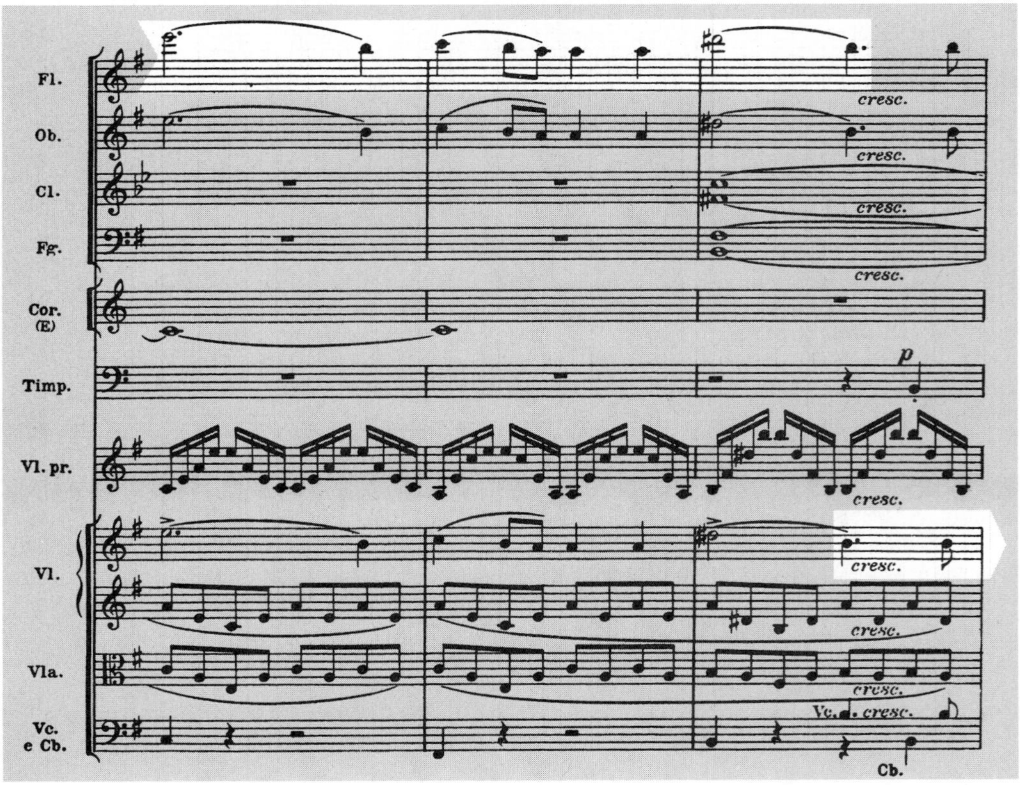
Fl.
cresc.
Ob.
cresc.
Cl.
cresc.
Fg.
cresc.
Cor.
(E)
p
Timp.
Vl. pr.
cresc.
Vl.
cresc.
cresc.
Vla.
cresc.
Vc. cresc.
Vc.
e Cb.
Cb.

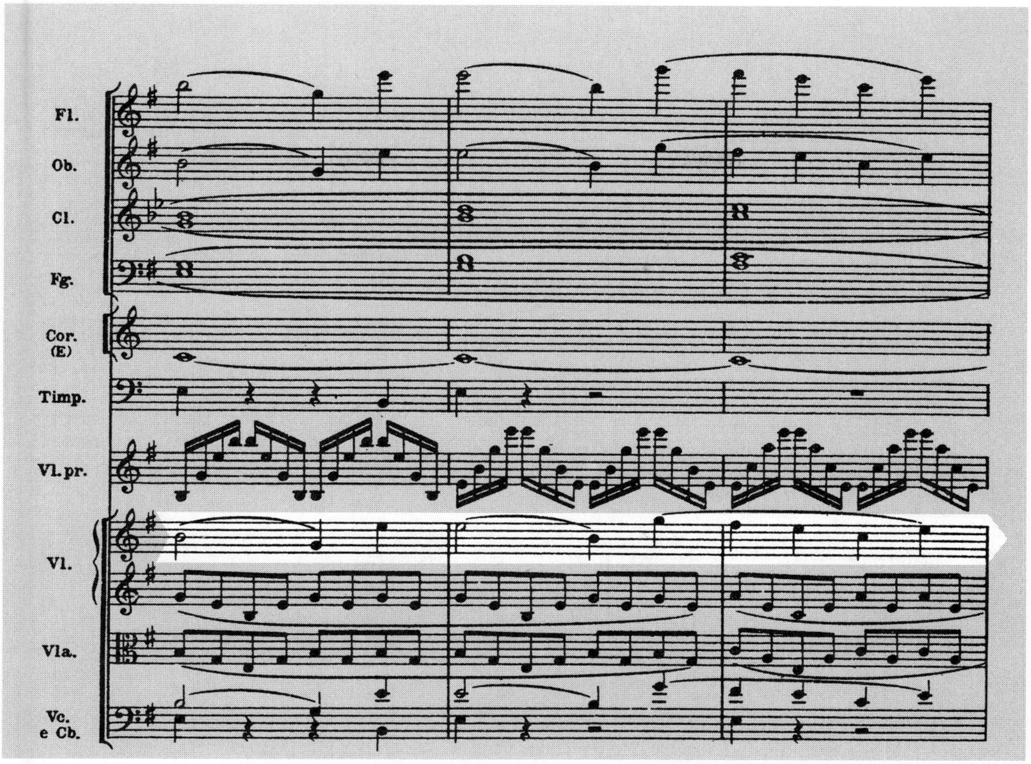
Fl.
Ob.
Cl.
Fg.
Cor. (E)
Timp.
Vl. pr.
Vl.
Vla.
Vc. e Cb.

Fl.
Ob.
Cl.
Fg.
Cor. (E)
Vl. pr.
ff
Vl.
cresc.
Vla.
cresc.
Vc. e Cb.
cresc.

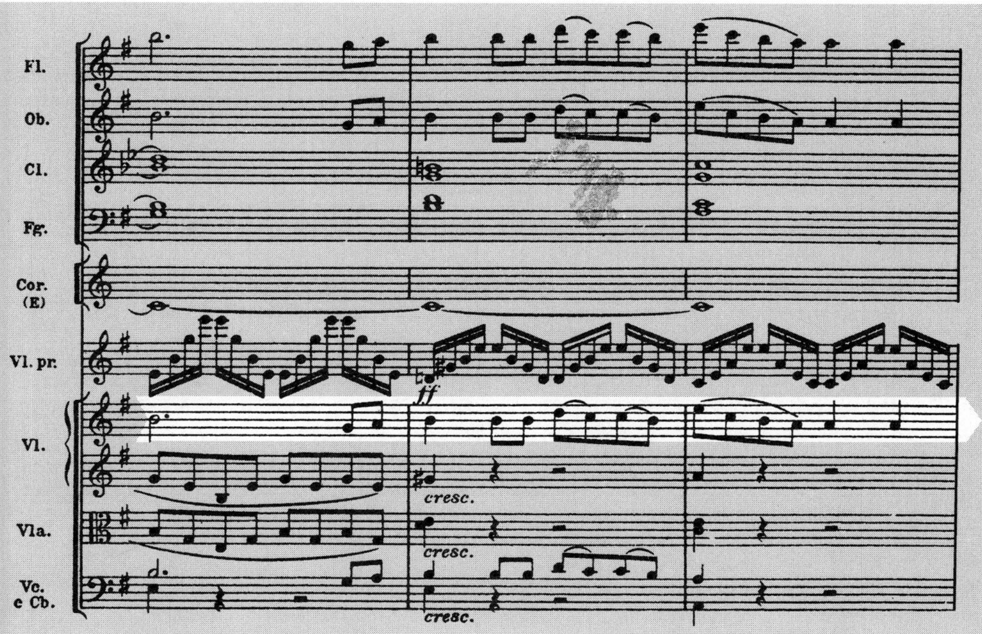

Tutti
zu 2
350
Fl.
ff
zu 2
Ob.
ff
Cl.
ff
Fg.
ff
Cor. (E)
ff
zu 2
zu 2
Tbe. (E)
ff
Timp.
ff
Vl.pr.
Vl.
ff
f
ff
Vla.
f
ff
Vc. e Cb.
Bassi f
ff

360
Fl.
Ob.
Cl.
Fg.
Cor. (E)
zu 2
Tbe. (E)
Timp.
Vl. pr.
Vl.
Vla.
Vc. e Cb.
ff
fp
mf
sf
sfp
370
dim.
sempre più tranquillo
pp

42
380
Fl.
Ob.
Cl.
Vl.pr.
zu 2
pp

390
Fl.
Ob.
Cl.
Cor. (E)
Vl.pr.
pp

Ob.
Cl.
Vl.pr.
cresc.
Vl.
Vla.
Vc. e Cb.
p

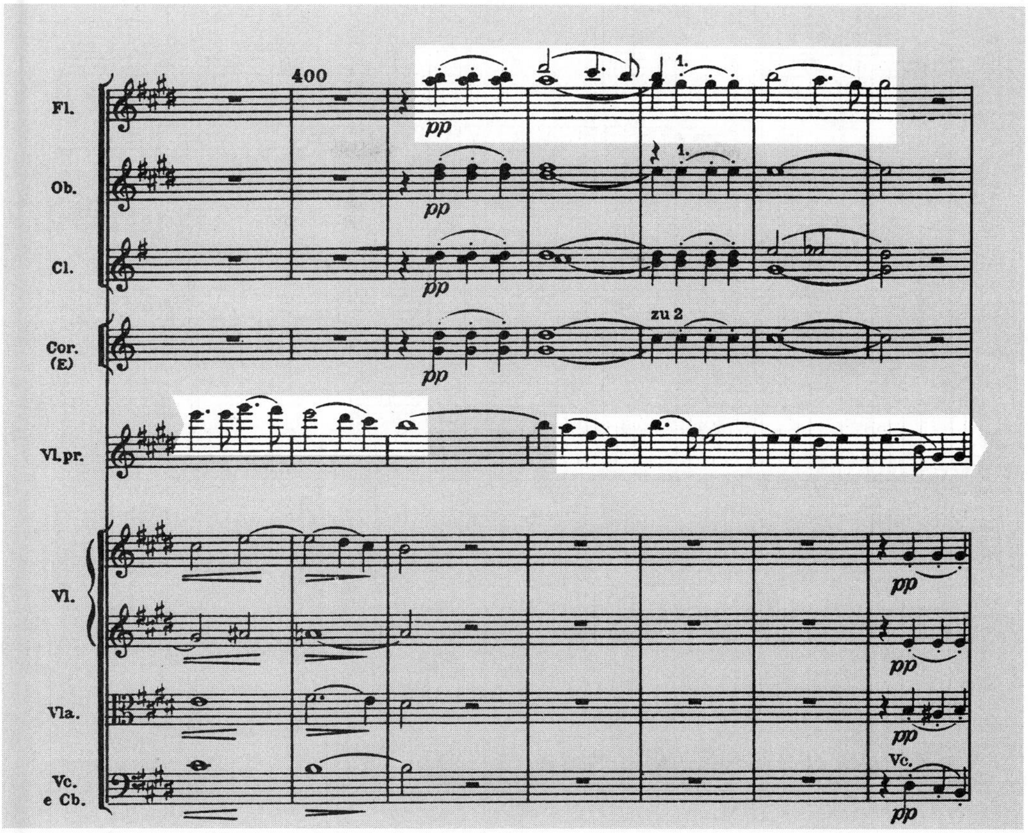
400
Fl.
pp
1.
Ob.
pp
1.
Cl.
pp
Cor. (E)
pp
zu 2
Vl. pr.
Vl.
pp
pp
Vla.
pp
Vc. e Cb.
Vc.
pp

410
Vl. pr.
dim.
pp
Vl.
Vla.
Vc. e Cb.
Bassi

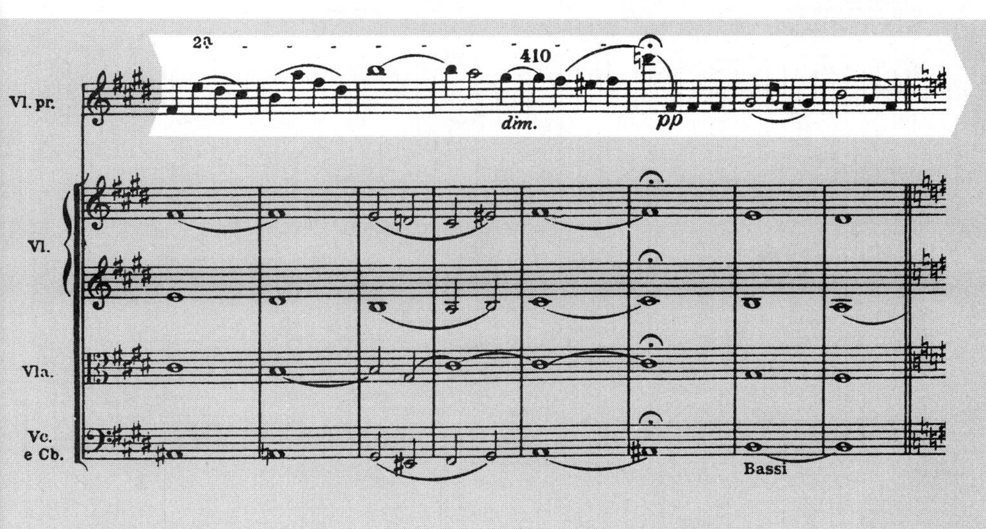

zu 2
Cor. (E)
pp
1.
Tbe. (E)
pp
Timp.
pp
Vl. pr.
3
cresc.
Vl.
pp
fsf
pp
fsf
Vla.
pp
fsf
Vc. e Cb.
pp
fsf
p

1.
420
Cl.
p
1.
Fg.
p
Vl.pr.
3
3
Vl.
p
p
Vla.
Vc. e Cb.

Cl.
Fg.
Vl. pr.
3
cresc.
Vl.
cresc.
cresc.
Vla.
cresc.
Vc. e Cb.
cresc.

Ob.
430
1.
p
Cl.
p
Vl. pr.
f
p
pizz.
Vl.
pizz.
pizz.
Vla.
pizz.
Vc. e Cb.

1.
Ob.
1.
Cl.
Cor. (E)
pp
Tbe. (E)
pp
Timp.
pp
Vl.pr.
pp
Vl.
pp
pp
Vla.
pp
Vc. e Cb.
pp
Ob.
Cl.
Cor. (E)
Tbe. (E)
Timp.
pp
Vl.pr.
cresc.
sf
sf
Vl.
arco
arco
arco
Vla.
arco
Vc. e Cb.

440
Cor. (E)
cresc.
Vl. pr.
sf
sf
più cresc.
Vl.
cresc.
cresc.
Vla.
cresc.
Vc. e Cb.
cresc.

Ob.
1.
p
Cl.
1.
p
Fg.
p
Cor. (E)
f
1.
p
Vl. pr.
f
sf
3
p
p
Vl.
f
p
f
p
Vla.
f
p
Vc. e Cb.
p

450
Ob.
Cl.
Fg.
Cor. (E)
Vl.pr.
p
cresc.
Vl.
Vla.
Vc. e Cb.
Fl.
zu 2
f
Tbe. (E)
Timp.
2a e 3a corda
ff

zu 2
Fl.
ff
zu 2
Ob.
ff
zu 2
Cl.
ff
Fg.
Cor. (E)
Tbe. (E)
imp.
l. pr.
3
3
Vl.
ff
ff
Vla.

460
Fl.
Ob.
Cl.
Fg.
Cor. (E)
Tbe. (E)
Timp.
Vl. pr.
Vl.
Vla.
Vc. e Cb.
zu 2
470
dim.

43
Più presto
Fl.
Cl.
Fg.
Cor. (E)
Tbe. (E)
Timp.
Vl. pr.
Vl.
Vla.
Vc. e Cb.
zu 2
p
sf
480
Sempre più presto
Ob.
sf cresc.

490
Fl.
Ob.
Cl.
Fg.
cresc.
p
zu 2
Vl. pr.
sf
ff
Vl.
Vla.
Vc. e Cb.
Presto
1.
f
Cor. (E)
Tbe. (E)
Timp.

500
Fl.
Ob.
Cl.
Fg.
Cor. (E)
Tbe. (E)
Timp.
Vl. pr.
f
cresc.
Vl.
cresc.
cresc.
Vla.
cresc.
Vc. e Cb.
cresc.
Fl.
1.
Ob.
Cl.
zu 2
Fg.
zu 2
Cor (E)
Timp.
Vl. pr.
ff
Vl.
p
cresc.
p
cresc.
Vla.
p
cresc.
Vc. e Cb.
p

510
Ob.
Cl.
zu 2
1.
zu 2
Fg.
cresc.
Vl. pr.
Vl.
Vla.
Vc. e Cb.
Tutti
Fl.
Ob.
Cl.
Fg.
Cor. (E)
Tbe. (E)
Timp.
Vl. pr.
Vl.
Vla.
Vc. e Cb.

520
Fl.
Ob.
Cl.
Fg.
Cor. (E)
Tbe. (E)
Timp.
Vl.
Vla.
Vc. e Cb.
zu 2
sf
tr

The Romantic concerto retained many of the traditional features of the Classical genre, including the three-movement structure and the general form of each movement. Distinctive new aspects of these concertos are the abbreviated first-movement structures, the general tendency toward cyclic unity, and the assimilation of the Romantic musical style. The brilliant Violin Concerto by Felix Mendelssohn (1809–1847) illustrates these tendencies well.

Each of the three movements is set in a traditional Classical form, but there are no pauses between the movements, and a musical quotation of the first movement in the second further enhances the cyclic quality. The first movement omits the opening *tutti* section that is standard in the Classical concerto; rather than waiting through an entire orchestral exposition, the soloist enters after one and a half measures. The movement then unfolds in a sonata-allegro form.

While the Classical framework is clearly evident, the movement as a whole projects the passion and virtuosity of Romanticism. Both the opening theme and the second theme are beautiful, lyric melodies. The latter is especially colorful, as the woodwinds initially present the tune over a sustained open G by the soloist. In a masterful stroke, Mendelssohn moves the cadenza from its traditional position at the end of the movement to the close of the development. In the cadenza, Mendelssohn exploits the violinist's technique with multiple-stopped chords and a rapid alternation of notes on all four strings. While the soloist is completing this passage, the orchestra quietly enters with the opening theme, creating an overlap of the development and recapitulation.

-wrote 24, in all major + minor keys

7. Frédéric François Chopin

8CD: 5/44–45

Prelude in E minor, Op. 28, No. 4
(published 1839)

-chromaticism.
-antecedent/consequent phrases w restricted range + simple ornaments

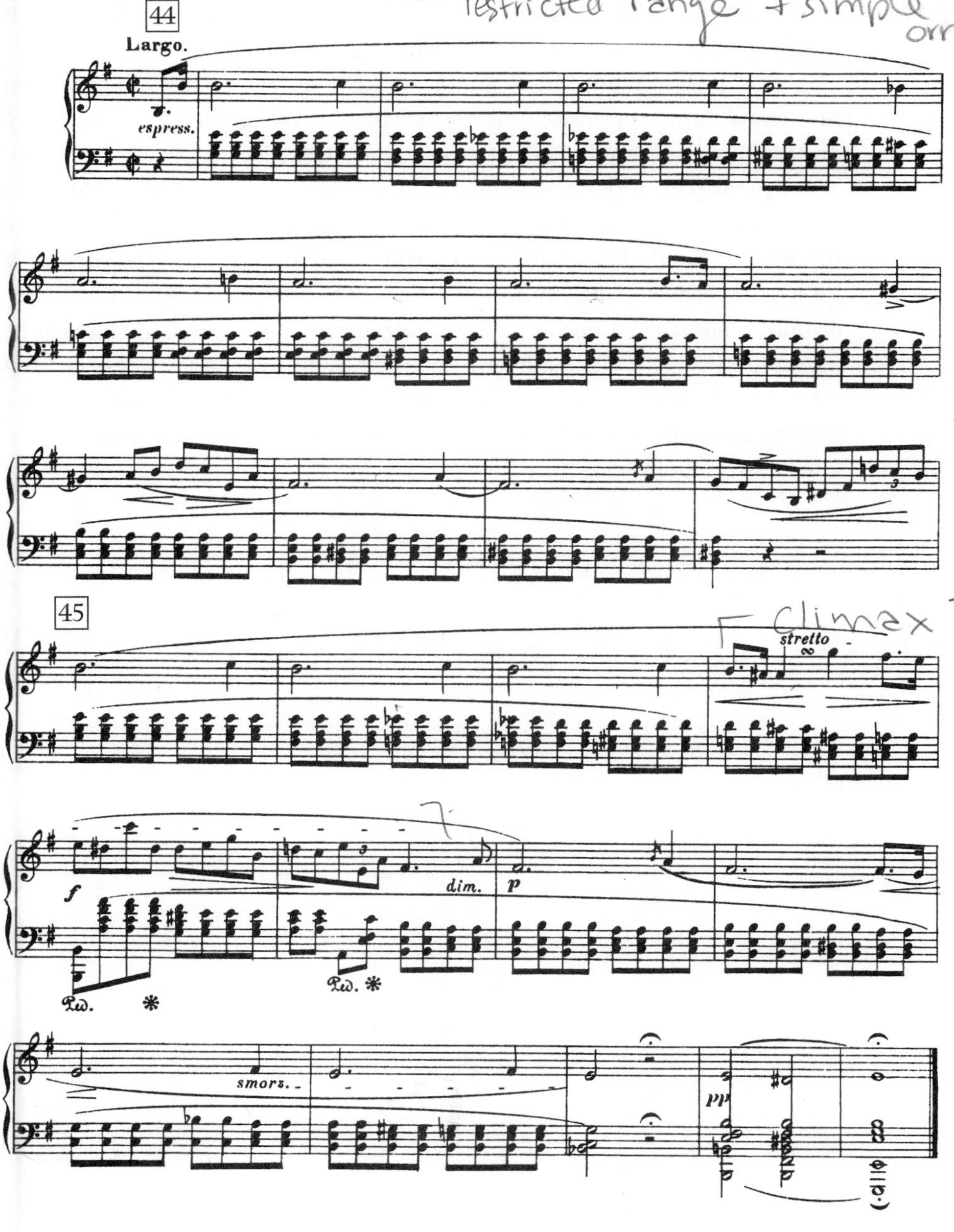
44
Largo.
espress.
45
stretto
f
dim.
p
Ped.
smorz.
pp

Climax

-lots of chromaticism
-rhythm increases

The preludes of Frédéric Chopin (1810–1849) stand as a Romantic counterpart to *The Well-Tempered Clavier* by J. S. Bach. Like its Baroque model, Chopin's set contains twenty-four works in all of the major and minor keys. But in keeping with the Romantic spirit, Chopin omits the learned fugues, allowing the preludes to stand by themselves. The twenty-four works, which provide a wide variety of moods, styles, and lengths, can either be performed as a unit or individually.

The fourth prelude, in E minor, is justifiably one of Chopin's most renowned compositions, primarily because of its brevity, chromaticism, and emotional potency. The melody, which can be heard as an antecedent-consequent pair of phrases, moves in a restricted range with simple ornamentation, suggesting the lyricism of a vocal line. The expressiveness of the prelude would be enhanced by a rubato performance, as the melody is set against repeated eighth notes that could be sped up or slowed down for dramatic effect. The accompaniment gradually descends with chromatic alternations, generally with one note changing in each successive harmony. The climax occurs in measures 16–18, where the range of the melody suddenly expands, the rhythmic activity increases, and the rate of harmonic change accelerates.

8. Frédéric François Chopin

Nocturne in C minor, Op. 48, No. 1 (1841)

8CD: 5/46–48
4CD: 2/61–63

46 61

Lento.
mezza voce.
p

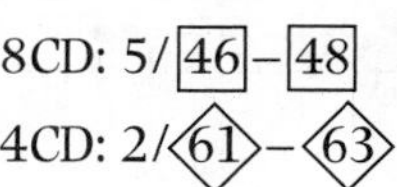

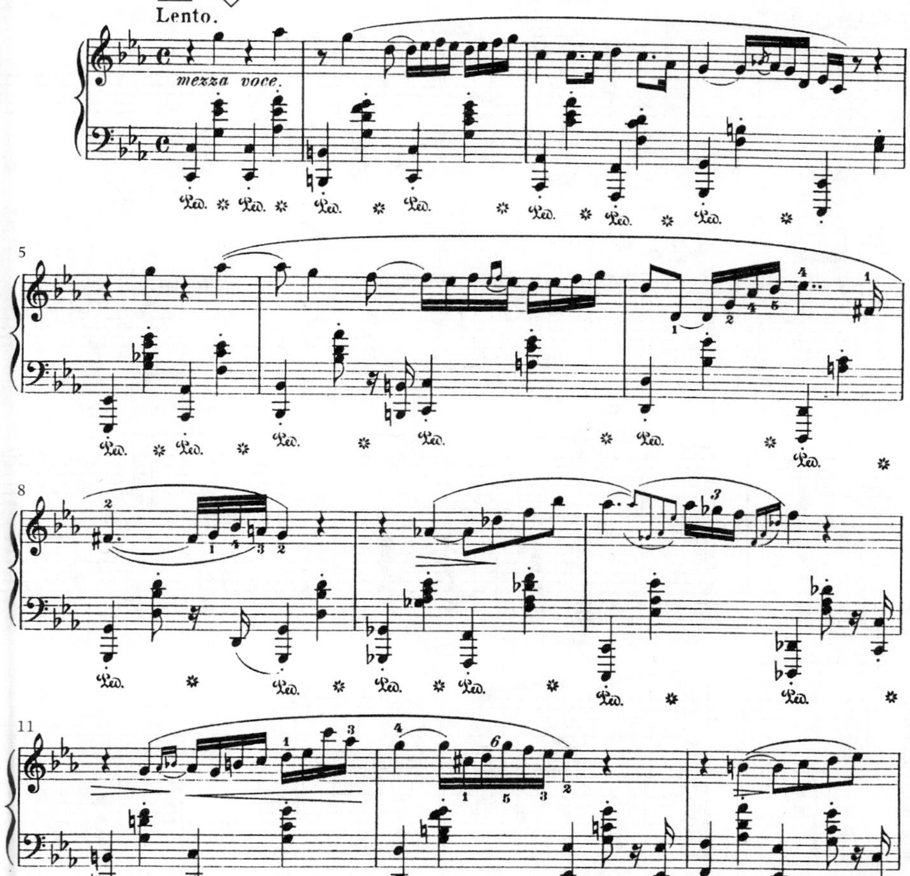

ten.
f
ten.
Poco più lento.
sotto voce.
sempre p
47
62

37
pp
cresc.
40
cresc.
f
cresc.
cresc.
cresc.
43
cresc.
cresc.
cresc.
ff
tr
riten.

46
8
Ped.
47
sempre
ff
Ped.
Ped.
Ped.
48
8
riten.
fz
p
accel.
Ped.
48
63
Doppio movimento.
pp agitato.
Ped.
Ped.
Ped.
Ped.
51
Ped.
Ped.
Ped.
Ped.
Ped.

53
55
cresc.
57
59
61
63
fz
cresc.

ten.
ten.
ff riten.
dim. e rall.
pp

During the nineteenth century, the piano was the most popular musical instrument in the home, and it was the preferred instrument for professional soloists. As a result, an impressive body of new literature was created in which piano miniatures replaced the formal sonatas of the Classical era. Many of these newer works pushed piano technique to virtuosic levels, as composers exploited the changes made to the instrument by piano manufacturers.

One of the major figures in Romantic piano music is the Polish-French virtuoso Frédéric François Chopin. Primarily active in Paris, Chopin devoted his compositional output almost exclusively to piano music. His oeuvre includes piano exercises (études), dances (waltzes, mazurkas, polonaises), and many other short, lyrical works. Typical qualities of these works include an emphasis on melody, often with elaborate embellishments, expressive chromatic harmony, and rubato, in which the right hand takes some liberties with the tempo while the left hand maintains a strict pulse.

Among Chopin's more evocative titles is the Nocturne, which suggests nighttime music. The Irish pianist John Field was the first to use this genre title in 1812. Chopin's Nocturne in C minor (1841), set in an **A-B-A** form, projects some of the quiet lyricism that is normally associated with the nocturne. But it is larger in scope and expression than the typical nocturne. Virtuoso flourishes, chromatic movement, and several emotional climaxes create a dramatic intensity that is not usually associated with the genre. An expressive coda brings the work to a quiet, poignant close.

9. Robert Schumann

"Und wüssten's die Blumen"
("And if the flowers knew"), from *Dichterliebe*
(A Poet's Love), No. 8 (1840)

8CD: 5/ 49 – 52
4CD: 2/ 57 – 60

9
wüß - ten's die Nach - ti - gal - - len, wie ich so trau - rig und
12
krank, sie lie - ßen fröh - lich er - schal - - len er -
15
51
59
qui - cken - den Ge - sang. Und wüß - ten sie mein
18
We - - he, die gol - de - nen Ster - ne - lein, sie

21
kä - men aus ih - rer Hö- - -he, und sprä- -chen Trost mir
52
60
24
p
ein. Sie al- - -le kön - nen's nicht wis- -sen, nur
27
Ei - ne kennt mei - nen Schmerz; sie hat ja selbst zer -
30
ritard.
ris-sen, zer-ris-sen mir das Herz.
sf
a tempo
ritard.
sf
sf

Text and Translation

Und wüssten's die Blumen, die kleinen Wie tief verwundet mein Herz, Sie würden mit mir weinen, Zu heilen meinen Schmerz.	And if the flowers, the little ones, knew how deeply my heart is wounded, they would weep with me to heal my pain.
Un wüssten's die Nachtigallen, Wie ich so traurig und krank, Sie liessen fröhlich erschallen Erquickenden Gesang.	And if the nightingales knew how sad and sick I am, they would happily sound out their life-affirming song.
Und wüssten sie mein Wehe, Die goldenen Sternelein, Sie kämen aus ihrer Höhe, Und sprächen Trost mir ein.	And if the little golden stars knew my hurt, they would descend from their heights and speak words of comfort to me.
Sie alle können's nicht wissen, Nur Eine kennt meinen Schmerz; Sie hat ja selbst zerrissen, Zerrissen mir das Herz.	All of these cannot know, only one understands my pain; because she herself has torn— has torn my heart in two.

Heinrich Heine

Robert Schumann (1810–1856) follows Franz Schubert as the second great composer of Lieder in the nineteenth century. Unlike Schubert, Schumann consistently chose high-quality poetry and conceived of the piano as an equal partner in his works, rather than as mere accompaniment. After avoiding Lieder composition for twenty-nine years, Schumann suddenly launched into the genre with a prodigious output in 1840, composing over one hundred Lieder, including the masterful song cycle *Dichterliebe (A Poet's Love)*. In this "year of the song," he also married the young piano prodigy Clara Wieck.

Based on poems of Heinrich Heine, *Dichterliebe* deals with the joys and pains of love. In "Und wüssten's die Blumen" ("And if the flowers knew"), the eighth song in the cycle, Schumann sets the four stanzas of the poem in a modified strophic form. The first three stanzas are identical, as the poet looks to the flowers, nightingales, and stars for comfort. But in an ironic turn that is typical of Heine, the mood changes in the last stanza when the forlorn lover resigns himself to his broken heart. Throughout the song, the piano provides a breathless accompaniment that both supports the voice and remains as a strong independent musical part.

10. Franz Liszt

8CD: 6/4–13

La campanella (The Little Bell), from *Transcendental Etudes after Paganini,* No. 3 (1838–39; rev. 1851)

7
p
cresc.

8
39
p
pp
43
47
poco rit.
sempre p
51
54
57

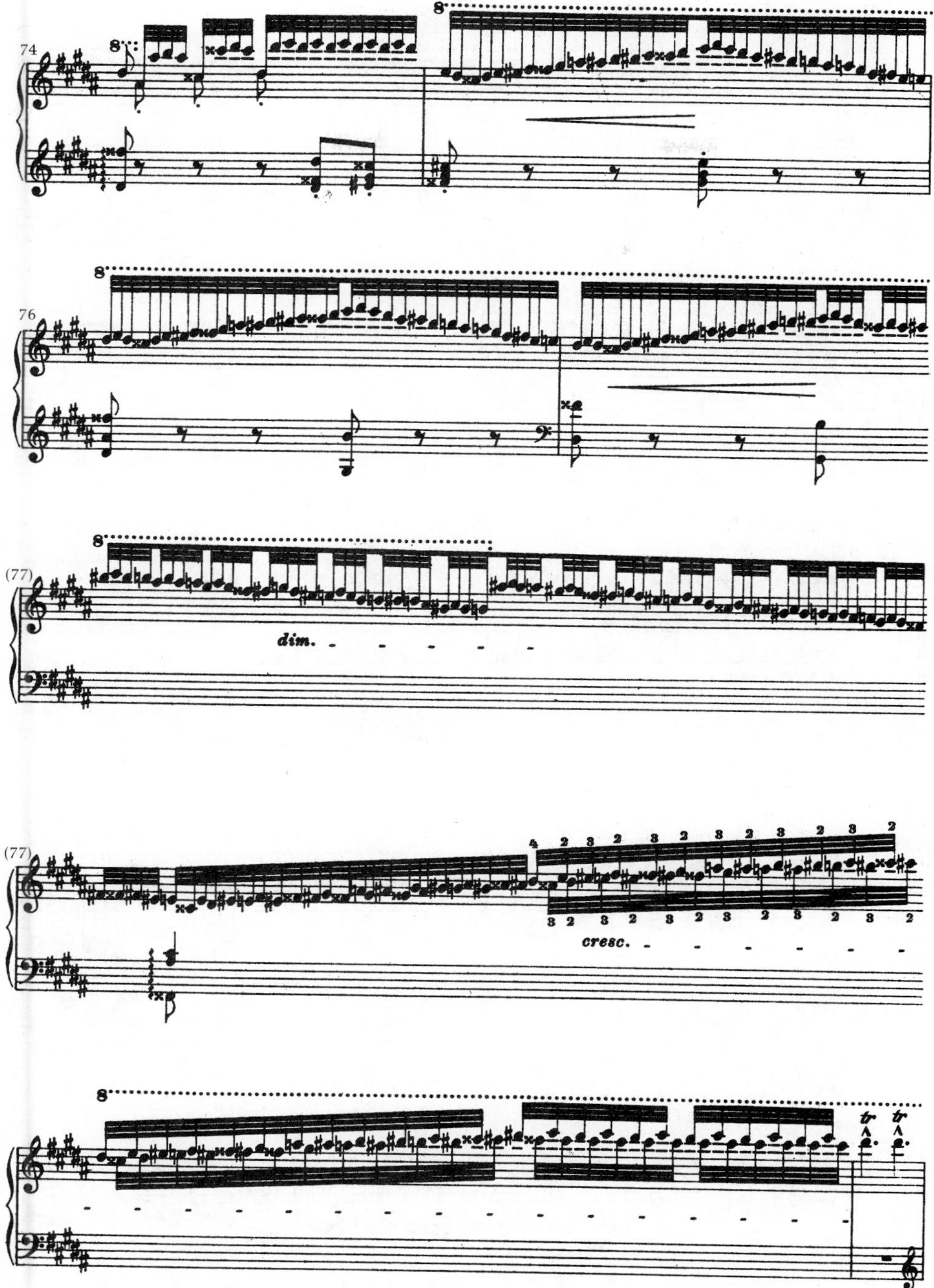
74
76
(77)
dim.
(77)
cresc.
tr
tr

10
79
p
82
84
sempre piano
smorz.
87
p
(89)

92
espressivo
94
p
pp
11
Più mosso.
(95)
staccato
98
102
p

106
8
p
Ped.
109
8
cresc.
112
più rinforzando
115
8
cresc.
Ped.
12
120
8

123
8
126
crescendo
molto
8
13
Animato.
129
ff
8
132
8
135
8
8

Instrumental virtuosity reached a peak in the performances and works of the Italian violinist Nicolò Paganini and the Hungarian pianist Franz Liszt (1811–1886). Paganini's dazzling technique and showmanship provided an inspiration for both violinists and pianists, an influence that can be seen in the numerous tributes to his works by other composers. Liszt assimilated Paganini's flamboyant style and raised it to new artistic levels. Paying homage to the violin virtuoso, Liszt created *Transcendental Etudes after Paganini* (1838–39, rev. 1851), which contains six works largely based on Paganini's 24 Caprices for solo violin.

Like Paganini's caprices and Chopin's études, Liszt's études are intended both as exercises to develop the performer's technique and as concert pieces. For Liszt, these études were literally intended to transcend the perceived limitations of the piano. The third étude, subtitled *La campanella (The Little Bell)*, borrows two thematic ideas from the finale of Paganini's Violin Concerto No. 2. The two themes, one in minor and one in major, are freely alternated and varied. The sound of a triangle in Paganini's concerto is imitated by repeated high pitches during the **A** sections, and the whole effect is light, colorful, and dazzling.

11. Richard Wagner

8CD: 5/53–57
4CD: 3/37–39

Die Walküre, Act III, Finale
(1856; first performed 1870)

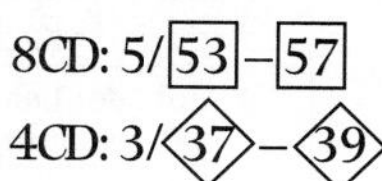

53

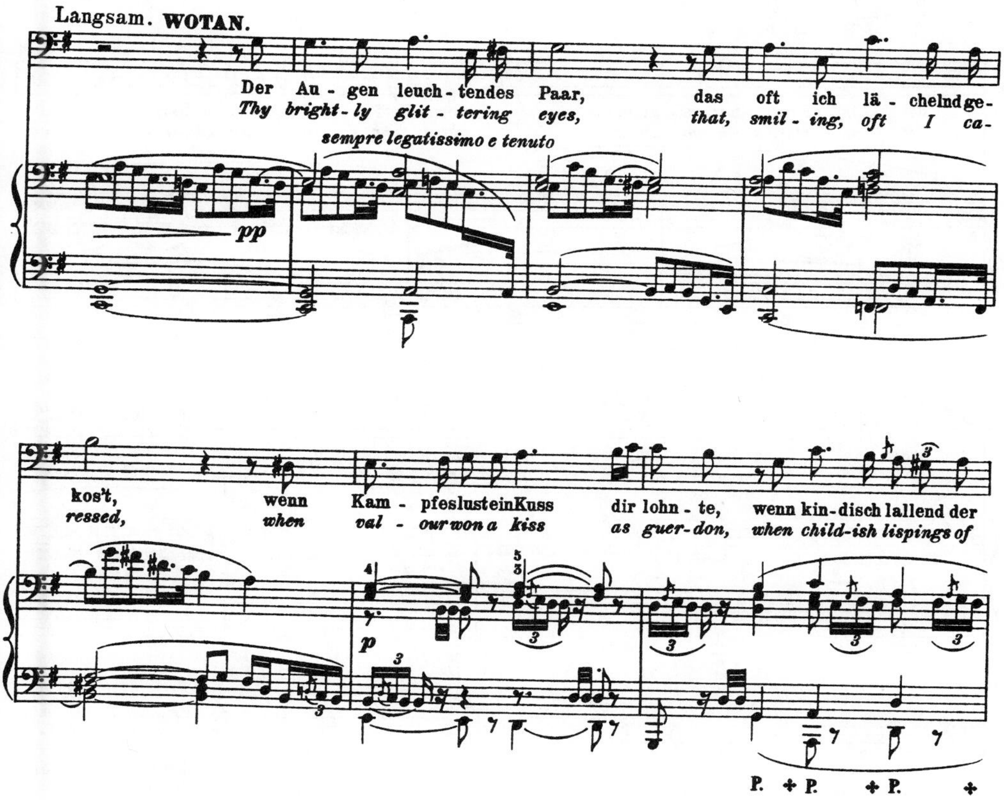

Langsam. WOTAN.
Der Au - gen leuch - tendes Paar, das oft ich lä - chelnd ge-
Thy bright - ly glit - tering eyes, that, smil - ing, oft I ca-
sempre legatissimo e tenuto
pp
kos't, wenn Kam - pfeslustein Kuss dir lohn - te, wenn kin - disch lallend der
ressed, when val - our won a kiss as guer - don, when child - ish lispings of
p
P. ✤ P. ✤ P. ✤

Editor's note: Shorter Norton recording begins on page **193.** This piano/vocal score includes pedal markings.

WOTAN.
Hel-denLob von hol - den Lippen dir floss: dieser Au-gen strahlendes Paar das
he-roes'praise from sweetest lips has flowed forth: those gleaming ra-di-ant eyes that
poco cresc.
mf
dim.
oft im Sturm mir ge-glänzt wenn Hoff - nungsseh-nen das Herz mir
oft in storms on me shone, when hope - less yearning my heart had
seng-te, nach Wel - ten-won-ne mein Wunsch ver-langte, aus wild we - bendem
wast-ed, when world's de-lights all my wish - es wakened, thro' wild wil - dering
fp
mf
Ban-gen: zum letz - ten Mal letz' es mich heut' mit des
sad-ness: once more to - day, lured by their light, my
poco rall.
dim.
dolce
più p

WOTAN.
pp
Le - be-woh-les letz - tem Kuss! Dem glück - licher'n Man-ne glän - ze sein
lips shall give them love's fare - well! On mor - tal more blessed once may they
pp
dolce
pp
P.
P.
cresc.
Stern: dem un - se - li - gen Ew' - - gen muss es schei-dend sich
beam: on me, hap-less im - mor - - tal, must they close now for
cresc.
dim.
f
(Er fasst ihr Haupt in beide Hände.)
(He clasps her head in his hands.)
schlies - sen. Denn so kehrt der Gott sich dir
e - - ver. For so turns the god now from
p
più p
pp espress.
54
(Er küsst sie lange auf die Augen.)
(He kisses her long on the eyes.)
ab, so küsst er die Gott - heit von dir!
thee, so kis-ses thy god - hood a - way!
pp
ppp
dolcissimo
P. (u.c.)

(Sie sinkt mit geschlossenen Augen, sanft ermattend, in seine Arme zurück. Er geleitet sie zart auf einen niedrigen Mooshügel
(She sinks back with closed eyes, unconscions, in his arms. He gently bears her to a low mossy mound, which is overshadowed
sempre pp
pp
(Er betrachtet sie und schliesst
(He looks upon her and closes
zu liegen, über den sich eine breitästige Tanne ausstreckt.)
by a wide-spreading fir tree, and lays her upon it.)
la melodia molto cantabile
l'accompagnamento sempre legatissimo e dolcissimo
più p
pp
poco cresc.
P.
ihr den Helm: sein Auge weilt dann auf der Gestalt der Schlafenden, die er nun mit dem grossen Stahlschilde der Walküren ganz
her helmet: his eyes then rest on the form of the sleeper, which he now completely covers with the great steel shield of the
dim.
ppp
zudeckt.__ Langsam kehrt er sich ab, mit einem schmerzlichen Blicke wendet er sich noch einmal um.)
Valkyrie.__ He turns slowly away, then again turns round with a sorrowful look.)
più pp
mf
dim.

pp
P.
più pp
pp
p
cresc.
f
tre corde
55
37
WOTAN
(Er schreitet mit feierlichem Entschlusse in die Mitte der Bühne, und kehrt die Spitze seines Speeres gegen einen mächtigen Felsstein.)
(He strides with solemn decision to the middle of the stage and directs the point of his spear towards a large rock.)
Mässig bewegt.
Lo - ge hör'!
Lo - ge hear!
fp
più p
lau - sche hie-her! Wie zuerst ich dich fand, als feu - ri - ge
List to my word! As I found thee of old, a glim - mering
Gluth, wie dann einst du mir schwandest, als schweifen-de Lo - he; wie ich dich band,
flame, as from me thou didst va-nish, in wan - dering fire; as once I stayed thee,
cresc

WOTAN.
bann' ich dich heut'!
stir I thee now!
Her - auf, wa - bern - de
Ap - pear! come, wav - ing
Lo - he,
fire
um - lod' - re mir feu - rig den
and wind thee in flames round the
poco cresc.
dim.
(Er stösst mit dem Folgenden dreimal mit dem Speer auf den Stein.)
(During the following he strikes the rock thrice with his spear.)
(Erster Stoss.)
(First stroke.)
Fels!
fell!
Lo - ge!
Lo - ge!
cresc.
più cresc.
(Zweiter.)
(Second.)
(Dritter.)
(Third.)
(Dem Stein entfährt ein Feuerstrahl.
(A flash of flame issues from
Lo - ge! hie - her!
Lo - ge! ap - pear!

der zur allmälich immer helleren Flammenglut anschwillt.)
the rock, which swells to an ever-brightening fiery glow.)
f
più f
56
38
(Hier bricht die lichte Flackerlohe aus.)
(Here flickering flames break forth.)
p
sempre stacc
cresc. poco a poco
sempre cresc.
f
Lichte Brunst umgiebt Wotan mit wildem Flackern. Er weis't mit dem Speere gebie-
Bright shooting flames surround Wotan. With his spear he directs the sea of fire
ff

terisch dem Feuermeere den Umkreis des Felsenrandes zur Strömung an; alsbald zieht es sich nach dem Hintergrunde, wo es nun
to encircle the rocks; it presently spreads toward the background where it encloses the mountain in flames.)
sempre stacc.
ff
dim.
fortwährend den Bergsaum umlodert.)
p dolce
sempre legato
sempre stacc.
57
39
WOTAN.
Wer mei - nes Spee - - - - res
He who my spear - - - - point's
cresc. poco
Spit - - - ze fürch - - - - - tet durch-
sharp - - - ness fear - - - - eth shall
a poco
schrei - te das Feu - - - er nie!
cross not the flam - - ing fire!

(Er streckt den Speer wie zum Banne aus.)
(He stretches out the spear as a spell.)
f
più cresc.
pesante
marcato
ff
(Er blickt schmerzlich auf Brünnhilde zurück)
(He gazes sorrowfully back on Brünnhilde.)
dim.
p
sehr ausdrucksvoll
dim.
più p

(Er wendet sich langsam zum Gehen.)
(Slowly he turns to depart.)
p dolce
più p
sempre più p
(Er wendet sich nochmals mit dem Haupt und blickt zurück.)
(He turns his head again and locks back.)
mp
pp
(Er verschwindet durch das Feuer.)
He disappears through the fire.
(Vorhang fällt.)
Curtain falls.
più pp
ppp

A cycle of four music dramas, *The Ring of the Nibelung* by Richard Wagner (1813–1883) stands as one of the most monumental achievements in Western music, both in its size and in its impact on opera, music in general, and all of the arts. One of the innovative features introduced by Wagner is the creation of a continuous dramatic flow. Rather than retaining artificial substructures such as arias, recitatives, and other musical numbers, Wagner developed an ongoing melodic style that he termed *Ewigemelodie* (endless melody). In order to create unity within this free dramatic flow, Wagner created a system of recurring *leitmotifs* (leading motives), which represent aspects of the drama. Among Wagner's other influential innovations are the sheer length of the works, his use of the low brass, and his exploration of the limits of functional harmony.

Die Walküre is the second music drama of the cycle. In this final scene, Wotan, the king of gods, must punish and bid farewell to his only real love, his daughter Brünnhilde. In a tender moment, he kisses her and thereby transforms her into a mortal. Brünnhilde enters into a magical sleep that can only be broken by a kiss. In order to ensure that a hero will awaken her, Wotan commands Loge (the god of fire) encircle her body with flames. Only a man without fear—a man truly worthy of his beloved daughter—will be able to penetrate the fiery circle and discover Brünnhilde. This scene contains the most extended solo singing of the Ring, as Wotan tenderly and sadly recalls the delights that Brünnhilde brought him. Leitmotifs abound, especially when Wotan is silent. Among the most prominent themes are Magic Sleep (a slow descent), Magic Slumber (a gentle, rocking theme), Magic Fire (crackling sixteenth notes in the woodwinds), Siegfried (a forceful melody sung by Wotan and played by the low brass), and Fate (a major/minor harmonic twist).

12. Giuseppe Verdi

Rigoletto, Act III, excerpts (1851)

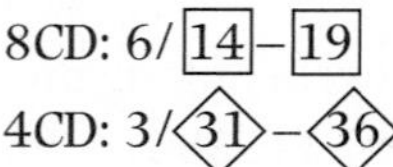

A lonely spot on the shore of the Mincio River, with the towers of Mantua in the background. On the left, a two-story house almost in ruins, the front of which, open to the spectator, shows a rustic inn on the ground floor: a broken staircase leads from this to a loft where stands a rough couch. On the side towards the street is a door, and a low wall extends backward from the house. Gilda and Rigoletto converse in great agitation along the road to the inn; Sparafucile is seated inside the inn. Upon reaching the inn, Rigoletto forces Gilda to watch through a fissure in the wall as the Duke enters, disguised as a cavalry officer.

Canzone (aria). "La donna è mobile" ("Woman is fickle")

Allegretto. (♪= 188)

14 31

Fl. & Vlns.

p Cl, Ob., Bn. & 'Cello Hn. *marcato*

p

Duke. *con brio* *legato* *pp*

La donna è mobile qual piuma al vento, muta d'accento
Woman's fidelity Turns like the weather, Sways like a feather

e di pensiero. Sempre un amabile leggiadro viso,
Tossed in the breezes. Fond of variety, She is beguiling,

pp
D.
in pianto o in ri - so, è menzo - gne-ro. La donna è mo-bil
Frowning or smil-ing, Just as she pleas-es. She is ca - pri-cious,
pp
p
qual piuma al ven-to, mu-ta d'ac-cen-to e di pen - sier,
Turns like the weath-er, Sways like a feath-er, Nev - er the same,
f
leggero
Fl.
Ob.
pp
e di pen - sier, e,
Nev-er, the same, nev -
p
pp
con forza
e di pen - sier.
er the same.
f
ff
p marcato

15 32

D.
p
pp
D.
È sempre mi-se-ro chi a lei s'af - fi - da, chi le con - fi - da
Blind in sim - plic - i - ty Men's hearts are cap-tured, Whol - ly en - rap-tured,
D.
mal cau-to il co - re! Pur mai non sen-te-si fe-li-ce ap - pie - no
Deaf to all warn-ing. Yet full-est hap-pi-ness No man has tast - ed
D.
chi su quel se - no non li-ba a - mo - re! La donna è mo - bil
Whose life is wast - ed Love-less and mourn-ing! Wom-an will wa - ver,
pp
p

(Re-enter Sparafucile with a flask of wine and two glasses, which he places on the table; then

with the hilt of his long sword he knocks on the ceiling twice. At this signal, a smiling young
dim.

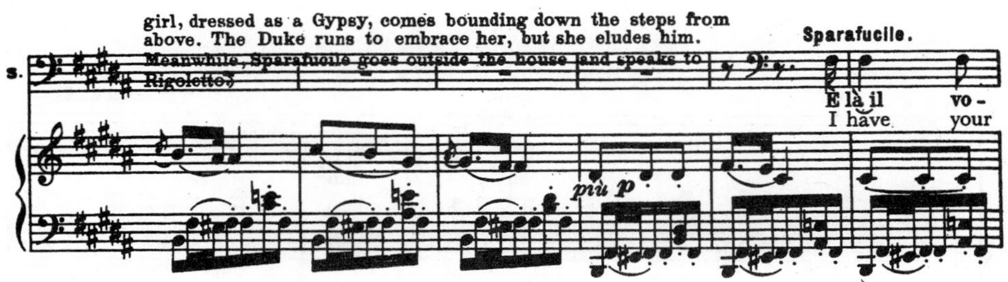
girl, dressed as a Gypsy, comes bounding down the steps from
above. The Duke runs to embrace her, but she eludes him.
Meanwhile, Sparafucile goes outside the house and speaks to
Rigoletto.)
Sparafucile.
S.
È là il vo-
I have your
più p

Rigoletto.
S.
R.
str'uo - mo... Vi-ver de - e o mo - ri - re? Più
man here. Give your or - ders, I o - bey you. De-
morendo

(Sparafucile goes off behind the
house, toward the river.)
R.
tar - di tor-ne - rò l'opra a com-pi - re.
tain him for a while, and then I'll pay you.

Quartet. "Un dì, se ben rammentomi" ("One day, if I remember right")

Gilda.
Maddalena.
G.
Ma.
In - i - quo! Ah, ah, e ven-t'altre ap-pres - so le
The trai-tor! Ha, ha! No one else be - fore me! You're
D.
do - ra!
dore you.
p
Ma.
scor - da for - se a-desso? Ha un' aria il si - gno - ri - no da ve - ro li - ber-
tell - ing me a sto-ry. A lib-er - tine, be - lieve me, Could nev-er once de-
Gilda.
G.
Ah pa-dre mi - o!
Ah, dear-est fa - ther!
Ma.
ti - no...
ceive me.
La-scia-te-mi, stor - di - to.
E-nough of that, it's sil-ly.
Duke (trying to embrace her).
D.
Sì!.. un mostro son,..
Yes, I'm ver-y bad . . .
Ih che fra-
Come, don't be
Fl.
Ob.
cresc.

Maddalena.
Duke.
casso! Stia saggio. E tu sii do-ci-le, non fa-re tan-to
naugh-ty! Be good now! Don't act so prud-ish-ly, Why sud-den-ly be
f
chias-so. O-gni sag-gez-za chiu-de-si nel gau-dio e nel-l'a-
haugh-ty? Cast all your fool-ish qualms a-way. My dar-ling, you must sur-
Strings
col canto
pp
Maddalena.
Scher-
You're
(takes her hand)
mo-re. La bel-la ma-no can-di-da!
ren-der. Your hand is white as i-vo-ry!
p
pp
Gilda.
za-te voi, si-gno-re. Son brut-ta. I-ni-quo!
mock-ing me, pre-tend-er! I'm ug-ly. Be-tray-er!
No, no. Ab-brac-cia-mi.
No, no! I long for you
f
p

Maddalena.
Ma.
Ebro! Signor l'in-dif - fe - rente, vi pia-ce canzo -
Li-ar! (laughing) It seems to be your fash-ion to jest your way through
D.
D'amor ar - den - te.
with glow - ing pas - sion!
Ma.
nar? Ne vo-glio la pa - ro - la..
life! Your prom-ise binds for - ev - er! (ironically)
D.
No, no, ti vo'spo - sar. A-ma-bi-le fi -
I want you for my wife! How lov-a-ble and
p
Gilda.
G.
I - ni - quo tra - di - tor!
Maddelena. My heart can bear no more!
Ma.
Ne voglio la pa - ro - la
Duke. Your prom-ise binds for - ev - er!
D.
gliuo - la! A ma - bi - le fi
clev - er! How lov - a - ble and
Rigoletto (to Gilda, who has heard all).
R.
E non ti basta an - cor? E non ti basta an -
You want to hear still more? You want to hear still

G.
I - ni - quo tra - di - tor!
My heart can bear no more!
Mn.
Ne vo-glio la pa - ro - la! ne voglio la pa - ro - la, ne voglio la pa -
Your prom-ise binds for - ev-er! Your promise binds for - ev-er! Your prom-ise binds for -
D.
gliuola!
clev-er!
a - ma - bi - le fi - gliuo - la! a - ma - bi - le fi -
How lov - a - ble and clev-er! How lov - a - ble and
R.
cor?
more?
e non ti basta an - cor? e non ti basta an -
You want to hear still more? You want to hear still
ff

17
34
G.
Ma.
ro - la!
ev - er!
Andante.
D.
gliuo - la! Bel - la fi - glia del - l'a - mo - re, schia - vo
clev-er! Mad-da - - le - na, I a - dore you, You en -
R.
cor?
more?
Andante. (♩ = 66)
Wood
pp
String pizz.

D.
son de' vez - zi tuo - i; con un detto, un det - to sol tu
slave me and en - chant me; On - ly this one fa - vor you must
puo - i le mie pe - ne, le mie pe - ne con - so - lar. Vieni, e
grant me, Come and love me, be my ra-diant guid-ing star. I im-
pp dolce
Cl. & Bn.
pp
sen-ti del mio co - re il fre - quente pal - pi - tar, con un
plore you, don't re - fuse me, Be my ra-diant, guid-ing star, grant me
stent.
Strings
detto, un det - to sol tu puo - i le mie pe - ne, le mie pe - ne con - so -
this one fa - vor, I im - plore you, Come and love me, be my ra-diant guid-ing
pp

18
35
G.
Gilda.
Ah! co-sì par-lar d'a-
Ah, I know his lips are
Maddelena.
Ma.
Ah!ah! ri-do ben di co-re, chè tai ba-ie costan po-co;
Duke. Talk is cheap, there's no de-ny-ing but your com-pli-ments a-muse me.
D.
lar.
star.
Fl.
Cl.
pp
Ob. & Vln.
G
mo-re
ly-ing.
Maddelena.
Ma.
quan-to val-ga il vo-stro gio-co, mel cre-de-te, so apprez-
Pret-ty speech-es don't con-fuse me, I know well how false they
G.
a me pur l'in-fa-me ho u-di-to!
Ah, to think I once be-lieved him!
In-fe-
How sin-
Ma.
R.
Rigoletto (to Gilda).
zar.
are.
Ta-ci, il pian-ge-re non va-
Qui-et, your cry-ing now is use-
Ob. & Vln.

G.
li - - ce cor tra - di - to, per an -
cere - - ly did I love him, and he
Ma.
Son av - vez - za, bel si - gno - - re,
Man - y times I heard that sto - - ry,
Duke.
D.
Con un det - to
Don't be heart - less,
R.
le; ta - ci, ta - ci, il pian - ge - re non va -
less! Nev - er mind him, your cry - ing now is use -
G.
go - - scia non scop - piar, no, no, non scop -
now be - trays me so. Ah, he scorned my
Ma.
ad un si - mi - le scherza - - re, mio bel si -
To be - lieve it would be mad - - ness, It's far too
D.
sol tu puo - i le mi - e
I im - plore you, Come and love,
R.
le, no, non val, no, no, non
less! No, the time for tears has
8

19
36
G.
piar.
love!
Ms.
gnor!
old!
D.
pe - ne con - so - lar. Bel - la fi - glia del l'a - mo -
ra - diant guid - ing star! Mad - da - le - na, I a - dore
R.
val.
passed.
col canto
pp
G.
In - - fe - li - ce
I be - lieved - him,
Ms.
Ah! ah! ri - do ben di co - re, chè tai ba - ie costan po - co,
Talk is cheap, there's no de - ny - ing but your com - pli - ments a - muse me
D.
re, schia - vo son de' vez - zi tuo -
you, You en - slave me and en - chant
R.
Ch'ei men - ti - va,
He was ly - ing,

G.
cor tra - -
now he be -
Ma.
quan - to val - ga il vo - stro gio - co, mel cre - de - te, so ap - prez -
Pret - ty speech - es don't con - fuse me, I know well how false they
D.
i; con un
me; On - ly.
R.
ch'ei men - -
He be - -
fp
G.
di - to, ah!
trays me! Ah,
Ma.
zar. Sono avvez - za, bel signo - re, ad un si - mi - le scher-
are. Man-y times I heard that sto-ry, To be-lieve it would be
D.
detto, un det - to sol tu puo - - i le mie
this one fa - vor you must grant me, Come and
R.
ti - - va sei si -
trayed you, I have

G.
— no, non scoppiar. In - fe - li - ce co - re, cor tra -
— it breaks my heart! All my trust and my de - vo - tion
Ma.
za - - re. Ah! ah! ah! ah! ri - - -
mad - - ness, Ha, ha, ha, ha! Ri - - -
D.
pe - ne, le mie pe - ne con - so - lar. Ah! con un
love me, be my ra-diant guid-ing star! Ah, Mad - da -
R.
con voce cupa
cu - - ra. Taci, e mia sa - rà la
proved it, But I give you my as -
Fl.
Ob.
G.
di - to, per an - go - scia non scop -
He has scorned, and now I am be -
Ma.
do di cor, ah, ah, ri - - -
dic - u - lous! Ha, ha! Ri - - -
D.
det - - - to sol tu
le - - - na, I a -
R.
cu - - ra la ven - det - ta d'af - fret -
sur - - ance That his crime shall be a -

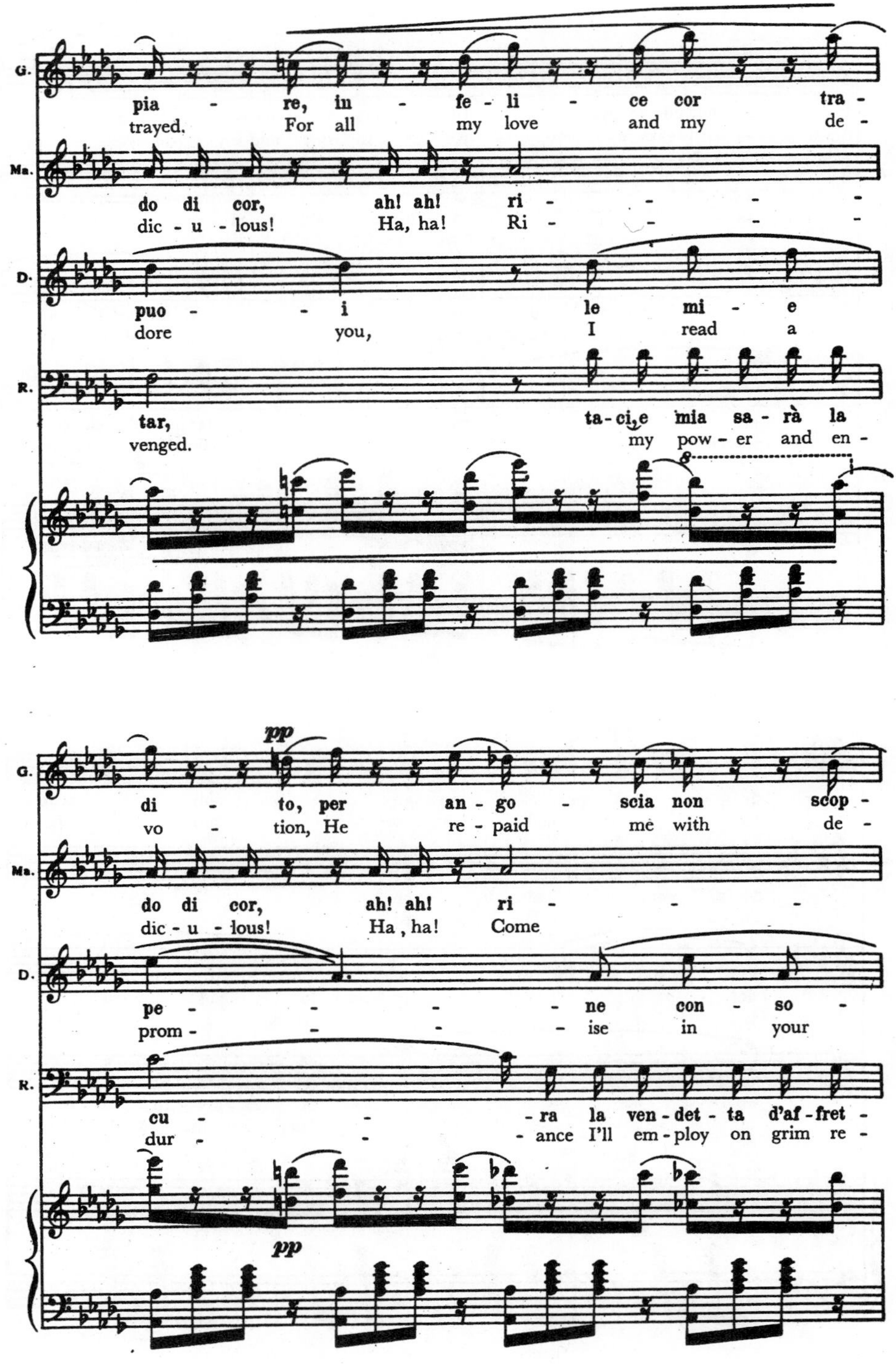
G.
pia - re, in - fe - li - ce cor tra -
trayed. For all my love and my de -
Ma.
do di cor, ah! ah! ri - - - -
dic - u - lous! Ha, ha! Ri - - -
D.
puo - - i le mi - e
dore you, I read a
R.
tar, ta - ci, e mia sa - rà la
venged. my pow - er and en -
G.
pp
di - to, per an - go - scia non scop -
vo - tion, He re - paid me with de -
Ma.
do di cor, ah! ah! ri - - -
dic - u - lous! Ha, ha! Come
D.
pe - - - ne con - so -
prom - - - ise in your
R.
cu - - ra la ven - det - ta d'af - fret -
dur - - ance I'll em - ploy on grim re -
pp

G.
pia - re, in - fe - li - ce cor tra -
cep - tion. How I loved him and a -
Ms.
do, ah! ah! ri - do ben di co - re, chè tai ba - ie co - stan
now, Talk is cheap, there's no de - ny - ing, But your com - pli - ments a -
D.
lar; vie - ni e sen - ti del mio
glance. I en - treat you don't re -
R.
tar. Sì, pron - - ta
venge. I am pre -
cresc.
G.
di - to, per an - go - scia non scoppiar, no, no, no, no, no,
dored him, And by him I am be-trayed, ah— And
Ms.
poco, quanto val - ga il vo - stro gioco, mel credete, so apprezzar, sì, sì,
muse me, Pret - ty speech - es don't con - fuse me, I know well how false they are, my friend.
D.
co - re il frequen - te pal - pi - tar, ah, sì,
fuse me, make me hap - py and be - mine, ah, my
R.
fia, sa - ra fa - ta - le,
pared to strike a fa - tal blow.
f

G.
no, no, non scop-
now he broke my
Ms.
so-no avvez-za, bel si-gno-re, ad un si-mi-le scher-
Man-y times I heard that sto-ry, To be-lieve it would be
D.
vie-
dar-
R.
io sa-prol-lo ful-mi-nar, io sa-prol-lo ful-mi-
I'll em-ploy all my en-dur-ance to strike a fa-tal
f
f
G.
pia-re, in-fe-li-ce cor tra-
heart, My trust and my de-vo-tion
Ms.
zar, ah, ah, ah, ah! ri-
hard, ha, ha, ha, ha! Ri-
D.
ni; ah! con un
ling. Ah, Mad-da-
con voce cupa
R
nar; ta-ci, e mia sa-rà la
blow. Yes, I give you my as-
p

G.
di - to, per an - go - scia non scop -
he for-got, and now I am be -
Ma.
do di cor, ah! ah! ri - - - -
dic - u - lous ha, ha! Ri - - - -
D.
det- - - - to sol tu
le - - - na, I a- -
R.
cu- - - - ra la ven - det - ta d'af - fret -
sur- - - - ance, That his crime shall be a -
pp
G.
pia - re, in fe - li - ce cor tra -
trayed. For all my love and my de -
Ma.
do di cor, ah! ah! ri - - -
dic - u - lous, ha, ha! Ri - - -
D.
puo - i le mi - e
dore you, I read a
R.
tar, ta - ci, e mia sa - rà la
venged. All my pow - er and en -

pp
G.
di - to, per an - go - scia non scop -
vo - tion, He re - paid me with de -
Ms.
do di cor, ah! ah! ri - - - -
dic - u - lous, ha, ha! Come
D.
pe - - - ne con - so -
prom - - - ise in your
R.
cu - - - ra la ven - det - ta d'af - fret -
dur - - - ance I'll em - ploy on grim re -
pp
G
pia - re, in - - fe - li - - ce cor tra -
cep - tion. How I loved him and a -
Ms.
do, ah! ah! ri - do ben di co - re, chè tai ba - ie co - stan
now, Talk is cheap, there's no de - ny - ing, But your com - pli - ments a -
D.
lar; vie - ni e sen - ti del mio
glance. I en - treat you, don't re -
R.
tar; sì, pron - ta
venge. I am pre - -
cresc.

G.
di - to, per an - go - scia non scop -
dored him, And by him I am be -
Ma.
po - co; quanto val - ga il vo - stro gio - co, mel cre - de - te, so ap - prez -
muse me; Pret - ty speech - es don't con - fuse me, I know well how false you
D
co - re il fre - quen - te pal - pi -
fuse me, make me hap - py and be
R.
fia, sa - rà fa -
pared to strike a
G.
piar, no, no, no,no, no, no,no, non scop -
trayed, ah And now he broke my
Ma
zar, sì, sì, sono avvez - za, bel si - gnore, ad un si - mi - le scher-
are, my friend, Man - y times I heard that sto - ry, To be - lieve it would be
D.
tar, ah sì, vie -
mine, ah, my dar -
R.
ta - le, io sa - prol - lo ful - mi - nar, io saprol - lo ful - mi -
fa - tal blow. I'll em - ploy all my en - dur - ance to strike a fa - tal

G.
piar, in - fe - li - ce cor tra - di - to, per ango - scia non scop-
heart. How I loved him and a - dored him, And he so— de-ceived my
Ms.
zar, il vo - stro gio - co— sò ap-prez -
hard. I know these sto - ries, — what they are
D.
ni. sen - ti del co - re il pal - pi -
ling, I read a prom - ise in your
R.
par, ta - ci, e mia sa - rà la cu - ra la ven-det - ta d'af-fret -
blow. Yes, I give you my as - sur-ance, That his crime shall be a -
G.
piar, in - fe - li - ce cor tra - di - to, per ango - scia non scop-
heart. How I loved him and a - dored him And he so — de-ceived my
Ms.
zar, il vo - stro gio - co— sò ap-prez -
worth. I know these sto - ries, — what they are
D.
tar, sen - ti del co - re il pal - pi -
glance, I read a prom - ise in your
R.
tar, ta - ci, e mia sa - rà la cu - ra la ven-det - ta d'af-fret -
venged. All my pow - er and en - dur-ance I'll em-ploy on grim re -

G.
piar, no, non scop-piar, non scop-
heart, he broke my heart, my
Ms.
zar, il vostro gio - co sò apprez-zar, il vo-stro gioco sò apprezza -
worth. How well I know what they are worth. How well I know these pret-ty sto -
D.
tar, vieni, vie-ni, vie-
glance. You shall be mine, be
R.
tar, ta-ci, ta-ci, ta-
venge, I shall em-ploy on
p
pp
G.
piar, ah no!
heart, ah, ah!
Ms.
re, ah sì!
ries, my friend!
D.
ni, vie - ni!
mine, be mine!
R.
ci, ta - ci!
grim re - venge!

In the nineteenth century, Italian opera maintained its traditional emphasis on the voice and the aria. Although changes occurred slowly during the course of the nineteenth century, a number of new qualities can be observed, including a more direct, cutting vocal line for tenors and more frequent ensemble singing in serious operas (an influence of *opera buffa*). Giuseppe Verdi (1813–1901) fashioned these musical elements into a dramatic flow and brought about a balance between musical and dramatic needs in opera. One of Verdi's most compelling and popular works is *Rigoletto.* Based on a play by Victor Hugo that was banned in France, *Le roi s'amuse (The King Is Amused),* Verdi's opera is a dark tale of seduction, revenge, and murder set in the Renaissance court of Mantua. Rigoletto, a hunchbacked court jester, seeks revenge against his employer, the Duke, for defiling his only valued possession, his daughter Gilda.

In Act III, the plot for vengeance unfolds in a brilliant musical and dramatic fashion. At the opening of this excerpt, the Duke sings his famous aria of seduction, "La donna è mobile" ("Woman is fickle") to Maddalena, while Rigoletto has Gilda watch through a window. The strophic aria is set to a waltz tempo with a guitarlike accompaniment. At the end of the aria, Rigoletto quietly completes a deal for the Duke's murder with Sparafucile, Maddalena's brother. In the ensuing quartet, four divergent moods are projected simultaneously: the ardor of the Duke, the playfulness of Maddalena, the lament of Gilda, and the resolve for vengeance by Rigoletto. Following this remarkable musical moment, Rigoletto's plans go astray. Ultimately, Rigoletto opens a large sack, expecting to see the Duke's body, only to find that Gilda has allowed herself to be killed for her unworthy lover. She dies in Rigoletto's arms as the curtains close.

13. Clara Schumann

Scherzo, Op. 10 (c. 1838) -quick tempo
-triple meter, lively mood

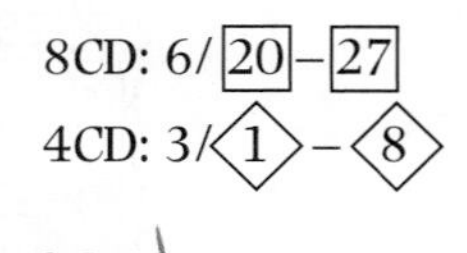

20 1 -lyrical, w intense passion

Presto 𝅗𝅥. = 80

p

mf

21 2

sf

(*f*)

p

sf

sf

sf

sf

26
8
sf
sf
31
p
mf
36
(f)
42
p
sf
f
sf
48
sf
sf
sf
8
dim.
(8
22
3
54
p
sf
sf

60
sf
sf
66
(sf)
8
sf
p
72
mf
78
f
p
84
sf
f
sf
sf
sf
90
sf
8
dim.
23
4
p

96
p
102
p
p
108
mf
cresc.
114
fp
p
120
dim.
126
cresc.
f

24
5
ben legato
un poco calando
assai dim.
doloroso
mf
ben marcato la melodia
stringendo
un poco ritenuto
p dolce
cresc.
Tempo I
f
ff
sf
sf

poco a poco crescendo
legato
tranquillo
25
6
ff
sf
mf
p

26
7
la melodia ben marcato
207
p
l'accompagnemento pp
mf
215
dim.
223
mf
231
rubato
un poco ritenuto
cresc.
pp
239
a tempo
leggierissimo
244

250
doloroso
pp
stringendo
258
poco a poco stringendo
265
cresc.
271
p
277
f
poco a poco dim.
283
sf
f

27
8
289
p
sf
295
f
301
8
307
pesante
ff
p leggieramente
(s)f

319
sf
sf
p
325
p
ff
sf
sf
331
sf
sf
fpp
misterioso
poco a poco
stringendo e
337
crescendo
ff
precipitato
342
6
sf
ff

Clara Schumann (1819–1896) was one of the most remarkable musicians of the nineteenth century. Married to Robert Schumann and a close friend to Johannes Brahms, Clara had contact with many of the leading performers and composers of the time. Called the "priestess" by her colleagues, she maintained a musical presence while supporting the career of her husband and raising seven children. After her husband's death, she concertized more extensively and championed Robert's works. Her own compositions include a piano concerto, a piano trio, and numerous Lieder and piano works.

One of the principal types of piano miniatures of the nineteenth century is the stylized dance movement, such as the waltz and scherzo. Clara Schumann's Scherzo, Opus 10, maintains the quick tempo, triple meter, and lively mood that are traditionally associated with the title. But the minor mode and passionate character lend a more dramatic tone to the work. Balancing the frenetic energy of the scherzo are two contrasting trio sections. The work as a whole is characterized by virtuosity, lyricism, and an intense passion, all qualities that reflect the considerable skill of its pianist-composer.

14. Bedřich Smetana

Vltava (The Moldau),
from *Má vlast (My Country)* (1874–79)

8CD: 6/28–35
4CD: 3/15–22

28 15

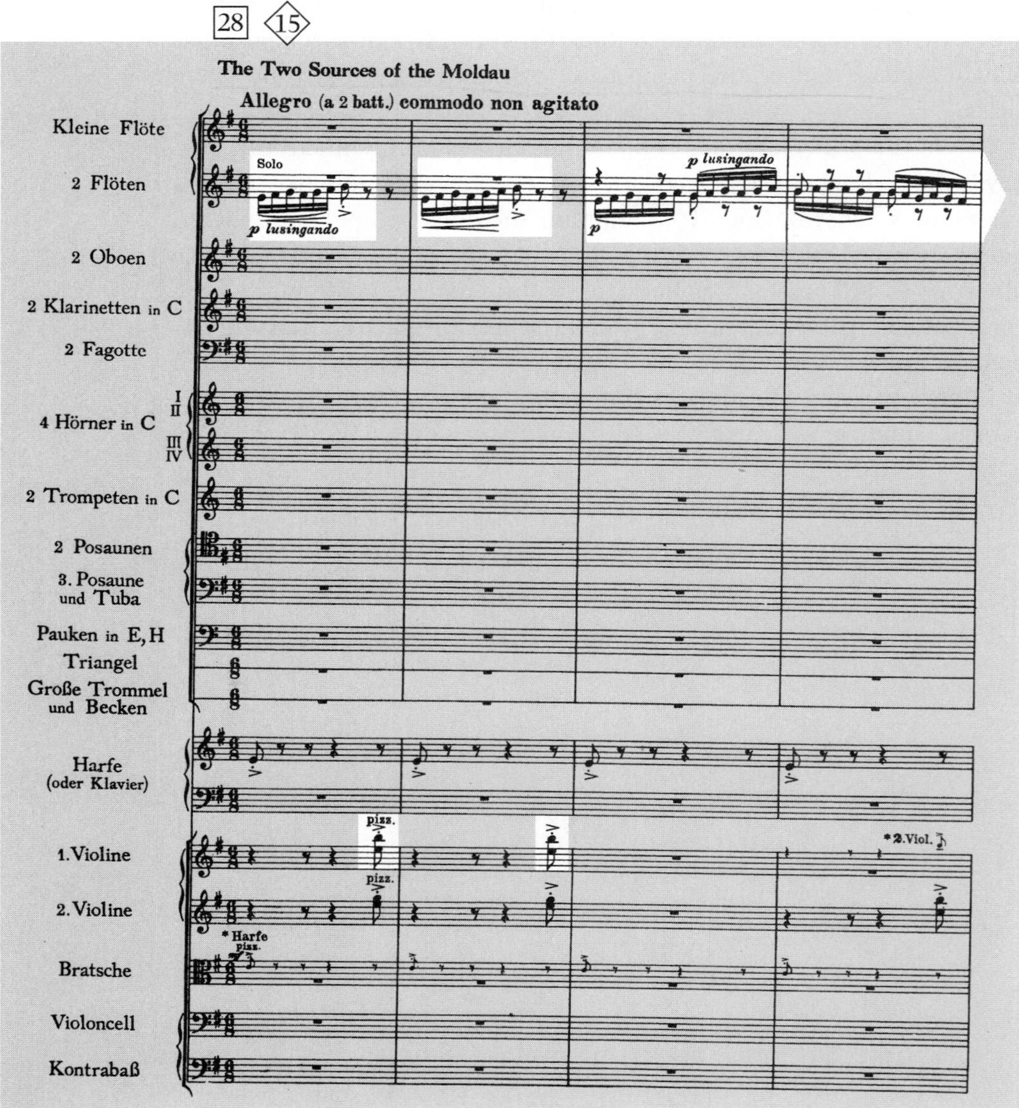

Editor's note: Smaller notes indicate an alternate version for reduced orchestra.

5
Fl.
Harfe
1.Viol.
2.Viol.
Br.
10
15
Klar. (C)
p
20

25
Fl.
Klar. (C)
1.Viol.
2.Viol.
Br.
p
30
35
29
16
Ob.
Hr. (C)
Trgl.
Vcll.
K.-B.
I.II.
a 2
p elegante
*2.Ob.
p
lusingando
arco
ondeggiante
p dolce
*2.Vcll.
pizz.

40
*1. Ob.
*2. Ob.
*3. Hr.
*2. Fag.
Fl.
Ob.
Klar. (C)
Fag.
Hr. (C)
Trpt. (C)
Pos. Tuba
Pk.
Trgl.
1.Viol.
2.Viol.
Br.
Vcll.
K.-B.
dolce
p dolce
a 2
dim.
sempre ondeggiante

45
Fl.
Ob.
dolce
dolce
Klar. (C)
*2. Ob.
Fag.
dolce
Hr. (C)
Trpt. (C)
Pos. Tuba
Pk.
Trgl.
glockenartig
1.Viol.
2.Viol.
sempre ondeggiante
Br.
sempre ondeggiante
Vcll
sempre ondeggiante
K.-B.

50
Fl.
Ob.
Klar. (C)
Fag.
Hr. (C)
Trpt. (C)
Pos. Tuba
Pk.
Viol.
Viol.
Br.
Vcll.
K.-B.
dim.
sf
p

55
Fl.
a 2
mf
cresc.
sf
Ob.
mf
mf cresc.
sf
Klar. (C)
mf cresc.
Fag.
mf
mf cresc.
Hr. (C)
p
cresc.
*4. Hr.
Trpt. (C)
p
Pos. Tuba
p cresc.
Pk.
Trgl.
p
Harfe
p
cresc.
sf
1.Viol.
mf
cresc.
sf
2.Viol.
mf cresc.
sf
Br.
mf cresc.
sf
Vcll.
mf cresc.
mf cresc.
sf
K.-B.
mf
sf

60
a 2
Fl.
Ob.
*2. Ob.
Klar. (C)
*2. Fl.
*2. Ob.
Fag.
Hr. (C)
*4. Hr.
Trpt. (C)
Pos. Tuba
Pk.
Trgl.
Harfe
Viol.
Viol.
Br.
Vcll.
K.-B.
cresc.

65
Fl.
Ob.
Klar. (C)
*2.Fl.2.Ob.
Fag.
Hr. (C)
Trpt. (C)
Pos. Tuba
Pk.
Trgl.
1.Viol.
2.Viol.
Br.
Vcll.
K.-B.
sf cresc.
cresc.
arco
pizz.
arco

70
Fl.
Ob.
Klar. (C)
*2.Ob.
*2.Vcll.
Fag.
Hr. (C)
*4.Hr.
Trpt. (C)
*3.Hr.
Pos. Tuba
*2.Fag.
Pk.
dopo la repetizione muta in C.G.
dim.
Trgl.
Harfe
1.Viol.
2.Viol.
dim.
Br.
dim.
Vcll.
pizz.
K.-B.

75
Fl.
Ob.
Klar. (C)
Fag.
Hr. (C)
Trpt. (C)
Pos. Tuba
Pk.
Trgl.
Harfe
1.Viol.
2.Viol.
Br.
Vcll.
K.-B.
sf
dim.
p

30
17
80
Forest Hunt
Fl.
Ob.
Klar. (C)
Fag.
Hr. (C)
Trpt. (C)
*2 Ob.
Pos. Tuba
*4. Hr.
Pk.
Trgl.
Harfe
1.Viol.
2.Viol.
Br.
Vcll.
arco
K.-B.

86
Fl.
Ob.
Klar. (C)
Fag.
Hr. (C)
Trpt. (C)
Pos. Tuba
Pk.
Trgl.
1.Viol.
2.Viol.
Br.
Vcll.
K.-B.
*2.Ob.
*3.Hr.
*4.Hr.

92
Fl.
Ob.
Klar. (C)
Fag.
Hr. (C)
Trpt. (C)
Pos. Tuba
Pk.
Trgl.
*4. Hr.
muta in A. D.
1.Viol.
2.Viol.
Br.
Vcll.
K.-B.

97
Fl.
Ob.
2. Ob.
Klar. (C)
Fag.
Hr. (C)
Trpt. (C)
3. Hr.
Pos. Tuba
Pk.
1.Viol.
2.Viol.
Br.
Vcll.
K.-B.

102
Fl.
Ob.
Klar. (C)
Fag.
Hr. (C)
Trpt. (C)
Pos. Tuba
Pk.
Trgl.
1.Viol.
2.Viol.
Br.
Vcll.
K.-B.
*2 Ob.
*3. Hr.
*4. Hr.
muta in E
*3. Hr.
f dim.
sf
f

107
Fl.
Ob.
Klar. (C)
Fag.
Hr. (C)
Trpt. (E)
Pos. Tuba
Pk.
1.Viol
2.Viol.
Br.
Vcll.
K.-B.
dim.
p dim.
sempre dim.

112
Fl.
Ob.
Klar. (C)
a 2
Fag.
Hr. (C)
Trpt. (E)
Pos. Tuba
Pk.
1.Viol.
2.Viol.
Br.
Vcll.
K.-B.
pp
ppp

Peasant Wedding
31
18
118
L'istesso tempo, ma moderato
Klar. (C)
Fag.
Hr. (C)
Trpt. (E)
3. Pos.
1. Viol.
2. Viol.
Br.
Vcll.
K.-B.
cresc.
128

136
Fl.
Ob.
Klar. (C)
Fag.
Hr. (C)
Trpt. (A)
*3.u.4.Hr.
Pos. Tuba
*2.Fag.
*2.Vcll.
Pk.
Trgl.
1.Viol.
2.Viol.
Br.
Vcll.
K.-B.

144
Fl.
Ob.
Klar. (C)
Fag.
Hr. (C)
Trpt. (A)
Pos. Tuba
Pk.
Trgl.
1. Viol.
2. Viol.
Br.
Vcll.
K.-B.
dim.
p

152
Fl.
a 2
p
Ob.
Klar. (C)
Fag.
*3.u.4. Hr.
Hr. (C)
Trpt. (A)
Pos. Tuba
Pk.
più p
Trgl.
1.Viol.
2.Viol.
Br.
Vcll.
K.-B.

160
a 2
Fl.
Ob.
Klar. (C)
Fag.
Hr. (C)
Pk.
1.Viol.
2.Viol.
Br.
Vcll.
K.-B.
dim.
sempre dim.
II.
più p
IV.
*4.Hr.
muta in E H
168
muta in B
muta in Es
muta in F
pp
ppp
*2.Fag.
pp Solo

32
19
Moonlight: Nymphs' Dance
L'istesso tempo
181
Fl.
Ob.
Klar. (B)
Fag.
Hr. (Es)
Trpt. (B)
1.Viol.
2.Viol.
Br.
Vcll.
K.-B.
plusingando
pp
ppp
*2.Ob.
*Die 1.Stimme blasen
*2.Ob.mit Dämpfer
in B
tranquillo
con sordini
dolciss.
pp ondeggiante
188
Fl.
Klar. (B)
(Es) Hr. (F)
Trpt. (B)
3. Pos.
Harfe
*3.Hr.ohne Dämpfer
*4.Hr.
1.Viol.
2.Viol.
Br.
Vcll.

192
Fl.
Klar. (B)
(Es) Hr. (F)
Trpt. (B)
3. Pos.
Harfe
1. Viol.
2. Viol.
Br.
Vcll.
sempre pp
ppp
*3. Hr.
*4. Hr.
p
196

200
Fl.
Klar. (B)
(Es)
Hr.
(F)
Trpt. (B)
3. Pos.
Harfe
1.Viol.
2.Viol.
Br.
Vcll.
sempre pp
sempre pp
*3.Hr.
sempre pp
*4.Hr.
sempre pp
p
p
*3.Hr.
pp
*Die 1.Stimme spielen
204
Fl.
Klar. (B)
(Es)
Hr.
(F)
3. Pos.
1.Viol.
2.Viol.
Br.
Vcll.
pp
*4.Hr.

208
Fl.
Ob.
Klar. (B)
Fag.
(Es)
Hr.
(F)
Trpt. (B)
Pos. Tuba
Pk.
Harfe
1. Viol.
2. Viol.
Br.
Vcll
K B
dim.
più pp
pp
*3.u.4.Hr.
*3.Hr.
*4.Hr.
p
8

212
Fl.
Ob.
Klar. (B)
Fag.
*4. Hr.
ppp possibile
(Es)
Hr.
(F)
ppp possibile
ppp possibile
*3. Hr.
*4. Pos.
Trpt. (B)
ppp possibile
Pos. Tuba
ppp possibile
*3. Pos. bläst die Tubastimme
ppp possibile
Pk.
Harfe
p
1.Viol.
2.Viol.
Br.
Vcll.
*2. Vell.
K.-B.
pp

216
Fl.
Ob.
Klar. (B)
Fag.
ppp
sempre pp
(Es)
Hr.
(F)
ppp
sempre pp
Trpt. (B)
*1.u.2. Pos.
ppp
sempre pp
Pos. Tuba
*3. Pos. bläst die Tubastimme
ppp
sempre pp
Pk.
Harfe
p
1. Viol.
pp
2. Viol.
pp
Br.
pp
Vcll.
pp
K.-B.
pp

220
Fl.
Ob.
Klar. (B)
Fag.
*2.Hr.
(Es)
Hr.
(F)
*3.Hr.
sempre pp
Trpt. (B)
Pos. Tuba
Pk.
Harfe
p
1.Viol.
2.Viol.
Br.
Vcll.
K.-B.

224
Fl.
Ob.
Klar. (B)
Fag.
(Es)
Hr.
(F)
Trpt. (B)
Pos.
Tuba
Pk.
Harfe
1. Viol.
2. Viol.
Br.
Vcll.
K.-B.
pp
p

228
Fl.
Ob.
Klar. (B)
Fag.
Hr. (Es) (F)
Trpt. (B)
Pos. Tuba
Pk.
Trgl.
Harfe
1.Viol.
2.Viol.
Br.
1.Vcll.
2.Vcll. K.-B.
*Die obere Stimme.
*Die obere Stimme
*3.u.1.Hr.
in E a 2
pp
p cresc.
pp cresc.
cresc.

231
Fl.
Ob.
Klar. (B)
Fag.
(Es)
Hr.
(F)
Trpt. (E)
a 2
Pos.
Tuba
Pk.
Trgl.
Harfe
1.Viol.
2.Viol.
Br.
1.Vcll.
2.Vcll. K.-B.
pp
cresc.
sf

234
Fl.
Ob.
Klar. (B)
Fag.
(Es)
Hr.
(F)
Trpt. (E)
Pos. Tuba
Pk.
1.Viol.
2.Viol.
Br.
1.Vcll.
2.Vcll. K -B.
cresc.
muta in C
muta in C
*2. Fag.

33
20
Tempo I
237
Fl.
*2.Ob.
dolce
*Die obere Stimme
Ob.
p
dolce
Klar. (B)
muta in C
p
Fag.
p dolce
Hr. (C)
p
Trpt. (E)
Pos. Tuba
*2. Fag.
pp dolce
Pk.
Trgl.
p
senza sordini
1.Viol.
p
dolce
senza sordini
2.Viol.
p
sempre ondeggiante
senza sordini
Br.
p
sempre ondeggiante
senza sordini
Vcll.
p
sempre ondeggiante
*2.Vcll.
senza sordini
p
sempre ondeggiante
pizz.
K.-B.
p

241
Fl.
Ob.
Klar. (C)
Fag.
Hr. (C)
Trpt. (E)
* 3. Hr.
Pos. Tuba
Pk.
1.Viol.
2.Viol.
Br.
Vcll.
K.-B.
dim.
f
sf
p

246
Fl.
a 2
mf cresc.
sf
Ob.
mf cresc.
*2. Ob.
Klar. (C)
Fag.
Hr. (C)
p
Trpt. (E)
*3. Hr.
Pos. Tuba
mf cresc.
Pk.
Trgl.
Harfe
p
cresc.
f
Viol.
mf
Viol.
Br.
Vcll.
K.-B.

251
a 2
Fl.
Ob.
*2. Ob.
Klar. (C)
Fag.
Hr. (C)
Trpt. (E)
Pos. Tuba
Pk.
Trgl.
Harfe
1.Viol.
2.Viol.
Br.
Vcll.
K.-B.
sf
cresc.
* Die obere Stimme
p
f

256
Fl.
Ob.
Klar. (C)
Fag.
Hr. (C)
Trpt. (E)
Pos. Tuba
Pk.
Trgl.
1.Viol.
2.Viol.
Br.
Vcll.
K.-B.
cresc.
arco
pizz.
arco

261
Fl.
Ob.
Klar. (C)
Fag.
Hr. (C)
Trpt. (E)
Pos. Tuba
Pk.
Trgl.
Harfe
1.Viol.
2.Viol.
Br.
Vcll.
K.-B.
*2.Vcll.
*2.Ob.
*2.Vcll.
*2.Fag.
mf
p
pp
sf
dim.
pizz.
tr

266
Fl.
Ob.
Klar. (C)
Fag.
Hr. (C)
Trpt. (E)
Pos. Tuba
Pk.
Trgl.
Harfe
1.Viol.
2.Viol.
Br.
Vcll.
K.-B.
*2.Ob.
sf
dim.
f
p

34
21
271
St. John's Rapids
bei kl. Bes. *1.Fl.nimmt Kl.Fl.bis Schluß
Fl.
Ob.
Klar. (C)
Fag.
Hr. (C)
Trpt. (E)
Pos. Tuba
*4.Hr.
Pk.
Trgl.
Gr.Tr.
Solo
mit Paukenschlägel
Harfe
1.Viol.
2.Viol.
Br.
1.Vcll.
2.Vcll. K.-B.
cresc.

276
Kl.Fl.
1.Fl.
2.Fl.
*1. Fl.
Ob.
Klar. (C)
Fag.
Hr. (C)
Trpt. (E)
*1. Pos.
*1.u.2. Pos.
Pos. Tuba
Pk.
mit Paukenschlägel
Gr. Tr.
1.Viol.
2.Viol.
Br.
1.Vcll.
2.Vcll. K.-B.

281
Kl. Fl.
1. Fl.
2. Fl.
*1. Fl.
Ob.
*2. Ob.
Klar. (C)
Fag.
cresc.
Hr. (C)
Trpt. (E)
Pos. Tuba
*4. Hr.
Pk.
1. Viol.
2. Viol.
Br.
1. Vcll.
2. Vcll. K.-B.

286
Kl.Fl.
1.Fl.
2.Fl.
Ob.
*2.Ob.
Klar. (C)
Fag.
Hr. (C)
Trpt. (E)
*1.Pos.
Pos. Tuba
Pk.
1.Viol.
2.Viol.
Br.
1.Vcll.
2.Vcll. K.-B.

291
Kl.Fl.
1.Fl.
2.Fl.
*1.Fl.
Ob.
Klar. (C)
Fag.
*1.u.3.Hr.
Hr. (C)
Trpt. (E)
Pos. Tuba
Pk.
Bck.
1.Viol.
2.Viol.
Br.
1.Vcll.
2.Vcll. K B.

296
Kl.Fl.
1.Fl.
2.Fl.
Ob.
Klar.
(C)
Fag.
Hr.
(C)
Trpt.
(E)
Pos.
Tuba
Pk.
1.Viol.
2.Viol.
Br.
1.Vcll.
2.Vcll.
K-B.
f
cresc.
sf
marc.
* Kl. Fl. loco
* 3. Hr.
* 4. Hr.
f * 3. Pos. bläst die Tubastimme

303
Kl. Fl.
1. Fl.
2. Fl.
Ob.
Klar. (C)
Fag.
Hr. (C)
Trpt. (E)
Pos. Tuba
Pk.
Bck.
1. Viol.
2. Viol.
Br.
1. Vcll.
2. Vcll. K.-B.
*1. Fl.
Kl. Fl. loco
cresc.
*3. Hr.
*4. Hr.
*3. Pos. bläst die Tubastimme

309
Kl. Fl.
1. Fl.
2. Fl.
Ob.
Klar. (C)
Fag.
marc.
Hr. (C)
Trpt. (E)
*1. u. 2. Pos.
rfz
Pos. Tuba
* 3. Pos. bläst die Tubastimme
Pk.
Gr. Tr.
Bck.
1. Viol.
2. Viol.
Br.
1. Vcll.
2. Vcll. K.-B.
marc.

315
Kl. Fl.
1. Fl.
2. Fl.
Ob.
Klar. (C)
Fag.
Hr. (C)
Trpt. (E)
Pos. Tuba
Pk.
Gr. Tr.
Bck.
Viol.
Viol.
Br.
Vcll.
Vcll. K.-B.
sempre cresc.
cresc.
f

321
Kl. Fl.
1.Fl.
2.Fl.
Ob.
Klar. (C)
muta in A
Fag.
Hr. (C)
muta in E
Trpt. (E)
*4. Hr.
Pos. Tuba
Pk.
dim.
sub. pp
Gr. Tr.
mit Schlägeln
Bck.
1.Viol.
2.Viol.
Br.
1.Vcll.
2.Vcll. K.-B.

328
Kl. Fl.
1. Fl.
2. Fl.
Ob.
Klar. (A)
Fag.
Hr. (E)
Trpt. (E)
Pos. Tuba
Pk.
1. Viol.
2. Viol.
Br.
1. Vcll.
2. Vcll. K.-B.
ff
pp
sub. cresc.
sub. cresc. molto
cresc. molto

The Moldau in its Greatest Breadth
333
Più moto
Kl.Fl.
1.Fl.
2.Fl.
Ob.
Klar. (A)
Fag.
Hr. (E)
Trpt. (E)
Pos. Tuba
Pk.
Trgl.
Harfe
1.Viol.
2.Viol.
Br.
1.Vcll.
2.Vcll.
K.-B.

341
Kl.Fl.
*Kl.Fl.loco
1.Fl.
*Kl.Fl.Okt.höher
2.Fl.
*1.Fl.
Ob.
Klar. (A)
Fag.
Hr. (E)
Trpt. (E)
Pos. Tuba
Pk.
Trgl.
Harfe
1.Viol.
2.Viol.
Br.
1.Vcll.
2.Vcll.
K.-B.

350
Kl.Fl.
1.Fl.
2.Fl.
Ob.
Klar.
(A)
Fag.
Hr.
(E)
Trpt.
(E)
Pos.
Tuba
Pk.
Trgl.
Harfe
Viol.
Viol.
Br.
Vcll.
Vcll.
K.-B.
fz
f
cresc.
marcatiss.

35
22
Vyšehrad Motive (Symphonic Poem No. 1)
359
Kl. Fl.
1. Fl.
2. Fl.
Ob.
Klar. (A)
Fag.
Hr. (E)
Trpt. (E)
Pos. Tuba
Pk.
Trgl.
Gr. Tr.
Bck.
Harfe
1.Viol.
2.Viol.
Br.
1.Vcll.
2.Vcll.
K.-B.

364
Kl. Fl.
1. Fl.
2. Fl.
Ob.
Klar. (A)
Fag.
Hr. (E)
Trpt. (E)
Pos. Tuba
Pk.
Trgl.
Gr. Tr.
Bck.
1. Viol.
2. Viol.
Br.
1. Vcll.
2. Vcll.
K.-B.
fz

369
Kl. Fl.
1. Fl.
2. Fl.
Ob.
Klar. (A)
Fag.
Hr. (E)
Trpt. (E)
Pos. Tuba
Pk.
Trgl.
Gr. Tr.
Bck.
1. Viol.
2. Viol.
Br.
1. Vcll.
2. Vcll.
K.-B.

374
sempre ff
Kl. Fl.
1. Fl.
2. Fl.
Ob.
Klar. (A)
Fag.
Hr. (E)
Trpt. (E)
Pos. Tuba
Pk.
Trgl.
Gr.Tr.
Bck.
1.Viol.
2.Viol.
Br.
Vcll.
K B.
fz
rfz
ff
*Kl.Fl.loco
8

383
Kl. Fl.
1. Fl.
2. Fl.
Ob.
Klar. (A)
Fag.
Hr. (E)
Trpt. (E)
Pos. Tuba
Pk.
Trgl.
Gr. Tr.
Bck.
Viol.
Viol.
Br.
Vcll.
K.-B.

392
Kl. Fl.
1. Fl.
2. Fl.
*1. Fl.
Ob.
Klar. (A)
Fag.
Hr. (E)
Trpt. (E)
Pos. Tuba
Pk.
Trgl.
Gr.Tr.
Bck.
1. Viol.
2. Viol.
Br.
Vcll.
K.-B.

401
Kl.Fl.
1. Fl.
2. Fl.
Ob.
Klar. (A)
Fag.
Hr. (E)
Trpt. (E)
Pos. Tuba
Pk.
Trgl.
Gr.Tr.
Bck.
1.Viol.
2.Viol.
Br.
1.Vcll.
2.Vcll.
K. B.
sf dim.
sempre dim.
*1. Fl.
*3. Hr.
*2. Fag.
*Die 2. Stimme bis Schluß

410
Kl. Fl.
1. Fl.
2. Fl.
Ob.
Klar. (A)
Fag.
Hr. (E)
Trpt. (E)
Pos. Tuba
Pk.
1. Viol.
2. Viol.
Br.
1. Vcll.
2. Vcll.
K.-B.
pp
p dim.
ppp
ff
dim.
sempre dim. al

419
rall.
Kl. Fl.
1. Fl.
2. Fl.
Ob.
Klar. (A)
Fag.
Hr. (E)
Trpt. (E)
Pos. Tuba
Pk.
1. Viol.
2. Viol.
Br.
1. Vcll.
2. Vcll.
K.-B.
pp
dim. al ppp
smorz.
ff
fz
rall.

Musical nationalism can most readily be seen in works that create an image or tell a story, such as operas, songs, and symphonic poems. One of the foremost nationalist composers in the nineteenth century was Bedřich Smetana (1824–1884), who came from eastern Bohemia (in the modern-day Czech Republic). He composed a set of six symphonic poems entitled *Má vlast (My Country)* that depicts various images of his homeland. These works can be performed as a group, but they are often heard individually, especially the second member of the set, entitled *Vltava (The Moldau)*. Smetana attached the following description to this movement:

> Two springs pour forth in the shade of the Bohemian forest, one warm and gushing, the other cold and peaceful. Coming through Bohemia's valleys, they grow into a mighty stream. Through the thick woods it flows as the merry sounds of a hunt and the notes of the hunter's horn are heard ever closer. It flows through grass-grown pastures and lowlands where a wedding feast is being celebrated with song and dance. At night, wood and water nymphs revel in its sparkling waves. Reflected on its surface are fortresses and castles—witnesses of bygone days of knightly splendor and the vanished glory of martial times. The Moldau swirls through the St. John Rapids, finally flowing on in majestic peace toward Prague to be welcomed by historic Vysehrad. Then it vanishes far beyond the poet's gaze.

Many of the images in this description are mirrored in the music, from the gentle murmur of two springs to the tumultuous St. John Rapids. Unifying the work is a recurring E-minor river theme that has its grandest statement, with a dramatic turn to major, as the river nears the city of Prague. Smetana's nationalism is not limited to patriotic visions of Bohemia. Folk-music traditions are also reflected in the melody and rhythm. The river theme has a distinct folk character with its limited range and repetitive patterns. Also distinctive are the folk-dance rhythms heard as the river passes the wedding feast.

15. Johannes Brahms

Ein deutsches Requiem (A German Requiem),
Fourth Movement (1868)

8CD: 5/ 58 – 62
4CD: 3/ 26 – 30

12
Ze - ba - oth, dei - ne Woh - nun -
Ze - ba - oth, dei - ne Woh - nun -
Ze - ba - oth, dei - ne Woh - nun -
Ze - ba - oth, dei - ne Woh - nun -
Fl.
Hob.
Hr.
Kl.
18
gen, Herr Ze - ba -
gen, Herr Ze - ba -
gen, Herr Ze - ba -
gen, Herr Ze - ba - oth, Herr Ze - ba -
Viol.
23
oth!
oth!
oth! Wie lieb - lich sind dei - ne Woh - nun -
oth!
p espress.
p espress.
con Ped.

30
p espress.
Wie lieb - - - -
p espress.
Wie lieb - - lich
gen, Herr Ze - - - ba oth! Wie
p espress.
Wie lieb - - - - - - - lich
37
- - lich sind dei - - ne Woh - - nun - gen, Herr Ze - - -
sind dei - - ne Woh - - nun - gen, Herr Ze - - -
lieb - - - - lich sind dei - - ne Woh - - nun - gen, Herr
sind dei - - ne Woh - nun - gen, Herr Ze - - -
59
27
42
- - - ba - oth! Mei - ne See - - -
- - - ba - oth! Mei - ne See - - -
Ze - - ba - oth! Mei - ne See - - -
ba - - - oth! Mei - ne See - - -
p
Holzbl.

48
cresc.
le ver -
le ver - lan - get und
le ver - lan - get und seh - net, ver - lan - - -
le ver - lan - get und seh - net, ver - lan - get und seh - net, ver - lan - - -
54
lan - get und seh - net, und seh - net sich nach den
seh - net, ver - lan - get und seh - - - net sich nach den
get und seh - - - - - - net sich nach den
get und seh - net, seh - net sich nach den
Fl. u. Kl.
60
Vor - hö - fen des Herrn; mein
Vor - hö - fen des Herrn; mein
Vor - hö - fen des Herrn; mein
Vor - hö - fen des Herrn; mein
Hob.

66
Leib und See - le freu - en sich in dem le - ben - - -
Leib und See - le freu - en sich in dem le - ben - di - gen
Leib und See - le freu - en sich in dem le - ben - di - gen
Leib und See - le freu - en sich in dem le - ben - di - gen
Str.
fp
mf
72
- - di - gen Gott,
cresc.
freu - en sich
Gott, mein Leib und See - le freu - en sich
Gott, mein Leib und See - le freu - en sich
Gott, mein Leib und See - le freu - en sich
78
in dem le - ben - - - - - - - di - gen
in dem le - ben - di - gen, in dem le - ben - - - - - - di - gen
in dem le - ben - - - - di - gen, in dem le - ben - - di - gen
in dem le - ben - - - - di - gen, in dem le - ben - di - gen

60
28
84
Gott.
Wie
Viol.
Fl.
Kl.
Hr.
90
lieb - lich sind dei - ne Woh - nun - gen, Herr Ze - - - ba -
lieb - - - lich sind dei - ne Woh - nun - gen, Herr Ze - ba -
Kl.
Viol.
96
oth, Herr Ze - ba - oth, dei - ne
oth, Herr Ze - ba - oth,
Fl.
Hob.
Hr.

102
Woh - nun - gen, Herr Ze - ba -
Woh - nun - gen, Herr Ze - ba -
Woh - nun - gen, Herr Ze - ba -
Woh - nun - gen, Herr Ze - ba - oth, Herr Ze - ba -
Kl.
Viol.
108
oth! Wohl de -
oth! Wohl de -
oth! Wohl de -
oth! Wohl de -
p
p legato espress.
con Ped.
113
nen, wohl de - nen, die
nen, wohl de - nen, die
nen, wohl de - nen, die
nen, wohl de - nen, die
p

61
29
119
cresc.
in dei - nem Hau - se woh - nen, die
in dei - nem Hau - se woh - nen,
in dei - nem Hau - se woh - nen,
in dei - nem Hau - se woh - nen,
124
lo - ben - dich im - mer - dar,
die lo - ben dich im - mer - dar, im - mer - dar, im - mer,
die lo - ben dich im - mer - dar, lo - ben dich, lo - ben
die lo - ben dich im - mer - dar, die lo - ben, die lo - ben, die
130
die lo - ben dich, die lo - ben dich im - mer -
im - mer-dar, im - mer-dar, die lo - ben dich im - mer - dar,
dich im - mer - dar, die lo - ben dich im - mer - dar,
lo - ben, die lo - ben dich, die lo - ben dich im - mer -

136
dar, im - mer - dar, die
die lo - ben dich im - mer -
die lo - ben dich im - mer - dar, die lo - ben dich im - mer -
dar, im - mer - dar, die lo - ben dich im - mer - dar,
141
lo - ben, die lo - ben, die lo - ben, die
dar, die lo - ben, die lo - ben, die lo - ben,
dar, die lo - ben, die lo - ben, die lo - ben, die lo - ben,
die lo - ben, die lo - ben, die lo -
147
62
30
lo - ben dich im - mer -
lo - ben dich im - mer -
die lo - ben dich im - mer -
ben, die lo - ben dich im - mer -
p dimin.
Fl.
Hob.
pp Str. pizz.
p es-

153
p dolce
dar! Wie lieb - - lich, wie lieb - - lich,
p dolce
dar! Wie
p dolce
dar! Wie lieb - - lich, wie lieb - - lich,
p dolce
dar! Wie
Viol.
espress.
press.
p
159
p
wie
lieb - - lich, wie lieb - - lich, wie lieb - - lich, wie
p
wie
lieb - - lich, wie lieb - - lich, wie lieb - - lich, wie
Fl.
Hob.
p
cresc.
Holzbl.
p
165
cresc.
f
lieb - - lich sind dei - - ne
cresc.
f
lieb - - lich, wie lieb - - lich sind dei - - ne
cresc.
f
lieb - - lich sind dei - - ne
cresc.
f
lieb - - lich, wie lieb - - lich sind dei - - ne
legato
cresc.
f
Str.

Text and Translation

Wie lieblich sind deine Wohnungen, Herr Zebaoth! Meine Seele verlanget und sehnet sich nach den Vorhöfen des Herrn; mein Leib und Seele freuen sich in dem lebendigen Gott.	How lovely is Thy dwelling place, O Lord of Hosts! My soul longs and even faints for the courts of the Lord; my flesh and soul rejoice in the living God.
Wie lieblich. . .	How lovely. . .
Wohl denen, die in deinem Hause wohnen, die loben dich immerdar!	Blessed are they that live in Thy house, that praise Thee evermore!
Wie lieblich. . .	How lovely. . .

The nineteenth century produced a rich and varied repertory of music for chorus. From simple part songs to colossal Requiems, choral music played an important role in European and American society. Johannes Brahms (1833–1897) contributed numerous works to the choral repertory for both amateur and professional ensembles. His masterwork, one of the landmarks of the era, is *Ein deutsches Requiem (A German Requiem)* (1868).

A Requiem Mass is generally based on the Latin text of the Catholic Church funeral service. But German Requiems, which have been composed since the time of Schütz and Praetorius, do not use the liturgical text of the Catholic service. Rather, the words are drawn freely from passages in the Lutheran Bible and are in the vernacular, German, instead of Latin. For his Requiem, Brahms chose a variety of texts from both the Old and New Testaments. A prominent theme in these verses is the comfort offered to those who mourn.

The seven movements of Brahms's Requiem can be viewed in an overall arch-like structure. At the heart of the work is the gentle fourth movement, based on a passage from Psalm 84. The opening lines appear three times in the movement, and they are set in a similar fashion each time. Contrasting with these sections are several passages of contrapuntal activity and vigorous rhythms. But the recurring principal theme evokes an ethereal serenity and creates an overall rondo-like form.

16. Johannes Brahms
Symphony No. 3 in F major, Third Movement (1883)

8CD: 6/1–3
4CD: 3/23–25

–melancholy waltz

10
Fl.
Kl.
Fg.
Vl.
Br.
Vc.
Kb.
p
m.v.
espress.
6

Kl.
Fg.
Vl.
Br.
Vc.
Kb.

20
Kl.
Fg.
Vl.
Br.
Vc.
Kb
pp
dolce
pp
pp
dolce
pp

Kl.
Fg.
Vl.
Br.
Vc.
Kb

30
Kl.
Fg.
Vl.
Br.
Vc.
Kb.
dim.
pp
dolce

Kl.
Fg.
Vl.
Br.
Vc.
Kb.
2.
p
dim.

40
Fl.
1.
mp espress.
Hb.
1.
mp espress.
Kl.
p
Fg.
1.
p
Hrn.
(C)
1.
mp espress.
Vl.
legg.
legg.
Br.
legg.
Vc.
p legg.
Kb.
p

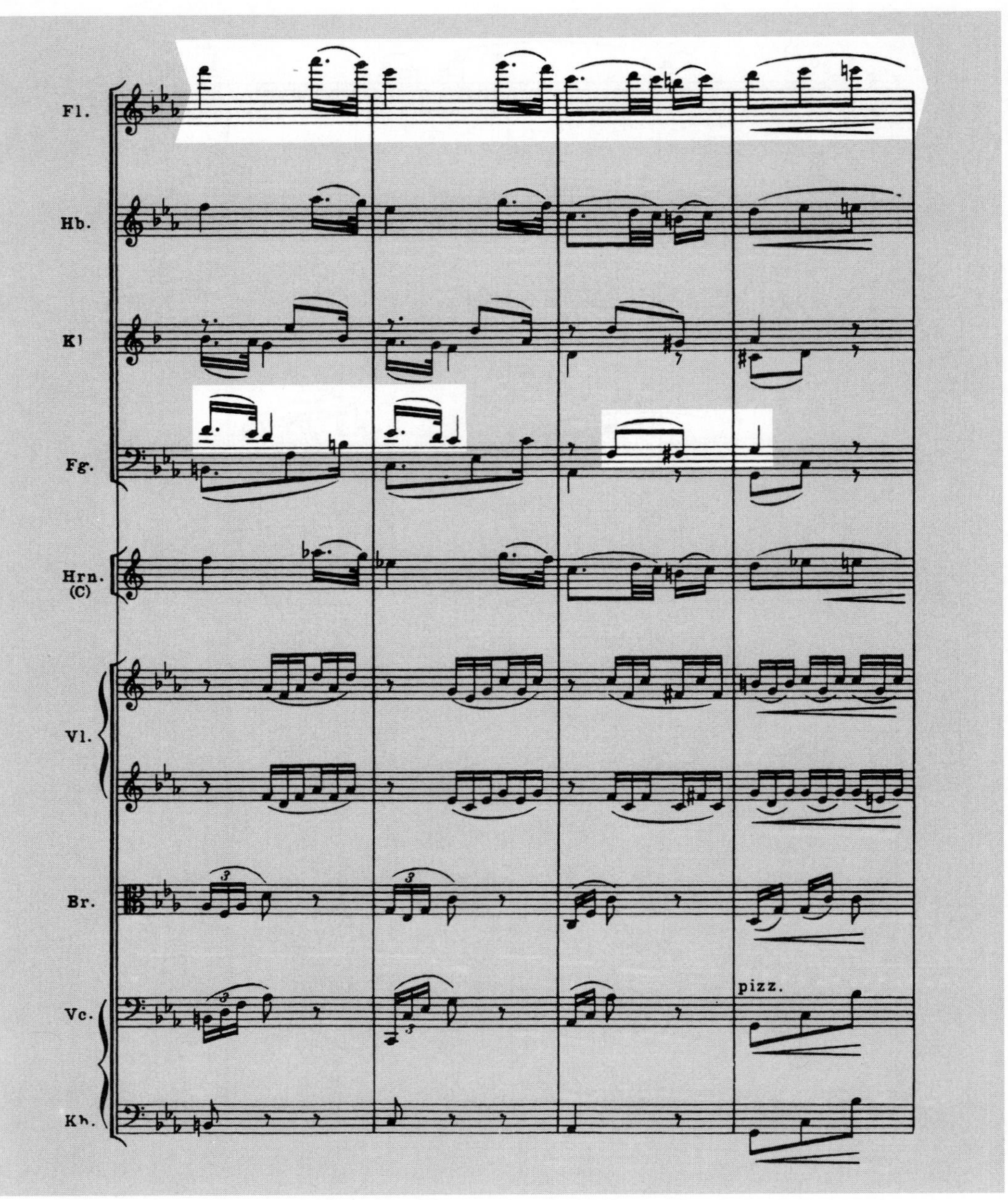
Fl.
Hb.
Kl
Fg.
Hrn.
(C)
Vl.
Br.
Vc.
pizz.
Kb.
3

50
Fl.
Hb.
Kl.
Fg.
Hrn. (C)
Vl.
Br.
Vc.
Kb.
p
dolce
2
24
1.
arco
p dolce

60
Fl.
Hb.
Kl.
Fg.
Hrn.
(C)
1.Vl.
Br.
Vc.
dolce
p dolce
p dolce

70
Fl.
Hb.
Kl.
Fg.
Vl.
Br.
Vc.
pp espress.
pp espress.
pp espress.
pp espress.

Vl.
cresc.
f
p dim.
Br.
Vc.
Kb.
arco
p
80
Fl.
Hb.
Kl.
Fg.
Hrn. (C)
1.
dolce
Vc.

90
Fl.
Hb.
Kl.
Fg.
Hrn.
(C)
Vl.
Br.
Vc.
p dim.
p dim.
p dim.
p dim.

Fl.
Hb.
Kl.
Fg.
Hrn.
(C)
Vl.
Br.
Vc.
1.
p
lunga
pp dim.
pp dim.
pp dim.
pp dim.

3
25
100
Fl.
p
1.
Hrn. (C)
p espressivo
3
Vl.
pp legg.
3
pp legg.
Br.
p
Vc.
p
pizz.
Kb.
p

Fl.
Hrn. (C)
Vl.
Br.
pizz.
Vc.
Kb.

110
Fl.
Hb.
Kl.
Fg.
Hrn. (C)
Vl.
Br.
Vc.
Kb.
1.
p espress.
dolce
p
5
arco

Hb.
Kl.
Fg.
Hrn. (C)
Vl.
Br.
Vc.
Kb.

120
Hb.
Kl.
Fg.
Vl.
pizz.
Br.
pizz.
Vc.
Kb.

Hb.
dolce
Kl.
1.
dolce
Fg.
dolce
Hrn. (C)
pp
Vl.
dolce
dolce
arco
Br.
dolce
Vc. Kb.
Bassi
dolce

130
Fl.
Kl.
Fg.
Hrn.
(C)
Vl.
Br.
Vc.
Kb
dim.
pp
dolce
p dim.
pp dolce
più p

Fl.
Kl.
Fg.
Hrn.
(C)
Vl.
Br.
Vc.
Kb

Fl.
Kl.
Fg.
Hrn. (C)
1. Vl.
Br.
Vc.
1.
p dim.
dim.
get.
mp espr.
Vc.
arco
p
mp espr.

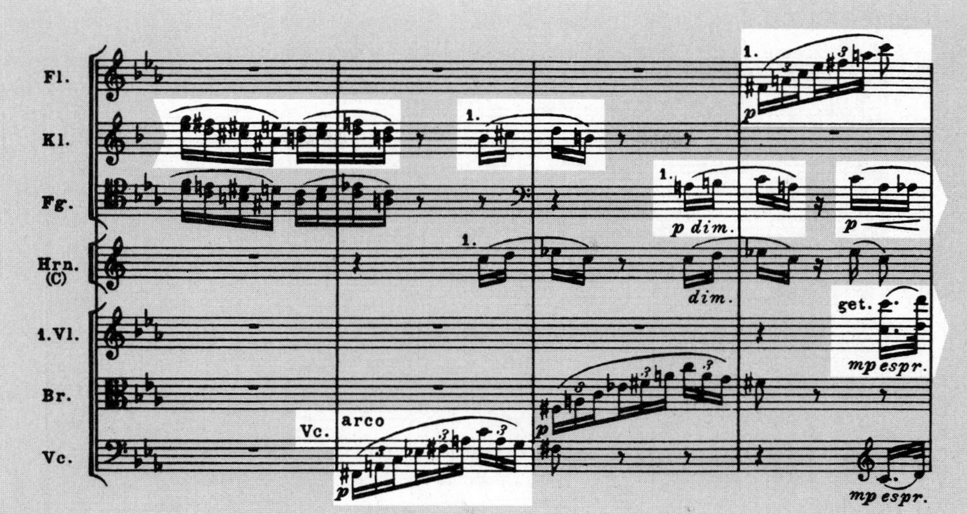

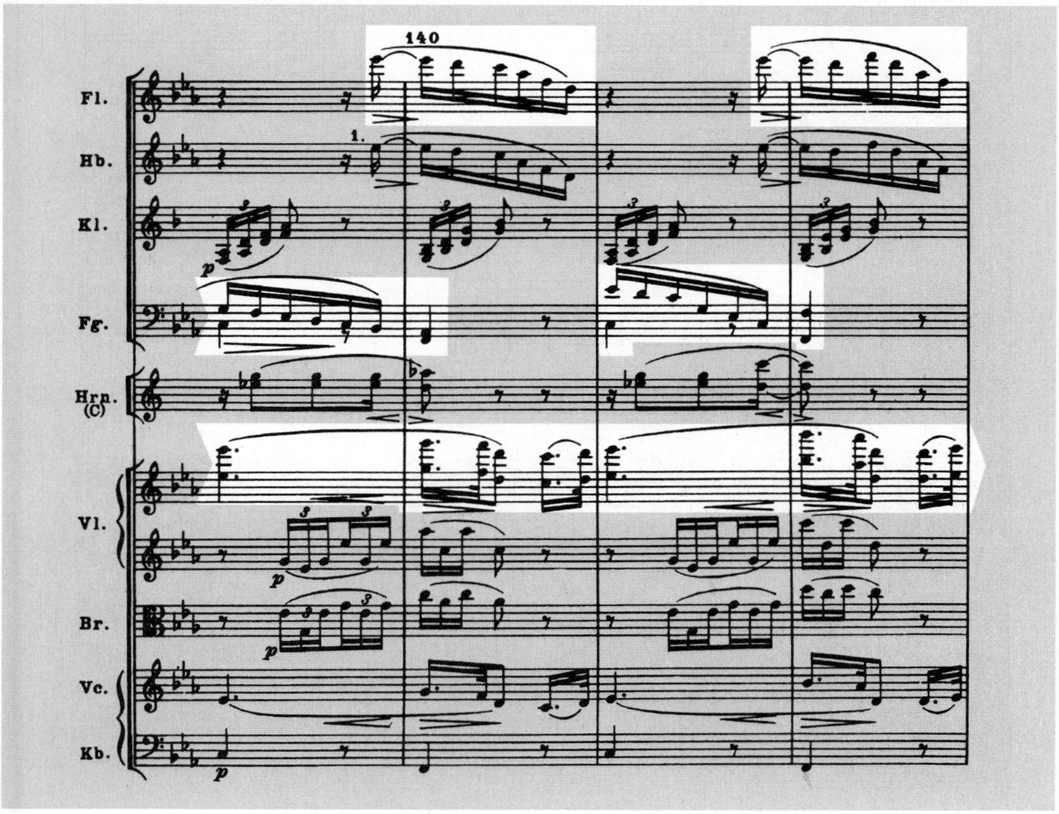
140
Fl.
Hb.
Kl.
Fg.
Hrn. (C)
Vl.
Br.
Vc.
Kb.
1.
p

Fl.
Hb.
Kl.
Fg.
Hrn. (C)
Vl.
Br.
Vc.
Kb.
150
zu 2
p
1.
dolce

160
Fl.
Hb.
Kl.
Fg.
Hrn.
(C)
zu 2
Vl.
get.
pizz.
Br.
Vc.
Kb.
arco
pp
f
p

Johannes Brahms, a leading figure in the second half of the nineteenth century, embraced the traditions of the Viennese Classical school. He mastered the Classical forms, including sonata and variation, and he composed significant works in all of the major Classical instrumental genres—symphony, concerto, piano sonata, and chamber music. Of these, the symphony was the last to be explored. Feeling the weight of Beethoven's masterworks, Brahms did not begin his first symphony until he was over forty-years old, and he completed only four symphonies during his lifetime.

In his symphonies, Brahms returns to the concept of absolute forms, without programmatic images. Each symphony contains four movements in standard Classical structures; cyclic elements are limited, and even the size of the orchestra is comparable to that of Beethoven. Within this framework, Brahms creates a distinctively Romantic sound by employing effective orchestrations, passionate melodies, complex harmonies, and blurred rhythmic effects.

The third movement of Symphony No. 3 retains the ternary structure of a scherzo, but Brahms replaces the traditionally lively tempo with a melancholy waltz. The cellos open the movement with a passionate, songlike melody accompanied by the murmuring of the upper strings. Each time the theme returns, it is presented in a different setting, most strikingly in the French horn solo at the reprise. The complexities of Brahms's textures, rhythms, and harmonies are particularly evident in the middle section.

17. Georges Bizet

Carmen, Act I, excerpt (1875)

8CD: 6/ 36 – 43

ten.
ten.
a
(The relief appears:
poco a poco cresc.
first a bugler and fifer, then a crowd of street-boys. — Following the latter, Lieutenant Zuniga and
ten.
ten.
Corporal Don José, then the dragoons. — During Street-boys' Chorus, the relief forms in front of the
mf
guard going off duty.)
3
f

poco a poco cresc. molto
f ben ritmato, quasi staccato.
A-vec la gar-de mon-tan-te, Nous ar-ri-vons, nous voi-là! Son-ne, trom-pette e-cla-tan-te! Ta ra ta ta ta ra ta ta. Nous mar-chons la tê-te hau-te Com-me de pe-tits sol-dats, Mar-quant sans fai-re de fau-te,
We are sol-diers marching proudly, Here we come to change the guard. Boys, blow your bu-gles loud-ly! See us march in per-fect man-ner, We are nev-er out of step. Fol-low the wav-ing ban-ner,
cresc.

(spoken.)
mf
Une, deux, mar - quant le pas. Les é - pau - les en ar - riè - re
One two, one two, hep, hep! Straight in line be - side our neigh-bors.
cresc.
f
pp
Et la poi - trine en de - hors, Les bras de cet - te ma - niè - re,
Shoul-ders back and heads up high. We raise our trust-y sa - bers,
Tom - bant tout le long du corps. A - vec la gar -
And sa - lute you go - ing by. We are sol - diers
cresc. molto.
de mon - tan - te, Nous ar - ri - vons, nous voi - là! Son - ne, trom -
march-ing proud-ly, Here we come to change the guard. Boys, blow your
cresc. molto.
ff
f
pette é - cla - tan - te, Ta ra ta ta ta ra ta ta, ta ra ta ta ra ta
bu - gles loud - ly,
p

ta, ta ra ta ta ra ta ta ta, ta ra ta ta ra ta ta ra ta ta ra ta ta ta ra
ta ta ra ta ta ta; Ta ra ta ta ra ta ta, ta ra ta ta ra ta ta ta, ta ra
ta ta ra ta ta ra ta ta ra ta ta ra ta ta ra ta ta ta.
mf unis.
Nous mar-chons la
See us march in
tê-te haute Comme de pe-tits sol-dats, Mar-quant sans fai-
per-fect man-ner, We are nev-er out of step, Fol-low-ing the
(spoken.)
re de faute, Une, deux, mar-quant le pas. Les é-pau-les
wav-ing ban-ner, One two, one two, hep, hep. Straight in line be-

cresc. molto.
en ar-rière Et la poi-tri-ne en de-hors, Les bras de cet-
side our neigh-bors, Shoul-ders back, heads up high. We pre-sent our
cresc. molto.
ff
te ma-niè-re, Tom-bant tout le long du corps. Nous ar-ri-vons!
trust-y sa-bers, And sa-lute you go-ing by. Com-pa-ny halt!
Nous voi-là!
Stand at ease!
Ta ra ta ta ra ta ta ra ta ta ta ta ta, ta ra ta ta.
fff
37
Recit.
Morales.
U-ne jeu-ne fil-le char-man-te Vient de nous de-man-
I have a mes-sage for you from a young and charm-ing
der si tu n'é-tais pas là! Ju-pe bleue et nat-te tom-
girl who asked to speak to you. Light blue skirt and ver-y long

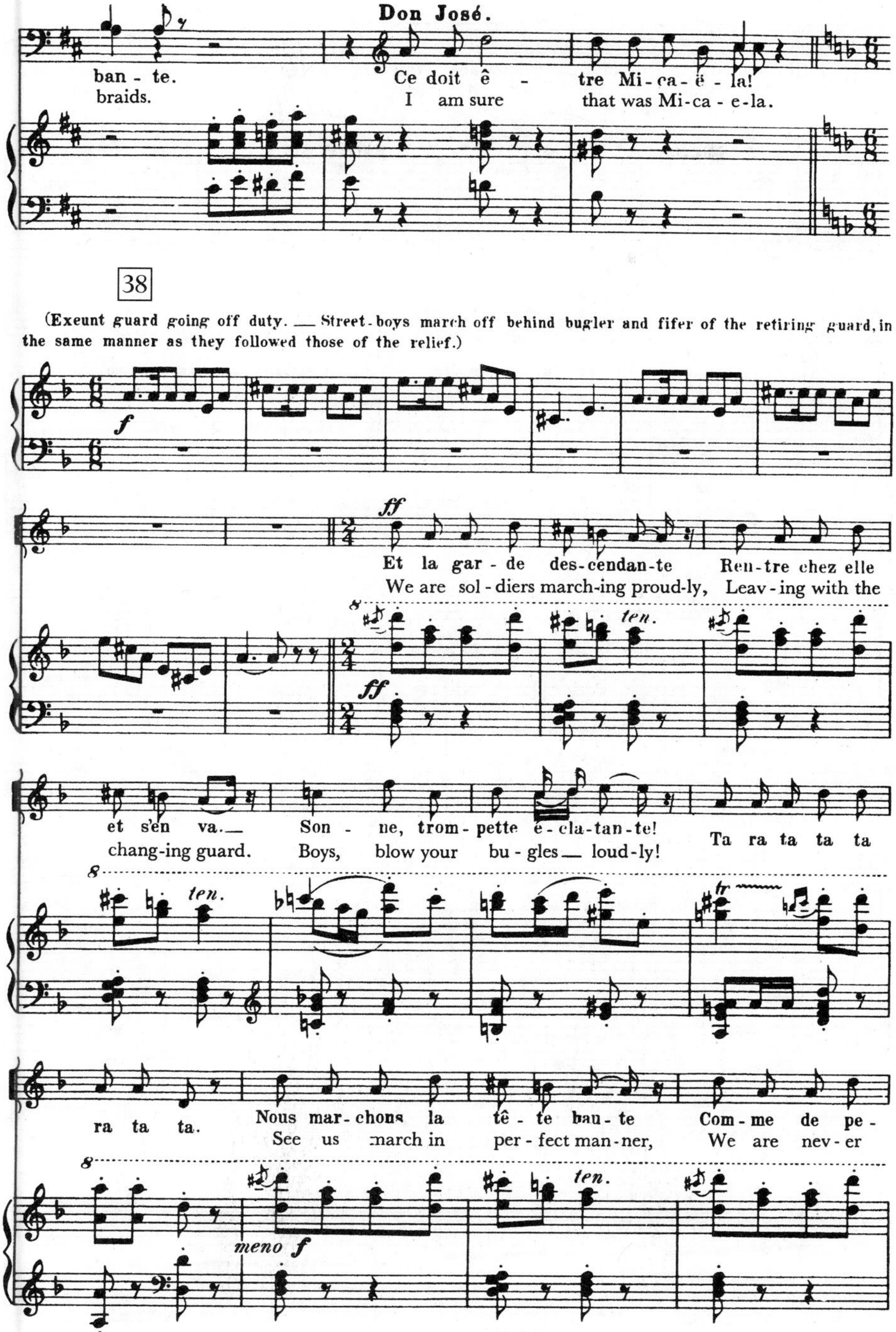

38

(Exeunt guard going off duty. — Street-boys march off behind bugler and fifer of the retiring guard, in the same manner as they followed those of the relief.)

f

ff

Et la gar - de des-cendan-te Ren-tre chez elle
We are sol - diers march-ing proud-ly, Leav - ing with the

ten.

ff

et s'en va. — Son - ne, trom - pette é - cla - tan - te!
chang-ing guard. Boys, blow your bu - gles — loud-ly!
Ta ra ta ta ta

ten.

ra ta ta. Nous mar - chons la tê - te hau - te Com - me de pe -
See us march in per - fect man - ner, We are nev - er

ten.

meno f

(spoken.)
tits sol - dats, Mar - quant sans fai - re de fau - te, Une, deux, mar -
out of step. Fol - low the wav - ing ban - ner, One two, one
ten.
quant le pas.
two, hep, hep!
Ta ra ta ta ra ta ta, ta ra ta ta ra ta ta
mf
ta, ta ra ta ta ra ta ta ra ta ta ra ta ta ra ta ta ra ta ta
unis.
ta, ta ra ta ta ra ta ta ta ra ta ta ra ta ta ta, ta ra
dim.
ta ta ra ta ta ra ta ta ra ta ta ra ta ta ra ta ta ta.
p

tr
sempre dim.
pp
pp possibile.

Recitative

39
Moderato.
Recit.
Zuniga.
Piano.
C'est bien là, n'est - ce
Don Jo - sé, is it
pas, dans ce grand bâ - ti - ment Que tra - vail - lent les ci - ga -
true that in that fac-to-ry there man - y pret - ty wom - en are
Don José.
riè - res? C'est - là, mon of - fi - cier, et bien cer - tai - ne -
work - ing? In - deed, sir, that is so, and ev - 'ry - bod - y
ment On ne vit nul - le part, fil - les aus - si lé -
knows that these cig - a - rette girls are of ver - y eas - y
Zuniga.
gè - res. Mais au moins sont - el - les jo -
vir - tue. Are they al - so eas - y to
alla misura e legg.

Don José.
li - es?
look at?
Mon of - fi - cier, je n'en sais
Sir, I don't know much a - bout
rien, Et m'oc - cupe as - sez peu de ces ga - lan - te - ri -
that, for I am not con - cerned with wom - en of that na -
es.
ture.
poco più allegro.
Zuniga.
Ce qui t'oc - cupe, a -
What con - cerns you, my
mi, je le sais bien, U - ne jeu - ne fil - le char-
friend, I think I know. You're in love with one charm-ing
man - te Qu'on ap - pel - le Mi - ca - ë - la,
girl. Mi - ca - e - la is her name.
p

Ju - pe bleue et nat - te tom - ban - te.
"Light blue skirt and ver - y long braids!"
Tu ne ré - ponds rien — à ce - la?
Don José.
Je ré - ponds que c'est
Well, am I right — a - bout that? I ad - mit you are
vrai, je ré - ponds que je l'ai - - me!
right. I con - fess, she's the girl I love.
Recit.
Quant aux ou - vri - è - res d'i - ci, Quant — à leur beau -
And as for the fac - to - ry girls, When — you hear the
té, les voi - ci! Et vous pou - vez ju - ger vous - mê - me.
bell, they'll be here. Then you can judge their looks quite well.
attacca subito.

Scene No. 4

40
Allegro.
Carmen.
Sopranos I & II.
(Cigarette-girls).
Chorus.
(The factory-bell is ringing.)
Tenors.
(Young men).
Basses.
(Townspeople)
(Don José sits down and pays no attention to the shifting scenes. He repairs the chain of his saber.)
Allegro. (♩. = 104.)
Piano.
pp
(the bell stops.)
cresc. molto.
ff
Allegretto moderato. (♩ = 104.)
pp

17. Bizet, *Carmen:* Chorus, "La cloche a sonné"

41
Andantino. (♩. = 60.)
BASSES. (Enter Cigarette-girls, smoking cigarettes, and slowly descending to the stage.)
Voy - ez les! re - gards im - pu - dents, Mi - ne co - quet - te! Fu - mant tou - tes, du bout des dents La ci - ga - ret - te.
Here they are, the bright - eyed co - quettes, Keen and au - da - cious, I - dly smok - ing their cig - a - rettes, And so flir - ta - tious!
pp
p
dim.
sf

(Beat 2/3).
SOPRANOS I.
p
Dans l'air nous sui - vons des yeux La fu -
Smoke rings make their la - zy way, Soft-ly
SOPRANOS II.
p
Dans l'air nous sui - vons des yeux
Smoke rings make their la - zy way,
pp
poco cresc.
mé - e, La fu - mé - e Qui vers les cieux Mon - te,
curl - ing, soft - ly curl - ing. Sky - ward they stray In a
poco cresc.
La fu - mé - e, La fu - mé - e Qui vers les cieux Mon - te,
Soft - ly curl - ing, soft - ly curl - ing. Skyward they stray In a
poco cresc.
dim.
p
mon - te par - fu - mé - e; Ce - la mon - te
fra - grant cloud un - furl - ing. Their per-fume per -
dim.
p
mon - te par - fu - mé - e; Ce - la mon -
fra - grant cloud un - furl - ing. Their per-fume
dim.
pp

gen - ti - ment A la tê - te, à la tê - te, Tout dou - ce -
vades the air, Gent - ly steal - ing, gent - ly steal - ing, Sooth - ing our
te gen - ti - ment A la tê - te, à la tê - te,
per - vades the air, Gent - ly steal - ing, gent - ly steal - ing,
poco cresc.
dim.
ment, Ce - la vous met l'â - me en fê - te!
mind To a mel - low pleas - ant feel - ing.
Tout dou - ce - ment, Ce - la vous met l'â - me en fê - te!
Sooth - ing our mind To a mel - low pleas - ant feel - ing.
pp e molto stacc.
Le doux par - ler, le doux par - ler des a - mants,
Those ten - der words you lov - ers say ev - 'ry day
mf
C'est fu - mé - e!
Fade a - way!
pp
Leurs trans - ports, leurs transports et leurs serments,
Your prom - is - es, too, like the smoke in the blue
C'est fu - mé - e!
Fade a - way!

17. Bizet, *Carmen:* Chorus, "La cloche a sonné"

cresc.
La fu - mé - e! Dans l'air
in the blue. See there,
cresc.
me - e! La fu - mé - e! Ah!
sky, of the sky. Ah!
f
mosso.
Ped.
Ped. dim.
nous sui - vons la fu - mé - e Qui monte en tour -
See them curl - ing and ris - ing and van - ish at
nous sui - vons la fu - mé - e Qui monte en tour -
See them curl - ing and ris - ing and van - ish at
dim.
p
nant, en tour - nant vers les cieux!
last in the blue of the sky.
nant, en tour - nant vers les cieux!
last in the blue of the sky.
p
La fu - mé - e!
See them rise
La fu - mé - e!
See them rise
dim.
pp
dim.

smorzando.
pp
La fu - mé
To the skies.
pp
smorzando.
La fu - mé
To the skies.
ppp
smorzando.
e!
e!
pppp
42
Allegretto molto. (♩. = 108.)
BASSES.
mf
Mais nous ne voyons pas
But where's Carmen to-day?
f
p

Allegro moderato. (♩. = 92.)
(Entrance of Carmen.)
la Carmen - ci - ta!
Why is she mis-sing?
ff
TENORS.
f
La voi-là!
There she is!
BASSES.
f
La voi-là!
Look at her!
p
cresc.
SOPRANOS.
ff
La voi-là!
Where she is
voi - là la Carmen-
there is al-ways ex-
TENORS.
ff
La voi-là!
Where she is
voi - là la Carmen-
there is al-ways ex-
BASSES.
ff
f
ff

ci - ta!
cite - ment!
(to Carmen.)
mf
ci - ta!
cite - ment!
Car - men! sur tes pas nous nous pres - sons
At last! We've been anx - ious - ly wait - ing for
(♩. = 100.)
p
tous!
you!
Car - men! sois gen - til - le au moins réponds-
We men want, at least, an an-swer from
nous,
you.
Et dis-nous quel jour tu nous ai - me - ras!
O Car-men, why must you tease us this way?
sf
dim.
p
Car - men, dis - nous quel jour tu nous ai - me - ras!
When will you give your love? Won't you name the day?
p
pp

Carmen.
quasi Recit.
mf gaily.
(after a swift glance at Don José.)
Quand je vous ai - me - rai? ma foi, je ne sais
When I'll give you my love? Who knows, it's hard to
a tempo Andantino.
colla voce.
p
colla voce.
a tempo.
f
p
pas, Peut - ê - tre ja - mais! peut - ê - tre de -
tell! Per - haps not at all. Per - haps ver - y
a tempo.
p
pp
(resolutely.)
main. Mais pas au - jour -
soon! But one thing I'll
pp
d'hui c'est cer - tain.
say: Not to - day.
pp
mf
attacca.

Scene No. 5
43
Allegretto, quasi Andantino.
Carmen.
Sopranos I & II. (Cigarette-girls).
Tenors. (Young men).
Basses. (Workingmen).
Chorus.
Allegretto, quasi Andantino. (♩= 72.)
Piano.
pp
p
L'amour
Love is
est un oi-seau re - bel-le Que nul ne peut ap-pri-voi - ser, Et c'est
free as the way - ward breeze, _ It can be shy, _ it _ can be bold. Love can
bien en vain qu'on l'ap - pel-le, S'il lui con - vient de - re - fu - ser. Rien n'y
fas-ci-nate, love can tease, _ Its whims and moods are _ thou-sand - fold. All at
portamento.
fait, menace ou pri - è-re, L'un par - le bien, _ l'au-tre se tait; Et c'est
once it ar-rives and lin-gers For just how long _ can't be fore - told. Then it
portamento.

l'au-tre que je pré - fè - re Il n'a rien dit; mais il me
deft-ly slips through your fin-gers, For love's a thing no force can
espress.
plait. L'a - mour! l'a -
hold. That's love for
Sopr.
pp legg.
L'a-mour est un oi-seau re - bel-le Que nul ne peut ap-pri-voi -
Love is free as the way-ward breeze, It can be shy, it can be
Ten.
pp legg.
L'a-mour est un oi-seau re - bel-le Que nul ne peut ap-pri-voi -
Love is free as the way-ward breeze, It can be shy, it can be
mour! l'a - mour!
you, That's love
ser, Et c'est bien en vain qu'on l'ap - pel - le S'il lui con -
bold. Love can fas - ci - nate, love can tease, Its whims and
ser, Et c'est bien en vain qu'on l'ap - pel - le S'il lui con -
bold. Love can fas - ci - nate, love can tease, Its whims and

p
l'a - mour! L'amour est en - fant de Bo - hême, Il n'a ja -
for you! A heart in love is quick-ly burned, It knows no
vient de re - fu - ser!
moods are thou - sand - fold.
vient de re - fu - ser!
moods are thou - sand - fold.
mais, jamais connu de loi, Si tu ne m'ai - mes pas, je t'ai - me; Si
law ex - cept its own de - sire. If I should love you and you spurn me, I'm
je t'aime, prends garde à toi! Si tu ne m'ai - mes pas, si
warning you, you play with fire! If I'm in love with you, don't
f
Prends garde à toi!
You play with fire!
Prends garde à toi!
You play with fire!
f
pp

cresc.
tu ne m'aimes pas, je t'ai - me! Mais si je t'ai-me, si je
ev-er, ev-er try to spurn me. My friend, re-mem-ber, if I
Prends garde à toi!
You play with fire.
Prends garde à toi!
You play with fire.
cresc.
t'aime, prends gar - de à toi!
love you, you play with fire.
L'amour est en - fant de Bo - hême, Il n'a ja -
A heart in love is quick-ly burned, It knows no
L'a - - - mour
A heart
mais, jamais con-nu de loi, Si tu ne m'ai - mes pas, je t'ai - me; Si
law ex - cept its own de - sire. If I should love you and you spurn me, I'm
est en - fant de Bo - - -
in love is quick - -

Carmen.
Si tu ne m'ai-mes pas, si
If I'm in love with you, don't
je t'ai-me, prends garde à
warning you, you play with
toi! Prends garde à
fire, you play with
toi!
fire!
hê - - - - me! Prends garde à
ly burned, you play with
toi!
fire!
tu ne m'aimes pas, je t'ai - me!
ev-er, ev-er try to spurn me.
cresc.
Mais si je t'ai-me, si je
My friend, re-mem-ber, if I
Prends garde à
You play with
toi!
fire!
Prends garde à
You play with
toi!
fire!
cresc.

t'ai - me, prends garde à toi!
love you, you play with fire.
à toi!
with fire.
à toi!
with fire.
cresc.
L'oiseau que tu croy - ais sur - prendre Battit de l'aile et s'en - vo -
Wait for love and you wait for - ev - er, Don't wait at all, it comes to
la; L'amour est loin, tu peux l'at - ten - dre; Tu ne l'at - tends plus, il est
you. Try to grasp it, It's far too clev - er, It flies a - way in - to the

portamento.
là! Tout au - tour de toi vi - te, vi - te, Il vient, s'en va, puis il re -
blue. Love has so man-y forms and shapes, Each day it wears a new dis -
portamento.
vient; Tu crois le te - nir, il t'é - vi - te; Tu crois l'é - vi - ter, il te
guise. Think you've caught it and it es - capes To catch you lat - er by sur -
tient! L'a - mour! l'a -
prise. That's love for
Sopr. pp legg.
Tout au - tour de toi vi - te, vite Il vient, s'en va, puis il re -
Love has so man-y forms and shapes, Each day it wears a new dis-
Ten. pp legg.
mour! l'a - mour! l'a -
you, That's love for
vient; Tu crois le te - nir, il t'é - vi - te; Tu crois l'é - vi - ter, il te
guise. Think you've caught it and it es - capes To catch you lat - er by sur -

p
mour! L'amour est en - fant de Bo - hême, Il n'a ja - mais, jamais connu de
you! A heart in love is quick-ly burned, It knows no law ex - cept its own de -
tient!
prise.
loi, Si tu ne m'ai - mes pas, je t'ai - me: Si je t'ai - me prends garde à
sire, If I should love you and you spurn — me, I'm warning you, you play with
toi! Si tu ne m'ai - mes pas, Si tu ne m'aimes pas, je
fire! If I'm in love with you, don't ev - er, ev - er try to
f
Prends garde à toi!
You play with fire!
Prends garde à toi!
You play with fire!
pp

cresc.
t'ai - me; Mais si je t'ai-me, si je t'ai-me prends gar - de à
spurn me, My friend, re-mem-ber, if I love you, you play — with
Prends garde à toi!
You play with fire!
Prends garde à toi!
You play with fire!
f
pp
cresc.
mf
toi!
fire!
L'amour est en - fant de Bo - hême, Il n'a ja - mais, jamais con-nu de
A heart in love is quick-ly burned, It knows no law ex - cept its own de -
L'a - - - mour est en -
A heart in
p

loi, Si tu ne m'ai - mes pas, je t'ai - me; Si je t'ai - me prends garde à
sire. If I should love you and you spurn _ me,. I'm warning you, you play with
fant _____ de Bo - - - hê - - - - -
love _____ is quick - - - ly
Carmen.
p
Si tu ne m'ai - mes pas. Si
If I'm in love with you, don't
f
toi! Prends garde à toi!
fire! You play with fire!
f
me! Prends garde à toi!
burned. You play with fire!
f
f
p

p cresc.
tu ne m'aimes pas, je t'ai - me; Mais si je
ev - er, ev - er try to spurn me. My friend, re -
Prends garde à toi!
You play with fire,
Prends garde à toi!
You play with fire,
t'ai - me, si je t'ai - me, prends garde à toi!
mem-ber, if I love you, you play with fire!
cresc.
à toi!
with fire!
cresc.
cresc.
ff

Opéra comique remained France's most unique operatic sound throughout the nineteenth century. Characterized by spoken dialogue and lighter, more popular arias, traditions of *opéra comique* extend back to the eighteenth century. Despite the genre title, operas in this tradition are not necessarily comedies; romanticism, revolution, and realism all impacted the genre. Georges Bizet (1838–1875) created *Carmen,* the greatest French opera of the nineteenth century, in 1875. Based on a powerful story by Prosper Mérimée, the opera portrays characters drawn from everyday life. Events and passions propel the plot, which culminates in the death of Carmen at the hands of Don José. Exoticism also plays a critical role in the story: the opera is filled with images of Spain and of gypsies, which had captivated the French public's imagination at that time.

At the beginning of this excerpt from Act I, the military presence is established by the changing of the guard. Trumpet fanfares and a light march tune accompany the movement of the soldiers, and street children follow, imitating the sounds of the march and of the bugles. In a few passages of dialogue (presented in recitative in this version of the opera), we learn of Don José's background and character.

At noon a bell rings, signaling a break for the girls working in the cigarette factory. They race out and are greeted by young men who gather daily to flirt and seek love. The men sing a gentle melody, and both the men and women sing of the enchanted qualities of cigarette smoke. The mood is suddenly broken, as the men ardently seek Carmen. She appears and sings her seductive *Habanera* aria. Literally a dance from Havana, the *habanera* is characterized by a moderate tempo and the alternation of triplets and duplets. Bizet enhances the folk quality of the aria by creating a simple guitar-like accompaniment and limiting the overall range, which features an alluring chromatic descent. The melodic material is exchanged between Carmen and a choir, as she quietly selects her next lover—Don José.

all – ABA form

18. Peter Ilyich Tchaikovsky

The Nutcracker, Three Dances (1892)

– duple meter

8CD: 6/[44]–[52]
4CD: 3/⟨43⟩–⟨45⟩

March

[44] ⟨43⟩

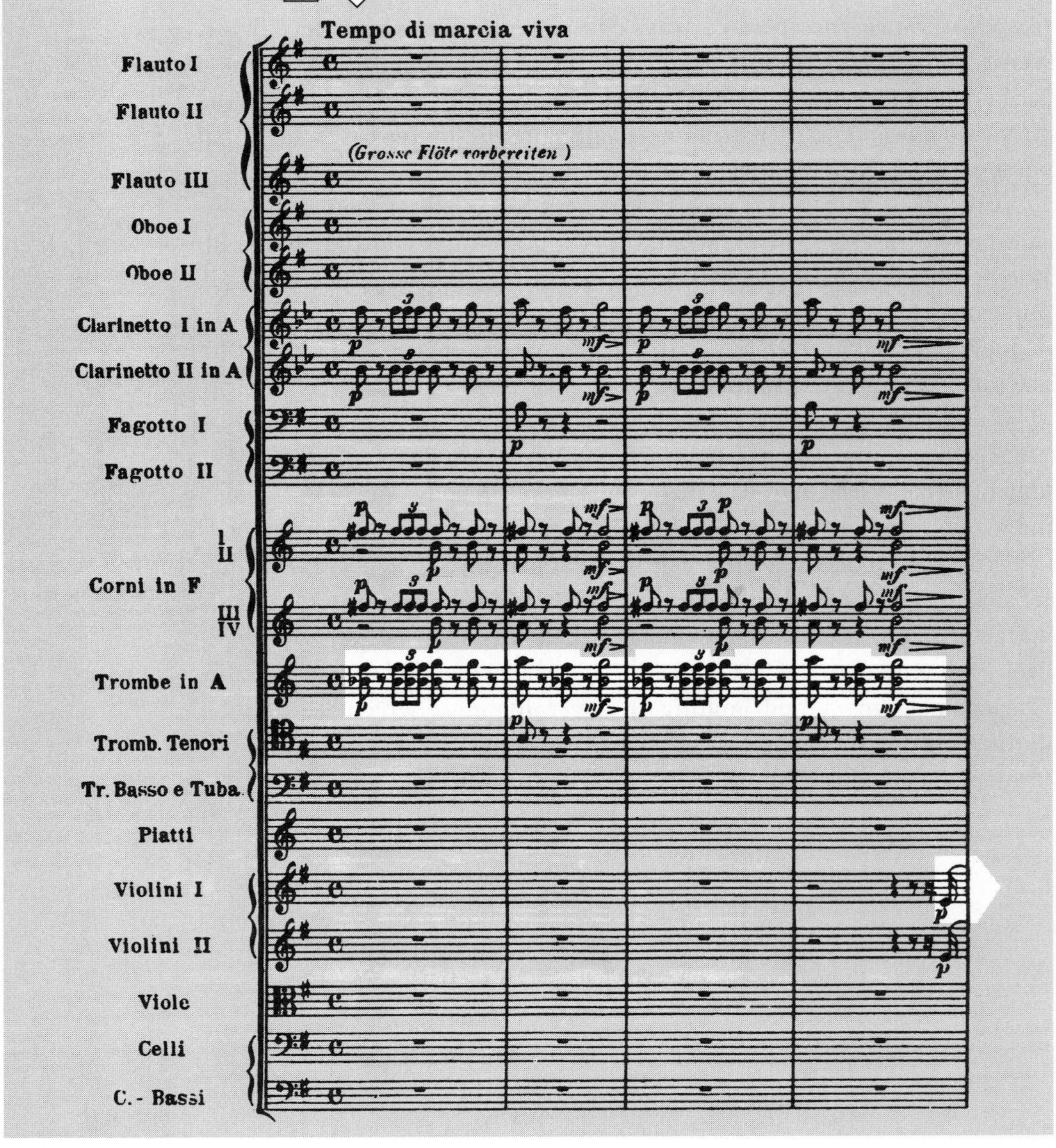

Tempo di marcia viva
Flauto I
Flauto II
(Grosse Flöte vorbereiten)
Flauto III
Oboe I
Oboe II
Clarinetto I in A
Clarinetto II in A
Fagotto I
Fagotto II
I II
Corni in F
III IV
Trombe in A
Tromb. Tenori
Tr. Basso e Tuba
Piatti
Violini I
Violini II
Viole
Celli
C.-Bassi

Fl.
Gr. Fl.
Ob.
Cl.
Fg.
pp
Cor. (F)
Trbe. (A)
Tbni.
Tuba
Mit Paukenschlägel.
Piat.
Vl.
Vle.
pizz.
Celli
C.-B.

10
Fl.
Ob.
Cl.
Fg.
Cor. (F)
Trbe. (A)
Tbni.
Tuba
Piat.
Vl.
Vle.
Celli
C.-B.
pizz.
pizz.

Fl.
Ob.
Cl.
cre - - - scen - - - do
f
Fg.
Cor. (F)
Trbe. (A)
Tbni. Tuba
Mit Paukenschlägel.
Piat.
Vl.
Vle.
Celli
C.-B.

20
Fl.
Ob.
Cl.
Fg.
Cor. (F)
Trbe. (A)
Tbni. Tuba
Piat.
Vl.
Vle.
Celli
C.-B.
pizz.
arco
mf
f

Fl.

Ob.

Cl.

Fg.

Cor. (F)

Trbe. (A)

Tbni. Tuba

Piat.

Vl.

Vle.

Celli

C.-B.

30
Fl.
Ob.
Cl.
mf
Fg.
p
pp
Cor. (F)
Trbe. (A)
Tbni, Tuba
Piat.
Vl.
Vle.
pizz.
Celli
C.-B.

Fl.
Ob.
Cl.
Fg.
Cor. (F)
Trbe. (A)
Tbni. Tuba
Mit Paukenschlägel.
Piat.
Vl.
Vle.
Celli
C.-B.

40
Fl.
Ob.
Cl.
pp
cre - - scen - - do
f
ff
Fg.
Cor. (F)
Trbe. (A)
Tbni. Tuba
Mit Paukenschlägel.
Piat.
Vl.
Vle.
pizz.
Celli
C.-B.
p

45
44
Fl.
Ob.
Cl.
Fg.
Cor. (F)
Trbe. (A)
Tbni. Tuba
Piat.
Vl.
Vle.
Celli
C.-B.
mf
marcato
arco

Fl.
Ob.
Cl.
Fg.
Cor. (F)
Trbe. (A)
Tbni. Tuba
Piat.
Vl.
Vle.
Celli
C.-B.
f
mf

46
45
Fl.
Ob.
Cl.
Fg.
marcato
marcato
Cor. (F)
Trbe. (A)
Tbni. Tuba
Piat.
Vl.
Vle.
Celli
C.-B.

50
Fl.
Ob.
Cl.
Fg.
Cor. (F)
Trbe. (A)
Tbni. Tuba
Piat.
Vl.
Vle.
Celli
C.-B.

Fl.
Ob.
mf
cresc.
Cl.
Fg.
Cor. (F)
Trbe. (A)
Tbni. Tuba
Piat.
Vl.
Vle.
pizz.
Celli
C.-B.

Fl.
Ob.
Cl.
Fg.
Cor. (F)
Trbe. (A)
Tbni. Tuba
Mit Paukenschlägel.
Piat.
Vl.
Vle.
arco
Celli
C.-B.

60
Fl.
Ob.
Cl.
Fg.
Cor. (F)
Trbe. (A)
Tbni. Tuba
Piat.
Vl.
Vle.
Celli
C.-B.
pizz.
pizz.

Fl.
Ob.
Cl.
Fg.
Cor. (F)
Trbe. (A)
Tbni. Tuba
Piat.
Vl.
Vle.
Celli
C.-B.
mf cresc.
cresc.
ff
Mit Paukenschlägel.

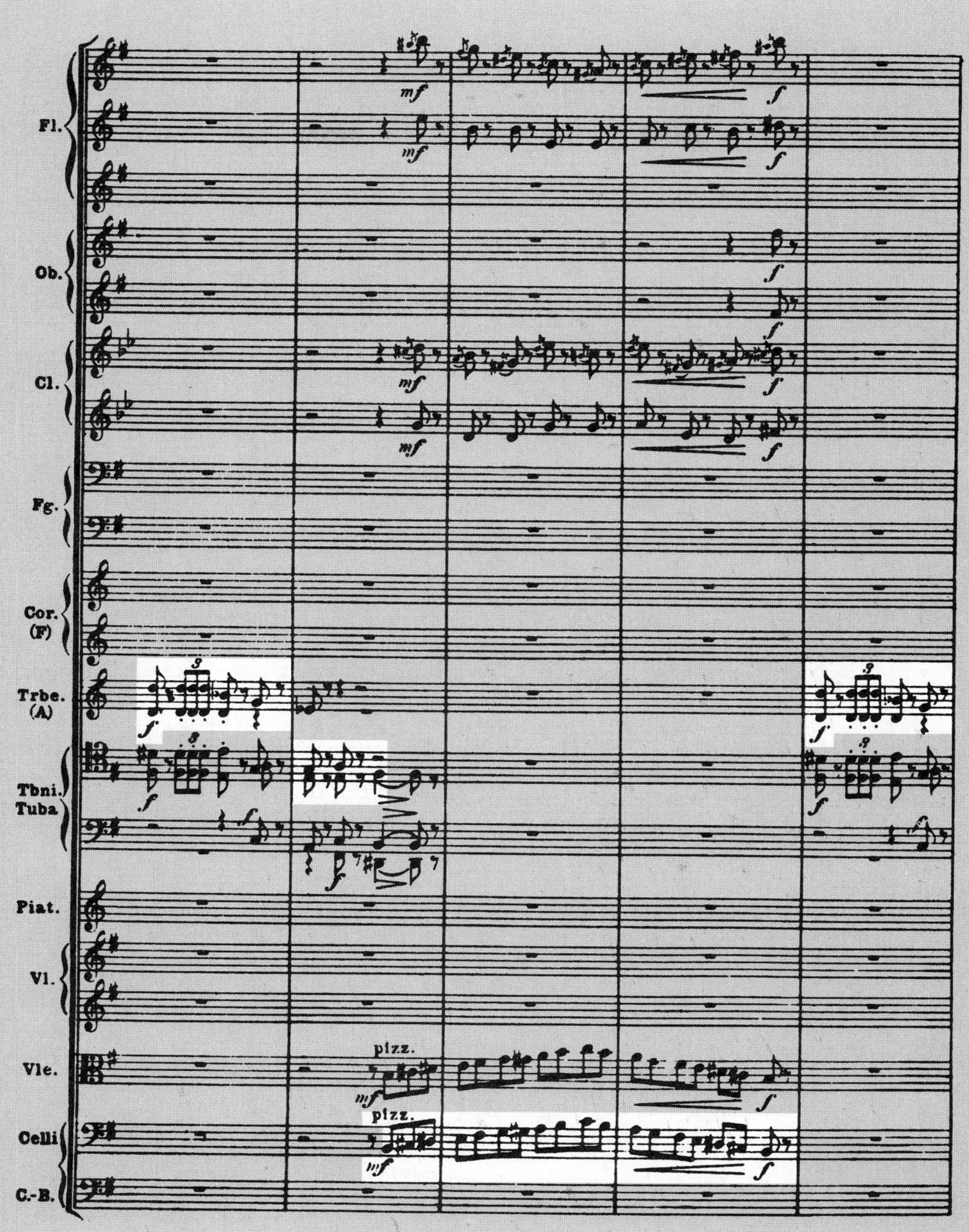
Fl.
Ob.
Cl.
Fg.
Cor. (F)
Trbe. (A)
Tbni. Tuba
Piat.
Vl.
Vle.
Celli
C.-B.
mf
f
pizz.

70
Fl.
Ob.
Cl.
Fg.
Cor. (F)
Trbe. (A)
Tbni. Tuba
Piat.
Vl.
Vle.
Celli
C.-B.
arco
arco
arco

Fl.
Ob.
Cl.
Fg.
Cor. (F)
Trbe. (A)
Tbni. Tuba
Piat.
Vl.
Vle.
Celli
C.-B.

Fl.
Ob.
Cl.
Fg.
Cor. (F)
Trbe. (A)
Tbni. Tuba
Piat.
Vl.
Vle.
Celli
C.-B.
mf
cresc.
pizz.

80
Fl.
Ob.
Cl.
Fg.
Cor. (F)
Trbe. (A)
Tbni. Tuba
Mit Paukenschlägel.
Piat.
Vl.
Vle.
Celli
C.-B.
arco
arco

Fl.
Ob.
Cl.
Fg.
Cor. (F)
Trbe. (A)
Tbni. Tuba
Piat.
Vl.
Vle.
Celli
C.-B.
pizz.
pizz.

Fl.
Ob.
Cl.
Fg.
Cor. (F)
Trbe. (A)
Tbni. Tuba
Piat.
Vl.
Vle.
Celli
C.-B.
mf
cresc.
f
ff
Mit Paukenschlägel.
arco

Dance of the Sugar Plum Fairy

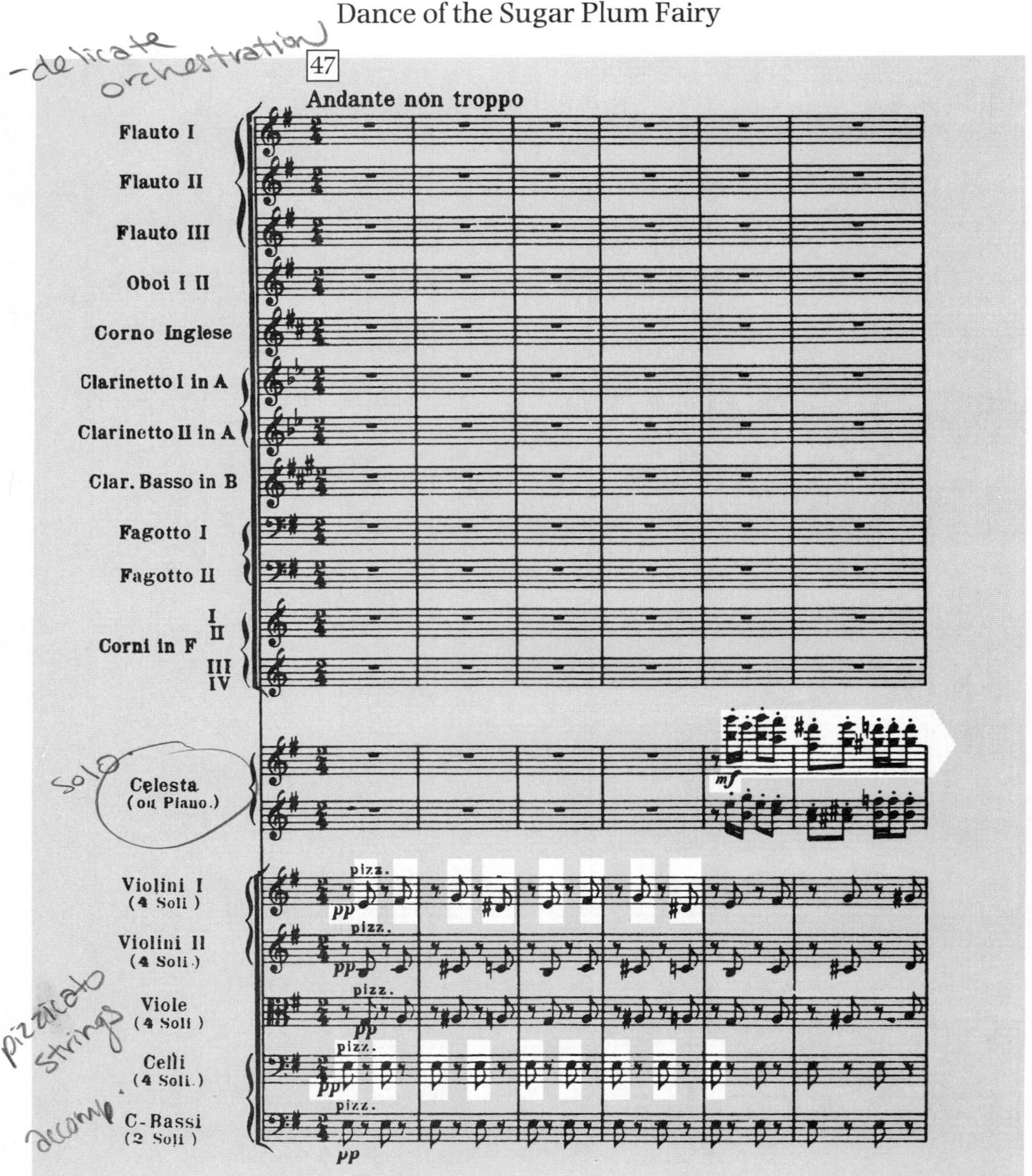

Cl.b.
Cel.
Vl.
Vle.
Celli
C.-B.
10
mf
fp
f
Cl.
I.
p
pp

20
Fl.
Ob.
C.Ingl.
Cl.
Cl.b.
Fg.
Cor.
(F)
Cel.
div.
Vl.
Vle.
Celli
C.-B.
arco
arco
arco
arco

48
Fl.
Ob.
C.Ingl.
Cl.
Cl. b.
Fg.
Cor. (F)
Cel.
Vl.
Vle.
Celli
C.-B.
pp
mf
sf
p
arco

Fl.
Ob.
C.Ingl.
Cl.
Cl.b.
Fg.
Cor. (F)
Cel.
Vl.
Vle.
Celli
C.-B.

30
Fl.
Ob.
C.Ingl.
Cl.
Cl.b.
Fg.
Cor. (F)
Cel.
Vl.
Vle.
Celli
C.-B.

Cel.
Cel.
49
Fl.
Fg.
Cel.
Vl.
Vle.
Celli
C.-B.
pp a punto d'arco
pp a punto d'arco
pp a punto d'arco
pp a punto d'arco

40
Cl.
Cel.
Vl.
Vle.
Celli
C.-B.
cresc.
Cl.
Cel.
Vl.
Vle.
Celli
C.-B.

50.
Fl.
Ob.
C.Ingl.
Cl.
Cl. b.
Fg.
Cor. (F)
Cel.
div.
Vl.
Vle.
Celli
C.-B.
pizz.

Trepak (Russian Dance)

10
Fl.
Ob.
C.Ingl.
Cl.
Cl.b.
Fg.
Cor.
(F)
Trbe.
(A)
Tbni.
Tuba
Timp.
Tamb.
Vl.
Vle.
Celli
C.-B.

20
Fl.
Ob.
C.Ingl.
Cl.
Cl.b.
Fg.
Còr.
(F)
Trbe.
(A)
Tbni.
Tuba
Timp.
Tamb.
Vl.
Vle.
Celli
C.-B.

Fl.
Ob.
C.Ingl.
Cl.
Cl.b.
Fg.
Cor. (F)
Trbe. (A)
Tbni. Tuba
Timp.
Tamb.
Vl.
Vle.
Celli
C.-B.

51
30
Fl.
Cb.
C.Ingl.
Cl.
Cl.b.
Fg.
Cor. (F)
Trbe. (A)
Tbni. Tuba
Timp.
Tamb.
Vl.
Vle.
Celli
C.-B.

Fl.
sempre staccato
sempre staccato
Ob.
C.Ingl.
Cl.
Cl. b.
Fg.
Cor. (F)
mf
Trbe. (A)
Tbni. Tuba
mf
Timp.
Tamb.
Vl.
Vle.
cresc.
Celli
cresc.
C.-B.
cresc.

40
Fl.
Ob.
a 2.
C.Ingl.
Cl.
Cl. b.
Fg.
Cor. (F)
Trbe. (A)
Tbni. Tuba
Timp.
Tamb.
Vl.
sempre *ff*
Vle.
Celli
C.-B.

50
Fl.
a 2.
Ob.
C.Ingl.
Cl.
Cl.b.
Fg.
Cor. (F)
Trbe. (A)
Tbni. Tuba
Timp.
Tamb.
Vl.
Vle.
Celli
C.-B.

Fl.
Ob.
Ingl.
Cl.
Cl. b.
Fg.
Cor. (F)
Trbe. (A)
Tromb. Tuba
Timp.
Tamb.
Vl.
Vle.
Celli
C.-B.
ff

52
60
Fl.
Ob.
C.Ingl.
Cl.
Cl.b.
Fg.
a 2.
Cor. (F)
Trbe. (A)
Tbni.
Tuba
Timp.
Tamb.
Vl.
Vle.
Celli
C.-B.
ff
sf

Fl.
Ob.
C.Ingl.
Cl.
Cl. b.
Fg.
Cor. (F)
Trbe. (A)
Tbni. Tuba
Timp.
Tamb.
Vl.
Vle.
Celli
C.-B.

stringendo
70
Fl.
Ob.
C.Ingl.
Cl.
Cl.b.
Fg.
Cor. (F)
Trbe. (A)
Tbni. Tuba
Timp.
Tamb.
Vl.
Vle.
Celli
C.-B.
sempre *fff*

Fl.
Ob.
C.Ingl.
Cl.
Cl.b.
Fg.
Cor. (F)
Trbe. (A)
Tbni. Tuba
Timp.
Tamb.
Vl.
Vle.
Celli
C.-B.

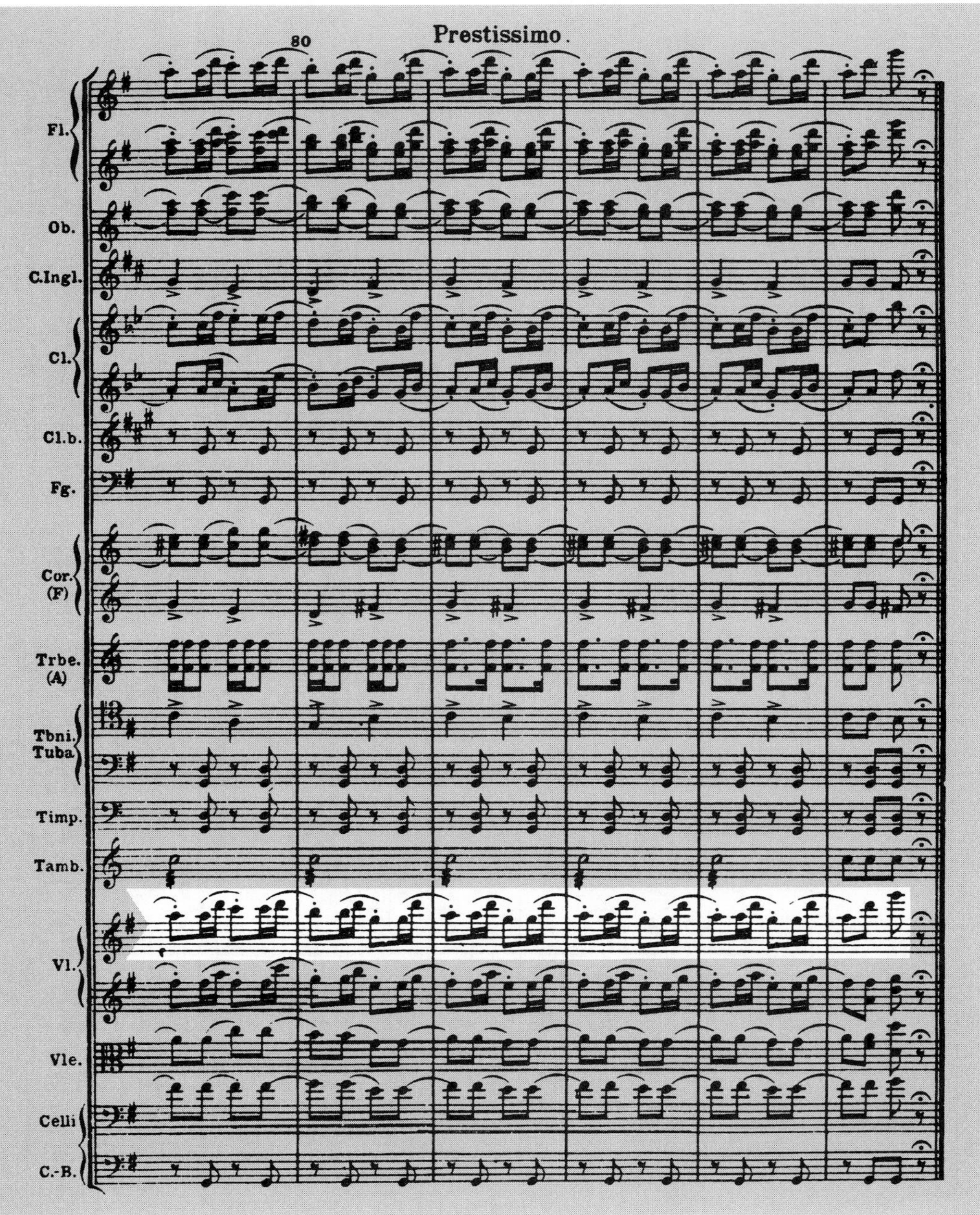
80
Prestissimo.
Fl.
Ob.
C.Ingl.
Cl.
Cl.b.
Fg.
Cor. (F)
Trbe. (A)
Tbni. Tuba
Timp.
Tamb.
Vl.
Vle.
Celli
C.-B.

In the second half of the nineteenth century, Russia became the principal center for ballet, and Peter Ilyich Tchaikovsky (1840–1893) emerged as its first great composer. Of his three masterworks in the genre, *Swan Lake, Sleeping Beauty,* and *The Nutcracker,* the last has become a popular tradition for December performances. The story, set at a Christmas party, is the product of two prominent literary figures: E. T. A. Hoffmann wrote the original story, and Alexandre Dumas *père* created an expanded version that was used as the basis for the ballet's scenario.

The essential elements of the plot occur in the first act. A handsome prince has been cursed, taking the shape of a grotesque nutcracker. The spell can only be broken if someone falls in love with him as he is, and if the evil Mouse King is killed. At midnight, a battle between toy soldiers and giant mice ensues, during which Clara kills the Mouse King. Coupled with her love for the nutcracker, this action breaks the spell, and the handsome prince reappears. The second act, set in the land of the sweets ruled by the Sugar Plum Fairy, is an extended celebration of Clara's heroic deed, in which dancers from all over the world appear in order to entertain and honor Clara.

The success of this ballet is a tribute to Tchaikovsky's ability to create memorable melodies and colorful, rich orchestrations. In keeping with the traditions of French ballet, Tchaikovsky incorporates a number of popular dances into the work. Each of the three excerpts included here is in **A–B–A** dance form. The *March,* which occurs at the beginning of the party scene in Act I, is a nineteenth-century popular dance in duple meter and a moderate tempo. The other two dances are from Act II. The delicate orchestration in the *Dance of the Sugar Plum Fairy* features a solo celesta, a pizzicato string accompaniment, and several brief woodwind solos. A cadenza for the celesta precedes the reprise of the **A** section. A number of the dances from Act II evoke the styles of exotic lands. The *Trepak* is based on a vigorous dance for men that is characterized by the distinctive Cossack *prisiadka* (kicking the legs from a squatting position).

19. Antonín Dvořák

CD8: 6/53–61

Symphony No. 9 in E minor
(From the New World), First Movement (1893)

7
fz
dim. p
fz
dim. p
p
ff
ff
ff
ff
ff
ff [z]
ffz
ff
ff
ff
ff
ff

12
p
p
p
f
pp
a 2
p
f
dim.
ff
p
f
p
f
32
pp
fz
fp
pp
pp
fz
fp
pp
pp

17
a 2
p
pp
f
fz
16

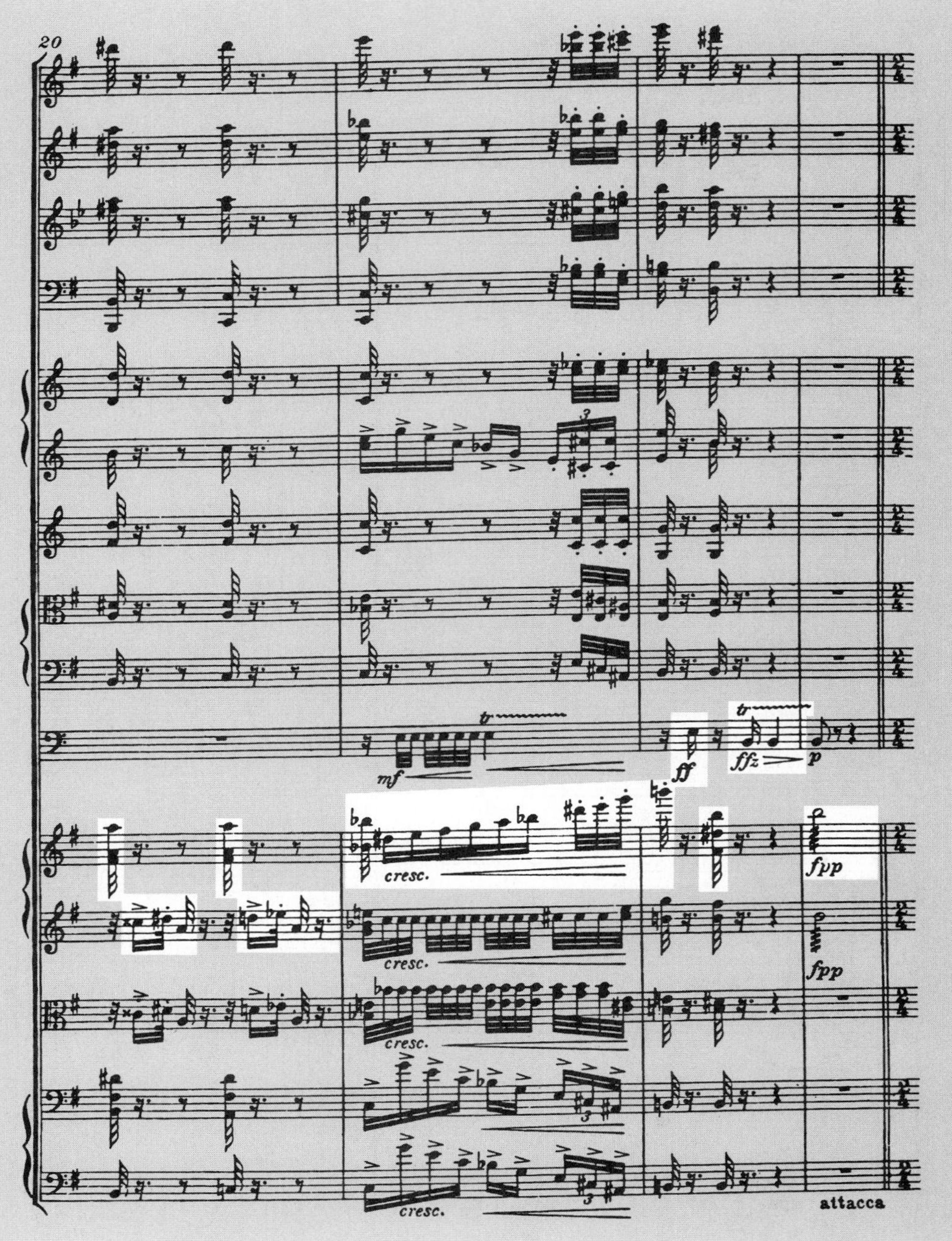
20
tr
mf
ff
ffz
p
cresc.
fpp
cresc.
fpp
cresc.
cresc.
attacca

54
24
Cl.
Allegro molto 𝅗𝅥 136
p
Fag.
p
Cor.III.IV
a 2
mf
[>]
f
Viol.
pp
pp
pp
pizz.
pp
arco
pp
pizz.
pp

32
Fl.
mp
Ob.
a 2
mf
fz
[mp]
Fag.
p
Viol.
pp
p
pp
arco

39
a 2
ff
f
tr

48
ff
ff
ff
ff
ff
ff
ff
ff
ff
ff
ff
ff
div.
fz
f
fz
f
fz
fz
f
fz
f
fz

54
fz
ff
a 2
p
fff
tr

61
a 2
fz
ff
a 2
f
tr
f
fz
f
fz
f
fz

67
a 2
ff
ff
ff
[f]
[f]
f
[f]
[f]
[f]
fz
fz
fz
fz
fz
fz
f
f
f

73
I.
fz
f[fz]
mp
mp
ff
ff
f
f
f
tr
f
tr
f
fz
fz
mf
dim.
f
f
mp
[f] fz
mf
ffz
mf
mp
ffz
mf
ffz
mf
mp
pizz.
ffz
ffz
mp

86 Fl.
p
Ob.
Cl.
pp
Fag.
pp
Viol.
pp
pp
pp
pp

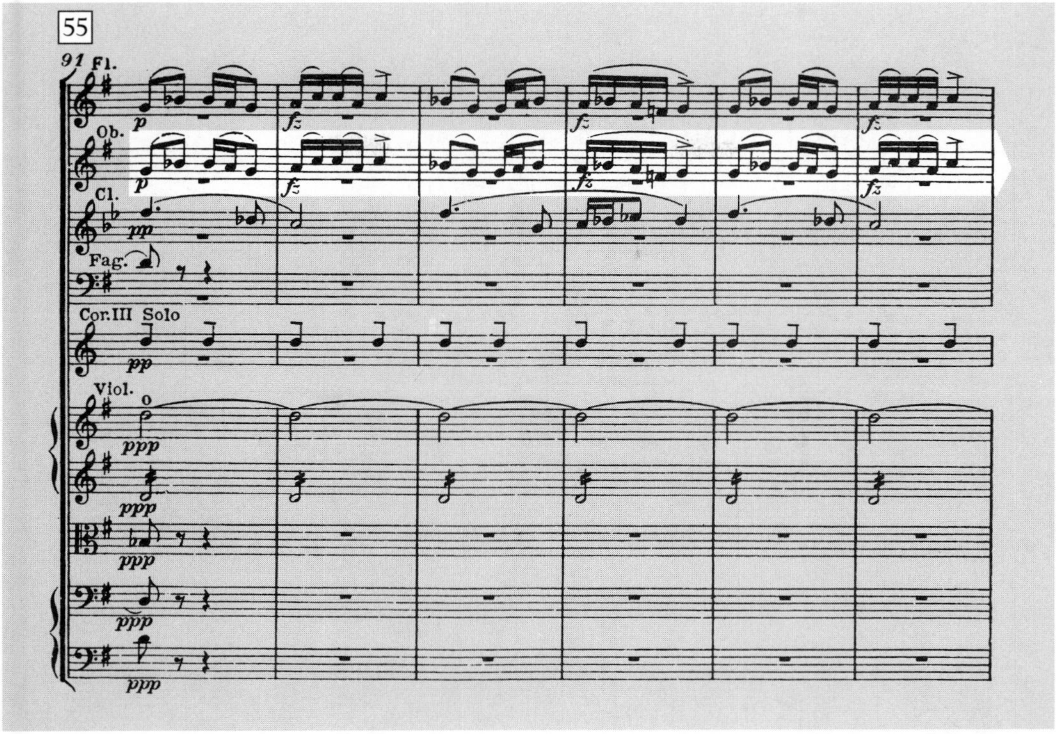
55
91 Fl.
p
fz
Ob.
Cl.
pp
Fag.
Cor.III Solo
Viol.
ppp

97 Fl.
fz
pp
Ob.
Cl.
Cor.
III.
Viol.
ppp
pizz.

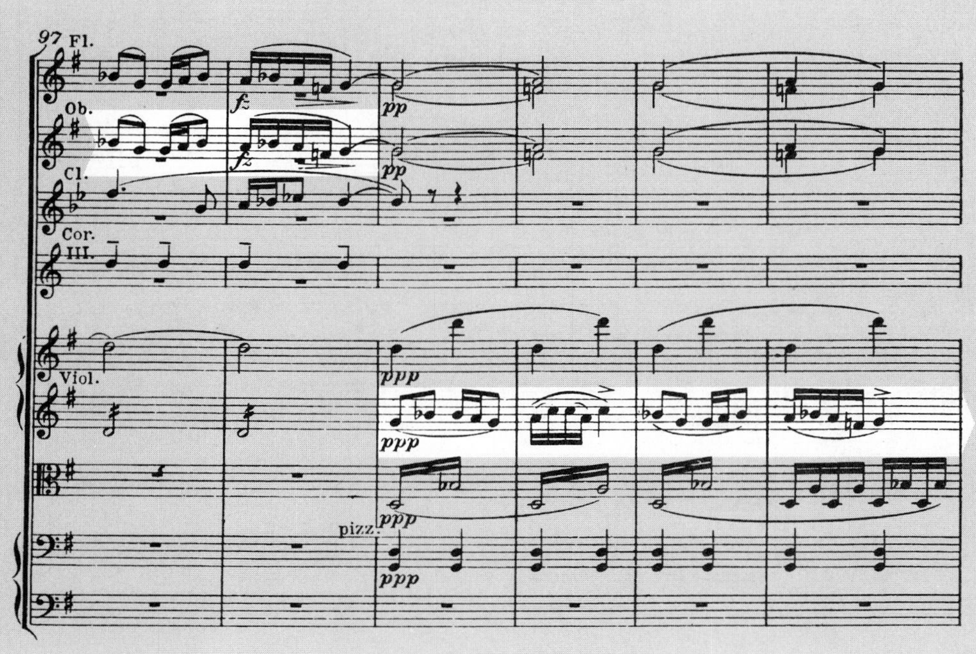

103
Fl.
cresc.
Ob.
cresc.
Viol.
molto
cresc.
molto
cresc.
non legato
arco
[pp]
molto
cresc.
arco
pp
molto
cresc.

115
Fl.
Ob.
Cl.
Fag.
Viol.
pizz.
cresc.
121
Fl
Ob.
Cl.
Fag.
Cor. III IV
Timp.
dim.
Viol.
arco

126
Fl.
Ob.
cresc.
f
p
Cl.
cresc.
Fag.
Viol.
fz
dim.

132
Fl.
Ob.
p
pp
cresc.
f
Cl.
Fag.
[p]
Viol.
ffz
fz

137 Fl.
Ob.
Cl.
Fag.
Viol.
p
pp
dim.

56
144 Fl.
Solo
Ob.
Cl.
Fag.
Viol.
pp
ppp

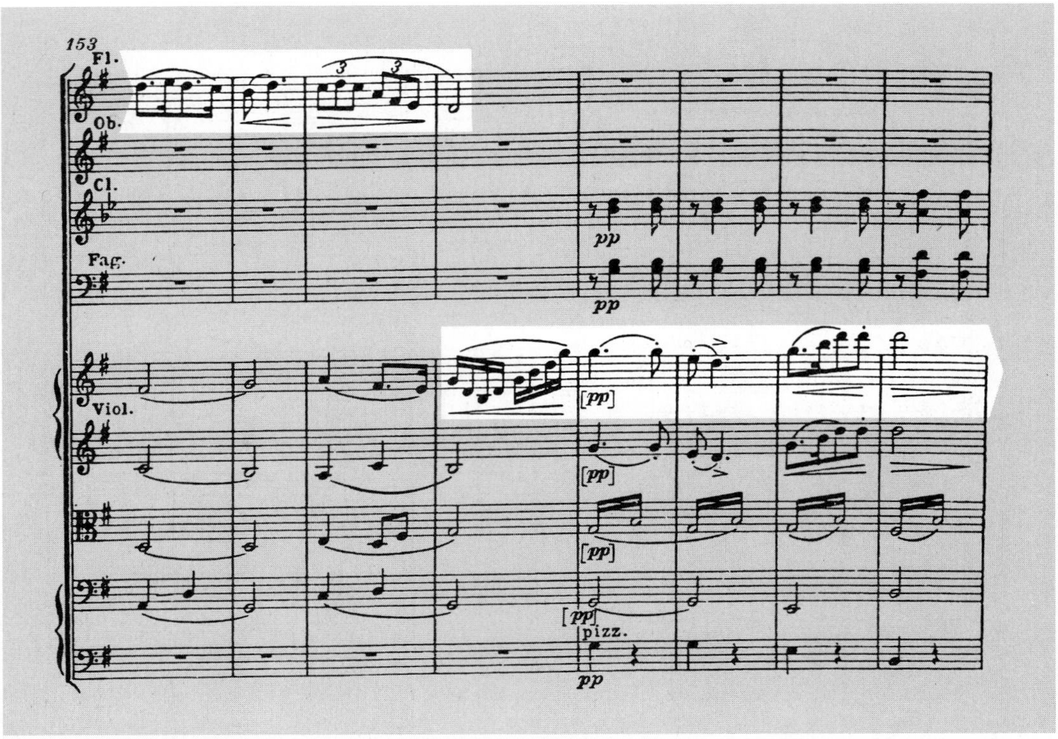

153
Fl.
Ob.
Cl.
pp
Fag.
pp
Viol.
[pp]
[pp]
[pp]
[pp]
pizz.
pp

167
ff
f
in C
a 2.
cresc.

174
1.
tr
fpp
fpp

57
177
2.
a 2
ff
fz
f
ffz

183
Cl.
Solo
Cor. III. IV.
Trb.
Viol.
dim.
leggiero
p
pp

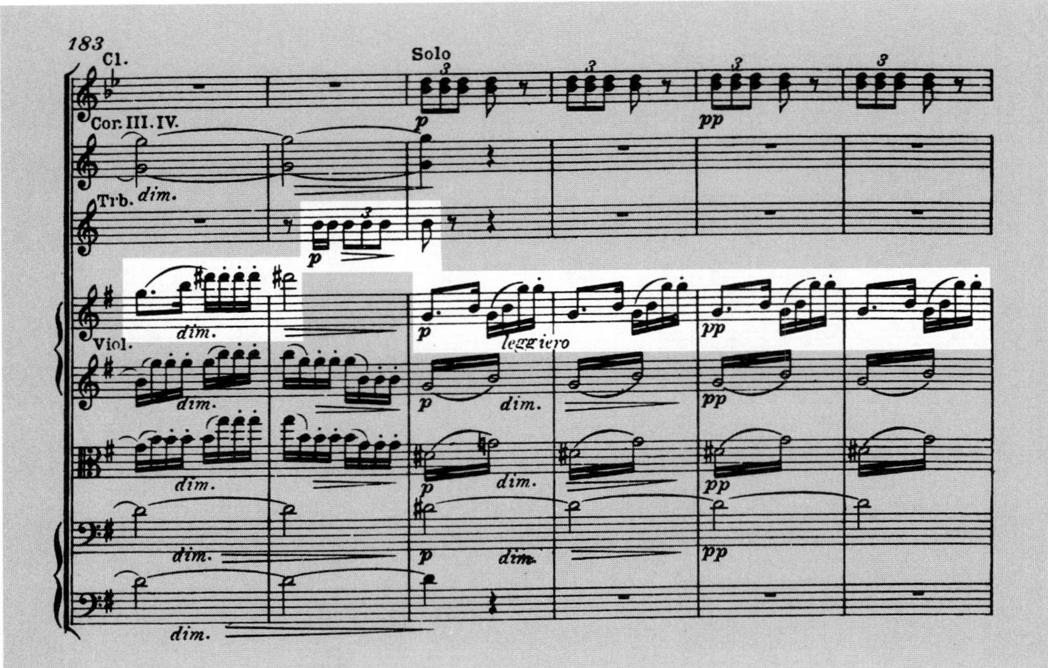

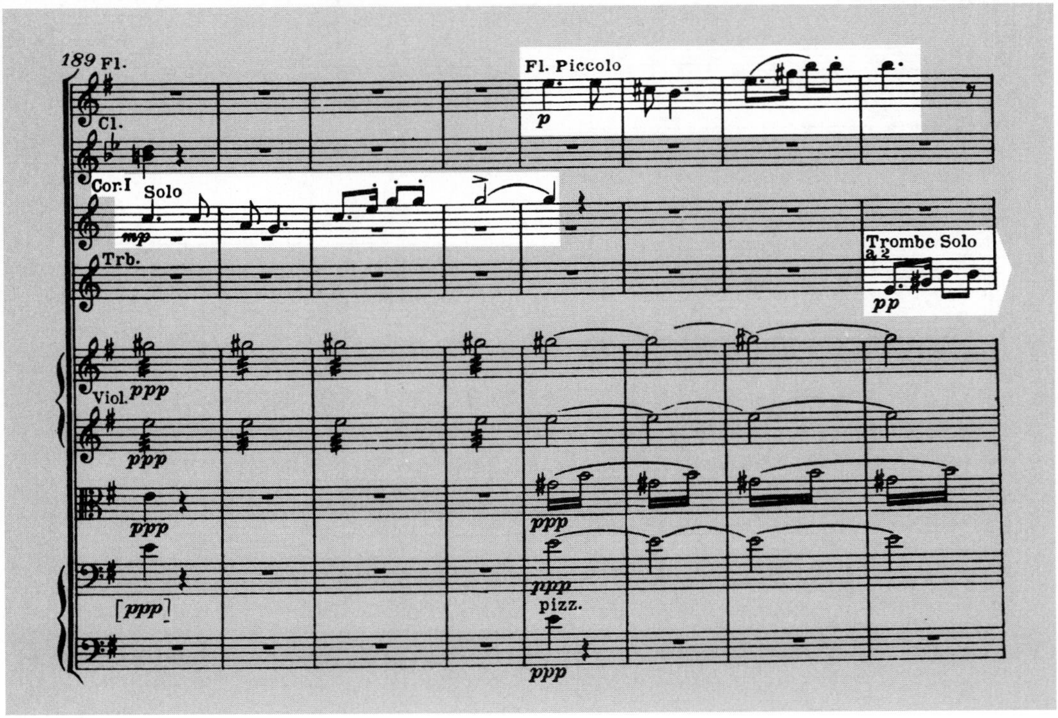
189
Fl.
Fl. Piccolo
Cl.
Cor. I
Solo
mp
Trb.
Trombe Solo
a 2
Viol.
ppp
[ppp]
pizz.
p
pp

197
p
pp
p
poco
pizz.
arco
pp
pp
fp
poco

202
Flauto gr. II
mf
mf
f
a
poco
cresc.
cresc.
mf
pp
cresc.
cresc.
cresc.
cresc.
cresc.
cresc.
fp
più
fz
f
a
poco
cresc.

208
a 2
a 2
sul G
div.
non div.
arco

215
a 2
ff
fz
a 2
ff
fz
fz
fz
div.
f
f
f

221
ff
a 2.
non div.
fz

228
fz
ff
fz

232
a 2
ff
f
[ff]
fz
[>]
[fz]

238
a 2

244
a 2
f
[ff]
a 2
f
a 2
f
ff
a 2
ff
[ff]
ff
f
f
fz
fz
ff
ff
ff

250
a 2
a 2
fz
fz
fz
fz
fz
fz
3
3
3
3

256
a 2
fz
p dim.
pp
ff
3
3
fz
a 2.
fz
p
pp
fp
p
pp
fp
p
pp
pp
fz

264
Solo
p
I.
p
pp
cresc.
pizz.
pp
cresc.

58
271
Fl.
Cl.
Fag.
Cor. III.IV
a 2
Timp.
Viol.
pizz.
arco
278
Fl.
Ob.
a 2
Cl.
Fag.
Timp.
Viol.

285
a 2
a 2
in E
a 2
arco

293
ffz
fz
f
fz
f

301
Viol. dimin.
dimin.
dimin.
dimin.
dimin.
p
dim.
pp
308 Fl.
59
Solo
[p]
Viol.
legato
dim.
ppp
legato
dim.
ppp
legato
dim.
ppp
pp
dim.
ppp
pizz.
[ppp]
ppp
314 Fl.
Viol.

320 Fl.
p
I.
Cl.
I.
p
Fag.
p
Cor.
II. pp
p
Viol.
ppp
ppp
pp
pp

326 Fl.
cresc.
fz
Ob.
cresc.
p
fz
Cl.
Fag.
cresc.
fz
Cor. I. II
cresc.
cresc.
f
cresc.
f
cresc.
f
cres.
f
arco
pp
cresc.
f

333
Cl.
mp
[mp]
p
Fag.
mp
[mp]
p
Viol.
f
p
pizz.

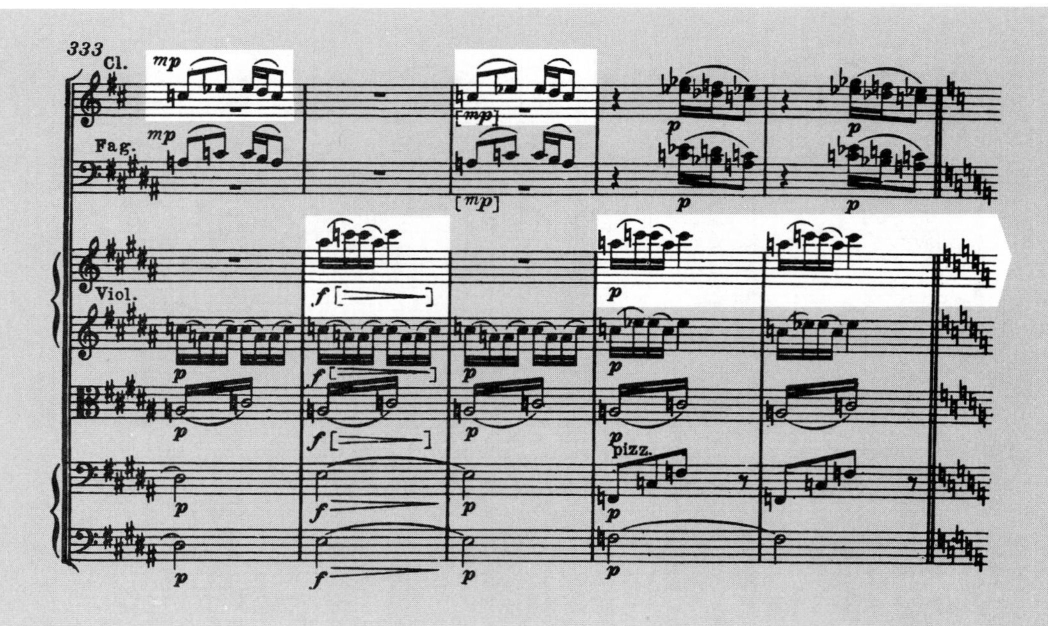

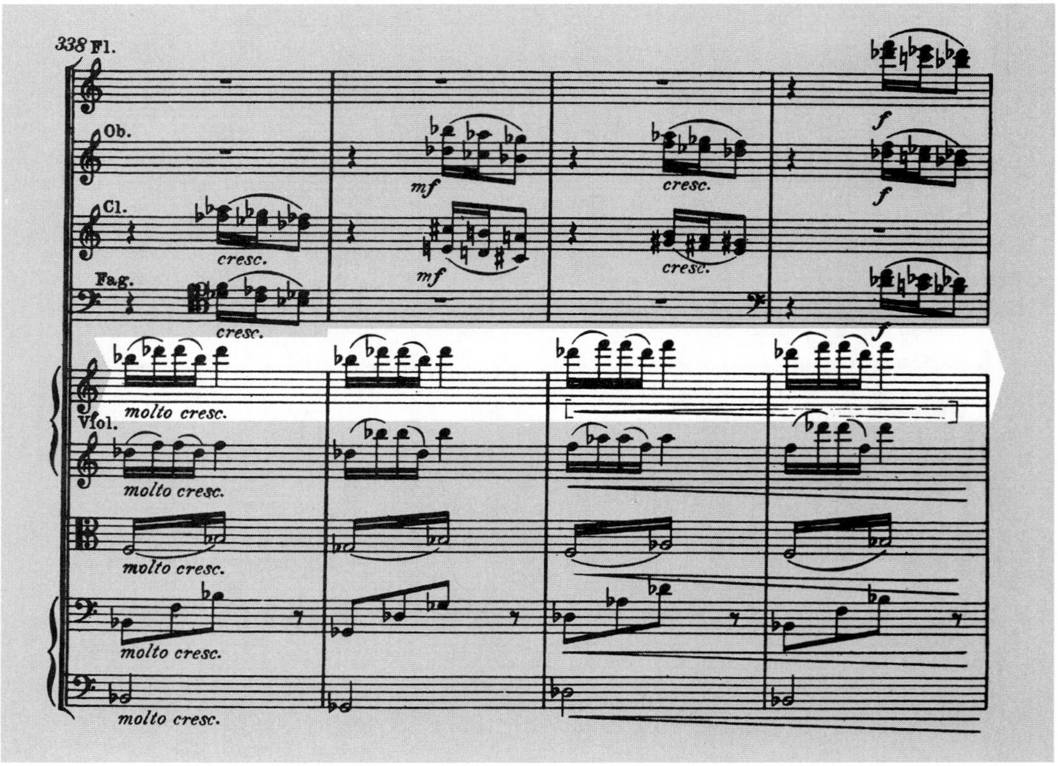

338
Fl.
f
Ob.
mf
cresc.
f
Cl.
cresc.
mf
cresc.
Fag.
cresc.
f
molto cresc.
Viol.
molto cresc.
molto cresc.
molto cresc.
molto cresc.

342 Fl.
Ob.
Cl.
Fag.
Cor.
Trb.
Viol.
arco
dim.
347 Fl.
Ob.
Viol. I
II
fz
dim.

352 Fl.
dim.
p
fz
Ob.
dim.
p
fz
Fag.
[>]
p
f[z]
dim.
Viol.
dim.
cresc.
fz
dim.
dim.
cresc.
fz
dim.
dim.
cresc.
fz
dim.
dim.
p
cresc.
fz
f
dim.
dim.
fz
f
dim.

358 Fl.
[p]
pp
pp
Ob.
[p]
pp
pp
Fag.
p
Viol.
p
dim.
pp
p
dim.
pp
p
dim.
pp
fp
dim.
pp
p
dim.
pp

60
365
Fl.
Ob.
p Solo
Viol.
ppp
ppp
ppp
ppp
ppp
374
Fl.
Ob.
p
Fag.
p
Viol.
pp
pp
pp
pp
pizz.
pp

382
Ob.
Cl.
Fag.
p
cresc.
mf
Viol.
arco
cresc.

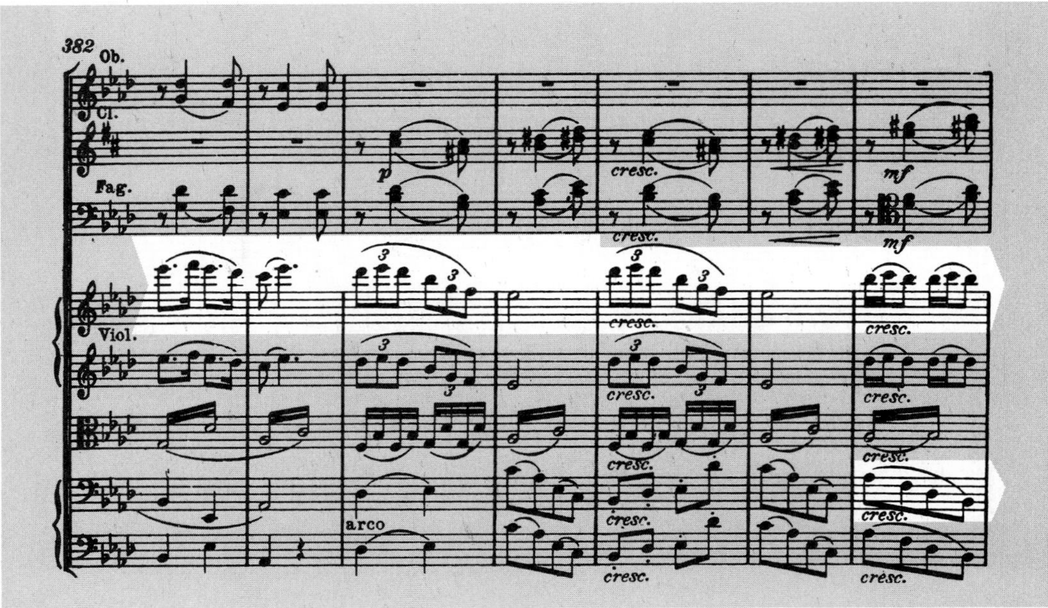

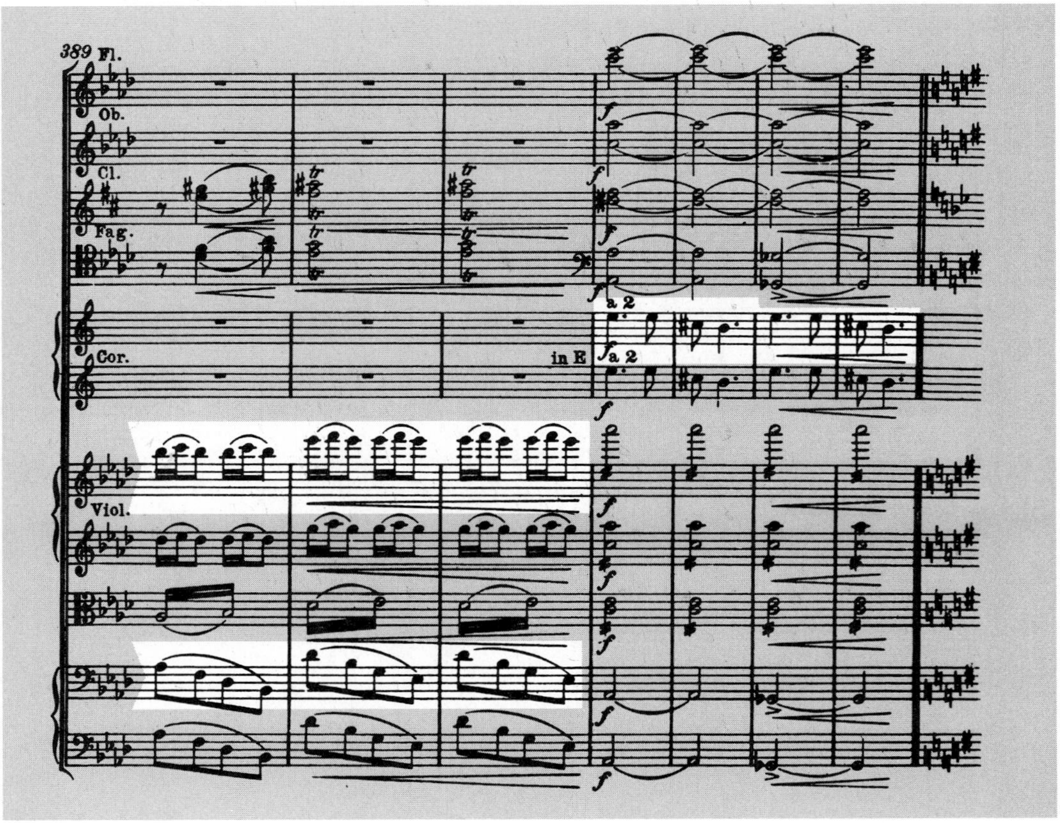
389
Fl.
Ob.
Cl.
Fag.
tr
f
a 2
Cor.
in E
Viol.

61
396
fff
ff
fz
in C.
a 2
tr
[>]

405
sfz
sfz
sfz
sfz
ffz
ffz
ffz
ffz
ffz
ff
fz
fz
fz
ff
fz
fz
fz
ff
sfz
sfz
sfz

412
ff
ff
f
f
f
f
f
f
f
f
fz
fz
fz
fz
fz
fz
fz
[fz]
fz
fz
fz
fz
fz
fz
fz
[fz]
fz
div.
fz
fz
fz
fz
fz
fz
fz
fz

420
a 2
a 2
a 2
a 2
a 2
a 2
fz
fz
fz
fz
[fz]

427
a 2
ff
fz
fz
fz
[fz]
f
fz
fz
[fz]

434
fz
a 2
ff
tr

441
a 2
tr
fz
[fz]
f[z]

Antonín Dvořák (1841–1904), like his contemporary Brahms, returned to the Classical traditions of the symphony, completing nine works in the genre. Unlike Brahms, however, Dvořák was also a strong nationalist and created a distinctively fresh folk character in his works. Late in his career, Dvořák left his homeland, Bohemia (now part of the Czech Republic), and lived in the United States for several years. He composed and premiered his last symphony in New York in 1893. The work, subtitled *From the New World,* follows the standard four-movement structure of the Classical symphony, but it also reflects some of the Romantic tendencies in the genre. Recurring themes create a strong sense of cyclic unity, and the middle movements, inspired by Longfellow's *The Song of Hiawatha,* suggest a programmatic conception.

This powerful symphony mixes elements of Classical structure, Bohemian folk music, and African-American spirituals. The first movement is a clearly defined sonata-allegro form with a slow introduction. American sounds can be heard in the syncopation of the opening somber melody and in the closing theme, which resembles the spiritual *Swing Low, Sweet Chariot.* Much of the other melodic material seems to be more Bohemian than American, but the overall energetic character has been linked to the untapped power that Dvořák saw in this country over one hundred years ago.

20. Giacomo Puccini

Madama Butterfly, Act II, "Un bel dì" ("One beautiful day") (1904)

8CD: 7/1–2

4CD: 3/40–41

dolcemente
rall.
But.
nu - to! Io non gli scen - do in - con - tro. Io no. Mi
told you! But I won't go to meet him. Not yet! I
dolcemente
rall.
pp
Tempo I
con semplicità
met-to là sul ci-glio del col-le e a-spet-to, e a-spet-to gran
wan-der to the rim of the hill-top and wait there. I wait for a
13
pp
rit.
a tempo
tem - po e non mi pe - sa, la lun-ga at - te - sa.
long time but I don't mind it, I'm used to wait-ing.
a tempo
pp rit.
p
animando un poco
E... u - sci - to dal - la fol - la cit - ta - di - na
A man e-mer-ges from the crowd-ed cit - y,
animando un poco

rall. un poco
But.
un uo-mo, un pic-ciol pun - to s'av - via per la col -
a dot on the hor - i - zon: he's set - ting out for our
rall. un poco
p
2
41
Sostenendo molto
Lo stesso movimento
li - na. Chi sa - rà? chi sa - rà? E co - me sa - rà
hill - top. Who on earth can it be? And when at last he
14 Lo stesso movimento
p
rall.
Lento
giun - to che di - rà? che di - rà? Chia - me - rà But - ter - fly dal - la lon -
gets here, what on earth will he say? He will call: "But - ter - fly." I hear him
rall.
ppp
ta - na. Io sen - za dar ri - spo - sta me ne sta - rò na -
faint - ly. But I don't think I'll an - swer, I'll stay a while in

con molto passione
rall. molto
But.
sco - sta un po' per ce - lia, e un po' per non mo-
hid - ing: at first to tease him, but then for fear to
rall. molto
col canto
Andante come prima
con forza
ri - re al pri-mo in-con - tro, ed e-gli al-quan-to in pe-na chia-me-
die in his em-brac - es! Then wor-ried by my si-lence he will
15
con molto passione
ff
p
rit.
rà, chia-me-rà: Pic - ci-na mo-gliet-ti-na o-lez-zo di ver-
call, he will call: "My lit-tle wife, my dar-ling, my fra-grant sweet ver-
pp
be - na, i no-mi che mi da-va al suo ve - ni - re
be - na..." the names he used to give me when first I met him.
r. h.
cresc.

(to Suzuki)
But.
Tut - to que-sto av-ver-ra, te lo pro-met - to. Tien - ti la tua pa-
That's the way it will be, you may be-lieve me. You have no right to
poco rall. e cresc.
Largamente
u - ra, io con si - cu - ra fe - de l'a - spet - to.
doubt it while I with faith un - shak - en a - wait him!
16
(Butterfly and Suzuki embrace, moved.)
dim.
meno f
rit.
(Butterfly dismisses Suzuki who exits through the door at the left. Butterfly gazes after her sadly.)
pp sostenuto

Giacomo Puccini (1858–1924), the leading figure in Italian opera at the turn of the century, composed some of the most popular operas of all time. He is often linked to *verismo* (realism), the Italian operatic movement in which the characters are drawn from everyday life and are subject to real-life passions. These qualities are most readily seen in his operas *La bohème* (1896) and *Tosca* (1900). *Madama Butterfly,* one of Puccini's most beloved works, combines verismo elements with the exoticism of Japanese culture.

The libretto for *Madama Butterfly,* by Giuseppe Giacosa and Luigi Illica, has a complex history. John Luther Long expanded Pierre Loti's original tale *Madame Chrysanthème* into a short story. David Belasco then adapted this story for a stage production, which in turn inspired Puccini to create the opera. Although the premiere for *Madama Butterfly* was a disaster, a revised version became a sensation in subsequent performances.

The plot centers on a young Japanese woman, Cio-Cio-San, who is a *geisha,* the equivalent to the Western courtesan. She renounces her profession and religion to marry an American naval officer, B. F. Pinkerton. After Pinkerton leaves for the United States, Cio-Cio-San gives birth to his son. When Pinkerton finally returns to Japan, Cio-Cio-San learns that he has married an American woman. She gives her child to him, and in a powerful scene, commits suicide rather than go back to the life of a geisha.

Throughout the opera, Puccini brilliantly combines the melody-oriented Italian opera style with Japanese colors, including pentatonic and whole-tone scales, traditional Japanese melodies, and the sound of a *gagaku* orchestra (harp, flute and piccolo, and bells). In the well-known aria "Un bel dì" ("One beautiful day"), Cio-Cio-San envisions the joy of Pinkerton's return to Japan. The aria begins in a dreamlike state, accompanied by a solo violin. As she imagines the arriving ship, the music becomes more intense and speechlike. Finally, the emotional level reaches a powerful climax, with the full orchestra supporting the vocal melody on the text "l'aspetto" (I will wait for him).

21. Gustav Mahler

8CD: 7/3–6

Das Lied von der Erde (The Song of the Earth),
Third Movement (1908–9)

III. *Von der Jugend* (*Of Youth*)

16
kl. Fl.
1.2. Fl.
1. Ob.
2. Ob.
1. Kl. in B
2. Kl.
1.2. Fag.
1. Vl.
2. Vl.
Br.
Ten.-St.
Vlc.
cresc.
zu 2
stacc.
lon aus grü-nem und aus wei-ßem Porzel-lan.
Wie der Rücken ei-nes Ti - gers wölbt die
24
1. Fl.
2. Fl.
1. Ob.
2. Ob.
1. Kl. in B
2. Kl.
1.2. Fag.
Ten.-St.
Vlc.
p subito
dim.
pizz.
Brücke sich aus Ja - de zu dem Pa-vil-lon hin-ü - - - ber.
interlude

4
32
kl. Fl.
sempre f
1.2. Fl.
zu 2
dim.
1. Ob.
2. Ob.
1.2. Kl. in B
1.2. Fag.
dim. - - - p
1.3. Hr.
in F
2.4. Hr.
1. Trp. in B
in B
mit Dämpfer
Trgl.
sempre pp
gr. Tr. Beck.
1. Vl.
Griffbrett
pp Zart, aber
2. Vl.
Br.
Ten.-St.
In dem
Theme 2
Vlc. get.
arco
pizz.
Kb.

40
kl. Fl.
1.2. Fl.
1.2. Ob.
1.2. Kl. in B
1.2. Fag.
1.3. Hr. in F
2.4. Hr.
1. Trp. in B
Trgl.
gr. Tr. Beck.
1. Vl.
2. Vl.
Br.
Ten.-St.
Vlc. get.
Kb.
zu 2
mit Empfindung.
arco
pizz.
Häus-chen sitzen Freun - de, schön ge-kleidet, trin - ken, plau - dern, man - che schreiben Verse nie - der.

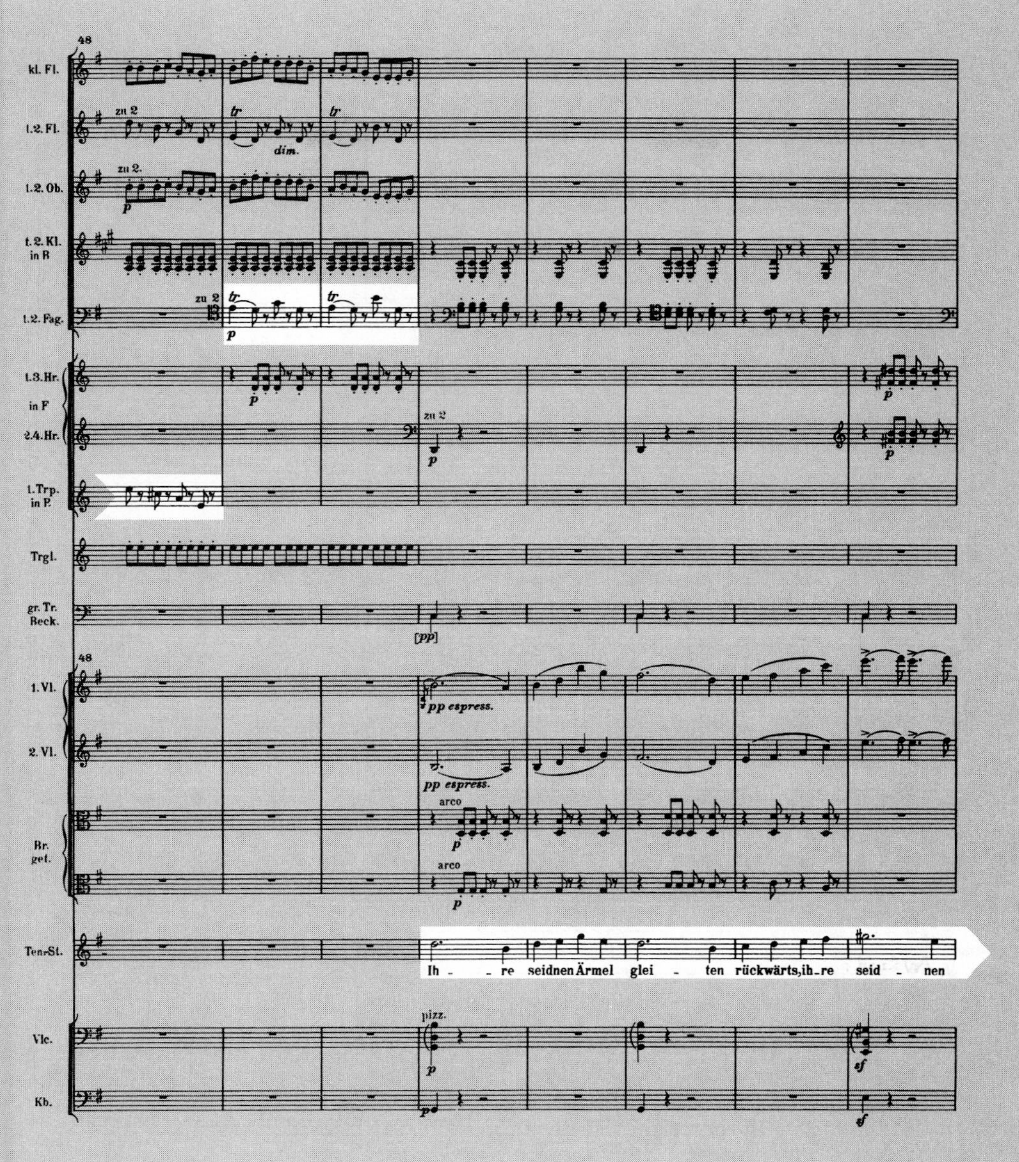
48
kl. Fl.
1.2. Fl.
zu 2
dim.
1.2. Ob.
1.2. Kl. in B
1.2. Fag.
1.3. Hr.
in F
2.4. Hr.
1. Trp. in F.
Trgl.
gr. Tr. Beck.
[pp]
1. Vl.
pp espress.
2. Vl.
Br. get.
arco
Ten-St.
Ih - re seidnen Ärmel glei - ten rückwärts, ih - re seid - nen
Vlc.
pizz.
Kb.

56
kl. Fl.
pp
1.2. Fl.
zu 2
sfpp
1. Ob.
sfp
f
p
2. Ob.
1. Kl.
in B
2. Kl.
sf
1.2. Fag.
1.3. Hr.
in F
2.4. Hr.
Trgl.
gr. Tr. Beck.
Vl. Solo
espress.
1. Vl.
2. Vl.
Br.
pizz.
Ten.-St.
Müt - zen hok - ken lu-stig tief im Nak - ken.
Vlc.
Kb.

5
Ruhiger
kl. Fl.
1.2. Fl.
1. Ob.
2. Ob.
1. Kl. in B
2. Kl.
1.2. Fag.
1.3. Hr. in F
2.4. Hr.
zu 2
gr. Tr. Beck.
Solo-Vl.
1. Vl.
2. Vl.
Br.
Ten.-St.
Vlc.
Kb.
cresc.
p espress.
pp espress.
arco
pizz.
Auf des klei - nen,

Langsam
kl. Fl.
1.2. Fl.
1.2. Ob.
1.2. Kl. in B
1.2. Fag.
1.2. Hr. in F
gr. Tr. Beck.
1. Vl.
2. Vl.
Br.
Ten.-St.
klei - nen Tei - ches stil - ler, stil - ler Was - ser - flä - che zeigt sich al - les wun - der -
Vlc.
Kb.
Poco rit. Rit. molto
Tempo (etwas mäßig)
1.2. Fl.
1.2. Ob.
1.2. Kl. in B
1.2. Fag.
1. Hr. in F
2. Vl.
Br.
Ten.-St.
lich im Spie - gel - bil - - de.
Vlc.
Kb.
mit Dämpfer
[mit Dämpfer]

6
Rit.
A tempo (mäßig)
Rit.
Molto rit.
Tempo I subito
(ohne Dämpfer)
espress. molto
p molto espress.
Dämpfer ab!
Al - les auf dem Kop - fe ste - hend in dem Pa - vil - lon aus grü - nem und aus wei - ßem

105
kl. Fl.
1.2. Ob.
1.2. Kl. in B
1.2. Fag.
Trgl.
1. Vl.
2. Vl.
Br.
Ten.-St.
Vlc.
zu 2
dim.
pp
f
get.
arco
stacc.
fp
p espress.
pizz.
sf
Por - zel - lan; wie ein Halb-mond scheint die Brük - ke, um - ge-kehrt der Bo - gen.

111
(118)
kl. Fl.
1.2. Fl.
1.2. Ob.
1.2. Kl. in B
1.2. Fag.
1. Vl.
2. Vl.
Br.
Ten.-St.
Vlc.
stacc.
zu 2
dim.
f stacc.
morendo
ppp
arco
Freun - de, schön ge - klei - det, trin - ken, plau - dern.

Text and Translation

Mitten in dem kleinen Teiche steht ein Pavillon aus grünem und aus weissem Porzellan.	In the middle of the little pool stands a pavilion of green and of white porcelain.
Wie der Rücken eines Tigers wölbt die Brücke sich aus Jade zu dem Pavillon hinüber.	Like the back of a tiger the bridge of jade arches over to the pavilion.
In dem Häuschen sitzen Freunde, schön gekleidet, trinken, plaudern, manche schreiben Verse nieder.	In the little house, friends are sitting beautifully dressed, drinking, chatting; several are writing verses.
Ihre seidnen Ärmel gleiten rückwärts, ihre seidnen Mützen hocken lustig tief im Nacken.	Their silken sleeves slip backwards, their silken caps perch gaily on the back of their necks.
Auf des kleinen Teiches stiller Wasserfläche zeigt sich alles wunderlich im Spiegelbilde.	On the little pool's still surface everything appears fantastically in a mirror image.
Alles auf dem Kopfe stehend in dem Pavillon aus grünem und aus weissem Porzellan;	Everything is standing on its head in the pavilion of green and of white porcelain;
wie ein Halbmond scheint die Brücke umgekehrt der Bogen. Freunde, schön gekleidet, trinken, plaudern.	like a half-moon stands the bridge, upside-down its arch. Friends, beautifully dressed, are drinking, chatting.

Gustav Mahler (1860–1911) primarily composed in two genres—symphonies and song cycles. Since the symphonies often include voices and the song cycles are generally arranged for orchestral accompaniment, the stylistic differences between the two are minimal. Both genres incorporate large orchestral forces, but, as evident in this work, Mahler skillfully uses the array of instruments as a colorful palette for delicate orchestration. Also typical of both genres are extended lyrical expressions and intricate contrapuntal textures.

Das Lied von der Erde (*The Song of the Earth*), Mahler's foremost song cycle, was composed near the end of his career. It is unique among his works in the genre in that he specifies two solo voices: a tenor and an alto/baritone. The texts of the six songs are based on Hans Bethge's *Chinese Flute.* Reflecting the growing interest and appreciation in nineteenth-century Europe for non-Western arts, this collection contains adaptations of Chinese poetry by a number of writers, most notably the revered eighth-century poet Li-Tai-Po. In the third song of the cycle, *Von der Jugend* (*Of Youth*), Mahler effectively evokes a Chinese character through the use of pentatonic scales and a delicate orchestration; the low brass are omitted, and the woodwinds, solo trumpet, staccato strings, and triangle play prominent roles in support of the tenor voice. The **A–B–A** form of the song, with a contrasting lyrical section in the middle, creates an arch form that can be seen as a musical counterpart to the bridge of jade described in the poem.

22. Claude Debussy

Prélude à "L'après-midi d'un faune"
(Prelude to "The Afternoon of a Faun") (1894)

8CD: 6/62–66
4CD: 3/46–50

62 46

5
HAUTB.
CL.
1°
p
più p
CORS
3°
p
p
p
più p
1re HARPE
glissando
2e HARPE
pp
pp
ppp
(sourdine)
Div.
pp
(sourdine)
Div.
pp
(sourdine)
pp
pp
Div.
(sourdine)
pp
pp
pp
pp

11
1re FL.
SOLO
HAUTB.
1°
expressif
CL.
Bons
1°
1°
CORS
3°
Div.
(sur la touche)
(sur la touche)
(sur la touche)
à 2

16
Fl.
1° et 2°
p cre - scen - do f f f
Hautb.
à 2
p cre - scen - do f f f
Cor Angl.
p cre - scen - do f f f
Cl.
1°
à 2
p cre - scen - do f f
1°
dim. et retenu
Bons
à 2
p cre - scen - do f
1. 2.
(1)
p cre - scen - do f f f
(2)
dim.
Cors
3. 4.
(3)
p cre - scen - do f f f
dim.
Div.
p cresc. - - - f f f
position nat.
cre - scen - do f f f
position nat.
cre - scen - do f f f
position nat.
cre - scen - do f f f
Unies.
cresc - - - f
12/8

21
1re FL.
SOLO
légèrement et expressif
p
2e
CORS
pp
4e
pp
1re HARPE
pp
2e HARPE
pp
pp
pp
Div.
pp
pizz.
pp

23
1er FL.
3
CL.
Bons
1°
1er COR
1°
p
1re HARPE
pp
2e HARPE
pp
Unis
pp
pizz.
pp
pizz.
pp
pizz.
Unis.
pp

26
p
FL.
2°
CL.
Bons
CORS
4°
pp
1re HARPE
5
2e HARPE p
Div.
arco
Div.
arco
arco

28
Cédez . . .
Fl.
Bons
Cédez . . .
Div.
Unis
Unis
Div.
dim.
dim.
dim.
arco
Div.
63
47
30
1re Fl.
au Mouvt
Cl
1o
sourdines
Cors
sourdines
1re Harpe
au Mouvt
ôtez vite les sourdines
ôtez vite les sourdines
ôtez vite les sourdines
pizz.

32
(Sans trainer)
1re FL.
CL.
Bons
CORS
1re HARPE
(Sans trainer)
pizz.
arco
Div.

35
64
48
En animant (M.M. ♩= 72)
1re FL.
HAUTB.
1° SOLO
doux et expressif
CL.
Bons
CORS
1re HARPE
En animant
pizz.
Div.
arco
Unis

38
HAUTB.
(à 2)
cre - - scen - - do
mf
COR ANGL.
cre - - scen - - do
mf
CL.
1°
cresc.
(2)
Bons
cresc.
mf
1. 2.
cresc.
CORS
3. 4.
3°
p
mf
arco
cresc.
mf
cre - - scen - - do
mf
cre - - scen - - do
mf
arco
cre - - scen - - do
mf
Div.
p
arco
mf

42
Toujours en animant
1°
FL.
2° 3°
cresc.
HAUTB.
2°
COR ANGL.
CL.
Changez en Sib
1°
à 2
B^ONS
CORS
Toujours en animant
Div.
Unis

45
FL.
HAUTB.
COR ANGL.
CL.
8ons
CORS
mf
f
f très en dehors
f (en dehors)
3o (en dehors)
1o
più f
dim.
Div.

49
retenu
1er mouvt (M.M. ♩ = 60)
1o
FL.
2o 3o
HAUTB.
COR ANGL.
CL.
Solo
p doux et expressif
Bons
CORS
1re HARPE
2e HARPE
(en dehors)
retenu
Div.
1er mouvt
dim.
pizz.

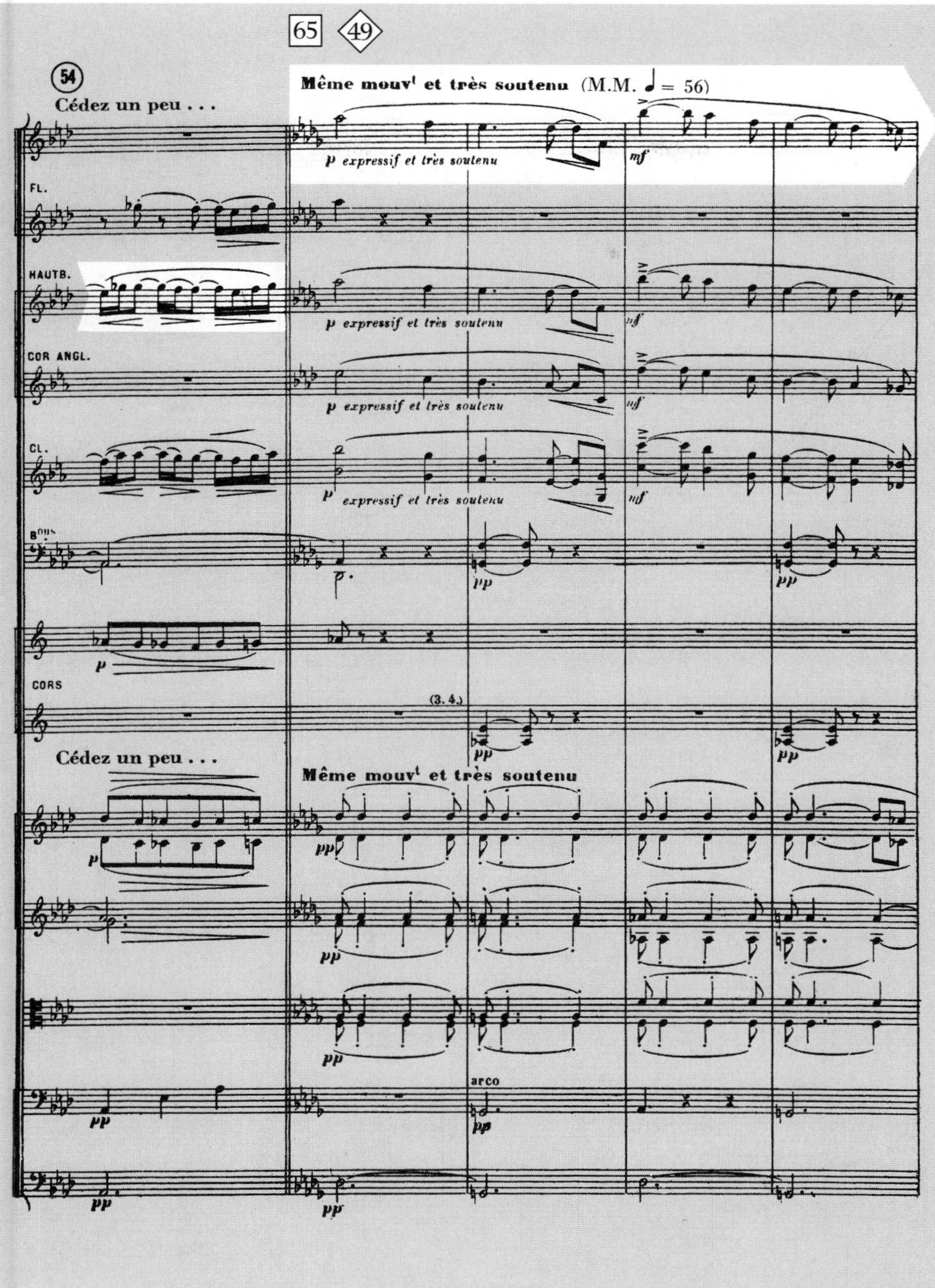
65
49
54
Cédez un peu . . .
Même mouvt et très soutenu (M.M. ♩ = 56)
p expressif et très soutenu
mf
FL.
HAUTB.
p expressif et très soutenu
mf
COR ANGL.
p expressif et très soutenu
mf
CL.
p expressif et très soutenu
mf
Bons
pp
pp
p
CORS
(3. 4.)
pp
pp
Cédez un peu . . .
Même mouvt et très soutenu
p
pp
pp
pp
arco
pp
pp
pp
pp

59
FL.
2° et 2°
HAUTB.
à 2
COR ANGL.
CL.
Bons
1°
1.2.
CORS
3.4.
4°
Unis
Div.
p
cre
scen
do
f
più f
mf
cresc
pp

63
En animant
pp subito
FL.
pp subito
HAUTB.
pp subito
COR ANGL.
pp subito
CL.
pp subito
Bons
pp
à 2
CORS
1re HARPE
pp
2e HARPE
pp
cre
En animant
Unis
très expressif et très soutenu
pp subito
pp subito
pp subito
pp subito
Div.
pp

66
Toujours animé
scen
do
cre
scen
do molto
FL.
HAUTB.
à 2
COR ANGL.
CL.
Bons
CORS
3o
4o
1re HARPE
2e HARPE
mp

69
FL.
HAUTB.
COR ANGL.
CL.
Bons
à 2
CORS
3o
1re HARPE
2e HARPE

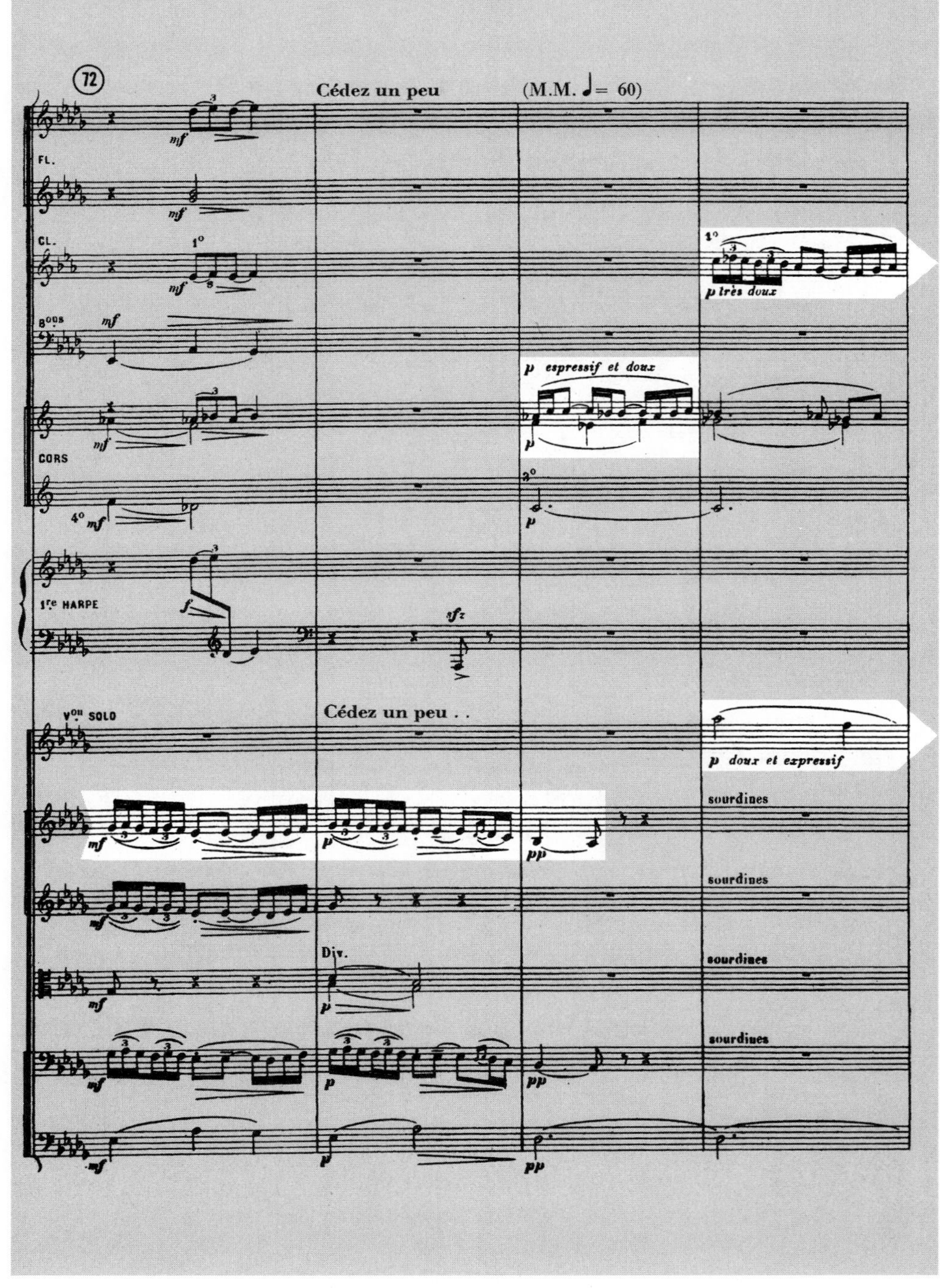
72
Cédez un peu
(M.M. ♩= 60)
Fl.
mf
Cl.
1°
mf
1°
p très doux
Bons
mf
p espressif et doux
p
Cors
4° mf
3°
p
1re Harpe
f
sfz
Von solo
Cédez un peu . .
p doux et expressif
mf
p
pp
sourdines
sourdines
Div.
p
sourdines
sourdines
pp

76
HAUTB.
1°
pp très doux
ppp
CL.
più p
pp
ppp
CORS
più p
Von SOLO
p
pp
66
50
79 (M.M. ♩= 84)
1re FL.
Mouvt du Début
doux et expressif
p
HAUTB.
CL.
CORS
1re HARPE
pp
Von SOLO
Mouvt du Début
(1rs Vns)
Div.
pp

82
1re FL.
Un peu plus animé
pp
HAUTB.
1o
p
sf
CL.
pp
Bons
pp
1. 2.
sourdines
pp
CORS
3. 4.
sourdines
3e
pp
1re HARPE
préparez le ton de Mib
Un peu plus animé
pizz.
pp

84
1
FL.
2, 3.
pp
HAUTB.
p
tr
sfz
pp
COR ANGL.
pp
CL.
p
pp
8ous
pp
1°
CORS
pp
sur la touche
arco
pizz
Div.
pp

86
HAUTB.
1er mouvt
doux et expressif
p
CORS
1re HARPE
pp
2e HARPE accordez sur SI#-DO♮, RÉ#-MI♭, FA#-SOL♭, LA#
1er mouvt
pos. nat.
pos. nat.
Div.
pos. nat.
Unis.
Div.
Div.

89
dans le mouvt plus animé
1.
FL.
2. 3.
p
1o
HAUTB.
3
p
COR ANGL.
p
sfz
CL.
Changez en La♮
pp
Bons
pp
pp
CORS
3o
pp
1re HARPE
2e HARPE
glissando
dans le mouvt plus animé
pizz.
pizz.
pizz.
pp
pizz.
pp

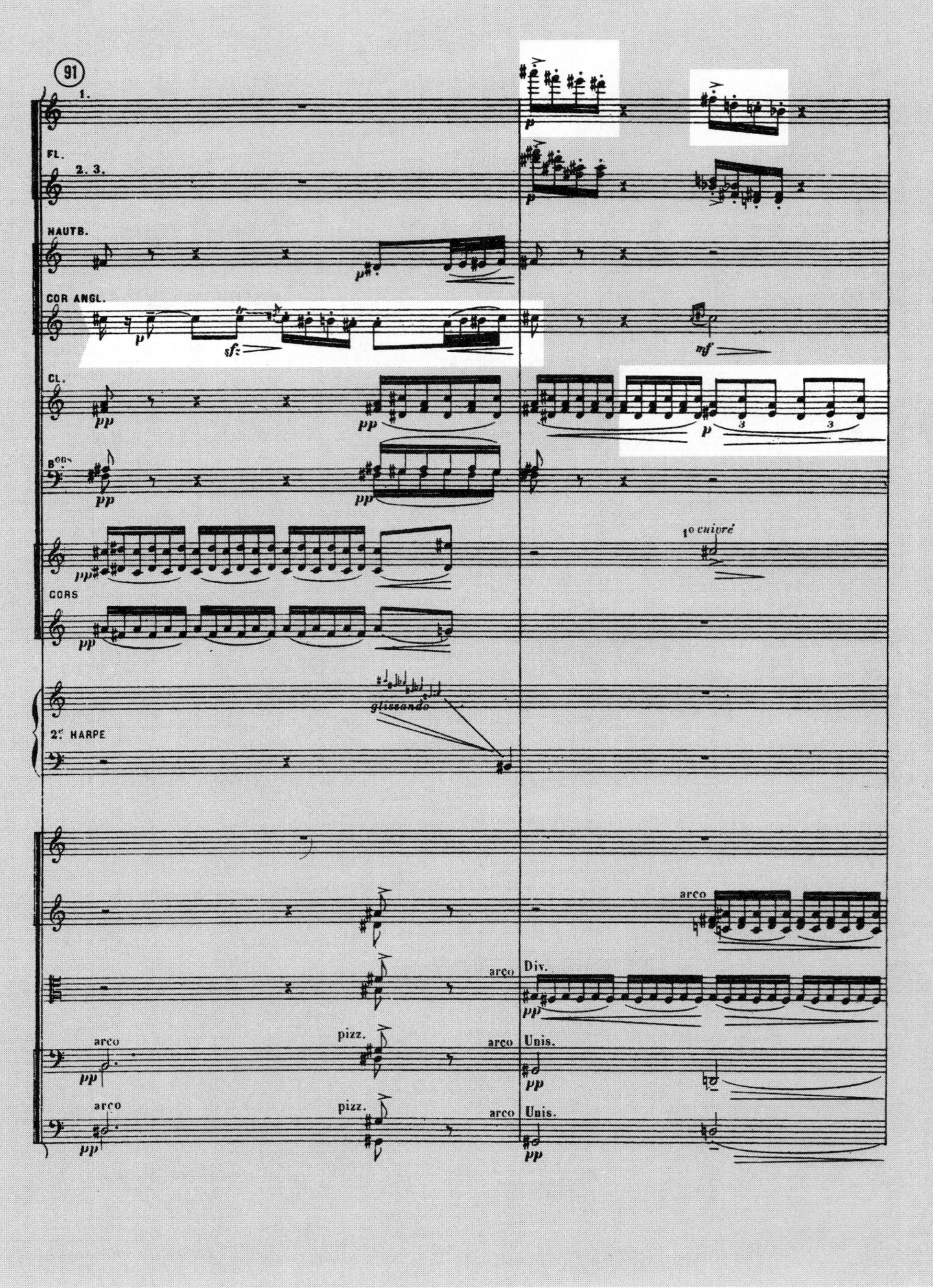
91
1.
FL.
2. 3.
HAUTB.
COR ANGL.
CL.
Bons
CORS
1o cuivré
glissando
2e HARPE
arco
Div.
Unis.
pizz.

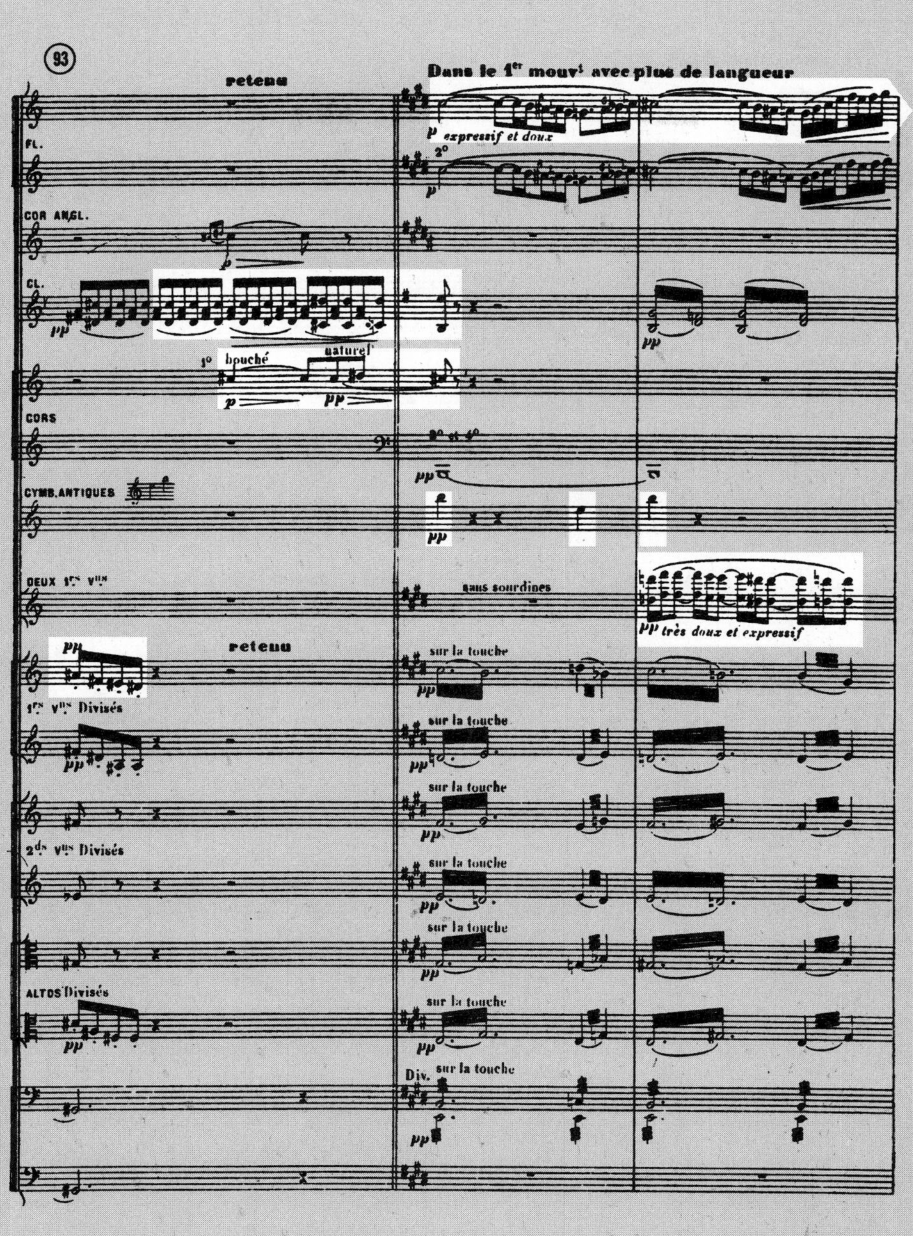
93
retenu
Dans le 1er mouv! avec plus de langueur
p expressif et doux
2o
FL.
COR ANGL.
CL.
1o bouché
naturel
CORS
2o et 4o
CYMB. ANTIQUES
DEUX 1rs Vns
sans sourdines
pp très doux et expressif
retenu
sur la touche
1rs Vns Divisés
2ds Vns Divisés
ALTOS Divisés
Div.

96
FL.
HAUTB.
CL.
Bons
CORS
1° sourdine
3° et 4°
CYMB. ANT.
1 Vlle SOLO
à 2

99
FL.
HAUTB.
CL.
B^ons
CORS
sourdine
2°
CYMB. ANT.
1re HARPE
pos. nat.
pos. nat.
pos. nat.
pos. nat.
pos. nat.
pos. nat.
expressif (un peu en dehors)
1 V^lle SOLO

102
Retenu
(a tempo)
Très retenu
1re Fl.
HAUTB.
1°
SOLO
COR ANGL.
CL.
Bons
2°
CORS
(sourdines)
Très retenu
Retenu
(a tempo)

106
Très lent et très retenu jusqu'à la fin
Fl.
2. 3.
Hautb.
1. 2. (sourdines)
Cors
3. 4. (sourdines)
Cymb. ant.
1res et 2es Harpes
1ère
Très lent et très retenu jusqu'à la fin
Unis
Div.
pizz.
pizz.

In the late nineteenth century, France was the principal center for modern arts. In painting, Monet created a new artistic vision in a movement called Impressionism. Capturing the interplay of light and objects, Impressionism broke with the long-standing Renaissance traditions of perspective. Similarly, French poets embraced a new literary style known as Symbolism, in which images and moods are suggested rather than described. Paralleling these developments, French composers explored innovative approaches to creating a musical work of art.

Claude Debussy (1862–1918) developed a distinctive musical style that is also known as Impressionism. Among the parallels to its artistic counterpart are Debussy's colorful, yet delicate timbres and the frequent vagueness of form, rhythmic pulse, melody, and harmony. The last of these is the most far-reaching innovation of the new style. Rejecting traditional functional harmony, Debussy explores new harmonic techniques, including whole-tone scales, parallel chords, ninth chords, and the establishment of tonal centers without relying on functional tonality.

The *Prélude à "L'après-midi d'un faune" (Prelude to "The Afternoon of a Faun")* is a seminal work in orchestral literature. Set as a single-movement symphonic poem, the composition was initially performed prior to a reading by Stéphane Mallarmé of his Symbolist poem "L'après-midi d'un faune." The poem describes a mythical faun (half man, half goat) who awakens from a dream. He struggles to recall a vague memory of an encounter with three nymphs, and is uncertain whether the event actually occurred or whether it was a dream. Fatigued by the process, the faun finally returns to sleep. The following excerpt is from the opening of the poem:

These nymphs I would perpetuate.
    So light
their gossamer embodiment, floating on the air
inert with heavy slumber.
    Was it a dream I loved?
My doubting harvest of the bygone night ends
in countless tiny branches; together remaining
a whole forest, they prove, alas, that since I am
    alone,
my fancied triumph was but the ideal
    imperfection of roses.
Let us reflect . . . or suppose those women that
    you idolize
were but imaginings of your fantastic lust!

Debussy brilliantly captures the moods of the poem in his prelude. The **A–B–A** form mirrors the arch structure that begins with the faun waking and ends with him returning to sleep. The delicate images are reflected in the subtle orchestrations, including an extended flute solo and a prominent harp part; the gentle rhythmic pulse; and the lack of tension that would normally result from functional tonality. The ardor of the faun can be heard in the extended melody from the middle section of the work. The movement comes to a quiet close, highlighted by the gentle sound of antique cymbals.

23. Amy Cheney Beach

8CD: 7/7–9

Violin Sonata in A minor, Second Movement (1896)

p
staccato
mf
1.
p
p
mf
p
Ped.
Ped.
Ped.
Ped.
Ped.

p
2.
p
sf p
p
p
p

cresc.
cresc.
Ped.
Ped.
Ped.
Ped.
Ped.

mf
poco rit.
a tempo
pp leggiero
mf
poco rit.
pp a tempo
Ped.
Ped.
Ped.
Ped.

cresc.
cresc.
Ped.
f
f
dim.
dim.
p
più dim.
più dim.
pp
pp
non legato senza cresc.

8
Più lento. (♩=96.)
sf
f
p
p legatissimo
Ped.
a tempo
rit.
pp
cresc.
p espressivo
mf
dim.
pp
espress.
sempre sul G
pp molto tranquillo
molto tranquillo
legatissimo
poco cresc.
dim.
Pedale sostenuto

sul D
dim.
pp
pp
sempre pp
sempre pp
Ped.
9
Tempo I.
accel.
accel.
p
cresc.
poco a poco cresc.

mf
rit.
a tempo
pp
mf
rit.
a tempo pp
scherzando
cresc.
cresc.
f
f
dim.
dim.
p
p

più dim.
pp
con delicatezza
Vivo.
leggierissimo
sempre pp
pp
f
rall.
ff

American society looked to Europe for cultural leadership in the nineteenth century. Appearances by composers and performing artists from across the ocean were seen as major events, and serious American-born musicians often traveled to Europe for instruction. By the end of the century, a number of individuals began to lay the foundation for the enormous growth of American music in the twentieth century. New England was a particularly strong center of activity, and one of the most prominent figures to emerge from this region was Amy Cheney Beach (1867–1944).

Beach was a child prodigy and contributed to the New England musical scene both as a concert pianist and as a composer. Encouraged by her husband, she completed a number of large-scale works, including a piano concerto, a Mass, and the *Gaelic* Symphony, all of which were performed by prestigious American ensembles. The concertmaster of the Boston Symphony Orchestra, Franz Kneisel, joined Amy Beach in the premiere of her Violin Sonata in A minor.

The sonata retains the four-movement structure found in some Beethoven sonatas and in the violin sonatas of Brahms, but the order of the inner movements is inverted. The second movement, cast in a traditional scherzo form, is in duple rather than the standard triple meter. Beach draws upon a rich harmonic palette, particularly in the trio, where the tranquil, lyrical mood provides an effective contrast to the lively and energetic scherzo sections that create a *perpetuum mobile* (perpetual motion) character.

Editor's note: The Norton recording, from a Joplin piano roll, features embellishments added by the composer.

f stacc.
12
25
1.
2.
f
p
r. h.
l.h.
l.h.
r. h.
mf
13
26

TRIO.
14
27
1.
2.
1.
2.

The son of a former slave, Scott Joplin (1868–1917) was the first prominent African-American composer. Although he posthumously received a Pulitzer prize for his opera *Treemonisha,* Joplin is primarily remembered for his piano rags. A gifted improviser and pianist who worked in St. Louis, Chicago, and New York, Joplin was the principal figure in the craze for ragtime. Characterized by lively syncopated melodies set against a steady left-hand accompaniment, these works flourished during the 1890s.

The pinnacle of popularity for ragtime was reached in 1899, when Joplin's *Maple Leaf Rag* sold over one million copies. The dance itself is sectional, similar to the popular waltzes of Johann Strauss, Jr. and the marches of John Philip Sousa. The dance contains four principal melodic sections, called strains. Each strain is sixteen measures in length, and each is repeated. The opening strain makes a brief reappearance after the second strain, creating the following formal pattern: **A–A–B–B–A–C–C–D–D.**

25. Arnold Schoenberg

Pierrot lunaire, Op. 21,
Nos. 18 and 21 (1912)

8CD: 7/[15]–[18]
4CD: 4/◇1–◇2

No. 18. *Der Mondfleck* (*The Moonfleck*)

[15] ◇1

Pic.
Kl. (B)
G.
Vcl.
mf quasi kadenzierend
quasi kadenzierend
f
pp
mf
sei_nes schwar - zen Rok - kes,
so spaziert Pier_
tr
sf

Pic.
Kl. (B)
G.
Vcl.
f
pp
sf
rot im lauen A_bend,
auf_zu_suchen Glück und A - ben_teu_er.
5

Pic.
Kl. (B)
G.
Vcl.
cresc.
Plötzlich stört ihn was an sei_nem An - zug, er be-
16
2
10
dim.
sieht sich rings und fin_det rich_tig- ei_nen wei_ßen Fleck

Pic.
Kl. (B)
G.
Vcl.
des hel_len Mon_ _des auf dem Rük_ken sei_nes schwarzen Rockes. War_te!
denkt er: das ist so ein Gips _ fleck! Wischt und wischt, doch

Pic.
Kl. (B)
G.
Vcl.
15
(ärgerlich)
bringt ihn nicht her- -un- ter!
(erregt)
Und so geht er
pp cresc.
sf
cresc.
gift- geschwollen wei- ter, reibt und reibt
bis an den frühen Morgen
(komisch bedeutsam)
ei- nen
hervor
fp
ff
pp
f

Text and Translation

Einen weissen Fleck des hellen Mondes
Auf dem Rücken seines schwarzen Rockes,
So spaziert Pierrot im lauen Abend,
Aufzusuchen Glück und Abenteuer.

With a fleck of white—from the bright moon—
on the back of his black jacket,
Pierrot strolls about in the mild evening
seeking his fortune and adventure.

Plötzlich stört ihn was an seinem Anzug,
Er besieht sich rings und findet richtig—

Suddenly something strikes him as wrong,
he checks his clothes and sure enough
finds

Einen weissen Fleck des hellen Mondes
Auf dem Rücken seines schwarzen Rockes.

a fleck of white—from the bright moon—
on the back of his black jacket.

Warte! denkt er: das ist so ein Gipsfleck!
Wischt und wischt, doch—bringt ihn nicht
herunter!
Und so geht er, giftgeschwollen, weiter,

Damn! he thinks: that's a spot of plaster!
Wipes and wipes, but—he can't get it
off.
And so goes on his way, his pleasure
poisoned,

Reibt und reibt bis an den frühen Morgen—
Einen weissen Fleck des hellen Mondes.

rubs and rubs till the early morning—
a fleck of white—from the bright moon.

- singer performs in quasi-speaking style - Sprechstimme

- each poem is a rondeau of 13 lines
- first line reoccurs in line 7 + 13
- explore new timbres

18
poco rit.
Tempo
rit.
Tempo
Fl.
Kl. (A)
nimmt Baß Klarinette in B
G.
nimmt Bratsche
Vcl.
sehr innig
Wünschen macht mich froh nach Freu - den, die ich lang ver - ach - tet. O
p espress.
Baß-Klarinette (B)
Bratsche.
p espress.
15
al - ter Duft aus Mär - chen - zeit, be - rau - schest wie - der mich. All meinen
ppp
Ped.

Fl.
B-Kl (B)
Br.
Vcl.
nimmt Piccolo
20
Un-mut geb ich preis; aus meinem sonnumrahm-ten Fenster beschau ich frei die lie-be Welt und
Piccolo.
rit.
Tempo
molto rit.
Dämpfer aufsetzen
mit Dämpfer
25
29
träum hin-aus in sel-ge Weiten... O al-ter Duft aus Mär-chen-zeit!

Text and Translation

O alter Duft aus Märchenzeit, *Berauschest wieder meine Sinne!* Ein närrisch Heer von Schelmerein Durchschwirrt die leichte Luft.	*O scent of fabled yesteryear,* *intoxicating my senses once again!* A foolish swarm of idle fancies pervades the gentle air.
Ein glückhaft Wünschen macht mich froh Nach Freuden, die ich lang verachtet: *O alter Duft aus Märchenzeit,* *Berauschest wieder mich!*	A happy desire makes me yearn for joys that I have long scorned: *O scent of fabled yesteryear,* *intoxicating me again.*
All meinen Unmut geb ich preis: Aus meinem sonnumrahmten Fenster Beschau ich frei die liebe Welt Und träum hinaus in selge Weiten . . . *O alter Duft aus Märchenzeit!*	All my ill humor is dispelled: from my sun-drenched window I look out freely on the lovely world and dream of beyond the horizon . . . *O scent of fabled yesteryear!*

Expressionism was a movement in literature, art, and music that sought to portray the dark side of the subconscious mind. The leading musical figure of this movement was Arnold Schoenberg (1874–1951), a Viennese composer who played a critical role in twentieth-century music as a composer, theorist, and teacher. The most important element of Schoenberg's Expressionistic style is his treatment of harmony, in which he pushes chromaticism, dissonance, and the lack of a tonal center (atonality) to new levels.

Schoenberg's early masterwork in Expressionism is the song cycle *Pierrot lunaire,* based on poems by the Belgian Symbolist poet Albert Giraud. Within these poems, the traditional clown figure of Pierrot is subject to nightmares and insanity, themes that are well suited for Expressionist settings. Each of the poems is a rondeau of thirteen lines, in which the first line recurs in lines 7 and 13, and the second line is repeated in line 8. The repetitive structure descends from the medieval rondeaux of Adam de la Halle and Guillaume de Machaut.

A critical element of Expressionism is the exploration of new timbres. Schoenberg creates a unique sound by setting the cycle for the accompaniment of a chamber group of eight instruments played by five performers: piccolo/flute, B-flat clarinet/bass clarinet, violin/viola, cello, and piano. Each of the twenty-one songs has a unique combination of instruments supporting the voice. In addition, Schoenberg treats the voice in a nontraditional manner. Rather than using a full singing voice, the singer is asked to perform in a quasi-speaking style, which Schoenberg termed *Sprechstimme.*

The two songs in this anthology typify the variety of individual treatments found in the cycle as a whole. Song No. 18, *Der Mondfleck (The Moonfleck),* is accompanied by the piccolo, B-flat clarinet, violin, cello, and piano. Pierrot, disturbed by a white spot on his collar (a patch of moonlight), frantically tries to rub it off. Supporting this image are scurrying musical lines that include a three-voice fugue and canons in diminution and retrograde. In the final song of the set, No. 21 *O alter Duft aus Märchenzeit (O Scent of Fabled Yesteryear),* Schoenberg employs all eight musical instruments. The reflective mood of Pierrot is supported by a more serene musical setting. As Pierrot thinks of old times, the harmony incorporates more thirds and hints of traditional sounds.

26. Charles Ives

8CD: 7/ 19 – 20

The Things Our Fathers Loved (1917)

11
faster and with more emphasis
in a gradually excited way
vil-lage cor-net band, play - ing in the square. The town's Red,White and Blue,
cresc.
14
ff
all Red,White and Blue Now! Hear the
più accel.
l.h.
ff
ff
16
songs! I know not what are the
l.h.
18
poco rall.
words But they sing in my
r.h.
l.h.
rit.

The New England composer Charles Ives (1874–1954) quietly created some of the most remarkable works in the history of American music. Staunchly nationalistic, Ives repeatedly drew inspiration from American events, transcendental ideas, and well-known popular, patriotic, and religious melodies. Today, he is recognized as a pioneer of the avant-garde, as many of his works anticipate future developments in American music.

Ives was a prolific composer of songs, writing over 150 works. *The Things Our Fathers Loved* (1917) typifies both his American spirit and innovative musical style. The text, written by Ives, is a nostalgic look at the American past through the melodies that linger in his memory. The vocal line is a pastiche of American tunes: *Dixie, My Old Kentucky Home, Nettleton, The Battle Cry of Freedom,* and *Sweet By-and-By.* Generally, the melodies are reshaped, but enough remains of the originals to be recognized. The piano accompaniment, which is separated from the vocal line both melodically and harmonically, creates a strong dissonant background.

27. Maurice Ravel

8CD: 7/ 21 – 26

Rapsodie espagnole (Spanish Rhapsody), Fourth Movement, *Feria* (1907–8)

21

Assez animé ♩. = 76

1°

pp

2 PETITES FLÛTES

2 GRANDES FLÛTES

1° Solo

pp

2 HAUTBOIS

1 COR ANGLAIS

2 CLARINETTES en SI♭

1 CLARINETTE BASSE en SI♭

3 BASSONS

1 SARRUSOPHONE

4 CORS (Chromatiques) en FA

3 TROMPETTES en UT

1er et 2e TROMBONES

3e TROMBONE et TUBA

4 TIMBALES FA♯, SOL, SI♭, DO

TAMBOUR DE BASQUE CASTAGNETTES

TRIANGLE, TAMBOUR

CYMBALES, GROSSE-CAISSE

TAM-TAM

XYLOPHONE

CÉLESTA

1re HARPE

2de HARPE

pp

Div. Assez animé ♩. = 76

Sourdines

ppp

VIOLONS

ALTOS

VIOLONCELLES

CONTREBASSES

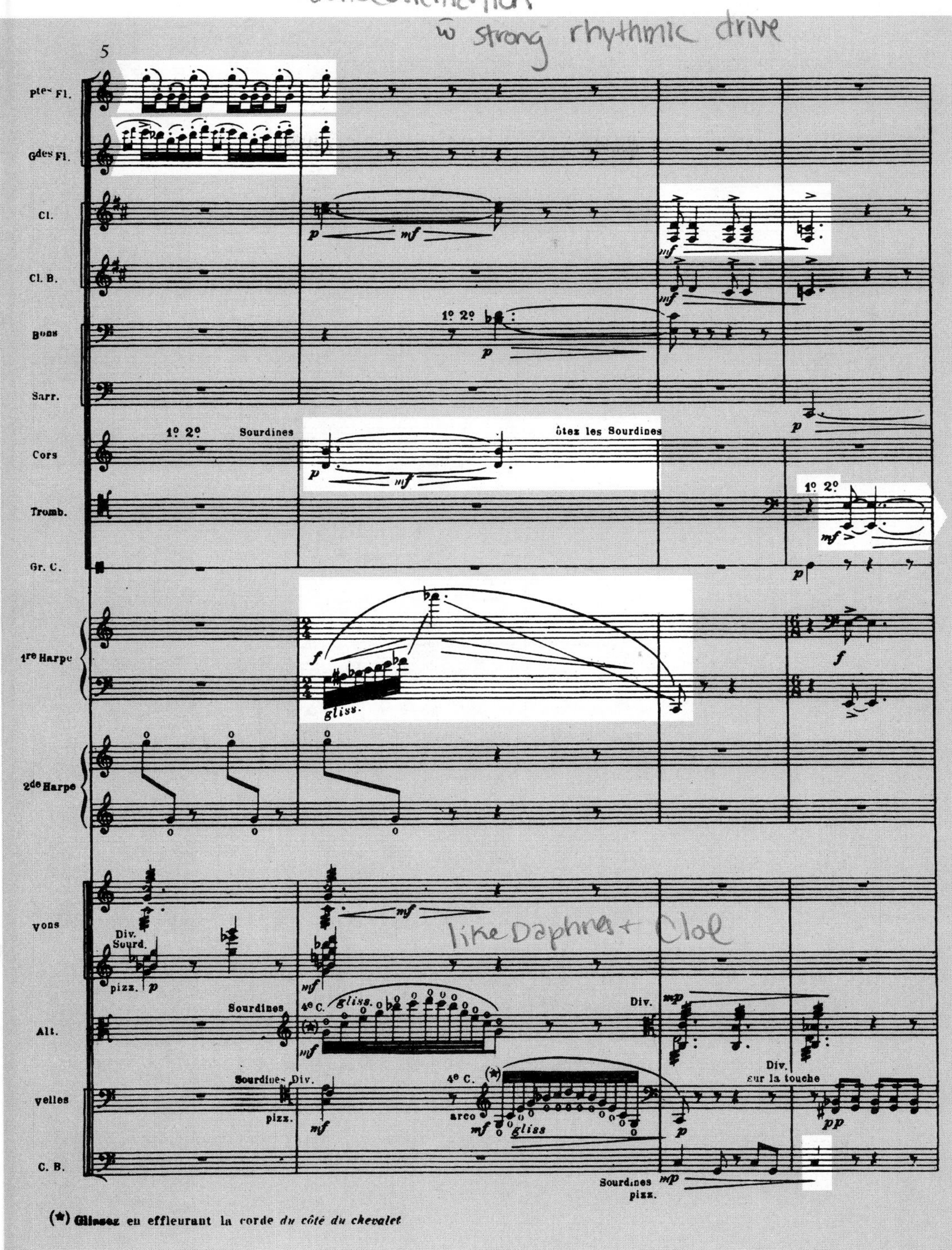

(*) Glissez en effleurant la corde *du côté du chevalet*

9
Bons
Sarr.
Cors
Tromb.
Timb.
1re Harpe
2de Harpe
Vons
Alt.
Vcelles
C. B.
mf
mf
mf
mf
ppp
mp
f
pp
f
Unis.
pizz.
f
Unis.
pizz.
f
mf
sur la touche
Div.
arco
ppp
mf

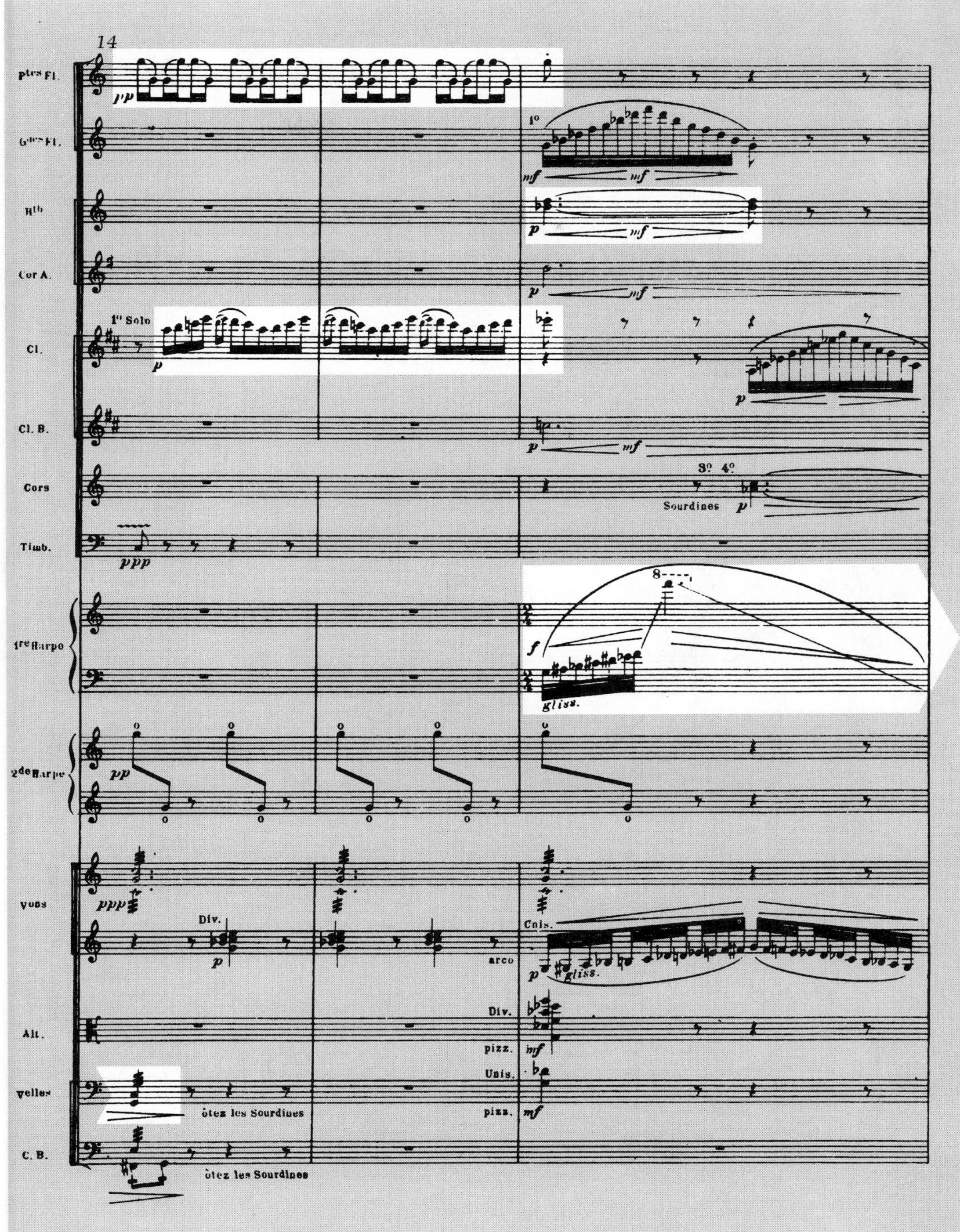
14
Ptes Fl.
Gdes Fl.
Htb
Cor A.
Cl.
Cl. B.
Cors
Timb.
1re Harpe
2de Harpe
Vons
Alt.
Velles
C. B.
pp
1º
mf
mf
p
mf
1º Solo
p
3º 4º
Sourdines
ppp
f
gliss.
pppp
Div.
Cnls.
arco
gliss.
Div.
pizz.
Unis.
pizz.
ôtez les Sourdines
ôtez les Sourdines

17
Cl.
Cl. B.
Bons
1. 2.
mf
p
Sarr.
p
Cors
mf
mettez les Sourdines
1r Solo
Tromb.
mf
Timb.
ppp
Gr. C.
p
1re Harpe
f
2de Harpe
pp
8a bassa
Vons
mp
arco
Alt.
mp
ôtez les Sourdines
Div. arco
Vcelles
mp
sur la touche
ppp
pizz.
C. B.
mp
sur la touche
ppp
arco

22
ptes Fl.
Gdes Fl.
Htb
Cl.
Cl. B.
Bons
Sarr.
Cors
Sourdines
ôtes les Sourdines
Tromb et Tuba
Timb.
1re Harpe
2de Harpe
Vons
gliss.
Alt.
Vcelles
C. B.

22
25
Htb.
Cor A.
Bons
Sarr.
Sourdines
Tromp.
Timb.
T. de B.
Xyloph.
1re Harpe
2de Harpe
ôtez les Sourdines
Vons
ôtez les Sourdines
Unis.
Div.
Alt.
pizz.
pizz.
velles
Unis. toujours sur la touche
B.

29
ptes Fl.
Gdes Fl.
Htb.
Cor A.
Cl.
Bons
Sarr.
Cors
Tromp.
Tromb.
Timb.
T. de B.
Cymb.
Xyloph.
Celesta
1re Harpe
Vons
Alt.
Vlles
C. B.
1o Solo
Sourdines
Unis.
pizz.
Div.
arco
jeu ordinaire
Ped.

32
Gdes Fl.
1° Solo
p en dehors
Cor A.
Solo
p en dehors
Cl.
mf
pp
Bons
Sarr.
Bouché
1° Solo
mf en dehors
mettez les Sourdines
Cors
Sons naturels
3°
ppp
Tromp
ôtez la Sourdine
Tromb. et Tuba
pp
Trg.
ppp
Tamb.
pp
1re Harpe
Vons
Div. arco
mf
sur la touche
ppp
Alt.
Div.
Unis.
p
Vcelles
pp
pizz.
C. B.
pp
pizz.

35
Ptes Fl.
Gdes Fl.
Htb
Cor A.
Cl.
Bons
Sarr.
Cors
Tromp.
Timb.
T. de B.
Trg.
1re Harpe
Vons
Alt.
Velles
C. B.
1o
à 2
Sourdines
1o 2o
ôtez les Sourdines
Div. à 3
pos. nat.
arco
ppp subit.

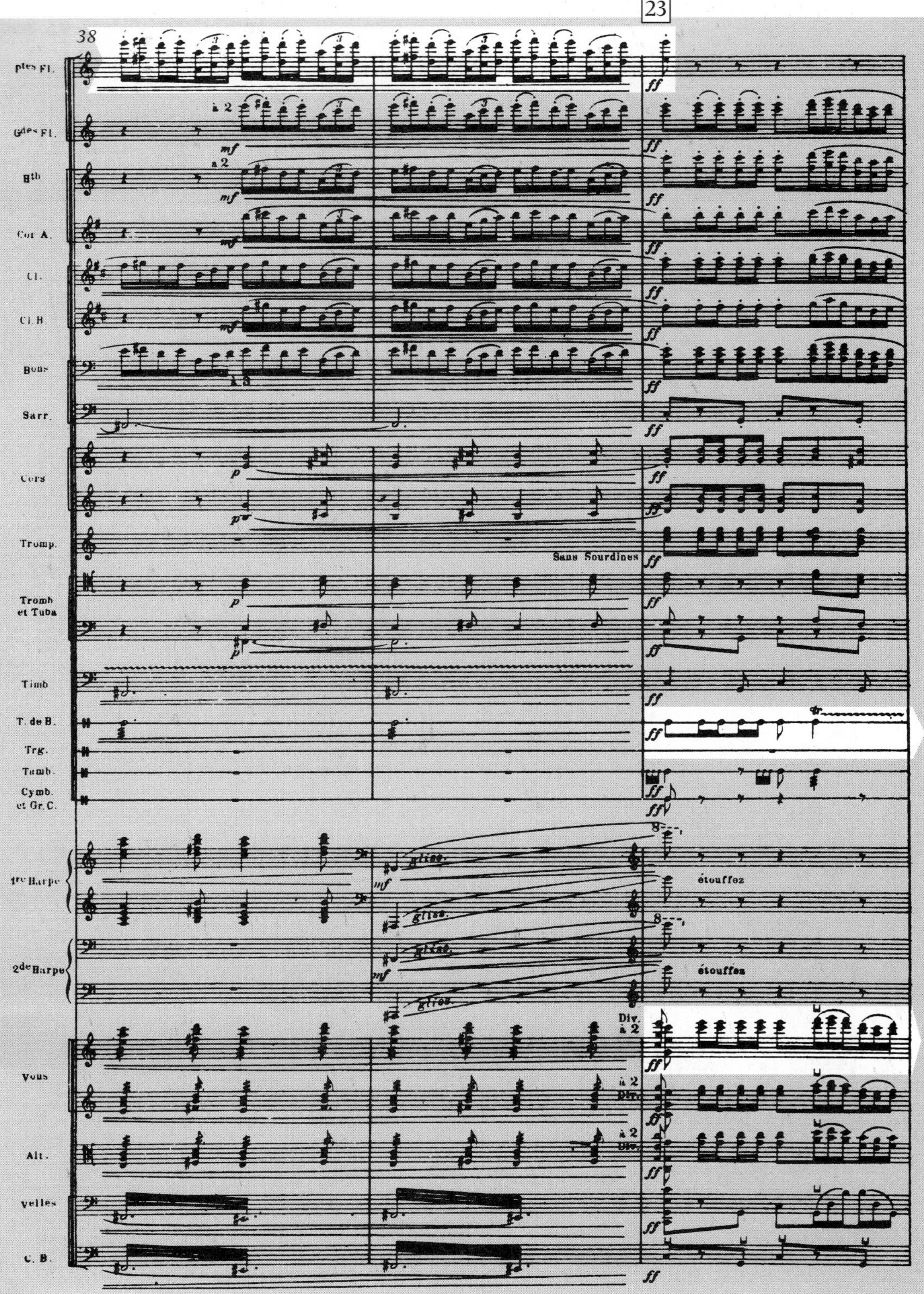

23
38
ptes Fl.
Gdes Fl.
Htb
Cor A.
Cl.
Cl. B.
Bons
Sarr.
Cors
Tromp.
Sans Sourdines
Tromb et Tuba
Timb
T. de B.
Trg.
Tamb.
Cymb. et Gr. C.
1re Harpe
gliss.
étouffez
2de Harpe
Div. à 2
Vons
Alt.
velles
C. B.

41
ptes Fl.
Gdes Fl.
Htb
Cor A.
Cl.
Cl. B.
Bons
Sarr.
Cors
Tromp.
Tromb. et Tuba
Timb.
T. de B
Cast
Tamb.
Cymb. et Gr. C.
Xyloph.
Vons
Alt
Velles
C. B.
1º 2º
pizz.
Unis.
Div.
gliss.

45
ptes Fl.
Gdes Fl.
Hb
Cor A.
Cl
Bons
Sarr.
Cors
Tromp.
1o 2o.
Tromb. et Tuba
3o
Timb.
T. de B.
Cast
Trg.
Tamb.
Cymb.
Xyloph
gliss.
Célesta
sans Ped.
gliss.
1re Harpe
vons
Div. à 3 arco
Div. à 2
pizz.
Unis.
Alt.
arco
Div.
vcelles
Div. arco
C. B.

49
ptes Fl
Gdes Fl
1° Solo
Htb
Cor A.
Cl.
Bons
Sarr.
Cors
Tromp.
Tromb. et Tuba
Timb.
T. de B.
Trg.
Tamb.
Cymb.
Célesta
gliss.
1re Harpe
Vons
Div. à 3.
arco
pizz.
Unis.
Div.
Alt.
Div. à 2
Vclles
C. B.

53
Gdes Fl.
Htb
Bons
Sourdine
1o Solo
Tromp.
Timb
1re Harpe
2de Harpe
Vons
Alt.
Velles
C B.
Div.
Unis.
1o
p
8

57
Ptes Fl.
Gdes Fl
Htb
Cor A.
Cl.
Bons
Cors
Tromp
Tromb et Tuba
Timb.
T. de B
Trg.
Tamb
Cymb.
1re Harpe
2de Harpe
Vons
Alt.
Velles
C. B.
sans Sourdines
Div.
sempre pizz.

61
ptes Fl.
Gdes Fl.
Htb
Cor A
Cl.
Cl. B.
Bons
Sarr.
Cors
Tromp
Tromb. et Tuba
Timb.
T de B.
Cast.
Trg.
Tamb.
Cymb.
Gr. C.
Vons
Alt
velles
C. B.
simili
Div. arco
arco
Div. arco
pizz.
Unis. pizz.

64
à 2
Ptes Fl.
Gdes Fl.
Htb
Cor A.
Cl.
Cl. B.
à 2
Bons
2e 3e
Sarr.
Cors
Tromp.
Tromb. et Tuba
Timb.
T. de B.
Cast.
Tamb.
Cymb.
Gr. C.
gliss.
1re Harpe
Div.
Vons
Div.
Alt.
arco
Unis.
pizz.
Div.
arco
Vcelles
Div.
arco
Unis.
pizz.
arco
C. B.
arco

67
Ptes Fl.
Gdes Fl.
Htb
Cor A.
Cl.
Cl. B.
Bons
Sarr.
Cors
Tromp.
Tromb. et Tuba
Timb.
T. de B.
Cast.
Trg.
Tamb.
Cymb.
Gr. C.
Vons
Alt.
Velles
C. B.
à 2
à 3
f
ff
fff

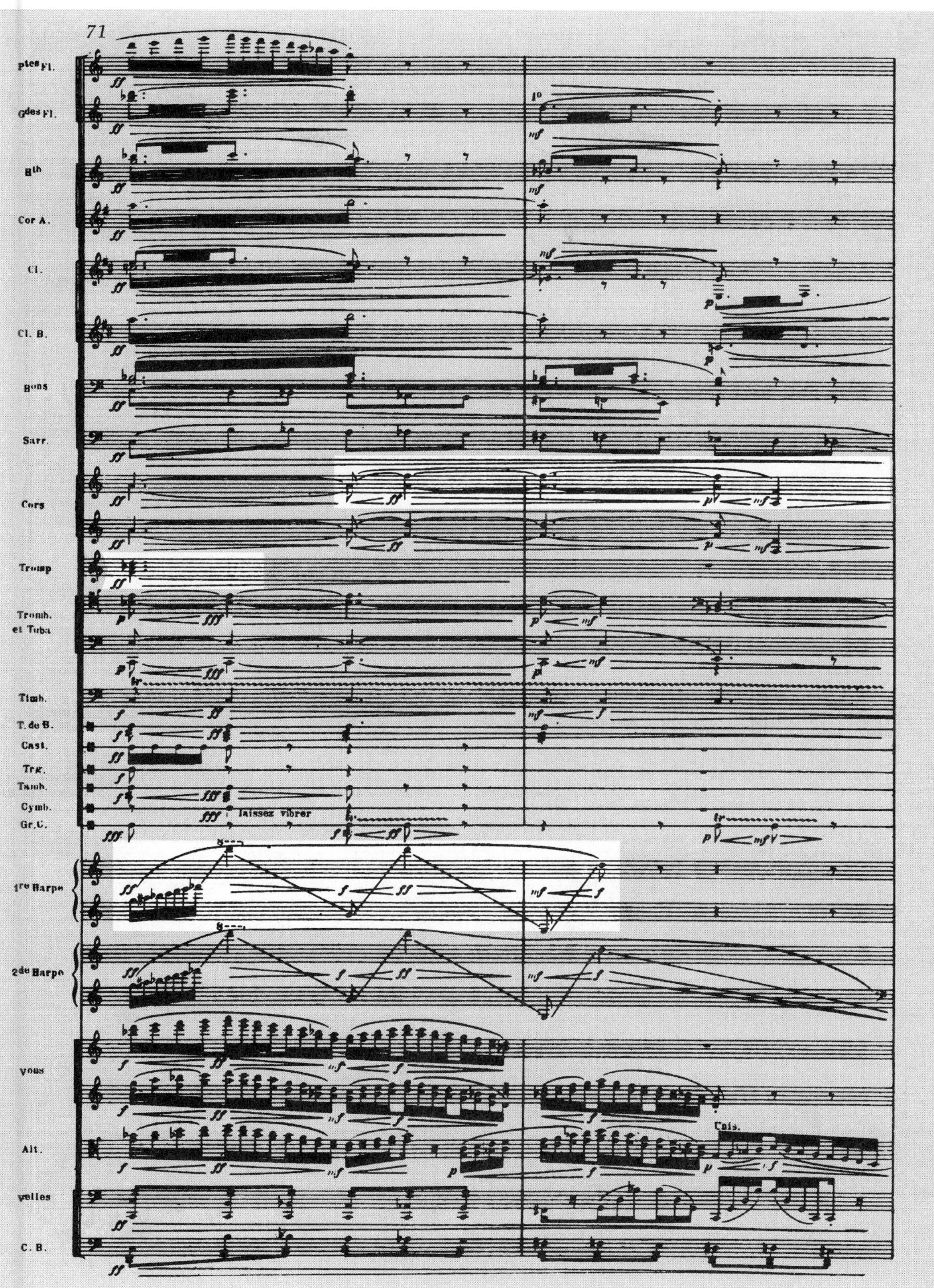
71
ptes Fl.
Gdes Fl.
Htb
Cor A.
Cl.
Cl. B.
Bons
Sarr.
Cors
Tromp
Tromb. et Tuba
Timb.
T. de B.
Cast.
Trg.
Tamb.
Cymb.
Gr. C.
laissez vibrer
1re Harpe
2de Harpe
Vons
Alt.
Velles
C. B.
Unis.

Eng. Horn Solo
73
24
Ralentissez beaucoup
Très modéré ♩= 80
Cor A.
Cl.
Cl. B.
Changez en La
Bons
Sarr.
Cors
Sourdines
Tromb
Timb.
Gr. C.
1re Harpe
2de Harpe
Vons
Alt.
2 Velles Soli
Div.
sur la touche
2e sur le Ré
gliss.
p en dehors
Velles
Unis
pizz.
1re C.B. Solo
2e et 3e C.B. Soli
C.B.
en se perdant

79
Cor A.
très expressif
Cl.
Cl.B.
Bons
1°. 2°
Cors
2de Harpe
Suivez le Solo
Vons
2 Alt. Soli
Div.
sur le Sol
sur l'Ut
gliss.
Alt.
2 velles Soli
Sourdines
velles
arco
Sourdines
1re C.B. Solo
2e et 3e C.B. Soli
C B.

85
Un peu retenu
au Mouvt
Ral.
Gdes F
Htb
Cor A.
Cl.
Cl B.
Bons
Sarr.
Cors
sans Sourdines
mettez les Sourdines
son naturel
Sourdines
Tromp.
1re Harpe
2de Harpe
Ut ♮
Ré ♮
2 Soli Div.
gliss.
4e C.
Tutti Unis
pizz.
sur la touche
Div.
arco
port.
Vons
Alt.
Unis
Velles
1re C.B.Solo
2e et 3e C.B. Soli
C.B.

91
au Mouvt
Ral.
au Mouvt
Ral.
au Mouvt
Gdes Fl.
Htb
Cl.
2o
1o Solo
mf
Cl. B.
p
Bons
Cors
Harpes
Unis
pizz.
Div.
arco
ppp
port.
vons
gliss.
Alt.
velles
C. B.
arco
pizz.

96
Ral.
au Mouvt
Ral.
au Mouvt
Gdes Fl.
Htb
Cor A.
Cl.
Cl. B.
Bons
Sarr.
Cors
ôtez les Sourdines
Tromp
Sourdines
Tromb.
Trg.
Célesta
1re Harpe
très rapide
presque en accord
gliss.
2de Harpe
Div.
arco
Unis
pizz.
ôtez les Sourdines
Vons
Alt.
Velles
C. B.
arco
pizz.
gliss.

102
25
Un peu plus animé
Gdes Fl.
Htb
Cor A.
Cl.
Cl. B.
Bons
Cors
Tromp.
2e Harpe
1ers vons
4 2ds vons Soli
2ds vons
Alt.
velles
C.B.
à 2
1º.2º Soli
Sourdines
aussi pp que possible
Div. arco
mf expressif
sur la touche
glissando
Div. pizz.
arco
pizz.
ôtez les Sourdines

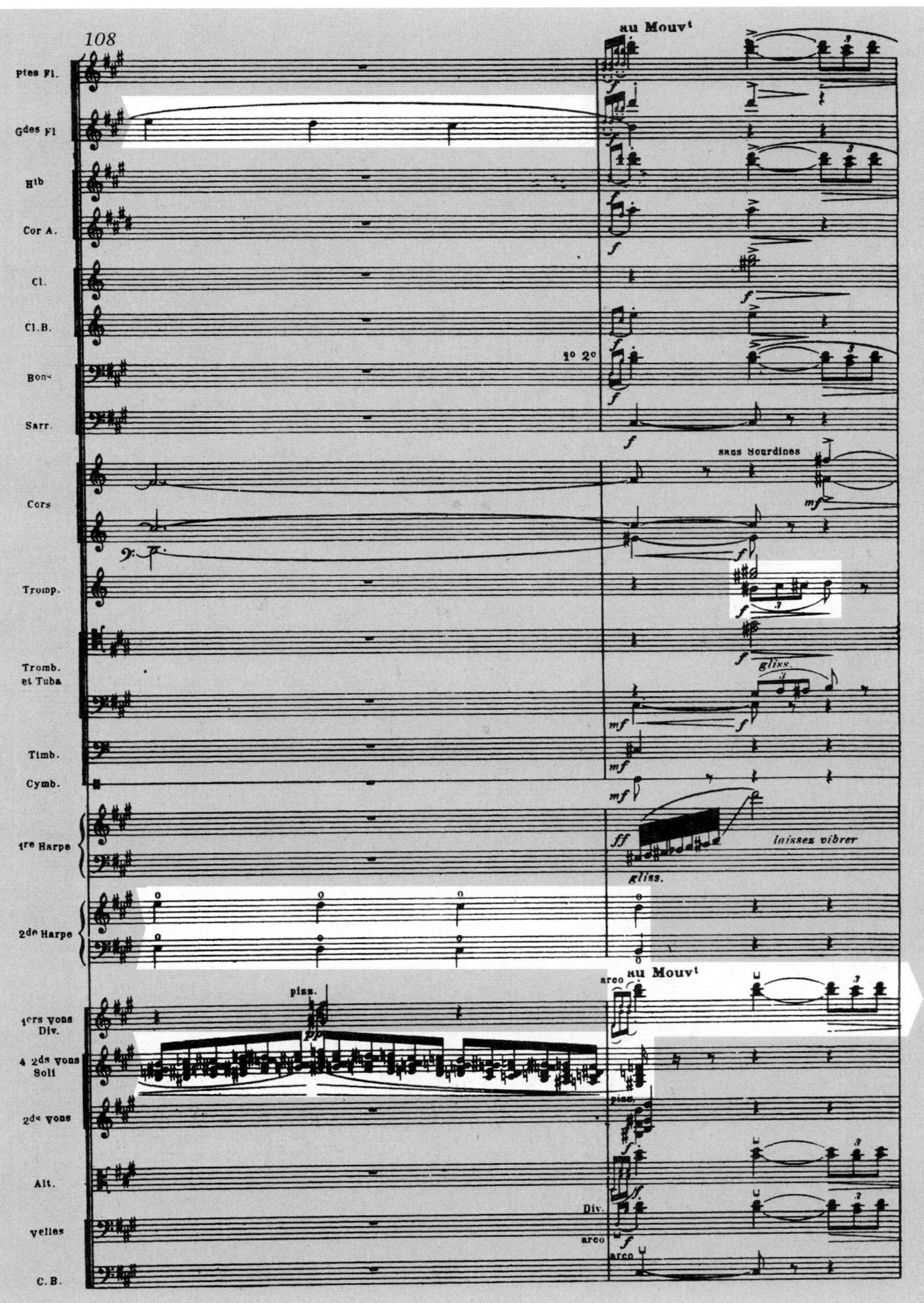
108
au Mouvt
Ptes Fl.
Gdes Fl
Htb
Cor A.
Cl.
Cl.B.
1o 2o
Bons
Sarr.
sans Sourdines
Cors
Tromp.
Tromb. et Tuba
gliss.
Timb.
Cymb.
1re Harpe
laissez vibrer
gliss.
2de Harpe
au Mouvt
arco
pizz.
1ers vons Div.
4 2ds vons Soli
2ds vons
pizz.
Alt.
Div.
arco
vcelles
arco
C.B.

110
Un peu plus animé
Ptes Fl.
Gdes Fl.
Htb
Cor A.
Cl.
Cl. B.
changez en Si ♭
Bons
Sarr.
mettez les Sourdines
Cors
sans Sourdines
Sourdines
Tromp.
Sourdines
Tromb. et Tuba
Tuba
Célesta
Un peu plus animé
1 1er von Solo
Sourdine
1ers vons
pizz.
2ds vons
Div.
gliss.
Unis
Div. à 4
1 Alt. Solo
Sourd.
Alt.
4 Alt. Soli arco
Sourdines
1 Velle Solo
Sourdine
Velles
C.B.
pizz.
arco

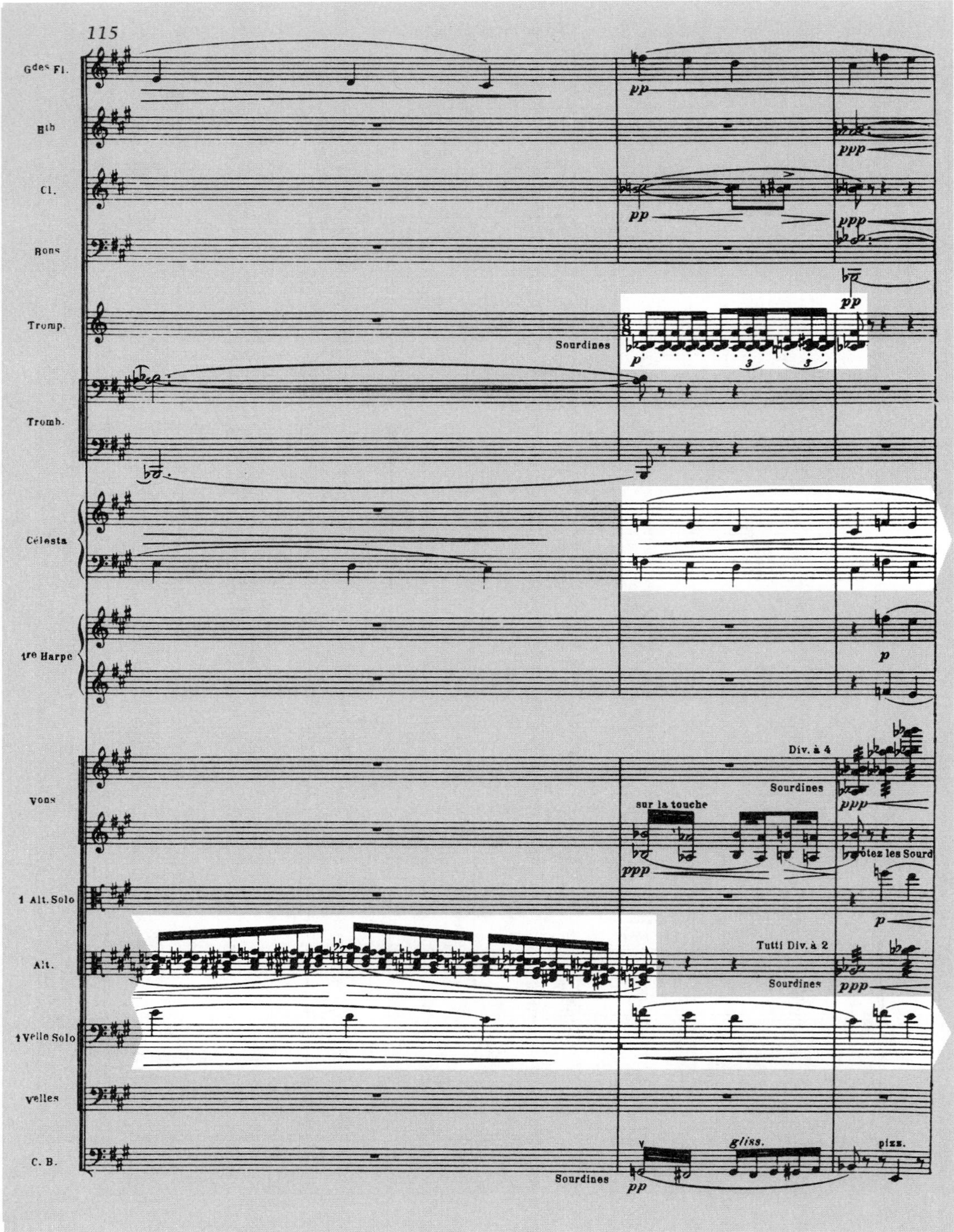
115
Gdes Fl.
Bth
Cl.
Bons
Tromp.
Sourdines
Tromb.
Célesta
1re Harpe
Vons
Div. à 4
Sourdines
sur la touche
ôtez les Sourd
1 Alt. Solo
Alt.
Tutti Div. à 2
Sourdines
1 Velle Solo
Velles
C. B.
gliss.
pizz.
Sourdines

118
Ptes Fl.
Gdes Fl.
Hth
Cl.
Bons
Cors
Sourd.
Célesta
1re Harpe
1 1er von Solo
1ers vons Div. à 4
ôtez les Sourdines
2ds vons
1 Alt. Solo
Alt.
ôtez les Sourdines
4 velles Soli
gliss.
1 velle Solo
Sourdines
velles
Sourdines
C. B.
ôtez les Sourdines

120
26
(Mouvt du début)
1o Solo
Gdes Fl.
Htb
Cl.
Bons
Sarr.
bouché
Cors
Sourdines
4o
Tromb.
1o
Sourdine
Timb.
Célesta
1re Harpe
1 1er von Solo
ôtez la Sourdine
1ers vons
2ds vons
sur la touche
sans Sourdines
1 Alt. Solo
Alt.
Div.
pizz
Velles Soli
Tutti
pizz.
ôtez les Sourdines
Div. arco
Velles
Div à 2
2 C.B.Soli
gliss.
Sourdines
C.B.
sans Sourdines

125
Pᵗᵉˢ Fl.
Gᵈᵉˢ Fl.
Hᵗᵇ
Cl.
Cl. B.
Bons
Cors
Sourdines
Sourdines
Tromp.
1º. 2º
Sourd.
Tromb
ôtez la Sourdine
Trg.
1ʳᵉ Harpe
gliss.
1º Solo
2º
1ᵉʳˢ Vons Div.
pizz.
Div. arco
Unis pizz.
2ᵈˢ Vons Div.
Div. arco
Div.
avec le dos de l'archet
Alt. Div
arco
Velles Div.
Div. à 2
C.B.

129
Ptes Fl.
Gdes Fl.
Htb
Cor A.
Cl.
Cl.B.
Bons
Sarr.
Cors
Tromp.
Tromb. et Tuba
Timb.
T. de B.
Tamb.
Cymb.
1re Harpe
1ers Vons
2ds Vons
Alt.
Vlles
C.B.
sans Sourdines
jeu ordinaire
pp subito
pizz.
arco
Unis

133
Ptes Fl.
Gdes Fl.
Htb
Cor A.
Cl.
Cl.B.
Bons
Sarr.
Cors
Tromp.
Tromb. et Tuba
Timb.
T.de B.
Cast.
Trg.
Tamb.
Cymb.
1re Harpe
Vons
Alt.
Velles
C.B.
mf gliss.
Div. à 2
pizz.
1° 2°

136
Ptes Fl.
Gdes Fl.
Cl.
1º Solo
p
Cors
pp
pp
Tromp.
Cast.
Trg.
Tamb.
ppp
Cymb.
Célesta
p
1re Harpe
2de Harpe
pp
Vons
Unis
arco
pizz.
pp
Alt.
arco
Div.
Vlles
arco
pizz.
pp
C.B.
pp

139
Gdes Fl.
Cor A.
Cl.
Bons
1° Solo
2°
Cors
Tamb
Célesta
1re Harpe
2de Harpe
Vons
Div.
arco
pizz.
Unis
Alt.
pizz.
Velles
C.B.

143
Ptes Fl.
Gdes Fl.
Htb
Cor A.
Cl.
Cl. B.
Bons
Sarr.
Cors
T. de B.
Tamb.
1re Harpe
2de Harpe
Vons
Alt.
Vclles
C. B.
arco gliss.
Div. arco

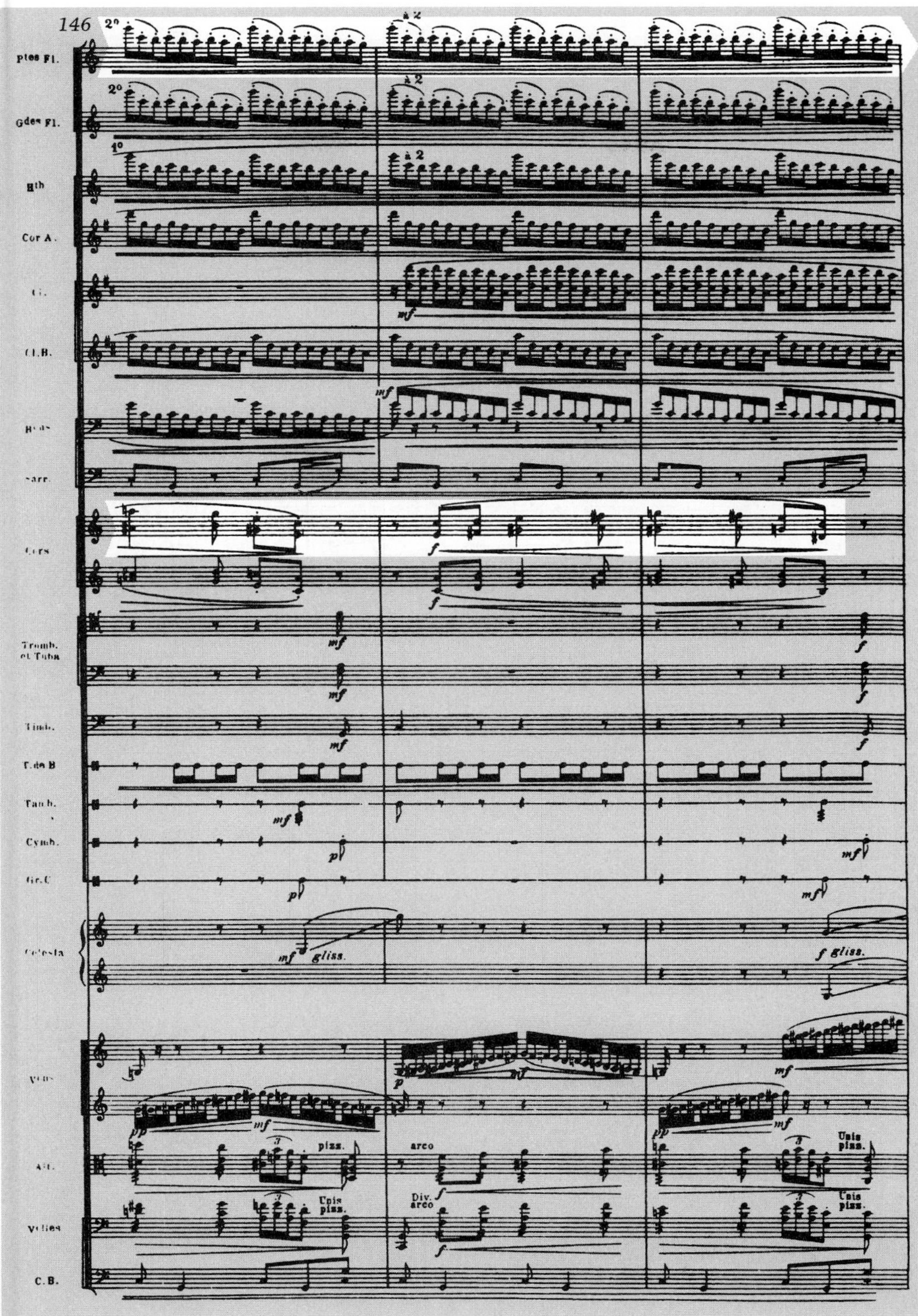
146
Ptes Fl.
Gdes Fl.
Hth
Cor A.
Cl.
Cl.B.
Bons
Sarr.
Cors
Tromb. et Tuba
Timb.
T. de B
Tamb.
Cymb.
Gr.C
Celesta
Vons
Alt.
Vlles
C.B.
à 2
mf
f
p
gliss.
pizz.
arco
Div. arco
Unis pizz.

149
p^{tes} Fl.
G^{des} Fl.
Htb
Cor A.
Cl.
Cl. B.
B^{ons}
Sarr.
Cors
Tromp.
Tromb. et Tuba
Timb.
T. de B.
Cast.
Trg.
Tamb.
Cymb.
Gr. C.
Celesta
Harpes
V^{ons}
Alt.
V^{elles}
C. B.
à 2
laissez vibrer
gliss.
Div.
pizz.
arco
Unis.

152
ptes Fl.
Gdes Fl.
Htb
Cor A.
Cl.
Cl. B.
Bons
Sarr.
Cors
Tromp.
Tromb et Tuba
Timb.
T. de B.
Cast
Tamb.
Cymb.
Gr. C.
Harpes
Vons
Alt.
Velles
C. B.
à 2
pizz.
arco
Unis. arco
Div.

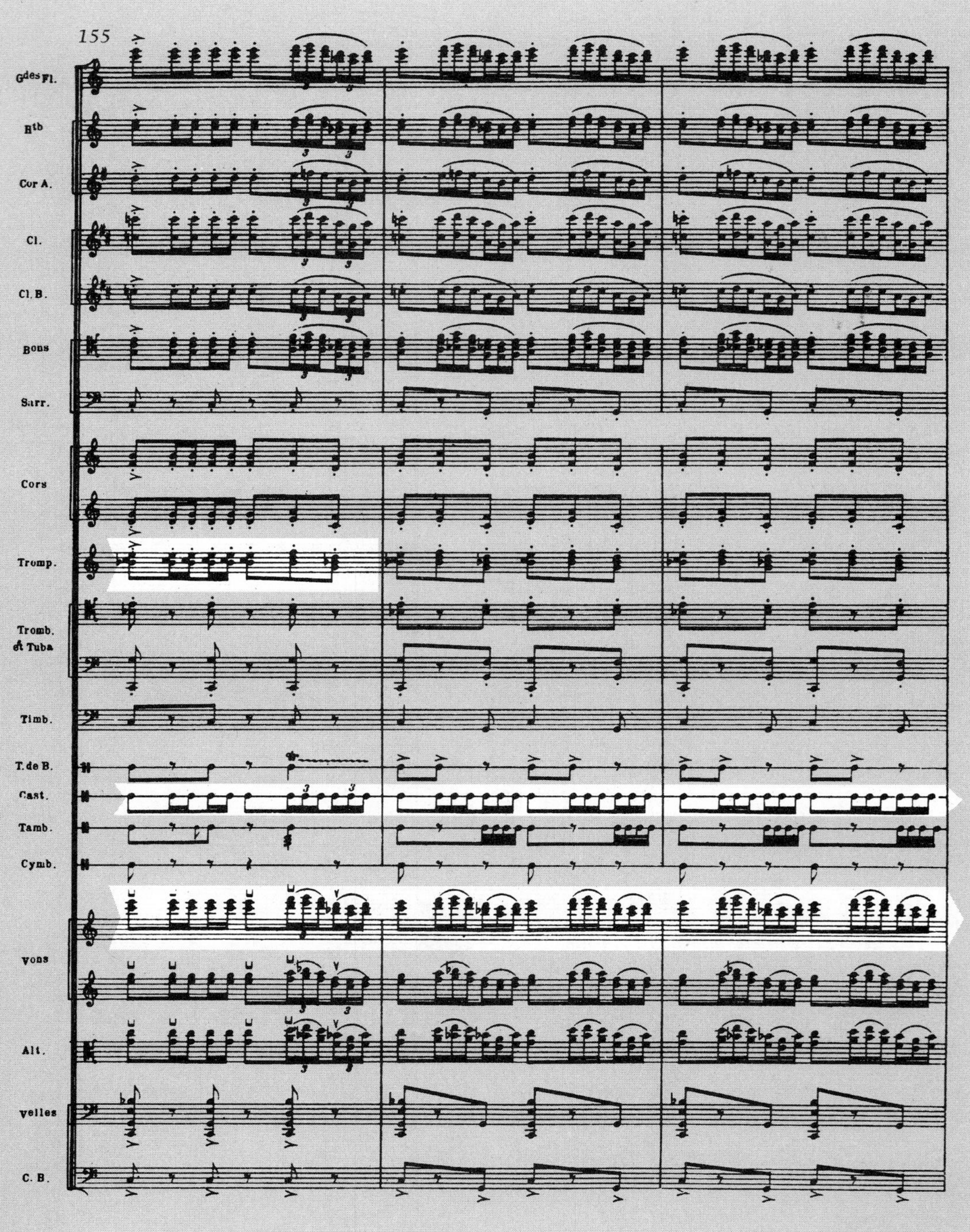
155
Gdes Fl.
Htb
Cor A.
Cl.
Cl. B.
Bons
Sarr.
Cors
Tromp.
Tromb. et Tuba
Timb.
T. de B.
Cast.
Tamb.
Cymb.
vons
Alt.
velles
C. B.

158
Un peu retenu
ptes Fl.
Gdes Fl.
Hb.
Cor A.
Cl.
Cl. B.
Bons
Sarr.
Cors
Tromp.
Tromb. et Tuba
Timb.
T. de B.
Cast.
Tamb.
Cymb.
Gr. C.
laissez vibrer
Harpes
gliss.
Un peu retenu
Vons
Alt.
Velles
C. B.

161
Plus animé
ptes Fl.
Gdes Fl.
Htb
Cor A
Cl.
Cl. B.
Bons
Sarr.
Cors
Tromp.
Tromb. et Tuba
Timb.
T de B.
Gr. C.
1re Harpe
Vons
Alt.
Velles
C. B.
1° espress.
mp
espress.
ppp
avec une baguette de Timbale
pp
Unis.
sur la touche
Unis.
Div.
port.
espress.
arco
pizz.
p

166
ptes Fl.
Gdes Fl.
Hth
Cor A.
Cl.
Cl. B
Bons
Cors
Tromp.
Timb.
Gr. C.
1re Harpe
2de Harpe
Vons
Alt.
Vlles
C. B.
Solo
1º
Solo
1º Solo
Sourdine
Unis.
Unis.

170
ptes Fl.
Gdes Fl.
1r Solo
à 2
Htb
Cor A.
Solo
Cl.
Cl B.
Solo
Bons
Sarr.
Cors
Tromp.
sans Sourdine 3o
Tromb. et Tuba
Timb.
Tamb.
Gr. C.
à 2
Harpes
Div.
Vons
Alt.
Velles
Unis.
arco
C. B.

173
Ptes Fl.
Gdes Fl.
Htb
Cor A.
Cl.
Cl. B.
Bons
Sarr
Cors
Tromp.
Tromb. et Tuba
Timb.
T. de B.
Trg.
Tamb.
Cymb.
Gr. C.
Harpes
Vons
Alt.
Velles
C. B.
à 2
à 3
le plus f possible
Unis.

176
ptes Fl.
Gdes Fl
Htb
Cor A.
Cl.
Cl. B.
Bons
Sarr.
Cors
Tromp
Tromb. et Tuba
Timb.
T. de B.
Trg.
Tamb.
Cymb.
Gr. C.
reprenez la Mailloche
1ers vons Div.
2ds vons Div.
Div.
Alt. Div
Div.
velles Div.
C. B. Div.

179
ptes Fl.
Gdes Fl.
Htb
Cor A
Cl.
Cl. B.
Bons
Sarr.
Cors
Tromp.
Tromb. et Tuba
Cast.
Tamb.
Cymb.
Gr. C.
1ers vons Div.
2ds vons Div.
Alt. Div.
Velles Div.
C. B. Div.
à 2
2°
tr
pizz.
Div.

182
Ptes Fl.
Gdes Fl.
Htb
Cor A.
Cl.
Cl. B.
Bons
Sarr.
Cors.
Tromp.
Tromb. et Tuba
Cast.
Tamb.
Gr. C.
f
fff
Vons
Alt.
Velles
C. B.

De plus en plus animé
185
ptes Fl.
Gdes Fl.
Htb
Cor A.
Cl.
Cl. B.
Bons
Sarr.
Cors
Tromp
Tromb. et Tuba
Timb
T. de B.
Cast.
Trg.
Tamb.
Cymb.
Gr. C.
De plus en plus animé
arco
Vons
Alt.
Vlles
C. B.

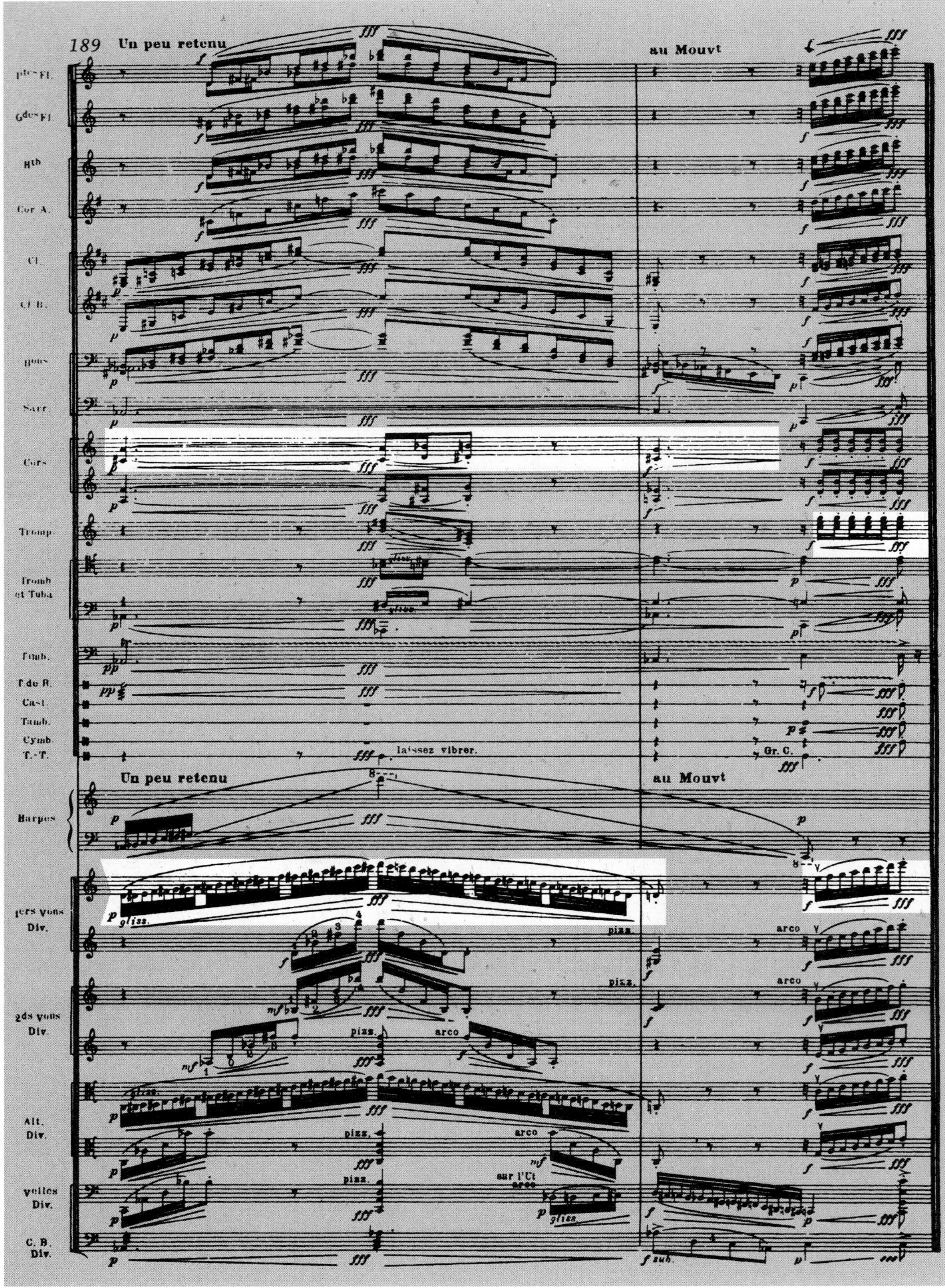
189 Un peu retenu
au Mouvt
Pltes Fl.
Gdes Fl.
Htb
Cor A.
Cl.
Cl. B.
Bons
Sarr.
Cors
Tromp.
Tromb et Tuba
Timb.
T. de B.
Cast.
Tamb.
Cymb.
T.-T.
laissez vibrer.
Gr. C.
Un peu retenu
au Mouvt
Harpes
1ers Vons Div.
gliss.
pizz.
arco
2ds Vons Div.
Alt. Div.
Vcelles Div.
sur l'Ut
C. B. Div.
f sub.

Maurice Ravel (1875–1937) absorbed much of the musical life of *fin de siècle* Paris. He was strongly influenced by the modernistic tendencies of Fauré and Debussy, but he was also well aware of the musical traditions of Paris. He maintained stronger ties to Classical forms than did Debussy, and he employed broader melodies and more incisive rhythms. Moreover, his orchestration techniques link back to Berlioz rather than to more recent figures. Tapping into the French tastes for the exotic, Ravel composed a number of works treating subjects in faraway lands. Foremost among these is his first major orchestral work, the suite *Rapsodie espagnole (Spanish Rhapsody).*

The suite contains four movements, resembling the structure of a symphony. The finale, entitled *Feria,* is based on the *jota,* a Spanish folk dance from Aragon. Characterized by a triple meter and a quick tempo, the dance features vigorous rhythms, often accompanied by tambourines and castanets. The movement is set in a vague **A–B–A** structure. The outer portions reflect the movement's dance orientation with their brilliant orchestration and strong rhythmic drive. The middle section presents a sultry melody and a quotation of a prominent theme from the first movement.

28. Béla Bartók

8CD: 7/ 27 – 33
4CD: 4/ 3 – 9

Concerto for Orchestra, Fourth Movement,
Interrupted Intermezzo (1943)

27 3

Oboe I
Violins I
Violins II
Violas
Violoncellos
♩ = ca 110
lunga
Allegretto, ♩ = ca 114
div.
pizz.
p sub.

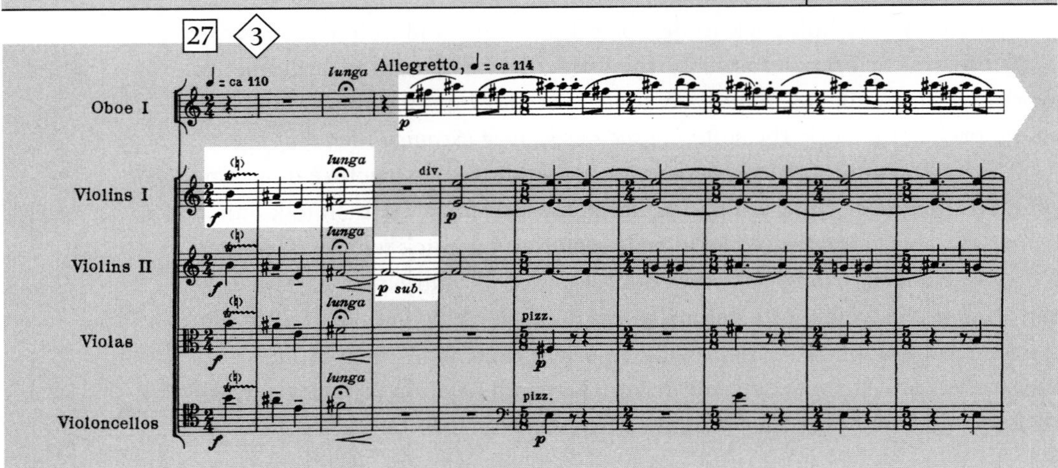

11
Fl. I
Ob. I
Cl. I in A
Bsn. I
Vlns. I
Vlns. II
Vls.
Vcs.
D. Bs.
unis.
div.
arco
pizz.

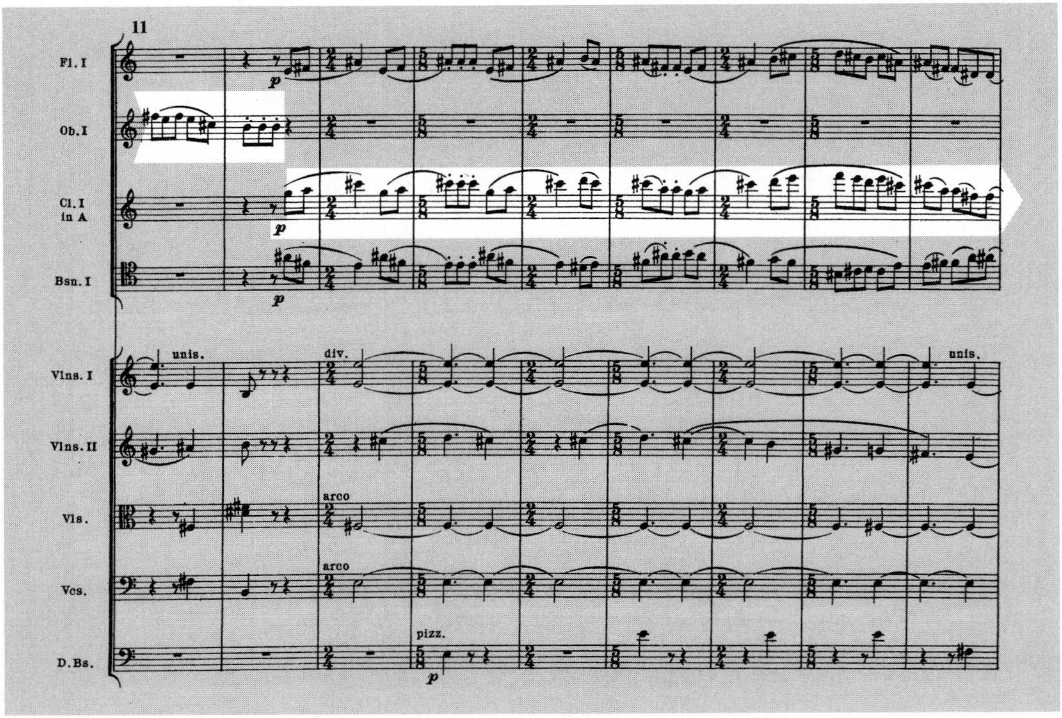

20
Fl. I
Cl. I in A
Bsn. I
Hn. I in F
Harp I
Vlns. I
Vlns. II
Vls.
Vcs.
D.Bs.
p
p, espr.
mp
* If the Flute has no low b, 1st Bassoon will play:
and Flute tacet.

29
rallent.
a tempo
Fl. I
Ob. I
Hn. I in F
Harp I
Vlns. I
Vlns. II
Vls.
Vcs.
D.Bs.
pp
p
arco
*real sound:

28
4
38
Calmo, ♩ = 106
Fl. I
Ob. I
Timp.
mf
Harps I,II
a 2
f
Calmo, ♩ = 106
Vlns. I
Vlns. II
Vls.
f, cantabile
Vcs.
D.Bs.
1'
47
C.A.
f
Timp.
Harps I,II
Vlns. I
f
Vls.
Vcs.
f
D.Bs.
f

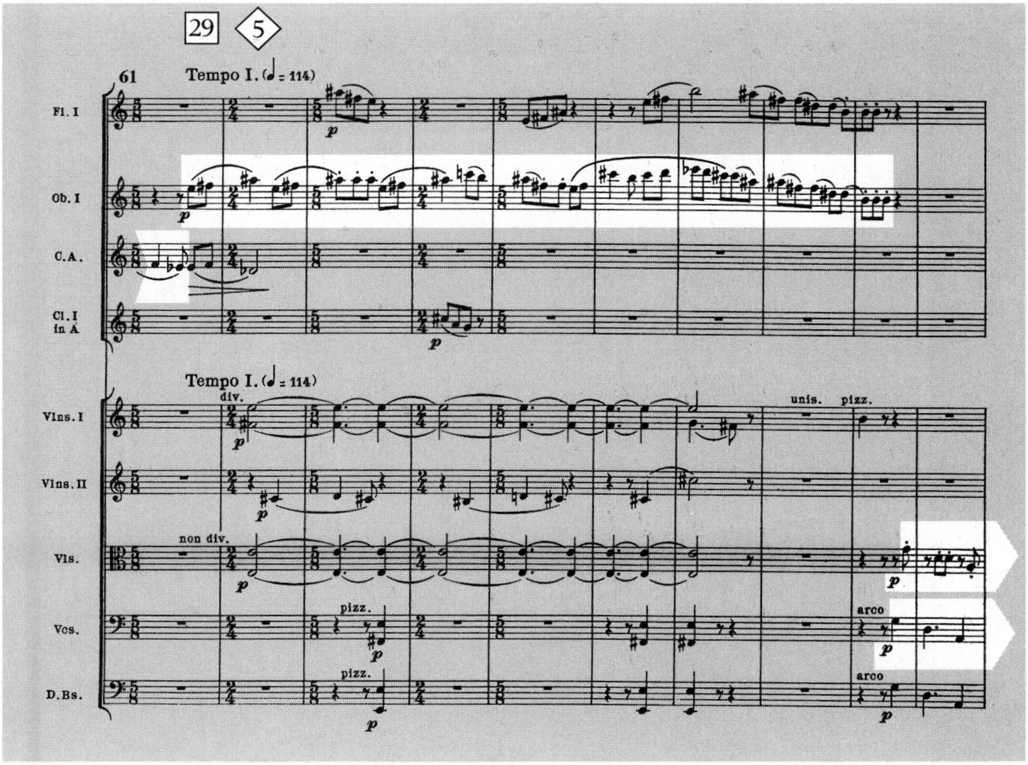

29 ◇5

61 Tempo I. (♩ = 114)

Fl. I

p

Ob. I

p

C.A.

Cl. I in A

p

Tempo I. (♩ = 114)

Vlns. I

div.

p

unis. pizz.

Vlns. II

p

Vls.

non div.

p

p

Vcs.

pizz.

p

arco

p

D.Bs.

pizz.

p

arco

p

30
6
71
accelerando
Obs. I, II
Cl. I in B♭
Bsn. I
Hns. I, II in F
Vlns. I
Vlns. II
Vls.
Vcs.
D.Bs.
arco
pizz.
1'
79
al Più mosso, 𝅗𝅥 = 94
Flts. I, II
Obs. I, II
Clts. in B♭
Trpts. I, II in C
con sord.
Trbs. I, II
Trb. III Tuba
sim.

87
I
Flts.
II, III
dim.
p
I
Obs.
II, III
I
Clts. in B♭
II, III
dim.
p
Bsns. I, II
Hns. I, II in F
Trb. II
Trb. III Tuba
gliss.
f
D. Bs.
mf
f

94
I
Flts.
II, III
I
Obs.
II, III
I
Clts. in B♭
II, III
Bsns. I, II
Hns. I, II in F
Tuba
Vlns. I
Vlns. II
D. Bs.
f

31
7
101
I
Flts.
II, III
a 2
ff
dim.
p
I
Obs.
II, III
I
Clts. in B♭
II, III
Bsns. I, II
Hns. I, II in F
(con sord.)
Trpts. I, II in C
I, II
Trbs.
III
f
Tuba
p, espr.
Trgl.
div.
unis.
gliss.
Vlns. I
Vlns. II
Vls.
D.Bs.

108
I
Flts.
II, III
I
Obs.
II, III
I
Clts.in B♭
II, III
Hns. I, II in F
senza sord.
I, II
Trpts.in C
III
con sord.
con sord.
I, II
Trbs.
III
Tuba
Cym.
with the thick end of a Side Drum stick
Tam-Tam
[laissez vibrer]
Vlns. I
Vlns. II
Vls.
gliss.
gliss.
gliss.

115

32 8

Calmo, ♩= 106

I Flts. II, III

dim.

I Obs. II, III

dim.

I Clts. in B♭ II, III

dim.

Hn. I in F

Trb. I

Harp I

Calmo, ♩= 106

Vlns. I

div. con sord.

Vlns. II

pizz.

Vls.

con sord.

Vcs.

pizz.

D. Bs.

1'

33
9
128
Tempo I. (𝅗𝅥 = 114)
Fl. I
Ob. I
C. A.
Cl. I in B♭
Vlns. I
Vlns. II
Vls.
Vcs.
senza sord.
arco
p
pp

137
rallent. - - a tempo
rallent.
Fl. I
C. A.
Cl. I in B♭
I, III
Hns. in F
II
con sord.
Vlns. I
Vlns. II
Vls.
Vcs.
p

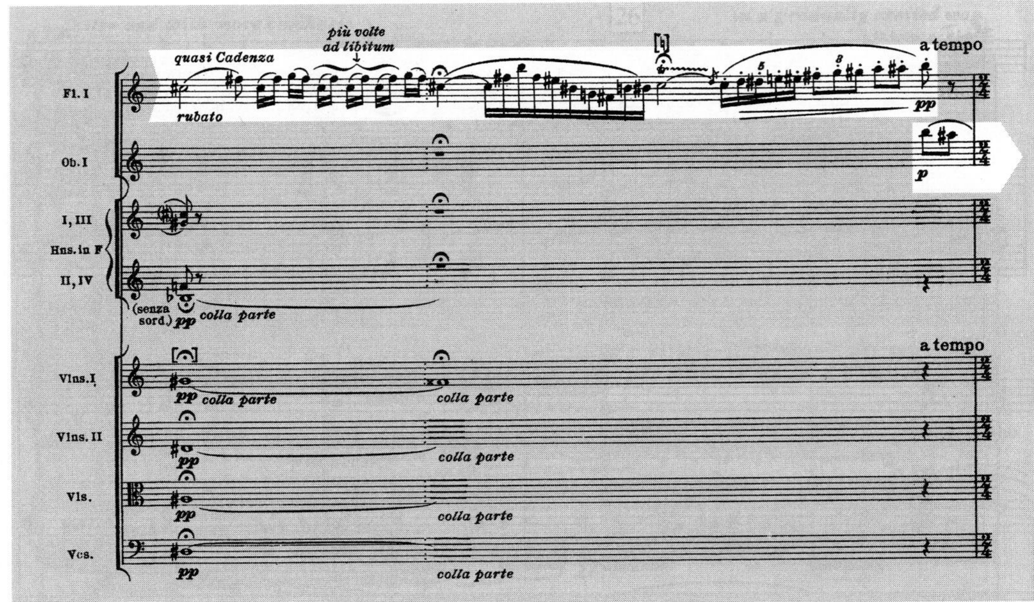

144
(♩ = 114)
Picc.
p
I
Obs.
II
p
p
I
Bsns.
II
p
p
p
(♩ = 114)
pizz.
Vlns. I
p
pizz.
Vlns. II
p
pp
pizz.
Vls.
p
pp
arco
p
pizz.
Vcs.
p
pp
arco
p
pizz.
D. Bs.
p
pp
arco
p

Béla Bartók (1881–1945) found a unique musical voice in the folk traditions of Eastern Europe. He studied the folk music of his native Hungary intently, writing numerous articles and collecting several anthologies of melodies. He then brought melodic, rhythmic, and harmonic aspects of these traditions into his own compositions. As a result, Bartók's music can be seen as a mixture of nationalist and neoclassical elements, along with his special gifts for color and dramatic flair.

Two years prior to his death, the terminally ill Bartók was commissioned by Serge Koussevitzky, the conductor of the Boston Symphony Orchestra, to write the *Concerto for Orchesta.* Bartók justified the title by explaining that he attempted "to treat the single orchestral instruments in a concertante or soloistic manner." In a very real sense, he composed a concerto for virtuoso orchestra.

The fourth movement, subtitled *Interrupted Intermezzo,* is set in a rondo pattern (**A-B-A′-C-B′-A′**). The **A** sections present a lively, folklike dance tune in the woodwinds. The shifting meters, reflecting the freedom of folk music, establish a playful mood. The beautiful lyrical melody in the **B** sections creates a striking contrast. Initially presented by the viola section with a harp accompaniment, the melody maintains the limited range and metrical variety of folk music. Section **C** centers on a theme from the Symphony No. 7 by Dmitri Shostakovich. Hardly a tribute to the Russian composer, the theme is mocked in a sarcastic, dissonant manner.

29. Igor Stravinsky

Le sacre du printemps (The Rite of Spring),
Part II (1913), excerpts

8CD: 7/34–42
4CD: 3/51–59

Editor's note: The Norton recording begins at the measure after 103 and ends with the downbeat at 142 (on p. 635).

Glorification de l'élue (Glorification of the Chosen One)

106
Fl. picc.
Fl. gr.
Fl. in Sol.
Oboi
Cor. ingl.
Clar. picc. (Mib)
Clar. (Sib)
Clar. basso
Fag.
C-Fag. 1.2.
Cor.
Tr. picc. in Re.
Tr. in Do
Tr-boni.
Tube.
Timp.
G. Cassa Tamtam.
Viol. 1.
Viol. 2.
V-le.
Celli.
Bassi.
Flatterz.
f cresc.
Les pavillons en l'air
gliss.
gliss. colla bacch. di Triang.
arco
pizz.
sempre f
glissando
arco
106

107
108
Fl. picc.
Flatterzunge
Fl. gr.
Flatterz.
Fl. in (Sol)
Oboi
Cor. ingl.
Clar. picc. (Mib)
Clar. (Sib)
Clar. basso
Fag.
C. Fag.
Cor.
come sopra
Tr. picc. (Re)
en dehors
Tr. (Do)
Tr-bone
Tube
Timp.
secco
Gr. C.
T. T.
arco
Viol. 1.
Viol. 2.
V.le.
Celli
Bassi
cresc.
a 2

109
Fl. picc.
Fl. gr.
Fl. in (Sol)
Oboi
Cor. ingl.
Clar. picc. (Mi♭)
Clar. (Si♭)
Clar. basso
Fag.
C. Fag.
Cor.
Tr. picc. (Re)
Tr. (Do)
Tr-bone.
Tube
Timp.
Gr. C.
T. T.
Viol. 1.
Viol. 2.
V-le.
Celli.
Bassi.
Flatters.
come sopra
a 2
etc.
pizz.
arco
div.
gliss.
unis.
div. a 3
109

110
Fl. picc.
Fl. gr.
1.
2.3.
Fl. in. (Sol)
Oboi
1.2.
3.4.
Cor. ingl.
Clar. picc. (Mi♭)
Clar (Si♭)
1.
2.3.
Clar. basso
Fag.
1.
2.3.
a 2
C. Fag.
Cor.
1.2.
3.4.
5.6.
7.8.
Tr. picc. (Re)
Tr. (C) 3.4.
Tube
sf
Timp. 3.
Viol.
div. a 3
arco
unis.
pizz.
V-le.
div.
Celli.
Bassi.
110

35 52

111
112
Fl. picc.
Fl. gr.
Oboi
Cor. ingl.
Clar. picc. (Mib)
Clar. (Sib)
a 2
Cor.
gliss.
Tr. picc. (Re)
Tr
3. Tr-bone
Gr. C.
arco
Viol.
V-le.
Celli.
Bassi.

113
Fl. picc.
Fl. gr. 1. 2. 3.
Oboi. 1.2. 3.4.
Cor. ingl.
Clar. picc. (Mib)
Clar. (Sib) 1. 2.3.
Clar. basso
Fag. 1.2.
C. Fag.
Cor. 1.2. 3.4. 5.6. 7.8.
Tr. picc. (Re)
Tr. 1.2. 3.4.
3 Tr-bone
2 Tube
Timp.
Gr. C.
Viol. 1. 2.
V-le.
Celli.
Bassi.
mf
sim.
ff
a 2
bacch. di Tamburo
8 4 etc.
p
bacch. di Timp.
a 3
pizz.
unis. arco
arco
113

114
Fl. picc.
Fl. gr.
1.
2.3.
a 2
Oboi.
1.2.
3.4.
Cor ingl.
Clar. picc. (Mi♭)
Clar. (Si♭)
1.
2.
3.
Clar. basso
sempre sim.
Fag.
1.
2.
3.
4.
C. Fag.
Cor.
1.2.
3.4.
5.6.
7.8.
Solo marc.
Tr. picc. (Re)
Tr.
1.2.
3.4
Tr-boni
2 Tube
Timp.
poco
poco
simile
Gr. C.
bacch. di Timp. (au bord)
pizz.
(enharm.)
Viol. 1.
div. a 3
Viol. 2.
div. a 3
V-le.
Celli.
simile
Bässe.
114

115
Fl. picc.
1.2. Fl.gr. 3.
F. in (Sol)
1.2. Oboi 3.4.
Clar. picc.(Mib)
1. Clar.(Sib) 2.3.
Clar. basso
1. 2. Fag. 3. 4.
C. Fag.
1. 3. Cor. 5. 7.
1.2. Tr. 3.4.
1.2. Tr-boni 3.
Timp.
Gr. C.
Viol. 1 e 2. div. a 3
V-le.
Celli.
Bassi.
mf
ff
f
a 2
simile
marc.
arco
pizz.
115

Molto allargando
116
Fl.picc.
Gr. Fl.
Fl.(Sol)
Oboi
Clar.(Mib)
Clar.(Sib)
Clar. basso
Fag.
C-Fag.
Fag. 4 : C. Fag. 2
Les pavillons en l'air.
Cor.
Tr-be
sempre sim.
Tr-boni
Tuba
Timp.
Timp 3 muta in La
Gr.C.
bachetta di Gr. C.
arco
pizz.
Viol. 1.2. div. a 3
V-le
Celli
Bassi
116
Molto allargando

36
53
117 a tempo
Fl. picc.
Gr. Fl.
Flatterz.
Fl. (Sol)
Oboi
Cor. ingl.
Clar. picc. (Mib)
Clar. (Sib)
Clar. basso
Fag. 1.2.3.
C-Fag. 1.2.
a 2
a 3
Les pavillons en l'air.
Cor.
Tr. picc. (Re)
Tr. (Do)
Tr-boni 1.2.
Tube
sempre sff
Timp.
Gr. C.
poco sf
T. T.
gliss. colla bacch. di Triang.
Viol. 1.
Viol. 2.
pizz.
arco
gliss.
V-le div.
détaché
Celli
Bassi
117 a tempo

118
119
Fl. picc.
1.2.
Fl. gr.
3.
Fl. (Sol)
1.2.
Oboi
3.4.
Cor. ingl.
Clar. picc.(Mib)
1.
Clar. (Sib)
2.3.
Clar. basso
Fag. 1.2.3.
a2
C. Fag. 1.2.
1.2.
3.4.
Cor.
5.6.
7.8.
Tr. picc.(Re)
1. 2.
3. 4.
Tr. (Do)
Tube
Timp.
pizz.
arco
div.
unis.
Viol. 1.
Viol. 2.
V-le
Celli
Bassi

120
Fl.picc.
1.2.
Fl.gr.
3.
Fl.(Sol)
1.2.
Oboi
3.4.
Cor. ingl.
Clar. picc.(Mib)
1.
Clar.(Sib)
2.3.
Clar. basso
Fag. 1.2.3.
C. Fag. 2 = Fag. 4.
C. Fag. 1.2.
1.2.
3.4.
Cor.
5.6.
7.8.
sim.
Tr. picc.(Re)
Tr. Do) 3.4.
Tube 1.2.
Timp. 3
muta in Sib
Timp. 1.2.
div.
arco
unis.
pizz.
1.
Viol.
2.
V.le
Celli
Bassi
120

Evocation des Ancêtres (Evocation of the Ancestors)

37 54

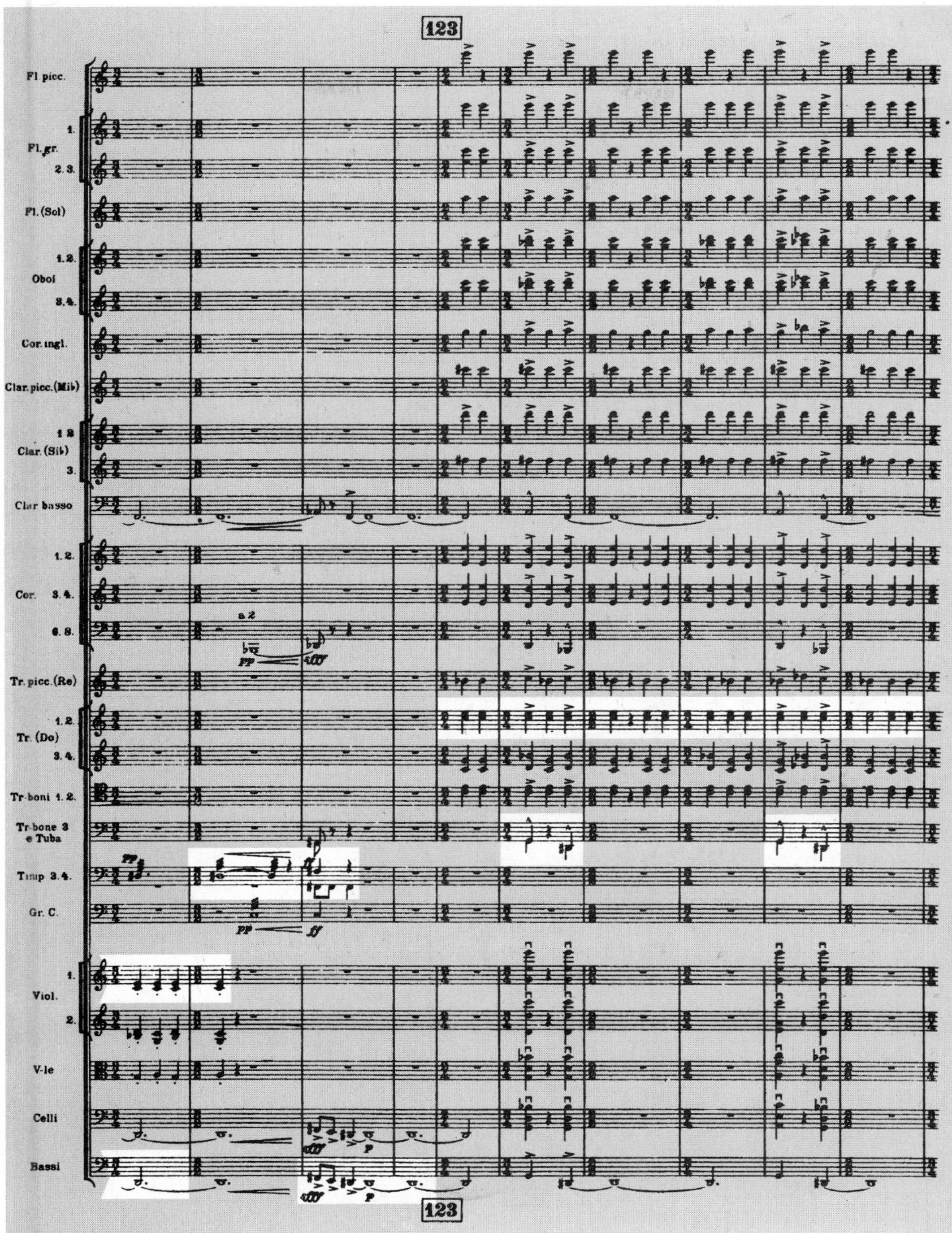
123
Fl picc.
1.
Fl. gr.
2. 3.
Fl. (Sol)
1. 2.
Oboi
3. 4.
Cor. ingl.
Clar. picc. (Mib)
1 2
Clar. (Sib)
3.
Clar basso
1. 2.
Cor. 3. 4.
5. 6.
a 2
pp
sff
Tr. picc. (Re)
1. 2.
Tr. (Do)
3. 4.
Tr-boni 1. 2.
Tr-bone 3 e Tuba
Timp 3. 4.
Gr. C.
pp
ff
1.
Viol.
2.
V-le
Celli
sff
p
Bassi
123

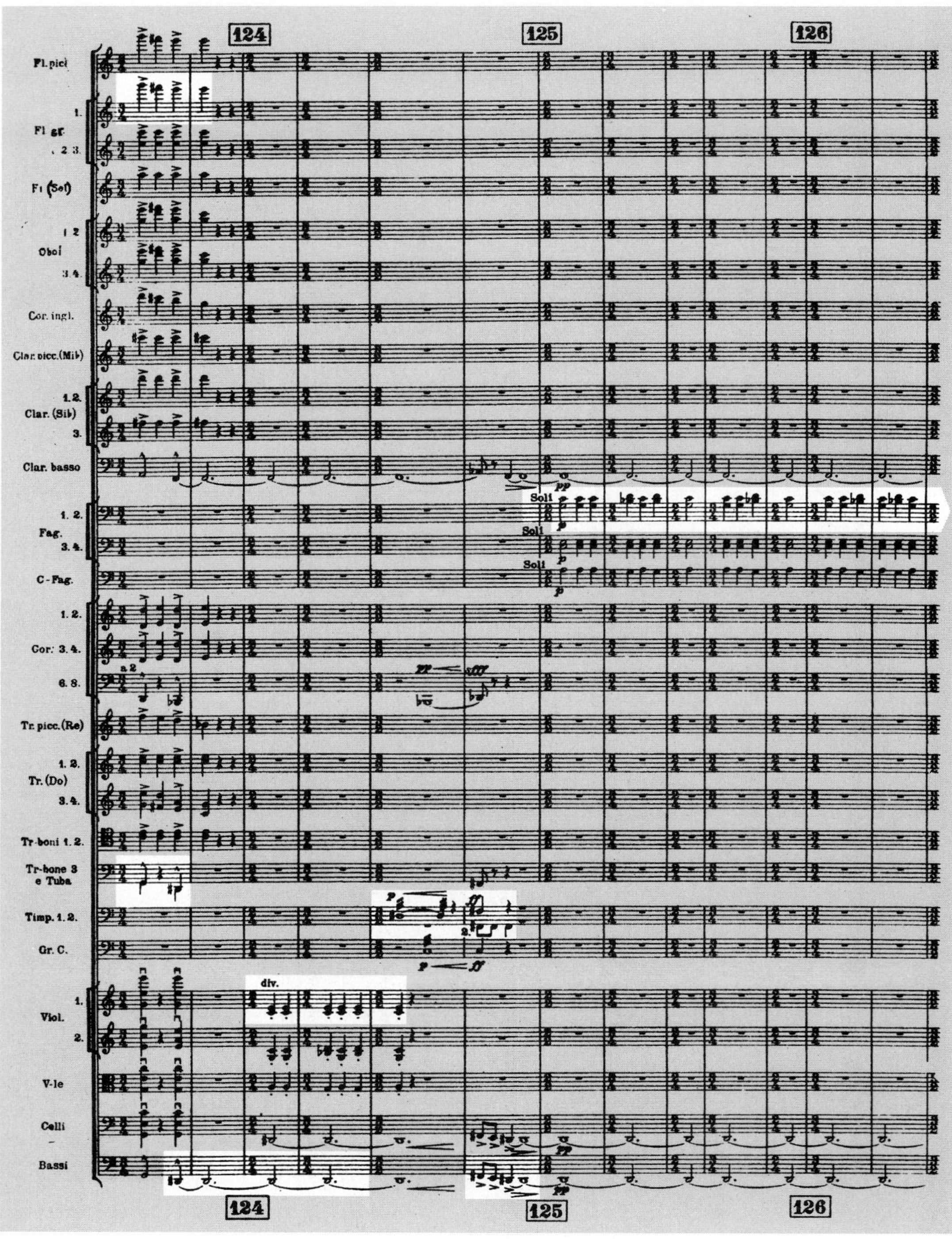
124
125
126
Fl. picc.
Fl. gr.
Fl. (Sol)
Oboi
Cor. ingl.
Clar. picc. (Mi♭)
Clar. (Si♭)
Clar. basso
Fag.
C-Fag.
Soli
Cor.
a 2
Tr. picc. (Re)
Tr. (Do)
Tr-boni 1. 2.
Tr-bone 3 e Tuba
Timp. 1. 2.
Gr. C.
div.
Viol.
V-le
Celli
Bassi

127
Lento ♩= 52
128
Fl. picc.
Fl. gr.
Fl. in Sol
Oboi
Oboe 4 : Cor. ingl. 2
Cor. ingl.
Clar. picc. (Mi♭)
Clar. (Si♭)
Clar. bassi
Fag.
C-Fag.
Cor.
a 2
Tr. picc. (Re)
Tr-be (Do)
Tromba 4 in Do: Tromba bassa in Mi♭
Tr-boni
Tr-bone 3 e Tuba
Timp.
Tamb. de Basq.
Gr. C.
Viol.
V-le
Celli
Bassi
127
128
Lento ♩= 52

Action Rituelle des Ancêtres (Ritual Action of the Ancestors)

38 55

39
56
131
Fl. in Sol.
Cor. ingl.
Clar. (Si♭) 1.
Fag. 1. 2.
Cor. 6. 8.
Timp
Viol. 1. 2.
V-le.
Celli.
Bassi.
poco più f
mettez les sourdines
132
Tr-be. (Do) 1. 2.
Tr. bassa (Mi♭)
con sord.
Solo.

133
Fl.gr.
Fl.in Sol.
Oboi.
Cor. ingl.
Fag.
Cor.
Tr-be. (Do)
Tr. bassa (Mi♭)
con sord.
div.
arco
con sord.
arco
Viol.
V-le.
Celli.
senza sord.

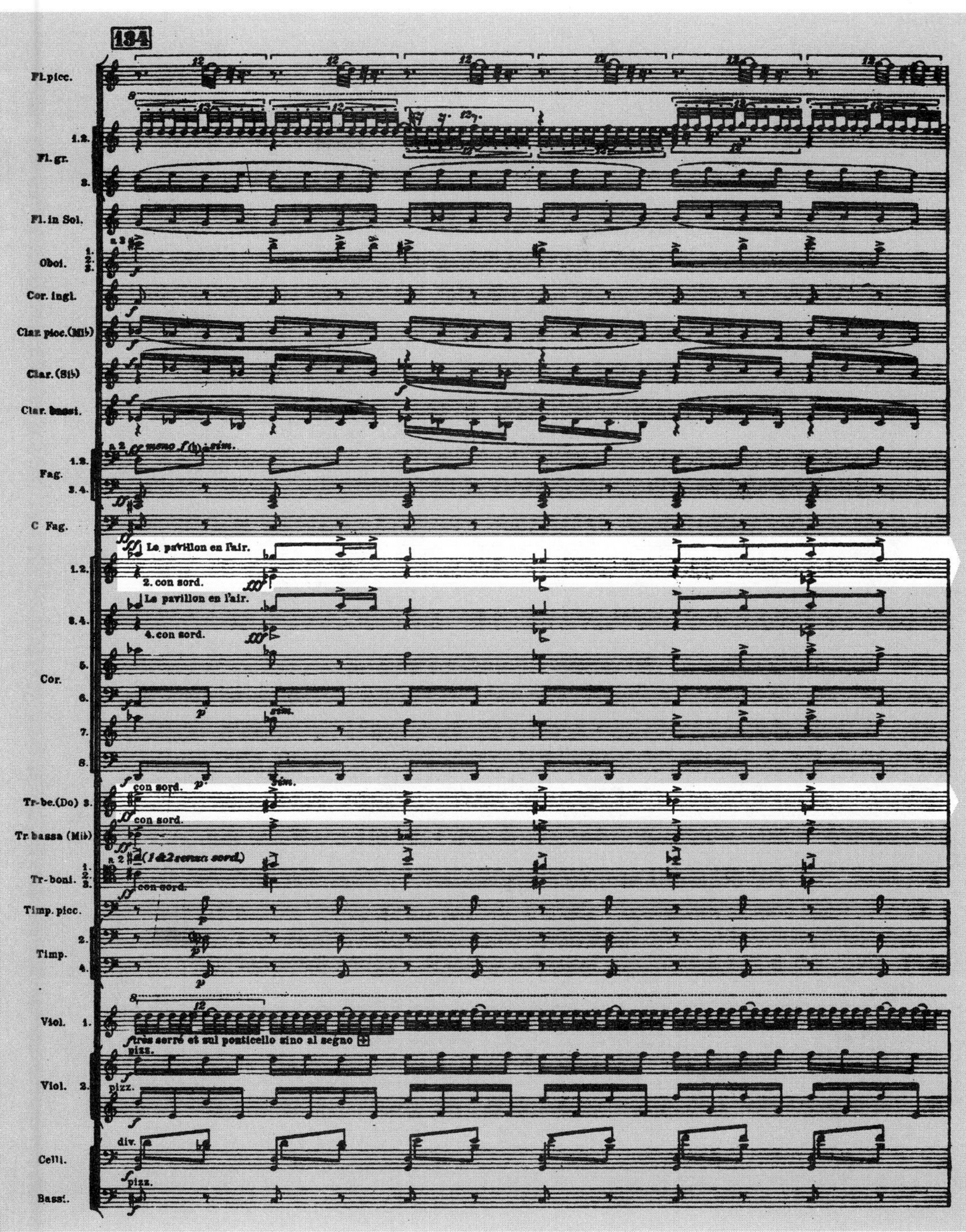
134
Fl. picc.
Fl. gr.
Fl. in Sol.
Oboi.
Cor. ingl.
Clar. picc. (Mib)
Clar. (Sib)
Clar. bassi.
Fag.
C Fag.
Le pavillon en l'air.
2. con sord.
Le pavillon en l'air.
4. con sord.
Cor.
sim.
Tr-be. (Do) 3.
con sord.
Tr. bassa (Mib)
con sord.
(1 & 2 senza sord.)
Tr-boni.
con sord.
Timp. picc.
Timp.
Viol. 1.
très serré et sul ponticello sino al segno
pizz.
Viol. 2.
pizz.
div.
Celli.
pizz.
Bassi.

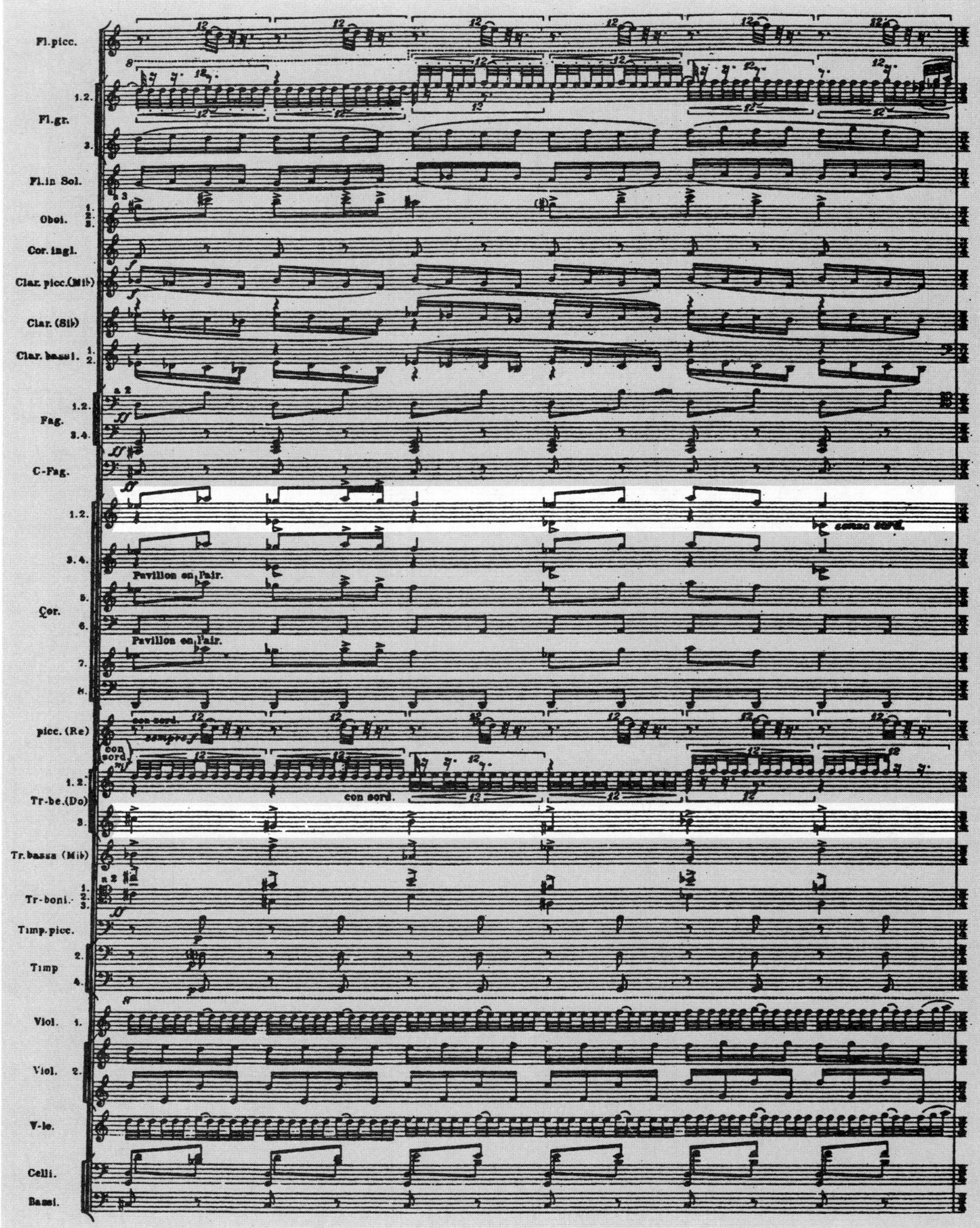

Fl. picc.
Fl. gr.
Fl. in Sol.
Oboi.
Cor. ingl.
Clar. picc. (Mib)
Clar. (Sib)
Clar. bassi.
a 2
Fag.
C-Fag.
senza sord.
Pavillon en l'air.
Cor.
Pavillon en l'air.
con sord.
sempre f
picc. (Re)
con sord.
con sord.
Tr-be. (Do)
Tr. bassa (Mib)
a 2
Tr-boni.
Timp. picc.
Timp
Viol. 1.
Viol. 2.
V-le.
Celli.
Bassi.

40
57
135
136
Fl. gr.
Fl. in Sol.
Oboi.
Cor. ingl.
Clar. picc. (Mi♭)
Clar. (Si♭)
Clar. bassi.
Fag.
C-Fag.
Cor.
Tr-be. (Do)
Tr. bassa (Mi♭)
Tr-boni.
Tube.
Viol.
V-le
Celli
Bassi.
ten.
cresc.
sim.
enharm.
mf cresc.
pesante
ten.
senza sord.
Solo.
mp cresc.
sul pont.
pizz.
arco
unis.
div.
unis. pizz.
div. arco

41
58
137
138
Fl. gr.
Fl. in Sol.
Ob.
Cor. ingl.
Clar. picc. (Mib)
Clar. (Sib)
Clar. bassi
Fag.
C-Fag.
Cor.
Tr. picc. (Re)
Tr-be. (Do)
Tr-boni.
Tube.
Timp. picc.
Timp.
Tamtam.
Tamb. de Basq.
Gr. C.
Piatti.
Viol.
V-le.
Celli.
Bassi.
pesante
sim.
mf cresc.
bouché
ouvert
senza sord.
1. Solo.
mp cresc.
sul pont.
sul ponticello sino al segno
pizz.
arco
div.
sempre sim.
mf sempre sim.

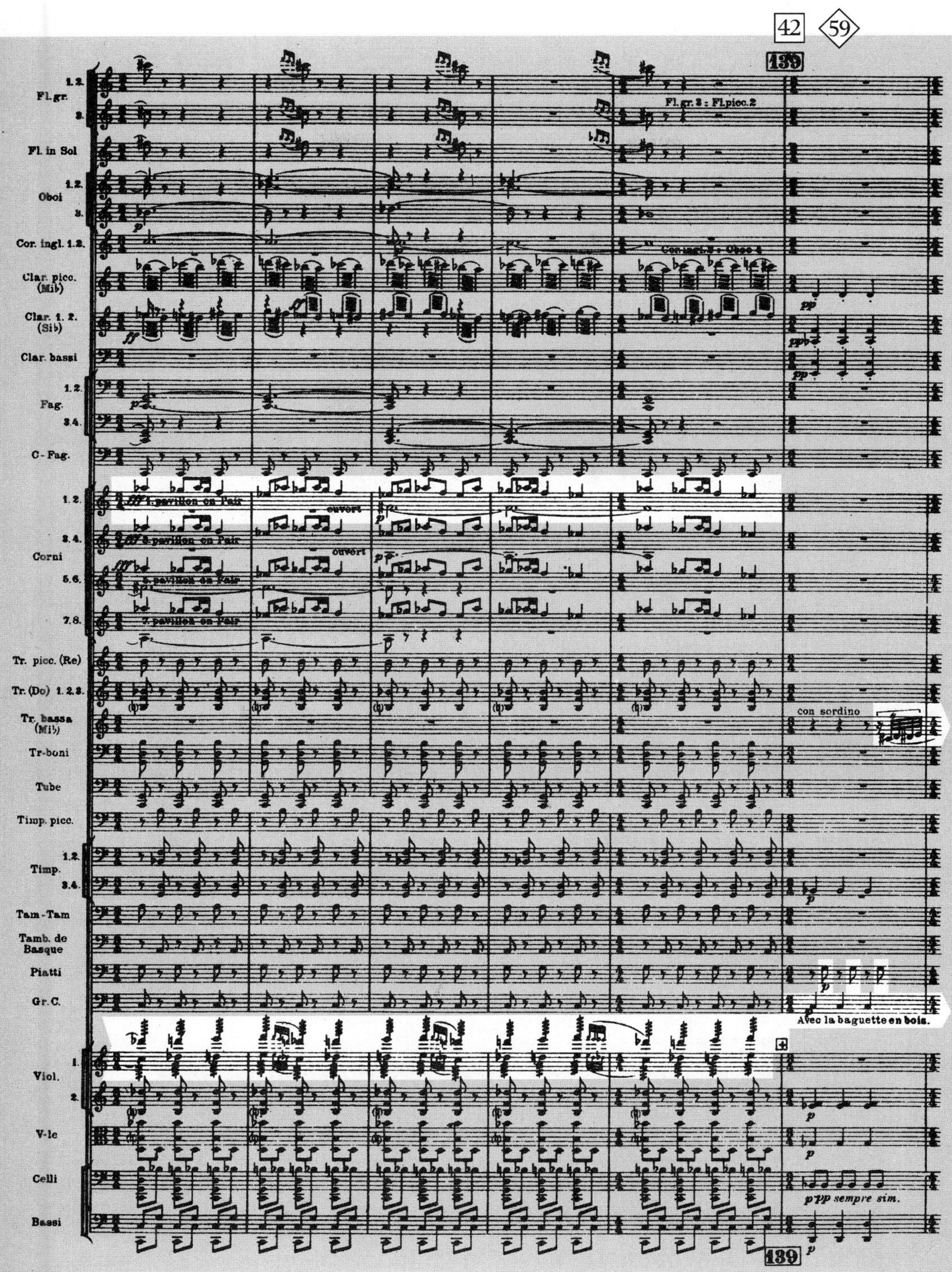

42
59
139
Fl. gr.
Fl. gr. 3 : Fl. picc. 2
Fl. in Sol
Oboi
Cor. ingl. 1. 2.
Clar. picc. (Mib)
Clar. 1. 2. (Sib)
Clar. bassi
Fag.
C - Fag.
Corni
1. pavillon en l'air
3. pavillon en l'air
5. pavillon en l'air
7. pavillon en l'air
ouvert
Tr. picc. (Re)
Tr. (Do) 1. 2. 3.
Tr. bassa (Mib)
con sordino
Tr-boni
Tube
Timp. picc.
Timp.
Tam-Tam
Tamb. de Basque
Piatti
Gr. C.
Avec la baguette en bois.
Viol.
V-le
Celli
ppp sempre sim.
Bassi

Fl. in Sol
Cor. ingl. 1.
Clar. picc. (Mib)
Clar. 1. 2. (Sib)
Clar. bassi 1. 2.
Tr. bassa (Mib)
Timp. 3.
Piatti
Gr. C.
pizz.
Viol. 1. 2.
V-le
Celli
Bassi

140
Cor. ingl. 1.
Clar. 1. 2. (Sib)
Clar. bassi 1. 2.
Timp. 2. 3.
pp
p pp sempre sim.
Gr. C.
Ordinairement (avec la mailloche de la Gr. C.)
V-le
Celli
Bassi
ppp

141
Clar. bassi 1. 2.
poco più f
Clar. basso 2 = Clar. 3 in Sib
pp
Timp. 2. 3.
Gr. C
V-le
Celli
Bassi

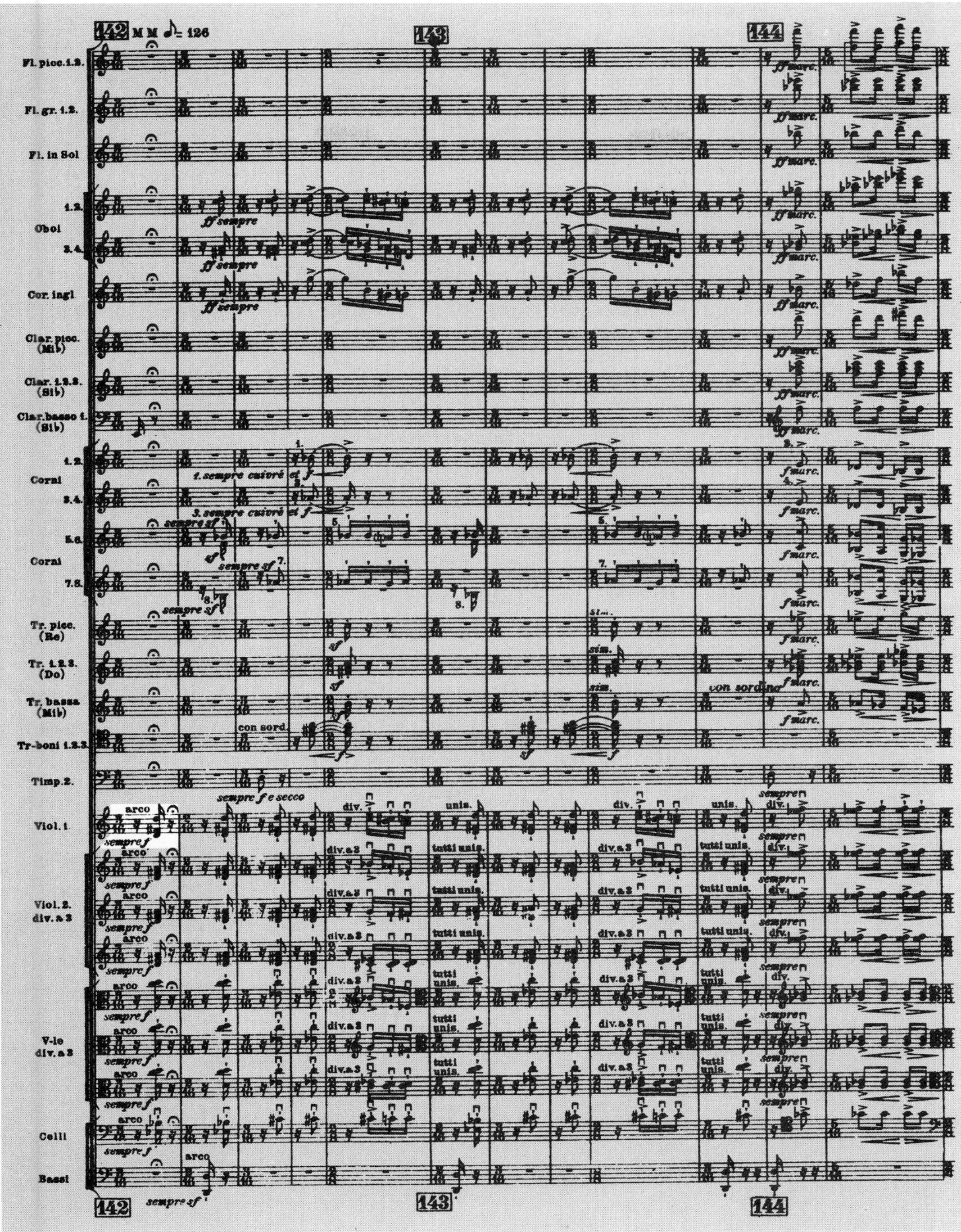
142
M M ♪= 126
143
144
Fl. picc. 1.2.
Fl. gr. 1.2.
Fl. in Sol
Oboi
Cor. ingl
Clar. picc. (Mib)
Clar. 1.2.3. (Sib)
Clar. basso 1. (Sib)
Corni
Tr. picc. (Re)
Tr. 1.2.3. (Do)
Tr. bassa (Mib)
Tr-boni 1.2.3.
Timp. 2.
Viol. 1.
Viol. 2. div. a 3
V-le div. a 3
Celli
Bassi
ff sempre
ff marc.
1. sempre cuivré et f
3. sempre cuivré et f
sempre sf
con sord.
con sordina
f marc.
sempre f e secco
arco
sempre f
div.
unis.
div. a 3
tutti unis.
sim.
sempre
sempre sf

The earliest creative period of Igor Stravinsky (1882–1971) saw a rapid transition from post-Romanticism through Impressionism to what is generally known as Primitivism. Unifying this period is a strong sense of nationalism that can be seen in the Russian models for Stravinsky's works, in the Russian stories of his ballets, and, especially with his later works, in a distinctive Russian style. The culminating point of this early phase is the landmark ballet *Le sacre du printemps (The Rite of Spring)*. Commissioned by the impresario Serge Diaghilev, *Le sacre du printemps* was premiered in 1913 by the Ballets Russes, causing a riot at the first performance. Modernisms dominated the production, with the stunning and energetic choreography by Nijinsky and the innovative costumes and scenic designs. But it is the modern musical sounds of Stravinsky that had the most enduring impact.

Stravinsky's Russian sound can most readily be heard in the melodies, with their limited ranges and repetition. Indeed, Stravinsky is able to interweave a number of authentic folk melodies unobtrusively into the work. Another critical link to Russian traditions is the work's static nature. Contrasts of moods are simply juxtaposed, and development, in the traditional Western sense, is absent. The most memorable features of the work are its primitive qualities, huge orchestral force, powerful dissonances, and pounding rhythms. The last, created by Stravinsky's innovative treatment of metric pulse, had the greatest impact on twentieth-century art music.

The ballet is based on Russian legends that describe a number of primitive spring rituals. In the first part, celebrations include a lustful abduction of women, a rivalry between two tribes, and a round dance. The second part of the ballet is more solemn. The women of the tribe, conducting a mysterious game, select a young maiden for sacrifice, whom they praise in the song *Glorification de l'élue (Glorification of the Chosen One)*. The elders appear, and preparation is made in *Evocation des ancêtres (Evocation of the Ancestors)* and *Action rituelle des ancêtres (Ritual Action of the Ancestors)* for the final sacrificial dance. A variety of rhythmic treatments can be heard in these excerpts, ranging from the regularity of a processional to the barbaric character at the opening of *Glorification de l'élue.*

30. Igor Stravinsky

8CD: 7/ 43 – 47

L'histoire du soldat (The Soldier's Tale), Marche royale (Royal March) (1918)

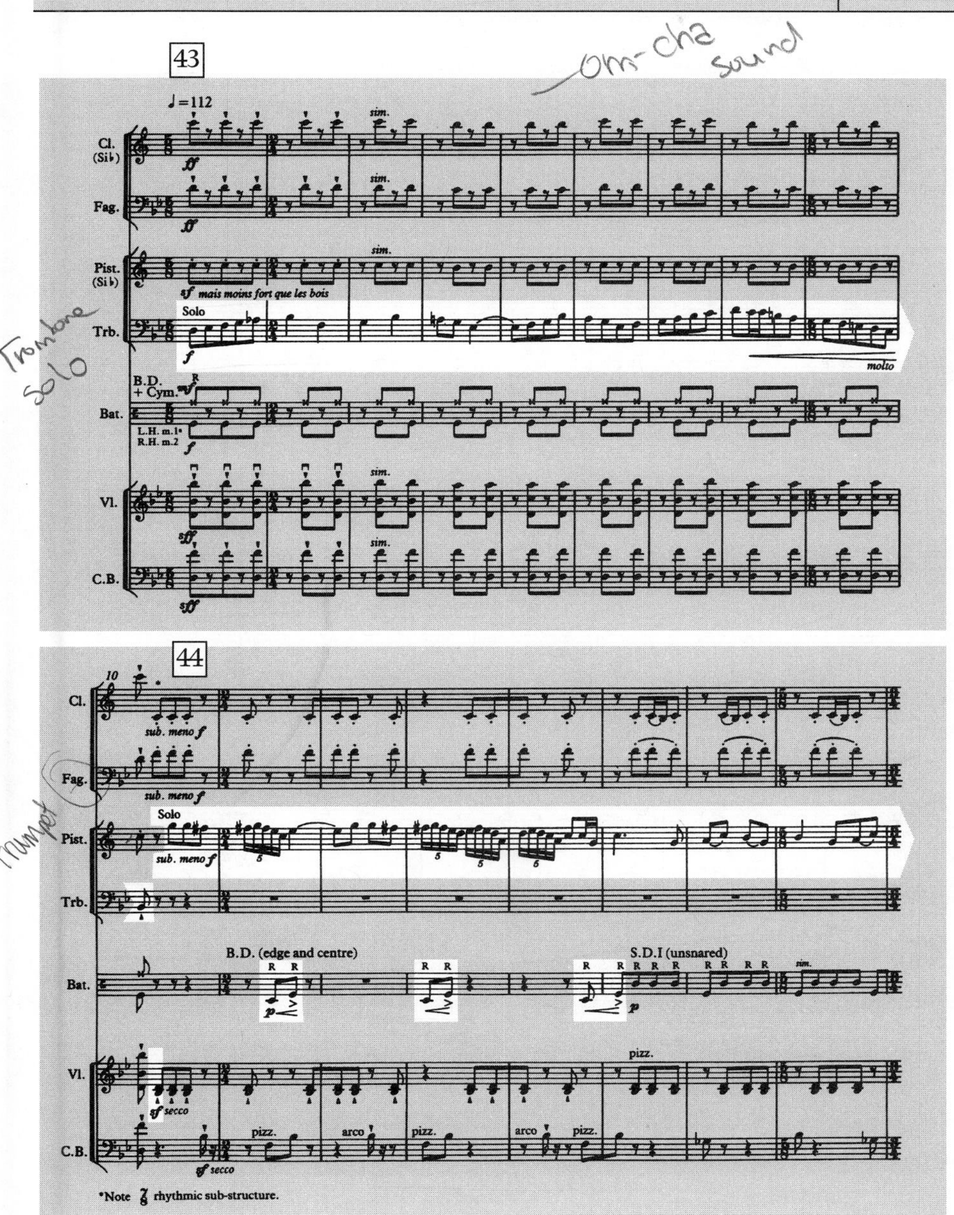

*Pist. 26[3-4]. These two staccato dots are in the 1924 score and part.

*Pist. 37-38. Phrasing thus in both mss. and 1924 part.

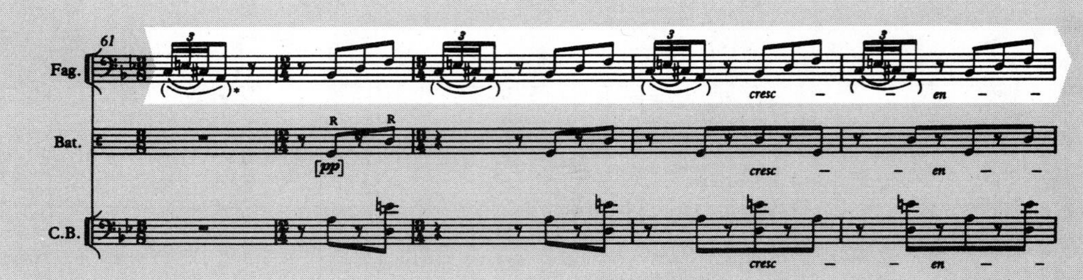

*Fag. 61, 63 etc. Phrasing thus in both mss.
**Pist. 68-70 Phrasing thus in both mss. and 1924 part.

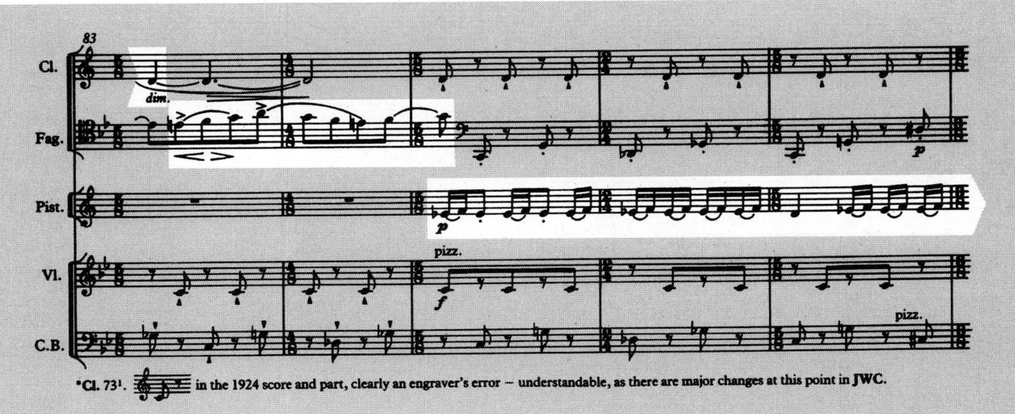

*Cl. 73[1]. in the 1924 score and part, clearly an engraver's error – understandable, as there are major changes at this point in JWC.

*Cl. 88–89. Phrasing thus in both mss. and 1924 part.
**Vl. 100. *p* from 1924 part.

46
101
Cl.
Fag.
Pist.
Trb.
Bat.
Vl.
C.B.
ff sub.
sub. meno f
Solo
f (mais moins fort que les bois)
f sub.
S.D.I (unsnared)
B.D. + Cym.
L
R R R
cresc.
sf secco

108
Cl.
Fag.
Pist.
Trb.
Bat.
Vl.
C.B.
Solo
B.D. (edge & centre)
[sim.]
S.D.I
leggiero
(accompagnando)
pizz.
arco

114
Cl.
Fag.
Pist.
Trb.
Bat.
Vl.
C.B.
Solo
poco
molto
B.D. + Cym.
R
p sub.
stacc.
(accompagnando)
arco
pizz.
sub. meno f

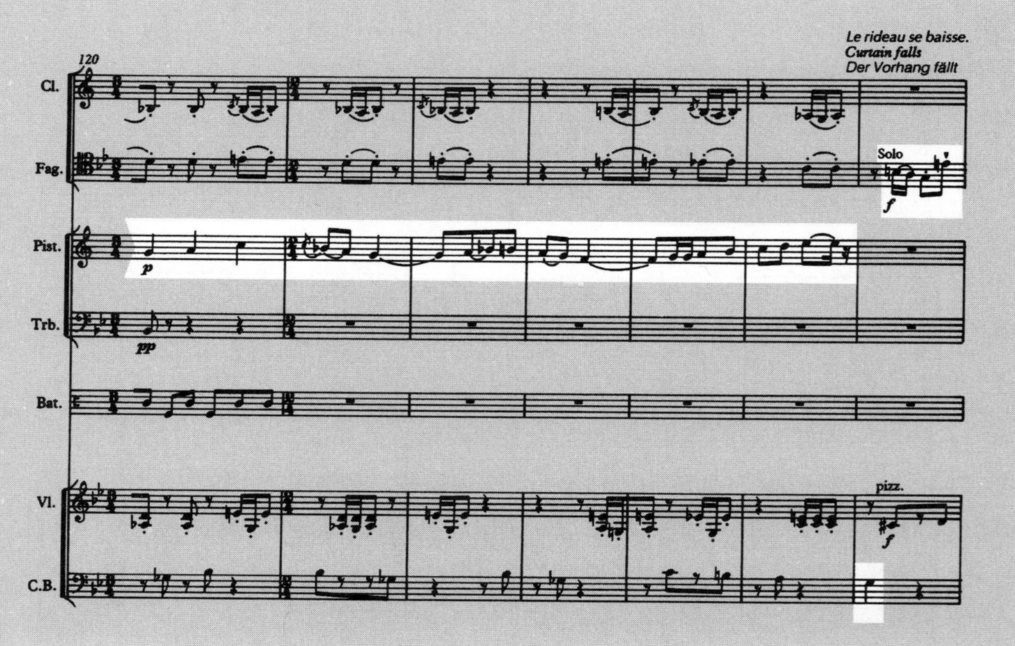
Le rideau se baisse.
Curtain falls
Der Vorhang fällt
120
Cl.
Fag.
Pist.
Trb.
Bat.
Vl.
C.B.
Solo
pizz.

*Fag. 127¹. in both mss. and in the 1924 part (but c.f. fig.3).

**129. Both mss. show that originally there was a break for dialogue at the end of this bar.

***139¹. in both mss.

L'histoire du soldat (The Soldier's Tale) is a dramatic work for narrator, dancers, and a small chamber ensemble. Created near the end of Stravinsky's Russian period (1918), the story is based on a Russian folk tale in which a soldier exchanges his violin (his soul) for a book that foretells the future. The soldier's life and soul are temporarily redeemed by the love of a princess, but eventually the devil is triumphant. In addition to the nationalistic story, Stravinsky retains the static quality and some of the melodic characteristics of his earlier works. At the same time, the work anticipates the imminent Neoclassical phase of Stravinsky's compositions, particularly in the sparse orchestration of just seven instruments, the clear tonal centers, the use of dance forms, and the generally detached emotions.

The *Marche royale* (*Royal March*) has a number of traditional features: it can be heard in an overall **A–B–A** form; there is a prevailing duple meter in a moderate tempo; and the trumpet, trombone, and drums—characteristic instruments of a march—are given prominent roles. But Stravinsky also plays with the most critical element of a march, the beat. Using polyrhythms and shifting meters, Stravinsky quietly creates an intricate rhythmic scheme that matches *Le sacre du printemps* in complexity. The detached humor and the B-flat tonality clearly suggest a Neoclassical conception.

31. Anton Webern

8CD: 7/48–50

Symphony, Op. 21, Second Movement (1928)

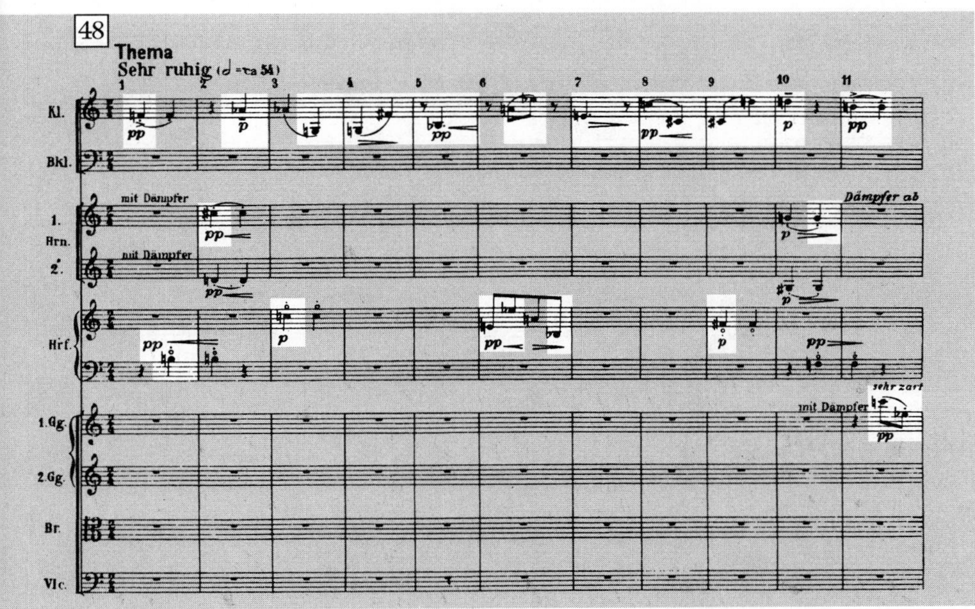

II. Var.
sehr lebhaft (𝅗𝅥 = ca 84)
Kl.
Bkl.
1. Hrn. 2.
ohne Dämpfer
Hrf.
1.Gg.
2.Gg.
Br.
Vlc.
pizz.
arco
rit.

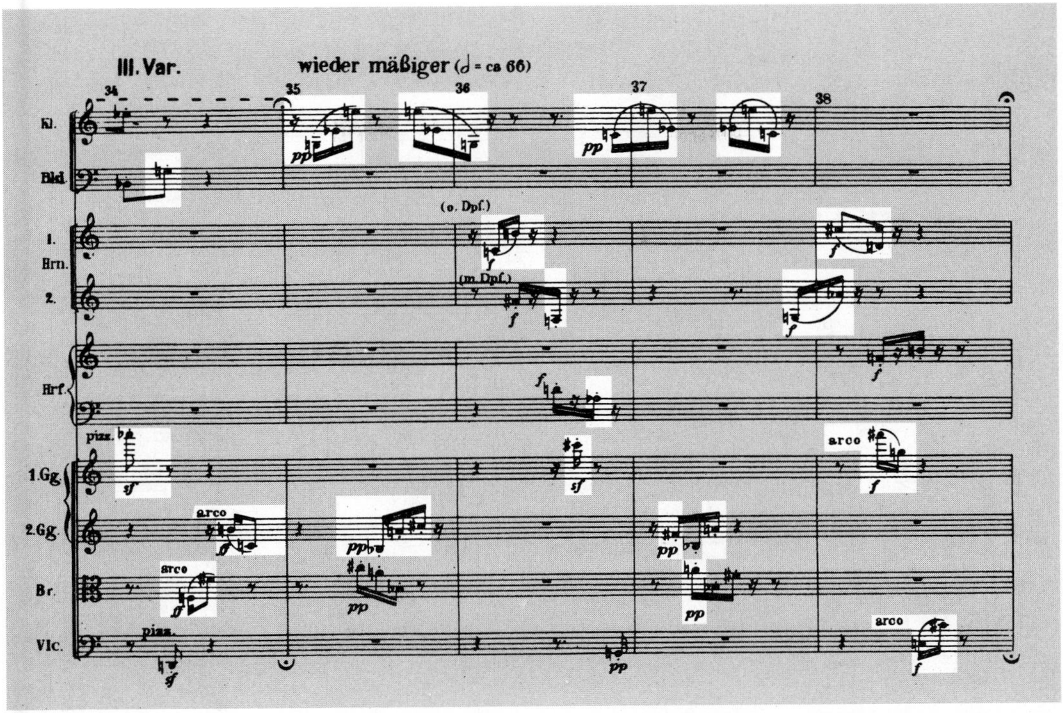

III. Var. wieder mäßiger (𝅗𝅥 = ca 66)

34 35 36 37 38

Kl.
Bkl.
(o. Dpf.)
1. Hrn. 2.
(m. Dpf.)
Hrf.
pizz.
1. Gg.
2. Gg.
arco
Br.
arco
Vlc.
pizz.
arco

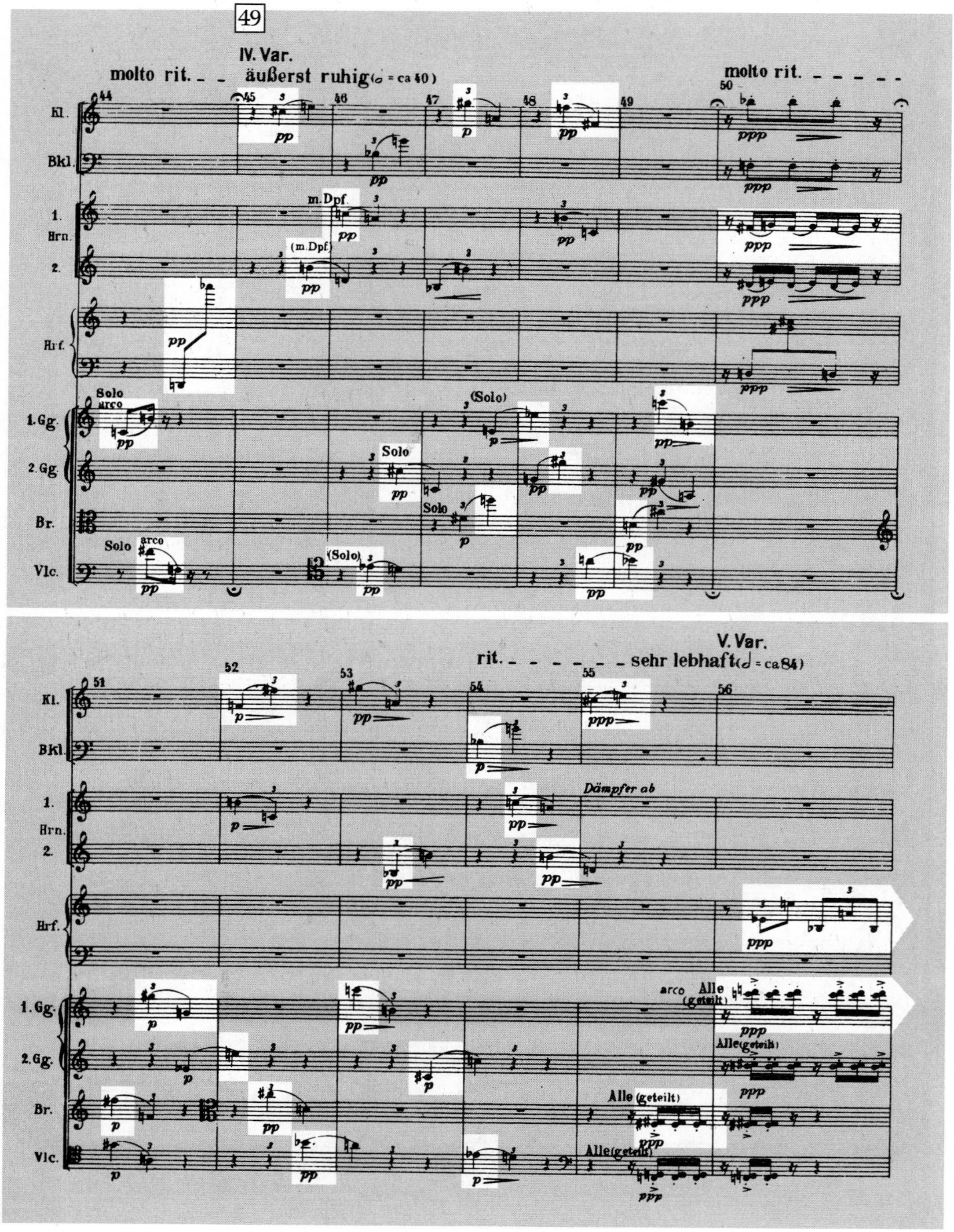

49

IV. Var.

molto rit. – – äußerst ruhig (o = ca 40)

molto rit. – – – – –

Kl.
Bkl.
1. Hrn. 2.
Hrf.
1. Gg.
2. Gg.
Br.
Vlc.

m.Dpf.
(m.Dpf.)
Solo arco
(Solo)
Solo

57
58
59
60
Kl.
Bkl.
1.
Hrn.
2.
Hrf.
1.Gg.
2.Gg.
Br.
Vlc.
pp
p
pp
cresc.
cresc.
cresc.
pp
cresc.
pp

61
62
63
64
Kl.
Bkl.
1.
Hrn.
2.
Hrf.
1.Gg.
2.Gg.
Br.
Vlc.
mf
p cresc.
mp cresc.
p cresc.
mp cresc.
p
cresc.
mp cresc.
p
cresc.
mp cresc.

VI. Var.
rit. marschmäßig (♩ = ca 66), nicht eilen
Kl.
Bkl.
1. Hrn. 2.
Hrf.
1. Gg.
2. Gg.
Br.
Vlc.
o. Dpf.
mf cresc.
gedämpft
offen
dim.
cresc.

50

VII. Var.
etwas breiter rit. tempo rit. tempo rit.

78 (𝅗𝅥 = ca 54)
79
80
81
82
83
Kl.
Bkl.
1.
Hrn.
2.
(o. Dpf.)
(m. Dpf.)
Hrf.
1.Gg.
2.Gg.
Br.
Vlc.
pizz.
arco
sf
ff
f
p
pp
mp

tempo
rit.
tempo
Coda
rit.
Kl.
Bkl.
Hrn.
Hrf.
1. Gg.
2. Gg.
Br.
Vlc.
(o. Dpf.)
(m. Dpf.)
(pizz.)
arco
pizz.
Solo
(Solo)
Solo pizz.
1928
10 Min.

Anton Webern (1883–1945) explored the more radical side of Schoenberg's Expressionistic vision. Unlike Berg, Webern created a style based on a stricter adherence to atonality and a concise and nonexpressive musical language. Instead of creating traditional structures from thematic units, Webern expanded upon Schoenberg's device of *Klangfarbenmelodie* (tone-color melody) and fashioned a colorful sound fabric out of touches of timbre, as individual instruments play only a few notes in succession, often separated by rests and large intervals. The disjointed effect has been termed pointillism, after the distinctive use of color dots in the paintings of Georges Seurat.

Webern's manipulation of serial techniques, and particularly his application of serialism to musical elements other than pitch, had a pronounced influence on composers of the post–World War II generation. His celebrated Symphony, Opus 21, reflects some Neoclassical qualities, particularly in the two-movement format featuring a sonata-allegro form with a double canon followed by a theme-and-variation structure. Both movements are based on the same dodecaphonic tone row. The row is a palindrome, so that intervals of the retrograde are identical to those of the prime. At the center of the row is a tritone, which is also the interval that separates the first and last note of the series. These characteristics are reflected in the structure of the second movement as a whole. Most notable is the palindrome structure, which can be seen within each variation and in the structure of the movement as a whole. The theme of the second movement, which spans eleven measures, is based on the transposed inversion and retrograde inversion of the tone row from the first movement. (A♮-F♯-G♮-G♯-E♮-F♮-B♮-B♭-D♮-C♯-C♮-E♭)

32. Alban Berg

8CD: 7/51–54

Wozzeck, Act III, Scene 4, Interlude, Scene 5 (1922)

Wozz
whispered loudly
da regt sich was.
Still!
Cel
As
(frog croaks)
(mp)
pp
230
accel
Etwas
(spoken)
(shouting)
Al-les still und tot.
Mör-der!
Str m D
Trp m D
pppp
Holz
ff
Hfe
gliss
(quasi Des-Dur)
rascher
235
again whispered
mf
poco rit
Mör - - - - der!!
Ha! da ruft's.
gest Hr
Str
gliss (C-Dur)
Hfe
Ces
(quasi Ces-Dur glissando)
Pos m D
— explores expressionistic themes of nightmares + insanity

(poco rit) - - - a tempo
poco string - - - - - poco rit - - molto
staggers a few more steps, searching, and comes upon the corpse
(spoken)
Wozz
Nein — ich selbst.
Ma-rie! Ma-
le-
gato
p non legato e poco cresc - - - mf
Str
molto pp
fehlende Akkordtöne
Kl
Solo Br
Trp
E H
Hr
Solo Vcl
etc
Beck
freihäng
Wieder langsamer, aber nicht schleppend
(quasi Hauptzeitmaß)
240
[quasi
rie! Was hast du für ei-ne ro - te Schnur um den Hals?
(Kl)
(Trp)
sempre pp
E H
p espr
2 Solo Gg
Hfe
sempre pp
(E H)
espr
(Kl)
port
etc

Walzertempo
poco string
(breaking into song)
Wozz
Hast Dir das ro - te Hals - band ver-dient, wie die Ohr - ring - lein,
(2 Gg)
(Hfe) hoch
Fl
Kl
p
poco cresc
H
richtige Lage
2 Solo Gg
(H)
poco cresc.
245
sempre string
mit Dei-ner Sün - de!
(spoken)
Wozz
mit Dei-ner Sün - de!
Rasch (♩ = 100-120)
Was hän - gen Dir die
Str
mf
f
Holz
K Bs allein
250
schwar - zen Haa - re so wild_?!_ Mör - der!_ Mör -
ff
(mit oberer 8va)
Holz
Pik
Xyl
Trp
(Holz)
Pauken

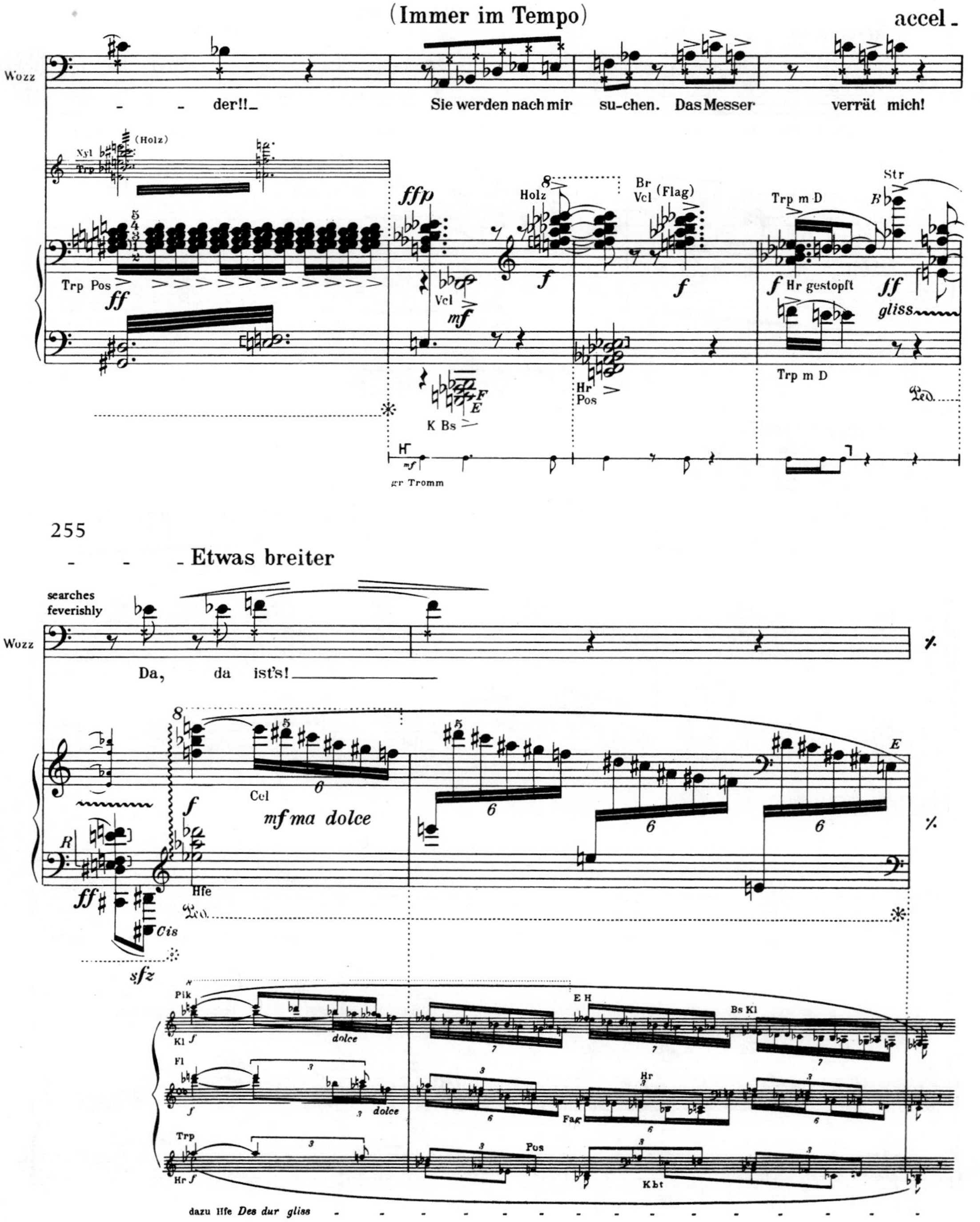

255

Etwas breiter

searches feverishly

Wozz

Da, da ist's!

Cel

mf ma dolce

f

Hfe

ff

sfz

Cis

E

Pik

Kl

dolce

E H

Bs Kl

Fl

Hr

Fag

Trp

Pos

Kbt

dazu Hfe *Des dur gliss*

Wie zu Anfang dieser Szene
(♩= ca 100)
ritard
quasi Hauptzeitmaß
(♩= 80)
am Teich
throws the knife in
Wozz
So! da hin-un-ter!
Es taucht ins
Holz Blech Holz
ff Str
dimin
p
Hfe
sfz
mf
poco a poco
260
dunk-le Was-ser wie ein Stein.
The moon rises blood-red from the clouds
Holz Blech Holz
Pos Hr
E H Kl
Pos
E H
Pos
Fag
Hr
dimin
verlöschend
Blech Holz Blech etc.
diminuendo
ppp
senza cresc
Hfe
pp
klcines Tamtam
freihängendes Becken
looks up
265
pp
A-ber der Mond ver-rät mich-
Der Mond ist blu-
6 Gg m D
Pos
alle 1. Gg ohne D
ppp
verlöschen
kl Tamtam
Becken
Hfe
verklingen lassen
gr Tamtam

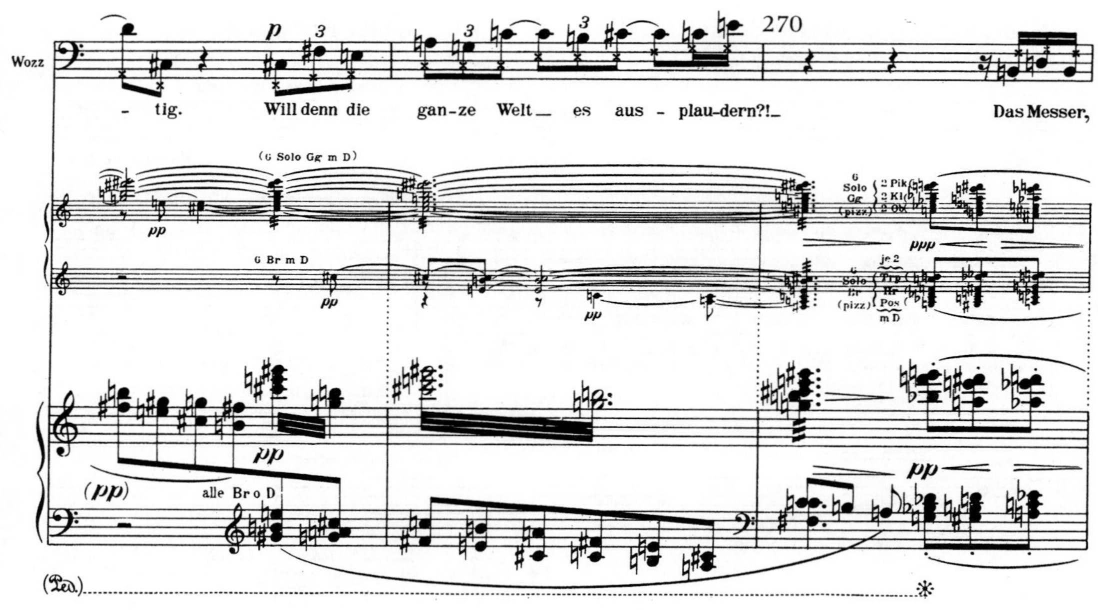
270
Wozz
-tig. Will denn die gan-ze Welt— es aus-plau-dern?!— Das Messer,
(6 Solo Gg m D)
6 Solo Gg (pizz) 2 Pik 2 Kl 2 Ob
6 Br m D
6 Solo Br (pizz) je 2 Trp Hr Pos m D
pp
ppp
(pp)
alle Br o D

Wozz
wades into
es liegt zu weit vorn, sie findens beim Ba-den o-der wenn sie nach Muscheln tauchen.
pp
p
etc
ppp

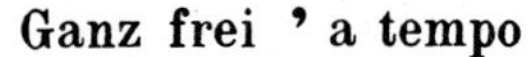
Ganz frei ' a tempo

the pond
275
(with a somewhat singing voice)
(spoken)
Wozz
Ich find's nicht.
A-ber ich muß mich wa-schen.
Ich bin blu-tig.
Gg m D
ppp ged Blech allein.
pp
f Holz
Pkn
mf
pp
tief
pp
Xyl
mf
1.Gg m D richtig
pp
2.Gg col legno gestr
(1.Gg)

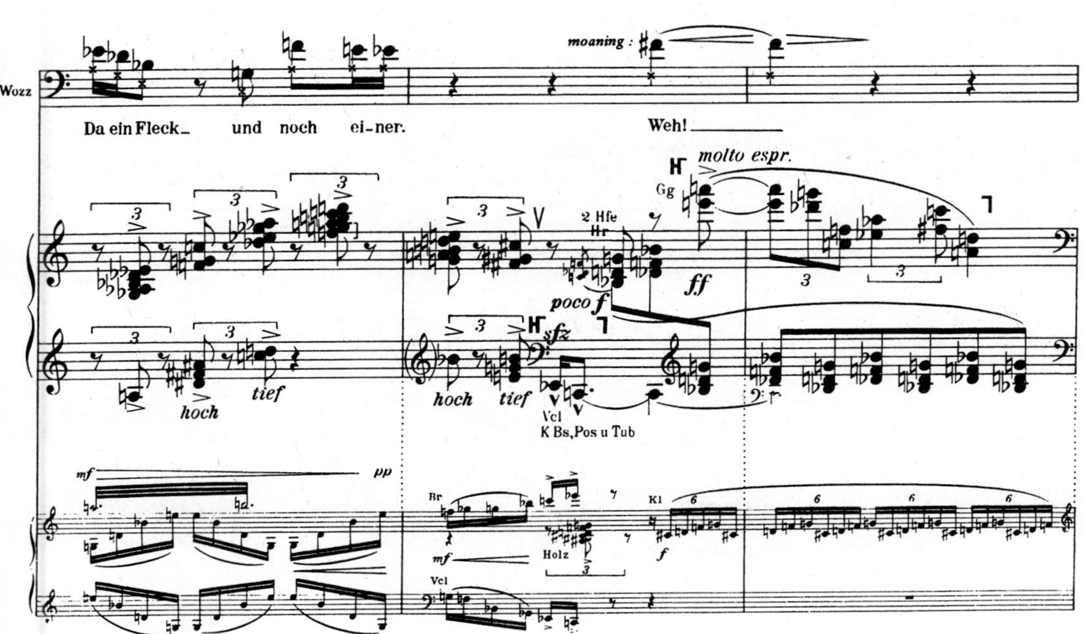
moaning:
Wozz
Da ein Fleck- und noch ei-ner.
Weh!
molto espr.
Gg
2 Hfe
Hr
poco f
ff
hoch
tief
sfz
Vcl
K Bs, Pos u Tub
mf
pp
Br
Kl
Holz
f
Vcl

280

Wozz

Weh! ich wa-sche mich mit Blut – das

hoch Vcl *f* *mf* (Hr Hfe) *f* K Bs, Tub *f* K Bs, Pos

hoch K Bs *mf* *mp* (Fag Hfe)

Kl *f* Bs Kl *f* *mf*

Fag *ff* K Fag

(he drowns . . .)

Wozz

Was-ser ist Blut . . . Blut . . .

p *pp* (*Beide Hände immer chromatisch*)

Str

Es 2. K Bs C C C

sempre Ped

Bs Kl *p* Holz u Hfe Vcl dazu *p* Br dazu (Str allein am Steg o D)

1. K Bs 3. K Bs

52
285
sempre pp
sempre pp
(ohne K Bs)
The Doctor enters
sempre pp
Holz
pp
Holz
ppp
(ohne Vcl)
p
Kl
Fag
Bs Kl
2 Fag
K Fag

The Captain follows the Doctor (speaks)
sempre pp
Fl dazu

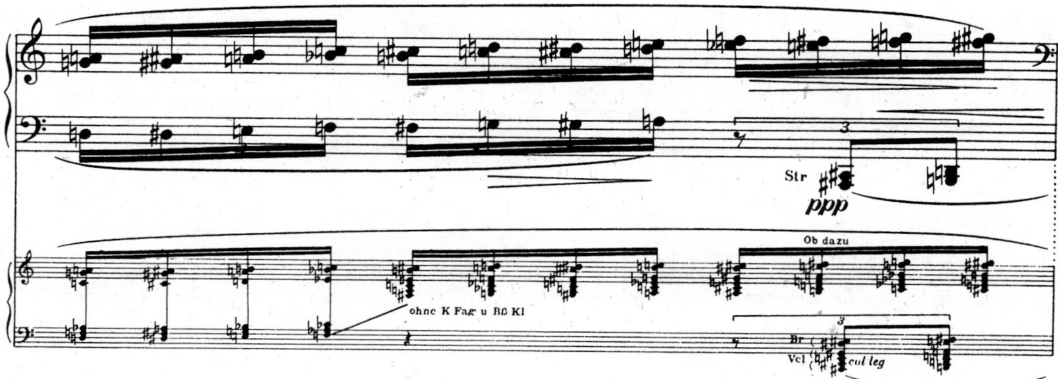
The Doctor (stands still): p Hören Sie? Dort!
Str
ppp
Ob dazu
ohne K Fag u Bß Kl
Br
Vcl
col leg

Hauptmann: p Jesus! Das war ein Ton. (also stands still)
290
Str 3
pp
ohne Fag
Ggn dazu

Doktor (pointing to the lake): **Ja, dort!** **Hauptmann:** Es ist das Wasser

im Teich. Das Wasser ruft. Es ist schon lange niemand ertrunken.

Hauptmann: Kommen Sie, Doktor! Es ist

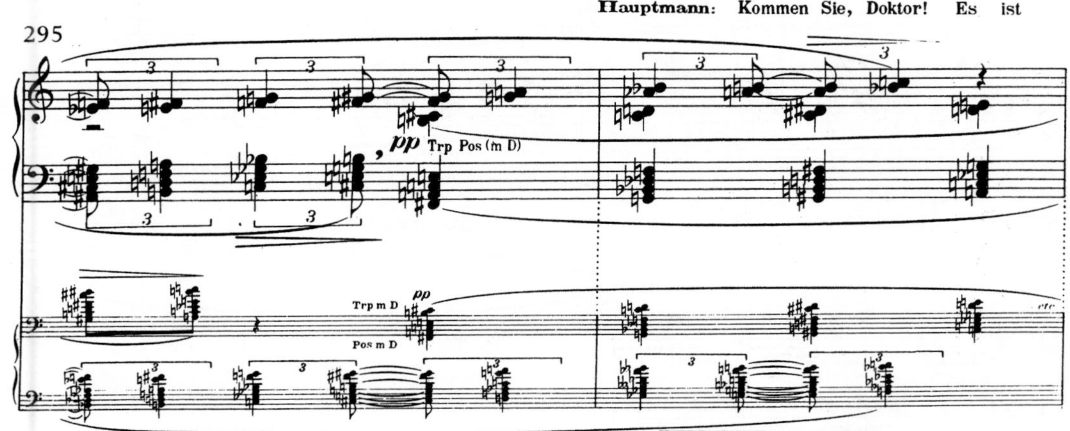

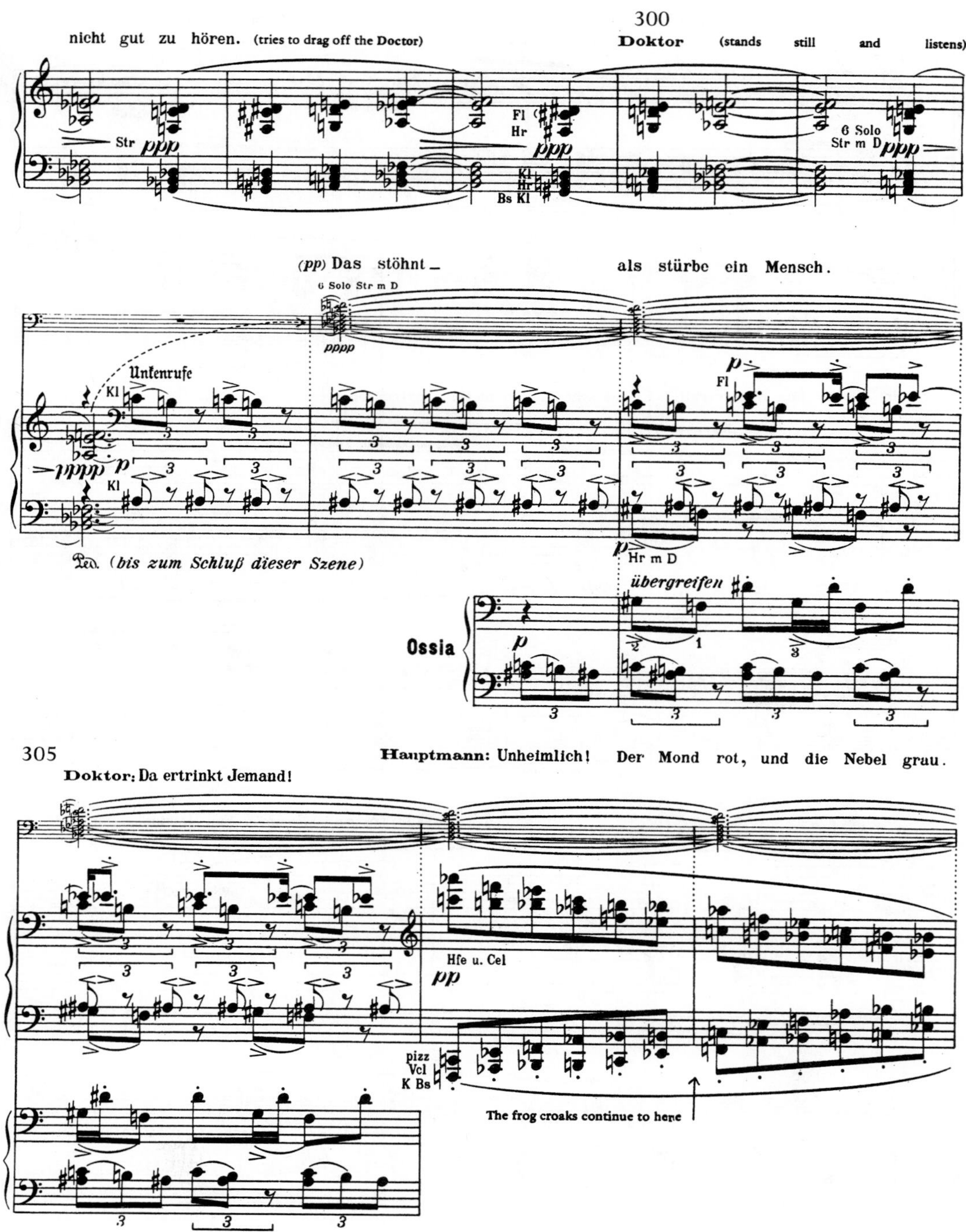
300
nicht gut zu hören. (tries to drag off the Doctor)
Doktor (stands still and listens)
Str
ppp
Fl
Hr
Kl
Hr
Bs Kl
6 Solo
Str m D
(pp) Das stöhnt _
als stürbe ein Mensch.
6 Solo Str m D
pppp
Unkenrufe
Kl
Fl
Ped. (bis zum Schluß dieser Szene)
Hr m D
übergreifen
Ossia
305
Doktor: Da ertrinkt Jemand!
Hauptmann: Unheimlich! Der Mond rot, und die Nebel grau.
Hfe u. Cel
pp
pizz
Vcl
K Bs
The frog croaks continue to here

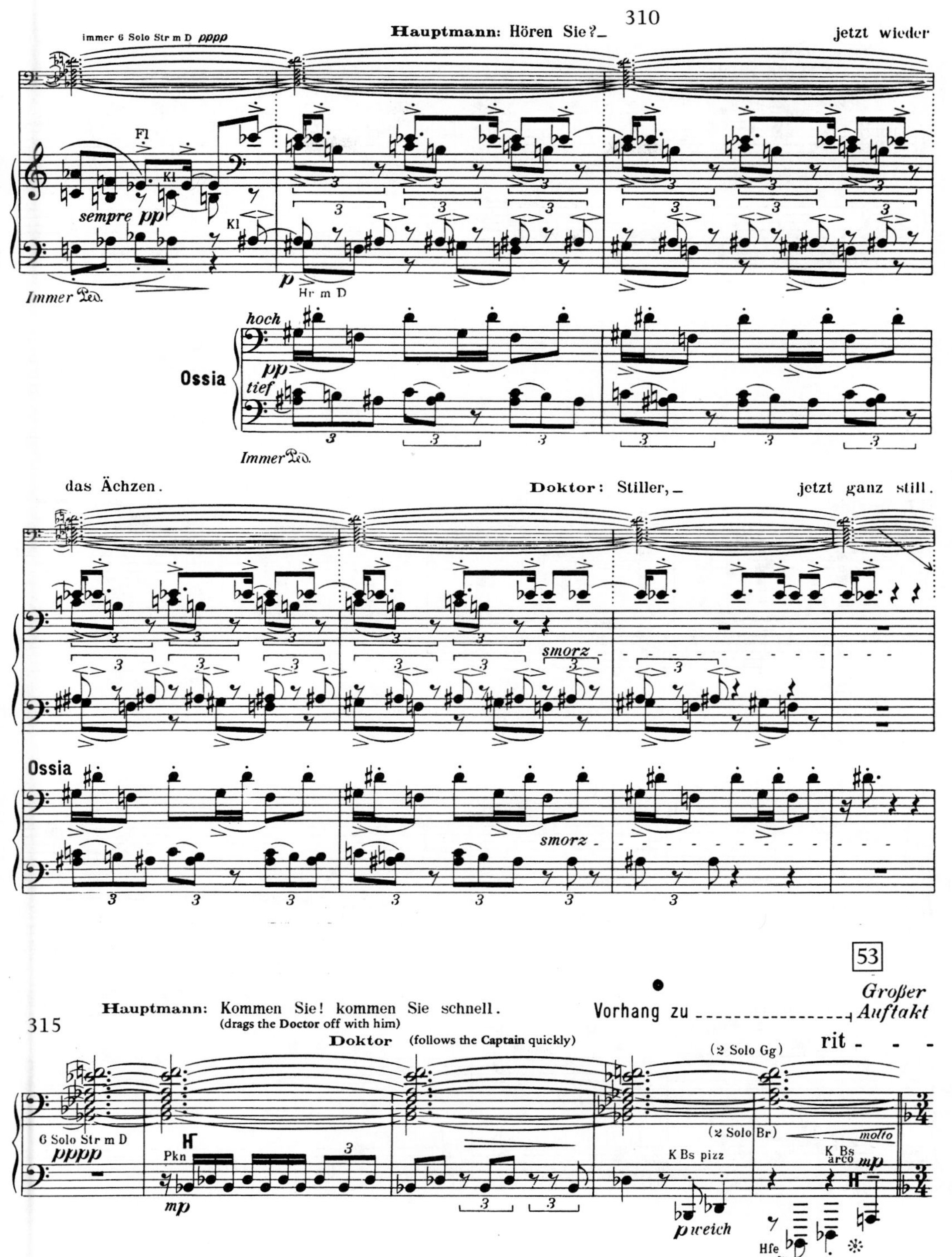
310
Hauptmann: Hören Sie?_
jetzt wieder
immer 6 Solo Str m D pppp
Fl
Kl
sempre pp
Kl
p
Hr m D
Immer Ped.
hoch
pp
Ossia
tief
Immer Ped.
das Ächzen.
Doktor: Stiller,_
jetzt ganz still.
smorz
Ossia
smorz
315
Hauptmann: Kommen Sie! kommen Sie schnell.
(drags the Doctor off with him)
Doktor (follows the Captain quickly)
Vorhang zu
53
Großer Auftakt
rit
(2 Solo Gg)
(2 Solo Br)
molto
6 Solo Str m D
pppp
Pkn
mp
K Bs pizz
p weich
K Bs arco
mp
Hfe
p (B Des)

320

Scene change

Adagio (♩= ♩= mindestens 46)

2.Gge
Br
p
Vcl dazu
2 Fag dazu
3
p
3
3. Fag u K Fag dazu
1.Ggn
p
(*mp*) (K Bs)

Solo Gg
pp
II. Spieler

I. Spieler

325

Kl 2.Gg
3
Str allein
p
Fag dazu

1. Hälfte Ggn
alle Ggn
330
p
mf
Ob dazu
3
Fl dazu
(Ob)
p
I
3 Fag
p
zurücktreten
mp Hr
3
mf
3
Pos
mp
3
II
Orig 8va
Hr
p
K Bs

I
II
1. Gg
Hfe
Pos u 2. Gg
Trp
Str
Pos
Hfe (Ganzton-Glissando)
335
nicht eilen
Holz u Trp
1. Gg u. Pos
molto
tief
sehr hoch
Pos
1. Gg dazu
Blech
2. Gg Trp
Br
Vcl dazu
Kbt Tamtam
340
klagend
Ggn
Str
allein
Br
(weg)
espress
Vcl
Fag
Hr
(gest)
wie aus der Ferne,
aber deutlich
meno p

string
molto
menop
1.Gg u 4 Ob cresc
mp
Fag
mp
mf
cresc
Vel
Holz
pp
Vel u. K-B
345
Bedeutend bewegter
(♩= 80-84)
ff furioso
Trp
(pizz)
Ob
(tief)
Pos
f
Str trem
Pk trem
(gr Trommschlag)
350
je 4
Kl, Fl
(pizz)
pizz
cresc
fp
Hr
Trp
f
Str
mf
3 Pos
m D
cresc

rall
Wieder etwas breiter (Andante)
(Fl Kl)
Str u Ob
Kl
f espr
(Trp)
(Pos) Hfe
rauschend
weg!
(cresc)
(Pke)
Hfe
355
Wieder drängend
Kl (Hfe)
(hoch) Ob
molto
col leg
Pos
Hrn u Fag (kl Tromm)
(tief)
(Br Vcl K Bs)
Wiede breiter
360
Ob
Trp Gg Xyl
f cresc
Br
alles übertönend
3 Pos
Hr Vcl
weg
Br Vcl
(3 Pos)
Hr Vcl
Hr
Pos
1 Pos
2 Pos
3 Pos
etc
Fag Bß Kl
cresc
Holz Str Tub gr Tromm

Breit
molto rit
365
Tempo I
12 Holzbl
Trp
(Tutti)
molto
Fl Kl Gg
(4 Pos)
Br
Hr
Schlagwerk
Hr Trp Br
Pos Hfe pizz 4 Pkn
Schon im neuen Tempo
(ohne Str)
dimin
weg
nicht hervortreten
(ohne Hr)
(ohne Pkn)
meno ff
espr
(quasi 4/4 Takt
ohne Pos Tb
54
Vorhang auf
370
molto p Str
Gg Fl Br
Cel
Ob Ggu
(Kl)
deutlich kadenzieren
molto
Hr Trp
Blech
Hfe
hoch
sehr hoch
Br u. Vcl
Pos Tub
Holz dazu
K Bß

5th (last) Scene In front of Marie's house (bright morning, sunshine)
Flowing 8ths, but with much rubato
= the previous triplet
(= 72 beginning)
parents dead - child alone
Mariens Knabe riding a hobby horse
children's voices
Kinder playing and shouting
Rin - gel, Rin - gel, Ro - sen-kranz, Rin - - - - gel-reihn!
Triangelschlag
Cel
Kl
sempre staccato
Flu
Gg pizz pp
zwei händig
2.Gg pizz
[richtig] pp
etc
375
Plötzlich schneller, aber sofort rall
Kinder playing
stop singing and playing
Rin - gel, Rin - gel, Ro - sen-kranz, Rin - - -
Other children rush in
Eins von ihnen (spoken)
Du, Käthe! – Die Marie...
Hfe
Kl Tamtam
freihäng Becken
Es Kl
Trp
m D
(sempre staccato)
Hr
Str
Tub

Zweites Kind: Was is?
Erstes Kind: Weißt' es nit? Sie sind schon Alle 'naus.
(rall)
(♩. = 58)
Noch etwas langsamer
Wieder voriges Tempo
380
Mariens Knabe (still riding)
Hopp, hopp!
Dritten Kind (to Marie's child): Du! Dein Mutter ist tot!
Pkn gedämpft
'poco rit
a tempo, ma sempre rubato
Mariens Knabe
Hopp, hopp! Hopp, hopp!
Zweites Kind: Wo is sie denn?
Erstes Kind: Draus liegt sie, am Weg, neben dem Teich.
(poco espr.)

385
riding
Mariens Knabe
Hopp,hopp! Hopp,hopp! Hopp,hopp!
Drittes Kind:
Kommt – anschaun!
Alle Kinder run off
(poco rit)
(Es Kl)
Bs Kl
Xyl
Solo Kl
ganz ohne Ausdruck
Str allein
Pke gedämpft
gr Tromm
dimin
p poco espress
Solo Vcl
Mariens Knabe (alone) hesitates for a moment, then rides off after the other children
Vorhang fällt
(ab) Leere Bühne
Etwas zögernd und molto rubato.
Allmählich wieder gleichmäßig fließend werden:
Quasi Tempo I
[rit. acc. rit. acc. rit. acc. rit. acc. rit] (♩. = ca 52)
poco espress
Solo Br
Trp m D
Solo Gg m D
Fl Cel
pp sempre senza cresc e dim
sempre pp, ma molto espr
Hr m D
Br
(Hr)
(Trp)
Fl Cel
nuendo
ppp
senza rit
390
(beide Hände hoch)
I
vierhändig
(tief)
II
Str m D ohne K Bß
pp
p
mp
molto p
ppp
(Hfe)
End of the opera

Text and Translation

Scene Four
Invention on a Chord of Six Notes

Path in the wood by the pond. Moonlight, as before.
(Wozzeck stumbles hurriedly in, then stops, looking around for something.)

Wozzeck

Das Messer? Wo ist das Messer? Ich hab's dagelassen. Näher, noch näher. Mir graut's . . . da regt sich was. Still! Alles still und tot.

The knife? Where is the knife? I left it there. Around here somewhere. I'm terrified . . . something's moving. Silence. Everything silent and dead.

(Shouting)

Mörder! Mörder!

Murderer! Murderer!

(Whispering again)

Ha! Da ruft's. Nein, ich selbst.

Ah! Someone called. No, it was only me.

(Still looking, he staggers a few steps further and stumbles against the corpse.)

Marie! Marie! Was hast du für eine
rote Schnur um den Hals?
Hast dir das rote Halsband
verdient, wie die Ohrringlein, mit deiner
Sünde! Was hängen dir die schwarzen Haare
so wild? Mörder! Mörder! Sie werden nach
mir suchen. Das Messer verrät mich!

Marie! Marie! What's that red cord around
your neck?
Was the red necklace payment for your sins,
like the earrings? Why's your
dark hair so wild about you? Murderer!
Murderer! They will come and look for me.
The knife will betray me!

(Looks for it in a frenzy)

Da, da ist's!

Here! Here it is!

(At the pond)

So! Da hinunter!

There! Sink to the bottom!

(Throws the knife into the pond)

Es taucht ins dunkle Wasser wie ein Stein.

It plunges into the dark water like a stone.

(The moon appears, blood-red, from behind the clouds. Wozzeck looks up.)

Aber der Mond verrät mich, der Mond ist
blutig.
Will den die ganze Welt es ausplaudern?
Das Messer, es liegt zu weit vorn, sie
finden's
beim Baden oder wenn sie nach
Muscheln tauchen.

But the moon will betray me: the moon is
blood-stained.
Is the whole world going to incriminate me?
The knife is too near the edge:
they'll find it when they're swimming
or diving for snails.

(Wades into the pond)

Ich find's nicht. Aber ich muss mich waschen.	I can't find it. But I must wash myself.
Ich bin blutig. Da ein Fleck—und noch einer.	There's blood on me. There's a spot here—and another.
Weh! Weh! Ich wasche mich mit Blut—	Oh, God! I am washing myself in blood—
das Wasser ist Blut . . . Blut . . .	the water is blood. . . blood . . .

(Drowns)
(The Doctor appears, followed by the Captain.)

CAPTAIN

Halt!	Wait!

DOCTOR *(Stops)*

Hören Sie? Dort!	Can you hear? There!

CAPTAIN

Jesus! Das war ein Ton!	Jesus! What a ghastly sound!

(Stops as well)

DOCTOR *(Pointing to the pond)*

Ja, dort!	Yes, there!

CAPTAIN

Es ist das Wasser im Teich. Das Wasser ruft.	It's the water in the pond. The water is calling.
Es ist schon lange Niemand ertrunken.	It's been a long time since anyone drowned.
Kommen Sie, Doktor!	Come away, Doctor.
Es ist nicht gut zu hören.	It's not good for us to be hearing it.

(Tries to drag the doctor away)

DOCTOR *(Resisting, and continuing to listen)*

Das stöhnt, als stürbe ein Mensch. Da ertrinkt Jemand!	There's a groan, as though someone were dying. Somebody's drowning!

CAPTAIN

Unheimlich! Der Mond rot, und die Nebel grau.	It's eerie! The moon is red, and the mist is grey.
Hören Sie? . . . Jetzt wieder das Ächzen.	Can you hear? . . . That moaning again.

DOCTOR

Stiller, . . . jetzt ganz still.	It's getting quieter . . . now it's stopped altogether.

CAPTAIN

Kommen Sie! Kommen Sie schnell! — Come! Come quickly!

(He rushes off, pulling the doctor along with him.)

SCENE CHANGE
INVENTION ON A KEY (D MINOR)

SCENE FIVE
INVENTION ON A QUAVER RHYTHM

In front of Marie's door. Morning. Bright sunshine.

(Children are noisily at play. Marie's child is riding a hobby-horse.)

CHILDREN

Ringel, Ringel, Rosenkranz, Ringelreih'n,	Ring-a-ring-a-roses,
Ringel, Ringel, Rosenkranz, Ring. . .	a pocket full of. . .

(Their song and game are interrupted by other children bursting in.)

ONE OF THE NEWCOMERS

Du, Käthe! Die Marie!	Hey, Katie! Have you heard about Marie?

SECOND CHILD

Was ist?	What's happened?

FIRST CHILD

Weisst' es nit? Sie sind schon Alle'naus.	Don't you know? They've all gone out there.

THIRD CHILD *(To Marie's little boy)*

Du! Dein'Mutter ist tot!	Hey! Your mother's dead!

MARIE'S SON *(Still riding)*

Hopp, hopp! Hopp, hopp! Hopp, hopp!	Hop, hop! Hop, hop! Hop, hop!

SECOND CHILD

Wo ist sie denn?	Where is she, then?

FIRST CHILD

Draus' liegt sie, am Weg, neben dem Teich.	She's lying out there, on the path near the pond.

THIRD CHILD

Kommt, anschaun!	Come and have a look!

(All the children run off.)

MARIE'S SON *(Continuing to ride)*

Hopp, hopp! Hopp, hopp! Hopp, hopp! Hop, hop! Hop, hop! Hop, hop!

(He hesitates for a moment and then rides after the other children.)

TRANSLATED BY SARAH E. SOULSBY

Schoenberg's two most eminent students, Alban Berg (1885–1935) and Anton Webern, each created a distinctive style bound only by the commonality of Expressionism and serialism. Berg maintained ties to the lyricism and emotional intensity of late Romanticism, which he exploits fully in his masterpiece, the opera *Wozzeck*. Based on an early nineteenth-century play by Georg Büchner, the opera tells the disturbing tale of Wozzeck, a common soldier in the army who is abused both by his captain and by the army doctor. The only love in his life is Marie, and they have a young child born out of wedlock. Marie has an affair, and this pushes Wozzeck over the edge. Near a lake, he brutally murders her. Eventually Wozzeck drowns in the lake, which he perceives as a pool of blood. The frustrations of Wozzeck's hopeless life, as portrayed in Büchner's play, symbolize the political repressions of the post-Napoleonic years; based on real-life events, the opera explores Expressionistic themes of nightmares and insanity.

Berg organizes the opera into three acts, each with five scenes. Orchestral interludes serve as transitions between the scenes. In Act III, Scene 4, Wozzeck has returned to the scene of the murder. After observing Marie's dead body and admiring the "red necklace" around her neck, he looks for and finds the murder weapon. He throws the knife into the lake, but then panics that the knife did not go deep enough. In his effort to retrieve it he drowns. In a chilling touch, the captain and the doctor—symbols of authority in society—appear at the lake, hear the sounds of death, and leave quickly, rather than helping. The music, which had supported the scene with gentle chromaticism, surges forth during the interlude. Berg employs the full brute force of the orchestra, mixing dissonances and tonal elements, to express anguish over the events.

The final scene provides a simple yet unsettling close to the opera. The young child of Wozzeck and Marie is playing in the street along with other children. An older child runs in with news that Marie has been found, and the children all race out to see the dead body. Too young to understand, Marie's child rides on his hobbyhorse after the other children to the sounds of "Hop, hop." We are left to imagine his reaction to the gruesome scene that awaits him. Throughout the final scene, the innocence of the music, with its childlike compound meter, enhances the tragedy of the story.

33. Sergei Prokofiev

8CD: 7/55–58

Alexander Nevsky, Seventh Movement (1939)

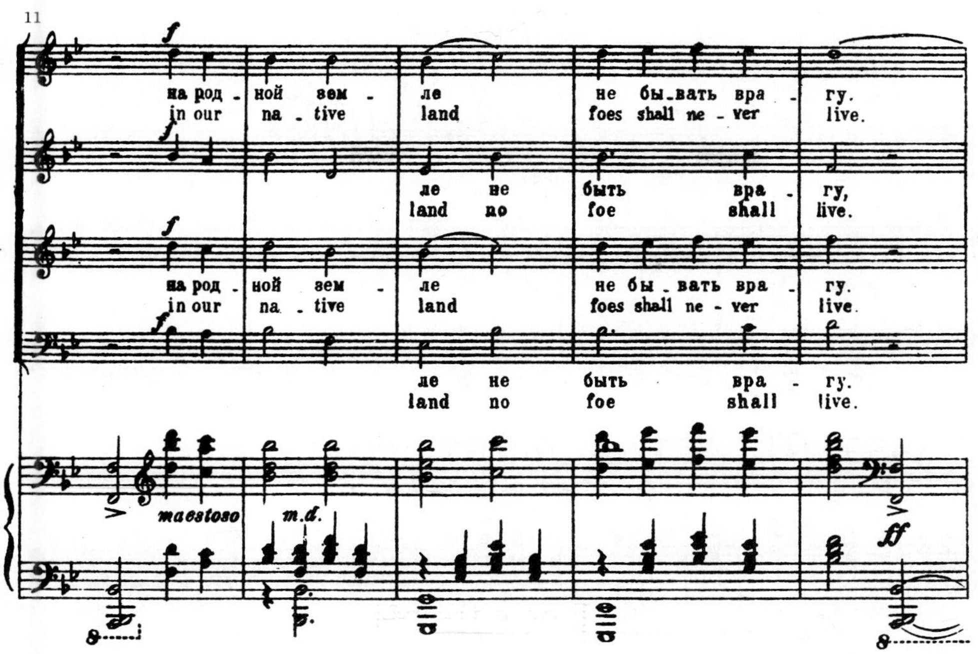
11
f
на род - ной зем - ле не бы-вать вра - гу.
in our na - tive land foes shall ne - ver live.
ле не быть вра - гу,
land no foe shall live.
на род - ной зем - ле не бы - вать вра - гу.
in our na - tive land foes shall ne - ver live.
ле не быть вра - гу.
land no foe shall live.
maestoso
m.d.
ff
8

16
f
ff
Кто при - дёт бу - дёт на смерть бит.
Foes who come shall be put to death.
Кто при - дёт бу-дет на смерть бит.
Foes who come shall be put to death.
бу - дет
shall be
8

56
Allegro, ma non troppo ♩= 84
Camp.
Xilof.
Legni, Tr-be
Arpa, Archi
simile
S.
Ве - се - ли - ся, пой, мать род - на - я Русь! На - род - ной Ру - си
Ce - le - brate and sing, na - tive mo - ther Russ! In our na - tive land
A.
Ве - се - ли - ся, пой, мать род - на - я Русь! На - род - ной Ру - си
Ce - le - brate and sing, na - tive mo - ther Russ! In our na - tive land

34
p subito
cresc.
не бы-вать вра-гу, не ви-дать вра-гу на-ших рус-ских сёл.
foes shall ne-ver live. Foes shall ne-ver see Rus-sian towns and fields.
p subito
cresc.
не бы-вать вра-гу, не ви-дать вра-гу на-ших рус-ских сёл.
foes shall ne-ver live. Foes shall ne-ver see Rus-sian towns and fields.
p
p subito
cresc.
37 S.
f
Кто при-дёт на Русь бу-дет на смерть бит!
They who march on Russ shall be put to death!
A.
f
Кто при-дёт на Русь бу-дет на смерть бит!
They who march on Russ shall be put to death!
T.
f
Не ви-дать вра-гу
Foes shall ne-ver see
B.
f
Не ви-дать вра-гу
Foes shall ne-ver see
f
V-ni
f espress.
m. d.
f

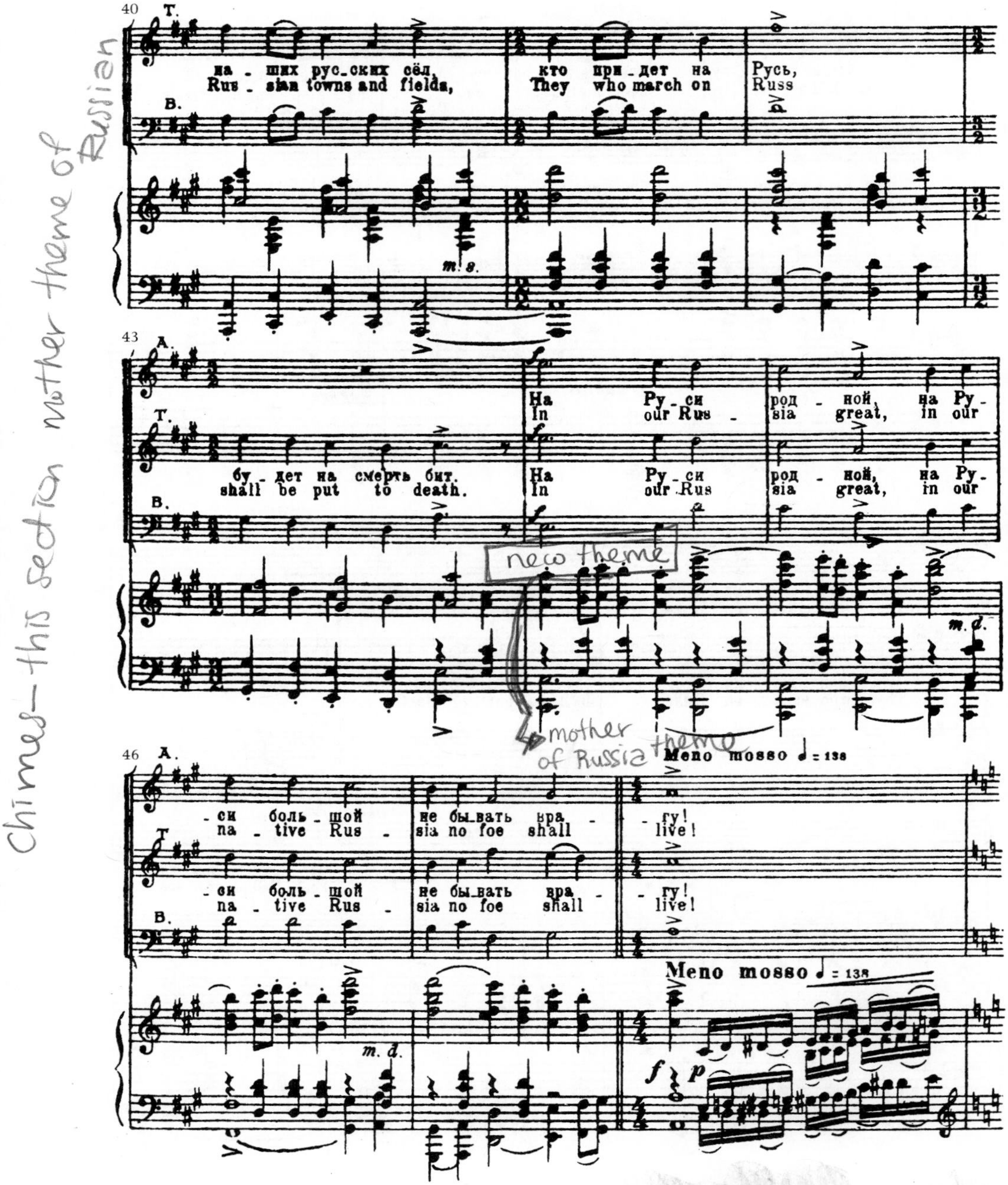

40

T.

на _ ших рус_ских сёл, | кто при_дет на | Русь,

Rus _ sian towns and fields, | They who march on | Russ

B.

m. s.

43

A.

На Ру_си | род _ ной, на Ру-

In our Rus _ | sia great, in our

T.

бу_дет на смерть бит. | На Ру_си | род _ ной, на Ру-

shall be put to death. | In our Rus | sia great, in our

B.

m. d.

46 A.

_ си боль_шой | не бы_вать вра _ | _ гу!

na _ tive Rus _ | sia no foe shall | live!

T

_ си боль_шой | не бы_вать вра _ | _ гу!

na _ tive Rus _ | sia no foe shall | live!

B.

Meno mosso ♩ = 138

m. d.

Meno mosso ♩ = 138

f *p*

57
Legni
Tr-be
Corni
Archi pizz.
Fl.
Fl.
Ob.

64
Fl.
Cl.
Cl.
p
66
Fl.
Archi
69
Fag.
mf
72
C. ing.
Ob.
mp
p
75
Sax.

58
Alti
Bassi
Fl
Cl.
Fg.
Sax.
На Ру -
In our
-си родной, на Ру -
Rus - sia great, in our
Ob.
-си боль - шой не бы -
na - tive Rus - sia no

84
-вать
foe
вра
shall
-гу.
live.
Cl.
Fl.
Cl.
86
Be
Ce
се
le
Sax.
Ob.
88
-ли
-brate
ся,
and
пой,
sing,
mf
mf
mf
Fl.
Fag.
Cl.

90
мать
na
род
tive
на
moth
Cl.
92
S.
A
T.
B.
На
In
Ру
our
си
Rus
род
sia
Русь!
Russ!
я
er
Ob.
Fl.
Fl., Archi
f espress.
Corni, Cl. b
Hymn-like, grand

95
-ной, на Ру - си боль - шой не бы - вать вра - - гу.
great, in our na - tive Rus - sia no foe shall live.
на Ру - си
in our
-ной, на Ру - си боль - шой не бы - вать вра - - гу.
great, in our na - tive Rus - sia no foe shall live.
на Ру - си
in our na-
100
Ве - се - ли - ся, пой, мать род-на-я Русь!
Ce - le - brate and sing, na-tive mo-ther Russ!
Ве - се - ли - ся, пой, мать род-на-я Русь!
Ce - le - brate and sing, na-tive mo-ther Russ!

105
Più largamente
S.
На ве - ли - кий празд - ник
To a fete in tri - umph
A.
T.
На ве - ли - кий празд - ник
To a fete in tri - umph
B.
Xil.
Camp.
Più largamente
Tr-be, Corni
Celli
Bassi
110
со - бра - ла - ся Русь.
all of Rus - sia came.
Be - се - ли - ся,
Ce - le - brate, re -
со - бра - ла - ся Русь.
all of Rus - sia came.
Be - се - ли - ся,
Ce - le - brate, re -
m.s.

115
Русь!
joice,
Ве се - ли - ся,
ce - le - brate and
Русь,
sing,
род -
our
Русь!
joice,
Ве се - ли - ся,
ce - le - brate and
Русь,
sing,
род -
our
Camp.
Tr-ni
m.s. m.d.
m.s. m.d.
f pesante
120
poco allarg.
на
moth
я
er
мать!
land!
на
moth
я
er
мать!
land!
poco allarg
m.s.m.d.
m.s.

After over fifteen years of self-imposed exile, Sergei Prokofiev (1891–1953) returned to his homeland, the Soviet Union, eventually settling in Moscow in 1936. Among the most important works created during his Soviet years are several film scores made in collaboration with the nation's foremost film director, Sergei Eisenstein. The first of these resulted in the classic film *Alexander Nevsky* (1938), which tells the story of the thirteenth-century hero who defeated both the Swedish army and, two years later, the Germans. The later event, which culminates with Nevsky's brilliant victory on the frozen Lake Chudskoye, provides the subject for the film's plot.

Prokofiev extracted and refined some of the musical sections of the film to create a seven-movement cantata for mezzo-soprano, chorus, and orchestra. The last movement, subtitled *Alexander's Entry into Pskov,* is taken from the triumphant final portion of the film. Prokofiev creates a distinctive Russian character by tapping into the strong choral tradition of the country and by employing a folklike melody, reminiscent of Musorgsky. This final movement of the cantata not only exhibits a nationalistic character, but also projects in its fullness of sound the Soviet government's view of the powerful working class.

34. George Gershwin

Piano Prelude No. 1 (published 1927)

8CD: 7/59–61
4CD: 4/41–43

60
42
pp
cresc.
f
p
mf
decresc.
Ped.
cresc.
f
p
mf
mf
p

f
p
p
f
f
poco a poco cresc.
8
Ped.

61
43
ff
p
ff
f

American popular music, especially jazz, provided a source of inspiration for a number of European and American composers. Among these figures was the American jazz pianist George Gershwin (1898–1937), who created the most successful synthesis of the popular and classical worlds. A master of popular songs, many of which were written for Broadway or Hollywood musicals, Gershwin sought to integrate jazz elements into art music with his first major orchestral work, *Rhapsody in Blue* (1924). Among his other celebrated works fusing the two styles are the piano preludes, the Piano Concerto in F, the symphonic poem *An American in Paris,* and the folk opera *Porgy and Bess.*

The renowned virtuoso violinist Jascha Heifetz was a close friend of Gershwin, and after Gershwin's untimely death, Heifetz transcribed a number of his works for piano and violin, including the three piano preludes, which were originally composed in 1927. The Prelude No. 1, set in **A–B–A** form, features a syncopated accompaniment and a jazz-like melody with wide leaps, quick runs, and the characteristic "blues" lowering of the seventh degree in the opening phrase. In the arrangement, the piano primarily functions as the accompaniment while the violin plays the melody or a new contrapuntal line against a piano melody. In this recording by Joshua Bell (violin) and John Williams (piano), Bell creates a jazz sound by sliding into notes, slightly flattening some pitches, and introducing a slap pizzicato near the beginning.

35. Silvestre Revueltas

8CD: 7/62–69

4CD: 4/15–22

Homenaje a Federico García Lorca (Homage to Federico García Lorca), Third Movement, *Son* (1937)

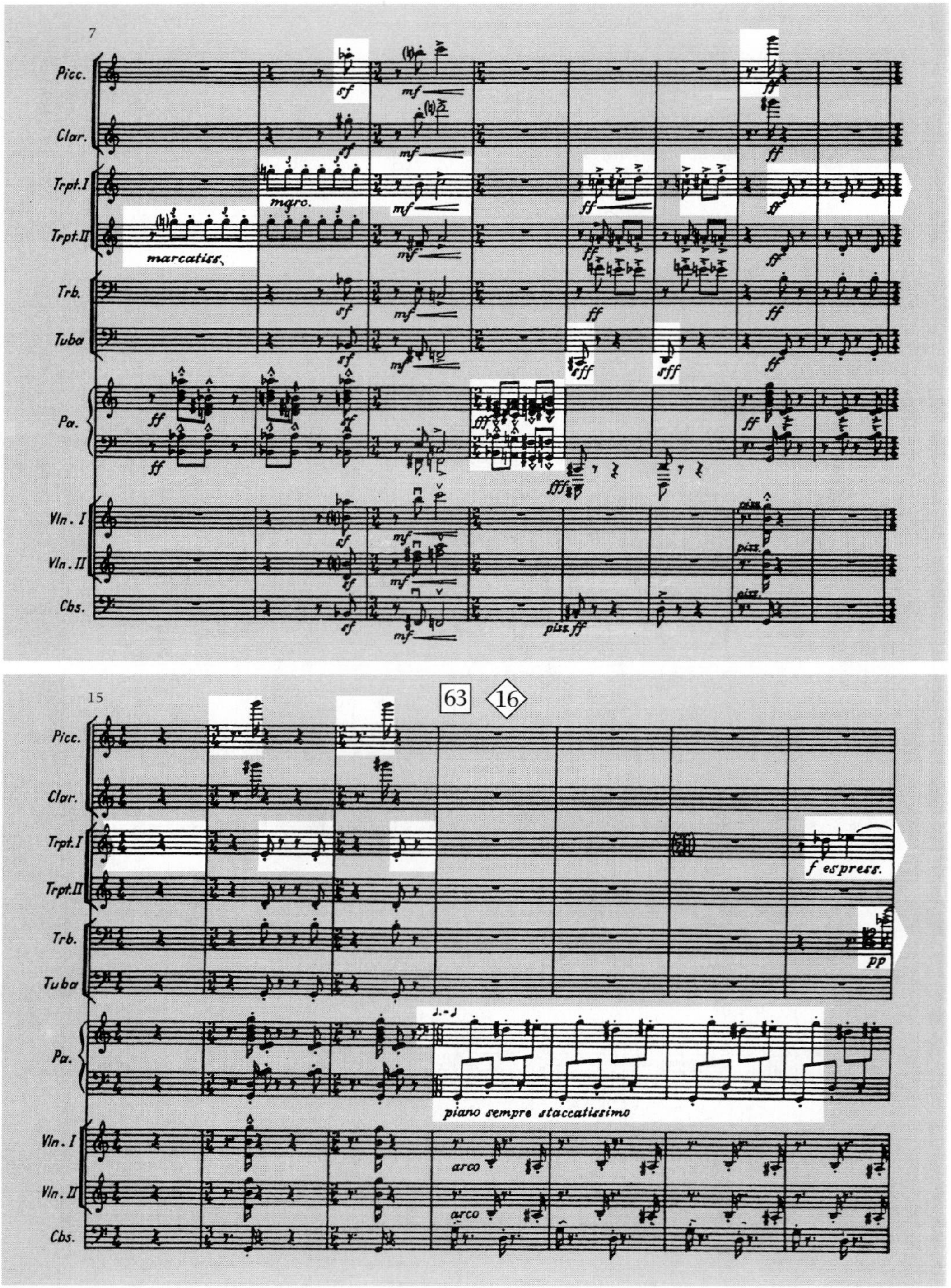

15
63
16
Picc.
Clar.
Trpt.I
Trpt.II
Trb.
Tuba
Pa.
Vln. I
Vln. II
Cbs.
f espress.
pp
piano sempre staccatissimo
arco
arco

22
Picc.
Clar.
Trpt. I
ma con sordino
Trpt. II
Trb.
molto espress.
Tuba
Pa.
Vln. I
Vln. II
Cbs.

28
Picc.
sff
mf
Clar.
sff
mf
Trpt. I
mf
sord.
Trpt. II
marc. ff
mf
Trb.
sempre pp
mf
Tuba
mf
Pa.
ff
sff
ff
Vln. I
ff
mf
Vln. II
ff
mf
Cbs.
ff
arco
mf

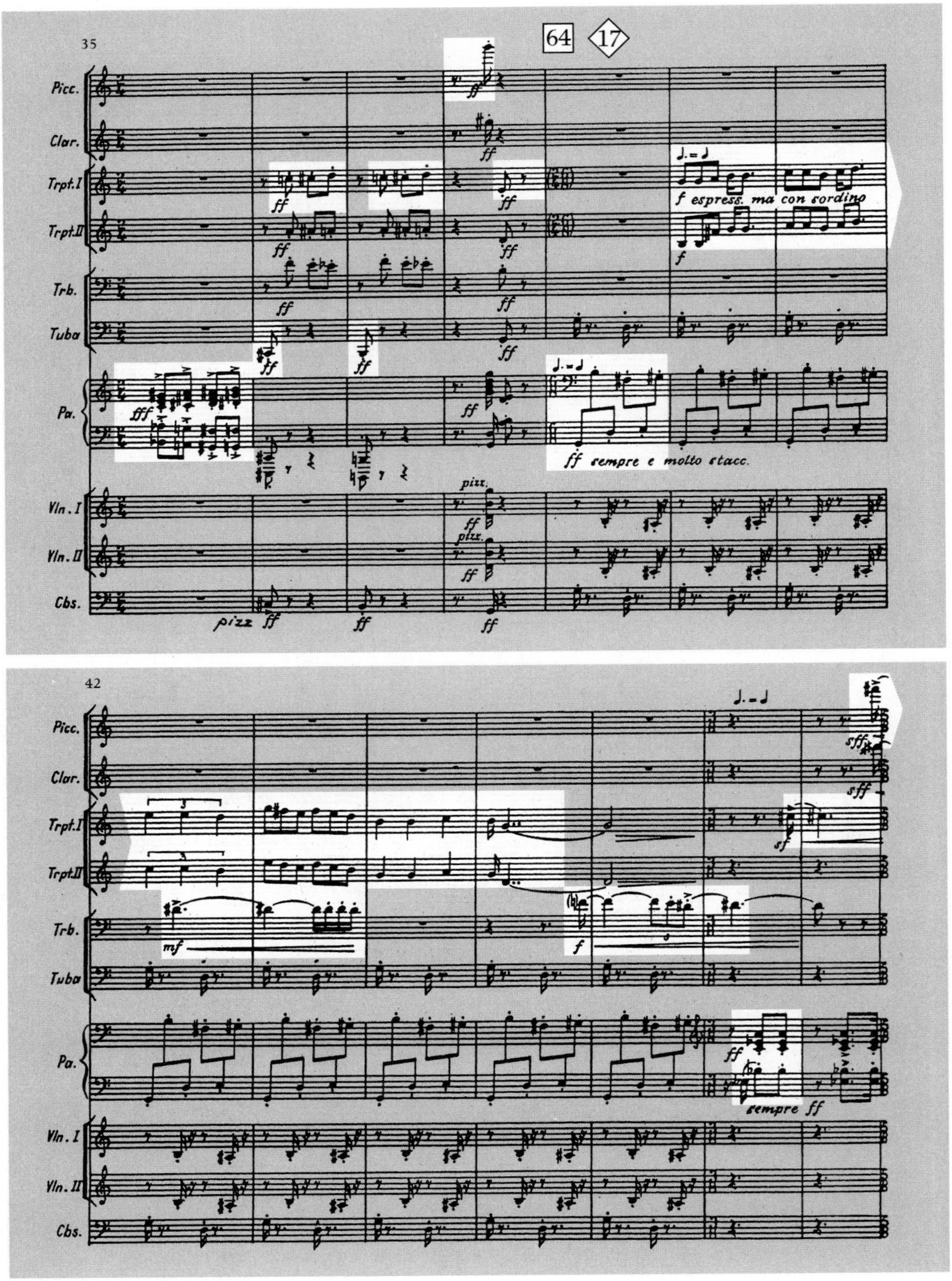

35

64 17

Picc.
Clar.
Trpt. I
Trpt. II
Trb.
Tuba
Pa.
Vln. I
Vln. II
Cbs.

f espress. ma con sordino

ff sempre e molto stacc.

pizz.

pizz

49
Picc.
Clar.
Trpt. I
Trpt. II
Trb.
Tuba
Pa.
Vln. I
Vln. II
Cbs.
ff
f
mf
arco
pizz
55
espress.
f espress.

62
Picc.
Clar.
Trpt. I
Trpt. II
Trb.
Tuba
Pa.
Vln. I
Vln. II
Cbs.
ff
sff
sempre staccatissimo
pizz.
pizz. sff

68
Picc.
Clar.
Trpt. I
Trpt. II
Trb.
Tuba
Pa.
Vln. I
Vln. II
Cbs.
f
mf
IV
gliss.

73
Picc.
Clar.
Trpt. I
Trpt. II
Trb.
Tuba
Pa.
Vln. I
Vln. II
Cbs.
gliss.
con sord.

79
Picc.
Clar.
Trpt. I
Trpt. II
Trb.
Tuba
Pa.
Vln. I
Vln. II
Cbs.
con sord.
pizz.
arco

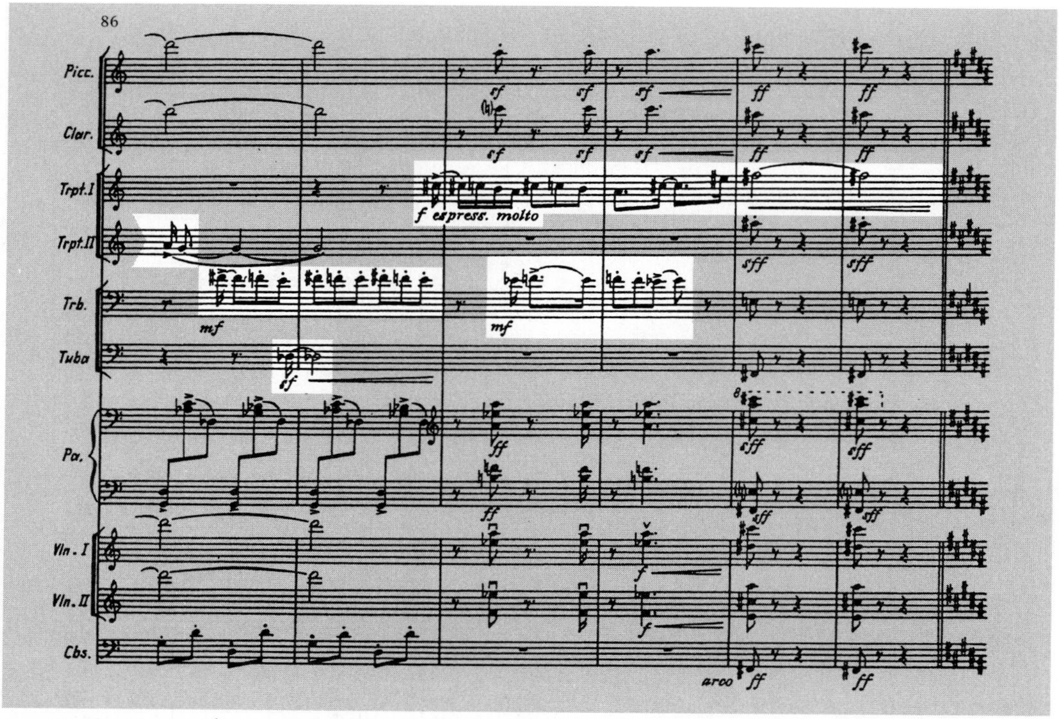
86
Picc.
Clar.
Trpt.I
Trpt.II
Trb.
Tuba
Pa.
Vln. I
Vln. II
Cbs.
f espress. molto
mf
ff
sf
sff
arco

92
65
18
Picc.
Clar.
Trpt.I
Trpt.II
Trb.
Tuba
Pa.
Vln. I
Vln. II
Cbs.
ff allegramente
allegramente
f
sff
ff
pizz.

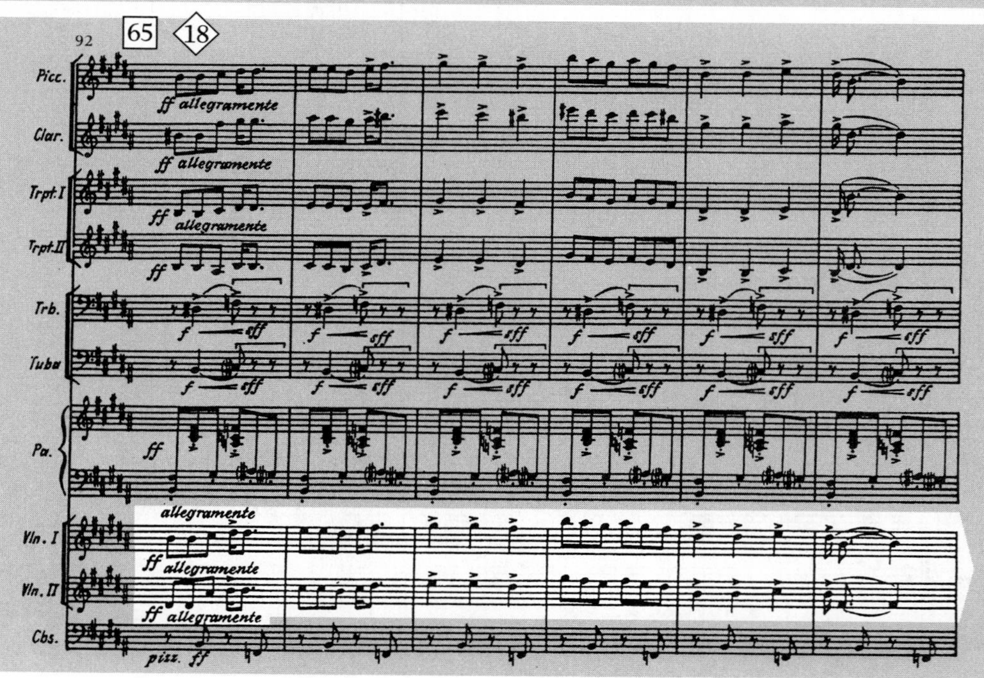

98
Picc.
Clar.
(ad lib. 8va bassa)
Trpt. I
Trpt. II
Trb.
Tuba
Pa.
Vln. I
Vln. II
Cbs.
pizz. ff

104
Picc.
Clar.
Trpt. I
Trpt. II
Trb.
Tuba
Pa.
Vln. I
Vln. II
Cbs.
pp
mf
f subito
stacc. e f subito
pizz. ff
pizz. f

110
Picc.
Clar.
Trpt. I
Trpt. II
Trb.
Tuba
Pa.
Vln. I
Vln. II
Cbs.
fff
sempre ff
Flatterzunge

116
Picc.
Clar.
Trpt. I
Trpt. II
Trb.
Tuba
Pa.
Vln. I
Vln. II
Cbs.
più fff
ff
pizz.

122
Picc.
Clar.
Trpt. I
Trpt. II
Trb.
Tuba
Pa.
Vln. I
Vln. II
Cbs.
ff
con sord.
f
pizz. sempre f
66
19
128
ff
pp con sord.
pp
ppp
p col legno ma

140
67
20
Picc.
sf
ff
Clar.
sf
ff
Trpt. I
ff marcatiss.
f
Trpt. II
sf
f
f
Trb.
sf
f
Tuba
sf
f
Pa.
ff
m. d.
gliss. sobre blancas
f
gliss.
Vln. I
arco sf
ff
Vln. II
arco sf
ff
Cbs.
arco sf
ff

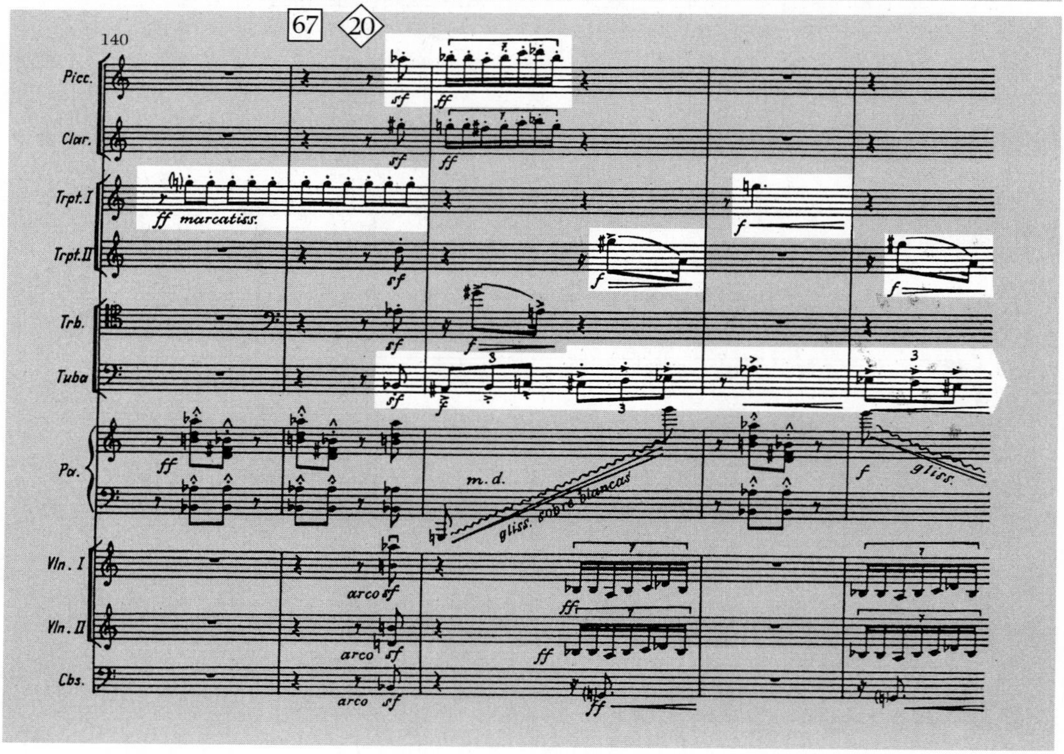

145

Picc. *ff* *sf* *mf* *sf*
Clar. *ff* *sf* *mf* *sf*
Trpt. I *f* *mf* *ff*
Trpt. II *sf* *mf* *ff*
Trb. *f* *sf* *mf* *ff*
Tuba *ff* *sf* *mf* *f*
Pa. *ff* sobre blancas *ff*
Vln. I *mf* pizz.
Vln. II *mf* pizz.
Cbs. *mf* pizz. pizz.

68
21
158
Picc.
ff
Clar.
ff
Trpt. I
f
Trpt. II
f
Trb.
f espress.
Tuba
f
Pa.
f
Vln. I
Vln. II
Cbs.
arco f

164
Picc.
ff
Clar.
ff
Trpt. I
f marc.
Trpt. II
f stacc.
Trb.
f
Tuba
marcatiss.
Pa.
più f
Vln. I
ff
Vln. II
ff
Cbs.

69
22

171

Picc.
Clar.
Trpt. I
Trpt. II
Trb.
Tuba
Pa.
Vln. I
Vln. II
Cbs.

ff
ad lib
ff
ppp
ppp
ppp
ff
staccatissimo
ff
ff
ff
ff
ff
ff
pizz.
ff

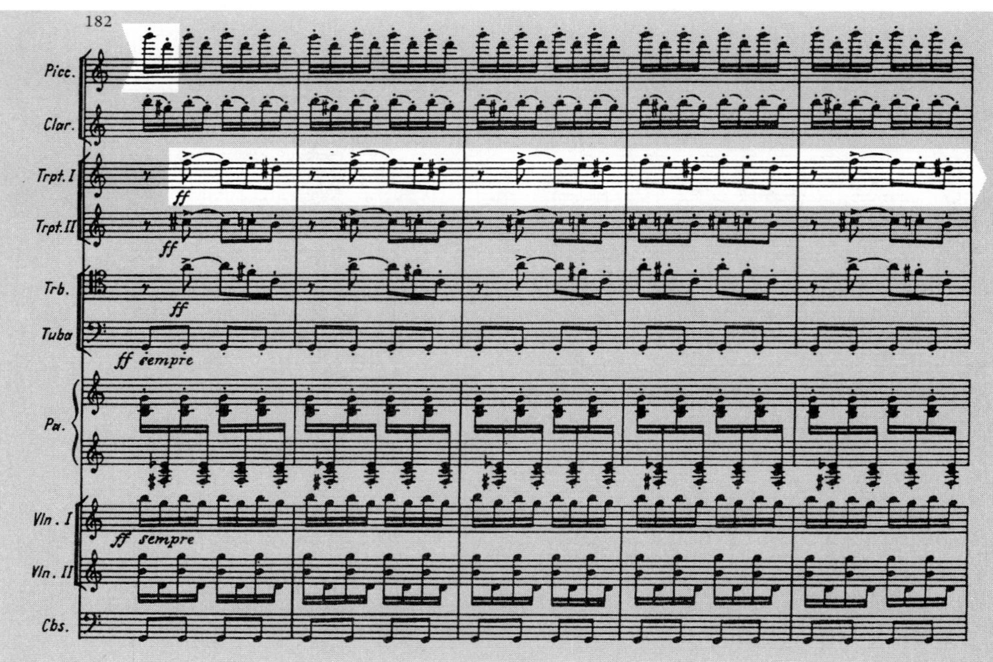
182
Picc.
Clar.
Trpt. I
Trpt. II
Trb.
Tuba
Pa.
Vln. I
Vln. II
Cbs.
ff
ff sempre

187
Picc.
Clar.
Trpt. I
Trpt. II
Trb.
Tuba
Pa.
Vln. I
Vln. II
Cbs.
staccatiss.
secco
arco
sff
ff

Mexico produced a number of outstanding nationalist composers in the twentieth century. The varied musical traditions from the Amerindian, Hispanic, and Western cultures provided a rich palette for art music composers such as Carlos Chávez and Silvestre Revueltas (1899–1940). Achieving international acclaim, Revueltas created a distinctive style that combines folklike melodies and captivating dance rhythms with a dissonant and chromatic harmonic language.

The Spanish Civil War had a major impact on Revueltas, who was a staunch supporter of the Loyalist government that was destroyed by the Fascists. In 1936, the great Spanish poet Federico García Lorca was executed by a Fascist firing squad, and Revueltas responded with a three-movement orchestral work, *Homenaje a Federico García Lorca (Homage to Federico García Lorca)*. The third movement is entitled *Son*, which is a traditional Mexican dance that alternates between 3/4 and 6/8 meter. Following the somber second movement, entitled *Duelo (Sorrow)*, the finale appears as a joyful celebration of life.

Son presents three principal themes in a rondo-like pattern. The unusual orchestration is largely indebted to the sound of the Mexican mariachi band. Pairs of melodic instruments—two trumpets, two woodwinds (piccolo and E-flat clarinet), and two violin parts—dominate. String basses, a trombone, and a tuba provide the bass support, and the piano plays an essential harmonic function. Absent are middle-register instruments, such as the violas and cellos. Percussion instruments add distinctive colors to the ensemble. The lively dance rhythm of the *son* appears in the third theme, and throughout, Mexican folk sounds are underscored by strong dissonant harmonies.

36. Aaron Copland

Billy the Kid, Scene 1, *Street in a Frontier Town* (orchestral suite) (1939)

8CD: 7/ 70 – 74
4CD: 4/ 10 – 14

Instrumentation

Piccolo	Timpani	Bass drum
2 Flutes	Glockenspiel	Triangle
2 Oboes	Xylophone	
2 Clarinets	Tin whistle	Piano
2 Bassoons	Sleigh bells	
	Wood blocks	Violins I, II
4 French horns	Gourd	Violas
3 Trumpets	Snare drum	Cellos
3 Trombones	Slapstick	Double basses
Tuba	Cymbals	

a tempo
rit.
Picc.
solo
stacc.
mp
Fl. 1
p
Clar. 1
pp solo
solo
stacc.
mp
Bsn. 1
2
solo
p
Trgl.
(Trgl.)
sfp
p
Harp.
sfp
Piano
p
7
a tempo
rit.
Vl. 1
2
pizz.
sf
(pizz.)
p
Vla.
Vlc.
C.b.
arco
p

Picc.
Fl. 1
Ob. 1
Clar. 1
Bsn. 1
Hr.
Trpt. 1
d = 126
mp
mp
mf
con sordino
mf
mp
8
d = 126
Vl. 1 2
Vla.
Vlc.
arco
mf
mf

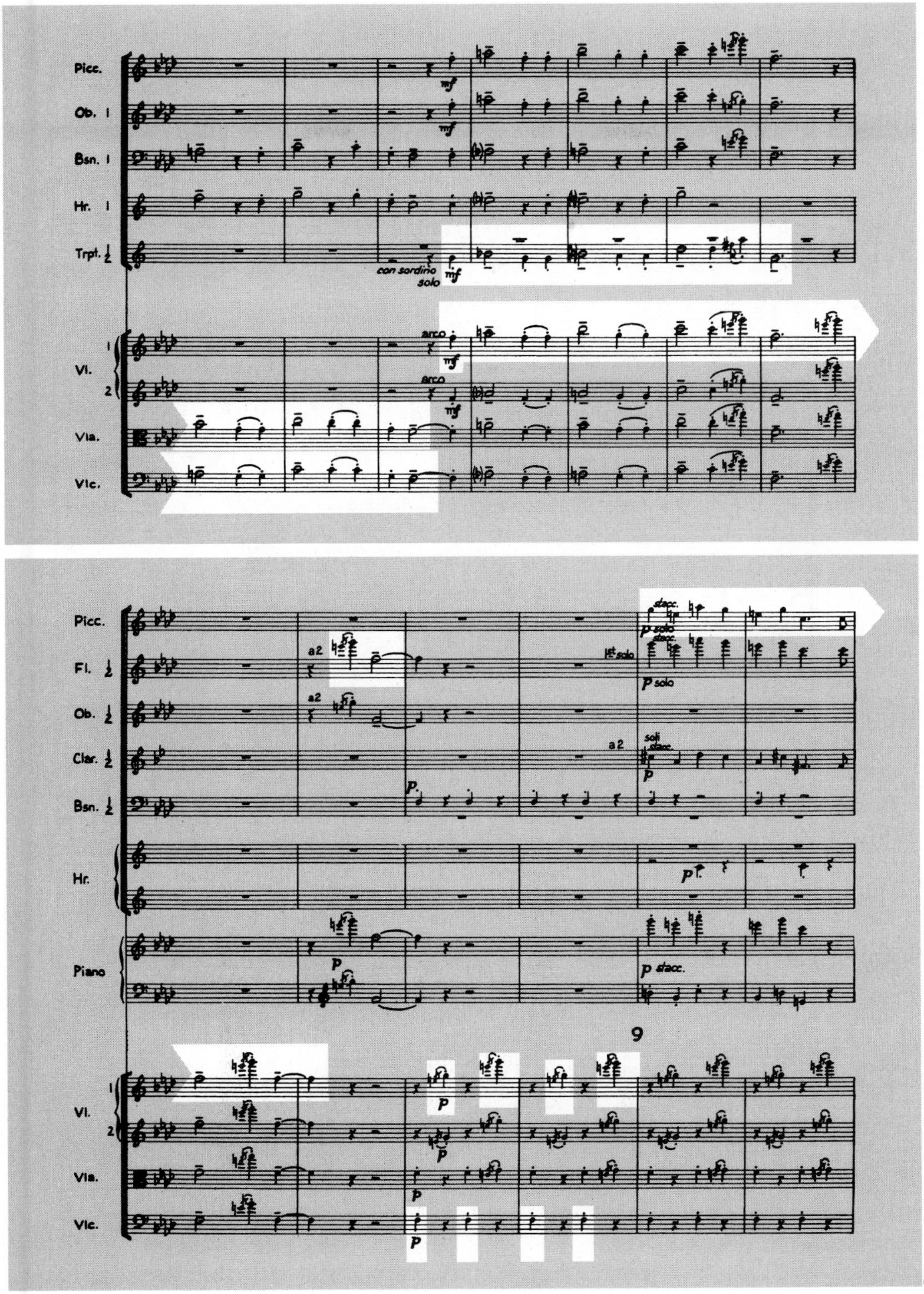

Picc.
Fl. 1 2
Ob. 1 2
Clar. 1 2
Bsn. 1 2
Hr.
Piano
Vl. 1 2
Vla.
Vlc.
a2
1st solo
stacc.
p solo
soli
p stacc.
9

Picc.
Fl.
Ob.
Clar.
(a2)
Bsn.
a2
f
(senza sord.)
pp
(senza sord.)
Hr.
Trpt.
con sordino
pp
con sordino
pp
Trb.
Tb.
Timp.
Piano
Vl.
Vla.
Vlc.
Cb.

Picc.
Fl.
Ob.
Clar.
Bsn.
Hr.
Trpt.
Trb.
Tb.
Timp.
Piano
Vl.
Vla.
Vlc.
Cb.
a2
f
senza sord.
stacc.
mp
pizz.
10

Bsn. 1 2
Hr.
Trb. 1
solo
mf poco marcato
Piano
mf stacc.
Vl. 1 2
Vla.
Vlc.
Cb.

Bsn. 1 2
Hr.
Trb. 1
Piano
Vl. 1 2
mp
Vla.
Vlc.
Cb.

71
11
Picc.
Fl. 1 2
Ob. 1 2
Clar. 1 2
Bsn. 1 2
Hr.
(senza sord.)
solo
mf
1
Trpt.
2 3
con sordino
p
1
Trb. 2
3
con sordino
Tb.
Timp.
stacc
Piano
11
Vl.
Vla.
Vlc.
Cb.

Picc.
Fl. 1 2
1° solo
f
Ob. 1 2
Clar. 1 2
1° solo
f
Bsn. 1 2
f
Hr.
f
f
Trpt. 1
f
2 3
Trb. 1 2 3
Tb.
Timp.
Perc.
Piano
Vl. 1 2
div.
f
pizz.
f
Vla
pizz.
f
Vlc.
arco
f
Cb.
arco
f

Picc.
Fl. 1 2
Ob. 1 2
Clar. 1 2
Bsn. 1 2
Hr.
Trpt. 1 2 3
solo
mp
Trb. 1 2 3
Tb.
Timp.
Perc.
Piano
f
12
Vl. 1 2
unis.
arco
Vla.
Vlc.
Cb.

Picc.
Fl. 1 2
Ob. 1 2
Clar. 1 2
Bsn. 1 2
Hr.
Trpt. 1 2 3
Trb. 1 2 3
Tb.
Timp.
Perc.
Piano
Vl. 1 2
Vla.
Vlc.
Cb.
solo
pizz.

Fl. 1 2
Clar. 1 2
Bsn 1 2
Hr.
Trpt. 1
Trb. 1
Piano
Vl. 1 2
Vla.
Vlc.
Cb.
13
solo
meno f
(senza sord.)
con sordino
(pizz.)
p dim. sempre
pp
ppp

Picc.
Fl. 1 2
Ob. 1 2
Clar. 1 2
Bsn. 1 2
Hr.
Trpt. 1 2 3
Trb. 1 2 3
Tb.
Timp.
Cymb.
B. Drum.
Piano
Vl. 1 2
Vla
Vlc.
Cb.
ff marcato
a2
senza sordino
with hard stick
arco
div.
14

Picc.
Fl. 1 2
a2
Ob. 1 2
a2
Clar. 1 2
Bsn. 1 2
Hr.
Trpt. 1 2 3
Trb. 1 2 3
Tb.
Timp.
Cymb.
B. Drum
Piano
Vl. 1 2
Vla.
Vlc.
Cb.

72
12
𝅗𝅥 = 𝅗𝅥 precedente. (𝅗𝅥 = 138)
Picc.
Fl. 1 2
Ob. 1 2
a2
Clar. 1 2
Bsn. 1 2
f stacc.
Hr.
f stacc.
Trpt. 1 2 3
Trb. 1 2 3
senza sordino
Tb.
Timp.
Wood-bl.
mf
Sn. Drum
Cymb.
B. Drum
Piano
15
Vl 1 2
div.
Vla.
Vlc.
pizz.
Cb.

Picc.
Fl. 1 2
Ob. 1 2
Clar. 1 2
Bsn. 1 2
a2 stacc.
f
Hr.
Trpt. 1
2 3
solo
solo
f
Trb. 1 2
3
Tb.
Timp.
Woodbl.
Cymb.
B. Drum.
Piano
Vl. 1
2
Vla.
Vlc.
arco
f
Cb.

Picc.
Fl. 1 2
Ob. 1 2
Clar. 1 2
Bsn. 1 2
Hr.
Trpt. 1 2 3
Trb. 1 2 3
Tb.
Timp.
Woodbl.
Cymb.
B.Drum
Piano
Vla. 1 2
Vla
Vlc.
Cb.
stacc.
mf
a2
soli
mf legato, cantabile
16
pizz.
unis.
arco
(pizz)

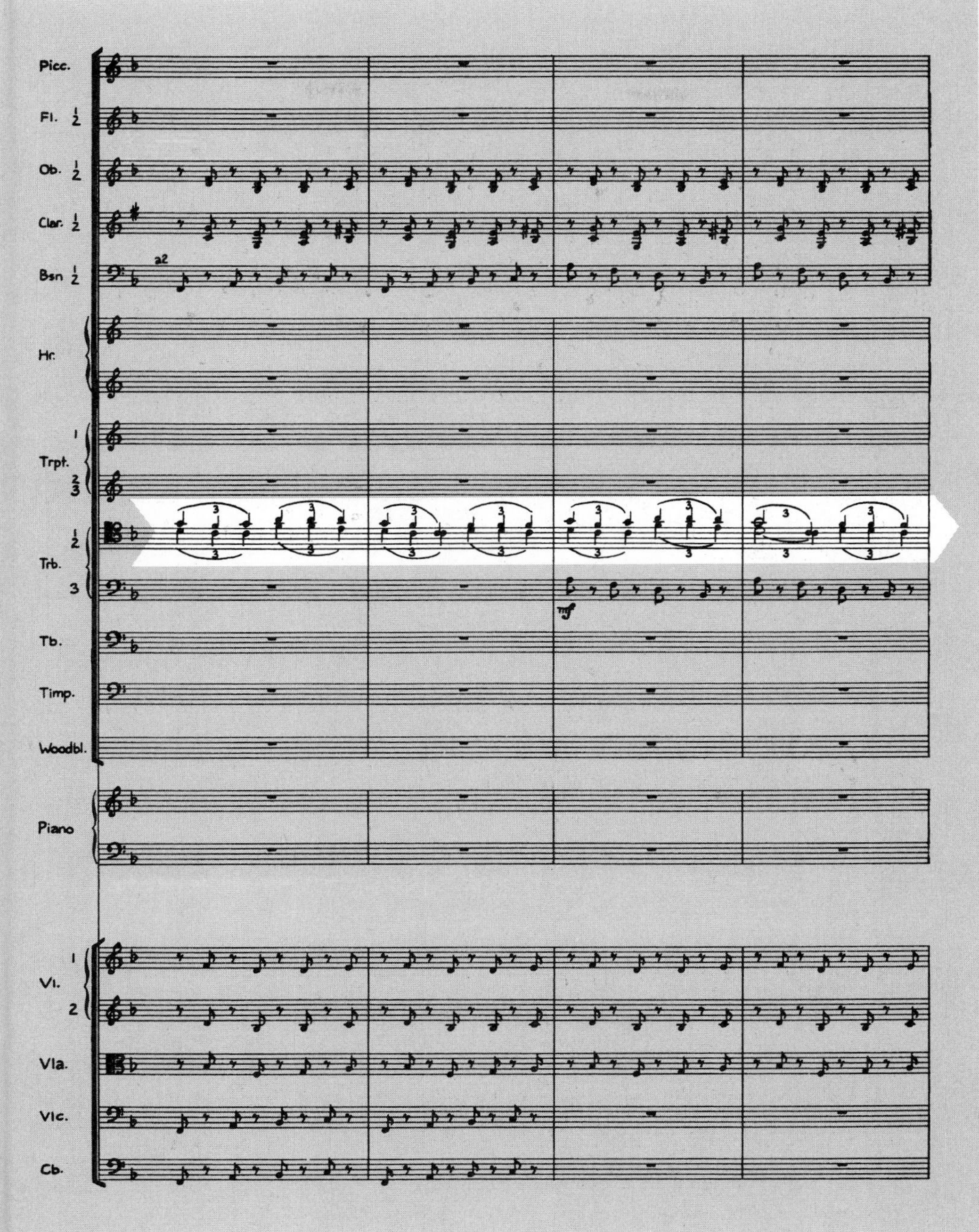
Picc.
Fl. 1 2
Ob. 1 2
Clar. 1 2
Bsn 1 2
a2
Hr.
1
Trpt.
2 3
1 2
Trb.
3
mf
Tb.
Timp.
Woodbl.
Piano
1
Vl.
2
Vla.
Vlc.
Cb.

Picc.
Fl. 1 2
a2
f
Ob. 1 2
Clar. 1 2
a2
f
Bsn. 1 2
a2
Hr.
f
Trpt. 1
2 3
Trb. 1 2
3
f
Tb.
f
Timp.
Woodbl.
Piano
Vl. 1
arco
f
div.
2
arco
Vla.
arco
Vlc.
(arco)
C.b.
(arco)

Picc.
Fl. 1 2
a2
Ob. 1 2
a2
mf
Clar. 1 2
a2
a2
mf
Bsn. 1 2
a2
Hr.
con sordino mf
Trpt. 1
con sordino
solo
mf
Trpt. 2 3
Trb. 1 2
Trb. 3
Tb.
Timp.
Woodbl.
Piano
17
Vl. 1
Vl. 2
Vla.
Vlc.
Cb.

a2
Ob. 1 2
Clar. 1 2
Hr. 1
Trpt. 1
Perc.
Piano
mf
Vl. 1 2
mf
Vla.
mf

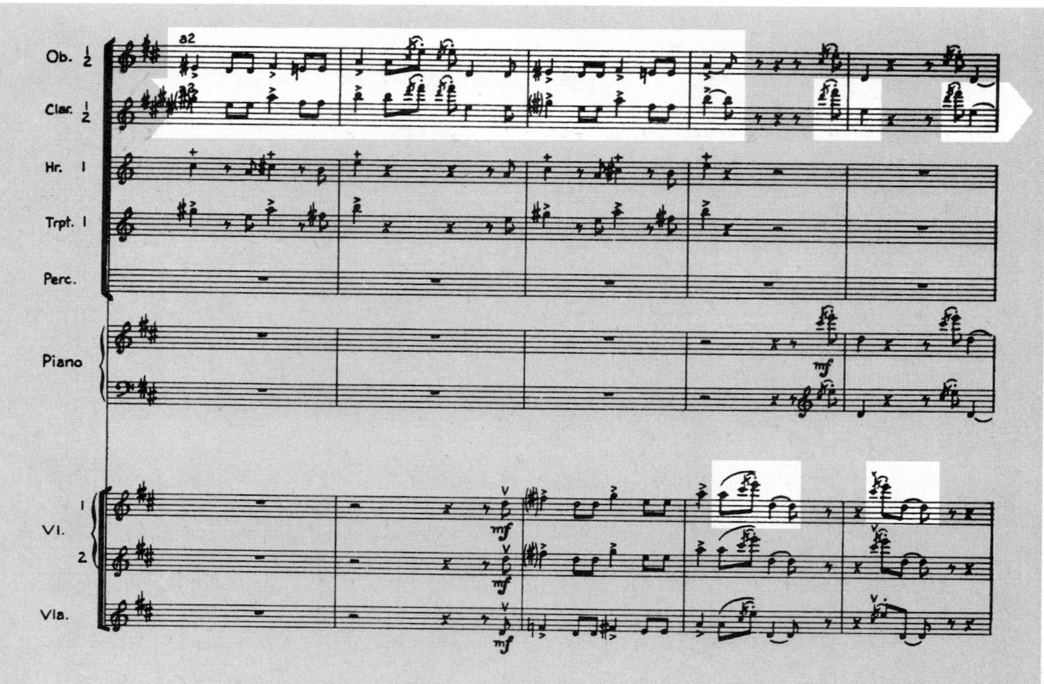

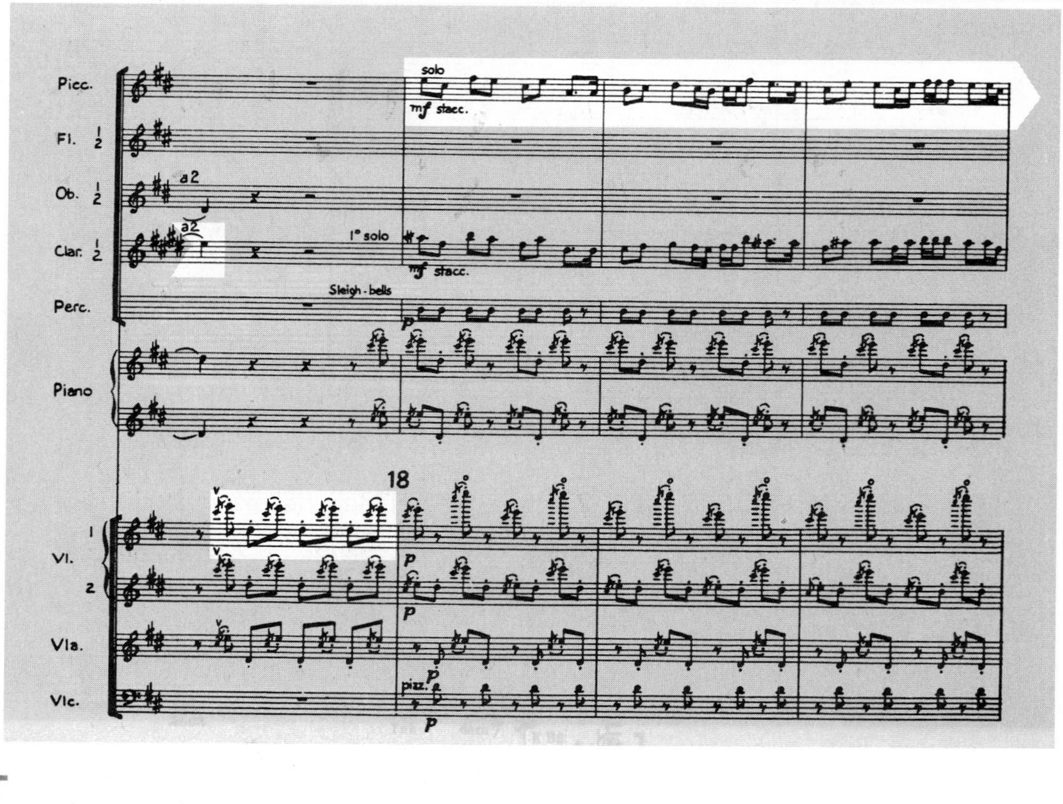

Picc.
solo
mf stacc.
Fl. 1 2
Ob. 1 2
a2
Clar. 1 2
a2
1° solo
mf stacc.
Perc.
Sleigh-bells
p
Piano
18
Vl. 1 2
p
p
Vla.
p
Vlc.
pizz.
p

Picc.
Fl. 1 2
mf
a2
Ob. 1 2
Clar. 1 2
Bsn. 1 2
Hr.
Trpt. 1 2 3
Trb. 1 2 3
Tb.
Timp.
Sleigh-b.
Woodbl.
Piano
Vl. 1 2
Vla.
Vlc.
Cb.

Picc.
Fl. 1 2
a2
Ob. 1 2
Clar. 1 2
Bsn. 1 2
Hr.
solo
cantabile
Trpt.
Trb.
Tb.
Timp.
Perc.
Piano
19
Vl.
Vla.
legato, cantabile
tenuto
Vlc.
arco
Cb.
div.

Picc.
Fl. 1 2
Ob. 1 2
Clar. 1 2
Bsn. 1 2
Hr. 1 2 3 4
Trpt. 1 2 3
Trb. 1 2 3
Tb.
Timp.
Perc.
Vl. 1 2
Vla.
Vlc.
Cb.

Mexican Dance and Finale

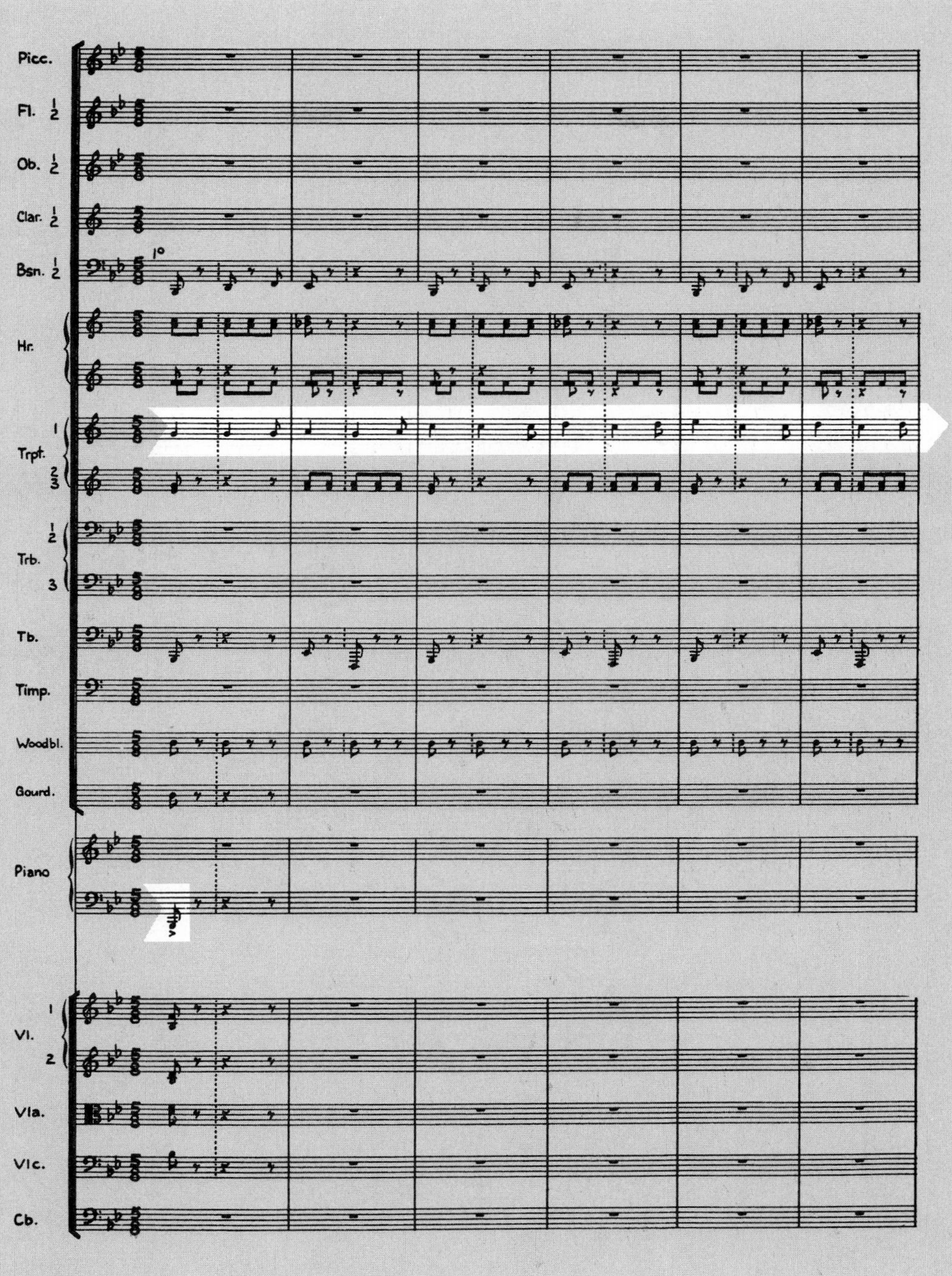
Picc.
Fl. 1 2
Ob. 1 2
Clar. 1 2
Bsn. 1 2
Hr.
Trpt. 1 2 3
Trb. 1 2 3
Tb.
Timp.
Woodbl.
Gourd.
Piano
Vl. 1 2
Vla.
Vlc.
Cb.

Picc.
Fl. 1 2
Ob. 1 2
Clar. 1 2
Bsn. 1 2
10
Hr.
1
Trpt.
2 3
1 2
Trb.
3
Tb
Timp.
Woodbl.
gourd.
Piano
21
1
Vl.
2
Vla.
Vlc.
Cb.

Picc.
Fl. 1 2
Ob. 1 2
Clar. 1 2
Bsn. 1 2
1°
Hr.
1
Trpt.
2 3
1 2
Trb.
3
Tb.
Timp.
Woodbl.
Gourd.
Piano
Vl. 1
2
Vla.
Vlc.
Cb.

Picc.
Fl. 1 2
solo
Ob. 1 2
Clar. 1 2
Bsn. 1 2
(10)
Hr.
Trpt. 1 2 3
Trb. 1 2 3
Tb.
Timp.
Woodbl.
Gourd.
Piano
22
Vl. 1 2
modo ordinario
Vla.
Vlc.
pizz.
Cb.

Picc.
Fl.
Ob.
Clar.
Bsn.
Hr.
Trpt.
Trb.
Tb.
Timp.
Woodbl.
Gourd.
Piano
23
Vl.
Vla
Vlc.
Cb.

Pict.
Fl. 1 2
Ob. 1 2
Clar. 1 2
Bsn. 1 2
1°
Hr.
Trpt. 1 2 3
Trb. 1 2 3
Tb.
Timp.
Woodbl.
Gourd.
Piano
Vl. 1 2
col legno
Vla
Vlc.
Cb.
(pizz)

Picc.
Fl. 1 2
Ob. 1 2
Clar. 1 2
Bsn. 1 2
10
Hr.
Trpt. 1
2 3
Trb. 1 2
3
Tb.
Timp.
Woodbl.
Gourd.
Piano
Vl. 1
2
Vla.
Vlc.
Cb.

74 14

Fl. 1 2
Ob. 1 2
Clar. 1 2
Hr.
Trpt. 1 2 3
24
Vl. 1 2
Vla.
Vlc.
mf
mp
arco
legato
modo ordinario
arco modo ordinario

Ob. 1 2
Clar. 1 2
Bsn. 1 2
Hr.
25
Vl. 1 2
Vla.
Vlc.
solo
sul G....
(dim.)

Ob. 1 2
Clar. 1 2
Bsn. 1 2
Hr.
Vl. 1 2
Vla.
Vlc.
(sul G)
pizz.
pizz.

Fl. 1/2
Ob. 1/2
a2
a2
mf
Clar. 1/2
senza sordino
p
(con sordino)
p
Hr.
senza sordino
p
(con sordino)
p
Glocksp.
Vl. 1
2
Vla.
Vlc.

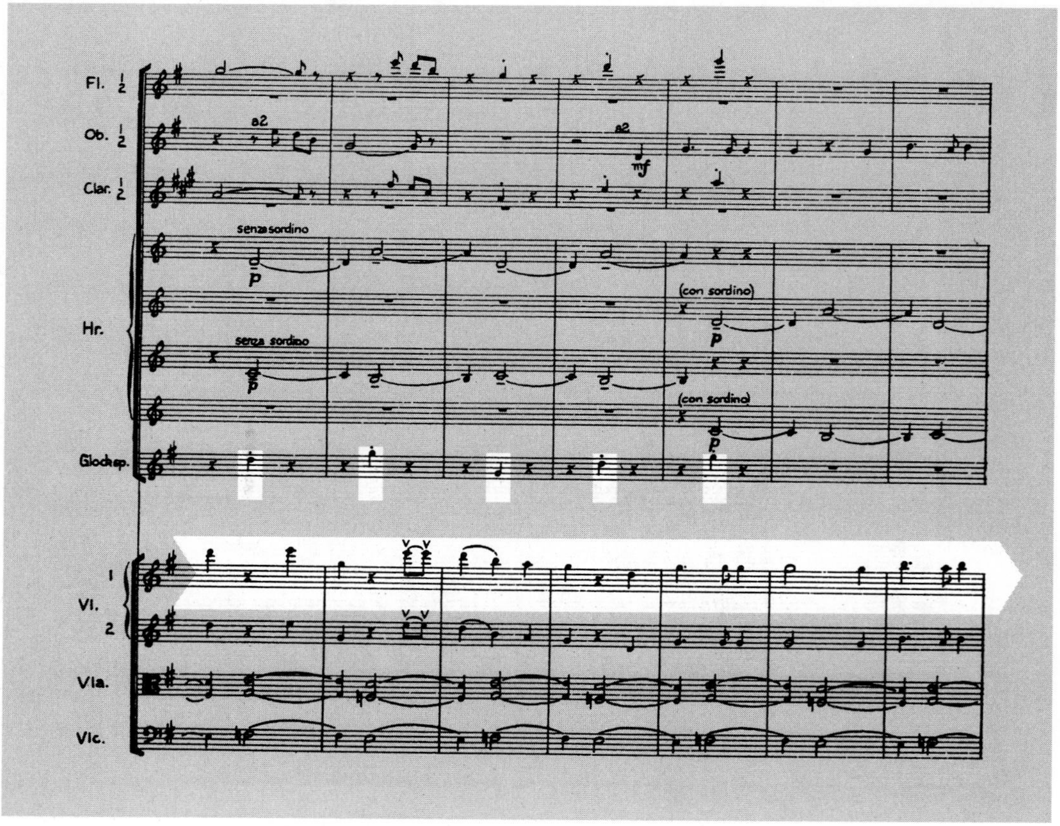

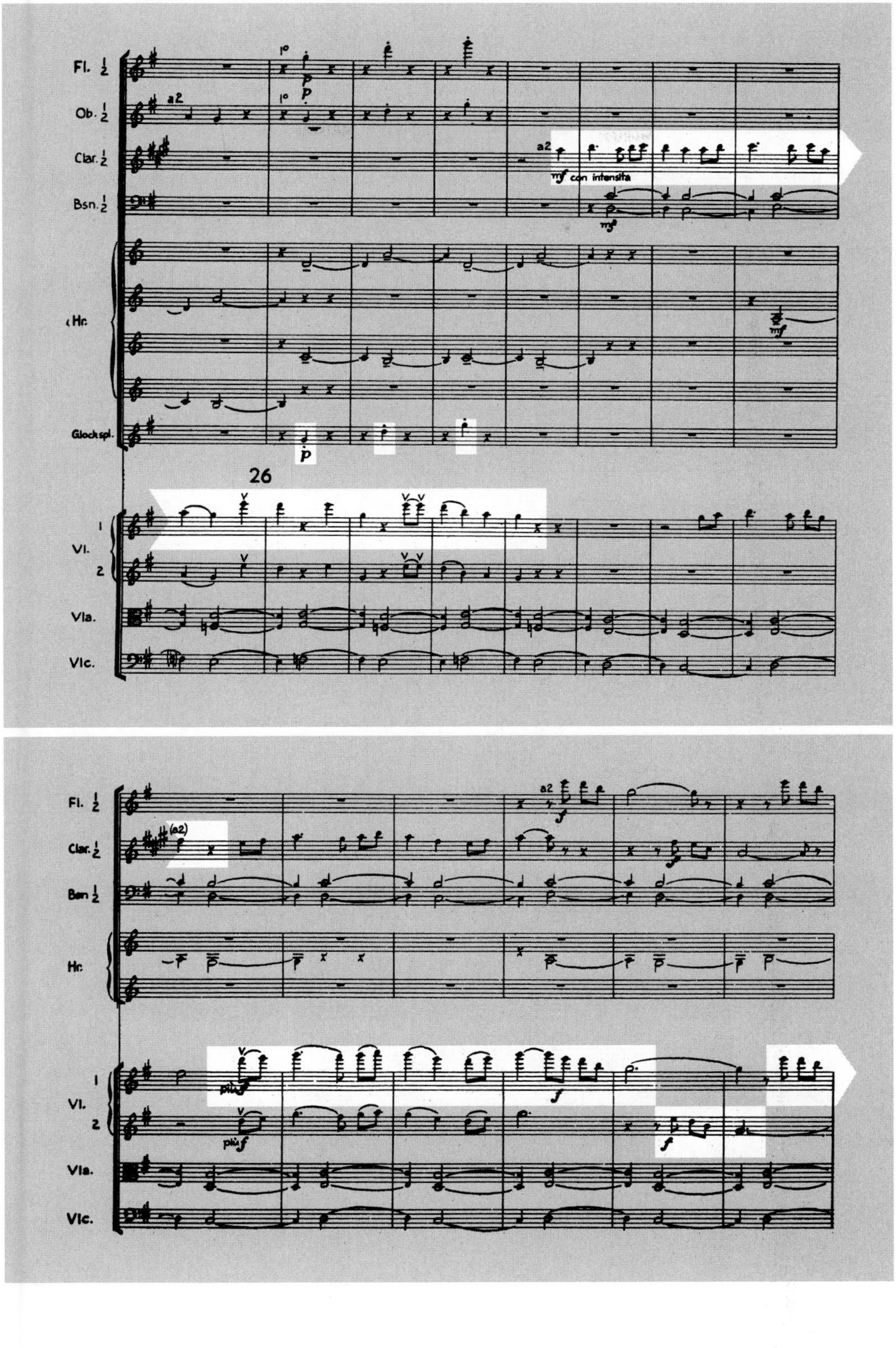

Fl. 1 2
1°
p
Ob. 1 2
a2
1°
p
Clar. 1 2
a2
mf con intensita
Bsn. 1 2
mf
Hr.
mf
Glock spl.
p
26
Vl. 1
Vl. 2
Vla.
Vlc.

Picc
Fl. 1 2
(a2)
Ob. 1 2
a2
Clar. 1 2
(a2)
Bsn. 1 2
Hr.
senza sordino
Trpt. 1 2 3
solo
Trb. 1 2 3
Tb.
Timp.
Perc.
Piano
26A
Vl. 1 2
Vla.
Vlc.
Cb.
(arco)

Picc.
Fl. 1 2
Ob. 1 2
Clar. 1 2
Bsn. 1 2
Hr.
Trpt. 1
2 3
Trb. 1 2
3
Tb.
Timp.
Perc.
Piano
Vl. 1
2
Vla.
Vlc.
Cb.
(a2)
stacc.
marc.
ff
a2.
senza sord.
senza sordino

Picc.
Fl. 1 2
(a2)
Ob. 1 2
Clar. 1 2
Bsn. 1 2
Hr.
Trpt. 1
2 3
Trb. 1 2
3
Tb.
Timp.
Glockspl.
Xyloph.
Cymb.
B. Drum.
Piano
8va
27
Vl. 1
2
Vla.
Vlc.
Cb.

Picc.
Fl. 1 2
(a2)
Ob. 1 2
Clar. 1 2
Bsn. 1 2
Hr.
Trpt. 1 2 3
Trb. 1 2 3
Tb.
Timp.
Glockspl.
Xyloph.
Cymb. B. Drum
Piano
8va
Vl. 1 2
Vla.
Vlc.
Cb.

meno mosso
Picc.
Fl. 1 2
(a2)
Ob. 1 2
Clar. 1 2
Bsn 1 2
Hr.
Trpt 1 2 3
Trb. 1 2 3
a2
Tb.
Timp.
Glockspl.
Xyloph.
Slapstick
Cymb. B. Drum.
Piano
27A
meno mosso
div.
Vl. 1 2
Vla.
pizz.
Vlc.
arco
Cb.

Aaron Copland (1900–1990) is generally recognized as America's foremost nationalist composer. This reputation largely rests on a series of ballets that he composed on American subjects, including the legend of Billy the Kid. Copland gives the following scenario for the opening scene of the ballet:

> The first scene is a street in a frontier town. Cowboys saunter into town, some on horseback, others on foot with their lassos; some Mexican women do a *jarabe*, which is interrupted by a fight between two drunks. Attracted by the gathering crowd, Billy is seen for the first time, a boy of twelve, with his mother. The brawl turns ugly, guns are drawn, and in some unaccountable way, Billy's mother is killed. Without an instant's hesitation, in cold fury, Billy draws a knife from a cowhand's sheath and stabs his mother's slayers. His short but famous career has begun.

The rest of the ballet treats Billy's later life, including a gun battle with his former friend Pat Garrett. At the end, a posse finally captures the tired and worn Billy.

Like Ives, Copland often quotes American tunes in his compositions. In this opening scene, he incorporates such traditional songs as *Goodbye, Old Paint; The Old Chisholm Trail; Git Along, Little Dogies; The Streets of Laredo;* and *Great Grand-Dad.* These songs of the Old West are woven into a general American sound that includes strong dance rhythms, syncopation, and a strong, effective orchestration. Copland sustains a lively, energetic mood with dissonances, polytonality, and polyrhythms. At the climax, the sound steadily builds in dissonance as *Goodbye, Old Paint* is obsessively repeated over a two-note ostinato.

37. Olivier Messiaen

8CD: 7/ 75 – 77

Quatuor pour la fin du temps (Quartet for the End of Time), Second Movement, *Vocalise, pour l'Ange qui annonce la fin du Temps (Vocalise, for the Angel who announces the end of Time)* (1941)

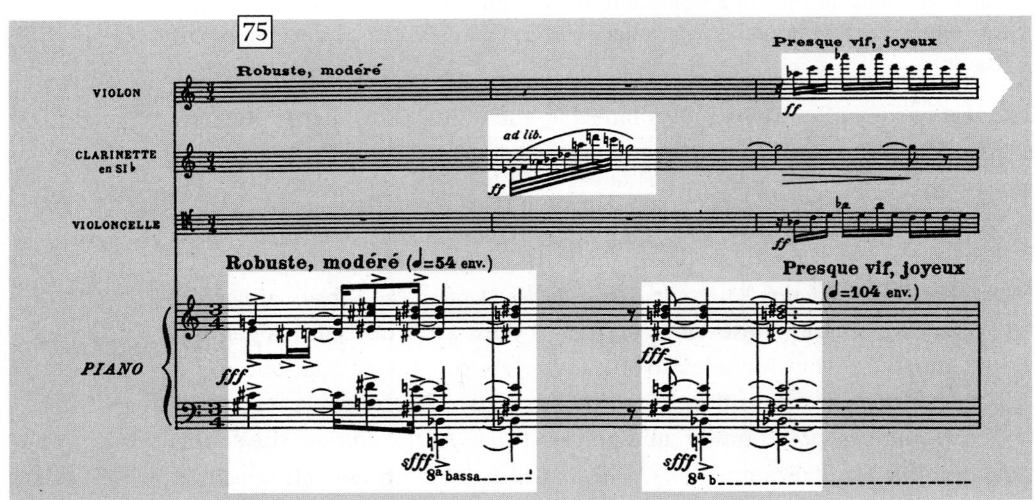

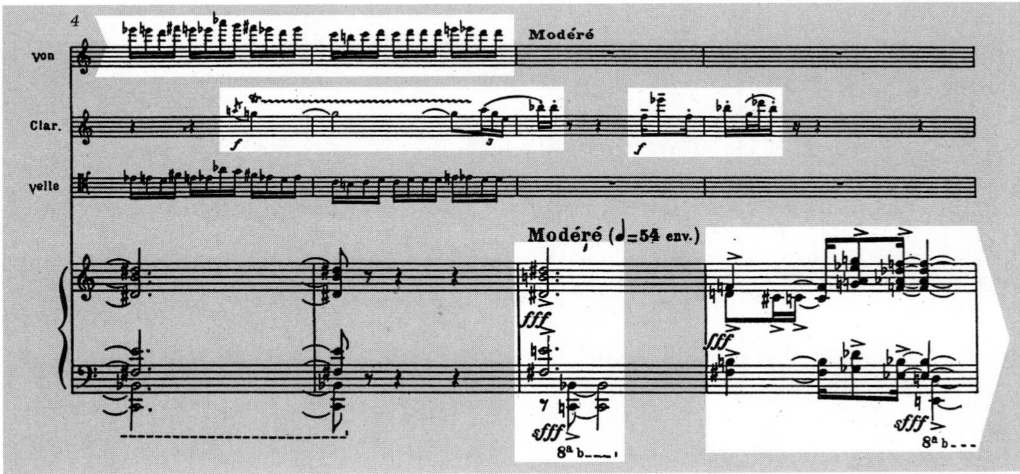

Presque vif
Modéré
ad lib.
Presque vif (♩=104 env.)
Modéré (♩=54 env.)
Presque vif
cresc. molto
Modéré
Presque vif (♩=104 env.)
Modéré (♩=54 env.)
fff (fulgurant, pressez ce trait)

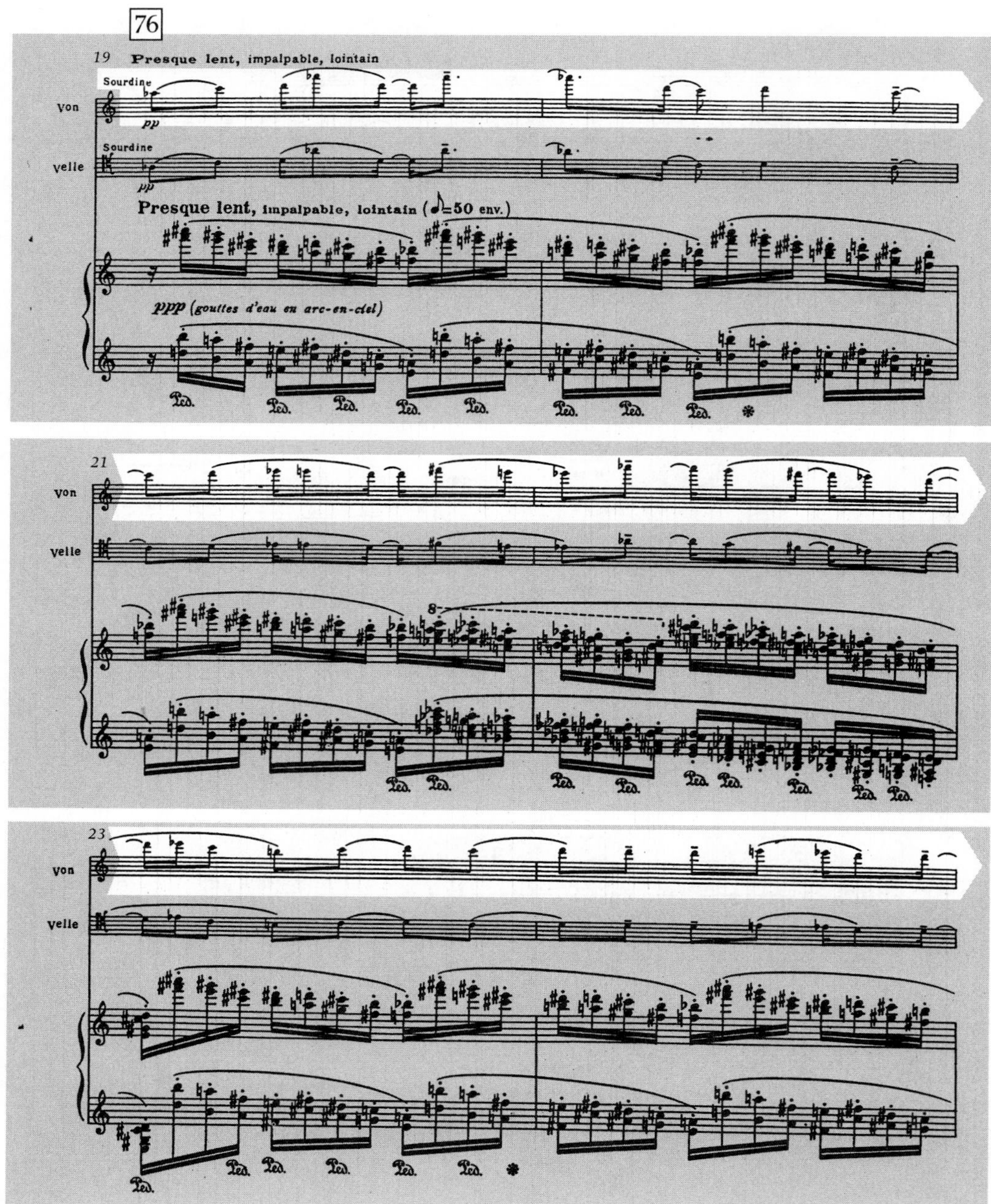
76
19
Presque lent, impalpable, lointain
Sourdine
Von
pp
Sourdine
velle
pp
Presque lent, impalpable, lointain (♪=50 env.)
ppp (gouttes d'eau en arc-en-ciel)
21
Von
velle
8
23
Von
velle

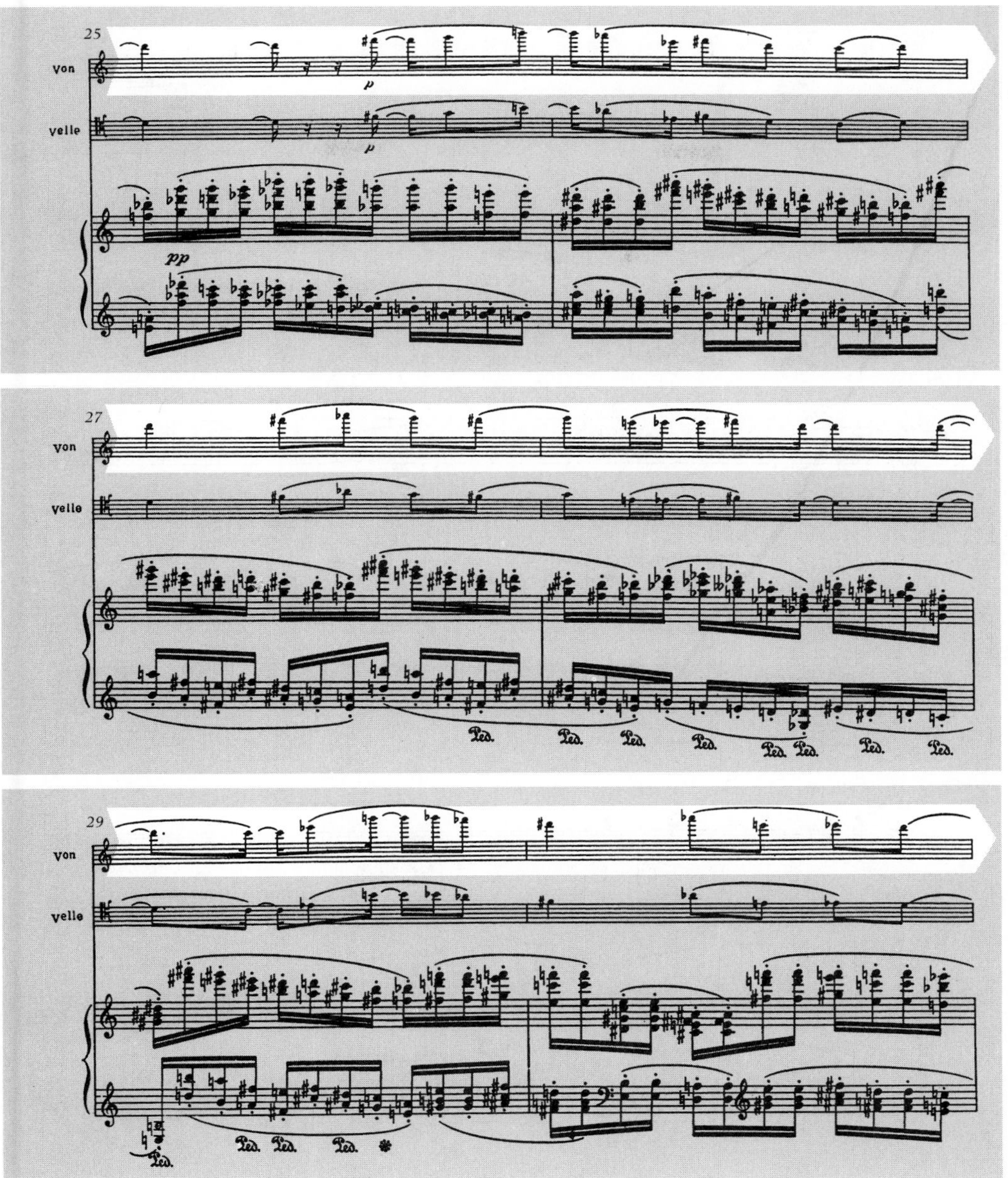

25
Von
p
velle
p
pp
27
Von
velle
Ped.
29
Von
velle
Ped.

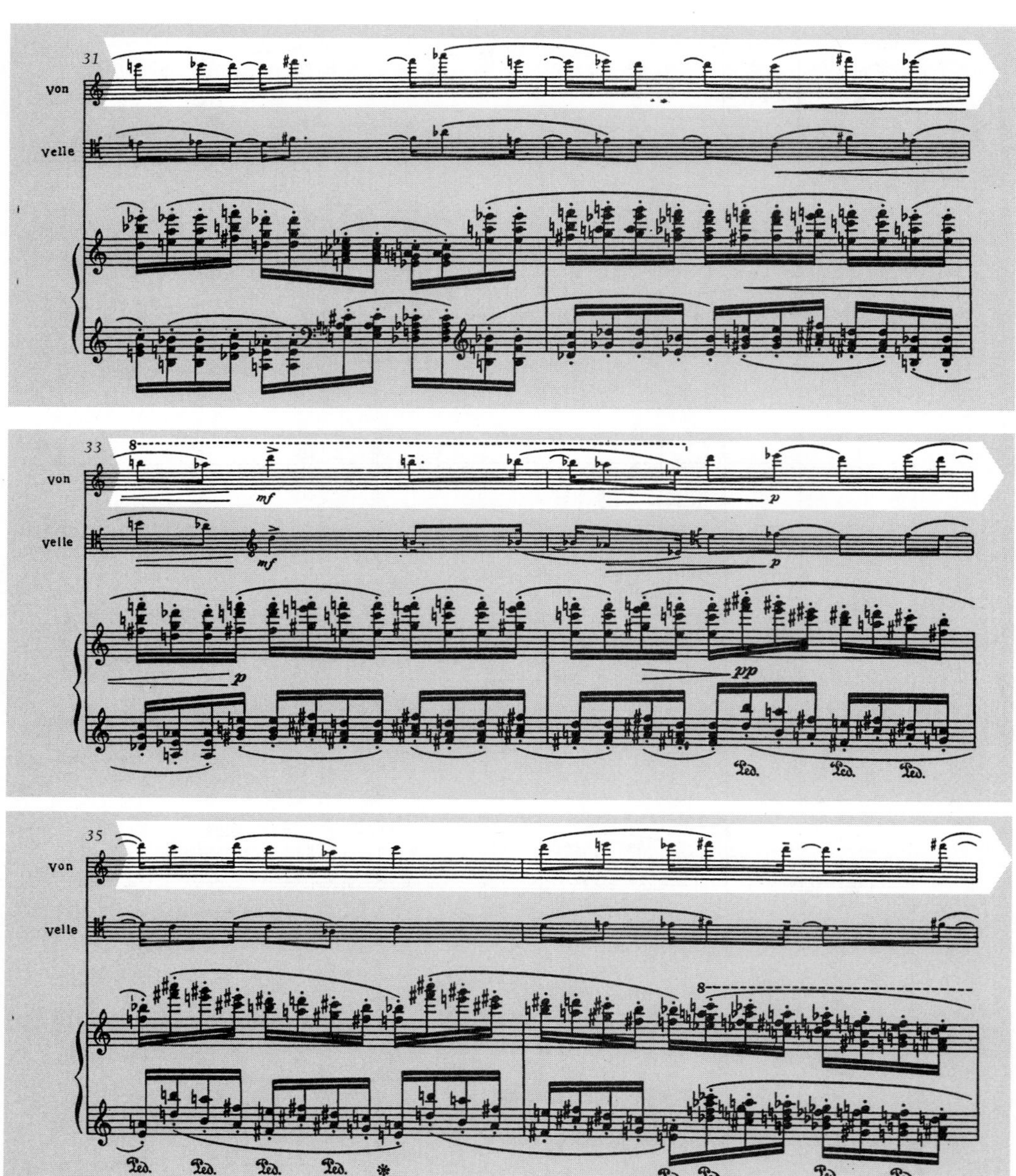
31
von
velle
33
8
mf
p
pp
Ped.
35
Ped.
8

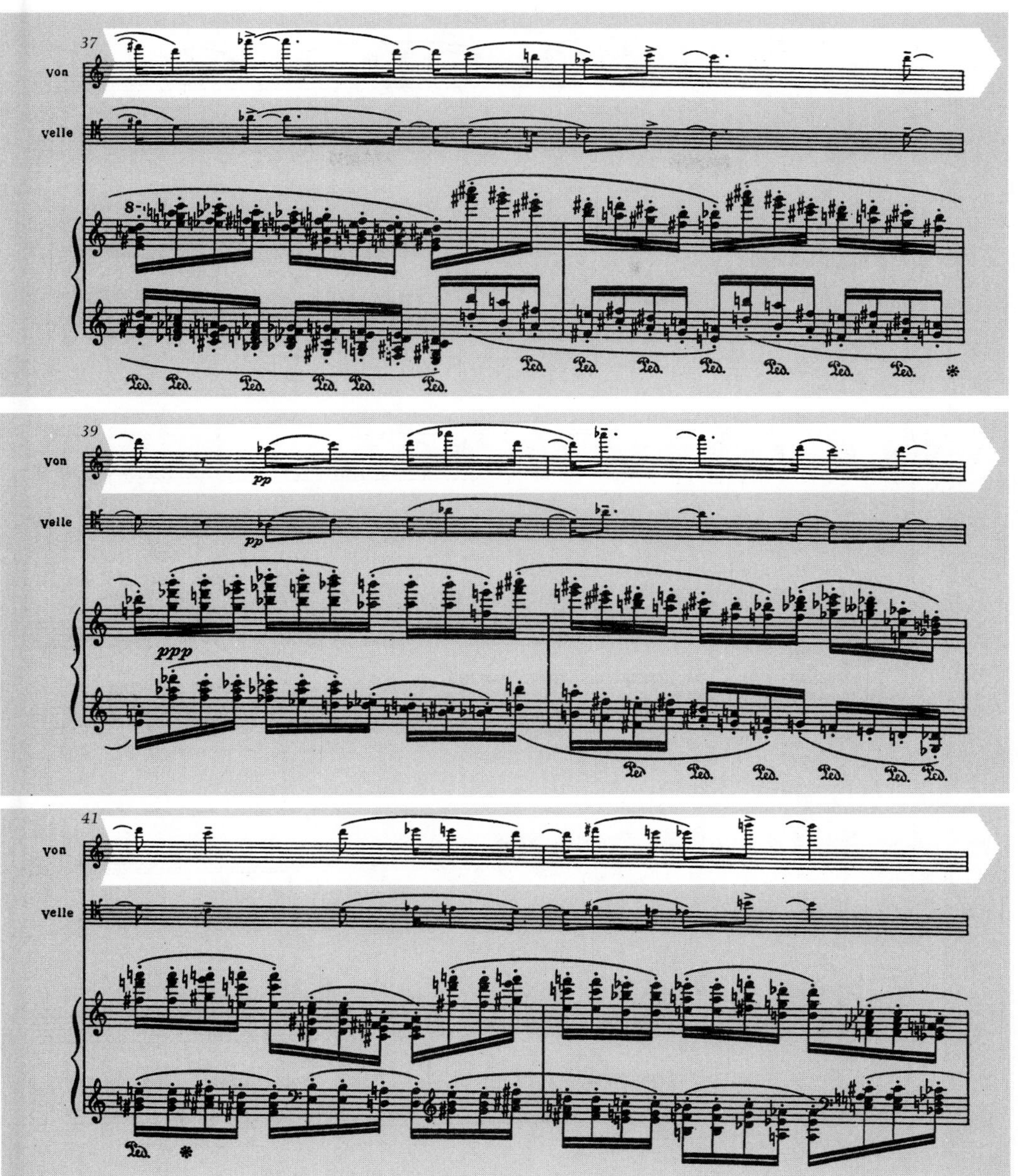
37
von
velle
8
Ped.
39
pp
ppp
41

43
Vᵒⁿ
Vᶜˡˡᵉ

45
Vᵒⁿ
Vᶜˡˡᵉ

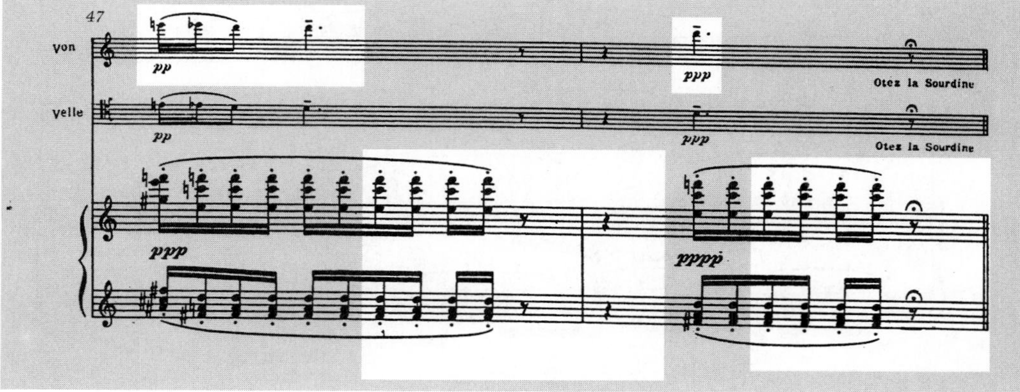
47
Vᵒⁿ
pp
ppp
Otez la Sourdine
Vᶜˡˡᵉ
pp
ppp
Otez la Sourdine
ppp
pppp

77
Presque vif
49
von
p cresc. molto
velle
p cresc. molto
Presque vif (𝅗𝅥=104 env.)

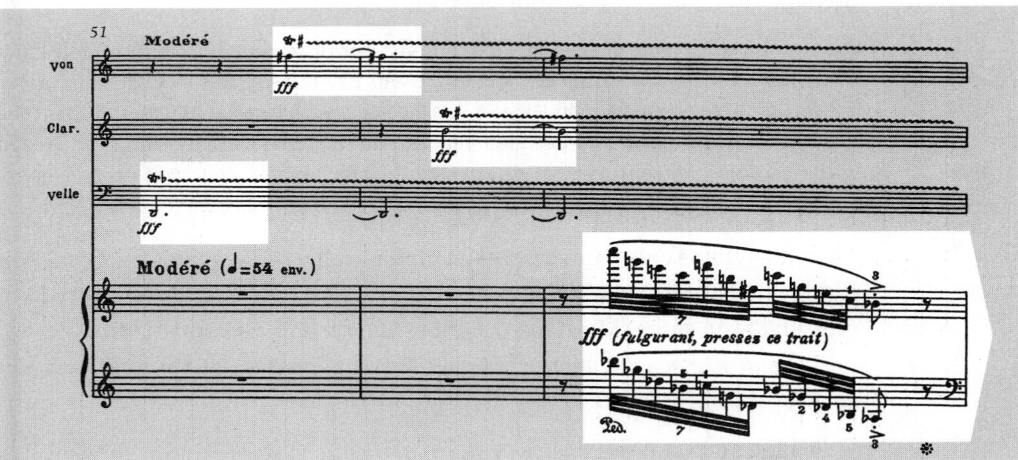
51
Modéré
von
fff
Clar.
fff
velle
fff
Modéré (𝅗𝅥=54 env.)
fff (fulgurant, pressez ce trait)
Ped.

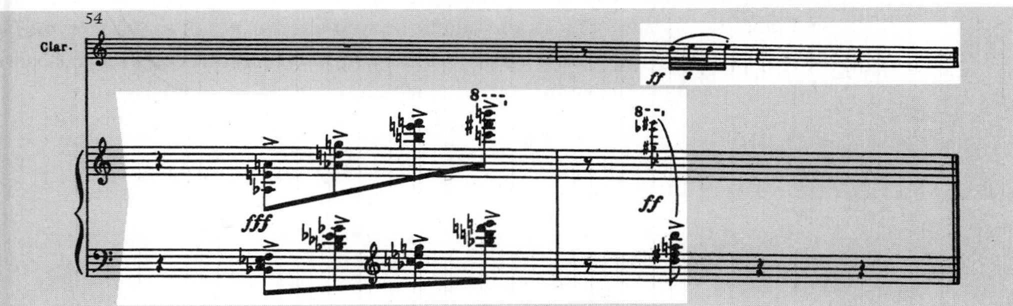
54
Clar.
ff
fff
ff

Olivier Messiaen (1908–1992), one of Europe's foremost avant-garde composers, created his celebrated *Quatour pour la fin du temps (Quartet for the End of Time)* while imprisoned in a Nazi war camp. Interned with three other musicians—a clarinetist, violinist, and cellist—Messiaen wrote the quartet for this unusual combination, with an additional piano part for himself. The ensemble performed the work in front of five thousand fellow prisoners on January 15, 1941.

The work typifies Messiaen's religious mysticism. It is inspired by a passage in the Revelation of St. John, Chapter 10, which describes the seventh angel whose trumpet will announce the end of time.

> I saw an angel full of strength descending from the sky, clad with a cloud and having a rainbow over his head. His face was like the sun, his feet like columns of fire. He set his right foot on the sea, his left foot on the earth, and standing on the ocean and the earth, he raised his hand to the sky and swore by Him who lives in the centuries of centuries, saying: *There shall be no more Time,* but on the day of the seventh Angel's trumpet the mystery of God shall be accomplished.

The quartet has eight movements, which parallel the seven days of creation (God rested on the seventh day) and the eighth day of timeless eternity. In a preface to the score, Messiaen describes the second movement, entitled *Vocalise, pour l'Ange qui annonce la fin du Temps (Vocalise, for the Angel who announces the end of Time):*

> The first and third sections, very short, evoke the power of this mighty angel, a rainbow upon his head and clothed with a cloud, who sets one foot on the sea and one foot on the earth. In the middle section are the impalpable harmonies of heaven. On the piano, soft cascades of blue-orange chords envelop in their distant chimes the song of the violin and cello, which is almost like plainchant.

38. John Cage

Sonatas and Interludes, Sonata V (1946)

8CD: 7/[78]–[79]

Table of Preparations

Material	Strings left to right	Distance from damper (inches)	Material	Strings left to right	Distance from damper (inches)	Material	Strings left to right	Distance from damper (inches)	Tone
			SCREW	2-3	1¼*				A
			MED. BOLT	2-3	1⅜*				G
			SCREW	2-3	1⅝*				F
			SCREW	2-3	1 13/16*				E
			SCREW	2-3	1¾*				E♭
			SM. BOLT	2-3	2*				D
			SCREW	2-3	1 9/16*				C♯
			FURNITURE BOLT	2-3	2 3/16*				C
			SCREW	2-3	2½*				B
			SCREW	2-3	1⅞*				B♭
			MED. BOLT	2-3	2⅜*				A
			SCREW	2-3	2¼*				A♭
			SCREW	2-3	3¾*				G
			SCREW	2-3	2 15/16*				F♯
SCREW	1-2	¾*	FURN. BOLT + 2 NUTS	2-3	2⅛*	SCREW + 2 NUTS	2-3	3¼*	F
			SCREW	2-3	1 13/16*				E
			FURNITURE BOLT	2-3	1⅞				E♭
			SCREW	2-3	1 15/16				C♯
			SCREW	2-3	1 1/16				C
(DAMPER TO BRIDGE = 4 5/16; ADJUST ACCORDINGLY)			MED. BOLT	2-3	3¾				B
			SCREW	2-3	4 9/16				A
RUBBER	1-2-3	4½	FURNITURE BOLT	2-3	1¼				G♯
			SCREW	2-3	1¾				F♯
			SCREW	2-3	2 5/16				F
RUBBER	1-2-3	5¾							E
RUBBER	1-2-3	6½	FURN. BOLT + NUT	2-3	6⅞				E♭
			FURNITURE BOLT	2-3	2 9/16				D
RUBBER	1-2-3	3⅝							D♭
			BOLT	2-3	7⅛				C
			BOLT	2-3	2				B
SCREW	1-2	10	SCREW	2-3	1	RUBBER	1-2-3	8¼	B♭
(PLASTIC (SEE G))	1-2-3	2 5/16				RUBBER	1-2-3	4½	G♯
PLASTIC (OVER 1-UNDER 2-3)	1-2-3	2⅞				RUBBER	1-2-3	10⅛	G
(PLASTIC (SEE D))	1-2-3	4¼				RUBBER	1-2-3	5 7/16	D♯
PLASTIC (OVER 1-UNDER 2-3)	1-2-3	4⅛				RUBBER	1-2-3	9¾	D
BOLT	1-2	15½	BOLT	2-3	11/16	RUBBER	1-2-3	14⅛	D♭
BOLT	1-2	14½	BOLT	2-3	⅞	RUBBER	1-2-3	6½	C
BOLT	1-2	14¾	BOLT	2-3	9/16	RUBBER	1-2-3	14	B
RUBBER	1-2-3	9½	MED. BOLT	2-3	10⅛				B♭
SCREW	1-2	5⅞	LG. BOLT	2-3	5⅞	SCREW + NUTS	1-2	1	A
BOLT	1-2	7⅛	MED. BOLT	2-3	2¼	RUBBER	1-2-3	4⅛	A♭
LONG BOLT	1-2	8¾	LG BOLT	2-3	3¼				G
			BOLT	2-3	11/16				D
SCREW + RUBBER	1-2	4 7/16							D (8va bassa)
ERASER (OVER D UNDER C♯ + E♭) AM. PENCIL CO. #346	1	6¾							D (16va bassa)

*MEASURE FROM BRIDGE.

[Mutes of various materials are placed between the strings of the keys used, thus effecting transformations of the piano sounds with respect to all of their characteristics.]

78
79

California-born John Cage (1912–1992) established himself as a major American avant-garde composer during the 1930s. Greatly influenced by Eastern philosophies and musical styles, Cage is best remembered as an advocate of indeterminacy and for his expansion of the boundaries of musical sound to include more of what had generally been considered as noise. In 1938, he invented the "prepared" piano, which is created by inserting various objects, such as nails, screws, wood, and leather, between the strings of a grand piano. Depending on the nature of the material and its placement, a great variety of sounds can be created, ranging from altered pitches to nonpitched effects.

Sonatas and Interludes is a set of works for prepared piano dating from 1946–48. These sixteen sonatas are grouped in sets of four. Between each group, Cage inserts an interlude. In the preface, Cage gives specific instructions on how to prepare the piano, indicating that forty-five of the eighty-eight strings are to be prepared with various materials at prescribed distances from the damper. *Sonata V*, set in a binary form, has a limited pitch content, primarily centering on the five pitches between B and E-flat. Because of the prepared alterations, many of these notes produce a nonpitched, percussive sound. The unusual timbre and hypnotic quality of the movement as a whole are reminiscent of the character of a Javanese gamelan ensemble; Cage's interest in Asian music is also apparent in his attempt to portray, in this set of piano works, the eight permanent emotions of [East] Indian aesthetics: the erotic, the heroic, the odious, anger, mirth, fear, sorrow, and the wondrous.

39. Billie Holiday

Billie's Blues (recorded 1936)

8CD: 8/ 1 – 7
4CD: 4/ 28 – 34

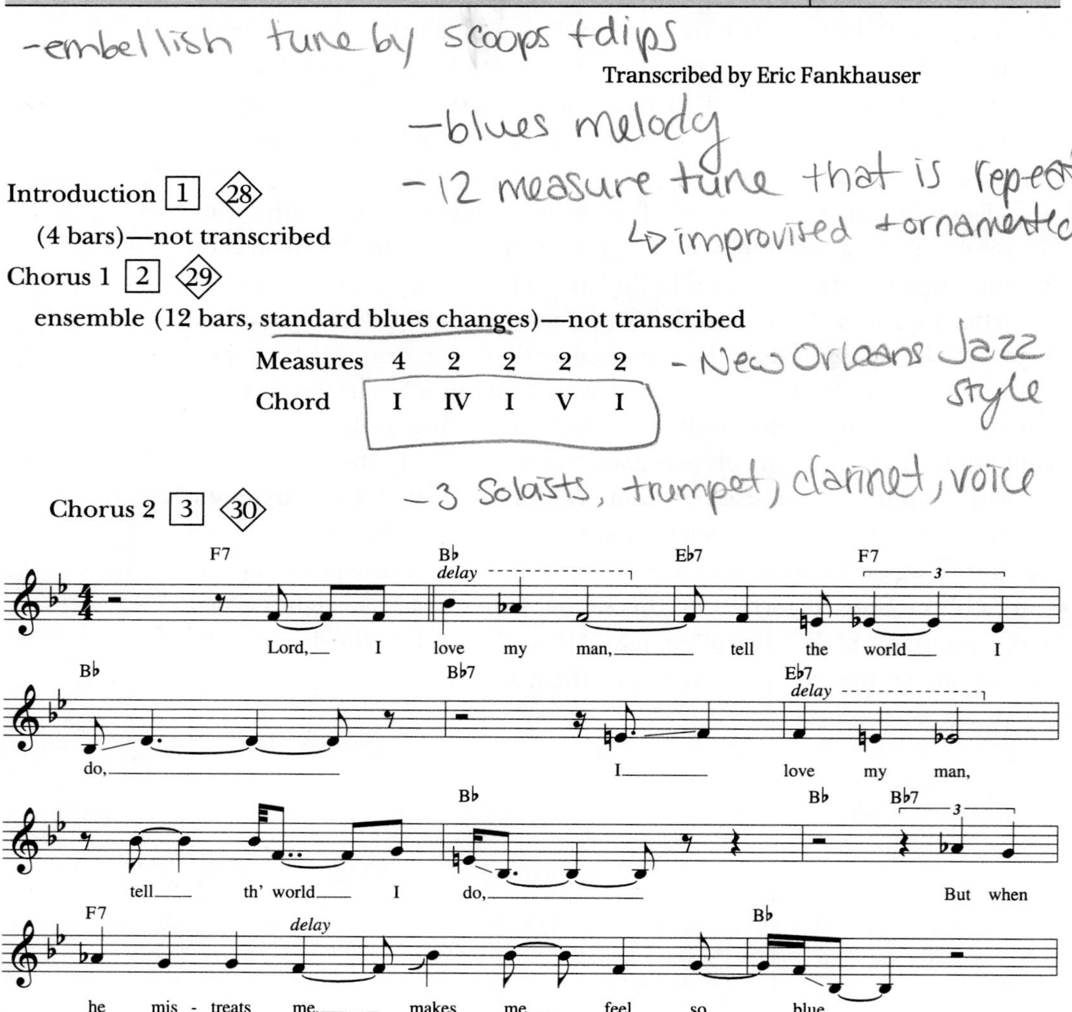

Editor's note: This transcription shows pitch inflections, such as wide vibrato, slides, glisses, and scoops into notes, as well as slight rhythmic alterations, including delays and anticipations.

Chorus 3 4 31
B♭ F7 B♭7 E♭7
delay ant.
My man woul-dn' gim-me no break-fast, Woul-dn' gim-me no din-ner,
Squawked a-bout my sup-per'n put me out-doors, Had the nerve to lay
a match-box on my clothes; I did-n't
have so man-y but I had a long, long ways to go.
Clarinet

Chorus 4 5 32
B♭ F7 B♭7 E♭7 B°7
vib.

Chorus 5
6
33
Bb
F7
Trumpet (growl)
Bb
Eb7
F7
Bb
Bb7
Eb7
vib.
Bb
Bb
B°7
smear
Cmi7
vib.
delay
F7
Bb
Clar.
Chorus 6
7
34
Bb
F7
Bb
delay
Some men like me 'cause I'm hap - py,
Some 'cause I'm snap - py,
Bb
Bb7
Eb7
Some call me hon - ey, oth - ers think I've got mon - ey,
Some tell me,
Bb
F7
delay
"Ba - by you're built for speed,"
Now if you put that all to - geth - er, Makes me
Bb
Tpt.
Eb7
Bb
ev' - ry - thing a good man needs.

The blues is a category of African-American folk music that expresses misery and unhappiness. Emerging as a specific song type after 1900, the blues exerted a strong influence on jazz, both as a model of performance style and as a source of melodies. The simple repetitive structure of the blues made it ideal for improvisation. A blues melody typically consists of a twelve-measure tune (three four-measure phrases) that is repeated in a strophic fashion, often with improvised ornamentation. The standard harmonic progression for the tune is as follows:

Phrase one	Measures 1–4	I chord
Phrase two	Measures 5–6	IV chord
	Measures 7–8	I chord
Phrase three	Measures 9–10	V chord
	Measures 11–12	I chord

The blues was a performance vehicle for a number of black female singers, including the remarkable Billie Holiday (1915–1959). Developing an original sound characterized by a flexible vocal quality, subtle melodic nuances, and great expressiveness, Holiday became the premier jazz singer of her time. She performed and recorded with some of the major figures in jazz history. In addition, Holiday became one of the first black singers to break through racial barriers when she appeared with the white Artie Shaw orchestra.

This recording of *Billie's Blues* from 1936 features three principal soloists: voice (Billie Holiday), clarinet (Artie Shaw), and trumpet (Bunny Berigan). Supporting this group are a piano, guitar, string bass, and drums. The style of performance is typical of New Orleans jazz. Following a four-measure introduction, the soloists improvise on the given melody (known as the chorus) six times, three of which are instrumental. The clarinet and trumpet have distinct improvising styles, and Holiday embellishes the tune with scoops and dips on notes. The text for Holiday's first stanza is a typical three-line strophe, but the subsequent two verses are more extended.

Text

Lord, I love my man, tell the world I do
I love my man, tell the world I do,
But when he mistreats me, makes me feel so blue.

My man wouldn't give me no breakfast.
Wouldn't give me no dinner,
Squawked about my supper and he put me outdoors,
Had the nerve to lay a matchbox on my clothes;
I didn't have so many but I had a long, long ways to go.

Some men like me 'cause I'm happy,
Some 'cause I'm snappy,
Some call me honey, others think I've got money,
Some tell me, "Baby you're built for speed,"
Now if you put that all together,
Makes me everything a good man needs.

40. Billy Strayhorn/Duke Ellington

8CD: 8/8–12

Take the A Train (recorded 1941)

Transcribed by Brent Wallarab; edited by Gunther Schuller.

9
5
Alto 1
Alto 2
Tenor 1
Tenor 2
Baritone
unis.
mf
mp
St. mute
Tpt. 1
Tpt. 2
Tpt. 3
f
p
Trb. 1
Trb. 2
Trb. 3
slow
mfp
Piano
Guitar
C6
D7(♭5)
Bass
Drums

9
Alto 1
Alto 2
Tenor 1
Tenor 2
Baritone
Tpt. 1
Tpt. 2
Tpt. 3
Trb. 1
Trb. 2
Trb. 3
Piano
Guitar
Bass
Drums
mf
f
p
G7
C6

13
Alto 1
Alto 2
Tenor 1
Tenor 2
Baritone
Tpt. 1
Tpt. 2
Tpt. 3
Trb. 1
Trb. 2
Trb. 3
Piano
Guitar
Bass
Drums
mf
mp
f
p
slow
mfp
C 6
D7(♭5)

17
Alto 1
Alto 2
Tenor 1
Tenor 2
Baritone
Tpt. 1
Tpt. 2
Tpt. 3
Trb. 1
Trb. 2
Trb. 3
Piano
Guitar
Bass
Drums
G7
C6
C9

21
Alto 1
Alto 2
Tenor 1
Tenor 2
Baritone
Tpt. 1
Tpt. 2
Tpt. 3
Trb. 1
Trb. 2
Trb. 3
Piano
Guitar
Bass
Drums
F6
mf

25
Alto 1
Alto 2
Tenor 1
Tenor 2
Baritone
mf
Tpt. 1
Tpt. 2
Tpt. 3
Trb. 1
Trb. 2
Trb. 3
25
Piano
Guitar
D7
G7
Bass
Drums

29
Alto 1
Alto 2
Tenor 1
Tenor 2
Baritone
Tpt. 1
Tpt. 2
Tpt. 3
Trb. 1
Trb. 2
Trb. 3
Piano
Guitar
Bass
Drums
p
mf
mp
f
C6/9
D9(♭5)

*Solo as played by Ray Nance

37
lightly
mp
Alto 1
Alto 2
Tenor 1
Tenor 2
Baritone
Tpt. 1
Tpt. 2
Tpt. 3
Trb. 1
Trb. 2
Trb. 3
Piano
Guitar
Bass
Drums
C6
D9
mf

41
Alto 1
Alto 2
Tenor 1
Tenor 2
Baritone
Tpt. 1
Tpt. 2
Tpt. 3
vib.
3
Trb. 1
Trb. 2
Trb. 3
41
Piano
Guitar
G7
D♭7
C6
Bass
Drums
mf

45
Alto 1
Alto 2
Tenor 1
Tenor 2
Baritone
Tpt. 1
Tpt. 2
Tpt. 3
slight bend
bend
Trb. 1
Trb. 2
Trb. 3
45
Piano
Guitar
C6
D9
Bass
Drums
mp

49
Alto 1
Alto 2
Tenor 1
Tenor 2
Baritone
Tpt. 1
Tpt. 2
Tpt. 3
Trb. 1
Trb. 2
Trb. 3
49
Piano
G7
D♭7
C6
Guitar
Bass
Drums
mf

53
Alto 1
Alto 2
Tenor 1
Tenor 2
Baritone
Tpt. 1
Tpt. 2
Tpt. 3
3
bend
vib.
3
vib.
Trb. 1
Trb. 2
Trb. 3
53
Piano
F6
Guitar
Bass
Drums

57
Alto 1
Alto 2
Tenor 1
Tenor 2
Baritone
Tpt. 1
Tpt. 2
Tpt. 3
bend
3
Trb. 1
Trb. 2
Trb. 3
57
Piano
mf
Guitar
D7
G7
Bass
Drums

61
Alto 1
Alto 2
Tenor 1
Tenor 2
Baritone
Tpt. 1
Tpt. 2
Tpt. 3
vib.
Trb. 1
Trb. 2
Trb. 3
61
Piano
Guitar
C 6
D 9
Bass
Drums
mp

65
Alto 1
Alto 2
Tenor 1
Tenor 2
Baritone
Tpt. 1
Tpt. 2
Tpt. 3
Trb. 1
Trb. 2
Trb. 3
Piano
Guitar
Bass
Drums
mf
f
G7
D♭7
C6

69
Alto 1
Alto 2
Tenor 1
Tenor 2
Baritone
open
Tpt. 1
open
Tpt. 2
Tpt. 3
open
Trb. 1
Trb. 2
Trb. 3
69
Piano
Guitar
Bass
to sticks
choke
Drums
(mf)

Solo as played by Ray Nance

77
Alto 1
Alto 2
Tenor 1
Tenor 2
Baritone
mp
mf
Tpt. 1
Tpt. 2
Tpt. 3
3
Trb. 1
Trb. 2
Trb. 3
77
Piano
Guitar
Fmi7
B♭7(♭9)
E♭6/9
Bass
Drums

81
Alto 1
Alto 2
Tenor 1
Tenor 2
Baritone
Tpt. 1
Tpt. 2
Tpt. 3
bend
squeeze
Trb. 1
Trb. 2
Trb. 3
81
Piano
E♭6
F7(♭5)
Guitar
Bass
Drums

85
Alto 1
Alto 2
Tenor 1
Tenor 2
Baritone
Tpt. 1
Tpt. 2
Tpt. 3
Trb. 1
Trb. 2
Trb. 3
Piano
Guitar
Bass
Drums
mp
mf
f
Fmi7
B♭7(♭9)
E♭6/9
E♭13

89
Alto 1
Alto 2
Tenor 1
Tenor 2
Baritone
Tpt. 1
Tpt. 2
Tpt. 3
shake
shake
Trb. 1
Trb. 2
Trb. 3
mf
p
Piano
Guitar
A♭6
Bass
Drums

93
Alto 1
Alto 2
Tenor 1
Tenor 2
Baritone
Tpt. 1
Tpt. 2
Tpt. 3
1-2
3
1-2
Trb. 1
Trb. 2
Trb. 3
93
Piano
Guitar
F9
B♭9
Bass
Drums

97
Alto 1
mf
mp
Alto 2
mf
mp
Tenor 1
mf
mp
Tenor 2
mf
mp
Baritone
mf
mp
Tpt. 1
mf
Tpt. 2
mf
Tpt. 3
mf
Trb. 1
mf
Trb. 2
mf
Trb. 3
mf
97
Piano
E♭6
F7(♭5)
Guitar
Bass
Drums
mf

101
12
Alto 1
Alto 2
Tenor 1
Tenor 2
Baritone
Tpt. 1
Tpt. 2
Tpt. 3
Trb. 1
Trb. 2
Trb. 3
Piano
Guitar
Bass
Drums
mf
mp
Fmi7
E13
E♭6
to brushes
dim.
mf

105
Alto 1
Alto 2
Tenor 1
Tenor 2
Baritone
in hat
Tpt. 1
Tpt. 2
Tpt. 3
mp
in hat
(or plunger)
Trb. 1
Trb. 2
Trb. 3
105
Piano
E♭6
F7(♭5)
Guitar
Bass
Brushes
Drums
2

109
Alto 1
Alto 2
Tenor 1
Tenor 2
Baritone
Tpt. 1
Tpt. 2
Tpt. 3
Trb. 1
Trb. 2
Trb. 3
Piano
Guitar
Bass
Drums
Fmi7
E13
E♭6

113
Alto 1
Alto 2
Tenor 1
Tenor 2
Baritone
Tpt. 1
Tpt. 2
Tpt. 3
Trb. 1
Trb. 2
Trb. 3
113
Piano
Guitar
E♭6
F7(♭5)
Bass
Drums
2

117
Alto 1
Alto 2
Tenor 1
Tenor 2
Baritone
Tpt. 1
Tpt. 2
Tpt. 3
Trb. 1
Trb. 2
Trb. 3
117
Piano
Guitar
Fmi7
E13
E♭6
Bass
Drums
pp

In the 1930s, the free improvisatory style of New Orleans jazz gave way to sophisticated arrangements for larger ensembles. Generally known as either the Big Band era or the Swing era, the period produced some remarkable musicians, one of the greatest of which was Duke Ellington (1899–1974). Born Edward Kennedy Ellington but known as "Duke," Ellington was a fine jazz pianist and a brilliant orchestrator. Ellington's band comprised of two trumpets, one cornet, three trombones, four or five saxophones (often doubling on clarinets), and a rhythm section consisting of two string basses, guitar, drums, vibraphone, and piano. In his distinctive orchestrations, Ellington treats each family of instruments as a unit, often having a soloist from one family accompanied by another group of instruments in close triadic harmonies.

Take the A Train was written and arranged by Billy Strayhorn (1915–1967), a frequent collaborator with Ellington. This recording, made on February 15, 1941, features Duke Ellington on the piano and Ray Nance on the trumpet. After Ellington's four-measure chromatic introduction, the saxophones present the principal theme, accompanied by the brass instruments. The thirty-two-measure chorus comprises four eight-measure phrases in the form **A–A–B–A.** In the remaining two choruses, Ray Nance improvises on the theme (both muted and unmuted), with bent notes, shakes (a wide vibrato produced by shaking the lip), and glissandi, while the saxophones either accompany or alternate with the soloist. An energetic four-measure interlude, interjecting a conflicting triple meter, separates the second and third choruses, and the coda contains two echoes of the final phrase of Chorus 3.

41. Dizzy Gillespie/Charlie Parker

A Night in Tunisia (recorded 1946)

8CD: 8/13–18
4CD: 4/35–40

*Editor's note: *The Norton Recording* performance of the Introduction is as follows: 8-bar ostinato (bass and percussion); 4-bar saxophone ostinato.

Solo break (alto sax, Charlie Parker)

13 35 Introduction (8 + 4 bar ostinato)

14 36 Chorus 1 (32 bars, **A-A-B-A**)

15 37 Interlude (12 bars)

16 38 Alto sax solo break; Chorus 2

17 39 Chorus 3 (32 bars, **A-A-B-A**)

18 40 Coda (8-bar ostinato)

New jazz styles, such as bebop, began to emerge in the late 1940s as a reaction to the controlled sounds of the Big Band era. Bebop, which features a small number of virtuoso soloists, returns to the original jazz emphasis on improvisation, but often with a frenetic character. Two bebop greats, Charlie "Bird" Parker (alto saxophone) and Miles Davies (trumpet), are featured in this 1946 recording of Dizzy Gillespie's popular *A Night in Tunisia.* Gillespie (1917–1993), also a trumpeter, was a founder of bebop and one of the greatest figures in jazz history. *A Night in Tunisia* is among a number of jazz classics that he composed.

The mood of the tune is established by a syncopated ostinato introduction. The thirty-two-measure chorus (**A-A-B-A**) is then presented by the trumpet (playing the **A** phrases) and saxophone (playing the **B** phrase). Following a brief saxophone interlude, the chord patterns of the chorus are repeated, featuring solos by the saxophone, guitar, and trumpet. Most notable are the extended improvisations, riffs (short melodic phrases), and Parker's famous break (a solo passage that interrupts the accompaniment). At the end of the work, the ostinato returns and gradually fades away.

42. Leonard Bernstein

8CD: 8/19–29
4CD: 4/48–58

Mambo and *Tonight* Ensemble, from *West Side Story* (1957)

Instrumentation

Woodwinds

Most musical theater scores call for woodwind players (called reeds) to double on a variety of instruments. In *Mambo*, five reed books (numbered I-V) appear in different positions in the score, depending on the range of the instrument played (highest on the top line, lowest on the bottom).

Reed I: Alto saxophone
B-flat clarinet
Flute

Reed II: E-flat clarinet
B-flat clarinet

Reed III: B-flat clarinet
Tenor saxophone
Flute

Reed IV: Piccolo
Bass saxophone
B-flat clarinet
Flute

Reed V: Bassoon

Brasses

2 French horns
3 B-flat trumpets
2 Trombones

Percussion

Timpani
Bongos
Timbales
Conga
Pitched drums

Maracas
Cowbells
Guiro
Xylophone
Piano

Trap set:
Snare drum
Tenor drum
Brass drum
Cymbals

Strings

7 Violins
4 Cellos
Double bass

19 48

Fast ♩ = 126

To Bass Saxophone

Reed IV Piccolo

Reed II E♭ Clarinet

To Tenor Saxophone

Reed III B♭ Clarinet

Reed I Alto Saxophone

Reed V Bassoon

F Horns 1 2

B♭ Trumpets 1 2 3

Trombones 1 2

Bongos

Timbales

Cowbells

*(snares off)

SD

Traps

BD

Piano

Fast ♩ = 126

Violins

Violoncellos

Contrabass

Editor's note: The Norton Recordings performance, which is the original Broadway cast recording, cuts the following five pages and resumes at measure 43 (p. 817).

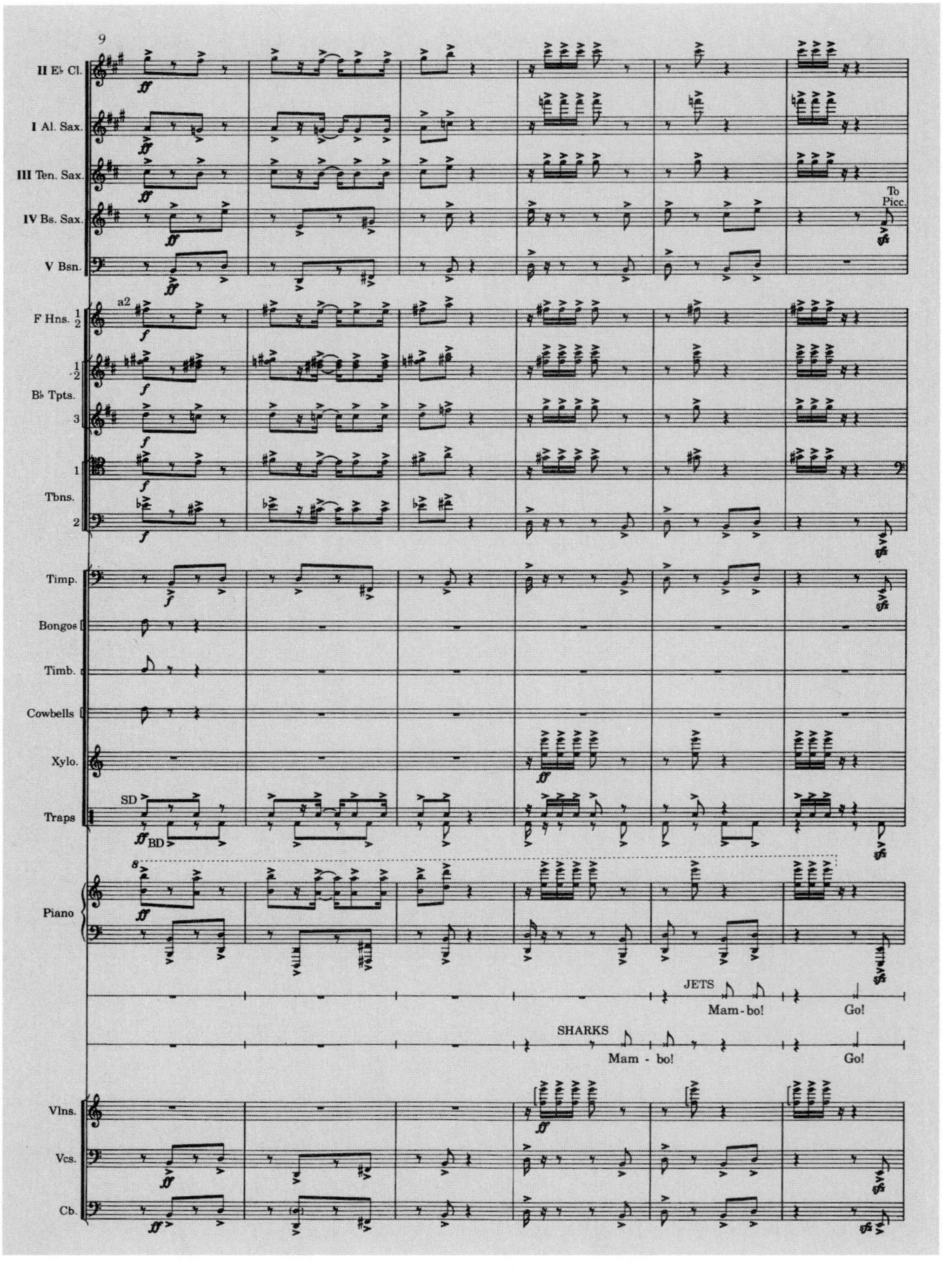

9

II E♭ Cl.
I Al. Sax.
III Ten. Sax.
IV Bs. Sax.
To Picc.
V Bsn.
a2
F Hns. 1 2
1 2
B♭ Tpts.
3
1
Tbns.
2
Timp.
Bongos
Timb.
Cowbells
Xylo.
SD
Traps
BD
8
Piano
JETS
Mam-bo! Go!
SHARKS
Mam - bo! Go!
Vlns.
Vcs.
Cb.

15
IV Picc.
II E♭ Cl.
I Al. Sax.
Ten. Sax.
V Bsn.
B♭ Tpts.
Tbns.
Bongos
Cowbells
Xylo.
Mambo ad lib.
SD (snares off)
BD
Traps
loco
Piano
Vlns.
Vcs.
pizz.
Cb.

22
II E♭ Cl.
I Al. Sax.
I Ten. Sax.
V Bsn.
f cresc.
F Hns. 1 2
ff cuivré
open
B♭ Tpts.
f
(p)
open
Tbns.
f cresc.
Bongos
Timb.
Cowbells
Traps
SD
BD
Piano
ff
Vlns.
Vcs.
arco
Cb.

29
II E♭ Cl.
I Al. Sax.
III Ten. Sax.
V Bsn.
f cresc.
F Hns. 1 2
ff cuivré
open
B♭ Tpts. 1 3
open
(p) f
Tbns. 1 2
f cresc.
Bongos
Timb.
Cowbells
Traps
SD
BD
Piano
Vlns. 1 2 3 4 5 6 7
Vcs.
arco
Cb.
ff

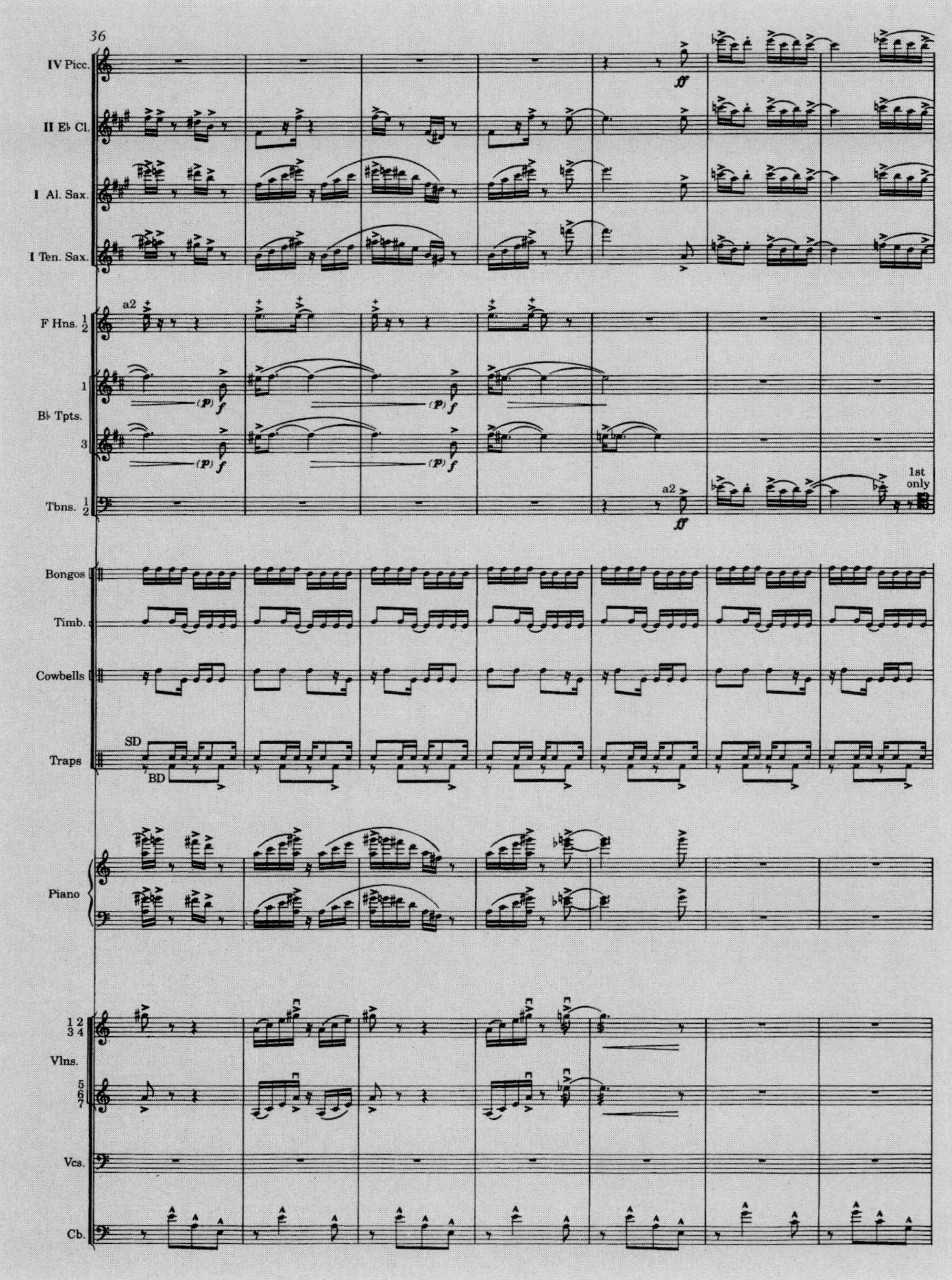
36
IV Picc.
II E♭ Cl.
I Al. Sax.
I Ten. Sax.
a2
F Hns. 1 2
1
B♭ Tpts.
3
(p)
f
ff
a2
1st only
Tbns. 1 2
Bongos
Timb.
Cowbells
SD
BD
Traps
Piano
1 2 3 4
Vlns.
5 6 7
Vcs.
Cb.

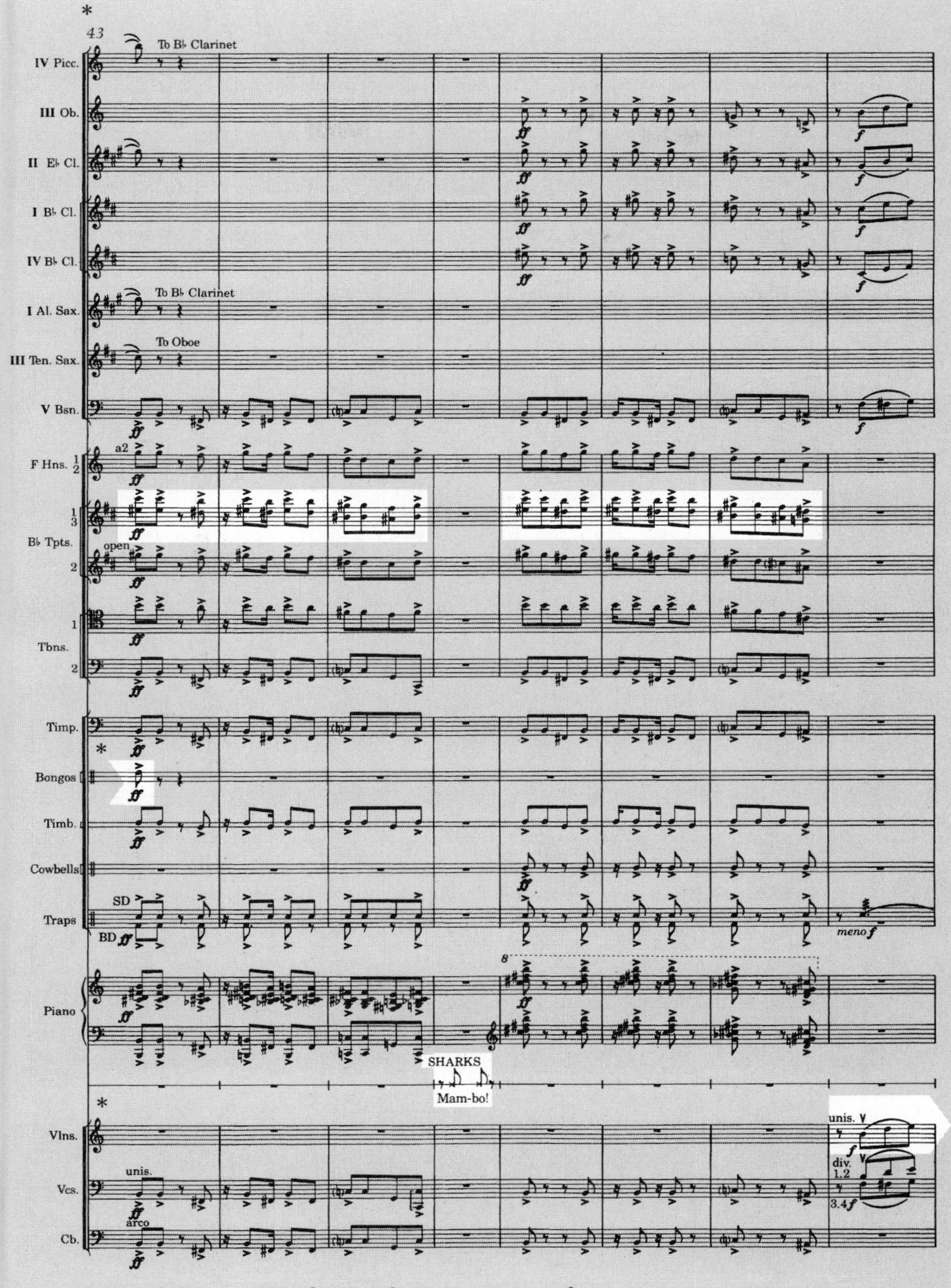

*Note: *The Norton Recordings* performance resumes here.

51
III Ob.
II E♭ Cl.
I B♭ Cl.
IV B♭ Cl.
V Bsn.
F Hns. 1 2
a2
B♭ Tpts. 1 3
2
Tbns. 1
2
Bongos
SD
Traps
loco
Piano
Vlns. 1 2 3
4 5
6 7
Vcs. 1 2
3 4
Cb.
molto
pp

59
IV Picc.
III Ob.
II E♭ Cl.
I B♭ Cl.
V B♭ Cl.
To Piccolo
V Bsn.
F Hns. 1 2
a2
♭ Tpts.
Tbns.
Timp.
Bongos
Timb.
Cowbells
Xylo.
SD
BD
Traps
Piano
Mam-bo!
Vlns.
pizz.
unis.
Vcs.
Cb.

20
49
67
IV Picc.
III Ob.
II E♭ Cl.
I B♭ Cl.
V Bsn.
F Hns. 1 2
B♭ Tpts. 1 2 3
Tbns. 1 2
Bongos
Conga
Pitched Drs.
Cowbells
Xylo.
Traps
Piano
Vlns. 1 2 3 4 5 6 7
Vcs. 1 2 3 4
Cb.
cresc.
To Flute
a2
fall-off
gliss.
rim shots
SD
BD
TD
L.H. gliss.
at frog
arco
pizz.

74
IV Picc.
I Fl.
III Ob.
II E♭ Cl.
V Bsn.
F Hns. 1 2
a2
B♭ Tpts.
Tbns. 1 2
fall-off
Bongos
Conga
Pitched Drs.
Cowbells
Xylo.
gliss.
Traps
TD
BD
Piano
Vlns.
pizz.
Vcs.
unis.
Cb.
To B♭ Clarinet

81
IV Picc.
III Ob.
II E♭ Cl.
I B♭ Cl.
V Bsn.
F Hns. 1 2
a2
♭ Tpts. 1 2 3
Tbns. 1 2
Bongos
Conga
Pitched Drs.
Cowbells
Xylo.
Traps
Mambo ad lib.
TD
BD
SD
Tem.Blk.
rim shot
Piano
142
Vlns. 1 2 3 4 5 6 7
Vcs. 1 2 3 4
Cb.
cresc.

88
IV Picc.
III Ob.
II E♭ Cl.
I B♭ Cl.
V Bsn.
F Hns. 1 2
a2
B♭ Tpts. 1 2 3
p ma marc.
Tbns. 1 2
a2
Bongos
Pitched Drs.
Cowbells
Xylo.
Traps
SD
Mambo ad lib.
TD
BD
(loco)
Piano
Vlns. 1 2 3 4 5 6 7
arco
Vcs. 1 2 3 4
Cb.
dim.

95
IV Picc.
III Ob.
II E♭ Cl.
I B♭ Cl.
V Bsn.
F Hns. 1 2
a2
poco f
cresc.
ff
fff
sfz
1
Tpts. 2
3
marc.
Tbns. 1 2
Bongos
Pitched Drs.
Cowbells
Xylo.
Traps
TD
BD
Piano
loco
Vlns.
unis.
Vcs.
Cb.

101
IV Picc.
III Ob.
II E♭ Cl.
I B♭ Cl.
V Bsn.
B♭ Tpts.
To D Trumpet
Solo
Tbn. 1
ad lib.
Conga
Cowbells
Guiro
Xylo.
Traps
BD
Piano
Vlns.
arco
Vcs.
Cb.

108
IV Picc.
III Ob.
II E♭ Cl.
I B♭ Cl.
V Bsn.
F Hns. 1 2
a2
B♭ Tpts. 1 3
open
shake
Tbns. 1 2
Timp.
with maracas*
Timb.
ad lib.
Conga
Cowbells
ad lib.
Guiro
Traps
SD
CYM
BD
TD
Piano
Vlns. 1 2 3
4 5
6 7
Vcs.
Cb.
cresc.
* maracas may be separate player.

114
21
50
IV Picc.
III Ob.
II E♭ Cl.
I B♭ Cl.
V Bsn.
F Hns. 1 2
D Tpt.
♭ Tpts. 1 3
Tbns. 1 2
Timp.
Bongos
Timb.
Pitched Drs.
Traps
Piano
Vlns.
Vcs.
Cb.
cresc.
To Tenor Saxophone
To Alto Saxophone
a2
(open)
shake
SD
TD
BD
ff
f
sfz

120
IV Picc.
II E♭ Cl.
I Al. Sax.
I Ten. Sax.
V Bsn.
a2
F Hns. 1/2
shake
D Tpt.
shake
shake
shake
B♭ Tpts. 1/3
Tbns. 1/2
Timp.
Bongos
Timb.
Pitched Drs.
TD
Traps
BD
Piano
Vlns.
Vcs.
Cb.

126
(Tony and Maria see each other)
IV Picc.
II E♭ Cl.
I Al. Sax.
I Ten. Sax.
V Bsn.
F Hns. 1 2
a2
D Tpt.
To B♭ Trumpet
B♭ Tpts. 1 3 2
open
Tbns. 1 2
gliss.
Timp.
with Maracas
ad lib.
Bongos
Timb.
Pitched Drs.
Traps
TD
BD
Susp. CYM
Piano
Vlns.
Vcs.
Cb.
pizz.

132
IV Picc.
II E♭ Cl.
I Al. Sax.
III Ten. Sax.
V Bsn.
F Hns. 1 2
a2
B♭ Tpts.
1 3
2
Tbns. 1 2
gliss.
a2
Timp.
Bongos
Timb.
Pitched Drs.
Traps
TD
BD
Piano
ALL
Go, Mam
Vlns.
Vcs.
Cb.

138
IV Picc.
II E♭ Cl.
I Al. Sax.
III Ten. Sax.
V Bsn
F Hns. 1 2
B♭ Tpts. 1 2 3
Tbns. 1 2
Timp.
Bongos
Timb.
Pitched Drs.
Traps
Piano
All
Vlns.
Vcs.
Cb.
a2
gliss.
valve gliss.
TD
BD
Susp. CYM
loco
- bo! Go, Mam - bo! Go, Mam - bo!

(The lights dim and the crowd disappears as Tony and Maria approach each other)
144
rall. molto
IV Picc.
To Flute
II E♭ Cl.
To B♭ Clarinet
I Al. Sax.
To Flute
III Ten. Sax.
To Flute
V Bsn.
F Hns. 1 2
a2
B♭ Tpts.
straight mute
straight mutes
Tbns.
Timp.
Bongos
Timb.
Pitched Drs.
Maracas
Traps
TD
BD
Piano
rall. molto
Vlns.
sul D
Vcs.
Cb.
dim.
SEGUE

-american theatre

Tonight

Ensemble melody A-A'-B-A'

Maria, Tony, Anita, Riff, Bernardo*

-beguine rhythm
(Latin American dance)

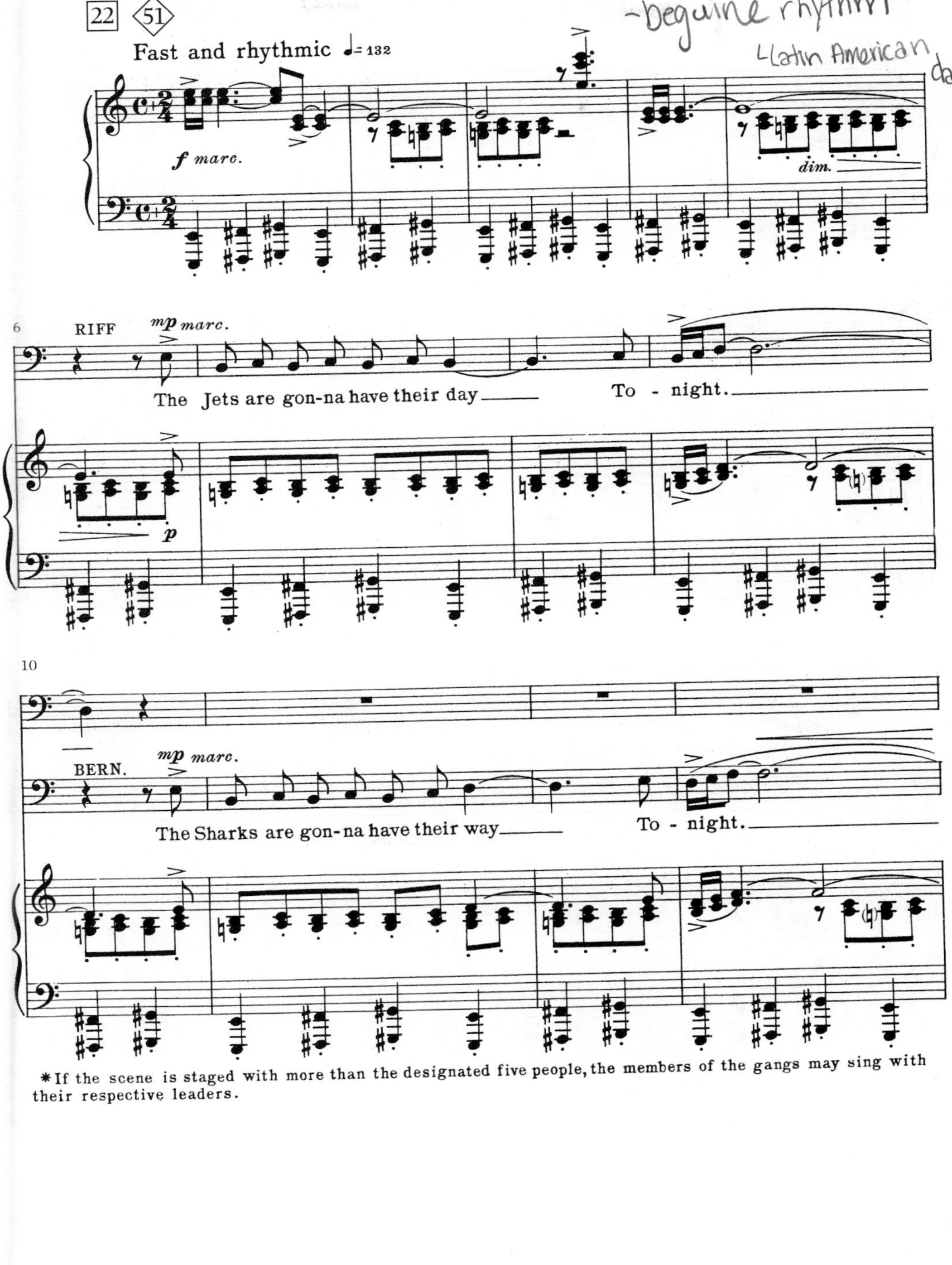
22
51
Fast and rhythmic ♩= 132
f marc.
dim.
RIFF
mp marc.
The Jets are gon-na have their day
To - night.
p
BERN.
mp marc.
The Sharks are gon-na have their way
To - night.

*If the scene is staged with more than the designated five people, the members of the gangs may sing with their respective leaders.

14
(RIFF)
mf
The Puer - to Ri - cans grum - ble: "Fair
(BERN.)
mp sempre staccato
17
fight." But if they start a rum - ble, We'll rum - ble 'em
20
right.
mp
We're gon-na hand 'em a sur-prise To -
p

24
We're gon-na cut 'em down to size______ To -
night. ______
28
night. ______
mf
We said,"O. K., no rum-pus, No
mp sempre staccato
32
tricks". But just in case they jump us, We're ready - y to

23
52
mix — To - night!
We're gon-na rock it to-night,
We're gon-na rock it to-night,
cresc.
f marc.
mf
— We're gon-na jazz it up and have us a ball! —
— We're gon-na jazz it up and have us a ball! —
f subito
They're gon - na get it to - night; — The more they turn it on, the
They're gon - na get it to - night; — The more they turn it on, the
mf subito

44
ff
hard-er they'll fall!
Well, they be-gan it!
ff
hard-er they'll fall!
Well,
cresc.
f
47
And we're the ones to stop 'em once and for all,
they be-gan it! And we're the ones to stop 'em once and for all,
49
ANITA (sexily)
24
53
An-
fff
To - night!
fff
To - night!
cresc.
p subito

53
i - ta's gon - na get her kicks
To - night.
56
We'll have our pri-vate lit-tle mix
To - night.
60
He'll walk in hot and ti - red,
So what? Don't
mp sempre staccato
64
mat - ter if he's ti - red, As long as he's hot

25
54
67
To - night!
TONY (warmly)
mf
To - night, to - night Won't be just an - y
mp
71
night, To - night there will be no morn - ing star.
75
più f
To - night, to - night, I'll see my love to -
cresc.

79
night And for us, stars will stop where they are.
26
55
83
f
To - day The min - utes seem like hours, The
3
f espr.
87
hours go so slow - ly, And still the sky is light.

91
mp
cresc.
Oh moon, grow bright, And make this end-less
cresc.
27
56
Come prima, in 4
95
f
day end-less night!
f
ff marcatissmo
99

102
RIFF (To Tony) mp
I'm count-ing on you to be there
sffz
dim.
p
105
To - night
When Dies-el wins it fair and square
109
mf
To - night.
That Puer-to Ri-can punk'll
mp
113
Go down And when he's hol-lered "Un-cle" We'll tear up the

28
57
MARIA (warmly)
To - night, to - night Won't
TONY (abstractedly)
All right.
(firmly)
town!
So I can count on you, boy?
be just an - y night, To - night there will be
(a bit impatiently)
All right.
(spoken) (gently)
We're gon-na have us a ball.
Womb to tomb!
simile

* The part of Anita may be augmented by voices in the wings from here to the end.

*The part of Maria may be augmented by voices in the wings from here to the end.

135
min - utes seem like hours, The hours go so
day, An - i - ta's gon - na have her day,
min - utes seem like hours, The hours go so
(lights on Riff)
fp
fp
sim.
They be - gan it,
sim.
gan it, they be - gan it
138
dim.
slow - ly, And still the sky is light.
Ber - nar - do's gon - na have his way To - night,
dim.
slow - ly, And still the sky is light.
They be - gan it.
f
And we're the ones To stop 'em once and for all!
dim.

141
pp
Oh moon, grow
to - night. To - night,
Oh moon, grow
f
We'll stop 'em once and for all! The Jets are gon - na have their
dim. molto
pp
The Sharks are gon - na have their
143
cresc. molto
bright, And make this end - less day end - less
this ver - y night,
bright, And make this end - less day end - less
way, The Jets are gon - na have their day,
way, The Sharks are gon - na have their day,

146
ff
night
To - night!
ff
We're gon-na rock it to - night!
ff
night
To - night!
ff
We're gon-na rock it to - night,
To - night!
ff
We're gon-na rock it to - night,
To - night!
f
ff
149

Leonard Bernstein (1918–1990), one of America's foremost musicians of the twentieth century, achieved critical success as a concert pianist, conductor, and composer. His masterwork is the Broadway musical *West Side Story,* which adapts Shakespeare's *Romeo and Juliet* to a modern New York setting. The musical centers on two rival gangs, the established Jets and the Puerto Rican Sharks, which are equivalent to the rival families in the Shakespeare tragedy. Bernstein emphasizes the ethnic differences between the gangs by incorporating elements of both American jazz and Latin American popular music. With these diverse styles, Bernstein creates a highly unified work that has immense popular appeal yet retains its ties to Western classical music.

The mambo is played at the neighborhood dance, which is equivalent to the masked ball in the Shakespeare drama. Bernstein uses this energetic Afro-Cuban dance, with its fast tempo and accented syncopation, to reflect the presence of the Sharks. Bongos, cowbells, shouts from the dancers, loud dissonances, and jazzy riffs contribute to the frenzied character of the dance. At the end, the music quickly fades as Tony and Maria see each other for the first time.

The *Tonight* Ensemble mixes popular elements within an operatic setting. The ensemble is in three sections. During the opening section, the two gangs sing an energetic melody over a menacing marching bass line. After alternating the material, the two gangs sing simultaneously. Anita joins in with a new verse, which closes this section. The second section is a reprise of Tony and Maria's balcony love song, *Tonight.* Set against a beguine rhythm (another Latin American popular dance), the melody is sung in its full **A-A′-B-A′** format. Upon the repetition of the tune by Maria, the final section emerges, and the two musical ideas are combined together. At the climax, both Tony and Maria sing of their love, while Anita and both gangs sing of hatred. The common element linking the two is the word "tonight."

43. György Ligeti

8CD: 8/30–32
4CD: 4/66–68

Désordre (Disorder), from *Etudes for Piano*, Book I (1985)

30 66

Composer's directions: Use the pedal very discreetly throughout the entire piece.
Editor's note: Measure numbers pertain to left hand.

29
36
43
31
67
52

62
8 bassa
crescendo poco a poco
71
8 bassa
8va
f più crescendo
81
8 bassa
32
68
8va
fff crescendo molto
poco
mf
fff sub.
f
p
simile
simile
91
fff
8 bassa
Ped.
hands together
loudest moment

Composer's directions:

*Dynamic balance: the right hand should play somewhat louder than the left, so that the accented chords in both hands sound equally loud (until the end of the piece).

Gradually add more pedal (but always sparingly).

*Gradual *crescendo* (until the end): the accents gradually become *ff*, then *fff* (with the right hand constantly louder), the eighth notes gradually *mp*, then *mf*.

8va
128
8va
135
8va
141
8va
8va
8va

György Ligeti (b. 1923) left his Hungarian homeland in 1956 and immediately began to add his own distinctive voice to the European avant-garde movement. He achieved quasi-celebrity status when three of his compositions—*Atmosphères,* the Requiem, and *Lux aeterna*—were used in Stanley Kubrick's classic film *2001: A Space Odyssey* (1968). In these works, Ligeti explored the use of fixed pitches to create large clusters of tones.

At the end of the 1970s, Ligeti's style began to change as he turned toward a complex polyrhythmic technique and moved away from the static quality of his earlier compositions. Among his later works are fifteen piano études, published in three books: Book I has six works (1985), Book II has eight works (1988), and Book III contains only one work—"White on White" (1995). In the tradition of fellow Hungarian Franz Liszt, each étude is given a subtitle. The first étude, *Désordre* (*Disorder*), presents a complex web of rhythmic patterns that, at a vigorous tempo, creates an effect well suited to its title. Two distinct rhythmic processes can be observed: additive metric patterns (5 + 3 or 3 + 5)—an influence of African rhythm—and the simultaneous playing of triple and duple patterns. With the quick tempo, the complexities of the rhythmic patterns are not heard, but rather the focus is on the overall effect that grows in intensity and diminishes only at the end.

44. Pierre Boulez

8CD: 8/33–35

Le marteau sans maître
(The Hammer Without a Master),
Nos. 1, 3, 7 (1953–54; revised 1957)

1. Avant "L'artisanat furieux" (Before "Furious Artisans")

Editor's note: The symbols between the staves are intended for the conductor.

a tempo
Fl. en sol
Vibr.
Guit.
Alto
pizz.
arco
B 10
poco rit.
a tempo
p sub.
pour 4

presser - - - a tempo
Fl. en sol
Vibr.
Guit.
Alto
arco
pizz.
pour 4
pour 6
mf
p
poco rit.
a tempo
cresc.
f

Fl. en sol
Vibr.
Guit.
Alto
pour 4
presser
a tempo
pour 6
arco
pizz.
(pizz.)
pp sub.
f sub.
p sub.

poco rit.
a tempo
Fl. en sol
Vibr.
Guit.
Alto
pour 6
sub.
pizz.
arco
poco rit.

a tempo
presser
a tempo
poco rit.
a tempo
presser
a tempo
poco rit.
a tempo
presser
Fl. en sol
Vibr.
Guit.
Alto
pour 4
pizz.
arco
arrêt assez court

3. L'artisanat furieux (Furious Artisans)

Fl. en sol
Voix
ca - da - vre dans le pa - nier
(♩ = 84)(♩. = 56)
(♩ = 126)
(♩. = 56) (♩ = 84)
senza dim.
cresc. al
tenuto senza dim.
Flzg.
Et che-vaux de
la - bours dans le fer à

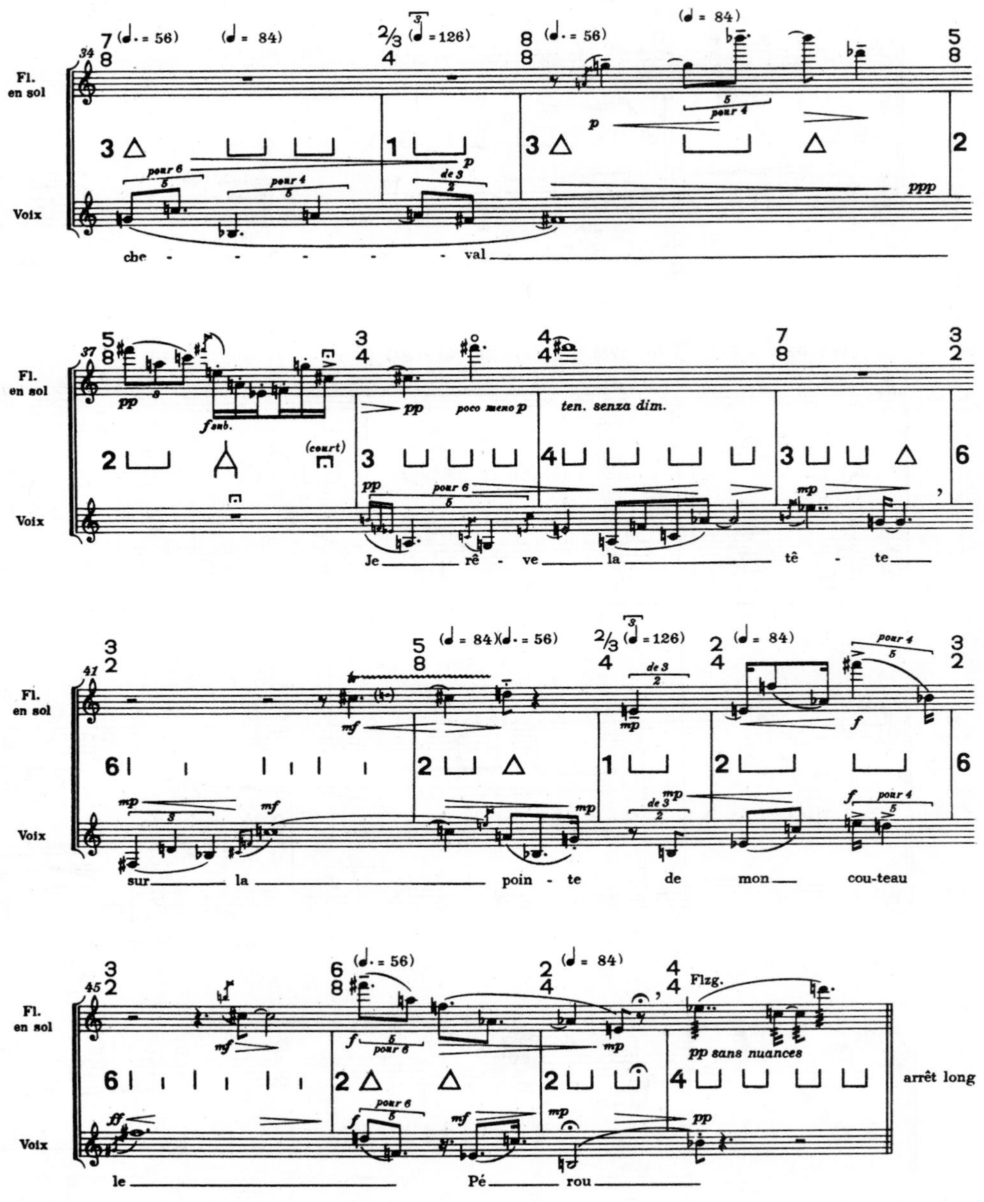

Text and Translation

La roulotte rouge au bord du clou	The red caravan at the prison's edge
Et cadavre dans le panier	And a corpse in the basket
Et chevaux se labours dans le fer à cheval	And the work horses in the horseshoe
Je rêve la tête sur la pointe de mon couteau le Pérou	I dream of Peru with my head on the point of my knife

7. Après "L'artisanat furieux" (After "Furious Artisans")

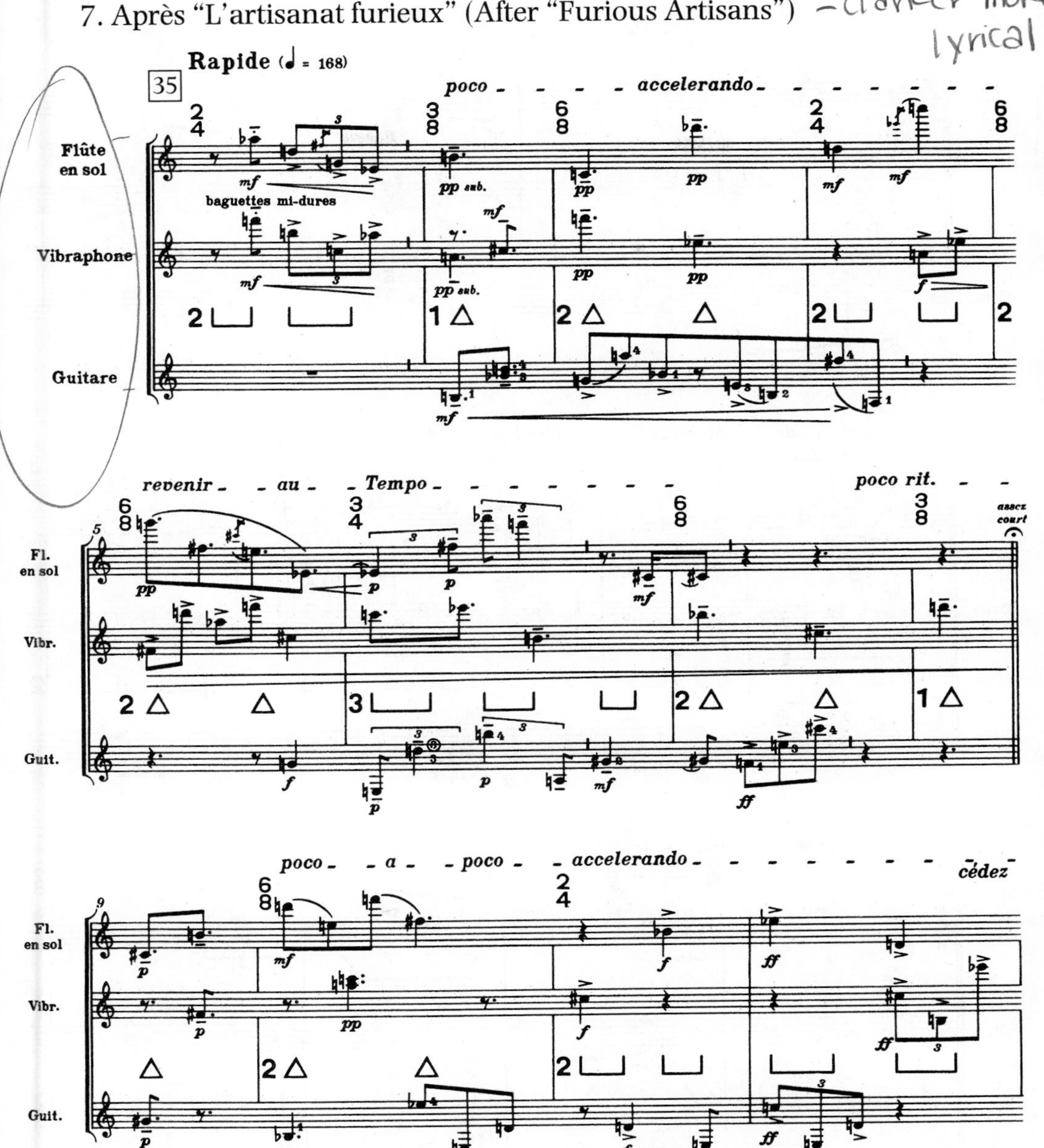

sempre accelerando
cédez
Fl. en sol
Vibr.
Guit.
(♩ = 208)
accelerando
molto
A tempo subito (♩ = 168)
très court
pour 4
sec
sempre ff
accelerando
pour 6
sempre f

(♩ = 208)
(♩. = 138)
beaucoup plus vif
poco rit.
accelerando
revenir au Tempo
Fl. en sol
Vibr.
Guit.
rit.
Tempo
più ritard.
accele
court
rando
poco
a
poco
accele
ff sempre
5 pour 6
pp sub.
f sempre
(non accentué)

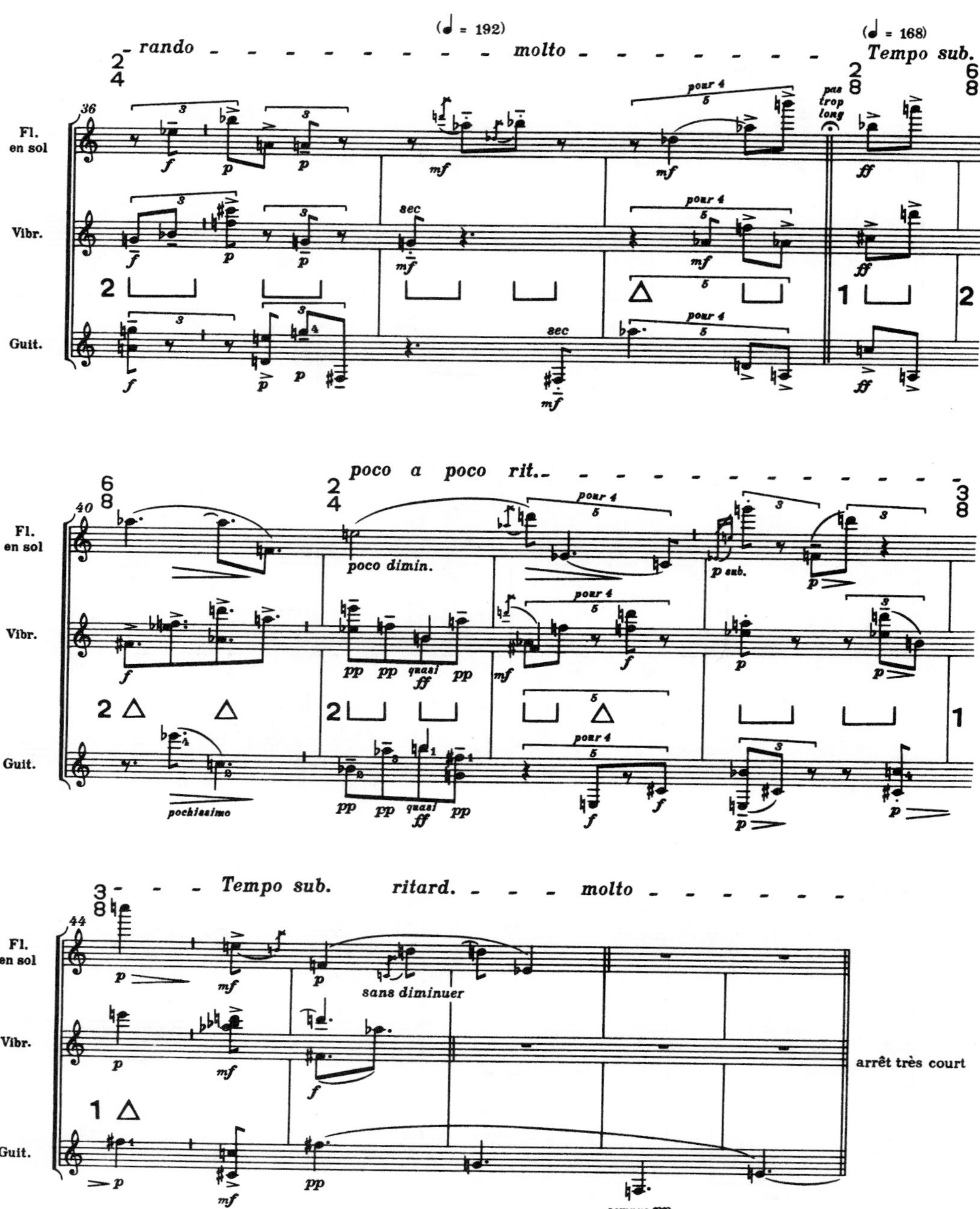

(♩ = 192)
(♩ = 168)
- rando - - - - - - - - - - molto - - - - - - - - - Tempo sub.
Fl. en sol
Vibr.
Guit.
pour 4
pas trop long
sec
f p mf ff
poco a poco rit.- - - - - - - - - - - - - - -
poco dimin.
pochissimo
p sub.
quasi ff
pp
- - - Tempo sub. ritard. - - - - molto - - - - - - - -
sans diminuer
arrêt très court
sempre pp

The avant-garde masterpiece *Le marteau sans maître (The Hammer Without a Master)* by Pierre Boulez (b. 1925) stands as a 1950s counterpart to Schoenberg's *Pierrot lunaire* of 1912. Both are song cycles accompanied by a small chamber group, and the advanced serial techniques employed by Boulez are descended from later innovations of Schoenberg. For each song, Boulez selects a unique combination of colors drawn from an alto voice, alto flute, guitar, viola, vibraphone, xylorimba, and other percussion instruments. The timbre is dominated by the middle and upper registers, creating a limpid and brilliant sound that suggests the influence of non-Western cultures.

The texts for the cycle are poems by the French surrealist René Char. Unlike Schoenberg, Boulez includes a number of purely instrumental movements that are either a prelude or a commentary on each song. These related movements are not presented in succession. Instead, the numbers are interwoven, so that the material overlaps. The three related movements in this anthology, *Avant "L'artisanat furieux" (Before "Furious Artisans")*, *L'artisanat furieux (Furious Artisans)*, and *Après "L'artisanat furieux" (After "Furious Artisans")* appear as movements 1, 3, and 7 in the cycle.

The musical style is similar in all three movements. A pointillistic texture is supported by wide intervals, shifting meters, constant dynamic changes, and frequent rests. These elements, combined with an overall dissonant sound, create a sense of randomness, in spite of the extensive calculations involved in the creation of the work. *Avant "L'artisanat furieux"* is set for alto flute, vibraphone, guitar, and viola. The percussive sound of the vibraphone, guitar, and pizzicato viola provide a contrast to the more sustained sounds of the flute and bowed viola. *L'artisanat furieux* is a duet for alto flute and alto voice. Both parts are virtuosic. The agile flute line often incorporates flutter tonguing, while the vocal line, which requires an extraordinarily wide range, has several extended phrases on a single syllable and features disjunct motion. *Après "L'artisanat furieux"* is similar in motivic material and general character to the opening prelude, but the darker and more lyric tones of the viola are omitted.

45. George Crumb

Ancient Voices of Children, First Movement,
El niño busca su voz (The Little Boy Is Looking for His Voice)
(1970)

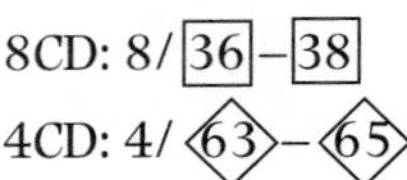

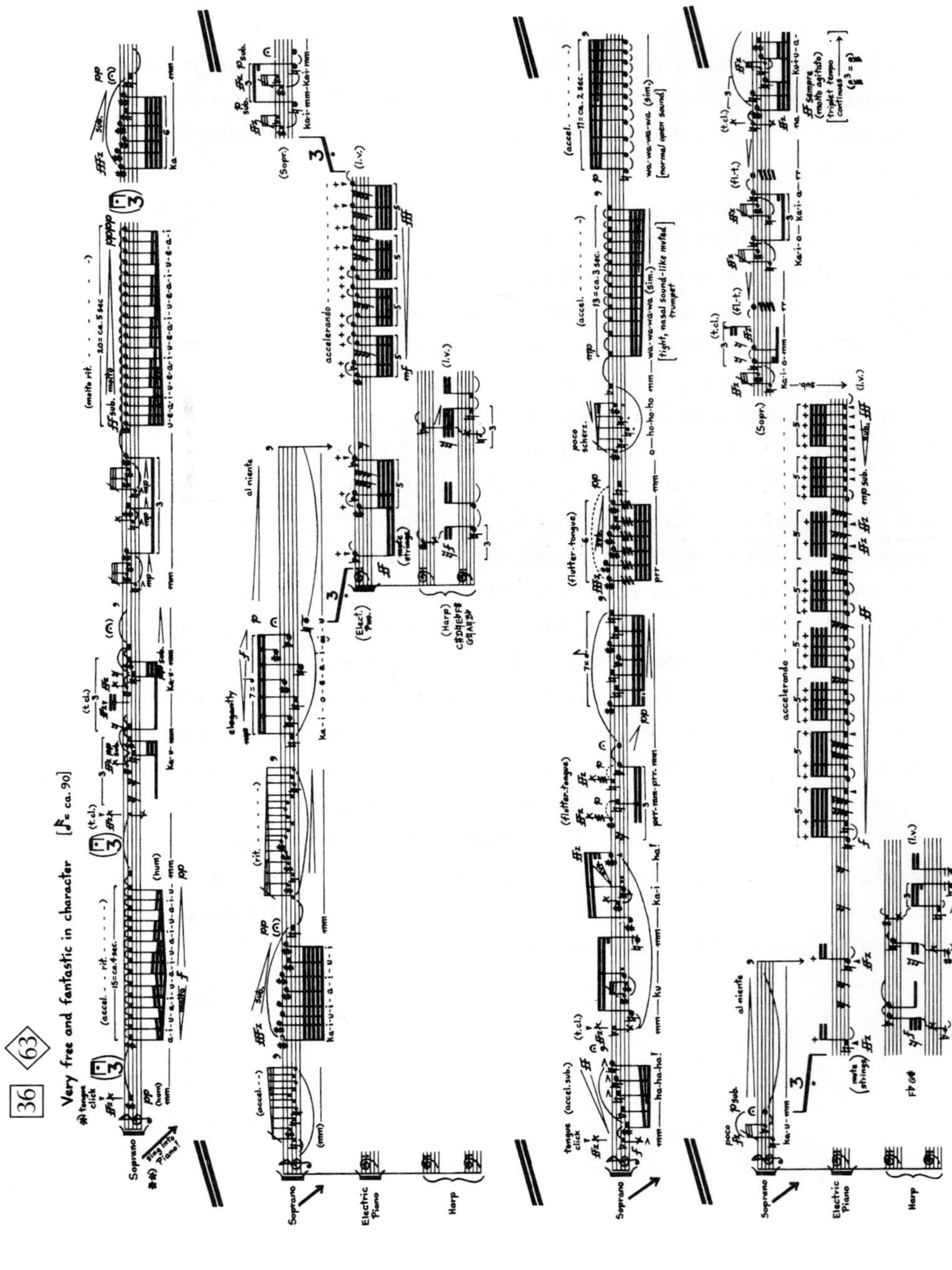

36 63 Very free and fantastic in character

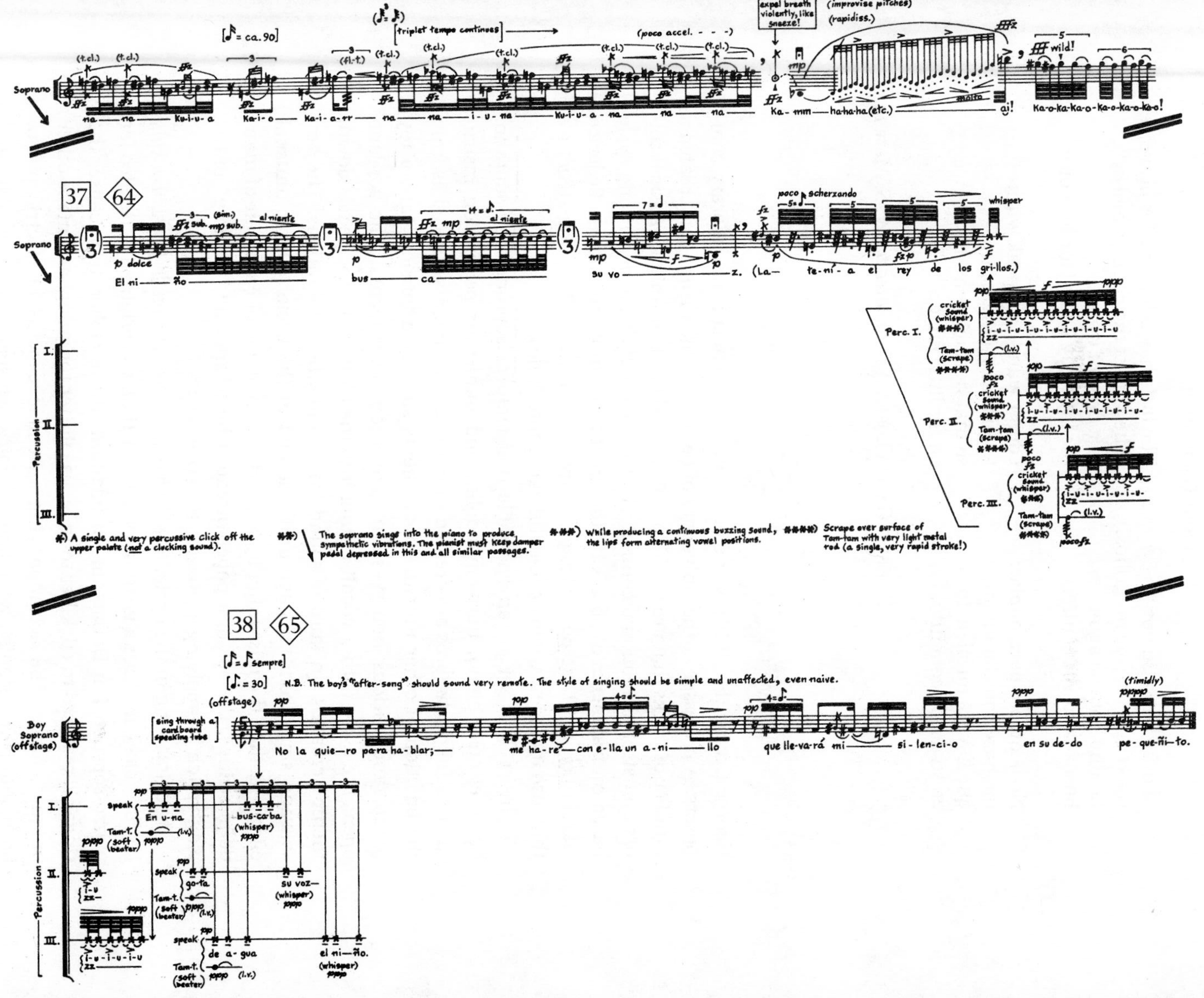
Soprano
(triplet tempo continues)
(poco accel. - - -)
expel breath violently, like sneeze!
(improvise pitches)
(rapidiss.)
wild!
na — na — Ku-i-u-a Ka-i-o — Ka-i-a-rr — na — na — i-u-na — Ku-i-u-a-na — na — na —
Ka-mm — ha-ha-ha (etc.) — ai! Ka-o-Ka-Ka-o-Ka-o-Ka-o-Ka-o!
37
64
p dolce
al niente
El ni — ño — bus — ca — su vo — z.
poco scherzando
whisper
(La- te-ní- a el rey de los gri-llos.)
Percussion
Perc. I.
Perc. II.
Perc. III.
cricket sound (whisper)
Tam-tam (scrape)
*) A single and very percussive click off the upper palate (not a clucking sound).
**) The soprano sings into the piano to produce sympathetic vibrations. The pianist must keep damper pedal depressed in this and all similar passages.
***) While producing a continuous buzzing sound, the lips form alternating vowel positions.
****) Scrape over surface of Tam-tam with very light metal rod (a single, very rapid stroke!)
38
65
N.B. The boy's "after-song" should sound very remote. The style of singing should be simple and unaffected, even naive.
Boy Soprano (offstage)
sing through a cardboard speaking tube
(timidly)
No la quie-ro para ha-blar; — me ha-ré — con e-lla un a-ni — llo que lle-va-rá mi — si-len-ci-o en su de-do pe-que-ñi-to.
speak
En u-na
bus-ca-ba (whisper)
go-ta
su voz — (whisper)
de a-gua
el ni — ño. (whisper)
Tam-t. (soft beater)

Text and Translation

El niño busca su voz.	The little boy is looking for his voice.
(La tenía el rey de los grillos.)	(The king of the crickets had it.)
En una gota de agua	In a drop of water
buscaba su voz el niño.	the little boy looked for his voice.
No la quiero para hablar;	I don't want it to speak with;
me haré con ella un anillo	I will make a ring of it
que llevará mi silencio	so that he may wear my silence
en su dedo pequeñito.	on his little finger.

FEDERICO GARCIA LORCA *Translated by W. S. Merwin*

George Crumb (b. 1929) is one of America's foremost contemporary composers. A professor at the University of Pennsylvania, Crumb has created a number of works that are justifiably acclaimed for their unique musical colors and strong emotional content. *Ancient Voices of Children* is a song cycle based on fragments of poems by the great Spanish literary figure Federico García Lorca. These poetic excerpts are grafted into a five-song structure that also includes two instrumental dance interludes.

The cycle is set for an ensemble that features soprano, boy soprano, oboe, electric piano, harp, mandolin, and numerous percussion instruments. Unique timbres are created from these instruments, as well as from the addition of other unusual instruments such as a musical saw, a toy piano, and various non-Western percussion instruments. The soprano opens the cycle with a vocalise sung into the piano with the pedals down, thereby creating an aura of sound from sympathetic vibrations. The boy soprano sings from off-stage until the end of the cycle. Other unusual effects include the mistuning by a quarter-step of one of each pair of mandolin strings, the use of a paper-threaded harp, and the "bending" of the piano pitch by applying a chisel to the strings.

The first song of the cycle, *El niño busca su voz (The Little Boy Is Looking for His Voice)*, features a virtuosic vocal line that was originally intended for mezzo-soprano Jan DeGaetani. In addition to the elaborate vocalise, the singer is required to click her tongue, use flutter tonguing, and make other unique sounds. The accompanying ensemble consists of electric piano, harp, and percussionist, who, like the voice, whisper and make additional vocal noises. At the end, the boy soprano enters from off-stage, singing through a cardboard speaking tube. The mixture of sounds from different cultures and time periods is described by Crumb:

> In composing *Ancient Voices of Children* I was conscious of an urge to fuse various unrelated stylistic elements. I was intrigued with the idea of juxtaposing the seemingly incongruous: a suggestion of Flamenco with a Baroque quotation (*Bist du bei mir,* from the Notebook of Anna Magdalena Bach), or a reminiscence of Mahler with a breath of the Orient. It later occurred to me that both Bach and Mahler drew upon many disparate sources in their own music without sacrificing "stylistic purity."

46. David Baker

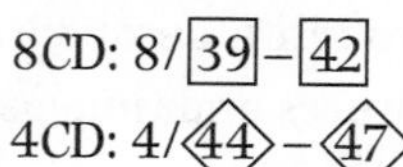

Through This Vale of Tears, Sixth Movement, *Sometimes I Feel Like a Motherless Child* (1986)

♩ = 58 39 44

ad libitum wordless vocal

mf

nor ice

n I

ı II

ɔla

llo

no

5

nor ice

n I

ı II

ɔla

llo

no

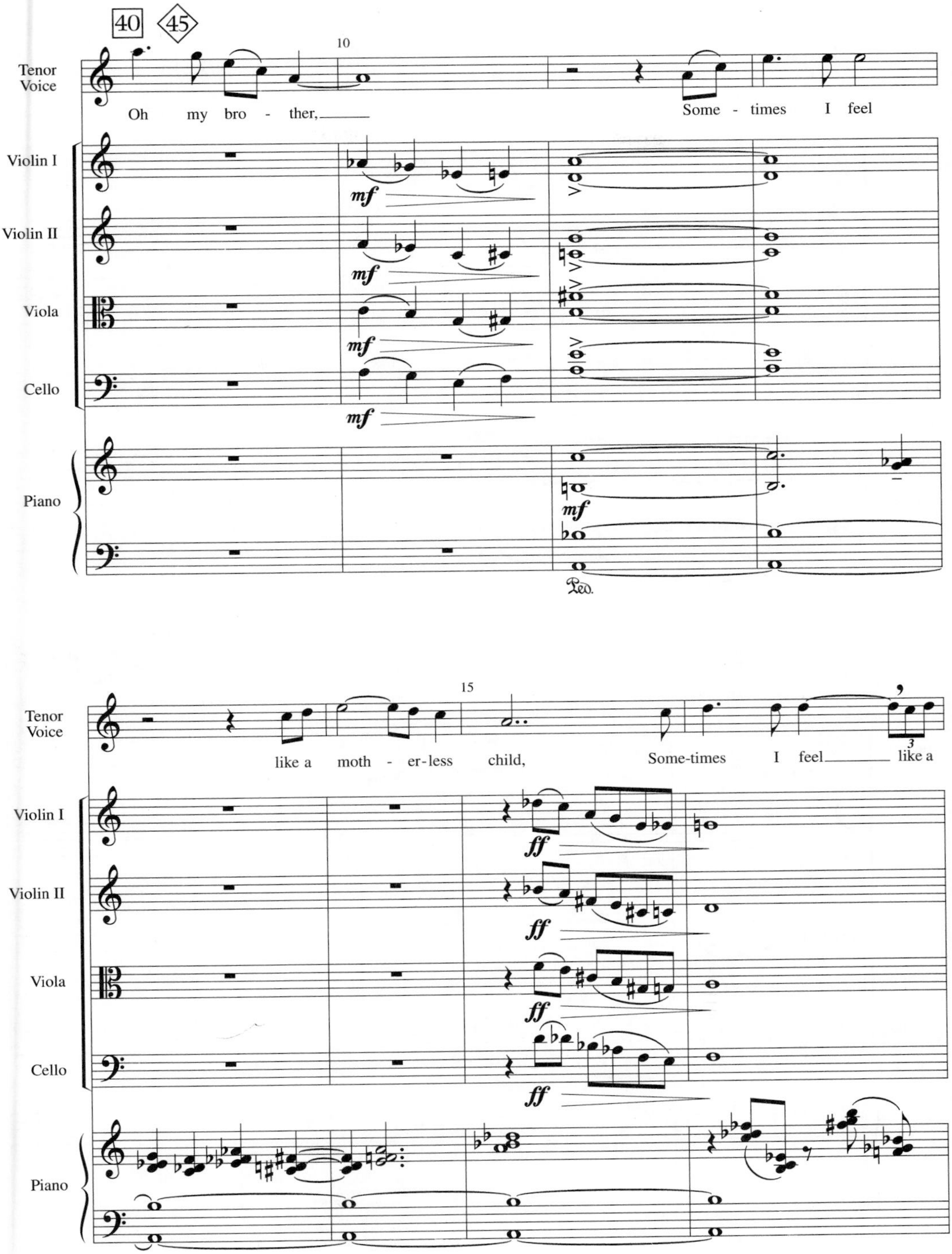

40 45

10

Tenor Voice

Oh my bro - ther, Some - times I feel

Violin I

Violin II

Viola

Cello

Piano

mf

Tenor Voice
moth - er less child,
Some-times I feel like a - moth-er-less child, A
Violin I
Violin II
Viola
Cello
decresc.
decresc.
decresc.
decresc.
Piano
20
Tenor Voice
long way from home,
a long way from home, a
Violin I
Violin II
Viola
Cello
Piano

41
46
25
Tenor Voice
long way— from home.
Violin I
Violin II
Viola
Cello
Piano
mp
mf
30
f
3

Tenor Voice
f
35
Some - times I feel like I'm al - most gone, Some-times I feel like I'm
Violin I
mp
Violin II
mp
Viola
mp
Cello
mp
Piano
Tenor Voice
40
al - most gone, Some - times I feel like I'm al - most gone, A long way— from
Violin I
Violin II
Viola
Cello
Piano

45
Tenor Voice
home, a long way from home, a long, long way from home.
Violin I
Violin II
Viola
Cello
Piano
Ped.
Ped.
42
47
50
Oh my bro - ther, oh my bro - ther, a long way from home.
sfz
ppp
8va
8va basso

The African-American composer David Baker (b. 1931) has distinguished himself as a performer, composer, and educator. Baker was born in Indianapolis, and studied music at Indiana University, where he now teaches. As a jazz musician on trombone and cello, he played with some of the leading jazz figures of the time. In addition to composing over a hundred works for jazz ensemble, he has combined a jazz idiom with Western art styles, including serial techniques and classical forms, creating what is called "third stream" music.

A number of Baker's compositions have dealt with the black experience in America. One of his most moving works is the song cycle *Through This Vale of Tears,* for tenor soloist, string quartet, and piano. The set of seven songs was created in response to the assassination of Martin Luther King, Jr. Commissioned by the African-American tenor William Brown, who performs on the recording, the cycle draws its texts from the Bible and from a number of African-American writers.

The sixth song, *Sometimes I Feel Like a Motherless Child,* is based on the traditional spiritual of the same name. The tenor opens the song with an unaccompanied wordless rendition of the melody. An outcry with the initial words "Oh, my brother!" precedes the instrumental entrance. Two varied stanzas of the tune follow, separated by an instrumental interlude primarily in triple meter. The movement ends with another dramatic outcry that is followed by a quiet close of somber resignation. The vocal line is frequently embellished, particularly near the cadences, but the modal melody primarily remains diatonic. This creates a harsh contrast with the strongly dissonant accompaniment, which is presented in parallel chords (in the first verse) and in a simple accompaniment pattern characteristic of a jazz song (in the second verse).

47. Arvo Pärt

Cantate Domino canticum novum
(O sing to the Lord a new song)
(1977; revised 1996)

8CD: 8/43–46
4CD: 4/91–94

R. Bourdon 8'	G.O. Bourdon Doux 8'
Flûte 4'	Flûte 4'
Octave 2'	

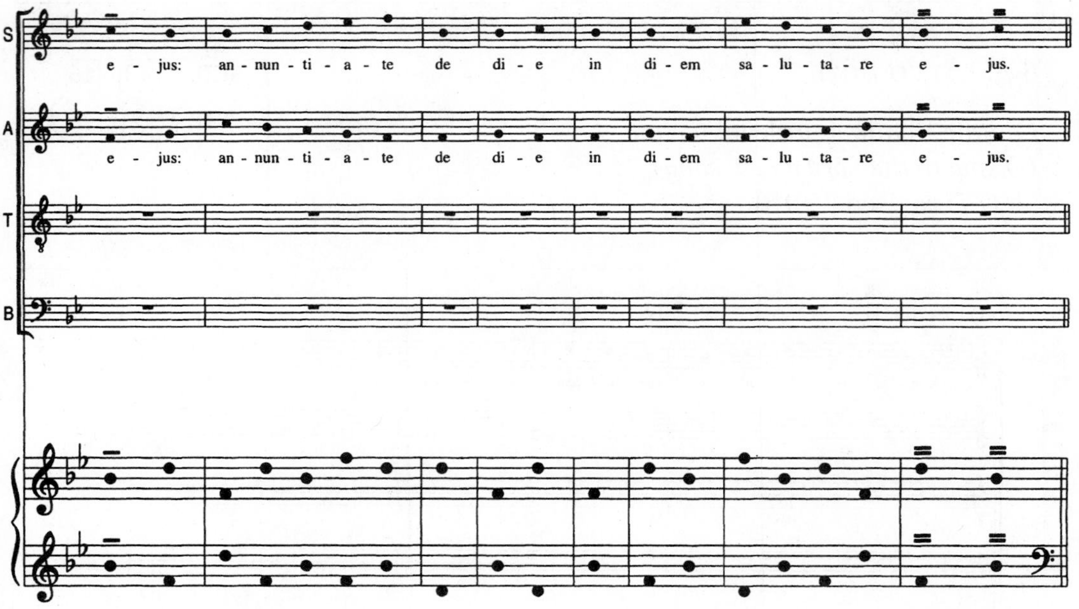
S
e - jus: an - nun - ti - a - te de di - e in di - em sa - lu - ta - re e - jus.
A
e - jus: an - nun - ti - a - te de di - e in di - em sa - lu - ta - re e - jus.
T
B

3
S
An - nun - ti - a - te in - ter gen - tes glo - ri - am e - jus, in o - mni - bus
A
An - nun - ti - a - te in - ter gen - tes glo - ri - am e - jus, in o - mni - bus
T
An - nun - ti - a - te in - ter gen - tes glo - ri - am e - jus, in o - mni - bus
B
An - nun - ti - a - te in - ter gen - tes glo - ri - am e - jus, in o - mni - bus
R.
R.

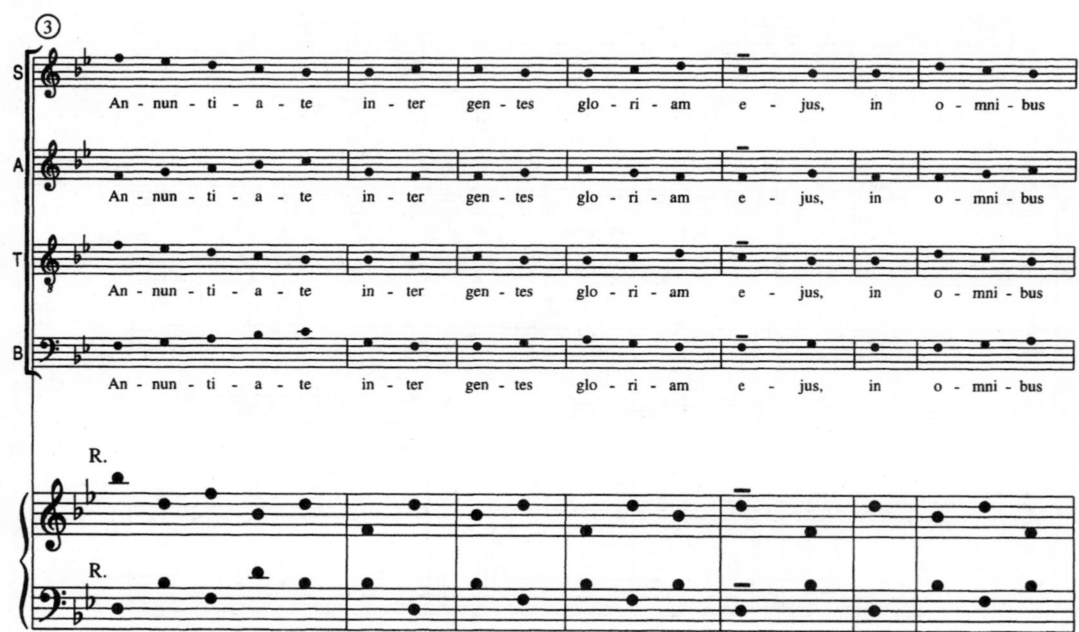

④ 44 92
S
po - pu - lis mi - ra - bi - li - a e - jus.
A
po - pu - lis mi - ra - bi - li - a e - jus.
T
po - pu - lis mi - ra - bi - li - a e - jus. Quo - ni - am ma - gnus Do - mi - nus, et
B
po - pu - lis mi - ra - bi - li - a e - jus.
G.O.

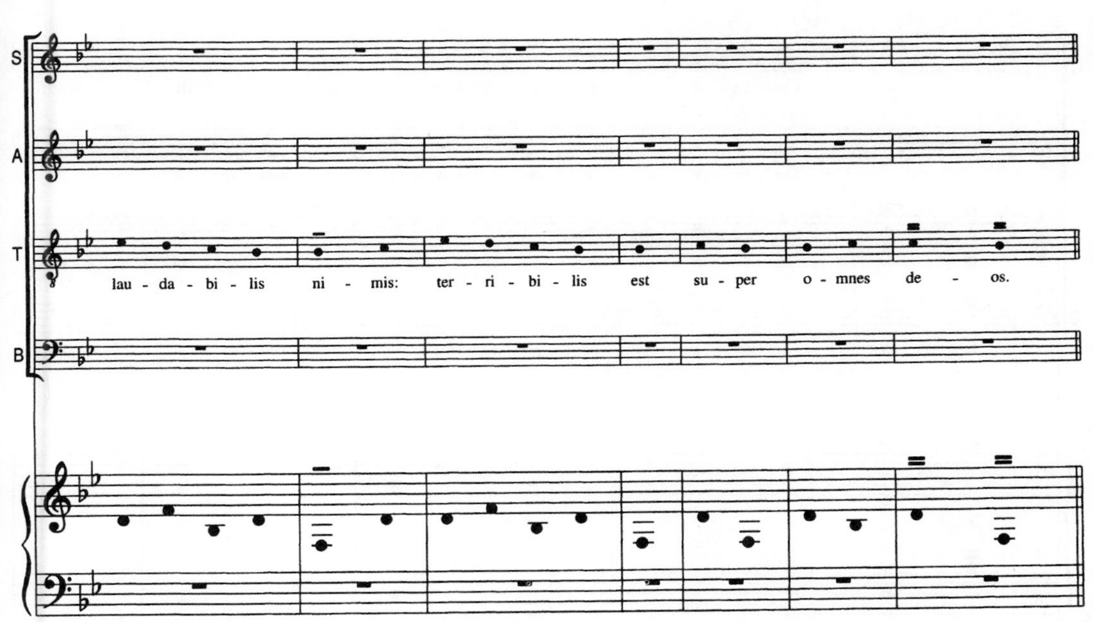
S
A
T
lau - da - bi - lis ni - mis: ter - ri - bi - lis est su - per o - mnes de - os.
B

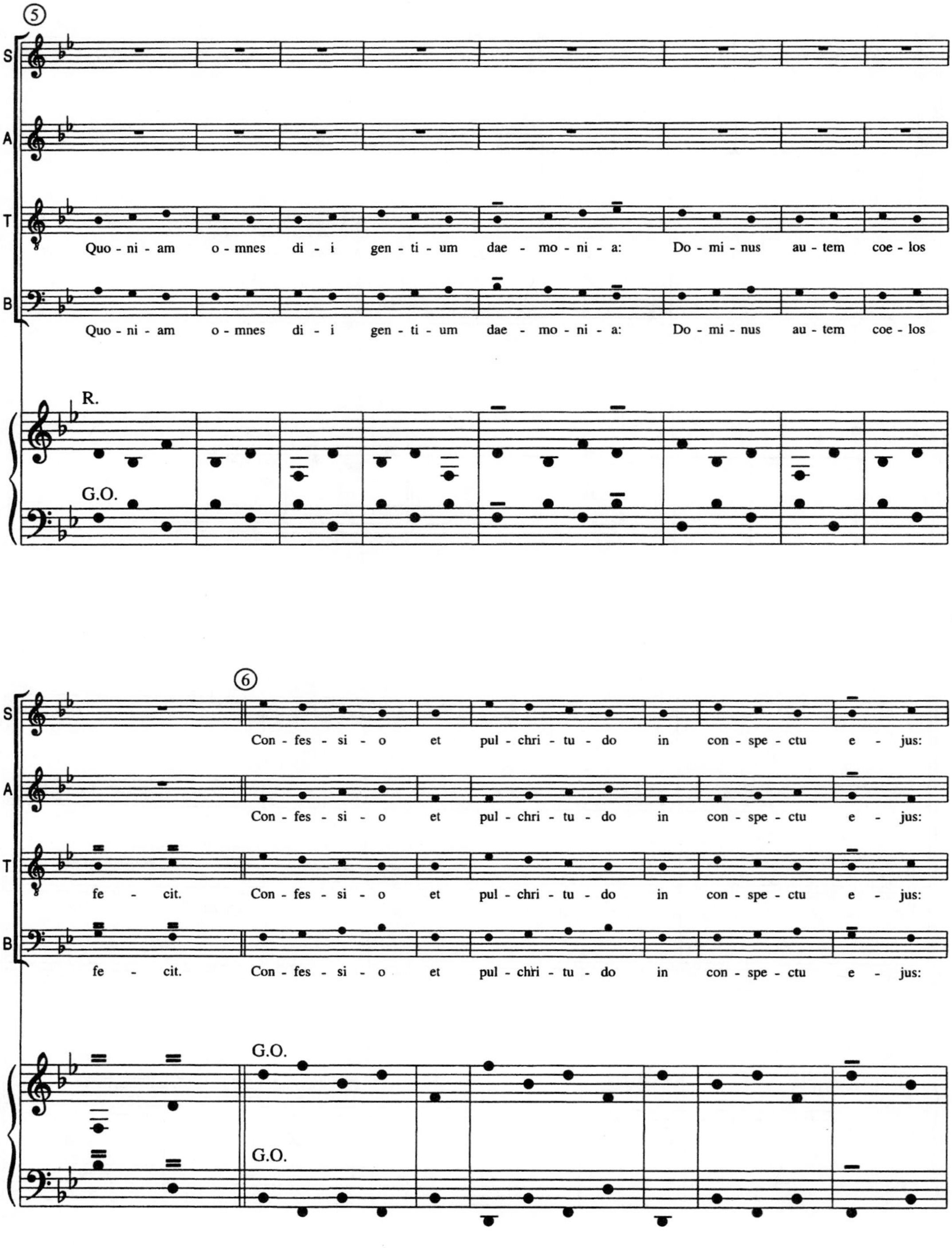

6

S
Con - fes - si - o et pul - chri - tu - do in con - spe - ctu e - jus:

A
Con - fes - si - o et pul - chri - tu - do in con - spe - ctu e - jus:

T
fe - cit. Con - fes - si - o et pul - chri - tu - do in con - spe - ctu e - jus:

B
fe - cit. Con - fes - si - o et pul - chri - tu - do in con - spe - ctu e - jus:

G.O.

G.O.

S
san - cti - mo - ni - a et ma - gni - fi - cen - ti - a in san - cti - fi - ca - ti - o - ne e - jus.
A
san - cti - mo - ni - a et ma - gni - fi - cen - ti - a in san - cti - fi - ca - ti - o - ne e - jus.
T
san - cti - mo - ni - a et ma - gni - fi - cen - ti - a in san - cti - fi - ca - ti - o - ne e - jus.
B
san - cti - mo - ni - a et ma - gni - fi - cen - ti - a in san - cti - fi - ca - ti - o - ne e - jus.
7
45
93
S
Af - fer - te Do - mi - no pa - tri - ae gen - ti - um, af - fer - te Do - mi - no glo - ri - am
A
T
B
R.

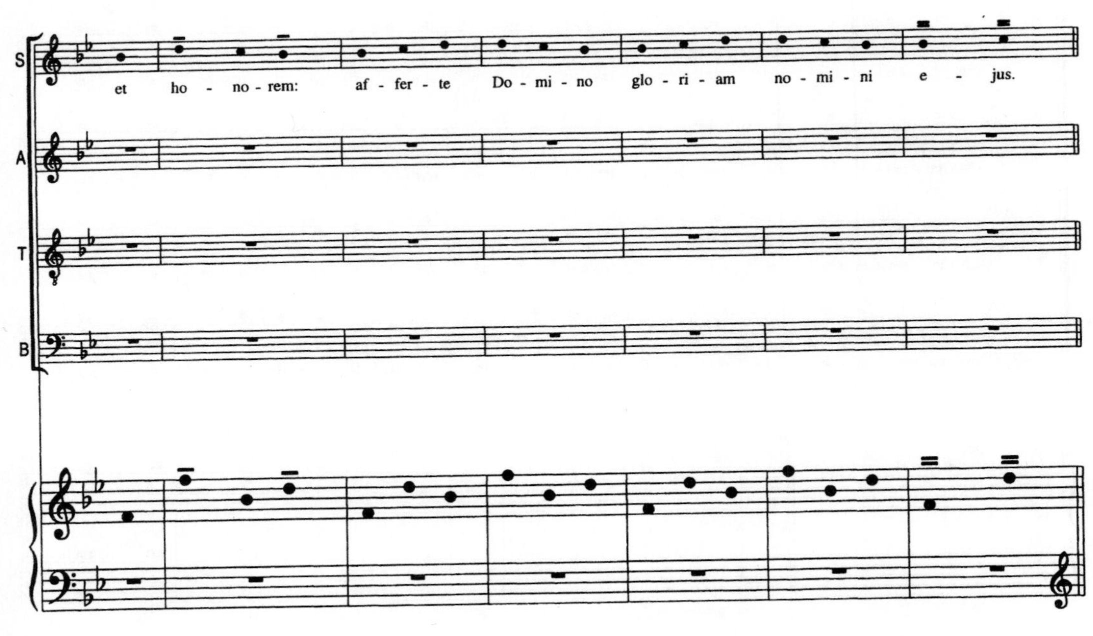

S
A
T
B
et ho - no - rem: af - fer - te Do - mi - no glo - ri - am no - mi - ni e - jus.

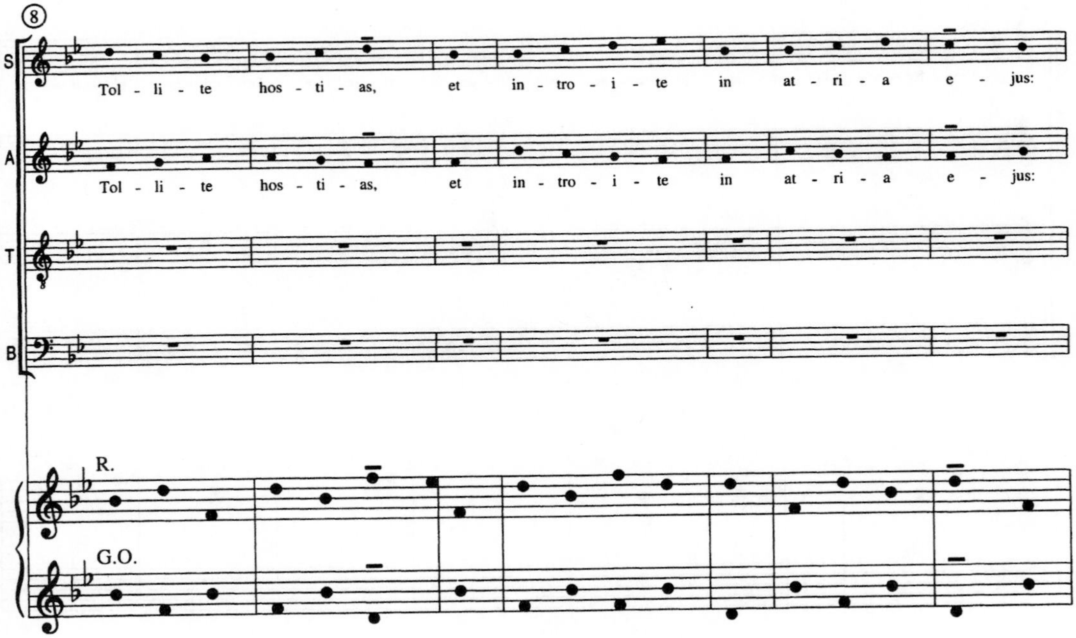
8
S
A
T
B
Tol - li - te hos - ti - as, et in - tro - i - te in at - ri - a e - jus:
Tol - li - te hos - ti - as, et in - tro - i - te in at - ri - a e - jus:
R.
G.O.

S
A
T
B
ad - o - ra - te Do - mi - num in at - ri - a san - cto e - jus.
ad - o - ra - te Do - mi - num in at - ri - a san - cto e - jus.
9
Com - mo - ve - a - tur a fa - ci - e e - jus u - ni - ver - sa ter - ra:
Com - mo - ve - a - tur a fa - ci - e e - jus u - ni - ver - sa ter - ra:
Com - mo - ve - a - tur a fa - ci - e e - jus u - ni - ver - sa ter - ra:
Com - mo - ve - a - tur a fa - ci - e e - jus u - ni - ver - sa ter - ra:
R.
R.

S di - ci - te in gen - ti - bus qui - a Do - mi - nus re - gna - vit.

A di - ci - te in gen - ti - bus qui - a Do - mi - nus re - gna - vit.

T di - ci - te in gen - ti - bus qui - a Do - mi - nus re - gna - vit.

B di - ci - te in gen - ti - bus qui - a Do - mi - nus re - gna - vit.

(10) [46] ◇94

S

A

T E - te - nim cor - re - xit or - bem ter - rae qui non com - mo - ve - bi - tur:

B

G.O.

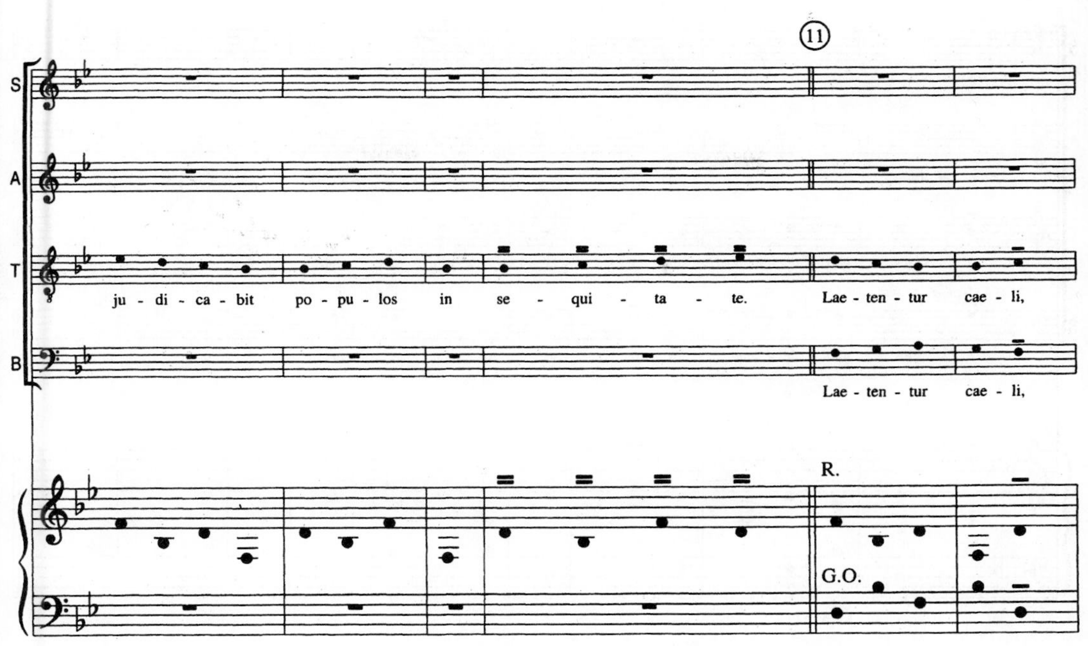
11
S
A
T
B
ju - di - ca - bit po - pu - los in se - qui - ta - te. Lae - ten - tur cae - li,
Lae - ten - tur cae - li,
R.
G.O.

S
A
T
B
et ex - sul - tet ter - ra: com - mo - ve - a - tur ma - re, et ple - ni - tu - do
et ex - sul - tet ter - ra: com - mo - ve - a - tur ma - re, et ple - ni - tu - do

S
A
T
e - jus: gau - de - bunt cam - pi, et o - mni - a quae in e - is sunt.
B
e - jus: gau - de - bunt cam - pi, et o - mni - a quae in e - is sunt.

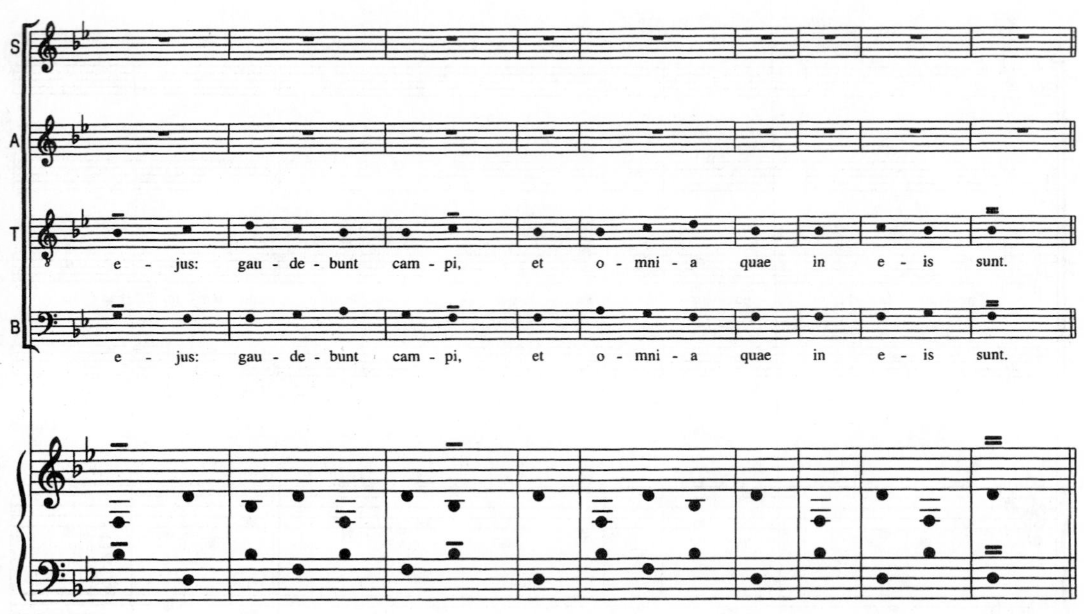

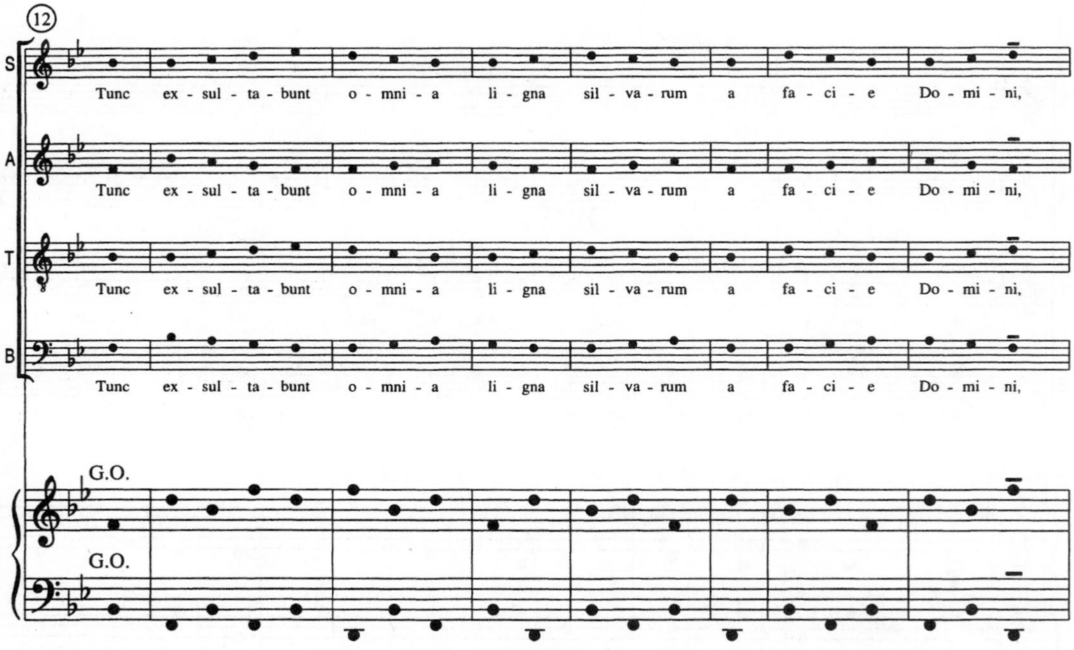

12
S
Tunc ex - sul - ta - bunt o - mni - a li - gna sil - va - rum a fa - ci - e Do - mi - ni,
A
Tunc ex - sul - ta - bunt o - mni - a li - gna sil - va - rum a fa - ci - e Do - mi - ni,
T
Tunc ex - sul - ta - bunt o - mni - a li - gna sil - va - rum a fa - ci - e Do - mi - ni,
B
Tunc ex - sul - ta - bunt o - mni - a li - gna sil - va - rum a fa - ci - e Do - mi - ni,
G.O.
G.O.

13
S
A
T
B
qui - a ve - nit: quo - ni - am ve - nit ju - di - ca - re fer - ram. Ju - di - ca - bit
G.O.
G.O. + Bourdon 16'
or - bem ter - rae in ae - qui - ta - te, et po - pu - los in ve - ri - ta - te su - a.

Text and Translation

Cantate Domino canticum novum:
Cantate Domino omnis terra.
Cantate Domino, et benedicite nomini ejus:
Annuntiate de die in diem salutare ejus.
Annuntiate inter gentes gloriam ejus,
In omnibus populis mirabilia ejus.

Quoniam magnus Dominus, et
laudabilis nimis:
Terribilis est super omnes deos.
Quoniam omnes dii gentium daemonia:
Dominus autem coelos fecit.
Confessio et pulchritudo in conspectu ejus:
Sanctimonia et magnifcentia in
sanctificatione ejus.

Afferte Domino patriae gentium,
Afferte Domino gloriam et honorem:
Afferte Domino gloriam nomini ejus.
Tollite hostias, et introite in atria ejus:
Adorate Dominum in atria sancto ejus.
Commoveatur a facie ejus universa terra:
Dicite in gentibus quia Dominus regnavit.

Etenim corexit orbem terrae qui
non commovebitur:
Judicabit populus in aequitate.
Laetentur caeli, et esultet terra:

Commoveatur mare, et plenitudo eius:
Gaudebunt campi, et omnia quae in
eis sunt.
Tunc exsultabunt omnia ligna
silvarium
A facie Domini, quia venit:
Quoniam venit iudicare terram.
Judicabit orbem terrae in aequitate,
Et populos in veritate sua.

O sing to the Lord a new song:
Sing to the Lord, all the earth.
Sing to the Lord, bless his name;
Tell of his salvation from day to day.
Declare his glory among the nations.
His marvelous works among all the peoples.

For great is the Lord, and greatly to
be praised.
He is to be feared above all gods.
For all the gods of the people are idols;
But the Lord made the heavens.
Honor and majesty are before him;
Strength and beauty are his
salvation.

Ascribe to the Lord, O families of the peoples.
Ascribe to the Lord glory and strength;
Ascribe to the Lord the glory due his name.
Bring an offering, and come into his courts.
Worship the Lord in holy array.
Tremble before him, all the earth;
Say among the nations, "The Lord reigns.

Yea, the world is established, it shall never
be moved.
He will judge the peoples with equity."
Let the heavens be glad, and let the earth
rejoice:
Let the sea roar, and all that fills it;
Let the field exult, and every thing in it.

Then shall all the trees of the wood
sing for joy
Before the Lord, for he comes;
For he comes to judge the earth.
He will judge the world with righteousness,
And the peoples with his truth.

Arvo Pärt (b. 1935) was born in Estonia, one of the republics of the former Soviet Union. Despite limited opportunities and lack of access to international music, Pärt rose to prominence as one of the region's leading composers. His early works combine serial techniques and a strong Neoclassical fascination with the traditions of Western music, particularly the music of Bach. After an extended break in composition, during which he studied medieval and Renaissance music, he developed a new sound that he calls tintinnabulation (after the Latin word for the ringing of bells). Because of his strong religious convictions, Pärt left the Soviet Union and settled in West Berlin, where he composed numerous sacred works.

Cantate Domino canticum novum (O sing to the Lord a new song) reflects both Pärt's interest in medieval traditions and his distinctive tintinnabular style. Based on Psalm 95, this work is set for SATB choir and organ. Reflecting the freedom of Gregorian chant, Pärt uses a free notation: measure lines do not mark off regular metric units, but rather separate individual words. Moreover, the rhythm is indicated by a notation system similar to that of Gregorian chant. Pärt uses black note heads only, without stem lines. Each note is of equal value (approximating an eighth note), but the addition of a single dash above a note doubles its value (quarter note), and two dashes triple the value (a dotted quarter note).

The work can be divided into four sections. Each section has three phrases: a monophonic opening phrase, a two-voice phrase moving primarily in contrary motion, and a four-voice phrase, in which the added voices double the homorhythmic contrary motion of the established voices. The overall effect of the work is similar to both Gregorian chant and early organum. The fullness of sound achieved by the expansion to a four-voice texture can be seen as word painting, as it reinforces images such as "declare his glory among the nations" and "all the trees of the woods sing for joy." The tintinnabular sound is created by the repetition of the pitch center (B-flat) and the triadic organ accompaniment. Pärt indicates specific organ registrations in the score.

48. Joan Tower

For the Uncommon Woman (1992)

8CD: 8/47–52
4CD: 4/85–90

Instrumentation

2 Flutes (2nd doubling Piccolo)
2 Oboes
2 Clarinets in B-flat
2 Bassoons

4 Horns in F
3 Trumpets in C
2 Trombones
Bass Trombone
Tuba

Timpani
Percussion (3 players)
I. Glockenspiel, wood blocks, temple blocks, cymbals, maracas, small dinner bell
II. Xylophone, snare drum, tenor drum, sleigh bells, tubular bells, castanets
III. Vibraphone, tambourine, cymbals, tenor drum, marimba, wood block

Strings

47
85
♩ = ca. 63
to Flute 2
a2
Fl. Picc.
Ob.
B♭ Cl.
Bn.
Hn. in F
Tpt. in C
st. mute
(open)
open
p cresc. molto
Tbn.
B. Tbn. Tba.
Timp.
W. Blk., small
L. Cym.
T. Blks.
T. Blk., high
(very fast roll)
Xyl.
S.D.
H. Cym., h.s.
Perc.
L. Cym., s.s.
(B.D.)
M. Cym., s.s.
B.D.
Vn.
Va.
Vc.
Cb.
*Unless indicated otherwise, play all dyads divisi.

48
86
♩ = ca. 138
Fl. 1 2
Ob. 1 2
B♭ Cl. 1 2
Bn. 1 2
Hn. in F
Tpt. in C
Tbn. 1 2
B. Tbn. Tba.
Timp.
Perc.
(T. Blk.)
H. Cym., h.s.
M. Cym. S. Bells
T.Dr.
H. Cym.
Tamb.
M. Cym.
Glock.
Vib.
Vn.
Va.
Vc.
Cb.
cresc.

15
Fl. 1 2
Ob. 1 2
B♭ Cl. 1 2
Bn. 1 2
Hn. in F 1 3
(2.)
2 4
Tpt. in C 1 2
3
Tbn. 1 2
B. Tbn. Tba.
Timp.
(Glock.)
1
Perc. 2
M. Cym., s.s.
(Vib.)
3
Vn. I
II
Va.
Vc.
Cb.
cresc.

22
Fl. 1 2
Ob. 1 2
B♭ Cl. 1 2
Bn. 1 2
a2
f
ff
Hn. in F
a2 brassy
Tpt. in C
cup mute
Tbn. 1 2
B. Tbn. Tba.
Timp.
mf
Perc. 2
(H. Cym.)
p
Tamb.
Vn.
I
II
p cresc.
Va.
Vc.
Cb.

28
Fl. 1 2
Ob. 1 2
B♭ Cl. 1 2
a2
ff
Bn. 1 2
a2
ff
(a2)
3.
Hn. in F
1 3
2 4
4.
(cup mute)
p
mf
Tpt. in C
1 2
3
1., cup mute
mf
Tbn. 1 2
B. Tbn. Tba.
Timp.
mf
p
T. Blk.
mp
Perc. 1 2 3
(Tamb.)
Vn. I II
Va.
ff
Vc.
ff
Cb.
ff

32
Fl. 1 2
Ob. 1 2
B♭ Cl. 1 2
Bn. 1 2
Hn. in F
1 3
2 4
4.
Tpt. in C
1 2
3
cup mute
Tbn. 1 2
B. Tbn. Tba.
Tuba.
Timp.
(T. Blk.)
Perc. 1 2 3
B.D.
Vn. I II
Va.
Vc.
Cb.

38
Fl. 1 2
a2
Ob. 1 2
B♭ Cl. 1 2
1.
Bn. 1 2
1.
Hn. in F 1 3
2 4
(4.)
Tpt. in C 1 2
3
Tbn. 1 2
B. Tbn. Tba.
(B. Tbn.)
Timp.
Marac.
Perc. 1
2
S.D.
ppp (barely audible)
3
non div.
Vn. I
II
non div.
Va.
Vc.
Cb.

49
87
42
to Piccolo
(a2)
a2
1.
(1.)
cresc.
Fl.
Ob.
B♭ Cl.
Bn.
Hn. in F
Tpt. in C
Tbn.
B. Tbn. Tba.
Timp.
(Marac.)
Glock.
(S.D.)
L. Cym., s.s.
Perc.
Vn.
Va.
Vc.
Cb.

47
Fl. 1 Picc.
Ob. 1 2
B♭ Cl. 1 2
Bn. 1 2
Hn. in F
Tpt. in C
Tbn. 1 2
B. Tbn. Tba.
Timp.
Perc. 2
(Glock.)
W. Blk.
T. Blk.
Glock.
Xyl.
T. Blk. H. Cym.
B.D.
M. Cym., h.s.
T.Dr.
M. Cym., H. Cym.
p sub. cresc.
p sub.
Vn.
Va.
Vc.
Cb.

55
Fl. Picc. 1
(a2)
to Flute
Ob. 1 2
a2
B♭ Cl. 1 2
Bn. 1 2
(a2)
Hn. in F 1 3
2 4
Tpt. in C 1 2
3
1.
cup mute
Tbn. 1 2
B. Tbn. Tba.
Timp.
mf
f
fp
Perc. 1
(Glock.)
T. Dr.
H. Cym.
Xyl.
M. Cym., s.s.
p cresc.
Sl. Bells
Perc. 2
Vib.
(H. Cym.)
B.D.
3
ff
Vn. I
Vn. II
Va.
Vc.
Cb.

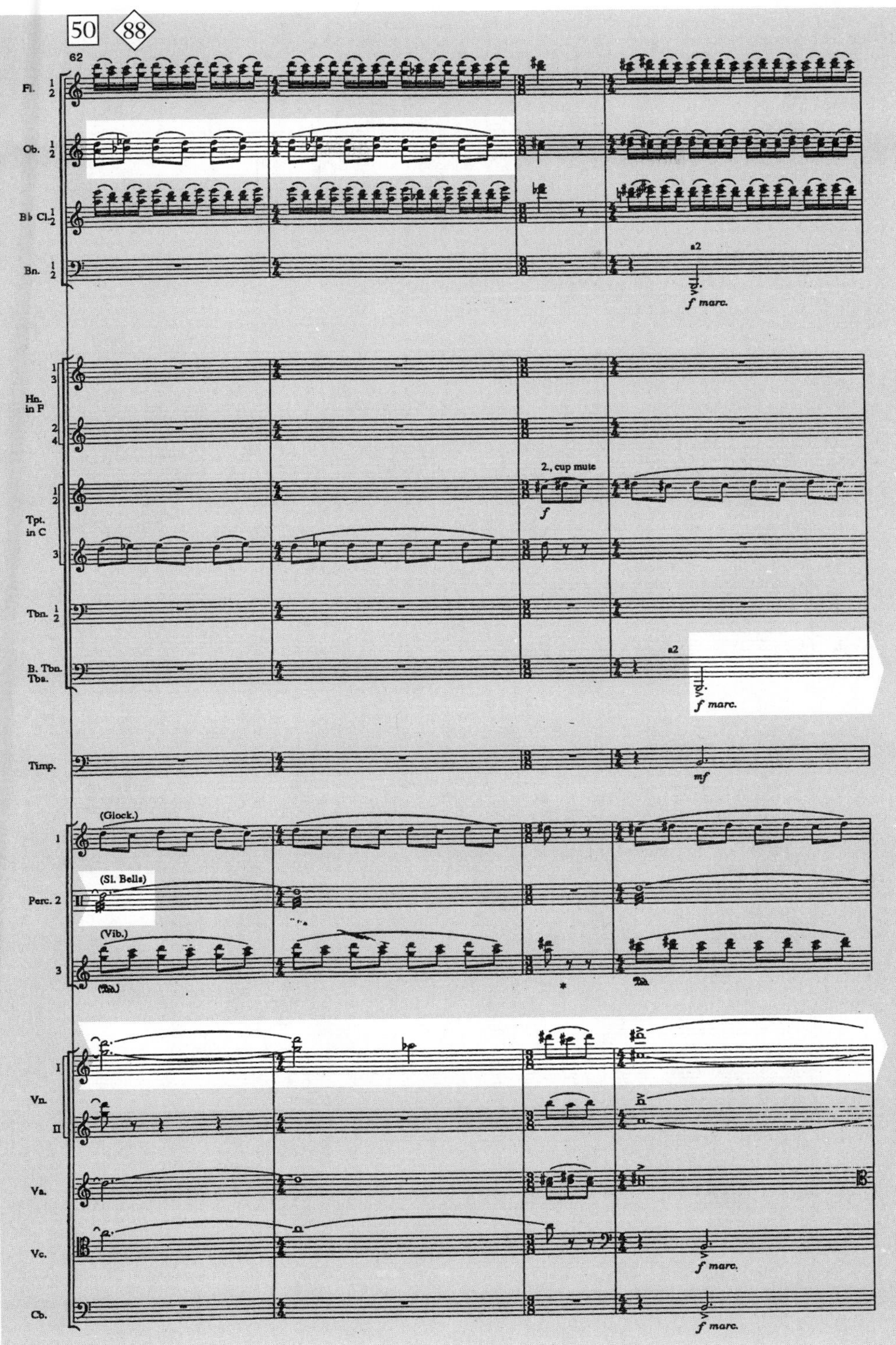
50
88
62
Fl. 1 2
Ob. 1 2
B♭ Cl. 1 2
Bn. 1 2
a2
f marc.
Hn. in F
1 3
2 4
2., cup mute
f
Tpt. in C
1 2
3
Tbn. 1 2
a2
B. Tbn. Tba.
f marc.
Timp.
mf
(Glock.)
(Sl. Bells)
(Vib.)
Perc. 1 2 3
Vn. I II
Va.
Vc.
f marc.
Cb.
f marc.

66
Fl. 1 2
Ob. 1 2
B♭ Cl. 1 2
Bn. 1 2
Hn. in F 1 3
2 4
cup mute
(1.)
Tpt. in C 1 2
3
Tbn. 1 2
(Tba.)
Tba.
Timp.
(Glock.)
(Sl. Bells)
(Vib.)
Perc. 1 2 3
Vn. I II
Va.
Vc.
pizz.
Cb.

70
Fl. 1 2
to Piccolo
Ob. 1 2
B♭ Cl. 1 2
Bn. 1 2
a2
f marc.
Hn. in F 1 3
a2
ff brassy
2 4
a2
ff brassy
Tpt. in C 1 2
(1., cup mute)
3
Tbn. 1 2
Tba.
Tuba
mf marc.
Timp.
mf
Perc. 1
(Glock.)
2
(Sl. Bells)
T. Blk.
Cast.
f
3
(Vib.)
T.Dr., h.s.
mfp
M. Cym.
f
Vn. I
ff energetic
II
ff energetic
Va.
ff energetic
Vc.
f marc.
ff energetic
Cb.
(pizz.)
f marc.

74
Fl. Picc. 1
Ob. 1 2
B♭ Cl. 1 2
Bn. 1 2
(a2)
Hn. in F 1 3
(a2)
2 4
Tpt. in C 1 2
3
Tbn. 1 2
Tba.
Tuba
pp
Timp.
pp
Sm. dinner bell
pp dolce
(Cast.)
Perc. 1 2 3
Maracas
pp
Vn. I
ffp
II
ffp
Va.
Vc.
p
arco
Cb.
p

79
51
89
Fl. 1
Picc.
Ob. 1 2
B♭ Cl. 1 2
Bn. 1 2
Hn. in F 1 3
2 4
Tpt. in C 1 2
3
Tbn. 1 2
Tba.
(Tuba)
Timp.
Perc. 1 2 3
(Din. bell)
M. Cym., h.s.
(Maracas)
Vn. I II
Va.
Vc.
Cb.
pp
mf
p cresc.
mp
p
cresc.

86
Fl. Picc.
Ob.
B♭ Cl.
Bn.
a2
Hn. in F
Tpt. in C
open
open
(1.)
Tbn.
mp cup mute
(Bs. Tbn.)
B. Tbn. Tba.
Timp.
(Din. bell)
(M. Cym.)
H. Cym., h.s.
Perc.
M. Cym., h.s.
non div.
Vn.
Va.
Vc.
Cb.

94
Fl.
Piccolo
Fl. 1
Picc.
Ob. 1/2
a2
Bb Cl. 1/2
Bn. 1/2
fp
Hn. in F 1/3
2/4
Tpt. in C 1/2
3
(1.)
Tbn. 1/2
mf
(Bs. Tbn.)
B. Tbn. Tba.
Timp.
Perc. 1
(H. Cym.)
M. Cym.
S.D.
Perc. 2
cresc.
(M. Cym.)
L. Cym.
3
(non div.)
Vn. I
II
ffp
Va.
Vc.
Cb.

99
Fl. Picc. 1
ff
ffp
cresc.
Ob. 1 2
ff
ffp
cresc.
B♭ Cl. 1 2
(a2)
Bn. 1 2
(a2)
f
Hn. in F 1 3
f
2 4
(a2)
f
Tpt. in C 1 2
f
fp
2.
fp
cresc.
3
f
Tbn. 1 2
(a2)
f
B. Tbn. Tba.
fp
cresc.
mf
Timp.
f
T. Blk.
1
pp
(S.D.)
Perc. 2
f pp
(Cym.)
3
Vn. I
f
II
f
Va.
f
Vc.
f
Cb.
f

103
Fl. 1
Picc.
Picc.
Ob. 1 2
B♭ Cl. 1 2
Bn. 1 2
Hn. in F 1 3
2 4
Tpt. in C 1 2
3
Tbn. 1 2
B. Tbn. Tba.
Timp.
Perc. 1 2 3
Vn. I II
Va.
Vc.
Cb.
ff
mf
1., st. mute
st. mute
a2
cresc.
p
(T. Blk.)
(S.D.)
Sm. W. Blk.
L. W. Blk.
M. Cym., s.s.
p cresc.

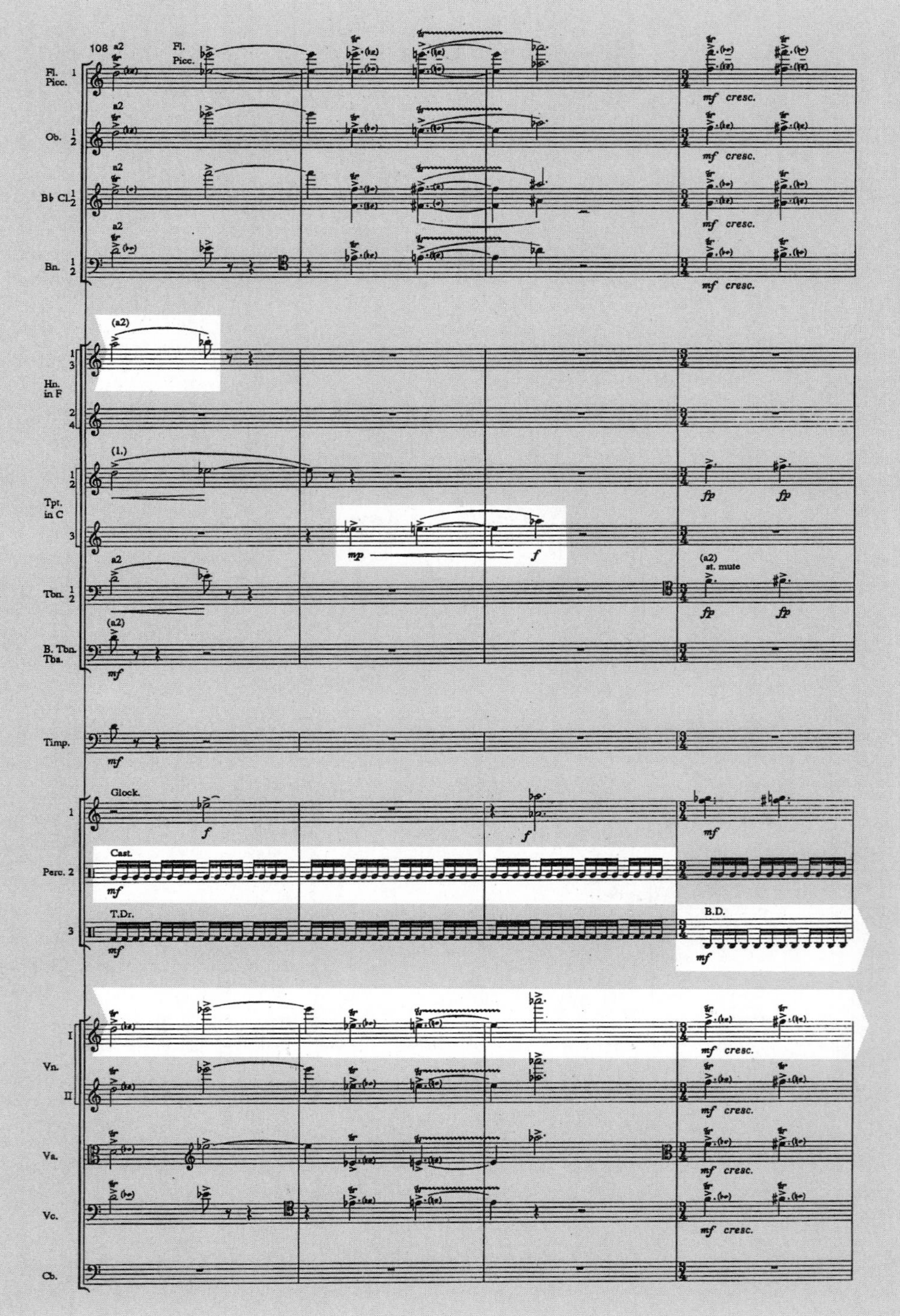
108
Fl. 1 Picc.
Ob. 1 2
B♭ Cl. 1 2
Bn. 1 2
Hn. in F
Tpt. in C
Tbn. 1 2
B. Tbn. Tba.
Timp.
Glock.
Perc. 2
Cast.
T.Dr.
B.D.
Vn. I
Vn. II
Va.
Vc.
Cb.
mf cresc.
st. mute

112
Fl. Picc.
Ob.
(a2)
ffp
cresc.
Bb Cl.
Bn.
(a2)
ff
Hn. in F
Tpt. in C
(1.)
fp
open
cresc.
Tbn.
(a2)
f
B. Tbn. Tba.
Timp.
p cresc.
Perc.
(Glock.)
(Cast.)
M. Cym.
(B.D.)
Vn.
Va.
Vc.
Cb.

52
90
117
Fl. 1
Picc.
ff brightly
Ob. 1 2
ff
B♭ Cl. 1 2
ff brightly
Bn. 1 2
ff
cresc.
a2
Hn. in F
1 3
f
cresc.
a2
2 4
cresc.
ff
open
f
Tpt. in C
1 2
3
f
a2, open
Tbn. 1 2
f
cresc.
B. Tbn. Tba.
Timp.
f
(Glock.)
1
ff
Sl. Bells
Perc. 2
ff
Tamb.
3
ff
Vn. I
ff bright
II
ff bright
Va.
ff bright
Vc.
ff bright
Cb.

121
Fl.
Picc.
Ob.
B♭ Cl.
Bn.
Hn. in F
Tpt. in C
Tbn.
B. Tbn. Tba.
Timp.
Perc.
Vn.
Va.
Vc.
Cb.
a2
(a2)
(Glock.)
(Sl. Bells)
Xyl.
Sl. Bells
(Tamb.)
Maraca
Tamb.

125
Fl. 1 Picc.
Ob. 1 2
B♭ Cl. 1 2
Bn. 1 2
Hn. in F
Tpt. in C
Tbn. 1 2
Tba.
Tuba
mf
cresc.
Timp.
pp
(Glock.)
M. Cym.
Xyl.
Perc. 2
Maraca
mf
cresc.
I.
marc.
Vn.
II
Va.
Vc.
Cb.
ff marc.

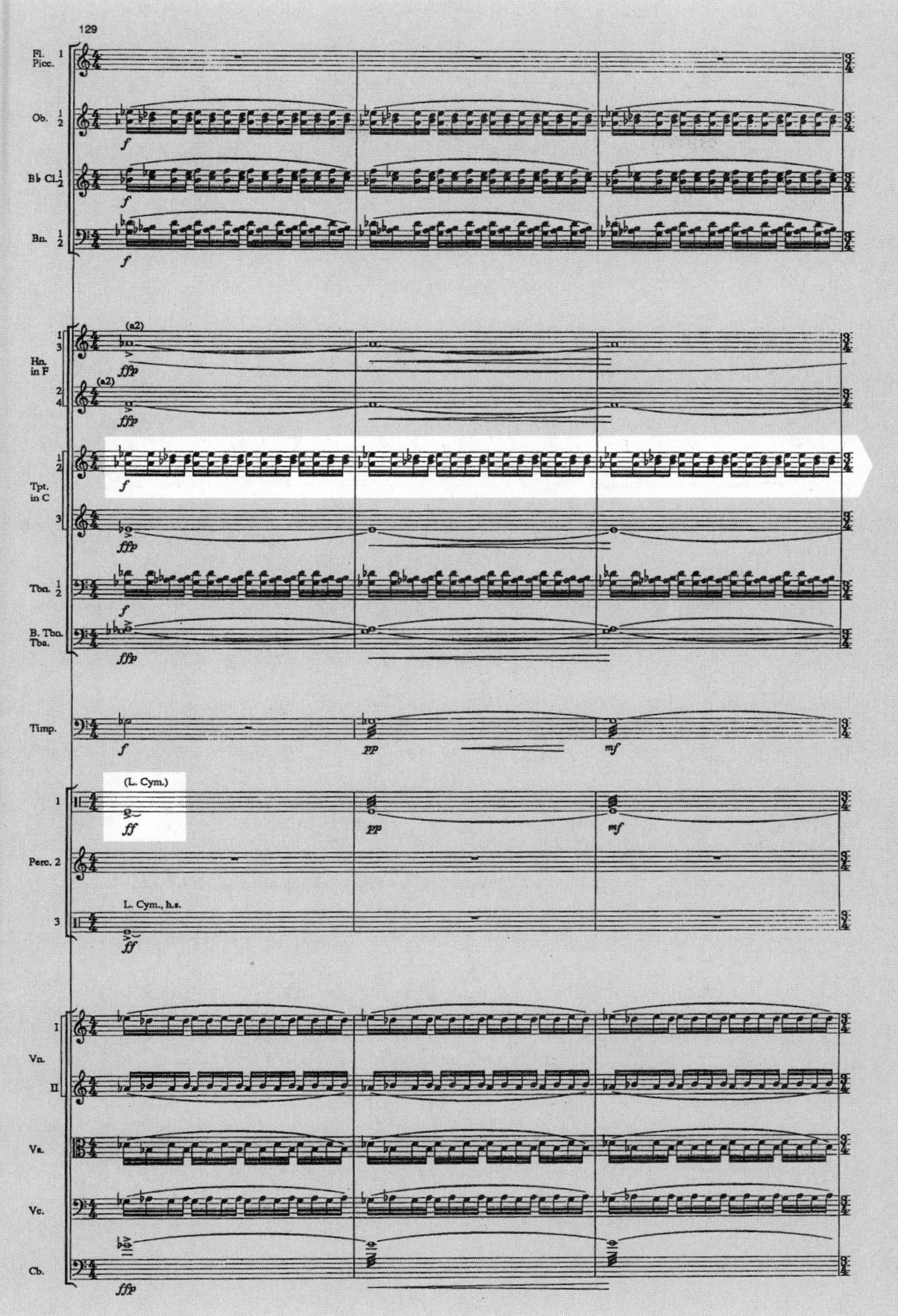
129
Fl. Picc. 1
Ob. 1 2
B♭ Cl. 1 2
Bn. 1 2
Hn. in F 1 3 2 4
(a2)
Tpt. in C 1 2 3
Tbn. 1 2
B. Tbn. Tba.
Timp.
Perc. 1 2 3
(L. Cym.)
L. Cym., h.s.
Vn. I II
Va.
Vc.
Cb.

132
Fl. 1
Picc.
Ob. 1 2
B♭ Cl. 1 2
Bn. 1 2
Hn. in F
Tpt. in C
Tbn. 1 2
B. Tbn. Tba.
Timp.
Perc.
(L. Cym.)
Glock.
L. Cym.
W. Blk.
Xyl.
S.D.
Tamb.
B.D.
(div.)
Vn.
Va.
Vc.
Cb.
a2
(a2)

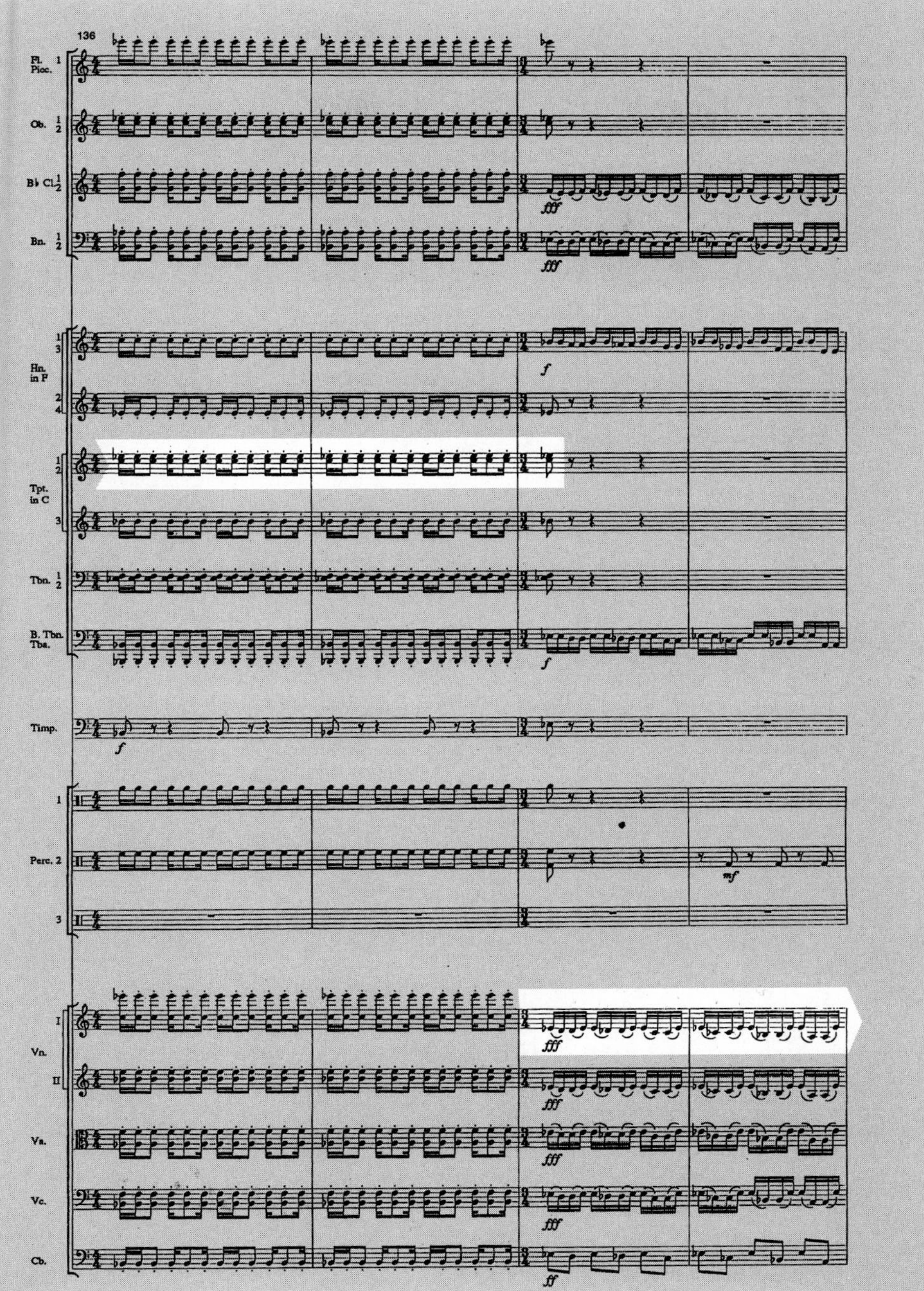
136
Fl. Picc.
Ob.
B♭ Cl.
Bn.
Hn. in F
Tpt. in C
Tbn.
B. Tbn. Tba.
Timp.
Perc.
Vn.
Va.
Vc.
Cb.

140
Fl. Picc. 1
Ob. 1 2
B♭ Cl. 1 2
Bn. 1 2
Hn. in F 1 3
2 4
Tpt. in C 1 2
3
Tbn. 1 2
B. Tbn. Tba.
Timp.
Perc. 1
2
3
Vn. I
II
Va.
Vc.
Cb.
ff
f
mf
cresc.

145
Fl. 1
Picc.
Ob. 1 2
B♭ Cl. 1 2
Bn. 1 2
Hn. in F
Tpt. in C
Tbn. 1 2
B. Tbn. Tba.
Timp.
Perc. 2
Vn. I
II
Va.
Vc.
Cb.
ff
fp
f

149
Fl. 1
Picc.
Ob. 1 2
B♭ Cl. 1 2
Bn. 1 2
Hn. in F 1 3
2 4
Tpt. in C 1 2
3
Tbn. 1 2
B. Tbn. Tba.
Timp.
1
Perc. 2
3
Vn. I
II
Va.
Vc.
Cb.

♩=ca.63
153
Fl. 1 Picc.
Ob. 1 2
B♭ Cl. 1 2
Bn. 1 2
Hn. in F
Tpt. in C
Tbn. 1 2
B. Tbn. Tba.
Timp.
Perc. 1 2 3
Vn. I II
Va.
Vc.
Cb.

157
Fl. Picc.
Ob.
B♭ Cl.
Bn.
Hn. in F
Tpt. in C
Tbn.
B. Tbn. Tba.
Timp.
Perc.
Vn.
Va.
Vc.
Cb.

Joan Tower (b. 1938) was born in New York and raised in South America. She later returned to the United States to attend Bennington College and Columbia University, where she received a doctorate in composition. She has won numerous awards in her distinguished career, and she can be seen as one of the most prominent contemporary American composers of orchestral and other instrumental music. Among her best-known works are *Petroushskates* (1980), *Sequoia* (1981), the Piano Concerto (1985), *Concerto for Orchestra* (1991), and a series of *Fanfares for the Uncommon Woman* (1986–93).

The *Fanfares for the Uncommon Woman* pay homage to the popular *Fanfare for the Common Man* written in 1942 by Aaron Copland. The first of this series quotes Copland and uses the same instrumentation (brass and percussion), but the intended focus is on "women who take risks and are adventurous." Currently, there are five works in the series. The most elaborate of these is number four. Because the extended nature of this work goes beyond the limitations of a fanfare, Tower changed the title to simply *For the Uncommon Woman.* Fanfare characteristics still appear, most notably in the use of brass and percussion and in the use of disjunct melodies, often incorporating the strong intervals of a fourth and a fifth. But the work, scored for a full symphony orchestra, is extended by nonfanfare material. The structure freely alternates between passages featuring sustained pitches and a wavering figure. Throughout, Tower creates strong dissonances, sometimes involving large sound masses, but she maintains clear tonal centers and a thoroughly accessible musical style.

49. Paul Lansky

8CD: 8/53–56
4CD: 4/81–84

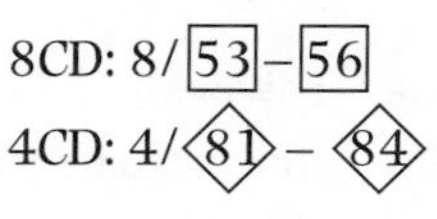

Notjustmoreidlechatter, excerpt
(1988)

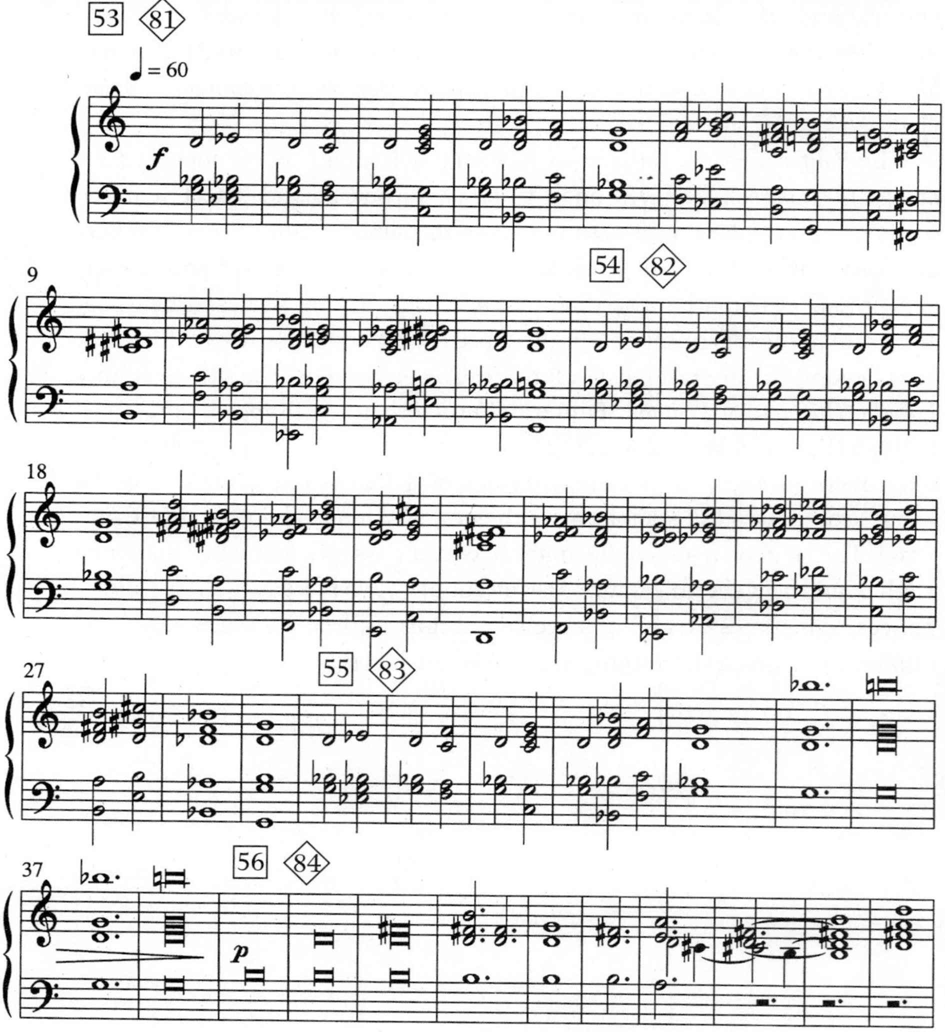

53
81
♩ = 60
f
9
54
82
18
27
55
83
37
56
84
p

Editor's note: The harmonic outline shown here was kindly prepared by the composer specially for this volume.

*Norton recording fades out here.

Paul Lansky (b. 1944) is a leading figure in computer music. A graduate of Princeton University, he has established himself as a composer, theorist, and critic, and he currently teaches at his alma mater. Lansky composed a trilogy of "idle chatter" pieces: *Idle Chatter* (1985), *just_more_idle_chatter* (1987), and *Notjustmoreidlechatter* (1988). These works feature the unintelligible sound of people talking. The effect is of a large chattering crowd that draws the ear into an attempt to understand the conversations.

In *Notjustmoreidlechatter,* Lansky employs a simple, recurring harmonic pattern, over which are superimposed thousands of synthesized word fragments. The rocklike chord progression moves slowly, as the harmony projects the character of "back-up voices." The randomness of the initial word fragments gives way to more humanlike utterances, but the words remain unintelligible throughout.

50. John Adams

Chamber Symphony, Third Movement, *Roadrunner* (1992)

8CD: 8/57–61
4CD: 4/95–99

Instrumentation

Flute
(doubling Piccolo)

Oboe

Clarinet in E-flat
(doubling Clarinets in B-flat & A)

Bass Clarinet in B-flat
(doubling Clarinet in B-flat)

Bassoon

Contrabassoon
(doubling Bassoon)

Horn in F

Trumpet in C
(with both metal and fiber mutes)

Trombone
(with both metal and fiber mutes)

Synthesizer*
(Yamaha SY77 or SY99)

Percussion
(Trap Set)†

Violin

Viola

Violoncello

Contrabass

*Synthesizer software is designed for a specific model of synthesizer, and is not interchangeable with other models or brands. Software included with rental materials is subject to change according to availability of synthesizer models. Consult the publisher for current status.

†

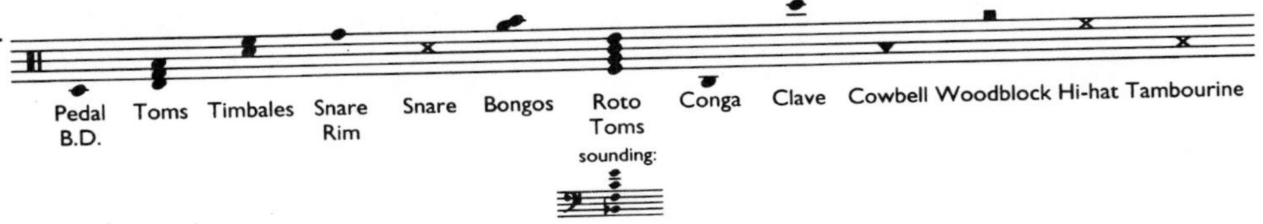

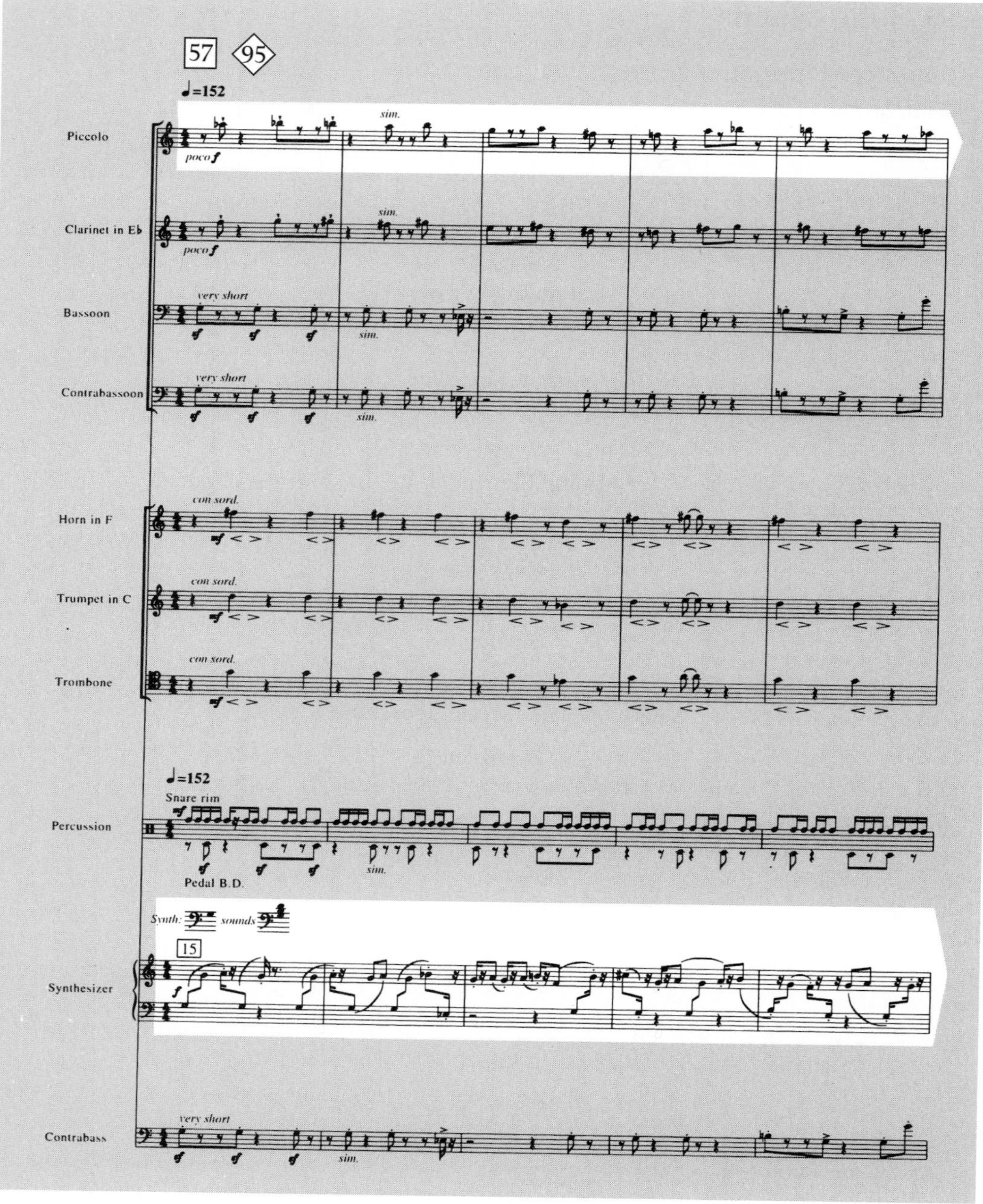
57
95
♩=152
Piccolo
sim.
poco f
Clarinet in E♭
sim.
poco f
Bassoon
very short
sim.
Contrabassoon
very short
sim.
Horn in F
con sord.
Trumpet in C
con sord.
Trombone
con sord.
♩=152
Snare rim
Percussion
sim.
Pedal B.D.
Synth:
sounds
15
Synthesizer
Contrabass
very short
sim.

6
Picc.
Cl. in Eb
Bsn.
Cbsn.
Hn. in F
Tpt. in C
Tbn.
Perc.
Synth.
short!
sim.
Vln.
Vla.
Vcl.
Cbs.

58
96
11
Picc.
Cl. in E♭
Bsn.
Cbsn.
Hn. in F
Tpt. in C
Tbn.
Perc.
Synth.
Vln.
Vla.
Vcl.
Cbs.
solo
tutta forza
pizz.

16
short!
Picc.
p
to Fl.
very short!
Ob.
mp
short!
Cl. in E♭
p
very short!
mp
very short!
Cl. in B♭
mp
very short!
Bsn.
p
mp
Cbsn.
p
Tambourine
Woodblock
Perc.
p
mp
Low Tom
Synth.
p
Vln.
Vla.
p
Cbs.
p

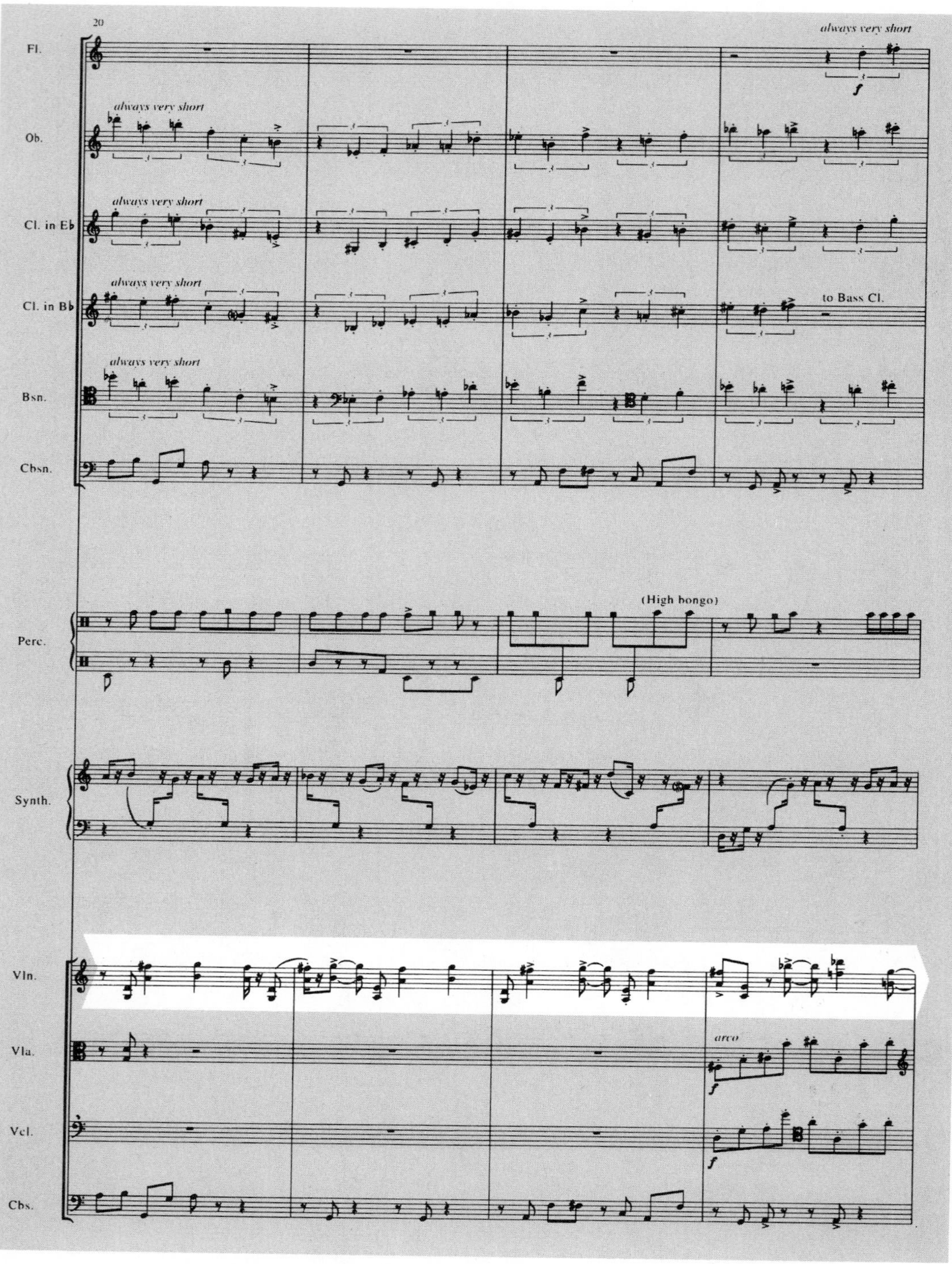
20
Fl.
always very short
Ob.
always very short
Cl. in E♭
always very short
Cl. in B♭
always very short
to Bass Cl.
Bsn.
always very short
Cbsn.
Perc.
(High bongo)
Synth.
Vln.
Vla.
arco
Vcl.
Cbs.

24
Fl.
Ob.
Cl. in Eb
Bsn.
Cbsn.
to Picc.
Hn. in F
Tpt. in C
Tbn.
(con sord.)
(con sord.)
Perc.
(Low bongo)
Roto Tom
Synth.
Vln.
Vla.
Vcl.
Cbs.

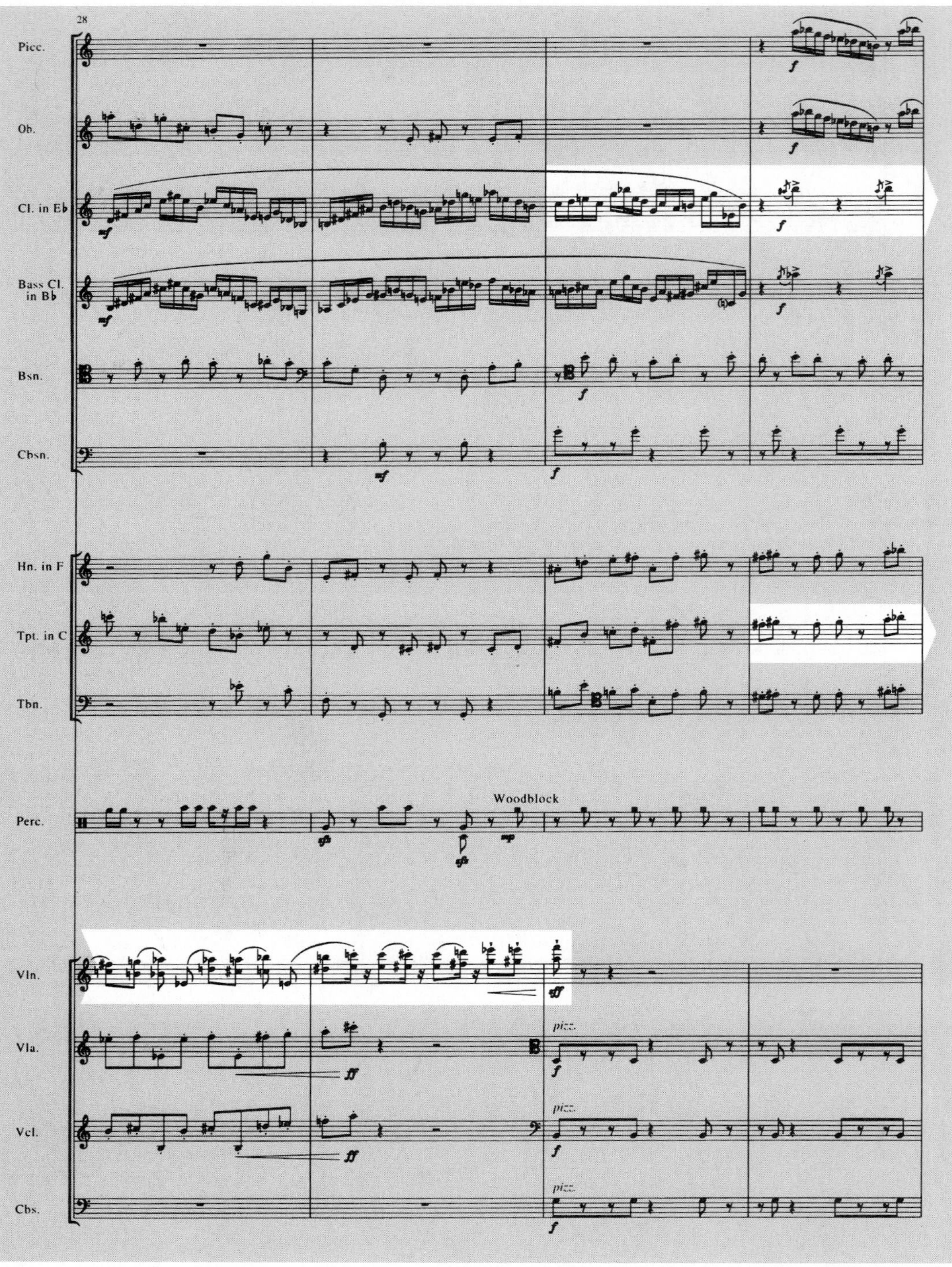
28
Picc.
Ob.
Cl. in E♭
Bass Cl. in B♭
Bsn.
Cbsn.
Hn. in F
Tpt. in C
Tbn.
Woodblock
Perc.
Vln.
Vla.
Vcl.
Cbs.
pizz.

32
Picc.
Ob.
Cl. in E♭
Bass Cl. in B♭
always very short
Bsn.
always very short
Cbsn.
Hn. in F
Tpt. in C
Tbn.
Perc.
Vla.
Vcl.
Cbs.
36
Picc.
Ob.
Cl. in E♭
Bass Cl. in B♭
Bsn.
Cbsn.
Vla.
Vcl.
Cbs.

40
Picc.
to Fl.
Ob.
Cl. in E♭
Bass Cl. in B♭
Bsn.
Cbsn.
Hn. in F
Tpt. in C
Tbn.
Vla.
Vcl.
Cbs.
44
59
97
Ob.
Cl. in E♭
Bass Cl. in B♭
sempre staccato
Bsn.
Cbsn.
Hn. in F
Tpt. in C
Tbn.
solo
Vln.
Vla.
Vcl.
Cbs.

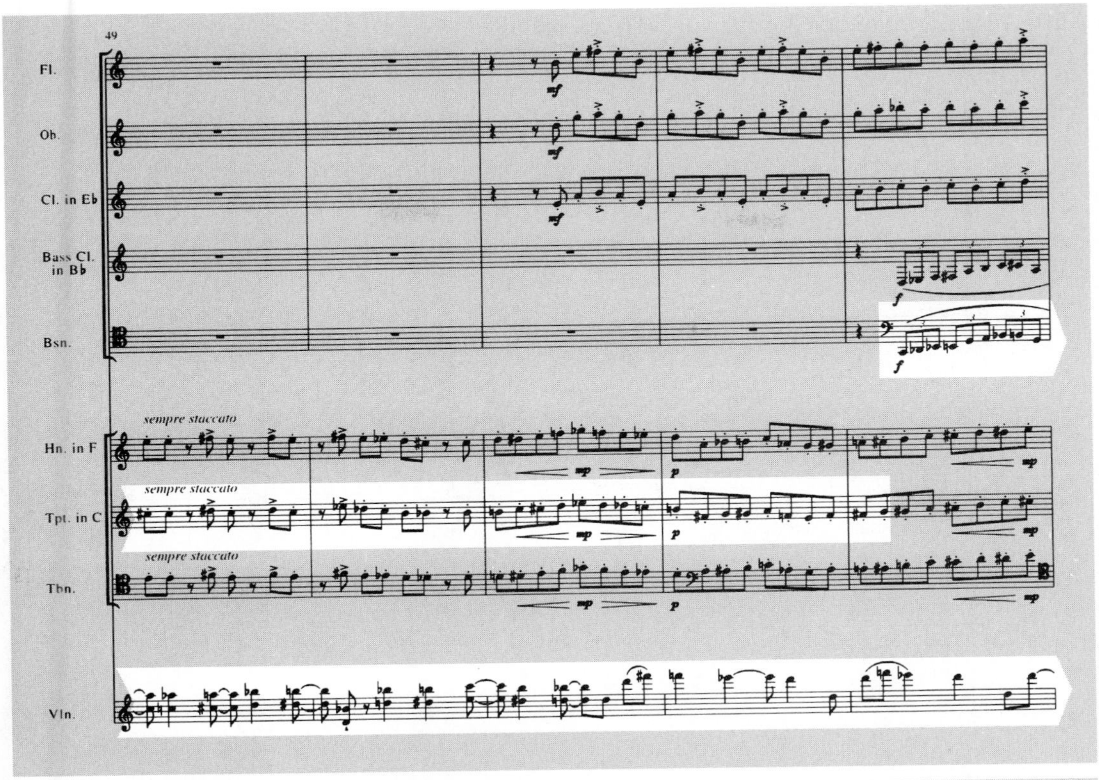
49
Fl.
Ob.
Cl. in Eb
Bass Cl. in Bb
Bsn.
Hn. in F
Tpt. in C
Tbn.
Vln.
sempre staccato
sempre staccato
sempre staccato
mf
mf
mf
f
f
mp
mp
mp
p
p
p
mp
mp
mp

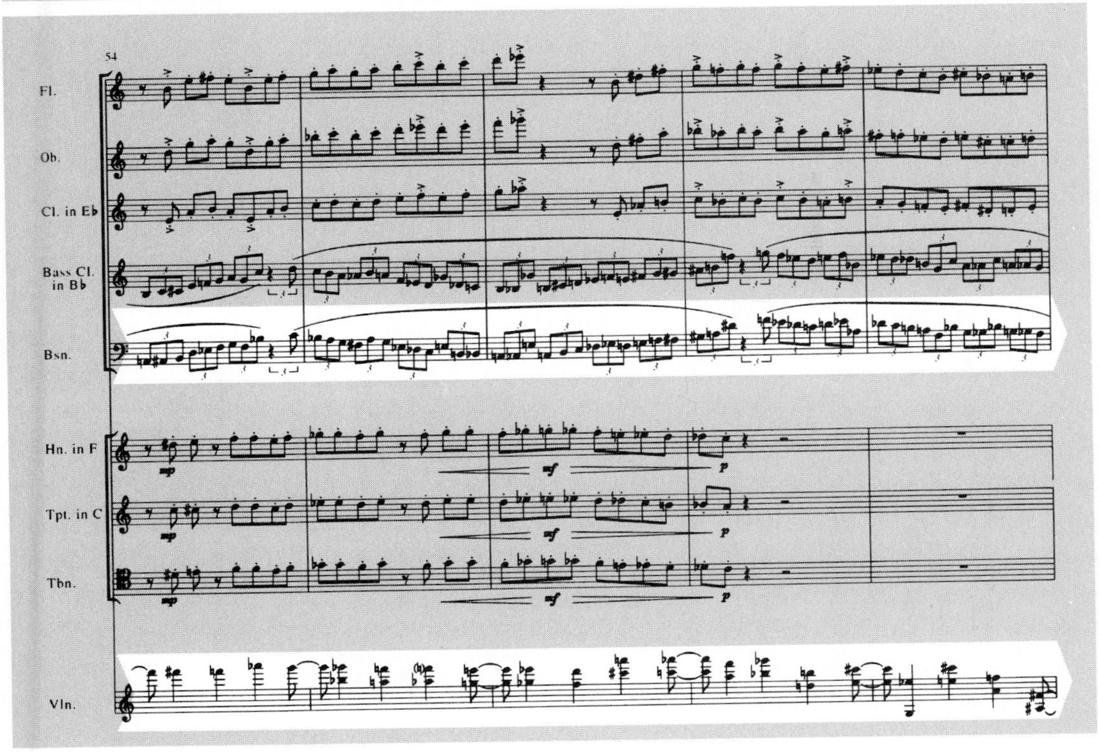
54
Fl.
Ob.
Cl. in Eb
Bass Cl. in Bb
Bsn.
Hn. in F
Tpt. in C
Tbn.
Vln.
mp
mp
mp
mf
mf
mf
p
p
p

59
Fl.
Ob.
Cl. in E♭
Bass Cl. in B♭
to Cl. in B♭
Bsn.
Cbsn.
Hn. in F
open
Tpt. in C
(mute)
High Hat
Perc.
Tambourine (with stick)
16
Synth.
Vln.
on the string
Vla.
arco
on the string
Vcl.
arco
Cbs.
arco

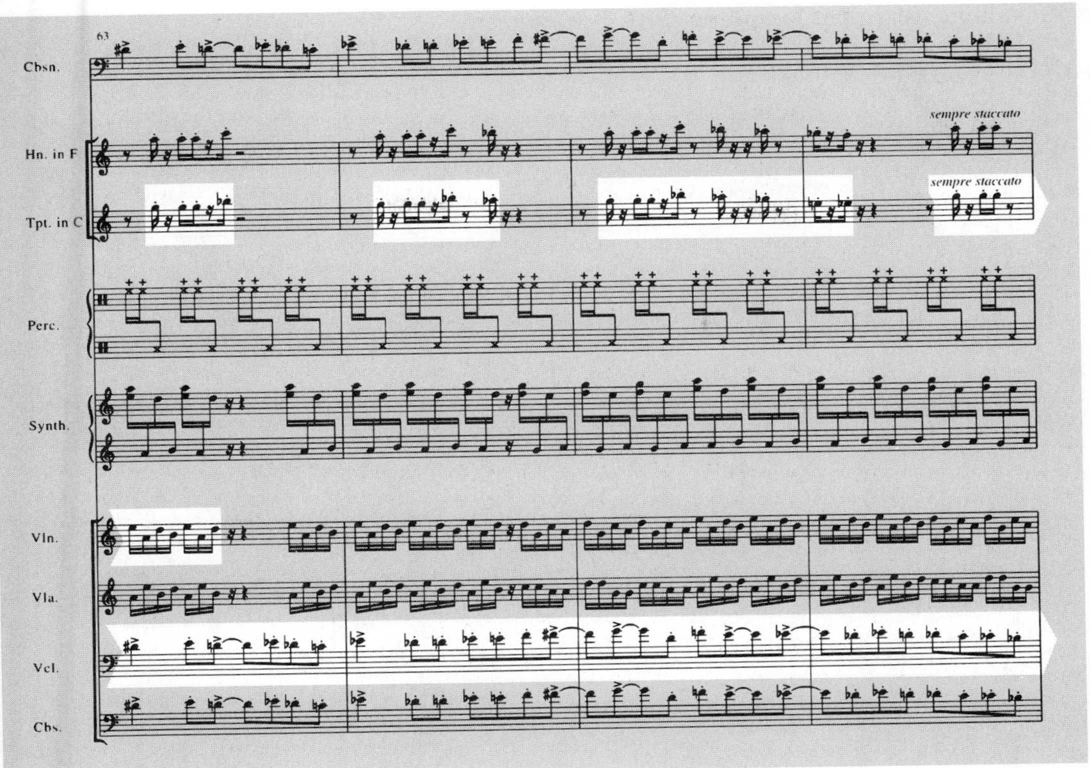

63

Cbsn.

Hn. in F

sempre staccato

Tpt. in C

sempre staccato

Perc.

Synth.

Vln.

Vla.

Vcl.

Cbs.

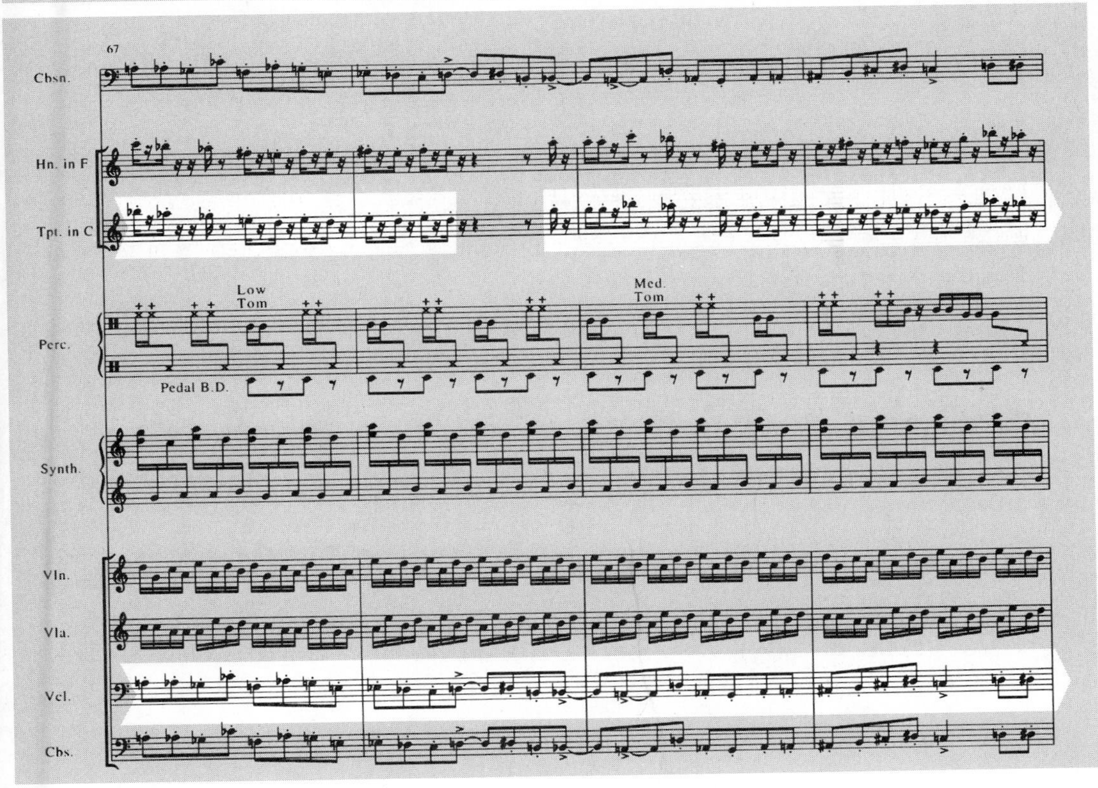

67

Cbsn.

Hn. in F

Tpt. in C

Perc.

Low Tom

Med. Tom

Pedal B.D.

Synth.

Vln.

Vla.

Vcl.

Cbs.

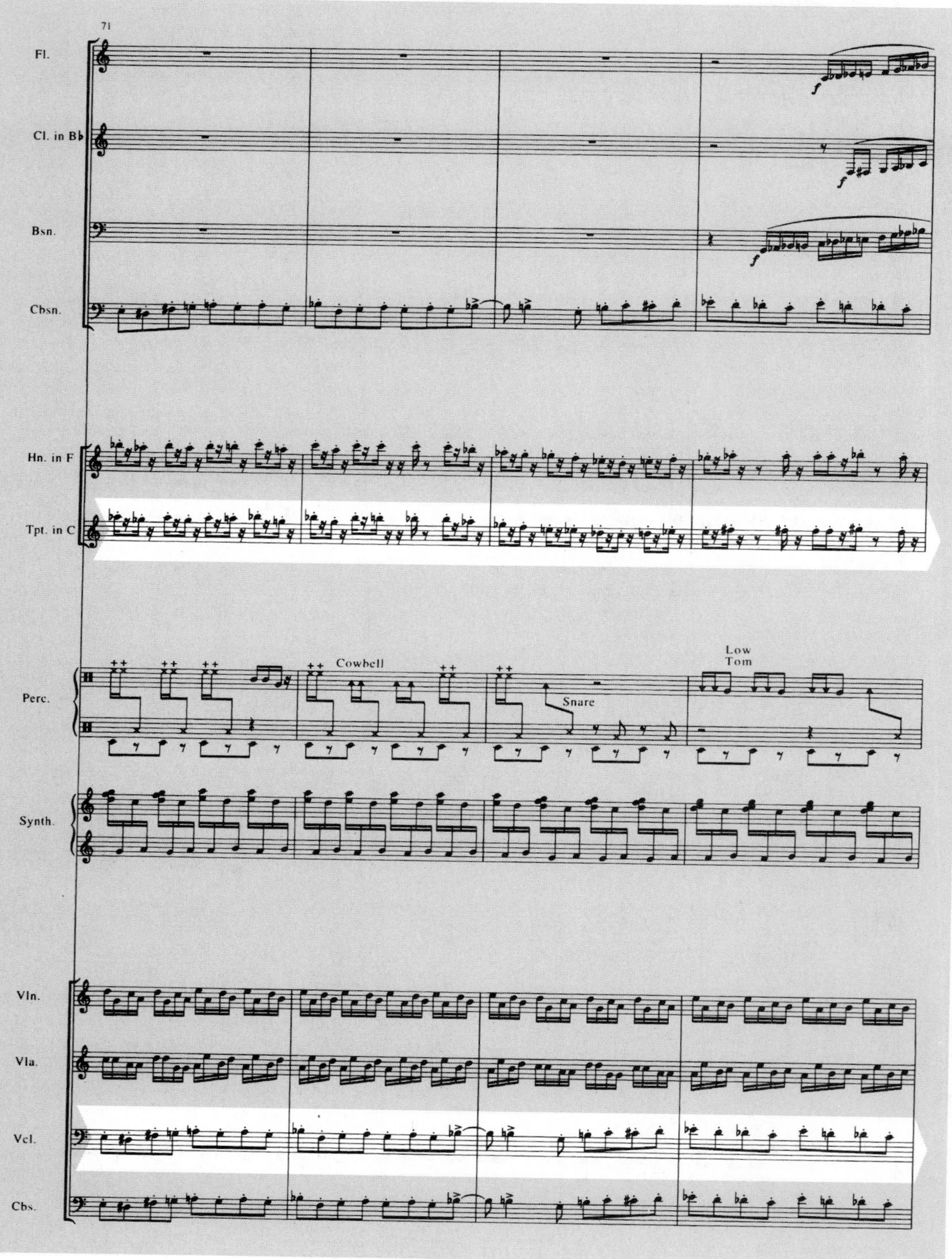
71
Fl.
Cl. in B♭
Bsn.
Cbsn.
Hn. in F
Tpt. in C
Perc.
Cowbell
Snare
Low
Tom
Synth.
Vln.
Vla.
Vcl.
Cbs.

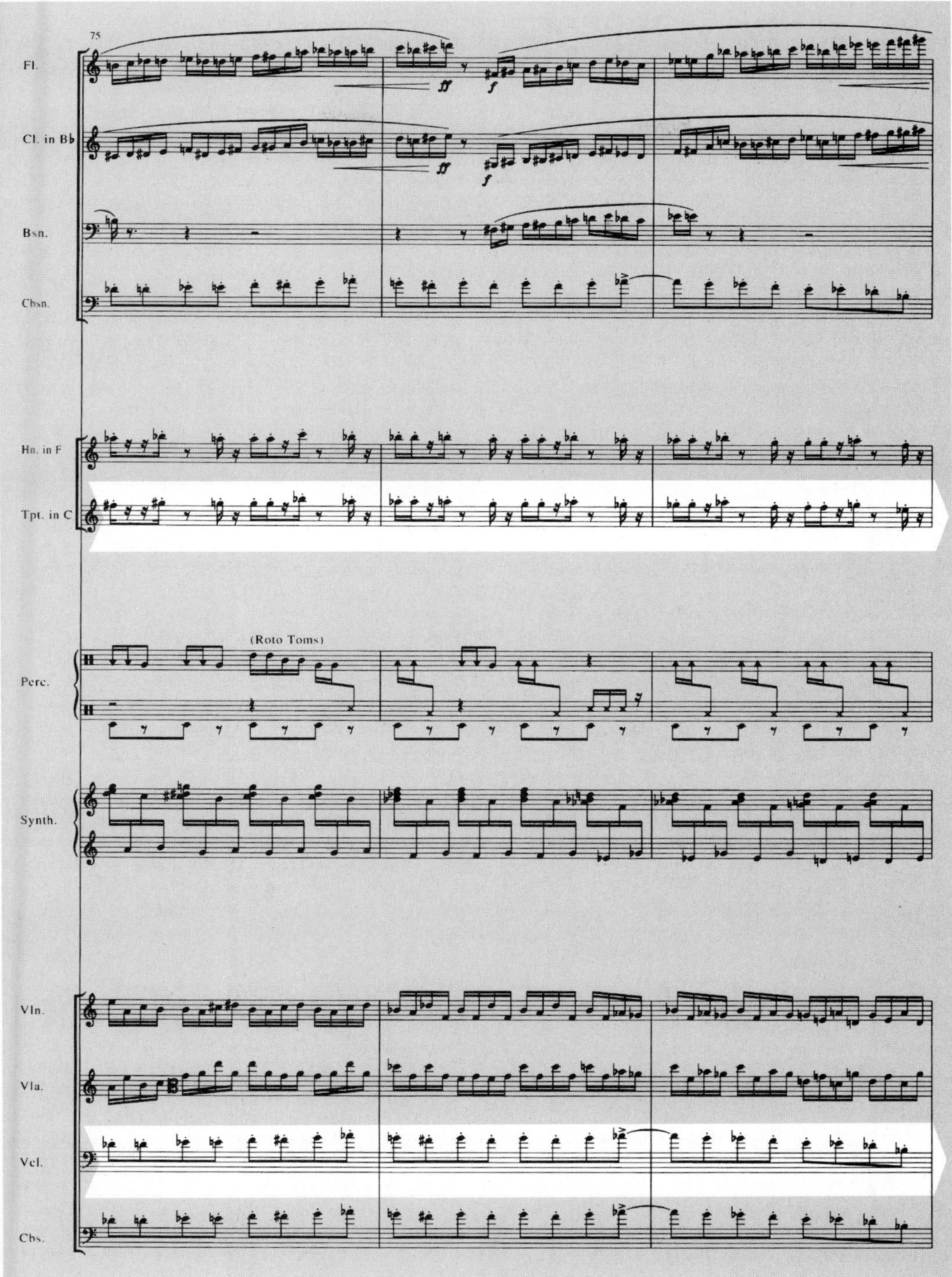
75
Fl.
Cl. in B♭
Bsn.
Cbsn.
Hn. in F
Tpt. in C
(Roto Toms)
Perc.
Synth.
Vln.
Vla.
Vcl.
Cbs.
ff
f

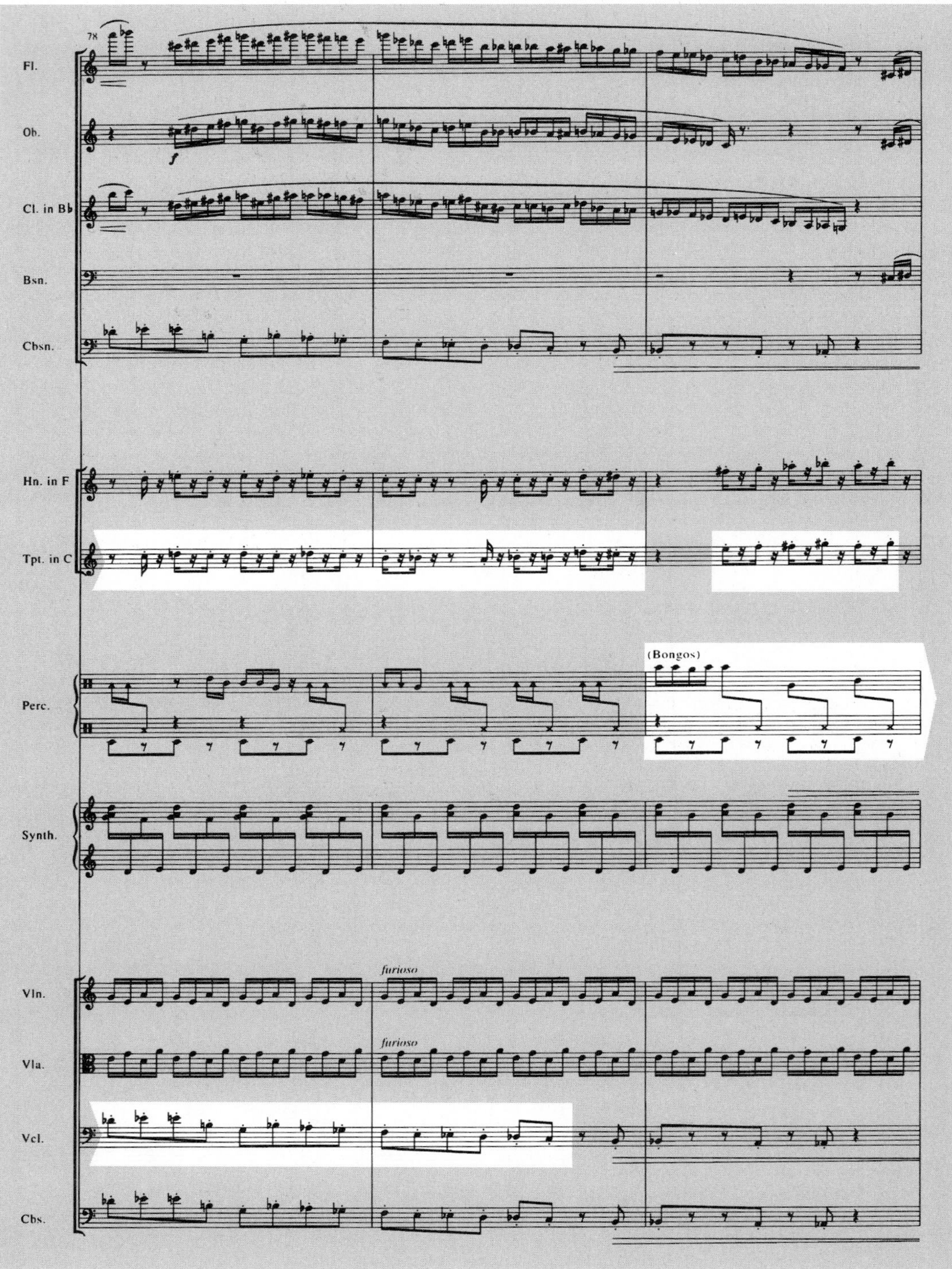
78
Fl.
Ob.
Cl. in B♭
Bsn.
Cbsn.
Hn. in F
Tpt. in C
(Bongos)
Perc.
Synth.
furioso
Vln.
furioso
Vla.
Vcl.
Cbs.

81
Fl.
Ob.
Cl. in B♭
Bsn.
Cbsn.
very short
sim.
Hn. in F
Tpt. in C
Tbn.
open
very short
sim.
Perc.
Snare rim
Synth.
15
(Synthesizer should be the prominent voice.)
Vln.
Vla.
Vcl.
Cbs.

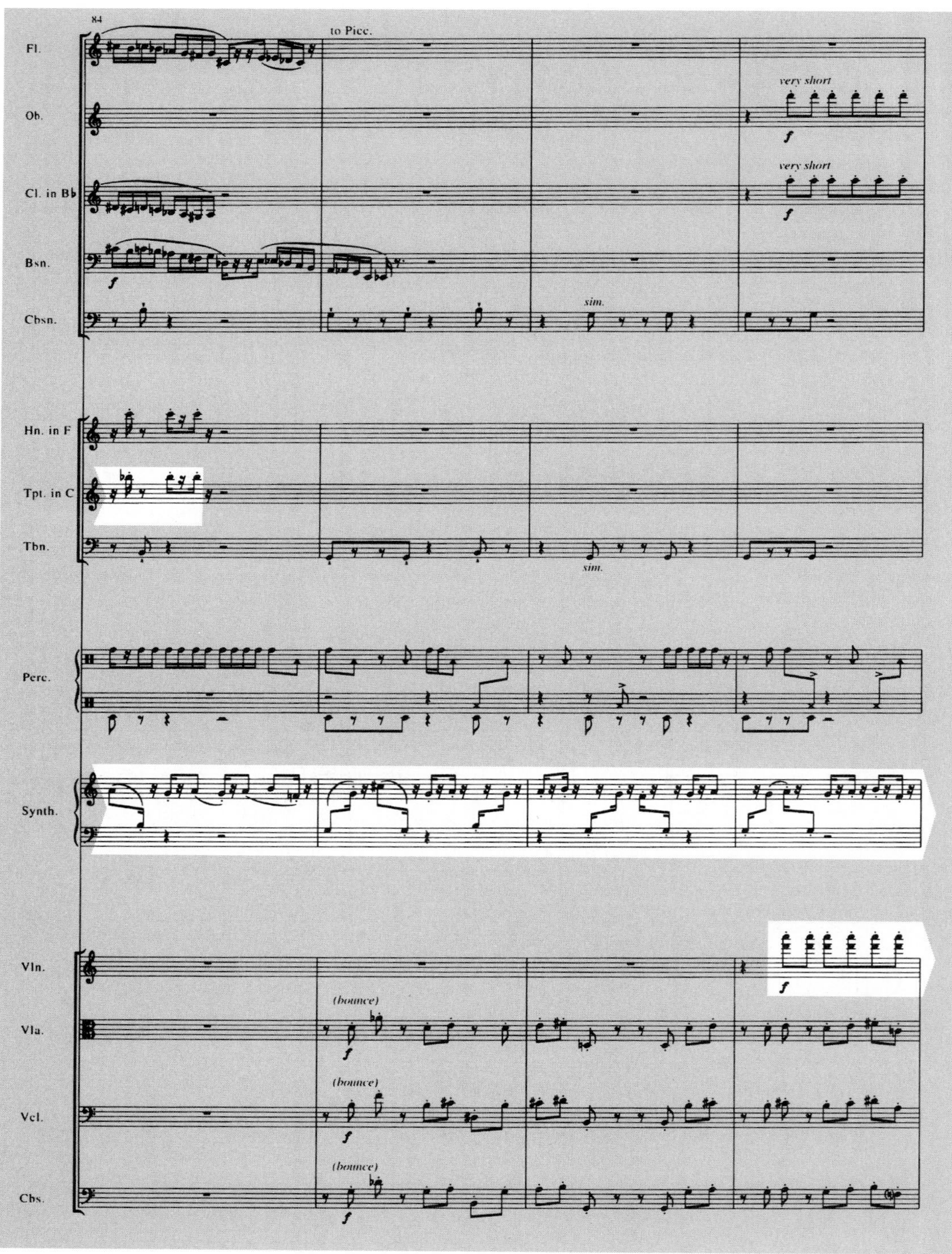
84
Fl.
to Picc.
Ob.
very short
f
Cl. in B♭
very short
f
Bsn.
f
Cbsn.
sim.
Hn. in F
Tpt. in C
Tbn.
sim.
Perc.
Synth.
Vln.
f
Vla.
(bounce)
f
Vcl.
(bounce)
f
Cbs.
(bounce)
f

88
Picc.
Ob.
Cl. in B♭
Bsn.
Cbsn.
Hn. in F
Tpt. in C
Tbn.
Perc.
Synth.
Vln.
Vla.
Vcl.
Cbs.
mf
f
sempre staccato
sempre staccato
(con sord.)

92
Picc.
Ob.
Cl. in Eb
Cl. in Bb
Bsn.
Cbsn.
Hn. in F
Tpt. in C
Tbn.
Perc.
Synth.
Vln.
Vla.
Vcl.
Cbs.
always very short
mf
always very short
very short eighths
always very short

95
Picc.
Ob.
Cl. in Eb
Cl. in Bb
Bsn.
Cbsn.
Hn. in F
Tpt. in C
Tbn.
High Bongo (with stick)
Perc.
Synth.
Vln.
Vla.
Vcl.
Cbs.

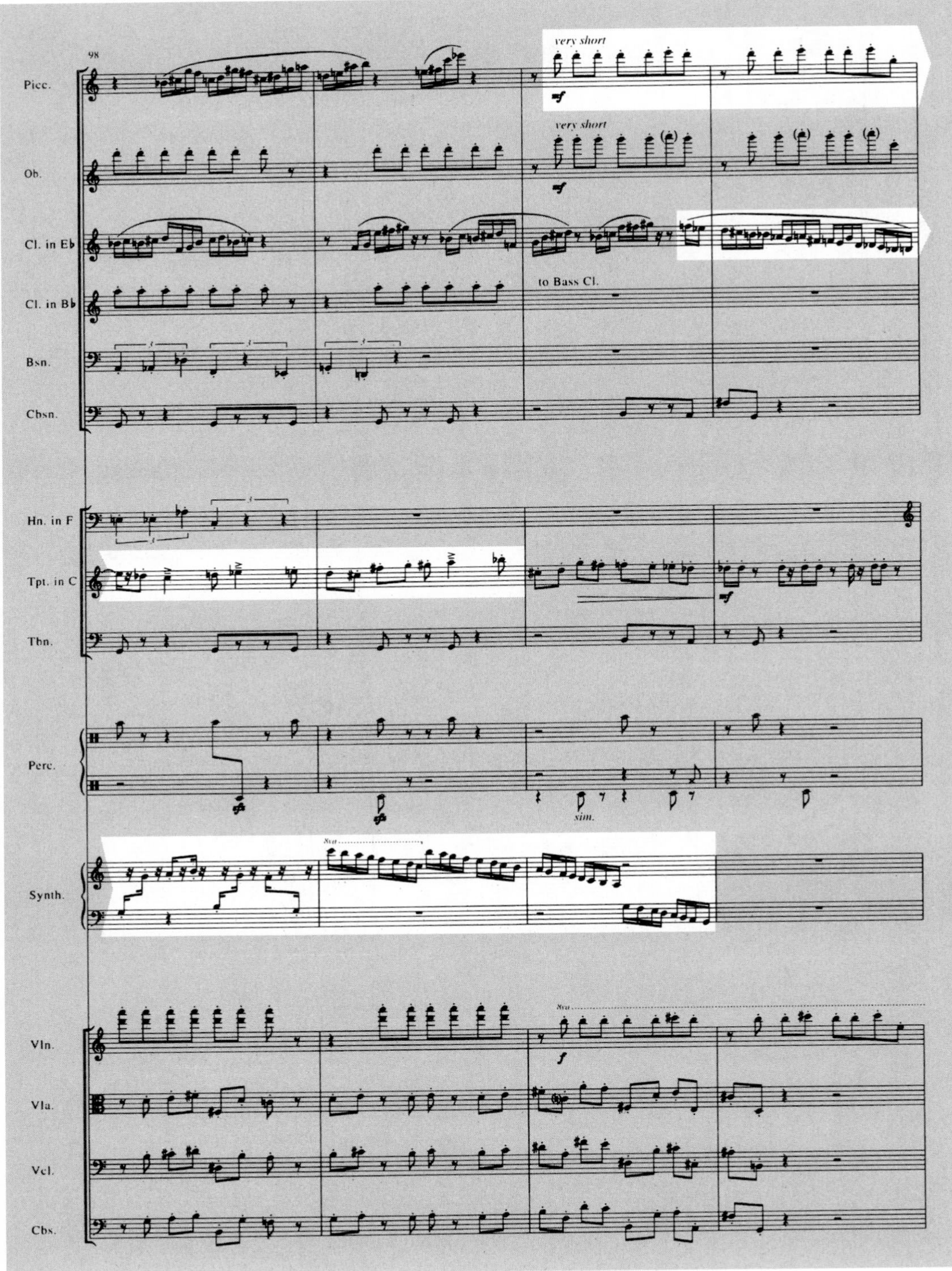
98
very short
mf
very short
mf
to Bass Cl.
sim.
8va
8va
f
Picc.
Ob.
Cl. in E♭
Cl. in B♭
Bsn.
Cbsn.
Hn. in F
Tpt. in C
Tbn.
Perc.
Synth.
Vln.
Vla.
Vcl.
Cbs.

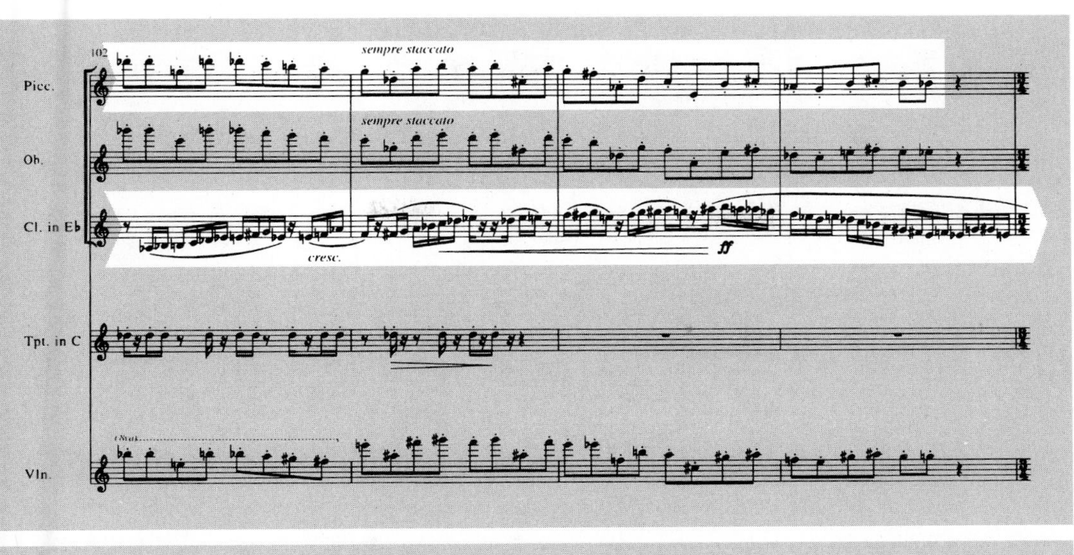

102
sempre staccato
Picc.
sempre staccato
Ob.
Cl. in Eb
cresc.
ff
Tpt. in C
Vln.

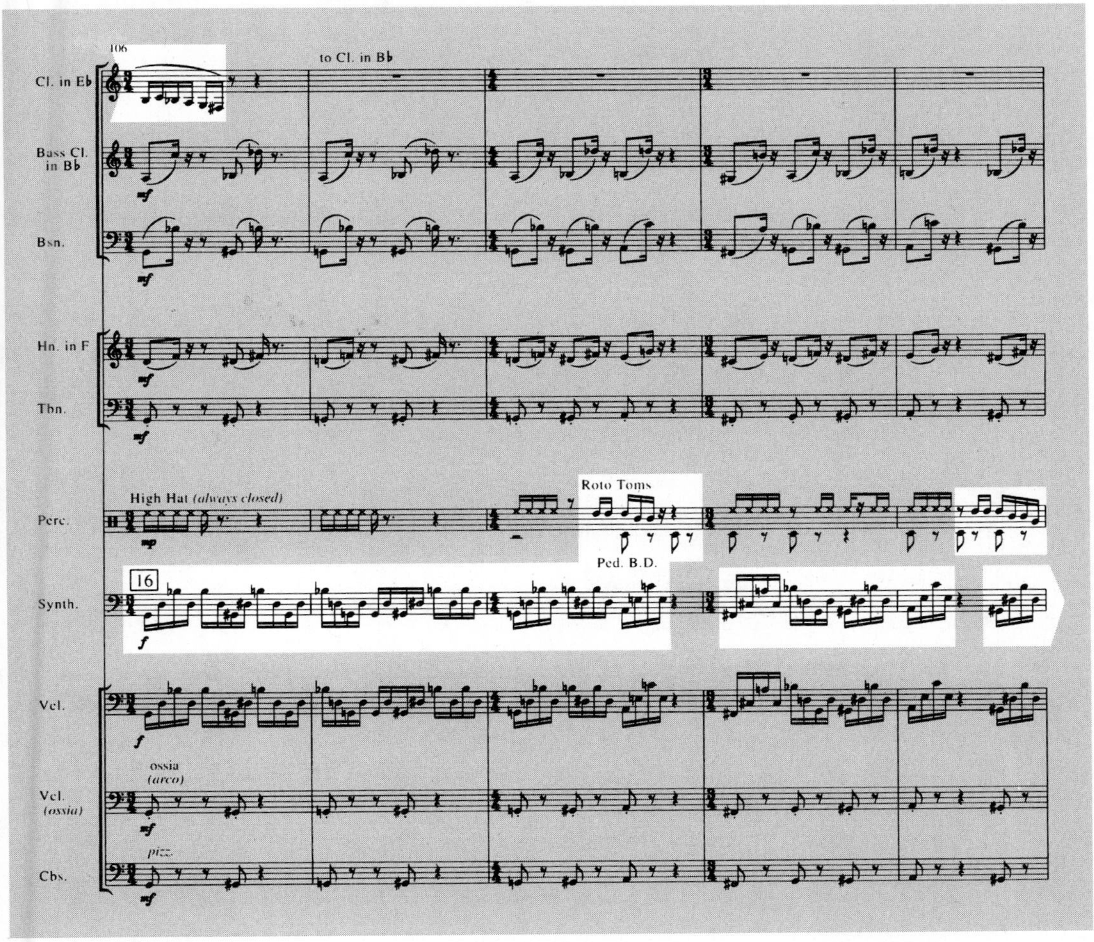
106
to Cl. in Bb
Cl. in Eb
Bass Cl. in Bb
mf
Bsn.
mf
Hn. in F
mf
Tbn.
mf
High Hat (always closed)
Roto Toms
Perc.
mp
Ped. B.D.
16
Synth.
f
Vcl.
f
ossia
(arco)
Vcl. (ossia)
mf
pizz.
Cbs.
mf

111
Bass Cl. in B♭
Bsn.
Hn. in F
Tbn.
Snare Rim
Perc.
Synth.
furioso
Vla.
Vcl.
Vcl. (ossia)
Cbs.
116
Bass Cl. in B♭
Bsn.
Hn. in F
Tbn.
sim.
Perc.
Synth.
furioso
Vln.
Vla.
Vcl.
Vcl. (ossia)
Cbs.

N.B.: The following section can be played on English Horn, if desired.

124
Ob.
Cl. in B♭
furioso
ff
Bass Cl. in B♭
Bsn.
Cbsn.
ff
Tpt. in C
High Bongo
Perc.
ff
Synth.
Vln.
Vla.
127
Begin gradual ritard.
Ob.
Cl. in B♭
to Cl. in A
Bass Cl. in B♭
Bsn.
Cbsn.
Hn. in F
ff
Tpt. in C
mute out
Low Bongo
High Timb.
Perc.
f
Synth.
Begin gradual ritard.
Vln.
Vla.
Vcl.
ff

60
98
♩=138 (steady)
to Cl. in B♭
Bass Cl. in B♭
Bsn.
Perc.
Low Timb.
Roto Toms
Synth.
♩=138 (steady)
solo
Vln.
on the string
(beat in two)
Tamb.
(stop beating)
gradual accelerando independent of the beat
gradually move to tremolo
off the string
sim.
Begin gradual ritard.
poco dim.

160
61
99
Cl. in A
Bsn.
Cbsn.
Synth.
Vln.
Cbs.
pesante
15
arco
pp

167
Begin gradual return to Tempo I
(♩=139)
Cl. in A
Bsn.
Cbsn.
Synth.
Vln.
Cbs.
mp

171
(♩=145)
(♩=150)
to Cl. in E♭
Cl. in A
Bsn.
Cbsn.
Synth.
Vln.
Cbs.
ppp

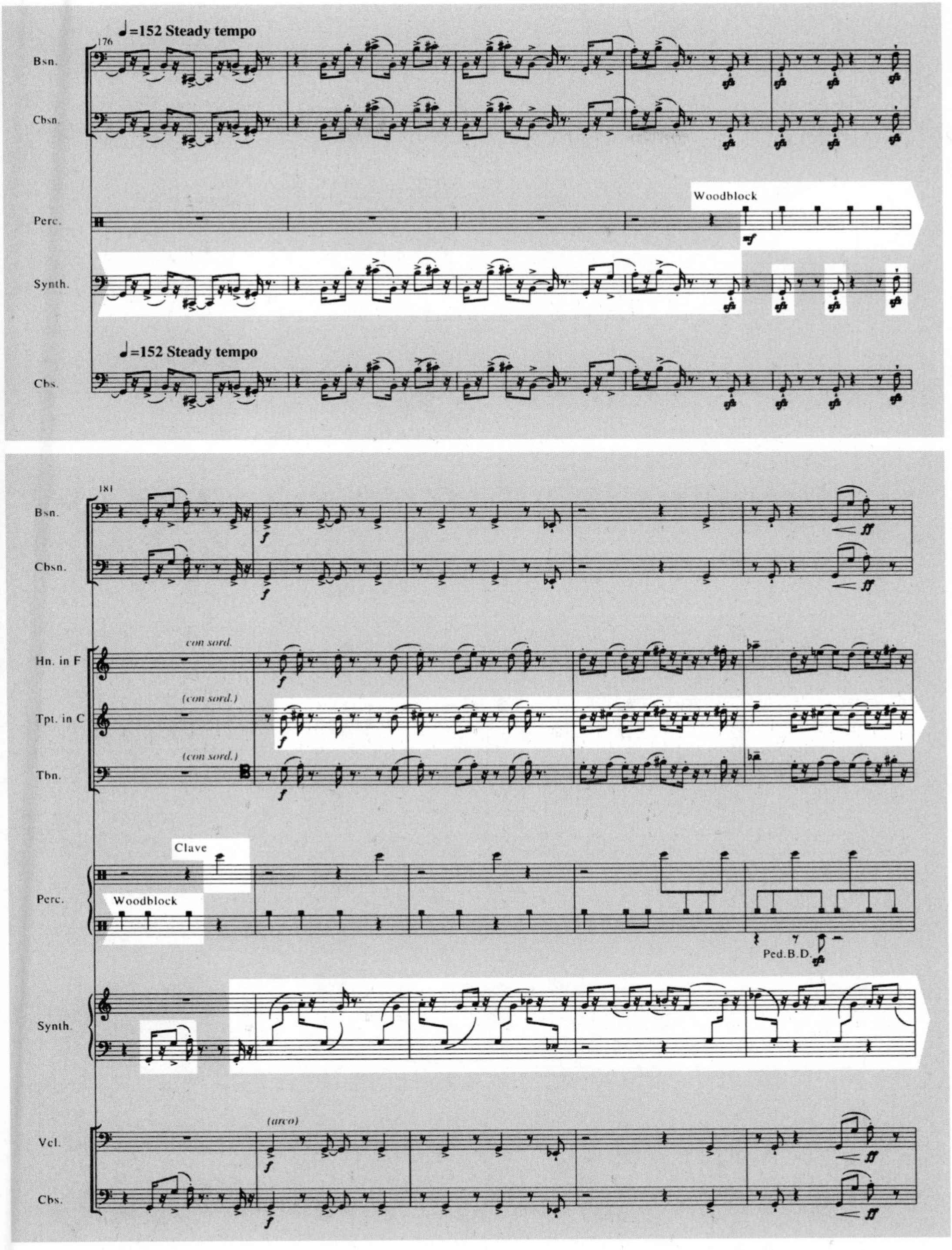

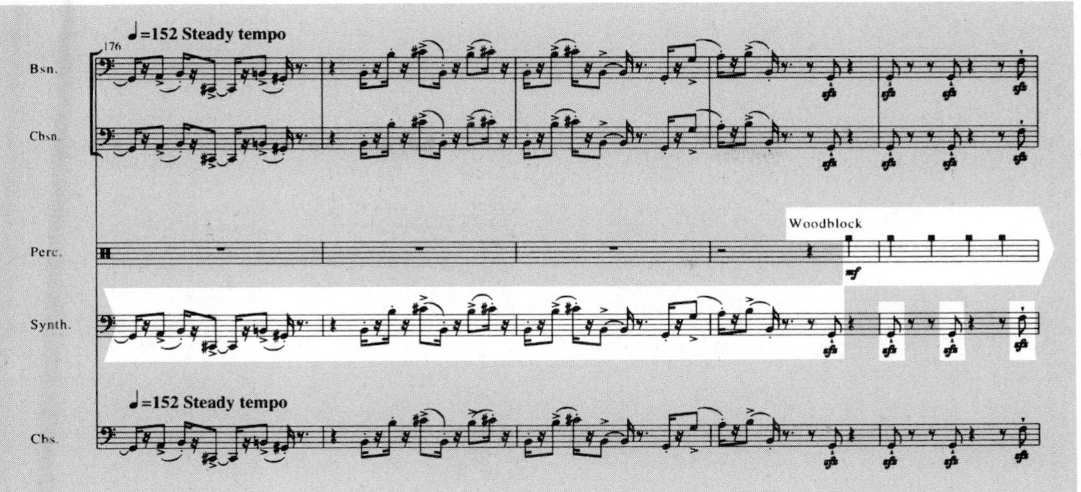

181
Bsn.
Cbsn.
con sord.
Hn. in F
(con sord.)
Tpt. in C
(con sord.)
Tbn.
Clave
Woodblock
Perc.
Ped.B.D.
Synth.
(arco)
Vcl.
Cbs.

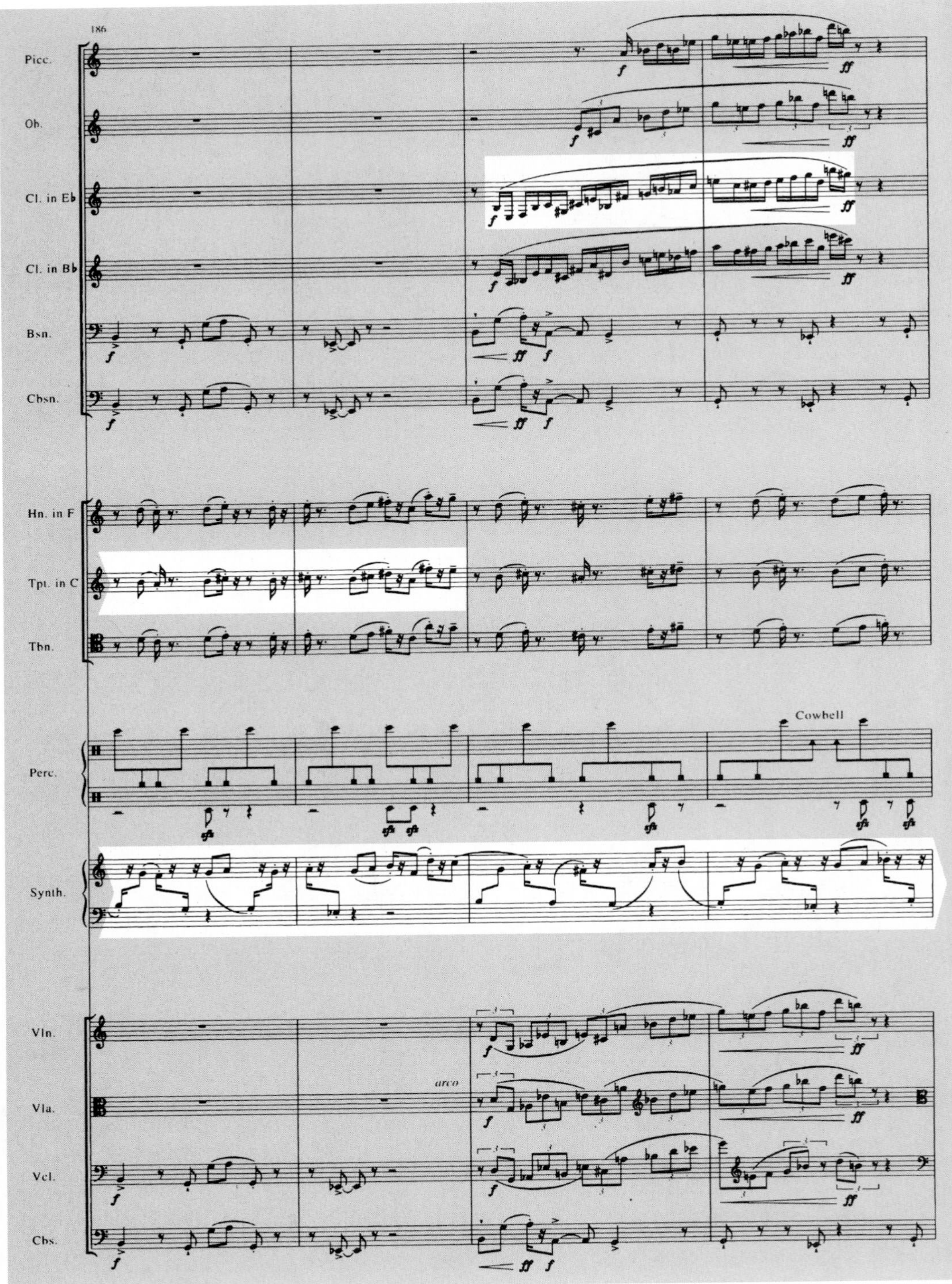
186
Picc.
Ob.
Cl. in E♭
Cl. in B♭
Bsn.
Cbsn.
Hn. in F
Tpt. in C
Tbn.
Cowbell
Perc.
Synth.
Vln.
arco
Vla.
Vcl.
Cbs.

190
Picc.
Ob.
Cl. in Eb
Cl. in Bb
Bsn.
Cbsn.
Hn. in F
Tpt. in C
Tbn.
Perc.
Roto Toms
sim.
Synth.
Vln.
Vla.
Vcl.
Cbs.

193
Picc.
Ob.
Cl. in E♭
Cl. in B♭
Bsn.
Cbsn.
Hn. in F
Tpt. in C
Tbn.
Timbale
(Roto Toms)
Perc.
Toms
Synth.
Vln.
Vla.
Vcl.
Cbs.

197
Picc.
Ob.
Cl. in Eb
Cl. in Bb
Bsn.
Cbsn.
Hn. in F
Tpt. in C
Tbn.
Perc.
Synth.
Vln.
Vla.
Vcl.
Cbs.
ff
f
sfz
very short
very short
very short

201
Picc.
Ob.
Cl. in E♭
Cl. in B♭
Bsn.
Cbsn.
Hn. in F
Tpt. in C
Tbn.
Snare
Perc.
Synth.
Vln.
Vla.
Vcl.
Cbs.

205
Ob.
Cl. in E♭
Cl. in B♭
Bsn.
Cbsn.
Hn. in F
Tpt. in C
Tbn.
Perc.
Synth.
Vln.
Vla.
Vcl.
Cbs.

209
Picc.
Ob.
Cl. in E♭
Cl. in B♭
Bsn.
Cbsn.
Hn. in F
Tpt. in C
Tbn.
Perc.
Synth.
Vln.
Vla.
Vcl.
Cbs.
cresc.
f
ff
soli

212
Picc.
Ob.
Cl. in Eb
Cl. in Bb
Bsn.
Cbsn.
Hn. in F
Tpt. in C
Tbn.
dampen immediately
Perc.
Synth.
Vln.
Vla.
Vcl.
Cbs.

In 1971, Harvard graduate John Adams (b. 1947) ventured away from the East Coast and settled in San Francisco, where he began teaching at the San Francisco Conservatory of Music. Within a decade, he rose to national prominence, and he received international acclaim for his opera *Nixon in China* (1987). A product of the postmodern climate, Adams's diverse influences include Schoenberg's Expressionism and rock music. He is a leading exponent of minimalist music, but his works are also steeped in the emotional freedom of New Romanticism.

Adams won the 1994 Royal Philharmonic Society Award for Best Chamber Composition for his three-movement Chamber Symphony. For this work, Adams drew inspiration from two sources, Schoenberg's Chamber Symphony, Op. 9, and cartoon music:

> The hyperactive, insistently aggressive and acrobatic scores for the cartoons mixed in my head with the Schoenberg music, itself hyperactive, acrobatic and not a little aggressive, and I realized suddenly how much these two traditions had in common.

Adams scored the work for eight wind players (many of which are asked to double on other wind instruments), four string players, a synthesizer, and percussion, including a trap set. The third movement is entitled *Roadrunner,* after the well-known cartoon character of the same name. Like the cartoon figure, this movement races at a frantic pace. Within this virtuosic setting, Adams creates a dense contrapuntal texture that retains the repetitive and syncopated qualities of minimalism. The violinist plays a major role in the movement, with several rhapsodic solos and a cadenza accompanied by percussion.

51. Abing (Hua Yanjun)

Er quan ying yue (The Moon Reflected on the Second Springs) (recorded 1950)

8CD: 8/66–69
4CD: 4/73–76

66 73 Statement (Variation) 1

67 74 Statement (Variation) 2

68 75 Statement (Variation) 3

69 75 Statement (Variation) 4

Editor's note: The music above is a notated version of the first statement of the melody as heard on the Norton recording; the following three statements represent elaborations or variations on the same melody.

According to the official Chinese biography, Abing (1883–1950) was born Hua Yanjun. Orphaned, he was adopted by a Daoist monk who taught him music. Abing was later expelled from the Daoist temple after performing sacred music in a secular setting. He wandered through China, singing and playing the erhu as a street musician, and, in his mid-thirties, he lost his sight. Near the end of his life, Abing recorded several works, of which *The Moon Reflected on the Second Springs* is the most famous.

The principal instrument of the work is an erhu, a two-stringed fiddle, generally tuned a fifth apart. The sound box, which rests on the lap, is covered with snakeskin and projects a strong, sometimes nasal sound. Lacking a fingerboard, the instrument creates a sound that moves in a continuum of pitch. The sound has a strong, vocal-like quality. In the recording, the erhu is accompanied by a yangqin, a hammered dulcimer. The melody has four phrases derived from a pentatonic scale. The entire melody is presented four times; each is varied with diverse ornamentation. The climax occurs in the third statement, when the erhu is played in the upper register.

52. Traditional Cajun Music

Jongle à moi (Think of Me)

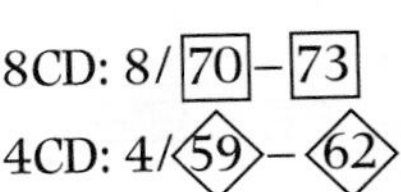

Transcription by Roger Hickman

70 59

Violin

5 Accordion 8va lower

9

13 Violin

17 Accordion

21

25

29

71 60

33 Voice 8va lower

O mais, o o o yé yail - le, Quoi faire t'es comme

37

ça? Jon - gle à moi, cat - in, bé - bé O, une fois par

Editor's note: The recorded performance includes trills, slides, scoops, double stops, and drones not notated in this transcription.

41
jour.
Yé, yé, yé, bé - bé,
Tu con - nais que moi je
45
t'ap - pelais.
Tous les same - dis soir, cat - in,
Jon - gle à moi
49
Violin and Guitar 8va lower
pen-dant la jour - née.
53
57
61
65
72
61
Violin
69
73
77

81
85
89
93
97
101
105
109
113
73
62
Voice
O___ O O, yé yail - le,___ Quoi faire t'es comme
117
ça?___ Jon - gle à___ moi, cat - in, bé - bé, Oué, une foir par

52. Traditional Cajun Music, *Jongle à moi*

Text and Translation

O mais, o, yé yaille,	O, but oh yé yaille,
Quoi faire t'es comme ça?	Why are you like that?
Jongle à moi, catin, bébé,	Think of me, darling baby,
O, une fois par jour.	At least once a day.
Yé, yé, yé, bébé,	Yé, yé, yé, baby,
Tu connais que moi je t'appelais	You know that I called for you
Tous les samedis soir, catin,	Every Saturday night, darling,
Jongle à moi pendant la journée.	Think of me during the day
O yé yaille,	O yé yaille,
Quoi faire t'es comme ça?	Why are you like that?
Jongle à moi, catin, bébé,	Think of me, darling baby,
Oué, une fois par jour.	At least once a day.
Yé, yé, yé, bébé,	Yé, yé, yé, baby,
Tu connais moi je t'aimais	You know that I love you
Jongle à moi, joline, bébé,	Think of me, darling baby,
Tous le soirs et toutes les journées.	Every night and every day.

In the middle of the eighteenth century, Acadian residents descended from French colonists were expelled from their home in Canada by the British and dispersed to various locations in the United States. In southwestern Louisiana, the so-called Cajuns intermingled with the Creoles, people of mixed French, Spanish, and African or Afro-Caribbean descent. Both Cajun music and Creole music, called *zydeco*, have maintained distinct characteristics, but each has also exerted strong influences on the other.

BeauSoleil, led by Michael Doucet, is one of the leading groups in the popular revival of Cajun music. The ensemble features traditional Cajun instruments—a fiddle, guitar, washboard, and drums, and the accordion, the principal instrument of zydeco. *Jongle à moi (Think of Me)* is a traditional Cajun fiddle tune, consisting of a pair of eight-measure phrases, sometimes alternating with an eight-measure phrase that acts as a bridge. The tune is sung twice in this performance.

The fiddle predominates in the instrumental sections, although the accordion and guitar occasionally vie for the lead. Typical Cajun fiddle techniques can be heard, including drones (playing a repeated pitch on one string while playing the melody on another), double stops (playing two notes at the same time), slides, and trills. The texture is sometimes heterophonic, with several instruments elaborating on the tune at the same time.

Appendix A

Reading a Musical Score

CLEFS

The music for some instruments is written in clefs other than the familiar treble and bass. In the following example, middle C is shown in the four clefs used in orchestral scores:

The *alto clef* is primarily used in viola parts. The *tenor clef* is employed for cello, bassoon, and trombone parts when these instruments play in a high register.

TRANSPOSING INSTRUMENTS

The music for some instruments is customarily written at a pitch different from its actual sound. The following list, with examples, shows the main transposing instruments and the degree of transposition. (In some modern works—such as Stravinsky's *Le sacre du printemps* included in volume two of this anthology—all instruments are written at their sounding pitch.)

Instrument	Transposition	Written note	Actual sound
Piccolo Celesta	sounds an octave higher than written	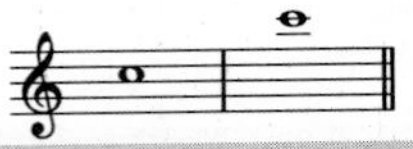	
Trumpet in F	sounds a fourth higher than written		
Trumpet in E	sounds a major third higher than written	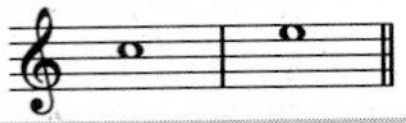	
Clarinet in E♭ Trumpet in E♭	sounds a minor third higher than written		
Trumpet in D Clarinet in D	sounds a major second higher than written	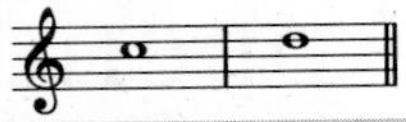	
Clarinet in B♭ Trumpet in B♭ Cornet in B♭ French horn in B♭, alto	sounds a major second lower than written		
Clarinet in A Trumpet in A Cornet in A	sounds a minor third lower than written		
French horn in G Alto flute	sounds a fourth lower than written		
English horn French horn in F	sounds a fifth lower than written		
French horn in E	sounds a minor sixth lower than written		
French horn in E♭ Alto saxophone	sounds a major sixth lower than written		
French horn in D	sounds a minor seventh lower than written		
Contrabassoon French horn in C Double bass	sounds an octave lower than written	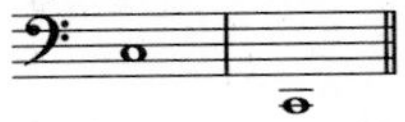	
Bass clarinet in B♭ Tenor saxophone (written in treble clef)	sounds a major ninth lower than written		
Tenor saxophone (written in bass clef)	sounds a major second lower than written		
Bass clarinet in A (written in treble clef)	sounds a minor tenth lower than written		
Bass clarinet in A (written in bass clef)	sounds a minor third lower than written	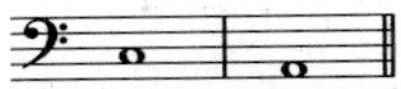	
Baritone saxophone in E♭ (written in treble clef)	sounds an octave and a major sixth lower than written	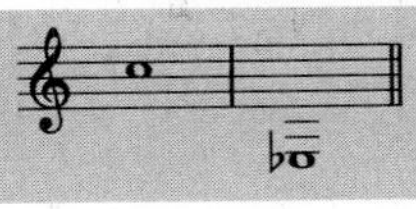	
Bass saxophone in B	sounds two octaves and a major second lower than written		

Appendix B

Instrumental Names and Abbreviations

The following tables set forth the English, Italian, German, and French names used for the various musical instruments in these scores, and their respective abbreviations (when used). Latin voice designations and a table of the foreign-language names for scale degrees and modes are also provided.

English	*Italian*	*German*	*French*
		WOODWINDS	
Piccolo (Picc.)	Flauto piccolo (Fl. Picc.)	Kleine Flöte (Kl. Fl.)	Petite flûte
Flute (Fl.)	Flauto (Fl.); Flauto grande (Fl. gr.)	Grosse Flöte (Gr. Fl.)	Flûte (Fl.)
Alto flute	Flauto contralto (fl. c-alto)	Altflöte	Flûte en sol
Oboe (Ob.)	Oboe (Ob.)	Hoboe (Hb.); Oboe (Ob.)	Hautbois (Hb.)
English horn (E. H.)	Corno inglese (C. or Cor. ingl., C.i.)	Englisches Horn (E. H.)	Cor anglais (C. A.)
E♭ clarinet	Clarinetto piccolo (clar. picc.)		

English	*Italian*	*German*	*French*
Clarinet (C., Cl., Clt., Clar.)	Clarinetto (Cl., Clar.)	Klarinette (Kl.)	Clarinette (Cl.)
Bass clarinet (B. Cl.)	Clarinetto basso (Cl. b., Cl. basso, Clar. basso)	Bass Klarinette (Bkl.)	Clarinette basse (Cl. bs.)
Bassoon (Bsn., Bssn.)	Fagotto (Fag., Fg.)	Fagott (Fag., Fg.)	Basson (Bssn.)
Contrabassoon (C. Bsn.)	Contrafagotto (Cfg., C. Fag., Cont. F.)	Kontrafagott (Kfg.)	Contrebasson (C. bssn.)
Alto saxophone Tenor saxophone Baritone saxophone	Sassofone	Saxophon	Saxophone
Surrusophone	Sarrusofano	Sarrusophon	Sarrusophone
		BRASS	
French horn (Hr., Hn.)	Corno (Cor., C.) [*pl.* Corni]	Horn (Hr.) [*pl.* Hörner (Hrn.)]	Cor; Cor à pistons
Trumpet (Tpt., Trpt., Trp., Tr.)	Tromba (Tr.) [*pl.* Tbe.]	Trompete (Tr., Trp.)	Trompette (Tr.)
Trumpet in D	Tromba piccola (Tr. picc.)		
Cornet	Cornetta [*pl.* Cornetti, Ctti.]	Kornett	Cornet à pistons (C. à p., Pist.)
Trombone (Tr., Tbe., Trb., Trm., Trbe.)	Trombone (Tromb.) [*pl.* Tromboni (Tbni., Trni.)]	Posaune (Ps., Pos.)	Trombone (Tr.)
Bass trombone Tuba (Tb.)	Tuba (Tb., Tba.)	Tuba (Tb.) [*also* Basstuba (Btb.)]	Tuba (Tb.)
Ophicleide (Oph.)	Oficleide	Ophikleide	Ophicléide
		PERCUSSION	
Percussion (Perc.), Battery	Percussione	Schlagzeug (Schlag.)	Batterie (Batt.)
Kettledrums (K. D.)	Timpani (Timp., Tp.)	Pauken (Pk.)	Timbales (Timb.)
Snare drum (S. D., sn.)	Tamburo piccolo (Tamb. picc.) Tamburo militare (Tamb. milit.)	Kleine Trommel (Kl. Tr.)	Caisse claire (C. cl.); Tambour militaire (Tamb. milit.)
Tenor drum (T. D.)	Cassa rullante	Rührtrommel	Caisse roulante
Bass drum (B. drum, B. D.)	Gran cassa (Gr. Cassa, Gr. C., G. C.) Gran tamburo (Gr. Tamb.)	Grosse Trommel (Gr. Tr.)	Grosse caisse (Gr. c.)
Cymbals (Cym., Cymb.) Tam-Tam (Tam.-T.)	Piatti (P., Ptti., Piat.) Cinelli	Becken (Beck.)	Cymbales (Cym.)

English	*Italian*	*German*	*French*
Tambourine (Tamb.)	Tamburino (Tamb.)	Schellentrommel; Tamburin	Tambour de Basque (T. de B., Tamb. de Basque)
Triangle (Trgl., Tri.)	Triangolo (Trgl.)	Triangel	Triangle (Triang.)
Glockenspiel (Glock.)	Campanelli (Cmp.)	Glockenspiel	Carillon
Bells; Chimes tubular bells, orchestral bells	Campane (Cmp., Camp.)	Glocken	Cloches
Antique cymbals	Crotali; Piatti antichi	Antike Zimbeln	Crotales; Cymbales antiques
Sleigh bells (S.bells)	Sonagli (Son.)	Schellen	Grelots
Xylophone (Xyl.)	Xilofono	Xylophon	Xylophone
Cowbells		Herdenglocken	
Crash cymbal			Grande cymbale chinoise
Siren			Sirène
Lion's roar			Tambour à corde
Slapstick			Fouet
Wood blocks			Blocs chinois
Castanet (Cast.)	Castagnette	Kastagnette	Castagnette
Bongos			
Bell tree			
Tom tom			
Conga			
Guiro			
Maracas (Marac.)			
	STRINGS		
Violin (V., Vl., Vln., Vi., Vn.)	Violino (V., Vl., Vln., Viol.)	Violine (V., Vl., Vln.); Geige (Gg.)	Violon (V., Vl., Vln.)
Viola (Va., Vl.) [*pl.* Vas.]	Viola (Va., Vla.) [*pl.* Viole (Vle.)]	Bratsche (Br.)	Alto (A.)
Violoncello; Cello (Vcl., Vc.)	Violoncello (Vc., Vlc., Vcllo.)	Violoncell (Vc., Vlc.)	Violoncelle (Vc.)
Double bass (D. Bs.)	Contrabasso (Cb., C. B.) [*pl.* Contrabassi or Bassi (C. Bassi, Bi.)]	Kontrabass (Kb.)	Contrebasse (C. B.)

OTHER INSTRUMENTS			
English	*Italian*	*German*	*French*
Harp (Hp., Hrp.)	Arpa (A., Arp.)	Harfe (Hrf.)	Harpe (Hp.)
Piano (Pa.)	Pianoforte (P.-f., Pft.)	Klavier	Piano
Celesta (Cel.)	Celesta	Celesta	Célesta
Harpsichord	Cembalo	Cembalo	Clavecin
Harmonium (Harmon.)			
Organ (Org.)	Organo	Orgel	Orgue
Synthesizer			
Guitar	Chitarra	Gitarre (Git.)	Guitare
Mandolin (Mand.)			
Marimba			
Vibraphone (Vib.)			
Sampler			
Uilleann pipes			
Accordion			
Concertina			
Erhu			
Yangqin			

Voice Designations

English	*German*
Soprano (S)	Sopran
Alto (A)	Alt
Tenor (T)	Tenor
Bass (B)	Bass
Voice	Singstimme
Voice in Sprechstimme	Rezitation
Chorus	Chor

Names of Scale Degrees and Modes

English	*Italian*	*German*	*French*
		SCALE DEGREES	
C	do	C	ut
C-sharp	do diesis	Cis	ut dièse
D-flat	re bemolle	Des	ré bémol
D	re	D	ré
D-sharp	re diesis	Dis	ré dièse
E-flat	mi bemolle	Es	mi bémol
E	mi	E	mi
E-sharp	mi diesis	Eis	mi dièse
F-flat	fa bemolle	Fes	fa bémol
F	fa	F	fa
F-sharp	fa diesis	Fis	fa dièse
G-flat	sol bemolle	Ges	sol bémol
G	sol	G	sol
G-sharp	sol diesis	Gis	sol dièse
A-flat	la bemolle	As	la bémol
A	la	A	la
A-sharp	la diesis	Ais	la dièse
B-flat	si bemolle	B	si bémol
B	si	H	si
B-sharp	si diesis	His	si dièse
C-flat	do bemolle	Ces	ut bémol
		MODES	
major	maggiore	dur	majeur
minor	minore	moll	mineur

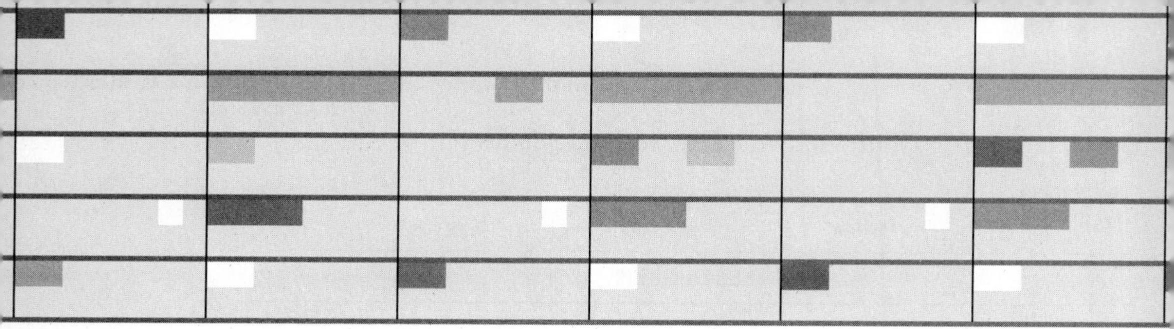

Appendix C

Glossary of Musical Terms Used in the Scores

The following glossary is not intended to be a complete dictionary of musical terms, nor is knowledge of all these terms necessary to follow the scores in this book. However, as listeners gain experience in following scores, they will find it useful and interesting to understand the composer's directions with regard to tempo, dynamics, and methods of performance.

In most cases, compound terms have been broken down and defined separately, as they often recur in varying combinations. A few common foreign-language words are included in addition to the musical terms. Note that names and abbreviations for instruments and for scale degrees will be found in Appendix B.

8va If written above a passage, an indication to play the passage an octave higher; if written below a passage, an indication to play the passage an octave lower.
16va If written above a passage, an indication to play the passage two octaves higher; if written below a passage, an indication to play the passage two octaves lower.
\+ Closed (hi-hat cymbals).
o Open (hi-hat cymbals).
𝄋 Sign (segno).

a The phrases *a 2, a 3* (etc.) indicate the number of parts to be played by 2, 3 (etc.) players; when a simple number (1, 2, etc.) is placed over a part, it indicates that only the first (second, etc.) player in that group should play.
ab Off.
aber But.
accelerando (accel.) Growing faster.

accentato, accentué Accented.
accompagnando Accompanying.
accompagnemento Accompaniment.
accordato, accordez Tune the instrument as specified.
adagio Slow, leisurely.
affettuoso With emotion.
affrettare (affrett.) Hastening a little.
agitando, agitato Agitated, excited.
al fine "The end"; an indication to return to the start of a piece and to repeat it only to the point marked "fine."
alla breve Indicates two beats to a measure, at a rather quick tempo.
allargando (allarg.) Growing broader.
alle, alles All, every, each.
allegramente Allegro, happily.
allegretto A moderately fast tempo (between allegro and andante).
allegrezza Gaiety.
allegro A rapid tempo (between allegretto and presto).
allein Alone, solo.
allmählich Gradually *(allmählich wieder gleich mässig fliessend werden,* gradually becoming even-flowing again).
alta, alto, altus (A.) The deeper of the two main divisions of women's (or boys') voices.
am Steg On the bridge (of a string instrument).
ancora Again.
andante A moderately slow tempo (between adagio and allegretto).
andantino A moderately slow tempo.
Anfang Beginning, initial.
anima Spirit, animation.
animando With increasing animation.
animant, animato, animé, animez Animated.
aperto Indicates open notes on the horn, open strings, and undamped piano notes.
a piacere The execution of the passage is left to the performer's discretion.
appassionato Impassioned.
appena Scarcely, hardly.
apprensivo Apprehensive.
archet Bow.
archi, arco Played with the bow.
arditamente Boldly.
arpeggiando, arpeggiato (arpegg.) Played in harp style, i.e., the notes of the chord played in quick succession rather than simultaneously.
arrêt Break (as in *arrêt long,* long break).
articulato Articulated, separated.
assai Very.
assez Fairly, rather.
attacca Begin what follows without pausing.
a tempo At the original tempo.
auf dem On the (as in *auf dem G,* on the G string).
Ausdruck Expression.
ausdrucksvoll With expression.
äusserst Extreme, utmost.
avec With.

bacchetta, bacchetti (bacch.) Drumsticks (*bachetti di spugna,* sponge-headed drumsticks).
baguettes Drumsticks (*baguettes de bois, wooden drumsticks; baguettes d'éponge,* sponge-headed drumsticks; *baguettes dures,* hard mallets; *baguettes midures,* medium-hard mallets or drumsticks.
bass, bassi, basso, bassus (B.) The lowest male voice.
battere, battuta, battuto (batt.) To beat.
beaucoup A lot.
Becken Cymbals.
bedeutend bewegter With significantly more movement.
behaglich heiter Pleasingly serene or cheerful.
beider Hände With both hands.
ben Very.
bend A slight alteration, or lowering, of the pitch.
bewegt Agitated.
bewegter More agitated.
bisbigliando, bispiglando (bis.) Whispering.
bis zum Schluss dieser Szene To the end of this scene.
blancos White keys (*glissando sobre blancos, glissando* on the white keys of the piano).
blasen Blow.
Blech Brass instruments.
bogen (bog.) Played with the bow.
bois Woodwind.
bouché Muted.
bourdon Organ stop of capped flue pipes producing a dark sound.

break A jazz term for a fast, solo passage, usually without accompaniment.
breit Broadly.
breiter More broadly.
bridge On a bowed string instrument, a wedge-shaped device that holds the strings in place and transmits the vibrations to the body of the instrument. On a piano, a rail that holds the strings and transmits vibrations to the soundboard.
brilliante Brilliant.
brio Spirit, vivacity.
brushes Fan-shaped wires that are bound together and used to play the snare drum and cymbals, especially in jazz.
burden Refrain.

cadenza (cad., cadenz.) An extended passage for solo instrument in free, improvisatory style.
calando (cal.) Diminishing in volume and speed.
calma, calmo Calm, calmly.
cantabile (cant.) In a singing style.
cantando In a singing manner.
canto Voice (as in *col canto,* a direction for the accompaniment to follow the solo part in tempo and expression).
cantus An older designation for the highest part in a vocal work.
capriccio Capriciously, whimsically.
cedendo Yielding.
cédez Slow down.
changez Change (usually an instruction to retune a string or an instrument).
Chinese ride A type of cymbals used particularly in jazz and popular music.
chiuso closed, stopped. See *gestopft.*
choke A sudden stopping of vibration, as on the cymbals.
chorus In jazz, a single statement of the melodic-harmonic pattern (e.g., 12-bar blues).
chromatisch Chromatic.
circa (ca.) About, approximately.
coda The last part of a piece.
col, colla, colle, coll' With the.
colore Colored.
come prima, come sopra As at first, as previously.
commodo Comfortable, easy.
con With.
corda String; for example, *seconda (2a) corda* is the second string (the A string on the violin).
corto Short, brief.
court Short.
crescendo (cres.) An increase in volume.
cuivré Played with a harsh, blaring tone.
cupa, cupo Gloomy, somber.

da capo (D.C.) Repeat from the beginning.
dal segno (D.S.) Repeat from the sign.
damper A felt-covered device on a piano that prevents a string from vibrating except when the key is depressed.
Dämpfer (dpf.) Mutes.
dazu In addition to that, for that purpose.
de, des, die Of, from.
début Beginning.
deciso Determined, resolute.
declamando In a declamatory style.
decrescendo (decresc., decr.) A decreasing of volume.
dehors Outside.
delay Playing behind the beat, common in blues and jazz.
delicato Delicate, delicately.
dem To the.
détaché With a broad, vigorous bow stroke, each note bowed singly.
deutlich Distinctly.
d'exécution Performance.
diminuendo, diminuer (dim., dimin.) A decreasing of volume.
distinto Distinct, clear.
divisés, divisi (div.) Divided; indicates that the instrumental group should be divided into two parts to play the passage in question.
dolce Sweetly and softly.
dolcemente Sweetly.
dolcissimo (dolciss.) Very sweetly.
dolore, doloroso With sorrow.
Doppelgriff Double stop.
doppio Double (as in *doppio movimento,* twice as fast).
doux Sweetly.
drammatico Dramatic.
drängend Pressing on.

dreifach Triple.
dreitaktig Three beats to a measure.
dur Major, as in G dur (G major).
durée Duration.

e, et And.
eilen To hurry.
ein One, a.
elegante Elegant, graceful.
Empfindung Feeling.
energico Energetically.
enharmonic Pitches that are the same but are spelled differently (e.g., C-sharp and D-flat).
espansione Expansion, broadening.
espressione With expression.
espressivo (espr., espress.) Expressively.
étouffez Muted, dampened.
etwas Somewhat, rather.
expressif Expressively.

facile Simple.
falsetto Male voice singing above normal range, with light sound.
feroce Fierce, ferocious.
fin, fine End, close.
Flatterzunge (Flatterz., Flzg.), flutter-tongue A special tonguing technique for wind instruments, producing a rapid, trill-like sound.
flebile Feeble, plaintive, mournful.
fliessend Flowing.
forte (f) Loud.
fortepiano (fp) Loud, then soft immediately.
fortissimo (ff) Very loud (*fff* indicates a still louder dynamic).
forza Force.
forzando (fz) Forcing, strongly accented.
forzandissimo (ffz) Very strongly accented.
fou Frantic.
frappez To strike.
frei Freely.
freihäng., freihängendes Hanging freely. An indication to the percussionist to let the cymbals vibrate freely.
frisch Fresh, lively.
fuoco Fire.
furioso Furiously.
furore Fury, rage.

ganz Entirely, altogether.
Ganzton Whole tone.
gedämpft (ged.) Muted.
geheimnisvoll Mysteriously.
geschlagen Pulsating.
gestopft (gest.) Stopping the notes of a horn; that is, the hand is placed in the bell of the horn to produce a muffled sound. Also *chiuso.*
geteilt (get.) Divided; indicates that the instrumental group should be divided into two parts to play the passage in question.
getragen Sustained.
gewöhnlich As usual.
giocoso Humorous.
giusto Moderately.
glissando (gliss.) Rapid scales produced by running the fingers over all the strings.
gradamente Gradually.
grande Large, great.
grande orgue (G.O.) The main division of an organ (great organ, English; *Hauptwerk*, German).
grandezza Grandeur.
grandioso Grandiose.
grave Slow, solemn; deep, low.
grazioso Gracefully.
Griffbrett Fingerboard.
grosser Auftakt Big upbeat.
growl A rough, "dirty" tone produced by brass and woodwinds instruments; used in jazz.
gut Good, well.

Hälfte Half.
harmonics Individual, pure sounds that are part of a musical tone; on string instruments, crystalline tones in the very high register, produced by lightly touching a vibrating string at a certain point.
hat A brass mute in the shape of a derby hat, held by the brim; used in jazz.
Hauptzeitmass Original tempo.
hauteur réelle In the octave notated, designation for transposing French horns.
head The tune and chord progression, in jazz.
hervortreten Prominent.
hi-hat Pair of cymbals suspended horizontally on a stand and operated

with a foot pedal; part of a drum set used in jazz.
hoch High, nobly.
Holz Woodwinds.
Holzschlägel Wooden drumstick.

im gleichen Rhythmus In the same rhythm.
immer Always.
impalpable Imperceptively.
in Oktaven In octaves.
insensibilmente Slightly, imperceptibly.
intensa Intensely.
interlude A connecting musical passage between movements or large sections of a work.
istesso tempo Duration of beat remains unaltered despite meter change.

jeté On a string instrument, the bow is thrown so that it bounces on the string with a series of rapid notes.
jeu Playful.
jusqu'à Until.

kadenzieren To cadence.
klagend Lamenting.
kleine Little.
klingen To sound.
komisch bedeutsam Very humorously.
kurz Short.

laissez To allow; *laisser vibrer*, to let vibrate.
langsam Slow.
langsamer Slower.
languendo, langueur Languor.
l'archet See archet.
largamente Broadly.
larghetto Slightly faster than largo.
largo A very slow tempo.
lasci, lassen To abandon.
lebhaft Lively.
lebhafter Livelier.
legatissimo A more forceful indication of *legato*.
legato Performed without any perceptible interruption between notes.
légèrement, leggieramente Lightly.
leggierissimo Very light.
leggiero (legg.) Light and graceful.
legno The wood of the bow (*col legno gestrich*, played with the wood).
lent Slow.
lentamente Slowly.
lento A slow tempo (between andante and largo).
l.h. Abbreviation for "left hand."
libetum Liberty (*ad libitum*, at liberty, at the pleasure of the performer).
licenzia License with tempo (*con licenzia*, with license or liberty).
liricamente Lyrically.
loco Indicates a return to the written pitch, following a passage played an octave higher or lower than written.
loin Distant, faraway.
Luftpause Pause for breath.
lunga Long, sustained.
lusingando Caressing.

ma, mais But.
maestoso Majestic.
mailloche Timpani mallet.
mano derecha Right hand (m.d.), in piano music.
mano izquierda Left hand (m.i.), in piano music.
marcatissimo (marcatiss.) With very marked emphasis.
marcato (marc.) Marked, with emphasis.
marcia March.
marschmässig, nicht eilen Moderate-paced march, not rushed.
marziale Military, martial, marchlike.
mässig Moderately.
mässiger More moderately.
melodia Melody.
même Same.
meno Less.
mettez With (as in *mettez les sourdines*, with the mutes).
mezza, mezzo Half, medium.
mezzo forte (mf) Moderately loud.
mezzo piano (mp) Moderately soft.
mezzo voce With half voice, restrained.
mindestens At least.
misterioso Mysterious.
misura Measured.
mit With.
moderatissimo A more forceful indication of *moderato*.
moderato, modéré At a moderate tempo.
moins Less.
molto Very, much.
mordenti Biting, pungent.

morendo Dying away.
mormorato Murmured.
mosso Rapid.
moto Motion.
mouvement (mouv., mouvt.) Tempo (as in au *mouvement*, a tempo).
movimento Movement, pace.
muta, mutano Change the tuning of the instrument as specified.

nach After.
naturalezza A natural, unaffected manner.
nel modo russico In the Russian style.
neuen New.
nicht Not.
niente Nothing.
nimmt To take; to seize.
noch Still.
node A point at which vibrations do not occur.
non Not.
nuovo New.

obere, oberer (ob.) Upper, leading.
oder langsamer Or slower.
offen Open.
ohne Without.
ondeggiante Undulating movement of the bow, which produces a tremolo effect.
open On a French horn, removing the hand or mute; unmuted.
ordinairement Ordinarily, normally.
ordinario (ord., ordin.) In the usual way (generally canceling an instruction to play using some special technique).
ossia An alternative (usually easier) version of a passage.
ôtez vite les sourdines Remove the mutes quickly.
ottava Octave (as in *8va*, octave higher than written; *8 basso, 8 bassa*, octave lower than written; *16 va*, two octaves higher than written).
ottoni Brass.
ouvert Open.

parte Part *(colla parte, colle parti*, the accompaniment is to follow the soloist[s] in tempo).
passionato Passionately.
passione Passion, emotion.
Paukenschlägel Timpani stick.
pavillons en l'air An indication to the player of a wind instrument to raise the bell of the instrument upward.
pedal, pedale (ped., P.) (1) In piano music, indicates that the damper pedal should be depressed; an asterisk indicates the point of release (brackets below the music are also used to indicate pedaling); (2) on an organ, the pedals are a keyboard played with the feet.
per During.
perdant fading (as in *en se perdant*, dying away).
perdendosi Gradually dying away.
pesante Heavily.
peu Little, a little.
piacevole Agreeable, pleasant.
pianissimo (pp) Very soft (*ppp* indicates a still softer dynamic).
piano (p) Soft.
piena Full.
più More.
pizzicato (pizz.) The string plucked with the finger.
plötzlich Suddenly, immediately.
plunger A plunger-shaped trombone mute that is held in the left hand and moved in front of and away from the bell; used in jazz.
plus More.
pochissimo (pochiss.) Very little, a very little.
poco Little, a little.
poco a poco Little by little.
ponticello (pont.) The bridge (of a string instrument).
portamento *Continuous* smooth and rapid sliding between two pitches.
portando Carrying.
position naturel (pos. nat.) In the normal position (usually canceling an instruction to play using some special technique).
possibile Possible.
precedente Previous, preceding.
precipitato Rushed, hurried.
premier mouvement (1er mouvt.) At the original tempo.
prenez Take up.
prepared piano A piano in which various objects have been inserted between the strings to alter the sound; introduced by John Cage.
préparez Prepare.

presque Almost, nearly.
presser To speed up.
prestissimo A more forceful indication of *presto.*
presto A very quick tempo (faster than allegro).
prima, primo First, principal.
principale First, principal, solo.
punto Point.

quarta Fourth.
quasi Almost, as if.
quinto Fifth.

ralentissez Slow down.
rallentando (rall., rallent.) Growing slower.
rapidamente Quickly.
rapide Rapid, fast.
rapidissimo (rapidiss.) Very quickly.
rasch Quickly.
rascher More quickly.
rauschend Rustling, roaring.
Recit A manual on the French organ for solo stops.
recitative, recitativo (recit.) A vocal style designed to imitate and emphasize the natural inflections of speech.
rein Perfect interval.
reprenez Take again, put on again.
resonante Resonating.
respiro Pause for breath.
retenu Held back.
revenir au tempo Return to the original tempo.
r.h. Abbreviation for "right hand."
rianimando Reanimating.
richtig Correct (*richtige Lage,* correct pitch).
rien Nothing.
rigore di tempo Strictness of tempo.
rigueur Rigor, strictness.
rinforzando (rf, rfz, rinf.) A sudden accent on a single note or chord.
risoluto In a resolute or determined manner.
ritardando (rit., ritard.) Gradually slackening in speed.
ritenuto (riten.) Immediate reduction of speed.
ritmato, ritmico Rhythmic.
ritornando, ritornello (ritor.) Refrain.
robuste Robustly.
rubato A certain elasticity and flexibility of tempo, consisting of slight accelerandos and ritardandos according to the requirements of the musical expression.
ruhig Quietly.

saltando Leaping.
sans Without.
scat A jazz vocal style that sets syllables without meaning (vocables) to an improvised vocal line.
Schalltrichter Horn.
scherzando (scherz.) Playful.
schlagen To strike in a usual manner.
Schlagwerk Striking mechanism.
schleppen, schleppend Dragging.
Schluss Cadence, conclusion.
schnell Fast.
schneller Faster.
schon Already.
Schwammschägeln Sponge-headed drumstick.
scorrevole Flowing, gliding.
sec, secco Dry, simple.
secunda Second.
segno Sign; used to mark the beginning or ending of a repeated section (*dal segno, D.S.,* from the sign; *sino al segno,* until the sign).
sehr Very.
semplice Simple.
semplicità Simplicity.
sempre Always, continually.
senza Without.
serre Short, pronounced (*tres serre,* very short or pronounced).
sforzando (sf., sfz.) With sudden emphasis.
sforzandissimo (sff, sffz) With very loud, sudden attack.
shake An effect on a brass instrument resembling an exaggerated vibrato, produced by shaking the instrument against the lips while playing; used in jazz.
simile (sim.) In a similar manner.
sin Without.
Singstimme Singing voice.
sino al Up to the . . . (usually followed by a new tempo marking, or by a dotted line indicating a terminal point).
si piace Especially pleasing.

smear An exaggerated bending of a semitone or tone down and then up again; often played with a harsh tone; used by brass instruments in jazz.
smorzando (smorz.) Dying away.
sobre On.
sofort Immediately.
soli, solo (s.) Executed by one performer.
son naturel Natural sound; on a brass instrument, played without valves.
sonoro Sonorous, resonant.
sopra Above; in piano music, used to indicate that one hand must pass above the other.
soprano (S.) The voice classification with the highest range.
sordini, sordino (sord.) Mute.
sostenendo, sostenuto (sost.) Sustained.
sotto voce In an undertone, subdued, under the breath.
sourdine (sourd.) Mute.
soutenu Sustained.
spiel, spielen Play (an instrument).
Spieler Player, performer.
spirito Spirit, soul.
spiritoso In a spirited manner.
spugna Sponge.
squeeze Squeezing the embouchure to raise the pitch; used in jazz.
staccatissimo Extremely detached or staccato.
staccato (stacc.) Detached, separated, abruptly, disconnected.
stentando, stentare, stentato (stent.) Delaying, retarding.
stesso The same.
Stimme Voice.
stimmen To tune.
stopped On a French horn, closing the opening of the bell with the hand or a mute.
straight mute (st. mute) A conical or pear-shaped brass mute in which the wider end is closed.
strascinare To drag.
straziante Agonizing, heart-rending.
Streichinstrumente (Streichinstr.) Bowed string instruments.
strepitoso Noisy, loud.
stretto In a non-fugal composition, indicates a concluding section at an increased speed.
stringendo (string.) Quickening.
subito (sub.) Suddenly, immediately.
suivez Follow (as in *suivez le solo*, follow the solo line).
sul On the (as in *sul* G, on the G string).
superius In older music, the uppermost part.
sur On.

tacet The instrument or vocal part so marked is silent.
tasto Fingerboard (as in *sul tasto*, bow over the fingerboard).
tasto solo In a continuo part, this indicates that only the string instrument plays; the chord-playing instrument is silent.
tema Theme.
tempo primo (tempo I) At the original tempo.
teneramente, tenero Tenderly, gently.
tenor, tenore (T.) The highest male voice.
tenuto (ten., tenu.) Held, sustained.
tertia Third.
tief Deep, low.
timbre Tone color.
timpanista Timpanist.
touche Key; note; fingerboard (as in *sur la touche*, on the fingerboard).
toujours Always, continually.
tranquillo Quietly, calmly.
tre corde (t.c.) Release the soft (or *una corda*) pedal of the piano.
tremolo (trem.) On string instruments, a quick reiteration of the same tone, produced by a rapid up-and-down movement of the bow; also a rapid alternation between two different notes.
très Very.
trill (tr.) The rapid alternation of a given note with the diatonic second above it. In a drum part, it indicates rapid alternating strokes with two drumsticks.
tromba Trumpet (as in *quasi tromba*, trumpet-like).
Trommschlag (Tromm.) Drumbeat.
troppo Too much.
tutta la forza Very emphatically.
tutti Literally, "all"; usually means all the instruments in a given category as distinct from a solo part.

übergreifen To overlap.
übertonend Drowning out.
umstimmen To change the tuning.
un One, a.
una corda (u.c.) With the "soft" pedal of the piano depressed.
und And.
unison (unis.) The same notes or melody played by several instruments at the same pitch. Often used to emphasize that a phrase is not to be divided among several players.
unmerklich Imperceptible.

velocissimo Very swiftly.
verklingen lassen To let die away.
vibrare, vibrer To sound, vibrate.
vibrato (vibr.) To fluctuate the pitch on a single note.
vierfach Quadruple.
vierhändig Four-hand piano music.
vif Lively.
vigoroso Vigorous, strong.
violento Violent.
viva, vivente, vivo Lively.
vivace Quick, lively.
vivacissimo A more forceful indication of vivace.
voce Voice (as in *colla voce*, a direction for the accompaniment to follow the solo part in tempo and expression).
volles Orch. Entire orchestra.
vorbereiten Prepare, get ready.
Vorhang auf Curtain up.
Vorhang zu Curtain down.
vorher Beforehand, previously.
voriges Preceding.

Waltzertempo In the tempo of a waltz.
weg Away, beyond.
weich Mellow, smooth, soft.
wie aus der Fern As if from afar.
wieder Again.
wie zu Anfang dieser Szene As at the beginning of this scene.

zart Tenderly, delicately.
Zeit Time; duration.
zögernd Slower.
zu The phrases *zu 2, zu 3* (etc.) indicate the number of parts to be played by 2, 3 (etc.) players.
zum In addition.
zurückhaltend Slackening in speed.
zurücktreten To withdraw.
zweihändig With two hands.

Appendix D

Concordance Table for Recordings and Listening Guides

The following table provides cross-references to the Listening Guides (LG) in *The Enjoyment of Music,* Ninth Edition, by Joseph Machlis and Kristine Forney (New York: Norton, 2003). The following abbreviations are used throughout: *Chr* for the Chronological version, *Std* for the Standard version, and *Sh* for the Shorter version. The table also gives the location of each work on both recording sets (see "A Note on the Recordings," p. xiv).

Chr LG#	*Std* LG#	*Sh* LG#	Score Number, Composer, Title	Score Page	*8-CD Set*	*4-CD Set*
41	2	21	1. Schubert: *Erlkönig (Erlking)*	1	5/1–8	1/80–87
40	33	—	2. Schubert: Lied, *Die Forelle (The Trout)*	9	5/9–11	—
40	33		3. *Trout* Quintet, fourth movement	15	5/12–18	—
48	9	25	4. Berlioz: *Symphonie fantastique*			
			Fourth movement	32	5/19–24	3/9–14
			Fifth movement	53	5/25–31	—
43	4	—	5. Fanny Mendelssohn Hensel: *Bergeslust (Mountain Yearning)*, Op. 10, No. 5	109	5/32–34	—
52	13	—	6. Felix Mendelssohn: Violin Concerto in E minor, Op. 64, first movement	115	5/35–43	—
45	6	—	7. Chopin: Prelude in E minor, Op. 28, No. 4	165	5/44–45	—
44	5	23	8. Chopin: Nocturne in C minor, Op. 48, No. 1	167	5/46–48	2/61–63

CHR LG#	STD LG#	SH LG#	SCORE NUMBER, COMPOSER, TITLE	SCORE PAGE	8-CD SET	4-CD SET
42	3	22	9. ROBERT SCHUMANN: "Und wüssten's die Blumen" ("And if the flowers knew"), from *Dichterliebe (A Poet's Love)*, No. 8	174	5/49–52	2/57–60
46	7	—	10. LISZT: *La campanella (The Little Bell)*	179	6/4–13	—
56	17	30	11. WAGNER: *Die Walküre*			
			Act III, Farewell and Magic Fire Music	189	5/53–57	—
			Act III, Magic Fire Music (only)			3/37–39
55	16	29	12. VERDI: *Rigoletto*, Act III			
			Aria, "La donna è mobile" ("Woman is fickle")	200	6/14–15	3/31–33
			Quartet, "Un dí, se ben rammentomi" ("One day, if I remember right")	205	6/16–19	3/34–36
47	8	24	13. CLARA SCHUMANN: Scherzo, Op. 10	225	6/20–27	3/1–8
49	10	26	14. SMETANA: *Vltava (The Moldau)*	236	6/28–35	3/15–22
54	15	28	15. BRAHMS: *Ein deutsches Requiem (A German Requiem)*, fourth movement	301	5/58–62	3/26–30
50	11	27	16. BRAHMS: Symphony No. 3 in F major, Op. 90, third movement	313	6/1–3	3/23–25
57	18	—	17. BIZET: *Carmen*, Act I			
			No. 3. Chorus, "Avec la garde montante" ("Along with the relief guard")	331	6/36–38	—
			Recitative, "C'est bien là" ("It's right there")	340	6/39	—
			No. 4. Chorus, "La cloche a sonné" ("The bell has rung")	343	6/40–42	—
			No. 5. *Habanera*, "L'amour est un oiseau rebelle" ("Love is a rebellious bird")	354	6/43	—
60	21	33	18. TCHAIKOVSKY: *The Nutcracker*			
			March	366	6/44–46	3/43–45
			Dance of the Sugar Plum Fairy	390	6/47–49	—
			Trepak (Russian Dance)	399	6/50–52	—
51	12	—	19. DVOŘÁK: Symphony No. 9 in E minor, *From the New World*, first movement	414	6/53–61	—
58	19	31	20. PUCCINI: *Madama Butterfly*, "Un bel dí" ("One beautiful day")	467	7/1–2	3/40–41
61	61	—	21. MAHLER: *Das Lied von der Erde (The Song of the Earth)*, third movement	473	7/3–6	—
62	62	34	22. DEBUSSY: *Prélude à "L'aprés-midi d'un faune" (Prelude to "The Afternoon of a Faun")*	485	6/62–66	3/46–50

CHR LG#	STD LG#	SH LG#	SCORE NUMBER, COMPOSER, TITLE	SCORE PAGE	8-CD SET	4-CD SET
53	14	—	23. BEACH: Violin Sonata in A minor, second movement	518	7/7–9	—
73	73	40	24. JOPLIN: *Maple Leaf Rag*	526	7/10–14	4/23–27
66	66	36	25. SCHOENBERG: *Pierrot lunaire*			
			No. 18, *Der Mondfleck (The Moonfleck)*	530	7/15–16	4/1–2
			No. 21, *O alter Duft ausMärchenzeit (O Scent of Fabled Yesteryear)*	536	7/17–18	—
70	70	—	26. IVES: *The Things Our Fathers Loved*	541	7/19–20	—
63	63	—	27. RAVEL: *Rapsodie espagnole (Spanish Rhapsody)*, fourth movement, *Feria*	544	7/21–26	—
69	69	37	28. BARTÓK: *Concerto for Orchestra*, fourth movement, *Interrupted Intermezzo*	596	7/27–33	4/3–9
64	64	35	29. STRAVINSKY: *Le sacre du printemps (The Rite of Spring)*, Part II			
			Glorification de l'élue (Glorification of the Chosen One)	608	7/34–36	3/51–53
			Evocation des ancêtres (Evocation of the Ancestors)	622	7/37	3/54
			Action rituelle des ancêtres (Ritual Action of the Ancestors)	626	7/38–42	3/55–59
65	65	—	30. STRAVINSKY: *L'histoire du soldat (The Soldier's Tale), Marche royale (Royal March)*	637	7/43–47	—
68	68	—	31. WEBERN: Symphony, Op. 21, second movement	647	7/48–50	—
67	67	—	32. BERG: *Wozzeck*, Act III			
			Scene 4	656	7/51–52	—
			Interlude	670	7/53	—
			Scene 5	675	7/54	—
90	90	—	33. PROKOFIEV: *Alexander Nevsky*, seventh movement	682	7/55–58	—
77	77	43	34. GERSHWIN: Piano Prelude No. 1	696	7/59–61	4/41–43
72	72	39	35. REVUELTAS: *Homenaje a Federico García Lorca (Homage to Federico García Lorca)*, third movement, *Son*	701	7/62–69	4/15–22
71	71	38	36. COPLAND: *Billy the Kid*, Scene 1, *Street in a Frontier Town*	718	7/70–74	4/10–14
82	82	—	37. MESSIAEN: *Quatour pour la fin du temps (Quartet for the End of Time), Vocalise*	760	7/75–77	—
85	85	—	38. CAGE: *Sonatas and Interludes*, Sonata V	769	7/78–79	—
74	74	41	39. HOLIDAY: *Billie's Blues*	772	8/1–7	4/28–34
75	75	—	40. STRAYHORN/ELLINGTON: *Take the A Train*	777	8/8–12	—
76	76	42	41. GILLESPIE/PARKER: *A Night in Tunisia*	808	8/13–18	4/35–40

CHR LG#	STD LG#	SH LG#	SCORE NUMBER, COMPOSER, TITLE	SCORE PAGE	8-CD SET	4-CD SET
79	79	45	42. BERNSTEIN: *West Side Story*			
			Mambo	810	8/19–21	4/48–50
			Tonight Ensemble	833	8/22–29	4/51–58
87	87	48	43. LIGETI: *Désordre (Disorder)*, from *Etudes for Piano*, Book I	850	8/30–32	4/66–68
83	83	—	44. BOULEZ: *Le marteau sans maître (The Hammer Without a Master)*			
			No. 1	856	8/33	—
			No. 3	862	8/34	—
			No. 7	865	8/35	—
84	84	47	45. CRUMB: *Ancient Voices of Children*, first movement	870	8/36–38	4/63–65
78	78	44	46. BAKER: *Through This Vale of Tears*, sixth movement, *Sometimes I Feel Like a Motherless Child*	874	8/39–42	4/44–47
94	94	54	47. PÄRT: *Cantate Domino canticum novum (O sing to the Lord a new song)*	881	8/43–46	4/91–94
93	93	53	48. TOWER: *For the Uncommon Woman*	894	8/47–52	4/85–90
92	92	52	49. LANSKY: *Notjustmoreidlechatter*, excerpt	928	8/53–56	4/81–84
95	95	55	50. ADAMS: Chamber Symphony, third movement, *Roadrunner*	931	8/57–61	4/95–99
89	89	50	51. ABING: *Er quan ying yue (The Moon Reflected on the Second Springs)*	969	8/66–69	4/73–76
80	80	46	52. *Jongle à moi (Think of Me)*, by BEAUSOLEIL	971	8/70–73	4/59–62

Acknowledgments

Page 9: Franz Schubert, *Die Forelle,* D. 550. From Schubert, *Lieder I, Sopran oder Tenor.* Used by permission of C. F. Peters Corporation. **Page 15:** Franz Schubert, Quintet in A major for Piano and Strings, D. 667. Edited by Anke Butzer and Jürgen Neubacher. © 1988 Ernst Eulenburg & Co GmbH. Used by kind permission of European American Music Distributors LLC, sole U.S. and Canadian agent for Ernst Eulenburg Ltd. **Page 109:** Fanny Mendelssohn Hensel, *Bergeslust.* © Breitkopf & Härtel, Wiesbaden. **Page 115:** Felix Mendelssohn, Violin Concerto in E minor, Op. 64. Used by kind permission of European American Music Distributors LLC, sole U.S. and Canadian agent for Ernst Eulenburg Ltd. **Page 167:** Frédéric François Chopin, Nocturne in C minor, Op. 48, No. 1. Reprinted with permission of Dover Publications. **Page 174:** Robert Schumann, "Und wüssten's die Blumen" from *Dichterliebe,* No. 8. From C. F. Peters No. 2383a, *Lieder I, Original-Ausgabe.* Used by permission of C. F. Peters Corporation. **Page 189:** Richard Wagner, *Die Walküre.* English translation by Frederick Jameson. Copyright © 1936 (Renewed) by G. Schirmer, Inc. (ASCAP). International Copyright Secured. All Rights Reserved. Reprinted by Permission. **Page 200:** Giuseppe Verdi, *Rigoletto.* Copyright © 1957 (Renewed) by G. Schirmer, Inc. (ASCAP). International Copyright Secured. All Rights Reserved. Reprinted by Permission. **Page 225:** Clara Schumann, Scherzo, Op. 10. Reprinted with permission of G. Henle Verlag. **Page 301:** Johannes Brahms, *Ein deutsches Requiem.* From Edition Peters No. 3672. Used by permission of C. F. Peters Corporation. **Page 313:** Johannes Brahms, Symphony No. 3 in F major. Used by kind permission of European American Music Distributors LLC, sole U.S. and Canadian agent for Ernst Eulenburg Ltd. **Page 331:** Georges Bizet, *Carmen.* English translation by Ruth and Thomas Martin. Copyright © 1958 (Renewed) by G. Schirmer, Inc. (ASCAP). International Copyright Secured. All Rights Reserved. Reprinted by Permission. **Page 414:** Antonín Dvořák, Symphony No. 9 in E minor. Edited by Klaus Döge. © 1986 Ernst Eulenburg & Co GmbH. All Rights Reserved. Used by kind permission of European American Music Distributors LLC, sole

U.S. and Canadian agent for Ernst Eulenburg & Co GmbH. **Page 467:** Giacomo Puccini, *Madama Butterfly.* English translation by John Gutman. Copyright © 1963 (Renewed) by G. Schirmer, Inc. (ASCAP). International Copyright Secured. All Rights Reserved. Reprinted by Permission. **Page 473:** Gustav Mahler, *Das Lied von der Erde.* Copyright 1912 by Universal Edition A.G., Wien. Copyright renewed, assigned 1952 to Universal Edition (London) Ltd., London. © This edition, revised by the Internationale Gustav-Mahler-Gesellschaft, copyright 1962 by Universal Edition A. G., Wien, and Universal Edition (London) Ltd., London. © copyright renewed. All Rights Reserved. Used by permission of European American Music Distributors LLC, sole U.S. and Canadian agent for Universal Edition A. G., Wien and Universal Edition (London) Ltd., London. **Page 530:** Arnold Schoenberg, *Pierrot lunaire,* Op. 21. Used by permission of Belmont Music Publishers, Pacific Palisades, CA 90272. **Page 541:** Charles Ives, *The Things Our Fathers Loved.* Words and Music by Charles Ives. Copyright © 1955 by Peer International Corporation. Copyright Renewed. This arrangement Copyright © 2002 by Peer International Corporation. International Copyright Secured. All Rights Reserved. **Page 544:** Maurice Ravel, *Rapsodie espagnole.* © 1908. Joint ownership Redfield and Nordice. Exclusive representation by Editions Durand, Paris, France. Reproduced by permission of Editions Durand. **Page 596:** Béla Bartók, *Concerto for Orchestra.* Reprinted with permission of Boosey & Hawkes, Inc. **Page 608:** Igor Stravinsky, *Le sacre du printemps.* Reprinted with permission of Boosey & Hawkes, Inc. **Page 637:** Igor Stravinsky, *L'histoire du soldat.* Copyright © 1987, 1992 Chester Music Ltd. International Copyright Secured. All Rights Reserved. Used by Permission of G. Schirmer, Inc. (ASCAP). **Page 647:** Anton Webern, Symphony, Op. 21. Copyright 1929 by Universal Edition. Copyright renewed. All Rights Reserved. Used by permission of European American Music Distributors LLC, sole U.S. and Canadian agent for Universal Edition. **Page 656:** Alban Berg, *Wozzeck.* Full score Copyright 1926 by Universal Edition A. G., Wien. Full score Copyright renewed. English translation Copyright 1952 by Alfred A. Kalmus, London. English translation Copyright renewed. All Rights Reserved. Used by permission of European American Music Distributors LLC, sole U.S. and Canadian agent for Universal Edition A. G., Wien. **Page 682:** Sergei Prokofiev, *Alexander Nevsky.* Copyright © 1941 (Renewed) by G. Schirmer, Inc. (ASCAP). International Copyright Secured. All Rights Reserved. Reprinted by Permission. **Page 696:** George Gershwin, Piano Prelude No. 1. Reprinted with permission of European American Music Distributors LLC-Warner/Chappell. **Page 701:** Silvestre Revueltas, *Homenaje a Federico García Lorca.* © Copyright 1958 by Southern Music Publishing Co., Inc. Copyright Renewed. Used by Permission. **Page 718:** Aaron Copland, *Billy the Kid.* Reprinted with permission of Boosey &

Hawkes, Inc. **Page 760:** Olivier Messiaen, *Quatour pour la fin du temps.* © 1941 by Editions Durand, Paris, France. Reproduced by permission of Editions Durand. **Page 769:** John Cage, *Sonatas and Interludes.* Copyright © 1960 by Henmar Press Inc. **Page 772:** Billie Holiday, *Billie's Blues.* Words and Music by Billie Holiday. Copyright © 1956, 1962 by Edward B. Marks Music Company. Copyright Renewed. This arrangement Copyright © 2002 by Edward B. Marks Music Company. International Copyright Secured. All Rights Reserved. Used by Permission. **Page 777:** Billy Strayhorn/Duke Ellington, *Take the A Train.* Words and Music by Billy Strayhorn. Copyright © 1941; Renewed 1969 DreamWorks Songs (ASCAP) and Billy Strayhorn Songs, Inc. (ASCAP) for the U.S.A. This arrangement Copyright © 2002 DreamWorks Songs (ASCAP) and Billy Strayhorn Songs, Inc. (ASCAP) for the U.S.A. Rights for DreamWorks Songs and Billy Strayhorn Songs, Inc. Administered by Cherry Lane Music Publishing Company, Inc. International Copyright Secured. All Rights Reserved. **Page 808:** Dizzy Gillespie/Charlie Parker, *A Night in Tunisia.* Reprinted with permission of European American Music Distributors LLC-Warner/Chappell. **Page 810:** Leonard Bernstein, *West Side Story.* Reprinted with permission of Boosey & Hawkes, Inc. **Page 850:** György Ligeti, *Désordre.* © Schott Musik International, 1986. All Rights Reserved. Used by permission of European American Music Distributors LLC, sole U.S. and Canadian agent for Schott Musik International. **Page 856:** Pierre Boulez, *Le marteau sans maître.* © Copyright 1954 by Universal Edition (London) Ltd., London. Final version: © Copyright 1957 by Universal Edition (London) Ltd., London. © Copyright renewed. Poèmes de René Char: © Copyright 1964 by Jose Corti Editeur, Paris. © Copyright renewed. All Rights Reserved. Used by permission of European American Music Distributors LLC, sole U.S. and Canadian agent for Universal Edition (London) Ltd., London. **Page 870:** George Crumb, *Ancient Voices of Children.* Copyright © 1970 by C. F. Peters, 373 Park Avenue South, New York, NY 10016. Reprinted with permission of the publishers who published the score of the complete work under Peters Edition No. 66303. **Page 874:** David Baker, *Through this Vale of Tears.* © 1986 MMB Music, Inc., Saint Louis. Used by Permission. All Rights Reserved. **Page 881:** Arvo Pärt, *Cantate Domino canticum novum.* © Copyright 1980, 1997 by Universal Edition A. G., Wien. All Rights Reserved. Used by permission of European American Music Distributors LLC, sole U.S. and Canadian agent for Universal Edition A. G., Wien. **Page 894:** Joan Tower, *For the Uncommon Woman.* Copyright © 1992 by Associated Music Publishers, Inc. (BMI). International Copyright Secured. All Rights Reserved, Reprinted by Permission. **Page 928:** Paul Lansky, *Notjustmoreidlechatter.* Copyright © 2002 by GrimTim Music. **Page 931:** John Adams, Chamber Symphony. Reprinted with permission of Boosey & Hawkes, Inc.

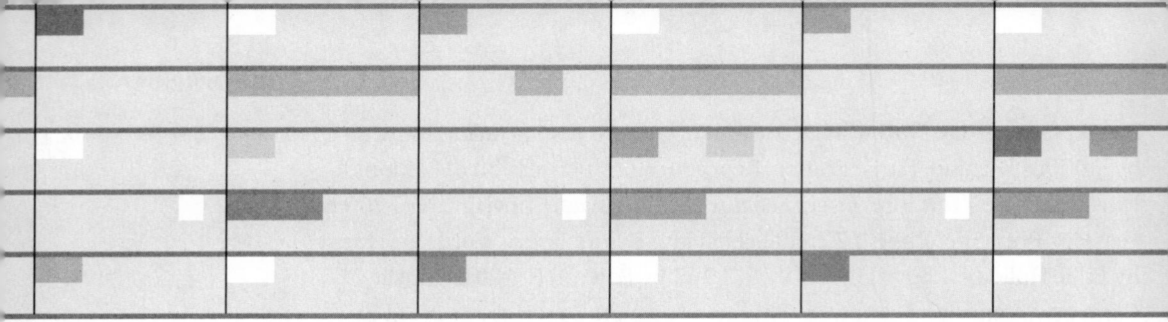

Index of Forms and Genres

A roman numeral following a title indicates a movement within the work.

A–B–A form: *see* ternary form

absolute music:
- BEACH, Violin Sonata in A minor (p. 518)
- BRAHMS, Symphony No. 3 in F major (p. 313)
- DVOŘÁK, Symphony No. 9 in E minor (*From the New World*) (p. 414)
- MENDELSSOHN, Violin Concerto in E minor (p. 115)

aria:
- BIZET, *Carmen,* Act I, *Habanera* (p. 354)
- PUCCINI, *Madama Butterfly,* "Un bel dí" (p. 467)
- VERDI, *Rigoletto,* Act III, "La donna è mobile" (p. 200)

art song: *see* song

ballet music:
- COPLAND, *Billy the Kid* (p. 718)
- DEBUSSY, *Prélude à "L'après-midi d'un faune"* (p. 485)
- STRAVINSKY, *Le sacre du printemps* (p. 608)
- TCHAIKOVSKY, *The Nutcracker* (p. 366)

big band jazz:
- STRAYHORN/ELLINGTON, *Take the A Train* (p. 777)

blues:
- HOLIDAY, *Billie's Blues* (p. 772)

cadenza:
- FELIX MENDELSSOHN, Violin Concerto in E minor, (p. 115)

Cajun music:
- *Jongle à moi* (p. 971)

cantata:
- PROKOFIEV, *Alexander Nevsky* (p. 682)

chamber music:
- ADAMS, *Chamber Symphony* (p. 931)
- BAKER, *Through This Vale of Tears* (p. 874)
- BEACH, Violin Sonata in A minor (p. 518)
- BOULEZ, *Le marteau sans maître* (p. 856)
- CRUMB, *Ancient Voices of Children* (p. 870)
- MESSIAEN, *Quatuor pour la fin du temps* (p. 760)
- SCHOENBERG, *Pierrot lunaire* (p. 530)

SCHUBERT, Piano Quintet in A major (*Trout*) (p. 15)
STRAVINSKY, *L'histoire du soldat* (p. 637)
Chinese traditional music:
ABING, *Er quan ying yue* (p. 969)
choral music:
BRAHMS, *A German Requiem* (p. 301)
PÄRT, *Cantate Domino canticum novum* (p. 881)
PROKOFIEV, *Alexander Nevsky* (p. 682)
chorus, operatic:
BIZET, *Carmen*, scene from Act I (p. 331)
computer music:
LANSKY, *Notjustmoreidlechatter* (p. 928)
concerto:
FELIX MENDELSSOHN, Violin Concerto in E minor (p. 115)
concerto, orchestral:
BARTÓK, *Concerto for Orchestra* (p. 596)

dance music:
BERNSTEIN, *West Side Story, Mambo* (p. 810)
Jongle á moi (p. 971)
JOPLIN, *Maple Leaf Rag* (p. 526)
RAVEL, *Rapsodie espagnole, Feria* (p. 544)
REVUELTAS, *Homenaje a Federico García Lorca* (p. 701)
TCHAIKOVSKY, *The Nutcracker*, (p. 366)
double-exposition form: *see* first-movement concerto form
durchkomponiert song: *see* through-composed song

electronic music:
LANSKY, *Notjustmoreidlechatter* (p. 928)
ensemble, operatic:
VERDI, *Rigoletto*, Act III, Quartet (p. 205)
étude:
LIGETI, *Désordre*, from *Etudes for Piano* (p. 850)
LISZT, *La campanella* (p. 179)

film music:
PROKOFIEV, *Alexander Nevsky* (p. 682)
first-movement concerto form:
FELIX MENDELSSOHN, Violin Concerto in E minor, I (p. 115)

interlude, orchestral:
BERG, *Wozzeck*, Act III (p. 670)

jazz:
GILLESPIE/PARKER, *A Night in Tunisia* (p. 808)
HOLIDAY, *Billie's Blues* (p. 772)
STRAYHORN/ELLINGTON, *Take the A Train* (p. 777)
jazz-influenced music:
BAKER, *Through this Vale of Tears* (p. 874)
GERSHWIN, Piano Prelude No. 1 (p. 696)

Lied: *see* song

march:
BERLIOZ, *Symphonie fantastique*, IV (p. 32)
STRAVINSKY, *L'histoire du soldat, Marche royale* (p. 637)
TCHAIKOVSKY, *The Nutcracker, March* (p. 366)
Mass, Requiem:
BRAHMS, *A German Requiem* (p. 301)
Mexican art music:
REVUELTAS, *Homenaje a Federico García Lorca* (p. 701)
musical theater:
BERNSTEIN, *West Side Story*, excerpts (p. 810)

nocturne:
CHOPIN, Nocturne in C minor, Op. 48, No. 1 (p. 167)
non-Western influences:
CAGE, *Sonatas and Interludes* (p. 769)
CRUMB, *Ancient Voices of Children* (p. 870)
LIGETI, *Désordre*, from *Etudes for Piano* (p. 850)

operatic scene:
BERG, *Wozzeck*, Act III, scenes 4 and 5 (p. 656)
BIZET, *Carmen*, scene from Act I (p. 331)
PUCCINI, *Madama Butterfly*, Act II, excerpt (p. 467)
VERDI, *Rigoletto*, Act III, excerpt (p. 200)
WAGNER, *Die Walküre*, Act III, scene 3 (p. 189)

orchestral music:
ADAMS, *Chamber Symphony* (p. 931)
BARTÓK, *Concerto for Orchestra* (p. 596)
BERLIOZ, *Symphonie fantastique* (p. 32)
BERNSTEIN, *West Side Story*, excerpts (p. 810)
BRAHMS, Symphony No. 3 in F major (p. 313)
COPLAND, *Billy the Kid* (p. 718)
DEBUSSY, *Prélude à "L'après-midi d'un faune"* (p. 485)
DVOŘÁK, Symphony No. 9 in E minor (*From the New World*) (p. 414)
FELIX MENDELSSOHN, Violin Concerto in E minor (p. 115)
RAVEL, *Rapsodie espagnole* (p. 544)
REVUELTAS, *Homenaje a Federico García Lorca* (p. 701)
SMETANA, *Vltava* (p. 236)
STRAVINSKY, *Le sacre du printemps* (p. 608)
TCHAIKOVSKY, *The Nutcracker* (p. 366)
TOWER, *For the Uncommon Woman* (p. 894)
WEBERN, Symphony, Op. 21 (p. 647)

piano music:
CHOPIN, Nocturne in C minor, Op. 48, No. 1 (p. 167); Prelude in E minor, Op. 28, No. 4 (p. 165)
GERSHWIN, Piano Prelude No. 1 (p. 696)
JOPLIN, *Maple Leaf Rag* (p. 526)
LIGETI, *Désordre*, from *Etudes for Piano* (p. 850)
LISZT, *La campanella* (p. 179)
CLARA SCHUMANN, Scherzo, Op. 10 (p. 225)
prelude:
CHOPIN, Prelude in E minor, Op. 28, No. 4 (p. 165)
DEBUSSY, *Prélude à "L'après-midi d'un faune"* (p. 485)
GERSHWIN, Piano Prelude No. 1 (p. 696)
prepared piano:
CAGE, *Sonatas and Interludes* (p. 769)
program music:
BERLIOZ, *Symphonie fantastique* (p. 32)
COPLAND, *Billy the Kid* (p. 718)
DEBUSSY, *Prélude à "L'après-midi d'un faune"* (p. 485)
SMETANA, *Vltava* (p. 236)
STRAVINSKY, *L'histoire du soldat* (p. 637); *Le sacre du printemps* (p. 608)
TOWER, *For the Uncommon Woman* (p. 894)
program symphony:
BERLIOZ, *Symphonie fantastique* (p. 32)
psalm setting:
PÄRT, *Cantate Domino canticum novum* (p. 881)

recitative:
BIZET, *Carmen*, "C'est bien là" (p. 340)
VERDI, *Rigoletto*, Act III, excerpt (p. 200)
rondo:
BRAHMS, *A German Requiem*, IV (p. 301)
rondo (modified):
BARTÓK, *Concerto for Orchestra*, IV (p. 596)
REVUELTAS, *Homenaje a Federico García Lorca* (p. 701)

scherzo and trio:
BEACH, Violin Sonata in A minor, II (p. 518)
CLARA SCHUMANN, Scherzo, Op. 10 (p. 225)
sectional form:
JOPLIN, *Maple Leaf Rag* (p. 518)
solo voice (in chamber ensemble):
BAKER, *Through This Vale of Tears* (p. 874)
BOULEZ, *Le marteau sans maître*, III (p. 856)
CRUMB, *Ancient Voices of Children*, I (p. 870)
SCHOENBERG, *Pierrot lunaire* (p. 530)
solo voice (in orchestral music):
BERNSTEIN, *West Side Story*, *Tonight* Ensemble (p. 833)
MAHLER, *Das Lied von der Erde*, III (p. 473)
sonata:
BEACH, Violin Sonata in A minor (p. 518)
CAGE, *Sonatas and Interludes* (p. 769)
sonata-allegro form:
DVOŘÁK, Symphony No. 9 in E minor (*From the New World*), I (p. 313)
song:
CRUMB, *Ancient Voices of Children*, I (p. 870)
HENSEL, *Bergeslust*, Op. 10, No. 5 (p. 109)

IVES, *The Things Our Fathers Loved* (p. 541)
MAHLER, *Das Lied von der Erde,* III (p. 473)
SCHOENBERG, *Pierrot lunaire* (p. 530)
SCHUBERT, *Erlkönig* (p. 1); *Die Forelle,* D. 550 (p. 9)
ROBERT SCHUMANN, "Und wüssten's die Blumen," from *Dichterliebe* (p. 174)

song-cycle (excerpt):
BOULEZ, *Le marteau sans maître* (p. 856)
CRUMB, *Ancient Voices of Children* (p. 870)
MAHLER, *Das Lied von der Erde* (p. 473)
SCHOENBERG, *Pierrot lunaire* (p. 530)

spiritual:
BAKER, *Through This Vale of Tears,* "Sometimes I Feel Like a Motherless Child" (p. 874)

strophic song form:
VERDI, *Rigoletto,* "La donna è mobile" (p. 200)

strophic song form (modified):
HENSEL, *Bergeslust,* Op. 10, No. 5 (p. 109)
SCHUBERT, *Die Forelle,* D. 550 (p. 9)
ROBERT SCHUMANN, "Und wüssten's die Blumen," from *Dichterliebe* (p. 174)

suite:
RAVEL, *Rapsodie espagnole* (p. 544)
TCHAIKOVSKY, *The Nutcracker* (p. 366)

symphonic poem:
DEBUSSY, *Prélude à "L'après-midi d'un faune"* (p. 485)
SMETANA, *Vltava* (p. 225)

symphony:
ADAMS, *Chamber Symphony* (p. 931)
BERLIOZ, *Symphonie fantastique* (p. 32)
BRAHMS, Symphony No. 3 in F major (p. 313)
DVOŘÁK, Symphony No. 9 in E minor (*From the New World*) (p. 414)
WEBERN, Symphony, Op. 21 (p. 647)

ternary form:
BRAHMS, Symphony No. 3 in F major, III (p. 313)
DEBUSSY, *Prélude à "L'après-midi d'un faune"* (p. 485)
GERSHWIN, Piano Prelude No. 1 (p. 696)
MAHLER, *Das Lied von der Erde,* III (p. 473)
RAVEL, *Rapsodie espagnole, Feria* (p. 544)
TCHAIKOVSKY, *The Nutcracker, March* (p. 366), *Dance of the Sugar Plum Fairy* (p. 390), *Trepak* (p. 399)

ternary form (modified):
CHOPIN, Nocturne in C minor, Op. 48, No. 1 (p. 167)

theater music:
STRAVINSKY, *L'histoire du soldat* (p. 637)

theme and variations:
LISZT, *La campanella* (p. 179)
SCHUBERT, Piano Quintet in A major (*Trout*), IV (p. 15)
WEBERN, Symphony, Op. 21, II (p. 647)

thirty-two-bar song form:
BERNSTEIN, *West Side Story, Tonight Ensemble* (p. 833)
GILLESPIE/PARKER, *A Night in Tunisia* (p. 808)
STRAYHORN/ELLINGTON, *Take the A Train* (p. 777)

three-part form: *see* ternary form

through-composed song:
CRUMB, *Ancient Voices of Children,* I (p. 870)
IVES, *The Things Our Fathers Loved* (p. 541)
SCHUBERT, *Erlkönig* (p. 1)

tintinnabular style:
PÄRT, *Cantate Domino canticum novum* (p. 881)

tone poem: *see* symphonic poem

traditional music:
ABING, *Er quan ying yue* (p. 969)
Jongle á moi (p. 971)

twelve-bar blues: *see* blues

twelve-tone music:
BOULEZ, *Le marteau sans maître* (p. 856)
WEBERN, Symphony, Op. 21, II (p. 647)

variation procedure:
ABING, *Er quan ying yue* (p. 969)
LISZT, *La campanella* (p. 179)

variations: *see also* theme and variations